"for anyone wanting to find out about and explore the full variety of North American skiing, ... Ski America & Canada is better. As a reader, I like a book I can use while traveling, for booking a room or dinner. Is this too much to ask? Charles Leocha puts his readers first. Other guides would be better if they followed his example."
—*The Sunday Telegraph*

"...a no-holds-barred look at ski resorts. Unlike snazzy brochures that claim their respective resorts are perfect for everyone, this guide offers the lowdown on which places are better for families, singles, honeymooners, beginners and experts."
—The Gannett Newspapers

"Ski vacationers will want to look at Skiing America and Ski Europe."
—*Consumer Reports Travel Letter*

"...a personal-experience feel, with insider tips."
—*USA Today*

"...convenient, indepth and portable...provides the down and dirty basics on major resorts."   —*Skiing Magazine*

"It provides independent evaluation of the ski terrain and offers more extensive information than found in other guides."
—*Skier News*

"If you're planning a ski vacation . . . this guide should serve you well."
—*Ski Magazine*

"Up-to-the-minute info, so accurate that even ski resort personnel peruse these pages . . . The only guidebook you'll ever need. The latest edition is packed chockablock with detailed information about the ski experience at every major resort in the United States and Canada."
—*Robb Report*

"Charlie Leocha is first a skier, then a writer. He shuns the party line of the big ski corporations, preferring instead to talk to locals. *Skiing America's* perspective is direct, credible, and no-holds-barred."
—*Daily Record,* NJ

"The flavor, feel and personality of each resort."
—*The Boston Globe*

Thanks

*No project as complex as this can be completed by
a single person or team without help from others.*

•

*Thank you to the public relations personnel at each of the ski resorts
reviewed in these pages: they carefully check facts,
phone numbers, prices and programs
even though they don't always agree with our reviews.*

•

*Special thanks to KLM, Northwest Airlines, Southwest Airlines and Air Canada
for getting our staff to resorts from California to the Alps.
These airlines serve almost every resort mentioned in this book,
and Northwest World Vacations^{SM} and Southwest Vacations offer
ski and snowboard packages to many of these resorts.*

•

*Thank you to Auto Europe for arranging automobile rentals
for the Ski America & Canada and Ski Europe staff
whenever they travel to Canada or Europe.
If you are planning to rent a car abroad,
this company is a secret all travelers
should know about—(800) 223-5555.*

•

*And thank you to Vail Resorts for hosting
our editorial conferences held at Vail and Beaver Creek, Colorado.*

SKI AMERICA AND CANADA

by Charles A. Leocha

Susan Graham Staples, Western Editor
Hilary Nangle, Eastern Editor

with

Steve Giordano, Lynn Rosen
Peggy McKay Shinn, Karen Cummings
Jeannie Patton, James Kitfield
Andrew Bill, Chris Elliott, Bob Aubrey
Karuna Eberl, Wade Nelson
Diane Slezak Scholfield
Claudia Carbone
Vanessa Reese

WORLD LEISURE CORPORATION

Hampstead, NH

Help us do a better job

Research for this book is an ongoing process. We have been at it for more than a decade. Each year we revisit many of these resorts, and every winter we speak with locals from every resort.

If you find a new restaurant, hotel, bar or disco that you feel we should include, please let us know. If you find anything in these pages that is misleading or has changed, please let us know. If we use your suggestion, we will send you a copy of next year's edition.

Send your suggestions and comments to:
Charlie Leocha, *Ski America & Canada*
World Leisure, Corporation
Box 160, Hampstead NH 03841, USA
or send e-mail to leocha@aol.com

Distributed to the trade in the U.S.A. by
Midpoint Trade Books, Inc., 27 W. 20th Street, Suite 1102,
New York, NY 10011, Tel. (212) 727-0190, fax (212) 727-0195.

Distributed to the trade in U.K. by
Portfolio, Unit 1c, West Ealing Business Centre, Alexandria Road,
London W13 0NJ. Tel. (0181) 579-7748, fax (0181) 567-0904.
Internet: www.portfoliobooks.com

Distributed to the trade in Canada by
Hushion House, 36 Northline Road, Toronto, Ontario, M4B 3E2, Canada
Tel. (416) 287-3146 fax (416) 287-0081 Internet: www.hushion.com.

Mail Order, Catalog, other International sales and rights, and Special Sales by
World Leisure Corporation, PO Box 160, Hampstead, NH 03841.
Tel. (877) 863-1966, fax (603) 947-0838.
E-mail: wleisure@aol.com; Internet: www.worldleisure.com.

ISBN: 0-915009-74-9   ISSN: 1072-8988   LCCN: 93-643936

Contents by geographical regions

We have organized this table of contents by geography—the way a skier might see geography. We start with the Rocky Mountains, stretching from Canada to New Mexico. We then cover California and several resorts in Nevada. Descriptions then follow about the Pacific Northwest resorts that include Alaska, British Columbia, Washington and Oregon. Finally, we shift to the East covering resorts from Quebec, Canada, in the north to Snowshoe, West Virginia in the south.

Within these four main sections, where resorts seem more logically organized according to geography rather than the alphabet, we have done so. For instance: Summit County with Breckenridge, Keystone and Copper Mountain, or Mt. Washington Valley that includes five or six resorts, depending on how one counts them.

Eastern Resorts

Contributors to *Ski America and Canada*

Charlie Leocha has skied virtually every major international resort. He writes about travel and skiing for magazines, newspapers and the Web. Charlie is a black-diamond skier, but a double-diamond après-skier. The rest of us bow to his energy and dancing ability. He's also the only *Ski America & Canada* staffer who knows which resorts have the best wine lists *and* the best bacon-and-eggs breakfasts. He is a member of the North American Snowsports Journalists Association (NASJA).

Susan Graham Staples lives in northern Vermont, where a day at the office often means sampling on-mountain conditions. She skis in the woods and launches off ledges with gusto. She first met Charlie when she was forced to zip down the trail edge to get a taste of the powder line that he was stealing. Susan, a former editor for *Snow Country* and *Snow Country Business*, is a member of NASJA. She is also Senior Web Editor for our Web site, www.resortspace.com.

Hilary Nangle dropped out of grad school to work at a ski area. She is a NASJA and the Society of American Travel Writers (SATW) member and writes regularly for ski and travel magazines. She has contributed to more than a dozen Fodor's Travel Guides. She has visited just about every B&B and country inn in Maine. A Mainer through and through, she believes the ideal skier's lunch is a bowl of lobster stew.

Steve Giordano is a veteran ski and travel journalist whose work has appeared in newspapers, magazines, books, radio and television. He used to be a ski patroller, but switched to ski journalism after pulling one too many drunks out of snowy creeks. A skier for more than 20 years, he switched to snowboarding a few years ago. He is a member of NASJA and SATW. He's also married to Lynn Rosen, and they make sure our Northwest entries are up-to-date.

Peggy McKay Shinn, a Westerner at heart, is now a resident Vermonter. She has skied at most major U.S. resorts where she seeks out the terrain that makes the rest of us grow weak in the knees. A NASJA member, she cast aside a graduate degree in environmental engineering to write full-time. She gives us the real scoop on child care and nursery facilities. Much to her mother's dismay, Peggy has vowed not to let motherhood slow her down.

Diane Slezak Scholfield, a near-native Southern Californian, remembers when getting off the chair lift without falling was her biggest challenge. She now skis black diamonds, but only on sunny spring days. She's our best scout for beginner and intermediate trails, mellow après-ski, microbrews on tap, and bagel-and-coffee breakfasts. She edits SnowLink.com and has won NASJA's Excellence in Snowsports Journalism–Writing award three times.

Lynn Rosen is an Emmy award-winning broadcaster, producer and writer at "border station" KVOS-TV in Bellingham. That's just her day job. She's also a theater critic and travel/ski writer. Mountain scenery is quite dramatic, so it's fitting that Lynn belongs to the American Theater Critics Association as well as NASJA. She also is one of the staff champion shoppers, a pushover for unique jewelry and clothing.

Karen Cummings has been writing about skiing for more than a decade. She lives life, balanced between Boston and Maine, with a smile. Karen began skiing at the tender age of 25 and immediately discovered après-ski—her specialty. These days her nightlife forays are "research." Karen is an expert shopper and has bought something at every resort she visits. She is also our cross-country aficionado who loves a workout with skating skis.

Claudia Carbone lives in the woods, minutes from Breckenridge in her native state of Colorado. For her, a great day is dancing through knee-deep Rocky Mountain powder. Claudia writes for many publications. Her groundbreaking book, *WomenSki*, established her as a national authority on women's skiing. Claudia is a founder of Snow Sports Association for Women and is the recipient of the Lowell Thomas Award from Colorado Ski Country and NASJA's Excellence in Snowsports Journalism–Writing award.

Andrew Bill has worked as a travel journalist for nearly 20 years, contributing to leading consumer magazines and newspapers on both sides of the Atlantic. Andy writes about adventure travel and alcoholic potables—such as, "The Best Bars Of The World" supplement for *Newsweek International* and so, ski writing was a natural progression. Our staff's witty Brit describes himself as "an avid if erratic skier."

Jeannie Patton was first published in 8th grade and she still sees life as a kid. She lived in Steamboat Springs as a ski bum, then worked for the ski area as Director of Public Relations. Author of hundreds of articles and a former editor at *Ski Magazine,* she knows that all good things come to those who hang out in high places.

James Kitfield is an expert après-skier who first met Charlie dancing in a conga line through a bar in Verbier, Switzerland. Life has been downhill since, at least as often as he can manage trips to the mountains. On the slopes he points his skis down double diamonds. Amazingly, he has a serious side. He has been awarded the Gerald R. Ford prize twice for distinguished defense reporting, and the Jesse H. Neal award for excellence in reporting.

Christopher Elliott is an accomplished travel journalist and a well-known travel curmudgeon. However, skiing is one activity that keeps him smiling. One of America's top travel journalists, his musings can be found at www.ticked.com as well in scores of magazines and newspapers. He has just moved to Key Largo but always makes time to get away to the slopes.

Mitch Kaplan took up the pen to support his inexhaustible ski habit and has been covering skiing, adventure and family travel ever since. He currently holds the unofficial New Jersey state record for the most consecutive days spent dreaming about playing in the snow. The author of several books and a member of NASJA, SATW and ASJA, he lives with his non-skiing wife, Penny, two college-age children who won't empty the nest and a gorgeous mutt named Callie.

Bob Aubrey is a snowboarder pure and simple. If there's snow piling up in the Rockies, you'll be sure to find him out riding. He's been just about everywhere you'd want to go on a board, and prides himself on the knowledge he's picked up over his 15+ years of riding. Always planning for the next session, he'll sometimes space his necessary journalistic duties, like paying his NASJA membership on time.

Karuna Eberl started snowboarding in the Colorado high country in 1988, before the hoards, and later took a sabbatical from college to be a snowboard bum in Utah. She now works from her home in Rollinsville, Colorado, as a full-time freelance writer, photographer and editor—that is, when she's not out showing up the guys on the hill. Oh, and she's also a member of NASJA.

Wade Nelson is a freelance writer living in Durango, Colorado. When snowboarding began to take off, Wade decided to catch that wave despite catching numerous edges. Never one to quit, he hasn't looked back—except at the "esses" he now leaves behind on his carving board. Wade is a founding member of Purgatory's over-35 snowboarding club: "Greys on Trays."

Vanessa Reese considers herself to be the world's first "black-diamond virtual skier." She has worked on *Ski America & Canada* and *Ski Europe* and helped develop our Web site. Until last year, the closest this Harvard graduate has ever come to a ski slope was Boston's blizzard of '78 until she visited Vail and Beaver Creek and took her first halting glides on cross-country skis and discovered snow tubing.

Katy Keck, our gourmet consultant, is recognized as one of the Top 30 Women Chefs in The World. **Scott Staples, Bradley Staples,** 14, and **Joshua Staples,** 11, were thumb-wrestled into contributing to the family and snowboarding coverage for the Lake Louise, Sunshine Village and Ski Banff @ Norquay, Marmot Basin in Jasper National Park, the Eastern Townships of Quebec, and Jay Peak Resort, Vermont. Avid snowboarders **Gavin Forbes Ehringer** and **Marie Daigle Thompson** also wrote some of our snowboarding coverage.

Plan your
winter vacation
with Ski America and Canada

Here's a book to help you branch out and to find the perfect ski resort (plus accommodations, restaurants and nightlife) to match your ability, your pocketbook and your interests. For overseas skiers, *Ski America and Canada* offers insights to help you locate the region and then the resort that matches your dream of an American ski vacation.

Not surprisingly, people take ski vacations for different reasons—for a romantic getaway, to have quality time with the family, to ski all-out with buddies, to ski a little and maybe shop a lot. And what happens when a hotshot skier travels with a never-ever or beginner? The average ski resort's brochure indicates that their resort is all things to all skiers—this is definitely not the case.

Ski America and Canada is as straightforward and honest a guide to North America's top resorts as you can buy. Our goal is to match you with the right vacation spot. Our staff includes experts and intermediates (including some who learned as adults), Generation Xers and Baby Boomers, skiers and snowboarders, eggs-and-bacon breakfast eaters and gourmet-coffee-and-bagel fans. Each skier and snowboarder has various likes and dislikes, and resorts have different personalities. We recognize this—that's why we include our opinions and personal observations. We detail the personality of each resort: where we found the best skiing and snowboarding, where we liked to eat and where we enjoyed the liveliest off-slope fun. And we give you the facts and current prices, plus hotel and restaurant descriptions, lift ticket and lesson prices, child care programs, nightlife hot spots, and where to call, fax, e-mail or write for more information.

A note about prices and older editions of this book

We make every attempt to include prices for the current ski season. Unfortunately, as of mid-August many resorts had not announced their new prices. Current prices have the 2001/02 notation. Where there is no notation, assume prices are from last season (2000/01). In recent years, ski resorts have created lift ticket prices for every occasion—prices for various age groups, various days, various times of the season, supermarket discounts, ad infinitum. It's getting to be just as complicated to purchase lift tickets as it is to buy your airline tickets.

Prices provided in this guidebook are in no way official and are subject to change at any time. In fact, prices do change with between high and low seasons; and resorts sometimes announce one price in July, change it by November, and change prices during the season.

Ski America and Canada is published every fall, but sometimes bookstores have older copies in their inventory. If you are reading this book in the fall of 2002 or after, get the latest edition. it can be found in most major bookstores or order through www.worldleisure.com, www.amazon.com, or www.barnesandnoble.com. Or, send a check to World Leisure, PO Box 160, Hampstead, NH 03841.

What's new in this edition

Of course, prices, programs, lessons and facilities have been updated to provide the most accurate information available at press time about each resort. Some of these resorts have been completely transformed through new developments and new hotels.

We have added a new chapter on the Eastern Townships of Quebec and its resorts—Mont Orford, Mont Sutton, Owl's Head and Bromont. We also have added chapters on both Snowshoe Mountain in West Virginia, and Panorama Mountain Resort in British Columbia. The chapters covering Canada's Banff Region (with Sunshine Village and Ski Banff @ Norquay), Lake Louise and Marmot Basin/Jasper National Park have been completely rewritten and expanded to include the family side of things. Big Sky Resort in Montana, and Utah's resorts, especially in the Olympic region, have been rewritten too. Perhaps the most noticeable change is our expanded snowboarding coverage for each major Western resort and many of those in the East, telling you where to ride, where the flats are and whether the terrain parks and features are any fun. For parents, we've made it easier to find out about children's programs by combining child care and lessons under the heading of Child Care.

Keeping up with area code, resort, hotel, restaurant and price changes always keeps us busy. There are literally thousands of changes to the book each year. We continue to add Web site addresses that will help you in your planning.

Using the Internet—www.resortspace.com

The development of the Internet has significantly changed the way people research and make reservations at ski resorts. Virtually every world-class resort now has a Web site with basic information including statistics, lift tickets, ski school prices, and how to contact them; you can even book online on some of the more savvy sites.

We have gathered more information than we can possibly stuff into this guidebook, so if you want to know more about any of the resorts we review here, visit our Web site, www.resortspace.com. There you'll find additional facts, advice and words of wisdom; often you'll find out more about a resort than at the resort's own site. Indeed, few resorts work to promote the surrounding areas, but www.resortspace.com offer details about the surrounding areas as well as much more economical lodging and dining options. As prices change and as activities are planned at each resort, we'll post that information.

During the coming months, *Skiing America & Canada* as well as *Ski Europe* will be made available for purchase by the chapter through our web site. Check online for details.

We have included the Web addresses for every resort listed in this book. Use them as well as www.resortspace.com to get the information you need.

Chapter organization

Each resort chapter has several sections. We begin by sketching the personality of the place—is it old and quaint, or modern and high-rise? Clustered at the base of the slopes, or a few miles down the road? Remote and isolated, or freeway-close? Family-oriented or catering to singles? Filled with friendly faces or an aloof herd of "beautiful" skiers?

The basic statistics of each resort include **addresses and phone numbers:** postal, e-mail, Internet, toll-free, fax—all of them that we could find.

A few important notes: The resort's **area code** is listed in the fact box and at the bottom of each even-numbered page. We don't list the local area code for every number in the chapter because you probably will use local numbers most often while you're at the resort (in the case of restaurants, for instance). Some of the fax numbers we list are for the ski area; others are for the central reservations office; some resorts don't have public fax numbers. In almost every instance, the Internet address we list is the officially sanctioned one maintained by the resort.

Next are terrain stats—the **base and summit altitudes,** important for those with altitude-related medical difficulties or for sea-level dwellers who plan to hit the slopes the same day they arrive; **vertical drop, skiable acreage** and **number and types of lifts,** all of which will give you a good idea of the resort's size.

Our terrain stats reflect *lift-served* terrain. Examples: Breckenridge, Colorado, lists its vertical as 3,398 feet; we list it at 2,546. If you want that maximum vertical, you must hike the extra 852 feet to the in-bounds summit. Grand Targhee has two mountains totaling 3,000 acres, but 1,000 of that acreage is reserved for snowcat skiing and snowboarding. Exceptions like these are explained where they occur.

Uphill lift capacity is the number of riders the lift system can carry each hour. **Bed base** is the approximate number of people who can be accommodated overnight near the resort. If the uphill capacity is much bigger than the bed base, the result is usually shorter lift lines. (Resorts with great uphill capacity/bed base ratios may still have long weekend lines if they are near major cities—we try to identify these.)

We tell you how close the **nearest lodging** is, if the resort has **child care** and the youngest age accepted, and if there are any restrictions on **snowboarding.** The **lift ticket** price in the fact box tells the per-day range of the adult lift ticket. The lower price usually is the per-day cost of the longest adult multiday ticket, or it is the midweek price. The higher price is the weekend walk-up-to-the-window cost. Ticket prices in the stat box are intended as an approximation; look in the chapter for more details.

Finally, **we rate the slopes** (based on five ability levels), the **dining,** the **nightlife** and the **other activities**. One star means it's poor, two is okay, three is good, four is very good and five is outstanding. Ratings are quite subjective, but they are a general consensus of the *Ski America and Canada* staff. We're simply trying to point you in the right direction.

Following the fact box is a detailed description of the mountain. **Mountain layout—Skiing** describe various sections of the mountain best for skiers at each of five ability levels. **Mountain layout—Snowboarding** tells riders where to go, where the flats are and whether the terrain parks and features are any fun. **Mountain rating** is a summary of the mountain's best and worst features, such as whether slopes may be too tough for the beginner or too mild for the expert.

Cross-country and snowshoeing information will tell you which resorts have Nordic trails, as well as significant cross-country and backcountry skiing opportunities nearby, and snowshoe rental and tour information.

The **Lessons** section details instructional programs for adults, including any special programs and recreational racing. The term "never-ever package" refers to a package with half-day or full-day first-time lesson, a lift ticket (often just for the beginner lift) and use of rental equipment. Some resorts charge more for first-time snowboarders than for skiers. Though it might appear that resorts are either cashing in on the trendy sport or discriminating against boarders, they tell us that the higher price is because fewer people sign up for first-time snowboard group lessons, and snowboard rental equipment takes a greater beating.

Child care covers non-skiing nursery and day-care programs, either at the resort or nearby, as well as the skiing and snowboarding lesson programs available for children.

Lift tickets are listed for adults, children, teens and seniors. We've organized them in a chart with one-day, three-day and five-day prices, followed by "Who skis free" and "Who skis at a discount" listed in paragraph form. Where prices are from last season, assume an increase of a couple of dollars. Be aware that resorts have various terms for children's lift tickets—"junior," "youth" and "young adult" are common.

Under **Accommodations** we list both the most luxurious places and many of the budget lodges, including features such as slopeside location, pools and spas, health clubs and intra-resort transportation. We also suggest lodging that is particularly suited to families, and our favorite B&Bs and inns.

Dining always includes the gourmet restaurants, but we don't leave out affordable places where a hungry family or a snowboarder on a budget can chow down and relax. We have compiled these suggestions from dozens of interviews with locals and tourists, plus our own dining experiences.

Après-ski/nightlife describes places to go when the lifts close, and where to find entertainment later in the evening. We tell you which bars are loud, which are quiet, what kind of music they play and whether they have live music.

Other activities covers off-slope activities—such as dogsledding, snowmobiling, ice skating, sleigh rides, shopping, fitness clubs and spas.

Getting there and getting around tells you how to get to the resort by air and car (and sometimes by train or bus), and whether a car is optional or necessary at the resort.

Types of accommodations

A **hotel** is relatively large, with 25 rooms or more, and comes without meals. If hotel rates include any meals, that is noted.

A **mountain inn** usually has fewer rooms than a hotel. Many have packages that include breakfast and dinner.

A **bed & breakfast (B&B)** tends to be even smaller, with just a few rooms. Most B&Bs have private baths now, so if guests must share a bath, we say so. Breakfast is included and some B&Bs also offer dinner.

Motels don't have the amenities of a hotel or the ambiance of a B&B, and often are further from the slopes. Motels are good for families and budget-minded skiers.

Condominiums have become the most affordable group lodging at American ski resorts because of their separate bedrooms and kitchen facilities. They usually have a central check-in facility. Most condominiums have daily maid service for everything but the kitchen.

When you call the resort's central reservations number, ask for suggestions. Most of the staff have been on lodging tours and can make honest recommendations based on your needs.

We use $$$ signs rather than listing the prices for restaurants and accommodations. Where you find $$$ signs, refer to this legend (also on the bottom of pages in each chapter):

Dining: $$$-Entrees $20+; $$-$10-20; $-less than $10.

Accommodations: (double room) $$$$-$200+; $$$-$141-$200; $$-$81-$140; $-$80 and less.

The following icon system to indicate a lodging's amenities is used mainly in the New England section of the book. The legend for these icons is as follows:

🚐	Airport Shuttle
⚡	Ski-in/ski-out
🏊	Indoor heated pool
🏊	Outdoor heated pool
🏋	Fitness center
✕	Restaurant
🐾	Pets OK
🚭	No Smoking
💈	In-room hairdryers
Ⓟ	Parking

High and low season

North American mountain resorts have several pricing seasons. The highest prices are during the Christmas-New Year holidays in late December. Regular season usually runs all of February and March, but at some resorts March is high season. Value Season is in January after New Year at some resorts. Low Season is usually the first couple of weeks in December, and April until closing. These vary from resort to resort, so ask for more information when you call. The most noticeable change is in the cost of accommodations, but some resorts also vary the prices of lift tickets, especially in pre-season and in spring.

Regional resorts

Throughout the book you'll find mini-sections on regional resorts. These resorts are best for weekend or short midweek visits by skiers and snowboarders who live in that region.

When a regional resort can be a side trip from a destination resort, we have included the description within that chapter. Regional resorts that are not near a large destination resort are in separate mini-chapters throughout the book.

These ski areas all have the following common features, *unless otherwise noted:*

•   lodging within a 20-mile radius (Note: Some of the phone numbers listed for lodging are reservations services; others just provide information about lodging in the area. If no phone number is listed for lodging, call the ski area.)

•   a day lodge with food service

•   adult and child ski and snowboard lessons (children usually start at age 4)

•   equipment rentals

We list toll-free phone numbers where available, plus the resort's recorded information line and Web site address. If you can't get a live voice from the info line, try the ski area's office number. (The toll-free numbers may not be applicable nationwide, since these resorts draw visitors primarily from the nearest urban areas.) Where we say, "None found," for Web site, that means we couldn't find an official site from the resort as of summer 2001.

Where two or more ski areas are close enough to be explored on the same weekend trip, they are presented together, but with separate contact information. Such ski areas are owned by different companies and do not have interchangeable lift tickets unless specifically noted.

Ability levels

These are the terms we use in the "Mountain layout—Skiing" and other sections:

● **Never-evers** are just what the name implies. We apply the term to novices during their first couple of days on skis or a snowboard.

●● **Beginners** can turn and stop (more or less) when they choose, but still rely on snowplow turns if on skis and sideslipping if on a snowboard. This group feels most comfortable on wide, fairly flat terrain.

■ **Intermediates** generally head for blue trails and parallel ski or link snowboard turns (more or less) on the smooth stuff. They return to survival technique on expert trails, and struggle in heavy powder and crud.

◆ **Advanced** skiers and boarders can descend virtually any trail with carved turns, but are still intimidated by deep powder, crud and super steeps. Advanced terrain by our definition includes moguls and glade skiing.

◆◆ **Experts** favor chutes, tight trees on steep slopes, deep-powder bowls and off-piste exploration. True experts are few and far between.

Skiing & snowboarding for everyone

Skiers and snowboarders come in all abilities, genders, interests and ages. Better equipment and slope-grooming techniques mean that skiing—and we use this as a catch-all phrase to describe Nordic or Alpine skiing, snowboarding, telemarking, snowskating and other forms of sliding on snowy slopes—is easier than ever to learn and you don't have to give it up as you age. As more people are attracted to snowsports, resorts are putting more emphasis on teaching you how much fun you can have participating in them. These are sports that combine the best of Mother Nature with the best of friendly people out to enjoy themselves.

Snowboarders, please don't take offense. We use the word "ski" in a general sense, meaning skiing or snowboarding. Our staff includes boarders who like to ride some days and ski on other days, as well as boarders who wouldn't be caught dead on two planks.

Ability levels

These are the terms we use in the "Mountain layout—Skiing" and other sections:

● **Never-evers** are just what the name implies. We apply the term to novices during their first couple of days on skis or a snowboard.

●● **Beginners** can turn and stop (more or less) when they choose, but still rely on snowplow turns if on skis and sideslipping if on a snowboard. This group feels most comfortable on wide, fairly flat terrain.

■ **Intermediates** generally head for blue trails and parallel ski or link snowboard turns (more or less) on the smooth stuff. They return to survival technique on expert trails, and struggle in heavy powder and crud.

◆ **Advanced** skiers and boarders can descend virtually any trail with carved turns, but are still intimidated by deep powder, crud and super steeps. Advanced terrain by our definition includes moguls and glade skiing.

◆◆ **Experts** favor chutes, tight trees on steep slopes, deep-powder bowls and off-piste exploration. True experts are few and far between.

Clinics for advanced skiers

Advanced skiers hardly ever take lessons, and it's no wonder. Until recently, advanced skiers were taught just like beginners: Groups of four to six make a few turns, then listen to the instructor give generalized tips on improvement. That format works well for lower-level skiers, all of whom need to learn the same skills. But while most skiers develop bad habits as they progress, not all develop the same ones. One skier may need to work on pole plants, another may need to keep his shoulders square to the hill and a third may be sitting too far back on her skis.

Just like World Cup racers, these skiers need fine-tuning. They need a coach, not an instructor: Someone who will observe the way they ski and then give very specific tips on breaking the habits that keep skiers from progressing to the next level.

Resorts have responded to advanced skiers' needs with coaching, not lessons. The terminology has changed—lessons are "workshops" or "clinics." Instructors are "coaches" or "pros." Ski school is "mountain development center" or some other politically correct term. Instead of the standard ski-stop-listen format, most of these clinics are heavy on ski, ski, ski and listening to the instructor as you go or while on the lift. Quite a few work on the "condition du jour"—powder, moguls, crud, etc. Other work on snowboard-specific skills, such as halfpipe tricks or carving. Many clinics have video feedback.

If you're at the intermediate or advanced level, look into these programs. But here are a few tips to be sure to get what you want:

• Don't use the word "lesson." Ask what type of clinics or workshops are offered for upper-level skiers or snowboarders.

• Be specific when asking about the format. How much time is spent moving on the hill? What skills will we work on?

• Insist that the instructor address each student's needs. Some instructors won't target individuals for fear of offending them. That's fine for beginners, but not for better skiers and snowboarders who need specific advice.

• If after the clinic you don't feel you got your money's worth, go to the ski school office and politely tell them why. ("I expected to actually ski moguls during the mogul clinic, not practice short turns on groomed slopes.") If they're smart, they'll get you in the right clinic.

Women's instruction

Nearly every major resort, and many of the smaller ones, has some sort of program just for women. Why segregate? Simply put, women ski differently than men; they are built differently than men; they approach the sport differently than men; and often their equipment must be set up differently than equipment for men.

Claudia Carbone, award-winning Colorado ski journalist and author of the book *WomenSki,* ($14.95; to order log into www.amazon.com, www.worldleisure.com or www.bn.com) observes, "There's more than one way to ski. The ultimate experience doesn't have to be a steep, fast, frightening run down back-bowl slopes. Some people experience exhilaration and satisfaction from a seamless sequence of perfectly carved arcs. Or a wintry waltz through fresh powder. Or smooth and easy gliding on a brilliant crisp day. You're not alone if you like to caress, rather than attack, the hill."

The goal of such seminars is not to segregate women from their male friends on the slopes permanently, but to provide an environment geared to eliminating learning barriers so that "women only" instruction ultimately becomes unnecessary.

Because lessons are usually with the same instructor each day, improvement is both dramatic and clearly recognizable. Most programs incorporate video sessions. When included, video instruction lets you see how you look when you ski and lets you see just how much you've improved.

Discussions address issues particular to women skiers and snowboarders, such as developing confidence and selecting proper equipment. Some seminars are as heavy on social fun as improving skills; others are for higher-ability skiers who want to learn to race or ski moguls, powder and steeps. Make sure to ask in-depth questions about a specific clinic before committing to it so you get what you're looking for. If you're an aggressive, athletic woman, you don't want to end up in a clinic that focuses on how to overcome fear; if you've always skied just because your husband does, you'll want to be in a clinic that lets you discover your own reasons for skiing.

There are women's programs that have received very high reviews at Squaw Valley, where Elissa Slanger originated this type of program a quarter-century ago; Telluride, where Annie Vareille Savath's influence as ski-school director shows through, and Crested Butte, where Kim Reichhelm, a former ski racer who also has been the Women's World Extreme Skiing Champion, operates her Women's Ski Adventures program.

The Snow Sports Association for Women (SSAW) normally holds its annual event to introduce women to snowsports—Take Your Daughter to the Snow Week—in late January or early February. Ski areas, cross-country skiing and snowshoe trail systems and shops across the country offer special programs and deals for those who bring a female friend or relative to the slopes that week. See the *SnowLink* Web site (www.snowlink.com) for a complete list of participants. (Resorts and shops are added as they commit, so check it often; the list is complete about two weeks prior to the event.)

Programs for the silver-haired crowd

Skiing (and snowboarding) isn't just for youngsters anymore. One of the fastest growing age groups in skiing is 55 and older. By the year 2010, 37 percent of all skiers are expected to be in that age group.

Some of those skiers learned when they were young and never stopped skiing, others returned to skiing after many years off snow and still others started late in life. Many resorts have started programs that cater to this upper-age group. Nearly every ski area in North America offers free or heavily discounted lift tickets to skiers when they reach 60, 65 or 70.

Thanks to clubs such as the Over the Hill Gang and the 70+ Club, older skiers always have companionship. The 70+ Club started in 1977 with 34 members; now it has more than 10,000—all 70 or older—in several countries. Here is a partial list of clubs and programs for older skiers. New programs are starting every season.

Clubs: Members of the **70+ Ski Club** wear distinctive red-and-white patches that identify them as part of this elite group. Annual dues are $10 for a single membership; $15 for husband and wife. Those 90 and older pay no dues. Founder Lloyd Lambert was a pioneer in getting discounts for older skiers. Lambert died in 1997 (well into his 90s), but his son, Richard Lambert, has taken over the administrative duties. For information, write to 1633 Albany St., Schenectady, NY 12304 or send e-mail to RTL70PLUS@aol.com.

The **Over The Hill Gang** is for skiers 50 and older. This international group has chapters all over the United States whose members not only ski, but also play tennis, go hiking and sailing and enjoy the outdoor life. Contact the Over The Hill Gang at 1820 W. Colorado Ave., Colorado Springs, CO 80904; (719) 389-0022; www.skiersover50.com.

Elderhostel, a non-profit organization that has educational travel adventures for those 55 and older, offers skiing programs at various resorts, mostly in New England and Western Canada. Skiing is combined with other academic courses. To request a catalog, call Elderhostel toll-free at (877) 426-8056 in the U.S. or Canada; (978) 323-4141 from other countries; or visit the excellent Web site at www.elderhostel.org.

Ski area programs: Special instruction or social programs for seniors are offered at many resorts, some of which are Purgatory, Colorado; Park City, Utah; Badger Pass, California; Northstar-at-Tahoe, California; Waterville Valley, New Hampshire; Aspen, Colorado; Stratton, Vermont; and Sun Valley, Idaho. Some are day programs, others are week-long vacations with big-band dances and wine-and-cheese parties.

The novice's experience

When you ski or snowboard, you escape from your everyday routine. No matter your level of expertise, you find challenge, beauty and a balance with nature. This is a sport where beginners *and* experts can have fun amid clean air and stunning scenery. It's also a sport where you'll easily meet other people.

Learning is not difficult if you don't try to teach yourself. We firmly believe that lessons are the only way to go for never-evers, whatever their athletic ability. Natural athletes may quickly develop balance, but they'll also develop bad habits that will hinder later progress. Toddlers can start as young as 3 and you're never too old to learn—*really*. Learning will not break the bank: Many resorts offer heavily discounted lessons for novices and advancing beginners. A few resorts even have free beginner lessons, either all the time or at certain times of the season. Where we know about these, we've noted them within the resort's chapter.

After only four or five lessons, most beginners have improved enough to safely negotiate their way down more than half the marked ski trails in North America. For cross-country skiing you need only a couple of lessons to begin gliding through the forests and across rolling meadows.

How do you get started? First, read the information about never-ever packages in our *Lessons* sections. Also pay attention to our notes on never-ever terrain in the *Mountain Layout* and *Mountain Rating* sections. Some resorts are not good for a first-timer's experience. Others may be good for learning to ski but not snowboard and vice versa. Call several resorts in advance and ask them to send you information on novice lessons. The best resorts will have a separate brochure or information sheet on the topic.

Most skiing and snowboarding Web sites are aimed toward those who already love these sports. One that also gives great advice for those just starting out is *SnowLink* (www.snowlink.com), the Web site of SnowSports Industries America. This Web site also has about 600 links to official Web sites for equipment and clothing companies, resorts and ski clubs, as well as a searchable database to find the ski or snowboard shop nearest your home.

While you're learning to ski or snowboard, rent your equipment. Renting is much less expensive than buying when you're a novice, because as you get better you'll need more advanced gear. Ski or snowboard shop employees will help you with the correct length and type, boots, bindings and adjustments. As you improve, they can suggest how to upgrade. The two principal places to rent are shops near home or at the resort. The choice will probably be based on how you get to the resort—flying or driving—and how much time you'll spend there. If possible, rent near home or at the resort the afternoon or evening before you start. You'll get better attention if you're not part of the masses the morning of your first lesson.

Proper clothing also is important. You don't need the latest, most colorful ski fashions—what you can find in your closet should do just fine, provided you can find such basics as a pair of long johns, a sweater, a waterproof or water-resistant jacket, wool or acrylic socks and a pair of wool trousers or nylon wind pants. One warning: Because your backside will be spending time in contact with the snow at first, don't wear jeans or other cotton pants. In fact, don't wear anything made of cotton, such as cotton socks or a T-shirt or sweatshirt. Cotton soaks up and holds moisture—either sweat or snow—and you'll soon be cold. If you're missing any of the basics, borrow from a friend, or call some shops to see if you can rent clothes. The secret to staying just warm enough is layering. A few lightweight garments are better than one heavy one, since layers trap the air. You can remove or add layers as temperatures change.

Wear a hat—50 percent of your body heat can escape through your head. Wear gloves—they will keep your hands warm and protected. Ski and snowboard gloves are padded and reinforced in ways different from any other gloves you're likely to have on hand, so these should be a specific purchase if you can't borrow them. Though you can get by with sunglasses, goggles are *vital* for seeing trail contours on overcast days or when skiing in falling snow. Use sunscreen—at high altitudes the sun's rays are stronger and the reflection of rays off the snow increases your total dose.

Your first lessons will teach you how to walk, slide and—most importantly—stop. Then the lessons focus on how to get up after falling (you may have already practiced that lesson on your own). You will learn the basic turn, called a "snowplow" or "wedge" turn for skiers and a "falling leaf" turn for snowboarders. With this turn you will be able to negotiate almost any groomed slope. Your instructor will show you how to use the lifts, and you'll be on your way.

You don't have to start with downhill skiing. Many skiers go right to cross-country or to snowboarding. Just pick the sport that suits you best. Enjoy!

Skiing for the physically challenged

At many areas, you're likely to see a few empty wheelchairs next to the ski racks in the base area. Skiing is a great sport for physically challenged people, because gravity plays such a major role. Special equipment is available for about any type of disability. If a resort doesn't have the right equipment, they'll invent it. There is no reason why an otherwise disabled skier can't ski as fast as an able-bodied one; in fact, sometimes they're faster—a real ego boost for those who must proceed a little slower than most on dry land.

Winter Park, Colorado, has been the pioneer in this area, and still has one of the best programs. Hal O'Leary, founder and director of the **National Sports Center for the Disabled,** began with a few sets of borrowed skis and a broom-closet office. Now a full-time staff of 13 and a volunteer organization of 850 handles 2,500 participants with 45 types of disabilities, and gives 14,500 lessons yearly.

Among those who can ski are amputees, wheelchair users, the blind and those with cerebral palsy and multiple sclerosis. Contact Hal O'Leary, Director, National Sports Center for the Disabled, Box 1290, Winter Park, CO 80482; (970) 726-1540; www.nscd.org.

Disabled Sports USA has chapters and programs in more than 60 cities and resorts, and reports that more than 12,000 individuals are in learning programs each year. Contact information: 451 Hungerford Dr., Suite 100, Rockville, MD 20850; (301) 217-0960; www.dsusa.org. A list of the DS/USA chapters with links to Web sites and contact information is at www.dsusa.org/links.html

Nearly every major destination resort has ties to a local organization that teaches physically disabled people to ski. Some of the resorts that have been big supporters of this type of instruction are Breckenridge, Colorado; Purgatory, Colorado; Big Bear Mountain, California; Park City, Utah; and Mt. Sunapee, New Hampshire.

SKI AMERICA
AND CANADA

Banff, Canada

Sunshine Village
Banff@Norquay

Banff Region Facts
Dining:★★★★
Apres-ski/nightlife:★★★★
Other activities:★★★★★

Internet: www.sblls.com (skiing)
www.banfflakelouise.com (tourism bureau)
www.canadianrockies.net/Banff (townsite)
Bed Base: 10,000 in Banff

While flying into Calgary during the day provides awe-inspiring views of the Canadian Rocky Mountains, perhaps the best surprise is to arrive late at night, when everything is enveloped in pitch black, and make the hour-and-a-half-long drive to Banff. The next morning when you draw back the curtains, the massive craggy mountains are suddenly *right* there, in your face. What a wake-up call!

The pristine beauty of Banff National Park is one of the reasons people are drawn to the region's three ski resorts. There is a true sense of being swallowed up by the wilderness—embraced by Mother Nature and then gently released to be part of her bountiful gifts here. Wildlife is plentiful, sightings of elk in town are common. Mule deer and bighorn sheep live in the Bow Valley, and sometimes bears and wolves can be seen along less-traveled roads.

From the castle-like Fairmont Banff Springs Hotel, one gazes down a densely wooded valley framed by towering mountain walls and dissected by a shimmering river. To see this scene is to understand the spell which must have overcome the builders of the Canadian Pacific Railway in the late 1800s.

The completion of the coast-to-coast railway in 1885 made one of the most picturesque and remote pockets in the Rocky Mountains suddenly accessible. This virgin landscape—formerly known only to Native Americans, fur traders and explorers—was now open to everyday travelers and tourists. That same year, Canada established its first national park, Banff. The scenery is still as magnificent as it was to the train travelers of the late 1800s with snow-capped mountain ridges, cliff faces pocked by glaciers, lakes and hot springs.

Contrast this with the beautifully designed, compact, yet very cosmopolitan town of Banff, filled with excellent restaurants, nightclubs, shops and lodging—a uniquely Canadian blend of quaint and rustic, set amid some of the most rugged scenery in the Rockies—sort of like a good Canadian whiskey sipped smooth but with enough bite to remind you of the point of the exercise.

Because summer is the high season here, crowds diminish in winter and lodging prices are rock bottom, even at the most luxurious hotels. The temperature can be numbingly cold, or pleasantly warm if a Chinook wind blows. Unlike the Canadian resorts closer to the Pacific Ocean, Banff receives a dry, fluffy powder that is the best thing this side of Utah.

And speaking of dry, fluffy powder, as much as we hate to say it, you won't catch first tracks at Sunshine Village and Lake Louise if you rely on the shuttlebuses—unless you wake up *really* early, in time for the first one of the morning. They make a lot of stops along the way before they head out to the resorts.

Sunshine Village Facts

Summit elevation:	8,954 feet
Vertical drop:	3,514 feet
Base elevation:	5,440 feet

Address: Box 1510, Banff, Alberta, Canada T0L 0C0
✆ Area code: 403
Ski area phone: 762-6500
Snow report: 760-7669
ⓘ Toll-free reservations: (877) 542-2633
Fax: 705-4015
Internet: www.skibanff.com
Number of lifts: 12–1 high-speed 8-passenger gondola, 4 high-speed quads, 1 quad, 1 triple chair, 2 double chairs, 3 surface lifts
Snowmaking: None **Skiable acreage:** 3,168
Uphill capacity: 21,300 per hour
Snowboarding: Yes
Nearest lodging: Slopeside, hotel
Resort child care: Yes, 19 months and older
Adult ticket, per day: $59.92 (2001/02, Cdn$)
Expert:★★★★ **Advanced:**★★★★
Intermediate:★★★★
Beginner:★★★★
Never-ever:★★★★

Ski Banff@Norquay Facts

Summit elevation:	7,000 feet
Vertical drop:	1,650 feet
Base elevation:	5,350 feet

Address: P.O. Box 219, Suite 7000, Banff, Alberta, Canada T0L 0C0
✆ Area code: 403
ⓘ Ski area phone: 762-4421
Snow report: 760-7704
Fax: 762-8133
Internet: www.banffnorquay.com
Number of lifts: 5–1 high-speed quad, 2 quad chairs, 1 double chair, 1 surface lift
Snowmaking: 90 percent
Skiable Acreage: 190 acres
Uphill capacity: 7,000 per hour
Snowboarding: Yes
Nearest lodging: Base of access road––ski-in only
Resort child care: Yes, 19 months and older
Adult ticket, per day: $47 (2001/02, Cdn$)
Expert:★★★★
Advanced:★★★★
Intermediate:★★★
Beginner:★★
Never-ever:★★

Tri-Area Lift Passes (2001/02, Cdn$ with GST)

The Banff/Lake Louise Region has an interchangeable lift ticket. It allows unlimited skiing at Sunshine, Ski Banff @ Norquay and Lake Louise and a free shuttle between Banff/Lake Louise hotels and the ski areas. It is available for those skiing at least three days. It also includes a free night-skiing ticket (Fridays only) when used at Ski Banff @ Norquay to make up the price difference.

	Adults	Children (6-12)
Three days	$175	$64
Five days	$292	$107
Seven days	$409	$150

Sunshine Village

Sunshine Village has long been known for its winding gondola ride that carries you almost 1,650 vertical feet from the parking lot—along the walls of a valley and box canyon—to the village base area and the rest of the lifts. That's why what's new for the 2001/02 winter seasons is *big* news. A new high-speed, eight-passenger gondola will whisk you from the parking lot to the mountain village in just about 13 minutes, instead of the previous 20, and you'll now get to Goat's Eye station in about 6 minutes. The amount of people that can be moved out of the base area is almost doubled, which means shorter lift lines too. Even more good news: The gondola loads and unloads at ground level, eliminating the need for stairs.

On the 13-minute ride to the rest of the lifts, you have plenty of time to survey the slopes where the real thrill rides begin. Much of the skiing on Sunshine's three peaks is wide-open, bowl-type skiing, but the bottom half of the slopes are covered in evergreens for those who like their runs cut through trees.

Though a restaurant and rental shop are near the parking lot at the gondola base, the real "base area" for Sunshine is at the top of the gondola at 7,082 feet, where you will find a mountain village with lodge, rental shop, general store, restaurant and the only slopeside lodging in the national parks. (A clarification: The base-elevation stat we list is for the gondola base; this book uses the term "base area" to mean the greatest concentration of shops and services.) From this point a half dozen lifts take off in all directions. Most people never head all the way down until the end of the day, and some not until their vacation ends. It's worth noting that Sunshine has the region's longest ski season, sometimes into June, because it gets up to three times the snowfall that the other Banff ski areas get. If the weather is clear, views across and down the canyon are nearly as breathtaking as the runs.

Mountain layout—Skiing

The 3-mile run at the end of the day on Banff Avenue—from the Village down to the parking lot—is a long, luscious trip for beginners, but it will seem tame for many intermediates. Advanced skiers can play on drops to the left, but they're short and eventually rejoin the trail. An alternative way down is Canyon Trail, which starts out intermediate and turns into a single-black diamond. You catch it near the base of the Jackrabbit Quad.

◆◆ **Expert** ◆ **Advanced:** There's plenty of terrain to explore. If you can't stand the thought of even a 13-minute gondola ride, plus another lift ride before being able to hit the slopes, do what we did. Get off at Goat's Eye station and board Goat's Eye Express, which whisks you to the top of 9,200-foot Goat's Eye Mountain and 1,900 vertical feet of black and double-black routes. There are even a couple of excellent blue cruisers thrown into the mix. At the top it's steep and wide-open until you crest a ridge into the glades, where the runs are cut fairly wide through trees with plenty of pitch. The glades here are lots of fun, make sure to dip in and out of them at will. Experts wanting to test their mettle can try Hell's Kitchen, a tree shot that's only a few shoulders wide at some points and eventually comes out directly under Goat's Eye Express. Any struggles on this gut-sucker will be viewed by the masses.

When you're ready to explore the rest of the resort, from the bottom of Goat's Eye Express, follow the signs down a short dip to Wolverine Express, ski Miss Gratz to Tee Pee Town chair and head up 8,954-foot Lookout Mountain. Advanced skiers searching for some untracked powder should follow the run under Tee Pee Town chair. When you hit the ridge, look to a traverse to your right that takes you to The Shoulder, a hard-to-find open slope known primarily to locals. There are some nice short glades here too.

The runs under Angel Express Quad—especially Ecstasy—have good pitch. At the top, the skiing is wide-open and above treeline, with spectacular views. Those in search of the steep-and-deep will not be disappointed, as the run splits into multiple fingers toward the midway point, some of which are short but quite steep chutes. You'll also find some delightful but short tree shots where Angel Flight, World Cup Downhill and Ecstasy converge, just above the base of Angel Express.

Heading right at the top of Angel Express will take you into a fairly steep bowl. Pick your poison, and shoot down to Continental Divide High-Speed Quad. This lift takes you a soaring 1,450 feet to the almost-summit of Lookout Mountain. At the top you cross the Continental Divide from Alberta to British Colombia. These descents also are wide-open, with moguls on North Divide and powder and open skiing in Bye Bye Bowl, which is convex instead of concave. Make sure to carry your speed to get out of the bowl.

From the top of the Continental Divide Quad skiers can climb a short distance for some truly extreme skiing. First you must rent an avalanche beacon at the base area or you will not be allowed through the control gate. After cresting the knoll of Lookout Mountain, you are rewarded with a gut-churning entrance into Delirium Dive. Be forewarned that the entrance is remarkably steep, though fairly wide. But after the first 30 or 40 yards, Delirium opens up into one of the finest and least skied bowls in the Rockies.

You'll also find interesting terrain to the left off Standish Double Chair, and into Paris Basin and Birdcage off Wawa T-bar.

■ **Intermediate:** There's terrain from every lift for skiers at this ability level; however, be sure you are confident at this ability level if you try the runs on Goat's Eye or the peak of Lookout Mountain. (Think twice if the weather's socked in, too.) If you're ready to try a few blacks, you'll find some short ones off Wolverine Express and JackRabbit Quad, both down-mountain from the other lifts. You can enjoy this area any time of the day, then either ride the gondola to the top from its midstation or take Miss Gratz to Tee Pee Town chair, but most people play here in the afternoon on their way back down.

●● **Beginner:** The Strawberry triple and Wolverine Express have gentle wide slopes good for those still perfecting their technique.

● **Never-ever:** Never-evers learn near the base village, where a tow rope pulls them to the top of a short gentle slope that is off to one side.

 ## Mountain layout—Snowboarding

The Dell Valley is a natural halfpipe near the Strawberry Triple Chair. The triangle formed by the Wawa T-bar and the Standish Chair is a natural terrain park with lots of air, natural hits, a quarterpipe, lips and drops. The boardercross is on Birdcage and the SilverBullet Halfpipe is on Strawberry Face.

If you like to hike for your turns, there are plenty of choices. You'll find lots of awesome cliffs, chutes and gullies, plus wide-open bowls. Start off with hiking up from the tops of Standish Chair, Wawa T-bar and Goat's Eye Express. The marked trails in these areas are also favorites with snowboarders.

Sunshine Village has one serious flat on Lookout Mountain when you're coming out of Bye Bye Bowl or South Divide. You need to *really* carry your speed, and even then, you'll probably have to hoof up the last section, which is actually a little hill that then drops you back into the main area so you can work your way to the lifts. Perhaps this is why so many riders avoid the top part of Lookout Mountain. Other flats and runouts you should be aware of (you'll be fine as long as you're ready for them): The beginning of Banff Avenue as you head out of the Village back toward the base, and the bottom section of Sunshine Coast, where all the runs on Goat's Eye dump you on the way back to the lift.

Mountain rating

Sunshine Village has a much-deserved reputation as a cruiser's mountain. Intermediates and advanced skiers and riders will find the most challenge, though Goat's Eye and Delirium Dive now up the ante for experts. This is a well-balanced mountain with fun for all levels, making it a good choice for families and groups of mixed abilities. There are some flats that make it difficult for snowboarders, but you can avoid most of them and still have enough mountain to play on. Many riders come here for the hike-to terrain.

Lessons (Cdn$ without GST)

Group lessons: $25 per session (2 hours).
Never-ever package: A 2-hour lesson, rentals and lift ticket is $53.
Private lessons: $65 an hour (no charge for an additional person). Multihour discounts are available.

Special programs: Sunshine Village encourages the traditional Ski Week, a week-long stay at the slopeside Sunshine Inn, by providing packages including classes with the same instructor. Groups can be divided by ability level or by family, and include evening activities. Call for prices which vary by season and size of room. Performance Seminars are $30 afternoon clinics that focus on moguls, steeps, powder, video or racing.

Sunshine Village participates in Club Ski and Club Snowboard, a three-day program featuring lessons with the same instructor and group, skiing one day each at three resorts (see *Lessons* in the Lake Louise chapter for details).

Child care (Cdn$ without GST)

Ages: 19 months to 6 years.
Costs: Full day is $23. Half day is $15. Lunch is $5 extra.
Reservations: Recommended; call 762-6560.

Children's lessons: Ages 3–6 just venturing onto the slopes can get a combo ski-and-play program for $51 for the full day (lunch is $5 extra) or $33 for half day. Equipment is included. Kids in that age group who already know how to ski can get a private one-hour lesson for $30, but equipment and lift ticket are extra. Young Devils is for kids ages 6–12 just starting or well on their way. The price is $46 for full day with lunch, $25 half day.

Lift tickets (2001/02, Cdn$ with GST)

	Adult	Child (6-12)
One day	$59.92	$21.40
Three days	$169.87 ($56.62/day)	$64.20 ($21.40/day)
Five days	$272.03 ($54.41/day)	$107 ($21.40/day)

Who skis free: Children ages 5 and younger.
Who skis at a discount: Students ages 13–25 and those 65 and older ski for $49.22. Students need ID to qualify for the discount.
Note: Check out the Tri-Area Pass if you're staying in Banff. It is valid at Sunshine Village, Ski Banff@Norquay and Lake Louise, and includes bus rides from hotels to the ski areas. The bus ride alone is about $15 round-trip between Banff and Sunshine Village, so the Tri-Area Pass can be a good deal even if you use it at Sunshine most of the time.

Ski Banff@Norquay

This small, but challenging, ski area is just a 10-minute drive from Banff and boasts some of the best grooming in Western Canada. It also has some of the gnarliest bump runs we've ever seen. There are virtually no lift lines here, so you can really rack up the vertical. The winding mountain road that takes you up to the base lodge can be fairly intimidating, but the views are incredible as you climb above the townsite of Banff. Be sure to look out for elk, we saw dozens of them. The Cascade Lodge at the base was built in 1996 after the previous lodge burned down. The beautiful log lodge includes an excellent restaurant, a bar, three large stone fireplaces and the other usual services.

Mountain Layout—Skiing

◆◆ **Expert** ◆ **Advanced:** The view of Banff and the Bow Valley from the North American chair is fabulous. This is the lift that takes you to those ribbons of bumps tumbling down the mountainside. Be positively sure you want to be here. This is very tough stuff, with no blue or green ways down. That said, we *must* tell you that these are quite possibly the most fun bump runs in all of skidom. And they are *long*! By the way, look closely at the tea house at the top of the lift—it's built to have avalanches roll right over the top of it.

Lone Pine is the name of that double-black mogul belt that plunges down a 35-percent gradient. There's a daily contest (when the lift is open) called Club 35,000 to see who can make the most consecutive runs in seven hours on this 1,360-foot, skeleton-jarring wall. It takes 26 runs to make the club—many have done it, which says a lot for local physical fitness. Another appeal for the adventure seeker is Valley of the Ten, a narrow drainage perfect for thrills. To get to it, skiers at the top of North American chair drop off (correct terminology) to the left into a drop-out (accurate again) called Gun Run, the steepest thing on the mountain. The easiest way down is Memorial Bowl, and it's still a tough black with monster moguls.

Off the Pathfinder Express, some chutes drop you off into a gully that feeds you back to the lifts. Black Magic and Ka-Poof are screaming cruisers. Like to earn your turns? Look up after you get off the lift, any lift, choose your medicine and start hiking. Just don't go alone and make sure someone knows where you've headed.

■ **Intermediate:** The terrain off the Pathfinder Express Quad, unseen from the base area, is mainly groomed intermediate. The intermediate runs here are pretty steep by most standards, so they're not for the timid, but excellent grooming makes them truly delightful. The mellower terrain is found off the Spirit quad. Start out on Hoodoo and work your way up to the tougher trails. Intermediates wanting to stay in the sun all day have a challenge. At midday none of the Pathfinder trails gets sun except the front two runs, Black Magic and Ka-Poof, which are both blacks.

● **Beginner:** One magic carpet and a short double chair serve three runs at the base. Adult beginners may get bored after a few runs. There's a big jump from beginner terrain to intermediate terrain here.

Mountain Layout—Snowboarding

Ski Banff@Norquay is a big supporter of snowboarding. The terrain park has a halfpipe, quarterpipe, tabletops, gap jumps and more. The park is groomed at least five nights a week, so you'll get the best riding experience they can give you. The park is conveniently located near the base and served by the Cascade Quad Chair; a reduced-rate Cascade lift ticket is available (see *Lift Tickets*).

Many snowboarders hate moguls, and if you're one of them, you won't find much black terrain unless you hike for it. The exceptions are Black Magic and Ka-Poof, off the Pathfinder Express. However, if consider moguls to be a challenge that will only improve your riding skills—and give you some true bragging rights, make a beeline for the bumps off the North American double chair.

The intermediate trails here are groomed to perfection, meaning lots of fun for riders who like to carve arcs or just let it rip. Some of the trails are rolling rides with occasional lips for catching air. You'll find some fun natural hits around the mountain if you look for them. Bruno's Gully is a must-try if it's open.

Mountain rating

Intermediates to experts will find plenty of challenge here, especially since even the blues are far more difficult than those found at most resorts. Excellent grooming on the intermediate runs makes them fun cruisers. If you're a mogul masher or want to improve your bump technique, this is the place to do it. Beginners are better off at Sunshine Village.

Lessons (2001/02, Cdn$ with GST)

Group lessons: $35 for two hours for skiing or snowboarding.
Never-ever package: $49 for a two-hour group lesson, lift ticket on the Cascade chair and rental equipment for skiers or snowboarders. Additional two-hour lesson in the afternoon, $20.

Private lessons: $69 per hour, each additional person $15. Ski Banff@Norquay participates in Club Ski and Club Snowboard, a three-day program of lessons with the same instructor and group, skiing one day each at three resorts (see *Lessons* in the Lake Louise chapter for details).

Child care (2001/02, Cdn$ with GST)

Ages: 19 months to 6 years.
Cost: Full day, without lunch, is $25. Half day, either morning or afternoon, is $18. Add a ski lesson, and costs are $35 and $30, respectively. Lunch, $5.

Reservations: Recommended; call 760-7709.

Children's lessons: Full day is $45; two hours, $30. Lunch is extra. A child's beginner package (lift, two-hour lesson and rentals) is $49.

Lift tickets (2001/02, Cdn$ with GST)

	Adult	Child (6-12)
One day	$47	$16
Noon-4 p.m.	$35	$14
Two hours	$25	$10

Who skis free: Children 5 and younger ski free when an adult buys a lift ticket.

Who skis at a discount: Students ages 13–24 with student ID and seniors 55 and older ski for $37. Ski Banff@Norquay has the region's only night skiing, on Fridays, $23 for adults, $12 for children, $21 for seniors and students with ID. If you only want to use the terrain park, a ticket for the Cascade lift costs $32 for adults, $12 for children, $25 for seniors and students with ID.

Although Ski Banff@Norquay also sells multiday tickets, we've given you the ticket prices we think destination visitors are most likely to use. The area sells hourly tickets for two to five hours, ranging in price from $25 to $41 for adults (discounts for kids, students and seniors). Our recommendation: Use the Tri-Area Lift Pass at Lake Louise and Sunshine Village, and buy a two- or three-hour ticket here. If you want to ski here again after two hours (and you may—it's a fun place, yet small), *then* use a day on your Tri-Area Pass.

Cross-country and snowshoeing

There are some lovely, easy loops **along the Bow River.** Take Banff Avenue to the end of Spray Avenue, or turn left and cross the river. Trails wind through the whole area. **Parks Canada** puts out a very informative booklet on the extensive Nordic skiing and snowshoeing in Banff National Park; you can get a copy for a small fee at the Banff Information Center, 224 Banff Ave., 9 a.m. to 5 p.m.

Fairmont Banff Springs Golf Course Clubhouse offers ski and skate rentals, plus group and private lessons. Maps and information on trails are available at the Clubhouse.

Several sports shops rent snowshoes, ask your lodging concierge. **White Mountain Adventures** (678-4099) is just one of many guide outfits that offers naturalist-guided snowshoe treks, guided backcountry tours and cross-country skiing tours.

Accommodations

Banff has accommodations to meet every taste and every budget. Rooms can be found for as little as $50 (Cdn$), and even the premier locations are within most budgets. In addition to the 7 percent GST, Alberta also has a 5 percent lodging tax, tacking on 12 percent to your cost.

The Sunshine Inn (762-6500; 800-661-1676; $$–$$$), at 7,200 feet in the center of Sunshine's base village, is the only slopeside lodging in Banff National Park. It's reached by riding the gondola up from the parking lot. All nightly rates include lift tickets; the hotel also runs a Ski Week program. Rooms are neat and simple. There's a giant outdoor hot tub where you and 19 others can relax while watching skiers whiz down the mountain. There's also a sauna, massage and chiropractic services, a family and game room, and an exercise room.

Ski Banff@Norquay now owns the cozy, spiffed-up, 1960s-era **Timberline Inn** (762-2281; www.banfftimberline.com; $–$$$$) at the bottom of its access road. Technically it's Banff's only ski-in hotel. You can ski in along a 1.5-kilometer trail, but you'll need the inn's shuttle to take you to the lifts. The shuttle also will run guests into town in the evening. Rates include Norquay lift tickets and are lower for triples and quads; higher for single travelers. You'll enjoy a good meal here at the Big Horn Steakhouse.

Other lodging is in Banff. We strongly recommend the experience of staying at the **Fairmont Banff Springs Hotel** (800-441-1414 in the U.S. and Canada, 762-2211; $$$–$$$$), the wine-colored, Scottish-influenced castle perched on a small hill, a short walk from downtown. You have seen this classic, rundle-rock monolith in many photos with its pointed, green-copper roofs rising from the nine-story walls, framed by evergreens and craggy peaks. Its public areas are expansive, designed for turn-of-the-century mingling—we're talking a ballroom for 16,000. Rates during the winter are a bargain compared to summer. The hotel has a full-service spa. Ski-lodging packages and ski-and-spa packages available. **Banff Park Lodge and Conference Center** (800-661-9266; 762-4433; $$$–$$$$) is an expanse of cedar buildings in a wooded area two blocks from downtown. It hosts many cultural activities.

Families will most definitely want to stay at the **Douglas Fir Resort and Chalets** (800-661-9267; 762-5591; Calgary direct, 264-2563; $$–$$$$). There are condo-style units with wood-burning fireplaces and full kitchens, two- and three-bedroom chalets, and a few suites. We nearly had to drag the kids off the two indoor waterslides here because they couldn't get enough of them. We're not talking little-dinky kiddy slides, we're talking huge, winding, fast waterslides like you would normally find at an outdoor water park. So we were forced to sit in the steam room, or the hot tub, or the wade pool at the bottom of the slides, watching them whoop it up. And a few times we even played on the waterslides ourselves. The waterslide area is open to the public for a cost, but it's free for hotel guests. In a separate area, for guests only, you'll find an indoor swimming pool, hot tub and saunas. There are also a coin laundry and a convenience store on site.

The **Mount Royal Hotel** (800-267-3035 Western Canada only; 762-3331; $$–$$$$) has a great location in downtown Banff, an excellent choice for those who enjoy nightlife. It gets a fair amount of street noise from Banff Avenue but has an exceptionally good restaurant. **The Inns of Banff** (800-661-1272; 762-4581; $$–$$$$) a modern, multi-level lodge with balconies in most rooms, is a 15-minute walk from downtown. **High Country Inn** (800-661-1244; 762-2236; $$–$$$) on Banff Avenue is one of the least expensive.

Banff International Hostel (762-4122; $) on Tunnel Mountain Road just added a 66-bed wing with two- and four-bed rooms with private bathrooms. Showers are shared. Facilities include a laundry, kitchen and cafe.

For lodging, contact **Banff/Lake Louise Central Reservations** (800-661-1676), a reservations service that books lodging and ski packages in Banff, Lake Louise and Jasper.

Dining

For those staying at Sunshine Village, the **Eagle's Nest Dining Room** ($$) in the Sunshine Inn offers fine dining with lobster and filet mignon. **The Chimney Corner Lounge** ($-$$), the inn's fireplace lounge, serves a very good sit-down lunch. Try the barbecue beef and a local-brewed ale. Ask to sit in the sunroom so you can watch the skiers and riders on Lookout Mountain. The **Creekside Restaurant** ($) at the base of the gondola serves a hearty breakfast, or choose a la carte. Like a flavored cappuccino? If you ask, they'll make one for you. Take time to wander around the restaurant to look at pictures from Sunshine's past, during the early glamorous days of skiing, as well as Native American relics and antique outdoor winter gear.

On-mountain at Ski Banff@Norquay, the food is excellent and affordable in the **Lone Pine Pub** ($), upstairs in the main lodge with gorgeous views. Try the lemon pepper salmon burger, the Alberta wild mushroom and bison stew, or the chicken souvlaki wrapped in a pita. The children's menu (ages 12 and younger) is $5.50 for your choice of pb&j, grilled cheese, chicken fingers, cheese burger or hot dog.

The Big Horn Steak House (762-2281; $$) in the Timberline Inn offers a cozy atmosphere with a spectacular view of the Valley and the Fairmont Banff Springs Hotel. The menu has a varied selection of pastas, fish and top-grade Alberta beef.

In the townsite of Banff, diners have a tremendous variety and number of restaurants from which to choose. You'll find almost every variety of ethnic food, as well as the familiar steak-and-seafood restaurants. Restaurants, especially those on Banff Avenue, often are on the second floor above the shops. Sometimes the entrances are obvious, sometimes not.

The Fairmont Banff Springs Hotel alone has 11 restaurants, including **The Samurai** (762-6860; $$–$$$), which serves Japanese cuisine. **Castello Ristorante** (762-6860; $$) serves

Italian dinners, while the **Bow Valley Grill** (762-2211, ext. 6841; $$–$$$) offers buffet or a la carte seafood and rotisserie-grilled meats. **Waldhaus** (762-6860; $$) serves fondue and other German, Austrian and Swiss fare at long tables that seat a dozen people. **Grapes** (762-2211, Ext. 6660; $$) is the 26-seat wine bar, but it also serves light meals. **Solace** (762-1772; $$), at the hotel spa, serves healthy, low-fat fare.

Le Beaujolais (on Banff Avenue at Buffalo Street, 762-2712; $$$) receives high praise for its French cuisine. Meals can be ordered à la carte, but the restaurant specializes in fixed-price three- or five-course meals. You are likely to see diners in coats and ties, though neither is required. **The Bistro** (on the corner of Wolf and Bear streets, 762-8900; $$) is owned by the same restaurateurs but is considerably more casual and cozy. It serves a variety of pastas and salads, as well as meat and poultry. Open for lunch and dinner.

Chef Werner Zullig from Ticino's has teamed up with Swiss Chef Mario Thom to create Canadian-themed fine dining at the **Pines** (537 Banff Ave., 760-6690; $$$) in Rundlestone Lodge. Creative contemporary food combined with beautiful presentation—such as a baked rack of venison with lemon pepper pears, sweet and sour red cabbage and blueberry spaetzli— is served in an atmosphere of rustic elegance. Don't miss the opportunity to eat at one of Banff's finest restaurants.

The dining room at **Buffalo Mountain Lodge** (Tunnel Mountain Road, 762-2400; $$$) offers relaxed elegance with hand-hewn beam construction and a massive fieldstone fireplace. Rocky Mountain Cuisine is their specialty, with a variety of wild game and fish. The wine list was awarded Wine Spectator's "Award of Excellence" several years in a row.

For gourmet Italian, you can try **Giorgio's Trattoria** (219 Banff Ave. 762-5114; $$), which serves Northern Italian pastas and pizzas, or **Guido's** (116 Banff Ave. above McDonald's, 762-4002; $$) for American Italian food, such as spaghetti, lasagna and chicken parmigiana. **Ticino** (415 Banff Ave., 762-3848; $$–$$$) specializes in dishes from the Italian part of Switzerland.

Bumper's The Beef House (762-2622; $$–$$$), with a cozy log interior, has been serving Alberta beef since 1975. We had melt-in-your-mouth prime rib (which comes in four cuts). Watch out, the horseradish sauce is very hot! Use it sparingly. The chicken cafoosalum has a very tasty maple sugar-lime sauce. Meals come with a good salad bar; try the mango jalapeno salad dressing or the creamy cuke. If you save room for dessert, order a large nut sundae and serve three people. There's a good kids' menu, plus they'll take most adult choices and make a smaller portion for children aged 12 and under.

Coyotes Deli & Grill (206 Caribou St., 762-3963; $–$$) serves breakfast, lunch and dinner at reasonable prices, with Southwestern, vegetarian and pasta dishes on the menu (also fresh-squeezed juices). **Grizzly House** (207 Banff Ave., 762-4055; $$–$$$) specializes in fondue and steaks as well as beef and wild game. **Earl's** (229 Banff Ave. at Wolf Street, 762-4414; $$) gets rave reviews for moderately priced Canadian beefsteak, fresh salmon, pasta and thin-crust pizza.

Aardvark Pizza & Sub (762-5500; $–$$), "the locals' choice in homemade pizza for over a decade," makes a great thick-crust pizza. We thought the kids were going to pass out with delight. The buffalo wings are tasty too; choose mild, medium, hot or suicide (mild is accurate). Open 11 a.m.-4 a.m. Free delivery; money-back guarantee if you're not satisfied.

One of the most fun places to eat is **Joe Btfsplk's Diner** (221 Banff Ave. 762-5529; $). Set in a 1950s-style diner decor complete with jukebox and Elvis posters, this restaurant serves huge portions. For gourmet coffees, huge gourmet sandwiches and light snacks, try **Evelyn's Coffee Bar** on Banff Avenue and **Evelyn's Too** on Bear Street. **Fine Grind** on

Banff Avenue and **Jump Start Coffee and Sandwich Place** on Buffalo Street also serve gourmet coffees and light snacks.

Après-ski/nightlife

Après-ski is more quiet than rip-roaring in Banff, but things really start hopping at night. Younger crowds probably will enjoy Banff nightspots, while older skiers might be happier at the Fairmont Banff Springs Hotel's many bars and lounges. The Happy Bus shuttles skiers to nightspots around Banff until midnight for $1, or you can walk between most lodging and town.

Après-ski, head to the bar at the **Mt. Royal Hotel.** Crowds also gather at the **Rose and Crown,** an English-style pub with draught ale, a fireplace, pool table, darts and live entertainment. **St. James Gate,** built in Dublin and assembled in Banff, is a traditional Irish pub with 33 draught beers and more than 65 single malt scotches.

At night, **Bumper's Loft Lounge** has a casual crowd, with live entertainment and ski movies. **Wild Bill's Legendary Saloon** on Banff Avenue has Country & Western bands and a huge dance floor. Locals flock to **Barbary Coast** on Banff Avenue for what is repeatedly hailed as the best live music, usually along the rock/blues lines. **Magpie & Stump** serves up great nachos and some of Banff's best après-ski. **Out'a Bounds** on Banff Avenue (but the entrance is on Caribou Street), with DJ dancing and occasional live bands, attracts 20-somethings. **Aurora,** in the basement of the Clocktower Mall, features a lounge, cigar bar and dance floor with DJs and bands. In the Fairmont Banff Springs Hotel, the **Rundle Lounge** has quiet music for hotel guests. At the **Waldhaus** by the Fairmont Banff Springs Golf Course, Happy Hans and Lauren, on accordion and trumpet, get everybody singing.

Other activities

Banff has so much to do, we can only begin to do it justice. We can't imagine anyone coming here and not finding the time to explore the natural beauty of the region and to view the abundant wildlife. Just a few of the ways to do that: Go **dogsledding** (Mountain Mushers, 762-3647) or **ice fishing** (Fishing Unlimited, 762-4936); take a **sleigh ride** (Warner Guiding and Outfitting, 762-4551); join a group for a **canyon icewalk** (White Mountain Adventures, 678-4099); or take an introductory course in **ice climbing** or **ski mountaineering** (Yamnuska; 678-4164).

One of the most famous **heli-skiing** companies, Canadian Mountain Holidays, is headquartered here (762-7100). You also can go **helicopter sightseeing** with Alpine Helicopters (678-4802) to view the magnificent mountain peaks. On a clear day, take the **Sulphur Mountain Gondola** (762-2523) for a beautiful vista of the Bow Valley.

If you aren't staying at the Douglas Fir Resort & Chalets (762-5591), you can still use their **two giant indoor waterslides, kiddy pool, hot tub, steam room, fitness room, arcade and pool tables** (see *Accommodations*). This is a great way to meet other families and for your kids to make new friends on vacation. Cost is Cdn$7.50 per person for non-guests of the hotel; kids 5 and younger free. **Banff Upper Hot Springs** (762-1515) is a wonderful way to wind down after a day on the slopes. Natural hot mineral waters fill a huge outdoor pool, and you're surrounded by beautiful mountain scenery. $5 for adults, $4 for children and seniors. Winter hours are 10 a.m.-10 p.m., Friday and Saturday until 11 p.m. Restaurant and gift shop on site. There's also a full-service spa here (760-2500 for spa reservations).

You should also find time to visit **Banff Park Museum** for the story of early tourism and wildlife management, and a taxidermy collection of animals indigenous to the Park; **Cave &**

Basin National Historic Site, where the hot springs were first discovered; **Whyte Museum of the Canadian Rockies,** for historic and contemporary art and historic homes; the **Buffalo Nations Luxton Museum,** for Plains Indians history; and the **Natural History Museum** for local geology.

Shopping here is almost an athletic activity, with hundreds of shops lining Banff Avenue and its side streets. Most are clustered in little malls where you can enter the shop from the inside on crummy days, or from the outside in good weather. Worth a drop-in: The Hudson's Bay Company, a department store famed for its blankets (and Canada's oldest company, founded in 1670); and Roots Canada, for fine leather-and-cloth backpacks and handbags, and casual clothing. For non-kitschy souvenirs: Orca Canada or Great Northern Trading Company (clothing, jewelry, knickknacks), Rocks and Gems (inexpensive jewelry made from native Canadian gemstones) or A Taste of the Rockies (smoked salmon, jams and honeys). The Fairmont Banff Springs Hotel has 18 specialty and boutique shops, featuring designer jewelry, gourmet kitchen accessories, toys and clothing. Our favorite here is the Canadian Pacific Store, with items that reflect the bygone elegance of luxury train travel.

Getting there and getting around

By air: Calgary Airport is served by major airlines, including Air Canada. Rocky Mountain Sky Shuttle (888-762-8754), Brewster Transportation (762-6700) or Laidlaw Transportation (762-9102) will get you from the airport to Banff.

By car: Banff is 85 miles west of Calgary on the Trans-Canada Highway, an hour-and-a-half drive. Ski Banff@Norquay is on Norquay Road, one exit past the Banff townsite. The Sunshine Village exit is 5 miles west of Banff; it's 5 more miles to the gondola base parking area. Free shuttles pick up skiers at 11 Banff hotels and the bus depot.

Getting around: It is possible to ski Banff and Lake Louise without a rental car by using free shuttlebuses to the ski areas or Happy Bus (evenings only, $1 a ride) within the town and region. Taxis are available, too, but that can add up quickly. For exploring, it's best to have a car.

Lake Louise Ski Area

Banff Region,
Canada

Summit elevation: 8,650 feet
Vertical drop: 3,250 feet
Base elevation: 5,400 feet

Address: P.O. Box 5, Lake Louise
Alberta, Canada T0L 1E0
☎ **Area code:** 403
Ski area phone: 522-3555
Snow report: 762-4766 (Banff)
ⓘ **Toll-free reservations:** (800) 258-7669
Fax: 522-2095
E-mail: vertical@skilouise.com
Internet: www.skilouise.com
Expert:★★★★
Advanced:★★★★
Intermediate:★★★★
Beginner:★★★★
Never-ever:★★★★

Number and types of lifts: 12—4 high-speed
quads, 1 quad, 1 triple, 2 doubles, 4 surface lifts
Skiable acreage: 4,200
Snowmaking: 40 percent
Uphill capacity: 16,400 per hour
Snowboarding: Yes
Bed base: 2,500 within 10 minutes
Nearest lodging: About 2 miles away
Resort child care: Yes, 3 weeks and older
Adult ticket, per day: $55-$59 (2001/02; CdnS)

Dining:★★★
Apres-ski/nightlife:★★
Other activities: ★★★★★ (includes region)

Lake Louise is Canada's second-largest ski area, behind Whistler Blackcomb in British Columbia, and is the third resort in Banff National Park. It's difficult to say what makes it more memorable: its colossal size with incredible terrain diversity or the truly jaw-dropping scenery. One visit is usually all it takes for Lake Louise to make virtually *everyone's* top 10 list of mountain resorts. Lake Louise is a great place to come for a taste of truly steep terrain. Warm-up on Lake Louise's Front Side and then tackle the Back Bowls.

The 36,000-square-foot Lodge of the Ten Peaks, and the corresponding remodeling of the original base lodge, has transformed the mountain's facilities. This massive, split-beam log building is one of the most handsome in the Rockies: Think of a log cabin built by Paul Bunyan. The lodge is constructed of some 2,500 fir, pine and spruce logs, most of them thinned from the Ptarmigan slope to open glade skiing and riding.

More and more U.S. skiers are discovering this resort and the phenomenal value that Canada offers the skier. The British have long known about Lake Louise. More British ski here than any other North American resort.

 ## Mountain layout—Skiing

Lake Louise is comprised of four mountain faces that create three distinct areas: the Front Face, the Back Bowls and the Larch Area. The Lake Louise trail map has an excellent synopsis of where different ability levels should head, so be sure to grab one. If you want sun all day and want to ski the whole area, go to the Back Bowls in the morning, Larch midday and end up on the Front Face. Take a free tour by the Ski Friends, a volunteer group, daily starting at Whiskyjack Lodge.

◆◆ **Expert** ◆ **Advanced:** On the Front Side, expert and advanced skiers can give the Men's Downhill or Ladies' Downhill a try to get an idea of what the big boys and girls ski when Lake Louise hosts World Cup races in early December. Plenty of runs directly below the Eagle Chair, Top of the World Express and especially the Summit Platter have excellent pitch and grade, as evidenced by the liberal smattering of black diamonds on the trail map. Grizzly Bowl, just off the Olympic Chair, has three or four different fall lines, trees and bumps all in one descent. It's a great last run of the day as you return from the back side.

The Summit Platter can become an expert challenge all by itself. The Platter used to be a T-bar until the folks at Lake Louise decided the steepness demanded concentration, not conversation. Whatever you do, don't skip Brown Shirt, it holds freshies for a week. It's totally worth working your way to skier's left a bit, toward the area's boundary. Be forewarned that while the top entrances to Shoulder Roll, Ridge Run and Whitehorn look relatively mild, things get steep very fast once you crest a ridge in the middle of the run. At that point, however, it's too late to turn back. Bonzai! The resort's steepest chutes, the Whitehorn 2 gullies, are off this lift too; they're not for the weak of heart and helmets are recommended.

After Whitehorn 2, probably the next-most-hair-raising area of the mountain is Diamond Mine, accessed off the Paradise Chair (you can't get here from the Summit Platter). The special attractions here include cornices and some of the steepest chutes in the area. Cornice-hoppers should go to the headwalls at the ER3 and ER7 gullies. Parachutes optional. You'll find some sweet, and often untouched, single-diamond terrain if you drop off Saddleback just before or after the intersection with Pika Connector.

You will also want to sample the double- and single-black diamonds under the Ptarmigan Chair. These tend to be steep, long and full of moguls. Bark-eaters should aim for the Fall Line Glades, a slew of glades to the right of Ptarmigan Chair. Awesome!

In the Larch area, there's great tree skiing directly under the lift between Larch and Bobcat runs. From the top of the Larch Chair, you'll see that some powder freaks have hiked up to the 8,900-foot summit to leave tracks down Elevator Shaft, between two rock outcroppings. The chute is within the ski area boundaries.

For a more modest thrill in a less traveled area, exit left off Larch Chair, then stay right and high on a gladed traverse until you find a deep powder bowl under Elevator Shaft. Called Rock Garden, it's a hidden playground of loops, swoops, moguls and Cadillac-sized rocks. You'll find bump thrills on Lynx.

■ **Intermediate:** On the Front Face, don't miss Meadowlark or Wapta, reached by the Eagle Chair; or Homerun and Gully, reached from Top of the World. The Front Face has a good web of intermediate trails served by Olympic, Glacier and Friendly Giant. Though lore holds that intermediates shouldn't take the Summit lift except to cross to the other side, don't believe it. There are some great Front Face drops down Skyline to Sunset Terrace and then back to the lifts. This run gives intermediates plenty of opportunities to dip into the ungroomed stuff and come back to safety.

Intermediates can reach the Back Bowls via the Top of the World quad or the Summit Platter, which will take you a little higher on the back side to a run called Boomerang, an immensely fun cruiser that seems to go on forever.

If the weather is socked in, however, skip Boomerang. The Larch Area has the best intermediate skiing, access by a high-speed quad. Wolverine, Larch and Bobcat are all long cruisers. And there are tons of trees in the Larch area that are perfect for any intermediate. Lynx has a black-diamond moniker, but can be handled by most intermediates. It's a gas.

●● **Beginner** ● **Never-ever:** Those with a little experience can ride the Friendly Giant quad chair and head down Wiwaxy, a 2.5-mile cruiser. Next step is Eagle Chair to try Deer Run and Eagle Meadows. If you're getting pretty confident and would like to try the Back Bowls, ride the Eagle Chair and take Pika down the back. You also can descend from the Top of the World quad on Saddleback, a cat track that can be a bit intimidating, especially if the snow's iffy. Definitely don't try Saddleback on a low-visibility day, there are no trees to guide you, and you must negotiate a couple of narrow spots. Beginners have a couple of nice runs in the Larch area, Marmot and Lookout. First-timers enrolled in lessons will start on the Sunny T-Bar, which serves an excellent beginner area separated from everything else.

Mountain layout—Snowboarding

Lake Louise gets huge kudos for its terrain park and halfpipe. The resort has built what it claims is the largest terrain park in North America—the Jungle. It features 2,000 feet of vertical drop with tabletops, big air jumps, halfpipes and a superpipe.

The Summit Platter is a Poma lift that's an expert challenge all by itself for snowboarders (and on windy or icy days, yikes!). If you can get over the trials and tribulations of riding the Platter—and you *really* should—there are some great hikes off the top to your left. Want guaranteed freshies? Head to the Back Bowls and stay far left to Brown Shirt, which holds snow for at least a week after a dump. It's worth it to work your way over to it. While you're over there, hike to Upper Boomerang, North Cornice and Wild Gully. The runout from the Back Bowls is kind of a drag, but it does have some pitch to it so just carry your speed and you'll be fine. For trees, head to Ptarmigan Chair and the Fall Line Glades, a slew of sweet tree runs that hold snow when you can't find it anywhere else. Off Larch Chair, hike in whichever direction draws you, you can't go wrong.

Carvers will find fresh cord on groomed runs for ripping arcs. Try Meadowlark, Home Run and Gully on the Front Side, and Larch and Bobcat in the Larch Area. There's nice beginner terrain on the Front Side and in the Larch Area. First-timers enrolled in lessons will start on the Sunny T-Bar, which serves an excellent beginner area separated from the rest of the runs. Too bad it's a T-Bar, a nightmare for snowboarders.

Mountain rating

All abilities have terrain suited to their skill level from all lifts except the Summit Platter. This makes it nice for families and groups of varying levels who want to ride together on the lifts. This is an excellent mountain for skiers and riders who want to improve to the next level. You'll need at least a week to explore the mountain and discover all the fun stashes.

Cross-country and snowshoeing

The **Fairmont Chateau Lake Louise** (522-3511) has about 150 km. of groomed trails and access to hundreds of miles of backcountry trails, with stunning views of the lake and mountains. The ungroomed, well-marked trail to Skoki Lodge, a rustic log cabin (meaning no electricity, no plumbing, wood-burning stove), begins just above Temple Lodge at the ski area and heads up the valley and over Boulder Pass, 7 miles one way. If you're not up for skiing so far into the wilderness, follow the gentle Shoreline Trail starting in front of the Fairmont Chateau Lake Louise, an easy mile and a half one way. Skiing *on* Lake Louise is not recommended.

A complex 20-km. network called **Pipestone Loops** starts 4 miles west of the Lake Louise Overpass on the Trans-Canada Highway. Although all are marked beginner, some are suitable for the intermediate. About 25 miles from Lake Louise, just over the border into British Columbia, is **Emerald Lake Lodge** (343-6321 or 800-663-6336). It has a 40-km. network of groomed trails with views of the Presidential Range, lodging in comfortable cabins and activities such as skating, snowshoeing and a games room. The lodge has a shuttle to the Lake Louise ski area.

Before setting out on any of the trails, check trail conditions at a park warden's office. Be aware that trail classification is done by healthy Canadians in good shape.

Lessons (2001/02; Cdn$ with GST)

Group lessons: $32 for 1.75 hours for skiers or snowboarders.
Never-ever package: $42 includes a 1.75-hour lesson, equipment rental and beginner lift ticket for skiers or snowboarders.

Private lessons: For skiers and snowboarders, $69 per hour, reduced to $49 if taken after 3 p.m.; extra skiers/snowboarders, $16 each.

Special programs: Lake Louise has a lot of special clinics, some two hours long, others several days long. Clinics cover bumps, freeride and freeskiing, style and technique, women's camps and more. The Club Ski program and Club Snowboard program operates at Lake Louise, Sunshine Village and Ski Banff @ Norquay. Groups of similar interest and expertise ski or ride together with the same instructor for four hours a day at each of the three areas, then dine at an optional closing-night dinner with prizes. The program starts Mondays and Thursdays, and one benefit is lift-line priority. The three-day program costs $169 (price includes GST, but not lift tickets or rentals).

Racing: There is a dual-slalom NASTAR course on Wiwaxy that is $5 for two runs.

Child care (2001/02; Cdn$)

Ages: 3 weeks to 6 years. Toddlers have their own play area.
Costs: Babies' care (younger than 19 months) is $25 per day or $4 per hour. Toddler care (19 months–3 years) is $4 per hour. Day care for kids ages 3–6 costs $3.50 per hour, with three-hour minimums. Hot lunch included.

Reservations: Infants younger than 19 months require reservations. Reservations are recommended for other ages. Call 522-3555.

Children's lessons: The Kinderski program, ages 3–4, provides supervised day care, one ski lesson and indoor and outdoor play at the beginning and end of the day. Cost is $36, or $46 for two one-hour lessons. In the Kids Ski program, children ages 5–12 are guided around the mountain with instruction along the way, $52 for a full day. The program includes a lift ticket. Optional lunch is $7. Children's snowboard lessons are for ages 7–12. The cost is $49 full day, lift ticket included. Rentals are an extra $11.

Lift tickets (2001/02; Cdn$ with GST)

	Adult	Child (6-12)
One day	$59	$15
Three days	$165 ($55/day)	$45 ($15/day)
Five days	$275 ($55/day)	$75 ($15/day)

Who skis free: Children younger than 6.

Who skis at a discount: Students ages 13–24 with student ID and ages 65 or older pay $47 per day. Skiers and boarders interested in visiting other Banff ski areas should buy the Tri-Area Pass (see Banff Region chapter for details).

Accommodations

Banff/Lake Louise Central Reservations (800-661-1676) books lodging and ski packages in Banff, Lake Louise and Jasper. **Resorts of the Rockies** (800-258-7669), which owns Lake Louise, books ski packages and lodging for these Western Canada resorts: Lake Louise, Nakiska, Fortress, Wintergreen, Fernie and Kimberley. You also can book online at www.skilouise.com.

The **Fairmont Chateau Lake Louise** (800-441-1414; 522-3511; $$$–$$$$) nests on the shore of Lake Louise, with the spectacular Victoria Glacier in the distance. This hotel dates back to a log chalet built in 1890. It has nearly 500 guestrooms, restaurants, shops, Nordic ski center, masseuse and free ski shuttles.

The **Post Hotel** (800-661-1586; 522-3989; $$$–$$$$) is a cozy, beautifully furnished, 93-room log lodge with great views on all sides and fireplaces in 38 of the rooms, two of which are lovely riverside cabins with heated slate floors. It's personal and quiet, with the warmth and elegance provided by Swiss innkeepers. The buffet breakfast is a board of tasty delights. There is a free ski shuttle. **Lake Louise Inn** (800-661-9237; 522-3791; $$–$$$$) is a simply decorated hotel that's good for families. Rooms range in size from economy double (2 double beds) to superior lofts that sleep six. Amenities include heated indoor pool, whirlpool, steam room and arcade room.

Deer Lodge (800-661-1595; 522-3747; $$–$$$) is the Fairmont Chateau's antithesis, though they are located quite close to each other. Deer Lodge has no television, for example, but it has a great rooftop hot tub. It's old and rustic, but well kept up.

The **Canadian Alpine Centre & International Hostel** (522-2200; $), on Village Road, is a very modern facility with two-, four- and six-bed rooms with private bathrooms and showers, laundry, kitchen and cafe. Nightly bed rates start at less than $20.

Dining

For breakfast on the mountain, the **Northface Restaurant** ($) in the Whiskeyjack Lodge serves a yummy and affordable breakfast buffet (however, beverages are extra which took us by surprise). On-mountain lunch options are the **Powder Keg** ($$) with nachos, sandwiches and pizza; the **Sitzmark** ($$), with more substantial fare like burgers and salads; the **Northface Dining Room**, with very affordable hot and cold luncheon buffets; and **Sawyer's Nook Restaurant** ($$) in Temple Lodge, known for its prime rib buffet.

By far, the most enjoyable time we've ever had dining on a mountain is at the **Lake Louise Torchlight Dinner & Ski,** held at the mid-mountain Whitehorn Lodge on Mondays and Fridays (522-3555; reservations required). Tables seat eight, which means everyone has to meet everyone else, because you're reaching across each other to grab appetizers of chicken-fried steak strips, mushrooms in pastry, and fried corn tortillas stuffed with spiced jalapeño cream cheese. Some couples are dancing while the band members leap around the room, jumping up on tables and falling to their knees as they sing the blues. Unfortunately, the fun has to end sometime. But not before you strap on a headlamp and follow a guide carrying a torchlight down the mountain, where buses take you back to your lodging. Cost is $49 per adult, $25 per child (Cdn$).

On Saturday evenings, the **Brewster Cowboy's Barbecue & Dance Barn** (800-691-5085; 762-5454) near the Fairmont Chateau provides hearty cowboy food and Western entertainment from mid-December to early April. It includes a sleigh ride to the barn.

For dinner in the **Fairmont Chateau Lake Louise** (522-3511 for reservations at all its restaurants), the most elegant dining room is the **Edelweiss** ($$$), serving such entrées as salmon and duckling. The **Walliser Stube Wine Bar** ($$–$$$) specializes in Swiss cuisine such as raclette and fondue. The **Poppy Room** is a family restaurant, the only one open for breakfast in winter, aside from the 24-hour deli. **Glacier Saloon** ($$) has steak sandwiches, finger food and salads.

The **Post Hotel** (522-3989; $$$) is recognized as serving the finest Continental cuisine in Lake Louise. For a special occasion, this is a wonderful place. **Deer Lodge** (522-3747; $$$) has homemade breads as well as innovative specials and pastries. **Lake Louise Station** (522-2600; $$–$$$) is a restored railway station with views of the mountains and freight trains that rumble past. The menu is quite extensive, with pastas, lamb, Alberta steaks and fresh salmon, among other dishes. Couples might like a table in the Killarney car, which was the private railroad car of a Canadian Railroad president.

Lake Louise Inn (522-3791) has three dining locations: The **Timberwolf** for pizza and pasta, the **hotel dining room** for lunch and dinner, and the **Explorer's Lounge**.

 ## Après-ski/nightlife

The **Sitzmark Lounge** is the après-ski spot at the mountain. It's in the Whiskeyjack Lodge and has live entertainment on weekends. On sunny spring days, hang out on the deck of the **Glacier Gazebo** near the base lifts.

Après-ski and nightlife in town center in the hotels. At the Fairmont Chateau Lake Louise, The **Glacier Saloon** has a lively atmosphere and dancing, while the **Walliser Stube** is serene. Quiet conversation is possible at the **Saddleback Lounge** in the Lake Louise Inn and the Post Hotel's **Outpost**.

 ## Other activities

The Banff/Lake Louise area has many opportunities for other winter sports such as **skating, ice fishing** and **ice climbing,** as well as **sightseeing, hot springs** and **museums;** see the Banff chapter for phone numbers.

 ## Getting there and getting around

By air: Calgary Airport is served by major airlines, including Air Canada. Rocky Mountain Sky Shuttle (888-762-8754; 762-5200), Brewster Transportation (762-6700) or Laidlaw Transportation (762-9102) will get you from the airport to Banff or Lake Louise.

By car: Lake Louise Village is 115 miles west of Calgary and 36 miles from Banff.

Getting around: Bus service is available from the airport to most hotels. The Lake Louise shuttlebus is free and operates from most hotels to the resort. Buy the Tri-Area ski pass and bus transportation is included. We really recommend a car for extensive sightseeing.

Dining: $$$-Entrees $20+; $$-$10-20; $-less than $10.
Accommodations: (double room) $$$$-$200+; $$$-$141-$200; $$-$81-$140; $-$80 and less.

Marmot Basin

Jasper, Alberta
Canada

Summit elevation: 8,534 feet
Vertical drop: 2,944 feet
Base elevation: 5,590 feet

Address: P.O. Box1300
Jasper, AB, Canada T0E 1E0
☎ **Area code:** 780
Ski area phone: 852-3816
Snow report: 488-5909 (Edmonton)
Fax: 852-3533
ⓘ **Toll-free reservations:** No central system
E-mail: info@skimarmot.com
Internet: www.skimarmot.com
www.discoverjasper.com
Expert:★★★★
Advanced:★★★★
Intermediate:★★★
Beginner:★★★
Never-ever:★★★

Number and types of lifts: 8–1 high-speed
quad, 1 quad, 1 triple chair, 3 double chairs,
2 surface lifts.
Skiable acreage: 1,000 acres
Snowmaking: 1 percent
Uphill capacity: 11,931 skiers per hour
Snowboarding: Yes
Bed base: 5,500
Nearest lodging: About 11 miles away in Jasper
Resort child care: Yes, 19 months and older
Adult ticket, per day: $44–$49 (01/02)

Dining:★★★
Apres-ski/nightlife:★★★
Other activities:★★★★

Far into the northland and separated from the hustle of Banff by a three-hour drive, Jasper is far enough north, and far enough from a major airport (Edmonton: three hours), that people aren't here by mistake or on a whim. They come for the scenery, the remoteness, the wonder of a herd of elk outside their hotel and the call of Canadian geese swooping over Lac Beauvert in the spring while the ski area still has winter snow.

The largest of the Canadian Rockies National Parks, Jasper has 4,200 square miles studded with lakes, dotted with wildlife, threaded by cross-country trails, and embroidered with spectacular drives such as the Icefields Parkway. Overloaded with tourists in the summer, it's delightfully uncrowded in the winter. You won't want to forget your camera for this vacation!

The townsite (local-speak for "town") of Jasper sprang up from a tent city in 1911, when the Grand Trunk Pacific Railway was laying steel up the Athabasca River Valley toward Yellowhead Pass, and its growth was rather helter-skelter. Hugging the Athabasca River and nestled against the train station, the town is relatively simple and nondescript, consisting of clapboard cottages, a steepled Lutheran church, stone houses and lodgings with no single architectural scheme. Here you'll find a friendly, relaxed and homey atmosphere. The townsite and its winter resort, Marmot Basin, are far less slick than the Banff resorts—the Alta to Deer Valley or the Mad River Glen to Stowe Mountain Resort.

Marmot Basin's base lodge, Caribou Chalet, is a beautiful 32,000-square-foot building that blends in with its surroundings. It houses a number of services including tickets, the ski and snowboard school, dining and restaurant facilities, the Marmot Shop, the nursery, guest services and the rental and repair shop.

Marmot's big news for 2001/02 is the development of Eagle Ridge, which was previously accessed only by hiking to earn your turns. There are two faces on Eagle Ridge: Eagle East and Chalet Slope. The 20 new runs off the ridge include expert, advanced and intermediate terrain, as well as one novice trail that winds its way down the mountain, adding a total of about 148 acres.

Mountain layout—Skiing

The area's one high-speed quad, Eagle Express, serves as the primary chair to the upper-mountain lifts. It can get somewhat crowded sometimes, so don't come back to the base during peak loading times, such as mornings before 9:30. Instead, try Caribou Chair on the lower mountain, far to the right, where there's rarely a wait. It has terrain for all abilities and also will get you to the upper-mountain lifts. You can purchase lift tickets here on the weekend. To reach it, drive past the main lodge and head for the farthest parking lot. Or park in any of the lots in this area and ski down to the base to buy your ticket if the Caribou Chair ticket office isn't open.

If you want to learn about the local history while you explore the mountain, join a mountain host for a complimentary tour.

◆◆ **Expert** ◆ **Advanced:** Marmot has tree-lined runs toward the bottom and wide-open bowls at the top. Generally, the higher you go, the tougher the skiing gets. The Knob Chair takes you to the highest lift-served terrain. From the top of that lift, the hardiest hike the last 600 feet up to Marmot Peak. (Our vertical-foot and summit stats reflect the *lift-served* terrain, while those advertised by the area include this hike.) It's all Alpine bowls up here, and they are really sweet.

Experts will want to drop into the fine powder in outrageously large Dupres Bowl, with Dupres Chute dividing it from Charlie's Bowl, which is even steeper and stays untracked longer. Charlie's Bowl, with its 50-plus-degree entrance that mellows out to perhaps 42 degrees, should be a double-black diamond. A straight shot across the bowl, where it is still so steep that you can reach out and practically touch the ground next to you, allows you to pick your descent.

Another good choice for bowls and untracked powder is to stay high and to the right of The Knob (facing down the mountain). Experts have several different playgrounds all to themselves here—including McCready's Choice and Thunder Bowl.

Head for the newly lift-served Eagle Ridge. Chalet Slope is a vast area of glades that are some of the most challenging and grin-inducing we've ever skied. Powder lasts the longest here. Unfortunately, the poor snow last season prevented us from sampling the bowl, chutes and glades on Eagle East, but they looked really enticing.

There's also excellent glade skiing off the Triple Chair and Kiefer T-bar, both of which serve Caribou Ridge. Off to the right, facing downhill, you'll have an absolute blast in the trees in a black area misnamed Milk Run. Further down the mountain, drop into any woods that look tempting, especially those off green-circle Old Road.

For mogul mashers, directly below the Eagle Express, Tranquilizer Chair and Triple Chair you'll find some super bump runs. Warm up here before heading to the right of Knob Chair, where the most challenging bumps are.

■ **Intermediate:** Every lift has an intermediate way down, even The Knob. Punch Bowl and Paradise are especially delightful runs. The Knob Traverse takes you high on the mountain where you'll have incredible views. On blustery days, stay low on the mountain, where trees provide shelter from winds that sometimes block visibility on the naked summit. The intermediate runs of Chalet Slope off the newly lift-served Eagle Ridge, which also hold snow longest, are excellent choices.

●● **Beginner** ● **Never-ever:** The three lifts at the base serve most of the lower-level terrain. Beginners have expansive mountain access, with 1,100 vertical feet on Eagle Express after they master terrain from the School House T-bar. They can even head up to Caribou Ridge for an above-treeline thrill where a wide trail, Basin Run, takes them safely back to the lower slopes. A novice run on the newly lift-served Eagle Ridge will provide gorgeous views from the top before you wind down the mountain.

Mountain layout—Snowboarding

Marmot Basin has a terrain park with a quarterpipe, a spine, rollers and tabletops. There's also a nice natural pipe on Marmot Run. But most riders come here for the freeriding. Off The Knob Chair, hike another 600 feet to catch freshies in Upper Basin or choose Peak Run to scoot over to the gully off High Traverse or Thunder Bowl. Don't skip Charlie's Bowl, which should really be designated a double-black diamond. There are so many lines to choose from, it's possible to literally spend all day here. Dupres Chutes are also quite the challenge.

Test yourself on the newly lift-served Eagle Ridge. Chalet Slope is a vast area of glades that will keep you challenged—and grinning. Powder lasts the longest over here, too. In a good snow year, don't miss the bowl, chutes and glades on Eagle East.

Like to ride the trees? There's excellent glade riding off the Triple Chair on Caribou Ridge. Off to the right, facing downhill, have an absolute blast in the trees in a black area misnamed Milk Run. Caribou Knoll is a real hoot, too. Further down the mountain, drop into any woods that look tempting, especially those off green-circle Old Road.

Intermediates have great choices all over. There's nice beginner terrain at the base of the mountain, though it's served by a T-bar, which can be a nightmare for snowboarders. After you feel comfortable on your board, you can head higher up the mountain via the chairs.

Mountain rating

Skiers and boarders of different levels can ride the same lifts, which makes Marmot great for family and group skiing. The terrain is fairly evenly divided between ability levels, with appropriate challenge, so everyone will enjoy themselves. If you're looking to improve your skills, Marmot is a perfect choice.

Cross-country and snowshoeing

This is prime ski touring and snowshoeing country, the scenery is guaranteed to delight and enthrall you.

Jasper Park Lodge trails, about 19 km., are unparalleled for beauty and variety. The gentle, groomed and easily accessible trails wind around lake shores, Alpine meadows and forests. The easiest is Cavell, a 5 km. loop with the elk. The perimeter loop samples a little of everything the Jasper Park Lodge trails offer.

Near Jasper Townsite, a good beginner trail is **Whistlers Campground Loop,** 4.5 km., which is level and lit for night skiing. **Pyramid Bench Trail** is 4.7 km., rated intermediate and overlooks the Athabasca River Valley. **Patricia Lake Circle,** 5.9 km. and rated intermediate (recommendation is to follow the trail clockwise), provides stunning views of Mt. Edith Cavell, the region's most dramatically sloped peak. Most lodges have trail maps.

For **guided cross-country skiing, backcountry and snowshoeing tours,** contact Edge Control, 852-4945; Beyond the Beaten Path, 852-5650; Maligne Tours, 852-3370; Overlander Trekking & Tours, 852-4056 (snowshoe tours only); or Alpine Art, 852-3709. Ask about rentals and/or instruction, too.

A full day's ski over Maccarib Pass from the Marmot Basin Road on the north shore of Amethyst Lake leads to Tonquin Valley Lodge, hearty home-cooked meals and welcome beds. Contact **Tonquin Valley Ski Tours,** Box 550, Jasper, Alberta T0L 1E0; 852-3909.

Lessons (2001/02 prices in Cdn$ with GST)

Group lessons: For all abilities, $29 for two hours, ski or snowboard (early bird, $23).

Never-ever package: With lift pass, two-hour lesson and ski or snowboard equipment for $54.

Private lessons: $53 an hour, with multi-hour discounts. Early-bird private costs $43.

Special programs: Moguls, carving, snowboard freestyle camps, seniors 50+. Meet at 1:30 p.m. daily, $29. Ski Improvement Weeks (Monday to Friday or Friday to Tuesday) include five two-hour sessions, video, a fun race and a Jasper Night Out. Cost is $114.

Racing: The Diet Coke Star Series is a dual slalom course, electronically timed, where your time is compared with a pacesetter's to determine if you qualify for a gold, silver, bronze or participant medal. Cost for two runs is $4.

Child care (2001/02 prices in Cdn$ with GST)

Ages: 19 months through 7 years.

Cost: All-day care is $30.

Reservations: 852-3816.

Children's lessons: Ages 4-5, 90-minute lesson in morning or afternoon, $25 includes rentals (five kids per instructor). For ages 6-12, there are several options. A full-day program, ski or snowboard, costs $55 (includes lunch). A two-hour group lesson, ski or snowboard, costs $22. Learn-to-ski or snowboard lessons are $54. One-hour private lessons are $53. Kids 13 and older do not have full-day programs: two-hour group lessons, specialty ski clinics and half-day snowboard freestyle camps cost $29; learn-to-ski or snowboard, including two-hour lesson, rentals and ticket, costs $54; a one-hour private costs $53 (early-bird, $43); Ski & Snowboard Weeks (Monday to Friday or Friday to Tuesday) include five two-hour sessions, video, a fun race and a Jasper Night Out for $84.

Lift tickets (2001/02 prices in Cdn$ with GST)

	Adult	Junior (6-12)
One day	$49	$20
Three days	$143 ($47+/day)	$60 ($20/day)
Five days	$237 ($47+/day)	$100 ($20/day)

Who skis free: Children ages 5 and younger.

Who skis at a discount: Youth/student prices (ages 13–25) are $41 for one day, with multi-day discounts; college-age students must be full time and present a valid student ID. Seniors ages 65 and older pay $35 for one day, with multi-day discounts. Early season rates are lower. During the Jasper in January winter festival, everyone aged 13 and older pays $35 per day, $20 for juniors.

Accommodations

Jasper Tourism and Commerce (Box 98, Jasper, Alberta, T0E 1E0; call 403-852-3858) will send a ski vacation planner that includes rates. The region has no central reservations service. Call the lodges directly. Many of the lodges have ski packages, so be sure to ask.

Although the **Fairmont Jasper Park Lodge** (852-3301 or 800-441-1414; $$–$$$$) is a grouping of traditional log cabins from the 1920s and new cedar chalets with spacious modern suites, the older buildings have all been renovated and are thoroughly modern in the areas that count, such as bathrooms. The lodging buildings are linked by pathways along Lac Beauvert to the main lodge that houses all the restaurants, night spots and shops. Nordic and downhill ski packages are available.

Other lodging is in Jasper Townsite, and many room rates are Cdn$100 or less a night because winter is considered the off-season.

Jasper Inn (852-4461; 800-661-1933; $–$$$$) has spacious standard rooms, studios, suites, loft units and one- to two-bedroom condo-style units. There's an indoor pool, steam room, sauna, Jacuzzi and coin laundry. Very good restaurant on premises.

The upscale **Royal Canadian Lodge—Jasper** (852-5644; 800-661-9323; $$–$$$$), formerly Chateau Jasper and now owned by Charlton Resorts, has an indoor pool and whirlpool, dining room, cocktail lounge and heated underground parking.

Pyramid Lake Resort (852-4900; $$–$$$) has skating and cross-country at your doorstep. Five miles from the town, it has a lovely view, whirlpools, kitchenettes and fireplaces.

The Astoria (852-3351; 800-661-7343; $$) is a small hotel of character with charmingly guestrooms. **Whistlers Inn** (852-3361; 800-282-9919; $$) has nice rooms, steam room, rooftop hot tub, two restaurants, pub and gift shops.

Marmot Lodge (852-4471; 888-852-7737; $–$$$) has rooms with kitchens and fireplaces. Indoor pool, sauna and whirlpool located on the premises. No charge for children under age 12. **The Athabasca Hotel** (852-3386; 800-563-9859; $–$$), one of Jasper's originals, is close to the bus and VIA RAIL station.

If you fly into or out of Edmonton, stay at the **Fantasyland Hotel** (800-661-6454; 444-3000; $$$–$$$$). Every floor is decorated in a theme such as Hollywood, Canadian Pacific Railway, Roman, African, and so forth. It's an experience. The hotel adjoins the West Edmonton Mall. Part shopping center, part amusement park with more than 800 stores, and includes (among other attractions) an indoor amusement park with a triple-loop roller coaster, a dolphin show, and an indoor water park with waterslides and 85-degree temperatures.

Dining

On the mountain, Marmot Basin has four places to eat. Upstairs in the Caribou Chalet, the **Caribou Café** ($-$$) has sit-down service, run by the Fairmont Jasper Park Lodge, with excellent sandwiches, burgers and salads. Ask to sit by the windows, you'll have spectacular views of the Athabasca River Valley and the mountain. There's also a **cafeteria** ($) in the base lodge. **Paradise Chalet** at mid-mountain, has a café and lounge ($), as well as a nice outdoor deck. On busy days, eat lunch before 11:45 or after 1:15. **Eagle Chalet** ($-$$) at mid-mountain is a cozy rustic restaurant with a fireplace to warm you. Or sit on its big outdoor deck that allows you to watch skiers and riders in the bowls as you eat a hearty meal. There's a shooter bar, too. Both Paradise Chalet and Eagle Chalet provide fabulous views of Jasper National Park.

Surprisingly, this little secluded town has some excellent restaurants and an incredible variety, too: Canadian, Chinese, French, Greek, Italian, Korean, Japanese, Mexican, continental and family-style dining are all available.

At Jasper Park Lodge, the **Edith Cavell** is the flagship restaurant, with white-glove tableside service (852-6052; $$$). French veal and shrimp in a pastry are specialties. For breakfast, the **Meadows** ($–$$) serves wholesome food in a country setting all day.

In town, the **Inn Restaurant** (852-4461; $$) at Jasper Inn offers a cozy, casual atmosphere. The creative menu includes such appetizers as citrus-marinated chicken brochettes with mushroom pierogies topped with tropical mango sour cream and pernod-soaked scallops served over a spring roll-wrapped potato triangle with wilted baby spinach and wasabi crème. Pasta entrees are very tasty. Also choose from Alberta beef, salmon, fish and chicken.

Tonquin Prime Rib Village (852-4966; $$) serves steaks, prime rib, barbecued ribs, seafood and Italian dishes. It has a bar and a beautiful view. Make reservations. **Fiddle River Seafood Company** (852-3032; $$–$$$) gets raves for creative fresh fish cooking. **Embers Steakhouse** (852-4471; $$) serves light and healthy cuisine (beef, local fish) in a casually elegant restaurant. The Royal Canadian Lodge's **Beauvallon Dining Room** (852-5644; $$$) serves elegant meals of Alberta steaks, British Columbia salmon, veal and wild game. Its Sunday brunch is popular so make reservations.

Families should consider **L&W Restaurant** (852-4114; $$), with an atrium setting and remarkably broad menu. Very good Greek cuisine. Also steaks, seafood, pasta and pizza. Kids' menu with prices from $5-$7 Cdn. **Caledonia Grill** (852-3361; $$) at Whistlers Inn is another good choice for families.

Miss Italia (852-4002; $$) is the spot for Italian. **Mountain Foods Cafe** (852-4050; $), a sit-down or take-out restaurant, has affordable deli items. Pizza and other Italian are at **Jasper Pizza Place** (852-3225; $). Japanese entrées and sushi bar at **Denjiro** (852-3780).

For breakfasts and other meals, try **Papa George's Restaurant** in the Astoria Hotel (852-3351; $–$$) or **Coco's Cafe** (852-4550; $), with fresh baked goods and gourmet coffees.

Après-ski/nightlife

Jasper is not known for rocking nightlife, but it's not dead, either. The **Atha-B Club** in Athabasca Hotel has the liveliest dancing in town. The hotel also has **O'Shea's,** an Irish pub. **Whistle Stop** at Whistlers Inn is a good pub-type nightspot with darts, pool and big-screen sports. **De'd Dog Saloon** in the Astoria Hotel is a locals' hangout. **Fireside Lounge** in Marmot Lodge has nightly entertainment.

At Jasper Park Lodge, the **Emerald Lounge** has hearty après-ski snacks, and **Tent City Sports Lounge** recalls the history of the lodge and has lively entertainment.

Other activities

Part of the reason visitors come to Jasper National Park is to enjoy the pristine wilderness and wildlife. There are a variety of ways to do this. Here are just a few:

Jasper in January is the area's annual winter festival. Lift tickets drop considerably, as do lodging rates. There's a long list of activities—let's just say it's a lot of fun!

One of the most unusual—and unforgettable—adventures is a **Canyon Icewalk,** a guided tour through Maligne Canyon a little over a mile through a 6- to 20-foot-wide gorge on the frozen river past ice caves, frozen waterfalls, towering canyon walls, fossils locked in time, and colors frozen into the ice. You'll need to be in reasonable physical shape to crawl up some

Dining: $$$-Entrees $20+; $$-$10-20; $-less than $10.
Accommodations: (double room) $$$$-$200+; $$$-$141-$200; $$-$81-$140; $-$80 and less.

head-high waterfalls and squeeze through narrow spots. At night this is a true other-world experience, with the moon and stars above, and absolute quiet enfolding you. The guides are a wealth of information about the geology, ice formations, wildlife and history. We cannot recommend this experience highly enough—just do it. Tours last two to three hours and are usually available from December through March. Winter boots and crampon-like soles provided. Call Overlander Trekking & Tours at 852-4056, Beyond the Beaten Path at 852-5650, or Jasper Adventure Center at 852-5595. Cost is about $35 per person.

Ice skating on a lake and **sleigh rides** are available at Jasper Park Lodge; go **dogsledding** with Overlander Trekking & Tours, 852-4056.

Heliskiing in Valemount, British Columbia, 56 miles away along a scenic drive, is available mid-February to mid-April. Overlander Trekking & Tours, 852-4056. Also Robson HeliMagic, 566-4700.

Sightseeing companies run bus tours to the more scenic vistas, including the Icefields Parkway, which has ragged peaks, frozen waterfalls and glaciers as attractions. Call Brewster Transportation, 852-3332, or Mountain Meadow Tours, 852-5595. Plan to take one day to drive along the Icefields Parkway (Hwy. 93)—you won't be sorry.

Wildlife spotting is a must-do. Mule deer, bighorn sheep, mountain goats and elk abound, as do moose, caribou, wolves and coyotes. Please remember: These are wild animals—use proper precautions not to make them feel threatened by your presence—keep your distance and don't make loud noises.

The exhibits at **Jasper-Yellowhead Museum and Archives** (852-3013) highlight Jasper's history and human heritage, such as the early explorers, the fur trade, the railway and skiing.

The **sports shop** at Marmot Basin has some very nice logo clothing, as well as the usual snowsports-related necessities. Downtown Jasper is a hodgepodge assortment of buildings and houses, but it's filled with **shops, boutiques** and **art galleries.** Don't leave Jasper without something to remind you of your visit.

Jasper Activity Centre (852-3381) has **swimming, curling, squash, racquetball, a weight room** and **indoor skating. Minor league hockey games** are played on Saturdays and Sundays. You can also go to the **movies** or **Arts Jasper** (852-3964) arts performances—dance, theatre and music. Pick up a **free winter guide** for a complete overview of activities.

Getting there and getting around

By air: Edmonton has the closest airport. Air Canada and Canadian Airlines have the most frequent flights from most North American cities, but Delta, American, Alaska and Northwest also fly here. If you don't rent a car, Greyhound operates daily service from Edmonton and Vancouver; call 421-4211.

By car: From Edmonton, Jasper is 225 miles west on Hwy. 16. The ski area is 12 miles south of Jasper via Hwy. 93, 93A and Marmot Basin Road. Jasper is about 170 miles north of Banff.

By train: VIA RAIL operates service to Jasper from Edmonton and Vancouver on its newly restored '50s-style art deco train, the Canadian. U.S. travel agents have more information.

Getting around: A car is best here. The ski area is a few miles from the town and lodging. Brewster Transportation operates the Banff-Jasper Ski Bus and the Marmot Basin Bus Service from Jasper; call 852-3332.

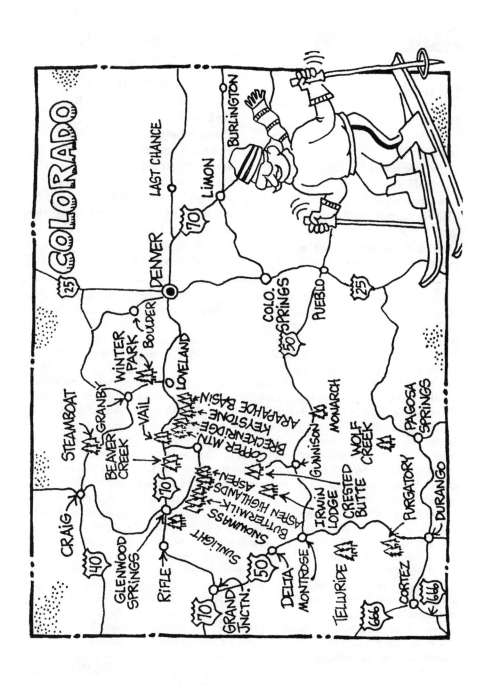

Aspen Area

Colorado

Aspen Mountain
Buttermilk
Highlands

Address: Aspen Skiing Company,
P.O. Box 1248, Aspen, CO 81612
Area code: 970
✆ **Ski area phone:** 925-1220
or (800) 525-6200
Snow report: 925-1221 or 888-ASPEN-SNO (277-3676)
h Toll-free reservations: (800) 262-7736
Fax: 925-9008
E-mail: info@stayaspen.com (reservations)
or info@aspensnowmass.com (ski info)

Bed Base: 9,000
Nearest lodging: Slopeside, hotels, condos
Resort child care: See Child Care section
Adult ticket, per day: $57–$65 (01/02 prices)
Internet: www.aspensnowmass.com (ski area)
www.aspenchamber.com (activities)
www.aspen.com (activities) www.aspen4u.com (lodging)
Dining:★★★★★
Apres-ski/nightlife:★★★★★
Other activities:★★★★★

Ask a crowd of non-skiing Americans to name a ski resort, and you can bet a bundle that Aspen will be one of those they name, though they will probably know more about the rich and famous who frequent the resort than about its equally notable skiing. With four mountains within a 12-mile radius (one of those, Snowmass, is detailed in its own chapter), offering 39 lifts, 270 trails and more than 5,900 skiable acres, a trip to Aspen just for the skiing would be well worth it. But Aspen has much more.

Aspen fits a niche unique among North American ski resorts. Sure, other resorts attract wealth, but Aspen's wealth glitters and sparkles with a "look-this-way" flamboyance. Here, the well-to-do seem to want everyone else to know it. You'll see the newest ski and city fashions on beautiful women as they pass turn-of-the-century brick façades. Private jets wait for their owners on the airport tarmac and create airport jet jams. Paparazzi aim their lenses at every celebrity in town so that supermarket tabloids can keep their pages filled.

Don't head to Aspen purely to observe celebrities, however. You may not find any. They are most common during the Christmas-New Year holidays and spring skiing, but are tough to spot when in ski clothes. Beyond downtown, the outward signs of wealth disappear.

If all your information about Aspen comes from *People* magazine, you probably think you can't afford to ski there. True, lift tickets are among the priciest in America, but it's a little-known fact that lodging and restaurants have a huge price range, starting out with inexpensive dorm accommodations and topping out at stratospheric luxury suites.

Aspen also draws skiers and snowboarders who could care less about the off-mountain scene. They come for the slopes, which have received rave reviews for decades. The region has four separate ski areas, all operated by Aspen Skiing Company (ASC). Aspen Mountain challenges intermediate through expert skiers, and snowboarders. Buttermilk is the perfect beginner and cruising mountain. It also will be home of the 2002 ESPN Winter X Games, Jan. 17–20. Highlands is the most varied for its size, with terrain for experts and beginners, cruisers and bumpers. Snowmass, larger than the other three combined, is several miles down the road. Though it is one of the four Aspen Skiing Company areas and included in the lift ticket, it has its own lodging, restaurants and shops, and is covered in the next chapter.

Here's a little-known freebie: Grab a free postcard at the ticket offices or Concierge Centers to let the folks back home know how much fun you're having, then give it back to the staff and Aspen Skiing Company will pay the postage. A fabulous freebie on Aspen Mountain is "First Tracks" with ski school pros. Early birds can bring their lift tickets and sign up for the 8 a.m. gondola at the concierge desk the day before. First Tracks is on a first-come basis, so sign up early. Ski or snowboard the first run of the day down empty, freshly groomed slopes!

 ## Mountain layout—Skiing

Aspen's four mountains are close to each other, but not interconnected. A free shuttle runs from base to base. This chapter covers Aspen Mountain, Highlands and Buttermilk. ASC runs a very efficient equipment transfer program between its four mountains. For $5, you hand over your skis, poles or snowboard to an attendant in the base area at the end of the day, tell him/her where you are skiing the next day, and your equipment will be waiting for you at that base area the next morning. We used this every day during our annual *Ski America* staff meeting; it worked beautifully.

If you're determined to see celebrities at Aspen, three sightings are guaranteed on Aspen Mountain. Look for shrines for Elvis Presley, Marilyn Monroe and Jerry Garcia. The Elvis shrine is in a grove of trees just below Back of Bell 3. Marilyn's shrine is on a cat-track above the Elvis shrine and Jerry is memorialized in a grove of spruce trees to skiers' right on Ruthie's Run after you unload from the FIS chair. Ask an Aspen ambassador for directions and be sure to take your camera. For a little romance, check out the Valentine's shrine between Walsh's and Hyrup's on Aspen Mountain where you'll find a secluded "porch swing" to canoodle between runs.

◆◆ **Expert: Highlands** is the best-balanced mountain of the three with slopes for every level, and it's the locals' favorite. No need for fur-trimmed outfits here, you can be comfortable if you appear for lunch at mid-mountain in jeans and gaiters. The vertical rise is one of the highest in Colorado. Highlands has three high-speed quads that dramatically cut the time needed to reach the summit and have changed the skiing in the mountain.

From the top of Loge Peak, the run back to the base is an uneven series of steeps, catwalks and gentle runouts. This mountain has some fantastic long cruises. The ridge, knifing directly to the summit, has thrilling pitches down both sides. Other than a few short blacks, such as Suzy Q and Limelight, the terrain makes a pronounced jump from intermediate to double-diamond expert.

Experts should head for the steeps at the top of Loge Peak in the Steeplechase (sunny in the morning) and Olympic Bowl (sunny in the afternoon) areas. These are very steep with no bail-out areas, so be sure you want to be here. Both areas have long cat trails back to the lifts.

Highlands ski patrol recently opened the Y- and portions of the B-Zones. A run accesses the very top of Highland Bowl. The steep terrain is reached by a 20- to 40-minute hike from the summit, or, if skiers and riders are lucky, they can catch a Snocat ride from Lodge Meadow to the top of Whip's Veneration, the only known free cat-skiing in North America.

Also check out the lower mountain. The Thunderbowl chair will take you from the base to the top of Bob's Glades or Upper Stein, or you can drop into double-black territory at several points along blue-square Golden Horn.

The basic guideline for **Aspen Mountain** is that the intermediate terrain is on the top knob around the summit and in the gullies between the ridges. The expert stuff drops from the ridges into the gullies. Of the blacks, take your pick and be sure you're up to it. These runs are very black. Take a trail map as you ride the lifts, and you'll be able to pick out what you'd like

Aspen Mountain Facts

Summit elevation: 11,212 feet
Base elevation: 7,945 feet
Vertical drop: 3,267 feet
Number of lifts: 8–1 gondola, 1 high-speed quad, 1 high-speed double, 2 quads, 3 doubles
Snowmaking: 31 percent **Skiable acreage:** 673 acres
Uphill capacity: 10,775 per hour **Snowboarding:** Yes
Expert:★★★★ Advanced:★★★★★
Intermediate:★★★★ Beginner:★ Never-ever:★

Buttermilk Facts

Summit elevation: 9,900 feet
Vertical drop: 2,030 feet
Base elevation: 7,870 feet
Number of lifts: 7–1 high-speed quad, 5 doubles, 1 surface lift
Snowmaking: 26 percent **Skiable acreage:** 415 acres
Uphill capacity: 7,500 per hour **Snowboarding:** Yes
Expert:★ Advanced:★★ Intermediate:★★★★
Beginner:★★★★★ Never-ever:★★★★★

Highlands Facts

Summit elevation: 11,675 feet
Vertical drop: 3,635 feet
Base elevation: 8,040 feet
Number of lifts: 4–3 high-speed quads, 1 triple
Snowmaking: 15 percent **Skiable acreage:** 714 acres
Uphill capacity: 5,400 per hour **Snowboarding:** Yes
Expert:★★★★ Advanced:★★★★★ Intermediate:★★★★
Beginner:★★★ Never-ever:★★

---

to ski. Watch for the ski patrol to open Walsh's after a storm. It can be powder heaven, a run you can brag about all week. Guided "Powder Tours" are offered on the back side of Aspen Mountain; call (800) 525-6200 for information.

◆ **Advanced:** If you consider yourself a confident advanced skier, read the expert section. If you feel you have recently reached advanced status, read the intermediate section. In our experience, there's a big jump from intermediate to expert terrain at **Highlands** and **Aspen Mountain. Buttermilk's** marked advanced terrain is really more advanced intermediate.

■ **Intermediate:** If you'd like to say you skied a black run on **Aspen Mountain,** Upper Little Percy or Red's Run are occasionally groomed. Ask at the base for a grooming report.

The gentlest intermediate terrain is at the summit—runs such as Dipsy Doodle, Pussyfoot and Silver Bell. Keep riding the Ajax Express and Gentlemen's Ridge lifts. Then head down Copper Bowl or Spar Gulch, two gullies that get packed as skiers funnel into them toward the base. Both runs join at Kleenex Corner, a sharp, narrow turn, then dump into Little Nell, a steep blue just above the gondola base. It's known as "Little Hell" because at day's end, it's crowded, usually a little slick and/or moguled, and smack in view of everyone. The blue cruisers in sight of Bonnie's outdoor deck, led by North American, are a delight.

At **Buttermilk,** intermediates will have fun on Jacob's Ladder and Bear, but the real playground is under the Tiehack chair. Much of this area is colored black on the trail map, but don't get too excited—it's just the toughest stuff on *this* mountain. You'll discover good upper-intermediate trails that make inspiring cruisers. In one day you can ride the Upper Tiehack chair a dozen times, taking a different cruise on each 1,500 vertical-foot run. Javelin is the best of the lot—a couple of tree islands to keep you awake and a lot of good dips and rolls. Smile in the evening when you overhear others scoffing about what a waste Buttermilk is for real skiers, and savor memories of 15,000 feet of vertical in just one afternoon.

At **Highlands**, intermediates will want to take these lifts: Cloud Nine, Olympic and Loge Peak. (The easiest of the intermediates are off Cloud Nine.) Don't miss Golden Horn and Thunderbowl on the lower mountain, very wide cruisers.

●● **Beginner: Aspen Mountain** may be the only mountain in America that has no designated green-circle runs. Don't try it if you're at this level.

Buttermilk is all that Aspen Mountain isn't. Beginners can experience top-to-bottom runs as soon as they master snowplows. The beginner terrain concentrates under the Buttermilk West chair. Tom's Thumb, Red's Rover, Larkspur, Westward Ho and Blue Grouse will keep beginners improving. The Homestead Road turns back to the Savio chair and lazily winds its way to the Main Buttermilk area.

At **Highlands**, beginners are best served by the trails from the Exhibition chair—Prospector, Nugget, Exhibition, Red Onion and Apple Strudel.

● **Never-ever:** Take your first few lessons at **Buttermilk**. Of Aspen's four mountains, this is by far the best for a first day on skis or a snowboard.

 ## Mountain layout—Snowboarding

At 673 acres, **Aspen Mountain** is not even one-fourth the size of Snowmass, but every acre is infinitely rideable. The mountain scenery is sublime—better, even, than Telluride or Crested Butte. This ain't a mountain for jibbers, bonkers or terrain park pilots—it's for expert riders who respect and even revere a pristine alpine playground. There are no beginner trails and scant few true intermediate runs. But if you have good skills, the mountain is replete with bumps, steeps, natural halfpipes and terrain features perfect for riders.

Aspen Mountain is comprised of three distinct ridges. To the west is Ruthie's, site of spine-tingling steeps and Aztec, the world-class downhill racing course. In the middle is Bell's Ridge (actually a separate mountain), offering mostly bumps and glades. And to the east is Gentleman's Ridge, which has easy groomers as well as the uncompromising steeps of Walsh's Gulch. For a long cruiser that forms a wild natural halfpipe, there's Spar Gulch, which cuts a steep "V" down the heart of the mountain to the patio of The Little Nell.

If you measure the quality of your riding by the perfection of the "esses" and the depth of the trenches you leave behind, **Buttermilk** is the place for you. Buttermilk has numerous constant-pitch, top-to-bottom fall line, groomed runs ideal for laying out perfect carves.

Buttermilk's biggest asset is its undeserved reputation as a "beginner" mountain. This ensures all the egos go to Aspen Mountain or Highlands, leaving Buttermilk largely deserted.

Midweek you and your buddies will often have entire trails to yourself. Buttermilk's solitude allows you to focus on improving your technique rather than constantly dodging skiers.

Buttermilk Mountain consists of the Main Buttermilk area, West Buttermilk and Tiehack. West Buttermilk is served by a rather slow double chairlift serving beginner terrain, but don't skip this area entirely. Larkspur can be one of the most fun carving runs on the mountain, allowing you to make one perfect carve after another, going into the trees on either side if you don't keep your turns tight. Carve Larkspur non-stop, top to bottom, and we guarantee you'll be high-fiving your buddies.

The mountain gets interesting over on Racer's Edge and Javelin, accessed from the Upper Tiehack lift. They'd probably be rated blues on other mountains, but they're labeled black diamonds here. These runs get groomed, meaning no moguls, but they're steep enough to force even advanced riders to concentrate on working their edges. Cutting down from Tiehack Parkway are the Ptarmigan and Timber Doodle Glades. Here's where intermediate boarders can learn to ride in the trees. The terrain is steep enough not to stall out, yet the trees are spaced far enough apart to learn. On a powder day you don't want to miss this area.

For 2001/02 Buttermilk will have a terrain park nearly 2 miles long, plus 30 new rail-slides. You'll also find the only 15-foot superpipe in the four Aspen mountains. Park designer and pro rider Jim Mangan designed the Drop Zone Terrain Park. It's geared towards intermediate and expert riders. At the bottom of the Drop Zone a gigantic kicker allows boarders with huge, and we're talking *huge*, air skills to put on a show for everyone at the base area. Hopefully, there's an ambulance standing by.

There also are a lot of runs at Buttermilk with gully-like sides that riders of all ages can swoop up and down, such as Bear. Riding at Buttermilk feels so much like playing you'll find yourself with a perpetual smile.

Buttermilk is home for the Pure Carve Expression Session. Last year the Expression Session brought over 100 carvers together. It's not a competition—there's no prize money— just a collection of individuals who know why snowboards have edges and how to have fun using them. And since Buttermilk is popular with snowshoers, there's a constant procession to the top of the mountain, making an excellent audience for showing off your carving skills.

Highlands attracts riders who are interested in riding blacks and double-blacks. While the resort's quick to point out they actually have more green and blue terrain than black, if intermediate cruisers or a great terrain park is what you're looking for, you'll be happier at Snowmass or Buttermilk. Highlands is where advanced and expert riders go to go steep on big powder days. At the peak, the snowcat- and hiking-accessed 12,500-foot Highlands Bowl gives riders with the legs—and the lungs—the ultimate in deep powder turns. A free snowcat ride from the top of Loge Peak takes riders halfway to the Highlands Bowl. You have to hike the rest of the way along a ridgeline that can give you a new perspective on "Into Thin Air." Don't ask for a map of the Highlands Bowl at the base area. They won't give you one. Once you've exhausted your last bit of lung power hiking to the 11,675-foot Fundeck Gate, *then* you can pick up your souvenir copy.

Get ready for a spectacular descent, one hundred or more turns in champagne powder up to your waist—or higher. Your best bet is to do the Highlands Bowl your first time with a guide who has ridden it several times before. Towards the bottom of the bowl, snowboarders need to stay high and rider's left to pick up the section of "Grand Traverse" where the least amount of cursing flats will be required. The "Grand Traverse" back from the Y-Zones and Steeplechase area can be a handful for riders, making you sorely wish you had poles. An icy curve marked with several signs admonishing you to slow down is followed by a slight uphill that will force those who do to unbuckle and skate. The catwalk itself is no wider than your average snowboard in many places, making skating, especially for goofy-footers, difficult.

The Olympic Bowl is intense, but short. Runs like Deception, Aces & Eights, and Why are serious steeps with trees, catwalk launches and powder stashes. And moguls.

Groomers suitable for carving include Thunderbowl and Golden Horn, on the lower part of the mountain. The Thunderbowl triple chair runs from the base of the mountain to the top of Golden Horn, making it easy to rack up vertical. Intermediate riders will want to ride the Cloud Nine, Olympic and Loge Peak lifts. The easiest intermediate runs are off Cloud Nine. Some of the most fun runs are directly beneath the lifts.

Highlands doesn't have a halfpipe or terrain park; however, Prospector Trail is known locally as Grommets Gulch and is a natural halfpipe. In summary, Highlands isn't for poseurs.

Mountain rating

Everyone gets something at Aspen. Beginners will have the most fun at Buttermilk. Intermediates probably will have a more varied day at Highlands, but the longest runs sweep down Aspen Mountain, and it's hard to beat the exhilarating cruising on Buttermilk. Experts have a tossup between Highlands and Aspen Mountain. Our advice to snowboarders: Carvers, riders learning trees and terrain park tricksters should head to Buttermilk, seekers of the pow and steeps will want to beeline it to Aspen Mountain or Highlands.

Cross-country and snowshoeing

Aspen/Snowmass has the most extensive free Nordic trail system in America, more than 80 km. of groomed trails called "Aspen's fifth mountain." The **Aspen Nordic Council's** free system is accessible from Aspen or Snowmass and includes easy golf-course skiing as well as more difficult trails rising up to Snowmass.

In addition to the free trails provided by Aspen's Nordic Council, **Ashcroft Ski Touring Unlimited** (925-1971) has 42 km. of groomed and set trails, and backcountry skiers can use summer hiking trails. Trail fees are $15 per day, and lessons and rentals are available.

Hut systems connect Aspen with Vail on the Tenth Mountain Trail and with Crested Butte over the Pearl Pass. Guides are available and recommended. Call Tenth Mountain Trail Association for more information, 925-5775.

Other centers are **Aspen Cross Country Center** (544-9246) on the Aspen Golf Course off Hwy. 82; **Ute Mountaineer** (925-2849); **Braun Hut System** (925-6618), with information on trails to Crested Butte; and **Snowmass Club Cross Country Center** (923-3148).

Snowshoeing is quite popular in town, so ask about those programs at any of the cross-country centers mentioned here. In conjunction with the Aspen Center for Environmental Studies (ACES), **Aspen Skiing Company** has naturalist-guided tours for $49 each day (including lift rides, equipment and snack) on Aspen Mountain and Snowmass. Call 925-1220 or ACES at 925-5756 for reservations. You also can snowshoe up Aspen Mountain or Buttermilk at certain times and on certain runs.

Lessons (2001/02 prices)

For brochures and information, or to make reservations for ski and snowboard school programs, call 925-1220 or (877) AT-ASPEN (282-7736).

Group lessons: Adult small group lessons cost $99 a day. They are offered at all the mountains, and are limited to an average of four per class for all levels. Unlimited extensions are $89 per day.

Never-ever package: Three-day first-time ski/snowboard packages (including lessons, lift tickets, rentals, and use of ski/snowboard simulator) run $327 and are offered at Buttermilk and Snowmass. One-day programs are $109. Unlimited extensions of the three-day program are $89 per day.

Private lessons: $309 for a half day for one to five people; $1,500 for five half days; and $2,100 for five full days. Other discounts are available. Reservations are required. Lessons are offered in several languages, include ski storage, lift line privileges, and demo discounts.

Special programs: Numerous, including clinics and/or ski and snowboard weeks for women, bumps, powder, off-piste, disabled skiers, video analysis, equipment assessment, shaped skis, and many more. Call (800) 525-6200 for a ski and snowboard school brochure.

Racing: NASTAR for adults is $6 for two runs or $10 per day, and for kids 12 and younger, $4. Courses are at Silver Dip Swing at Aspen Mountain (daily), Nugget at Highlands (Wednesday–Sunday) and Cabin Trail at Snowmass (Monday, Wednesday, Friday, Saturday). Weekly passes are $20.

 # Child care (2001/02 prices)

Ages: 8 weeks to 4 years.
Costs: $95 for a full day; $399 for five full days.

Reservations: Recommended. Child care in Aspen is offered by Kids' Club in the Yellow Brick Building, 315 Garmisch St. Call 925-3136. The state-licensed program offers indoor and outdoor (non-skiing) activities.

Other options: Also try **Aimee's Angels** (923-2809) for child-care needs. **Baby's Away** (800-948-9030; 920-1699) rents and will deliver baby needs to your lodge, such as crib, stroller, car seat and toys. Reservations are recommended for all of these services. Children from 5th through 12th grade can mingle with local kids in the afternoons at the **Aspen Youth Center** (hotline with weekly activities information, 925-7091) in downtown Aspen. The center has games, ping-pong, pool tables, movies and a dance room. The center does special programs depending on the season. Admission is free.

Children's lessons: Aspen Skiing Company has a completely different program for young children at each mountain (except for Aspen Mountain, where only adult lessons are taught). The programs at Snowmass are detailed in that chapter. Ages 7–12 skiing and ages 8-12 snowboarding pay $69 per day at Buttermilk (920-0935) or Aspen Highlands (544-3025). These programs include instruction and lunch, but rentals are extra.

 # Lift tickets

Aspen lift ticket prices had not been set as of late August 2001. According to a spokeswoman, they are committed to "variable" pricing based on the weather and snow conditions. Aspen promises not to exceed $65 a day for lift tickets. These prices reflect Aspen's maximum price. If the weather is bad and snow conditions miserable you may ski for less; if you can make plans months in advance (like advance-purchase airline tickets) you can pay less; there are also lift/lodging packages that offer savings.

Who skis free: Ages 6 and younger.

Who skis at a discount: Those 70 years and older get unlimited skiing or riding with The Silver Pass for $119 all season long. Ages 65 to 69 pay $177 for three days, $295 for five and $354 for six.

 ## Accommodations

Aspen Central Reservations, (888) 290-1325 or (970) 925-9000 can reserve nearly all properties listed here. Multiday lift-and-lodging packages are the best deal. Or log on to www.aspensnowmass.com and check out the "Virtual Hostel" for last-minute, discounted lodging packages.

Hotel Jerome, 330 East Main Street, (800-331-7213 or 920-1000; $$$$) is on the National Register of Historic Places, and it has been restored to more elegance than the silver barons ever knew. The lounges are furnished with overstuffed chairs and framed in etched glass. Rooms are filled with antiques. Baths feature Jacuzzis and marble counters.

The **Sardy House** (920-2525 or 800-321-3457; $$$$) on East Main Street is a restored Victorian mansion. A modern addition has been tacked onto the rear, but we suggest you try to get one of the original rooms.

The **Little Nell** (920-4600 or 888-843-6355; $$$$) is just steps from the Silver Queen Gondola at the base of Aspen Mountain. It has received the highest rating (five on a 1–5 scale) from several rating services, such as AAA and Mobil. All rooms have fireplaces, sofas, oversized beds with comforters, and marble bathrooms. There is a spa and a heated outdoor pool.

The **St. Regis, Aspen** (920-3300 or 800-241-3333; $$$$) is richly appointed, with a tasteful decor that brings to mind an exclusive hunting club. It has a fitness center and various ski packages, and its restaurants are top-flight.

The **Residence** (920-6532; $$$$) has world-class European suites in an historic downtown landmark building. Also luxurious are the **Aspen Club Lodge** (800-882-2582; $$$$) and the small **Hotel Lenado** (800-321-3457; $$$$).

The **Snowflake Inn** (925-3221 or 800-247-2069; $$$), a block from the transportation center on East Hyman Avenue is clean, roomy and is walking distance from the Ajax gondola, the buses to the other areas, and the downtown area. And it has a very friendly staff, laundry facilities, a heated pool and spa, and a free continental breakfast and après-ski snacks. What more does one need?

Our favorite place in Aspen, a lodge of a kind that's disappearing all too fast, is **The Mountain Chalet** (925-7797 or 800-321-7813; $–$$$). This place is just plain friendly to everyone, including families. If you can't stand a 3-year-old crawling over a lounge chair in the lobby or families howling over a game of Monopoly, then don't stay here. Rates are reasonable and include a hearty breakfast served family-style. It's a few blocks from Aspen Mountain's Silver Queen gondola, and across the street from the transportation center (ideally situated, in other words). Call early for rooms, because folks reserve space here well in advance. Package deals for lodging, lift tickets and full breakfast are as low as $60 per person per day in a dorm bunk or a four-person room; about $130 per person per night for two to a room. To get these prices, call the chalet directly.

Other places that treat guests very well are the **Mountain House Lodge** (920-2550; $$), **The Beaumont** (925-7081 or 800-344-3853; $$), the **Hotel Aspen** (800-527-7369; $$) and the **Molly Gibson Lodge** (800-356-6559; $$).

Also try **Skier's Chalet** (920-2037; $–$$) across from the Shadow Mountain Lift (formerly Lift 1-A) with a heated outdoor pool, the **Limelight** (925-3025 or 800-433-0832; $$), the **Christiana** (925-3014; $$) at 501 West Main Street and the **St. Moritz Lodge** (925-3220; $), a hostel only five blocks from the center of town.

You can still find some inexpensive rooms at the **Christmas Inn** (925-3822; $$), **Innsbruck Inn** (925-2980; $$), **Ullr Lodge** (925-7696; $$) and budget champion **Tyrolean Lodge**

(925-4595 or 800-321-702; $). The **Heatherbed Lodge** (925-7077; 800-356-6782; $) is a good place to stay near Highlands. Rates are about $120 per night and include a full breakfast.

Several management companies rent condominiums. For luxury, three-bedroom unit, condos right on the slopes, try **Mountain Queen Condominiums** (925-6366). The **Gant** (800-345-1471) is another choice in condo lodging. **Coates, Reid and Waldron**, 720 East Hyman Ave. (925-1400 or 800-222-7736), is the largest management company in the area, with condos and homes. Chateau Eau Claire and Chateau Roaring Fork are two of their popular units. Shadow Mountain is not so luxurious, but has a ski-in/ski-out location. Condominiums directly on the slopes are the **Fasching Haus** (925-5900), **Fifth Avenue** (925-7397) and **Durant Condominiums** (925-7910). They are available through Aspen Central Reservations.

Dining

Let's start with *the* place to eat breakfast, **The Wienerstube** (a.k.a. "the Stube") at 633 E. Hyman and Spring. Come here for Eggs Benny, omelettes, Austrian sausages and homemade Viennese pastries. **Main Street Bakery Cafe,** 201 E. Main St., has homemade baked goods, granola, fruit, eggs and great coffee for reasonable prices. Another recommended breakfast spot is the contemporary cafe, **Poppycock's**, 609 E. Cooper. For the best coffee in town, head to **Bagel Bites**, Aspen's only bagel shop at 300 Puppy Smith St.; or **Ink! Coffee** inside the D&E Snowboard Shop in the Aspen Mountain Building.

Aspen has enjoyed an unparalleled culinary revolution that has bypassed sole meunière for a more exotic "beach party" shellfish. Exotic ingredients and foods are definitely trendy. Over the past few years, we've seen black trumpets and white truffles, edible nasturtiums and a veal dish called "@*#?&!." Aspen is a place where you can enjoy the fine restaurants thoroughly, knowing that the next day you'll ski off those calories.

The Montagna at the Little Nell at 675 E. Durant (920-6330) is newly renovated and specializes in contemporary American Alpine cuisine. It was voted tops in Colorado by the readers of *Gourmet* and is a Grand Award recipient, the highest achievement from *Wine Spectator*. Open for breakfast, lunch and dinner, as well as Sunday brunch.

Syzygy's menu combines French, southwestern, Oriental and Italian cuisines. Don't be put off by the hard-to-pronounce name (Siz i je) or the obscure explanation of its meaning on the menu. At 520 E. Hyman Avenue (925-3700, reservations required); the atmosphere is intimate yet casual. Open daily 6 to 10 p.m.

Go to **Piñons** (second floor at 105 S. Mill; 920-2021) to dine in a cozy western ranch decor, with stucco walls, a leather bar and menus and huge brass bowls. All meats and fish are grilled over mesquite and cherry wood. Desserts vary daily. Open daily 6 to 10 p.m.

If you think that at these prices, you should be entertained and have your apartment cleaned for a year, one man will at least do the former. Owner Mead Metcalf has been playing to **The Crystal Palace** sellout crowds each evening at 6 and 9 p.m. for more than four decades. At 300 East Hyman Avenue (925-1455; reservations may be necessary several weeks in advance), the Crystal Palace's talented staff not only cranks out a full dinner and bar service, but then belts out a cabaret revue spoofing the media's latest victims. You can choose from perfectly pink beef tenderloin with Madeira sauce, roast duckling, rack of lamb or prime rib. The food doesn't have to be good, but it is.

On the outside chance there's still a platinum card burning a hole in your parka, try **Renaissance**, 304 East Hopkins (925-2402). Chef-owner Charles Dale (who grew up in the palace in Monaco with Caroline and Albert) claims his is one of three restaurants in the world to have a daily changing degustation or tasting menu (five courses), as well as offering course-by-course, by-the-glass wine pairings. Wine gets special attention at Renaissance. The list has won the *Wine Spectator* Award of Excellence. Reservations recommended.

Cache Cache (925-3835; $$–$$$) on the lower level of the Mill St. Plaza gets a thumbs up from locals for Mediterranean and French cuisine, especially their half-price early-bird specials. The polenta nicoise, wild mushroom cannelloni and perfectly grilled yellowtail are favorites. On their bar menu, salads begin at about $3 and all entrees are under $11.

Outstanding gourmet Italian restaurants are **Farfalla,** 415 E. Main (925-8222; $$$) and **Campo de Fiori,** 205 E. Mill (920-7717; $$). For Italian fare with an Asian twist, check out **Mezzaluna** at 624 Cooper (925-5332; $$).

Matsuhisa (544-6628; $$$) (named for the chef) is the latest "don't-miss," world-class classic Japanese restaurant in town. Other recommended newer restaurants include: **Vihn Vihn** (920-4373; $$) for Vietnamese food; **Blue Maize** (925-6698; $$) features Southwest and Latin American food.

Eateries recommended by locals and visitors: **L'Hostaria** (925-9022; $$–$$$) with decor and recipes direct from Italy. Their special is a two-pound Chilean sea bass Fed-Exed-in daily and baked with olive oil, herbs, clams and mussels; **The Big Wrap** (544-1700; $) features burrito-like wraps but with a variety of exotic fillings; **Hickory House** for ribs and barbecue; and the **Motherload**.

La Cocina (925-9714; $), 308 E. Hopkins, is popular with locals—they call it "Lah-co". Enjoy great homestyle Mexican food and low prices (no credit cards accepted). **The Cantina** (925-3663, $–$$) at the corner of Mill and Main is a trendier Mexican alternative.

Boogie's Diner (925-6610; $), 534 E. Cooper, is a real '50s diner with oldies music like Elvis' "Hound Dog," blue plate specials and meatloaf (great milkshakes, too). **Little Annie's Eating House** (925-1098; $$), 517 E. Hyman, is still the ribs, chicken, burger and potato pancake champ. Try Annie's daily specials. The **Skier's Chalet Steak House** (925-3381), 710 S. Aspen, has been around since 1951 serving traditional steak, seafood and salad. **The Steak Pit** (925-3459; $$) at the corner of Hopkins and Monarch has also been in business for a time. Since 1960, they've served some of the best steaks in Aspen along with a sumptuous all-you-can-eat salad bar. **Little Ollie's** (544-9888, $) at 308 S. Hunter, is the place for healthy Chinese food. It has free delivery for dinner, or you can dine at the restaurant. Try to make time for **Mirabella** and **Bently's**.

For a real adventure, head out to the **Pine Creek Cookhouse** (925-1044) for a casual evening and solid fare. At an elevation of 9,725 feet, this rustic log cabin is in the midst of towering pines beneath Elk Mountain peaks some 11 miles from Aspen. It is accessible by a one-and-a-half-mile cross-country trek or by a sleigh drawn by a team of Percherons. Views are outstanding. Reservations are essential (at times two to four weeks in advance), as the logistics of running a kitchen not reached by road in winter is no small matter. The Cookhouse feeds several hundred people each day, and all that food (wild game is its specialty) comes in by snowmobile. Meals are prepared right in front of you in the open kitchen and are served by one of your cross-country guides.

On the mountains:

Bump's (925-4027), at the Buttermilk base area, features foods from a wood-fired rotisserie, brick ovens and a pit smoker, as well as huge salads, pastas and stews. The same managers operate the **Ajax Tavern**, 685 E. Durant Ave. (920-9333) at the base of Silver Queen Gondola. The menu boasts Mediterranean influences in a clubby room. Lunch is a hearty selection of Colorado lamb, roasted mussels, pastas, salads and sandwiches with a Napa Val-

Dining: $$$-Entrees $20+; $$-$10-20; $-less than $10.
Accommodations: (double room) $$$$-$200+; $$$-$141-$200; $$-$81-$140; $-$80 and less.

ley wine list and outdoor seating. At the top of the gondola is **The Sundeck Restaurant,** a favorite spot for spectacular views, people-watching and innovative cuisine.

While not a sit-down restaurant, **Bonnie's,** just above Lift 3 on Aspen Mountain, feeds some 1,500 hungry skiers per day between 9:30 a.m. and 2:30 p.m. Go before noon or after 2 p.m., unless you love lines. Owner Bonnie Rayburn's gourmet pizza on freshly made crust is a huge crowd pleaser. Homemade soups, such as the Colorado white-bean chili, are served with large crusty pieces of fresh French bread. Save room for apple strudel.

Long-time local Gwyn Gordon Knowlton moved **Gwyn's** and her queen-of-ski-food reputation to the base of Ruthie's high-speed double a few seasons ago. Diners may settle at dining room tables for chef Jeff Kennedy's Asian-inspired specialities, such as tempura scallop and seared sashimi salad, or grab a seat on the deck. Last season, Gwyn's opened **Joe's Crab Shack.** Chef Joe Hope serves up a delicious assortment of fresh seafood and sushi on the deck at Gwyn's, weather permitting, and inside when it's snowing.

Some on-mountain options at Buttermilk and Highlands include the **Cliffhouse,** with a new outdoor deck atop Buttermilk that serves Mongolian Barbecue, a "salad bar" from which guests custom their own stir-fries; **Cloud Nine Cafe,** a European-style that began a new tradition in 1998 with the beginning of a fixed-price menu; and the **Merry-Go-Round,** located mid-mountain at Highlands, that serves grilled brats, burgers and Mexican fare.

Après-ski/nightlife

Ajax Tavern, adjacent to The Little Nell, draws a big crowd as the lifts start to close. If you don't find what you want there, the crowd spreads out to **The Little Nell Bar, Mezzaluna,** the **Aspen Club Lodge, Little Annie's,** Cooper Street Pier, the **J-Bar,** the **Red Onion** and O'Leary's. Après-ski comes in all varieties here, from **The Cantina,** with its very happy hour (have a margarita in the compadre size), to the quiet and genteel **Hotel Jerome Bar.**

At night, the music and dance beat begins to take over. Earlier in the evening, the high-energy place to find out who's in town is **Mezzaluna,** with its brassy horseshoe-shaped bar. **St. Regis** has live music in the lounge, and **The Little Nell** bar and **Syzygy** have jazz.

For a good singles bar and the best in upscale people-watching, head to **Mezzaluna.** **Eric's Bar, Cigar Bar** and **Aspen Billiards** also attract singles, and have lots of microbrews on tap (great scotch, too). Another upscale beer spot is **McStorlie's Pub.** A relatively mixed crowd with normal tastes congregate in the **Red Onion, Little Annie's** and O'Leary's.

Cooper Street Pier is very much a local and college student hangout. **Shooter's,** on Hyman Avenue, is a very dark and smoky bar with great deals on shooters and beer. For the best "last call," try **Mother Lode.** There are many other night spots in town; pick up a copy of Aspen Magazine's Traveler's Guide for a list, or local papers for current happenings.

Other activities

Ice skating is across from the transportation center at Silver Circle Ice Rink (925-6360) and indoors at Aspen Ice Garden (920-5141). For winter **fly-fishing** trips call Aspen Outfitting Co. (925-3406), Oxbow Outfitting Co. (925-1505) or Aspen Sports (925-6332). **Sleigh rides** take place at the T-Lazy-7 Ranch (925-7040). The T-Lazy-7 also leads **snowmobile tours** around the Maroon Bells and through the ghost town of Independence.

Cooking School of Aspen offers classes from Aspen's finest chefs for adults and kids (920-1879). **Spas and athletic clubs** offer relaxation after a tough day on the hill. Try the Aspen Club and Spa (925-8900), and the Aspen Athletic Club (925-2531).

Many winter visitors to Aspen never touch the slopes during their stay. The place is a **shopper's paradise,** and even if you can't afford the mostly high-end merchandise, browsing is part of the fun. High on the browsing scale is Boogie's, 534 E. Cooper St. In addition to funky clothes and other stuff, you'll find Elvis Presley's 1955 red Corvette (but not for sale).

Great shops for kitchen and home: Devonshire, 220 S. Mill St., for French and English antiques; Les Chefs D'Aspen, on the corner of Cooper and Hunter, sells imported kitchenware plus local gourmet foods and coffee. Of course, clothing stores are abundant and filled with unusual items. Some of our favorites: Hildegard's, 228 Mill St., for unique accessories; Limited Additions on the Mill Street Plaza for one-of-a-kind designer clothing; Goldies and the Kids, 205 S. Mill, for delightful kids' clothing. We usually stop by Gracy's and Susie's Ltd., both on E. Hopkins, to check out what the wear-it-once crowd has on consignment. Stefan Kaelin for Women is the first full-service ski shop for women only.

Most of Aspen's 30 **art galleries** are within a four-by-three-block area between Spring and Monarch Streets and Hopkins Ave. and Durant St. Our favorites are Omnibus Gallery for vintage poster art; Galerie Du Bois for Impressionism; Highline Gallery for glass art; and Pam Driscol Gallery for life-size bronze sculptures.

This last activity is a good way to segue into our transportation section. **The Ultimate Taxi** is a unique way to tour Aspen. This disco on wheels probably will top your list of Aspen Memorable Experiences. Check it out at www.ultimatetaxi.com or for a ride call 927-9239.

 # Getting there and getting around

By air: Aspen/Sardy Field is served by regular flights from four cities: Denver (United), Phoenix (America West), Memphis and Minneapolis/ St.Paul (Northwest Jet Airlink) and Los Angeles (United). Our staff flew in on the Sunday that ended Christmas vacation, just as some 150 private jets were stacked up waiting to fly out. Some of our staff got in, but with no luggage; others had to be bused from Denver and Glenwood Springs. It was a mess. Expect delays.

Eagle County airport, about 70 miles away, is becoming the best-served airport for this resort. It hosts scores of flights across the country. Colorado Mountain Express (800-525-6363 or 949-4227) takes skiers from Eagle to Aspen.

If you find yourself in Aspen without your gear or outdoor clothing, make sure to ask the airlines for a voucher to rent what you need until they show up with your luggage. All the airlines hand out coupons for equipment in case yours is delayed. These vouchers are accepted at virtually every sports shop in town.

Regular ground transportation also leaves the Denver International Airport for Aspen, but it's a very long drive on I-70, about 150 miles away. Rental cars are available at both Denver and Eagle County Airport.

By train: Amtrak has service to Glenwood Springs, where skiers can get ground transportation the rest of the way.

Getting around: Aspen has a free bus system, RFTA, with several routes in town and to Glenwood Springs. There also is a separate, free shuttle between the various ski mountains. Downtown is enjoyably walkable. Thank goodness a car is unnecessary—parking is a pain.

Nearby resorts

Sunlight Mountain Resort, Glenwood Springs, CO; (800) 445-7931

Internet: www.sunlightmtn.com

4 lifts; 440 acres; 2,010 vertical feet

Not only is this a less pricey ski option if you're headed to nearby Aspen, but Glenwood Springs is the home of the world's largest hot springs pool, two blocks long and kept at a toasty 90 degrees. Most of Ski Sunlight is intermediate terrain, though the double black diamond Sunlight Extreme provides steep and gladed challenges for the best of skiers and riders.

Lift tickets: Adults, $30; Junior (6-12) and Senior (60-69), $20; 70+ and younger than 5, free.

Distance from Denver: About 175 miles west on I-70 and Hwy. 82. The closest airport is Vail/Eagle, about 30 miles east of Sunlight Mountain. Aspen is about 50 miles south. Glenwood Springs is a daily stop on Amtrak's California Zephyr route from San Francisco to Chicago.

Lodging information: Call (800) 445-7931 for a free vacation planner.

Snowmass

Snowmass Village, Colorado

Summit elevation: 12,510 feet
Vertical drop: 4,406 feet
Base elevation: 8,104 feet

Address: Aspen Skiing Company
P.O. Box 1248, Aspen, CO 81612 or
Snowmass Resort Association,
P.O. Box 5566, Snowmass Village, CO 81615
✆ **Area code:** 970
Ski area phone: 925-1220 or
(800) 525-6200
Snow report: 925-1221 or (888-ASPEN-SNO, 277-3676)
ⓘ **Toll-free reservations:** (800) 598-2005
Fax: 920-0771
E-mail: info@aspensnowmass.com
Internet: www.aspensnowmass.com or
www.snowmassvillage.com
Expert:★★★★ **Advanced:**★★★★
Intermediate:★★★★★
Beginner:★★★ **Never-ever:**★★

Number of lifts: 20–7 high-speed quads,
2 triples, 6 doubles, 3 surface lifts, 2 magic carpets
Snowmaking: 6 percent
Skiable acreage: 3,010 acres
Uphill capacity: 27,978 per hour
Bed Base: 6,000 rentable units
Nearest lodging: slopeside, condos
Resort child care: Yes, 6 weeks and older
Snowboarding: Yes, unlimited
Adult ticket, per day: $29–$65 (00/01 prices)

Dining:★★★ (at resort)
★★★★★ (in the region)
Apres-ski/nightlife:★★(at resort)
★★★★★ (in the region)
Other activities:★★★

Though it is lumped into the Aspen experience by geography, Snowmass can stand on its own as a winter destination. Measuring by skiable acreage, Snowmass is one of the top 10 resorts in America in size, and it's the second-largest in Colorado (after Vail). It covers more than 3,010 acres—more than Ajax, Buttermilk and Highlands combined. And thanks to a surface lift to the top of the Cirque (formerly reached by a hike or snowcat), Snowmass lays claim to the highest lift-served skiing in North America, and the longest vertical drop in the United States, 4,406 feet. (Big Sky, MT, has a 4,180-foot vertical; Jackson Hole, WY, 4,139 feet. Now you have your après-ski bar conversation opener.)

Snowmass is a wonderful intermediate and advanced area. The Big Burn allows you to activate your autopilot, and the run from the top of Elk Camp to Fanny Hill is a four-mile-plus cruise. But Snowmass has steeps such as Hanging Valley that pucker up intermediates and delight experts.

Snowmass village seems to stretch forever. Like Keystone or Copper Mountain, this is a purpose-built winter resort. A village mall has shops, restaurants, bars and ski administration facilities. Hundreds of condos line the lower part of the resort, and about 95 percent of the lodging is ski-in/ski-out. It doesn't get much more convenient than Snowmass. A note to those staying in a ski-in/ski-out condo unit: Turn around and look at your unit before you head down to the lift for your first run. Try to find and remember a landmark, though it will be difficult in this land of brown condos. We had a heck of a time knowing where to leave the ski run to return to our condo at the end of the day.

A tip for those staying in Aspen and skiing here for a day: Park at the Two Creeks base area, which is closer to Aspen. The Two Creeks quad connects to the Elk Creek high-speed quad lift, getting you to the top of Elk Camp in less than 20 minutes.

A cool freebie is "First Tracks" on Wednesday and Friday at 8 a.m. Simply sign up the day before at the concierge desk and you can be one of the day's first to ski or ride down empty, freshly groomed slopes with a Ski & Snowboard School pro!

Mountain layout—Skiing

◆◆ **Expert:** Get a rush dropping through trees in the Hanging Valley Glades or into the bowl at Hanging Valley Wall—both double-blacks. To get there quickly on powder morns, take Wood Run, Alpine Springs and High Alpine Chairs. The ski school offers guided tours back here.

Another extreme playground is the Cirque, a scooped-out place between Sheer Bliss and High Alpine lifts. This is served by a surface lift, at the top of which you'll find the "Rocky Mountain High" run, named in memory of the late singer John Denver. Don't try this area unless you're comfortable on Hanging Valley Wall. You'll have to be deft of foot on Rock Island and KT Gully. Even more challenging is AMF at the top. A local says it stands for "Adios, My Friend," but we think he gave us the "this-is-a-family-guidebook" version.

◆ **Advanced:** Skiers ready to burn up steep-pitched cruising will think they've found nirvana when they make the first descent into the Campground area. Here is a wonderful long run: To come off the top of Big Burn on Sneaky's, tuck to avoid the uphill stretch at Sam's Knob, cut south around the Knob and head into the blacks of Bear Claw, Slot, Wildcat or Zugspitze to the base of the Campground lift. All offer great cruises and patches of moguls normally of the mellow sand-dune variety.

■ **Intermediate:** In addition to its black runs, Sam's Knob also is a great intermediate area, as are Elk Camp and the new Two Creeks area. The Big Burn is legendary cruiser fun. It's an entire side of a mountain that was allegedly set aflame by Ute Indians in the 1880s as a warning to advancing white settlers. The pioneers settled anyway, but the trees never grew back thickly, so the run, dotted by a few spruces, is a mile wide and a mile-and-a-half long. On low visibility days, though, watch out.

If the pitch at Big Burn is not quite to your liking, head over to High Alpine, which is perhaps five degrees steeper. If you ride the new surface lift to the Cirque and find it too challenging, ski the intermediate ridge back to the Big Burn.

●● **Beginner:** Beginners have a wide gentle area parallel to the village. Fanny Hill eases down by the mall, Wood Run lift opens another easy glide around the Wood Road side of the village, and further to the left a long straightaway, Funnel, will give beginners the feeling they're really covering terrain.

Beginners who want to see more of the mountain can head up to Sam's Knob and try Finestra with its spectacular views and great menu, enjoy the view and head down a meandering trail bearing the names Max Park, Lunchline and Dawdler, which turns back to Fanny Hill. (Avoid the blue runs on the face of Sam's Knob because they are not for beginners.) The next step up would be Elk Camp, labeled blue but very gentle.

● **Never-ever:** We would give the beginner terrain here a higher rating but for one important fact: Many of the ski-in/ski-out condos are along the green runs, so at the beginning and end of the day, they often are used by skilled skiers and snowboarders in a hurry to get to either the lifts or the hot tub. If you're just starting, we recommend a trip to Buttermilk.

Mountain layout—Snowboarding

Snowmass is so huge there's excellent terrain for riders of all levels—and persuasions. Expert riders should head to the Cirque. From the top of the lift, adrenaline seekers access the Cirque Headwall, AMF and Gowdy's.

The Campground area's snow generally stays untracked days after a big snowfall, delighting advanced riders who continue to discover fresh tree lines and bottomless powder stashes. To access Campground, go to the top of The Big Burn and stay rider's left to Sneaky's.

Intermediate boarders seeking to get avoid crowds on Fanny Hill should head for Elk Camp, where groomed intermediate slopes and a high-speed quad that let you rack up the vertical. From the top of the Elk Camp lift, a short 5- to10-minute hike takes you to Long Shot, a backcountry-like, ungroomed run that winds 3 miles through the National forest—getting you even further away from the bubbas. Long Shot was recently voted "2nd Favorite Snowboard Run" by readers, mostly locals, of the Aspen Times, right behind The Big Burn.

The Big Burn is a gigantic open area on the mountain, intermediate in pitch, approximately a mile wide by a mile long. A few trees here and there disrupt an otherwise completely open snowfield. On a powder day you can make endless turns, until your thighs also feel the big burn. There's nothing like it at any other ski area in North America. Eventually you'll end up on Dallas Freeway or Wineskin, which will take you back to The Big Burn Lift.

If you are so lucky as to get powder so deep that even The Big Burn isn't steep enough, head over to the High Alpine lift for steeper terrain. From the top of High Alpine, ambitious riders hike 10 minutes to get hang time on Hanging Valley Wall. The Alpine Springs and Naked Lady lifts serve a variety of intermediate runs including Lunkerville and Coffee Pot. The Naked Lady offers some fun rollers.

If you think tricks are for kids, Snowmass has two halfpipes and two terrain parks with features suitable for freestylers of all levels. Park designer and pro rider Jim Mangan designed both parks. The Sam's Knob and Coney Glade lifts, both high-speed quads, provide dedicated lift access to Trenchtown, home to a halfpipe and terrain park geared for advanced riders (the Coney Glade lift gives you full view of freestylers in action). There's a booming sound system and the Trenchtown yurt is an upbeat warming hut. The Trenchtown halfpipe is 300 feet long and is cut with a 12-foot Pipe Dragon. The Trenchtown Park, separated by the pipe into upper and lower sections, has a variety of tabletops, spine ramps, rail-slides and fun boxes. For 2001/02 there will also be a boardercross course on Upper Velvet Falls, directly to rider's left of the Trenchtown halfpipe. Beginner and intermediate snowboarders will want to take the Funnel chairlift to the Funnel halfpipe and terrain park.

Assay Hill is a good spot for learning to snowboard. You'll find it near the Funnel lift, to the left of Fanny Hill, the Snowmass Village Mall and the ticket office.

Mountain rating

This is an intermediate mountain, even though it has pockets of excellent advanced terrain and beginner smoothies. If experts know where to go, they will love it here. Skiers and riders who crave cruising will think they have arrived in heaven. Few competent skiers and riders who have returned from Snowmass have been heard complaining. That's the best recommendation of all.

Cross-country and snowshoeing

Nordic skiing at Snowmass is on the golf course at the **Snowmass Cross Country Center** (923-3148). It offers lessons and rentals, plus its trails connect with the most extensive free Nordic trail system in America, which runs between the towns of Aspen and Snowmass and covers more than 80 km. of groomed trails. For other information on cross-country skiing opportunities, see the Aspen chapter.

Snowshoe tours leave daily at 10 a.m. and 1 p.m. from Two Creeks for a naturalist-led tour of a secluded loop through the woods. Tours including lifts, equipment and a snack are $49 for adults, $29 for ages 8–19 and 65 and older. Call 800-525-6200 or 925-5756.

Lessons (2001/02 prices)

Group lessons: Adult small group lessons cost $99 a day and $62 for a half day. Limited to an average of four per class for all levels. Unlimited extensions are $89 per day.

Never-ever package: Three-day first-time skier packages, including equipment rental, run $327 and are offered at Snowmass and Buttermilk. One-day programs are $109. Unlimited extensions of the three-day program are $99 per day.

Private lessons: $309 for a half day for one to five people; $1,500 for five half days; and $2,100 for five full days. Other discounts are available. Reservations are required. Lessons include ski storage, lift line privileges, and demo discounts.

Special programs: Numerous, including clinics and/or ski weeks for women, bumps, powder, disabled skiers, video analysis, equipment assessment, shaped skis, and many more. Call ASC at (800) 525-6200 and ask for a ski and snowboard school brochure.

Snowmass has one other instruction program that we believe is unique among U.S. ski resorts: speed skiing. On Fridays, skiers can pay $5 for three runs down Slot, a black-diamond run in the Sam's Knob area, or $15 for the day. Basic instruction and a helmet are included, and participants can rent specialized skis for an extra fee. You'll get a certificate indicating your speed, often as high as 65 miles per hour.

Racing: NASTAR is offered for $6 for two runs or $10 for the entire day for adults; children pay $4 for two runs or $8 for the entire day. Clinics also are offered.

Child care (2001/02 prices)

Ages: 8 weeks to 3 years.
Costs: $57 half day, $89 a day with multiday discounts.
Reservations: Required; call 923-0563 or (800) 525-6200.

Other options: Little Red School House (923-3756) offers licensed day care for ages 3–5; **Aimee's Angels** (923-2809) has care for ages 12 months–3 years. **Nighthawks** is an evening child care program (923-0470) for ages 3–10; $12/hour for the first child; half that price for additional children in the same family. For other suggestions, see the Aspen chapter.

Children's lessons: We've listed the children's programs at Snowmass here; kids' lessons at Buttermilk and Aspen Highlands are in the Aspen chapter. To make reservations for the following lessons, call (800) 525-6200.

Snow Cubs is for ages 8 weeks–3 years. Toddlers get daycare, lunch and brief ski lessons. Toilet-trained 3-year-olds take group lessons, while the others must enroll in private lessons. The cost is $89 for a full day, plus $65 if a private lesson is needed. Big Burn Bears is for ages 3–4 years. They have a segregated learning area and indoor area. The cost is $89 for a full day (all full-day lessons include equipment and lunch); $57 for a half day. One-hour private lessons are $99. Grizzlies is the same price, but for ages 5–6. Bears on Board is a snowboard program for ages 5–7. It costs $159 for a full day, and includes rental equipment, which is extra in the other programs. Ages 7–12 for skiing, and 8–12 for snowboarding, have full-day classes for $69 (with lunch); $52 for half-day.

Teens ages 13–19 can enroll in "Too Cool for School" every day of the season, where groups are formed by age, ability and "personality." The program includes races and mountain picnics with evening activities such as ice skating. The cost is $64 per day, $174 for three days, $320 for five days and $55 for a half day.

Lift tickets (2001/02 prices)

Aspen/Snowmass lift ticket prices had not been set as of late August 2001. According to a spokeswoman, they are committed to "variable" pricing based on the weather and snow conditions. Aspen promises not to exceed $65 a day for lift tickets. These prices reflect Aspen's maximum price. If the weather is bad and snow conditions miserable you may ski for less; if you can make plans months in advance (like advance-purchase airline tickets) you can pay less; there are also lift/lodging packages that offer savings.

Who skis free: Ages 6 and younger.

Who skis at a discount: Those 70 years and older get unlimited skiing or riding with The Silver Pass for $119 all season long. Ages 65 to 69 pay $177 for three days, $295 for five and $354 for six.

Accommodations

Snowmass has few hotels but thousands of condominiums, many of which are slopeside. Hotel and lodge prices generally start at $150 and up a night (condos about $50 more). For other recommendations, and reservations, call **Snowmass Central Reservations** (800-598-2004). That agency uses four price categories: economy, moderate, deluxe and luxury. Economy lodging-lift packages start at less than $100 per person per night, while luxury packages will run more than $200.

Hotel accommodations are relatively limited: **The Snowmass Lodge and Club** ($$$$), below the village, offers condos with health club access and serves as the Nordic center. There are regular shuttles to the slopes. **The Silvertree Hotel** ($$$$) is the other luxury hotel, open since the ski area began in 1967. Less expensive hotel or lodge accommodations include the **Pokolodi Lodge** ($-$$$), **Snowmass Inn** ($-$$$), **Stonebridge** ($-$$$), in the center of the village, **Snowmass Mountain Chalet** ($-$$$), which includes a full breakfast and soup lunch and slopeside convenience or **Wildwood Lodge** ($$-$$$$). We're particularly impressed with the Wildwood Lodge and the Silvertree. Both are comfortable with beautiful rooms, and close to everything in Snowmass.

Our staff stayed at **The Crestwood Condominiums** (www.thecrestwood.com; $$$-$$$$) and found them comfortable, roomy, right next to the slopes and well-designed for groups. In the deluxe category, these condos have fireplaces, a bathroom for every bedroom, laundry facilities, a swimming pool, exercise room and airport shuttle service.

Snowmass Lodging Company (800-365-0410 or 923-3232) books some of the most upscale condos, including **Woodrun V** ($$$$) and **Chamonix** ($$$$). In the economy category, we like **Willows**, two levels below the village mall. In the moderate category, try

Terracehouse ($$$-$$$$) or **Lichenhearth** ($$$-$$$$), which are close to Willows. The **Top of the Village** ($$$-$$$$) and the **Timberline** ($$-$$$$) condos are a good five- to 10-minute climb above the village mall. The **Sonnenblick** ($$$$) has only large units, three to five bedrooms in the deluxe price category.

Dining

Snowmass Village claims some of the best restaurants in the area. Known for its dogsledding and kennels, **Krabloonik,** (923-3953; $$$) has an even bigger reputation for its restaurant's wild-game selection and extensive wine list. In a rustic log house at Snowmass, this venue offers panoramic views of Mt. Daly and Capitol Peak.

The Snowmass Club bistro, **Sage** (923-5600; $$$), offers distinctive food with a casual unpretentious atmosphere and at more moderate prices.

Most other eateries are in the Village Mall (if we don't tell you, that's where you'll find them). The chef at **La Provence** (923-6804), Maurice Couturier, was once the late King of Jordan's chef. It serves southern French fare. **The Magarita Grill** (923-6803), also run by the same chef, serves southwestern cuisine influenced by Central America. Other quality spots are **Il Poggio** (923-4292; $$$) and **The Conservatory** ($$$), in the Silvertree Hotel.

Midrange dining can be found at **The Stonebridge Restaurant** ($$-$$$), **Butch's Lobster Bar** ($$$; located at the top of the village), **Brothers' Grille** ($-$$), which reportedly has the best hamburgers in the valley, and **Mountain Dragon** ($-$$) for Chinese.

Every restaurant in Snowmass has children's menus. **The Stew Pot** ($-$$) features soups, tasty and unusual stews and sandwiches. For other soups and sandwiches, try **Paradise Bakery** ($) in Silvertree Plaza. Or go to **S'no Beach Café** ($-$$) featuring "eggs S'noBeach" for breakfast. **Café Rolf**, owned and operated by a Swiss chef, is a good family-style place.

Spend a family evening at the **Burlingame Cabin** (923-0575; $$$) or the **Lynn Britt Cabin** (923-0575) nestled in aspen groves on Snowmass. At both, a heated snowcat and well-blanketed open-air sleigh transport guests to a cabin with wood stove, western-style meal, bluegrass entertainment and sing-alongs.

For a quick breakfast on the way to the slopes, try **Moondogs Cable Car. Café D&E** serves gourmet coffee from inside D&E Snowboard shop. The afore-mentioned **S'no Beach Café** is where our staff—hearty-breakfast fans that we are—chowed down. Locals stop at the **Wildcat**, in the shopping center, for a massive (and inexpensive) breakfast. Try the cream chip beef or have a giant omelette with pancakes, sausage and bacon.

Snowmass Village excels with mountaintop cookery. **Gordon's High Alpine Restaurant** (reservations are essential, 923-5188), at the top of Alpine Springs (Lift 8), is the spot for fine dining. Gordon's offers a sit-down breakfast daily from 9:30 to 10:30 a.m. Lunch is served from 11:30 a.m. to 2:30 p.m. **Krabloonik** (923-3953), mentioned earlier as a dinner choice, is also open for lunch. It is at the base of Campground off the Dawdler Catwalk.

Another on-mountain option is **Up 4 Pizza** ($) at the top of the Big Burn in Snowmass. For quick "power food," head to one of the **yurts** near the snowboard halfpipes and the terrain park, or at the bottom of Assay Hill.

At the base of **Two Creeks** ($), you can get made-to-order wraps and New York deli-style sandwiches. **Finestra** at Sam's Knob has sitdown dining or head to the **cafeteria.** The **Cirque Café** ($-$$), slopeside at the Snowmass Village Mall, has a buffet breakfast for a fast exit to the slopes in the morning, and a more leisurely sit-down lunch and dinner service.

Après-ski/nightlife

The **Cirque Café** and the **Brothers' Grille** are the hubs of après-ski. The Cirque Café tends to be more crowded and rowdier. Brothers' has five different draft beers and almost a dozen hot drinks for quick warmups. **Zane's Tavern** is a sports bar with après-ski drink specials. At night Snowmass Village is quiet. The best action in town is at the **Tower**, where Doc Eason performs magic throughout the night.

Other activities

The **Anderson Ranch Arts Center** (923-3181) in Snowmass Village exhibits work by visiting and resident artists during the winter. The center also offers a series of workshops in ceramics, woodworking and photography from January through April. Call for current events.

Krabloonik Kennels in Snowmass Village (923-4342) is known for its daily tours through the Snowmass wilderness area, led by Iditarod-experienced huskies. Morning or afternoon rides include a four-course gourmet lunch at the kennel's restaurant in Snowmass Village. Rides last about two hours and cost about $195 per person; $125 for children aged 3-8.

A **sledding hill** at the Snowmass Cross Country Center (923-3148) is open from 9 a.m. to 5 p.m. daily. Plastic sleds and wooden toboggans can be rented for $5 or $15 per day, respectively. A **tubing hill** at Tube Town, on Assay Hill operated from noon until 8 p.m. daily. Cost is $15 for unlimited runs, and the use of tubes.

For more information about off-slope activities, see "Other Activities" in the Aspen chapter or contact Snowmass Village Resort Association (800-598-2006; 923-2000).

Getting there and getting around

See the Aspen chapter for information on getting to the region. Getting around Snowmass Village is a little more involved than getting around Aspen, so we'd like to share some tips based on our experience (and we still recommend that you use public transportation because of limited parking):

Getting around: The Roaring Fork Valley's (mostly) free bus system, RFTA, will shuttle you between Snowmass and Aspen. At Snowmass Village, you board the RFTA bus at the transportation center at the Snowmass Village Mall. Between 8 a.m. and 4:30 p.m., the RFTA bus is free. After 4:30 p.m., however, the charge is $3 per person, one way, between Aspen and Snowmass Village. (RFTA buses within Aspen are free in the evening.) If you have been skiing at one of the three mountains in Aspen and you relax in the bar afterward, keep a close eye on the clock so the charge doesn't take you by surprise.

Snowmass Village has a separate, free shuttle system with several routes that run throughout the village. To get to Aspen, you ride a Snowmass Village shuttle to the transportation center, then transfer to an RFTA bus. Although the system is very efficient (and you can't beat the price), it takes about an hour to get from a Snowmass Village condo to Aspen, and vice versa. If you expect to make two round trips per day into Aspen (one for skiing and the second for nightlife), stay in Aspen. Otherwise, you will feel as if you spent most of your vacation riding a bus.

Summit County

Colorado

Some winter vacationers aren't satisfied with skiing and riding at just one place. When they return to the office, they want to drop resort names and compare the black-diamond plunges. For these skiers, we suggest Summit County.

Summit County, about a 90-minute drive from downtown Denver, has four well-known ski areas—Breckenridge, Copper Mountain, Keystone and Arapahoe Basin. Each resort—except A-Basin—has its own village with lodging, shopping and restaurants.

If you plan to do most of your skiing at just one area, stay at that resort, but if you want to experience them all and save some money, then set up your base camp in Dillon, Frisco or Silverthorne, three small towns off I-70 that surround Lake Dillon, a reservoir.

This tri-town area is smack in the center of the ski action. Breckenridge is about 9 miles in one direction, Copper Mountain 5 miles in another, Keystone 7 miles away in a third, and A-Basin just a little farther than Keystone. Having a car is nice, but not really necessary. The reliable Summit Stage, the free bus system subsidized by sales tax revenue, runs between the towns and the ski areas all day.

Summit County deserves its lofty name. It has a base elevation above 9,000 feet. (If you have problems with high altitudes, take note. If you like spring skiing, also take note: High elevations usually mean a longer ski season.) Each of these areas stays open at least until late April most years, and Arapahoe Basin—with its base lodge above 10,000 feet—often stays open until July 4.

Vail Resorts Inc. owns Keystone and Breckenridge. It has an interchangeable lift ticket that includes Vail, Beaver Creek, Keystone and Breckenridge, or you can buy a multi-day ticket for Keystone and Breckenridge alone for a little less. Your Keystone-Breckenridge ticket also is valid at Arapahoe Basin, or you can buy that ticket separately. You'll have to buy a separate ticket to ski at Copper Mountain, which is owned by rival ski-resort corporation Intrawest.

This chapter lists accommodations, dining, nightlife and non-ski activities in the tri-town area of Frisco, Dillon and Silverthorne. You can pick up information and helpful brochures at two Summit County Chamber Visitors' Centers, one at 150 Tenderfoot (off Lake Dillon Drive) in Dillon and another in Frisco on North Summit Boulevard. Or call the chamber at 800-530-3099 or 668-0376. They'll act as matchmaker for you and your lodging needs. Some helpful Web sites are www.summitchamber.org, www.summitnet.com, www.TownofDillon.com or www.friscocolorado.com.

Separate chapters detail skiing, lodging, dining and nightlife at Breckenridge, Copper Mountain and Keystone. For information on A-Basin, refer to the Keystone chapter.

 ## Accommodations

Frisco: This is our first choice for a home base, for several reasons. One, it is the closest town to Breckenridge and Copper Mountain, and Keystone isn't far away. Two, its downtown area along Main Street has lots of funky shops and restaurants, perfect for a late afternoon or evening stroll. And three, we like friendly mountain inns, and found three good ones.

The **Galena Street Inn** (800-248-9138 or 668-3224; $–$$), First Avenue and Galena Street (one block off Main Street), was built just a few years ago. Its 15 rooms have private baths, televisions and phones, and all are nicely furnished. A hot tub and sauna are among the amenities. A full breakfast with hot entrée is included, as are après-ski refreshments. No smoking or pets. For each extra person in the same room, it's $20 each.

The gurgling of Ten Mile Creek is the wake-up call for guests at **Creekside Inn** (800-668-7320 or 668-5607; $–$$$). Innkeepers Vince and Jill Pierse found this quiet setting at the west end of Main Street the ideal spot to build a quintessential mountain inn with a touch of the Old World. Afternoon snacks, special-diet and early-bird breakfasts, ski storage and wheelchair access are a few of the amenities. The seven guest rooms each have a private bath, and a fireplace in the great room and deck hot tub make this a tempting home away from home. No Smoking, no pets, no children younger than age 12.

Hotel Frisco (800-262-1002 or 668-5009; $–$$$) was completely remodeled a few years ago. The cozy ski lodge, located at 308 Main Street, has 16 nicely decorated rooms, a huge river-rock fireplace in the lobby and an outdoor hot tub.

If you're looking for super-budget lodging, try **Just Bunks** (668-4757; $), a "home-style hostel." For moderately inexpensive rooms, try the **Open Box H Bed & Breakfast** (970-668-0661; $–$$), four rooms all with private bath, television, phone and full breakfast.

Dillon/Silverthorne: Lodging here is mostly chain hotels and motels.

The **Best Western Ptarmigan Lodge** (800-842-5939 or 468-2341; $$–$$$) in the Dillon town center is one of the best bargains, particularly during the early and late seasons and in January. Another moderately priced motel is the **Dillon Inn** (800-262-0801 or 262-0801; $$–$$$), which has an indoor pool. **The Lodge at Carolina in the Pines** (262-7500; $$–$$$$) is a B&B that overlooks Lake Dillon and has a serene setting.

Off the interstate in Silverthorne are side-by-side chain hotels: **Four Points by Sheraton Hotel** (800-321-3509 or 468-6200; $$–$$$) and **Days Inn** (800-329-7466 or 468-8661; $$–$$$). The Summit Stage stops at their doors, and they are convenient to the Factory Stores (see *Other Activities*).

Budget travelers should stay at the **Super 8** (800-800-8000; 468-8888; $$–$$$) in Dillon, across from the Summit Place Shopping Center. Most of the best cheap restaurants are in this center. Or, try the **Alpen Hutte Lodge** (468-6336; $–$$), 471 Rainbow Drive. Both the Greyhound bus from Denver and the Summit County shuttle buses stop there, and for about $27, you get a bed in an eight-person dorm room. There are also private rooms that sleep two and private family rooms that sleep four. The lodge has a nice kitchen, is clean and it's walking distance from restaurants (especially the brewery) and shopping.

The towns have many more B&Bs, chain hotels, private homes and condos. For reservations, call **Summit County Central Reservations**, 800-365-6365, or **Reservations for the Summit** at 800-999-9510.

Dining

Frisco: Perhaps the best restaurant in Frisco is **Uptown Bistro** (668-4728) on Main Street. A '90s bistro atmosphere complements an uptown á la carte menu. Main courses include such delights as pumpkin squash ravioli with sage brown butter and garlic-ginger-flavored seared ahi tuna with a spicy mushroom spring roll. Great desserts and wood-oven-baked gourmet pizzas. Make reservations and ask to be seated in the back, away from the front-door draft.

A longtime favorite is the **Blue Spruce Inn** (668-5900; $$$) in a historic log cabin at the corner of Madison and Main. Entrées include such dishes as filet béarnaise, vegetables en croûte, grilled venison and scallops dijonaise. The food is good, though a little sauce-heavy, and the atmosphere and service are excellent. Reservations recommended.

People flock to **Tuscato** (668-3644; $$$) on Main Street, which serves an eclectic collection of excellent Italian cuisine. A Southwestern-styled restaurant is **Golden Annie's** (668-0345; $$) on the corner of 6th and Main. **El Rio Cantina & Grill** (668-5043; $$), 450 W. Main, has the most complete Mexican menu and a lively happy hour, and **Barkley's** (668-3694; $$) at 620 Main St. serves good prime rib and Mexican food. **Ti Amo** (668-1993) dishes out creative Italian meals and excellent wines.

Budget eats: Locals recommended **Ge-Jo's** (668-3308), upstairs at 409 Main St., for inexpensive Italian fare and **Szechuan Taste** (668-5685) at 310 Main St. for Chinese food (dine in or take out). Frisco also has many fast-food chain restaurants, most along Summit Boulevard. **Deli Belly's** has giant sandwiches at 275 Main Street in Frisco.

Halfway between Frisco and Breckenridge, in an area called Farmer's Korner, are neighboring restaurants that are quite different. **The Blue River Inn** (547-9928; $) is a no-frills local hangout with great burgers, inexpensive draft beers and a 10-ounce sirloin that is probably still less than $10. **The Swan Mountain Inn** (453-7903; $$$) offers an elegant, nightly four-course meal in a seven-table dining room with a fireplace. The inn also has a weekend brunch.

Dillon & Silverthorne: Locals and visitors alike rave about **Silverheels Southwest Grill** (468-2926; $–$$$) at 81 Buffalo Drive in Silverthorne. Fine Southwestern fare and a Spanish tapas bar are the specialties here. The restaurant, in a hacienda-style building in the Wildernest area, is a bit off the main drag but worth the search. When you call for reservations ask for directions.

Another choice for finer dining is **Ristorante Al Lago** (468-6111; $$) in the Dillon town center. It serves Northern Italian meals. **The Old Chicago Restaurant** (468-6200; $–$$) with 110 different beers and great happy hours is at the Four Points Hotel.

For more casual dining in Dillon, try the **Dillon Dam Brewery** (262-7777; $$), which lives up to its slogan, "the best dam brewery in town"; **Pug Ryan's** (468-2145; $) in the Dillon town center; or **Wild Bill's Stone Oven Pizza** (468-2006; $), also in the Dillon town center. Some of the best deli sandwiches we've ever had are at **Gastronome's Gourmet Catering & Deli** (469-0218; $), upstairs from Wild Bill's.

In Silverthorne, you can cook your own meat over an open grill at **The Historic Mint** (468-5247; $$) or enjoy Tex-Mex food at **Old Dillon Inn** (468-2791; $), which was relocated to Silverthorne just before Lake Dillon was created. Budget diners: the Summit Place Shopping Center on Highway 6 on the Dillon-Silverthorne border has several great restaurants, including **Sunshine Cafe** (468-6663), jammed with locals; and **Nick-N-Willy's** (262-1111) for very good bake-your-own take-out pizza.

The best breakfast in the tri-town area is **Claimjumper** (668-3617), on Summit Boulevard across the street from Wal-Mart in Frisco. Not only does it have an extensive omelet-and-pancake menu, it has breakfast specials that taste great and fill the plate. A close second is the **Arapahoe Cafe** (468-0873) on Lake Dillon Drive in the Dillon town center, a huge favorite with locals. The cafe building used to stand in the old town of Dillon, but was moved in the 1960s when the reservoir flooded the area. The service is great, the menu names are creative

(Arapahuevos Rancheros, Hans and Franz Power Breakfast, etc.) and eavesdropping on the other tables will fill you in on local politics. Both restaurants also have inexpensive lunch and dinner menus.

Definitely in the running for the Best Breakfast title are **Sunshine Cafe** in the Summit Place Shopping Center and **Log Cabin Cafe** (668-3847) on Main Street in Frisco.

For those who prefer a lighter breakfast, head for the **Butterhorn Bakery** (668-3997), 408 W. Main Street in Frisco. Across the street is **Pika Bagel Bakery** (668-0902), and in the Summit Place Shopping Center in Silverthorne is **Blue Moon Baking Company** (468-1472).

Après-ski/nightlife

Mountain resorts and brew pubs seem to go hand in hand. Summit County has five, three of which are in the tri-town area. **Backcountry Brewery** is on the corner of Summit and Main in Frisco, **Pug Ryan's** is in the Dillon Town Center and **The Dam Brewery** is in Dillon. (The others are in Breckenridge and Keystone; read about them in those chapters.) The current trend is to end a day on the mountain with a freshly drawn Colorado specialty brewski. All three places serve food and have lively happy hours.

The leading sports bar is **High Mountain Billiards**, an upscale game room with pool tables, dart boards, shuffleboard, chess, checkers, backgammon and sports TV. This no-smoking, richly decorated bar serves a mostly over-30 clientele. It's next to the Backcountry Brewery in Frisco. **Barkley's West** in Frisco varies its entertainment from live music to dance classes to Under 21 nights.

Old Dillon Inn in Silverthorne has live Country & Western music on weekends, and the best margaritas in town. Its 120-year-old bar definitely has authentic Old West atmosphere. The building was pieced together from bits of defunct establishments, and the whole thing was moved in 1961 when the old town of Dillon disappeared under the aforementioned lake. Other popular choices are the **Pub Down Under**, underneath the Arapahoe Cafe in Dillon, or the **Corona St. Grill,** in the Dillon Town Center.

Child care

Services of the Summit, Inc. (668-0255) in Frisco has professional babysitters ages 18–65 who are insured, bonded and child-care trained. They will come to your hotel or condo anywhere in the county. **Baby's Away** (800-979-9030) rents and will deliver baby needs to your lodge, such as crib, stroller, car seat and toys.

Other activities

Companies that offer **snowmobiling** and/or **sleigh and dogsled rides** are Tiger Run Tours, 453-2231; Good Times Tours, 453-7604; and Two Below Zero Dinner Sleigh Rides, 453-1520. In the Dillon/Silverthorne area, call Eagles Nest Equestrian Center, 468-0677. **Summit Activities Center** offers an activity concierge service at 888-230-2844.

Cross-country skiing is available at the Frisco Nordic Center on Highway 9 about one mile out of town toward Breckenridge. Trail passes are $10, with discounts for those aged 55 and older or 12 and younger. Rentals and instruction are available. Call 668-0866.

Pack an extra suitcase for **shopping.** Better yet, buy a bag at one of the luggage stores in the **Silverthorne Factory Outlets.** Then start filling it with bargains at nearly 80 brand-name stores. This is probably the largest factory outlet center in Western ski country. Among the

Dining: $$$-Entrees $20+; $$-$10-20; $-less than $10.
Accommodations: (double room) $$$$-$200+; $$$-$141-$200; $$-$81-$140; $-$80 and less.

stores are Carole Little, Anne Klein, Liz Claiborne, Levi, Nike, Bass Shoes, American Tourister and Samsonite.

Collectibles and antiques lovers will go nuts at **Junk-Tique,** 313 Main St. in Frisco. It has an excellent inventory of collectible housewares, clothing and furniture. The store also stocks some new jewelry and knickknack items. Kids will love the huge black locomotive that is the centerpiece of the store. Cigar lovers can stop by **Antler's Liquor Store** in Frisco, which has what the owner claims is the largest humidor room in Colorado.

 ## Getting there and getting around

By air and car: Frisco, Dillon and Silverthorne are just off I-70, about 75 miles west of downtown Denver and 90 miles from Denver International Airport. Resort Express vans transport from Denver International Airport, 800-334-7433 or 468-7600. The airport is about two hours away.

Getting around: Frisco is laid out nicely for walking along Main Street or you can take the free Frisco Flyer from 7 a.m. to 7 p.m. Otherwise, take the Summit Stage, the free bus system that links the towns with each other and the ski areas.

A car is an option here; most distances are too far for walking, but the Summit Stage is reliable. Call 668-0999 for route info, or pick up a route map and schedule from the Chamber of Commerce or the stores that carry them. Note that the bus takes about an hour to get from one resort to another. If you really enjoy nightlife and want to do extensive exploration of the restaurants and bars, we recommend a car. For car rental once you get to Summit County, call Summit Car Rental (453-8212 or 888-677-1949).

Nearby resorts

Loveland, Georgetown, CO; (800) 736-3754 or (303) 569-3203

Internet: www.skiloveland.com
11 lifts; 1,365 acres; 2,410 vertical feet
One of our Colorado-based contributors keeps the daily snow report on her e-mail update, the Loveland Cam on her browser, and is ready to jump into her car at a moment's notice and drive an hour to some of the best big-mountain skiing in the state. The snow is reliably deep (the base at 10,600 feet means this is *real* high in the mountains) from mid-October through about mid-May.

You see the area as you approach the Eisenhower Tunnel along I-70 west from Denver. It looms into the distance right up to the Continental Divide, and spreads out on both sides of the interstate. A ski area in two parts, Loveland Basin and Loveland Valley are connected by a lift and a shuttle service. Loveland Valley, on the left as you approach the tunnel, is great for beginners, intermediates and anyone who wants to hide from the stiff winds that sometimes plague Loveland Basin. The Basin is a real stash, jammed with enough expert and advanced terrain to challenge the best and stuffed with intermediate runs and long cruisers, most of which you can't see from I-70. By the way—snowboarding accounts for more than 25-percent of lift ticket sales—the highest ratio of any Colorado area.

Experts can get high here—The Ridge, with its 400 acres of wild terrain, tops out at 13,010 feet, and is an above-timberline alpine garden of glades, chutes and bowls. A few seasons ago the area opened Chair 9, the highest four-passenger chair lift in the world, so you no longer have to hike up to get the goodies. **Advanced** skiers should head for Chair 1 for bumps and chutes. Avalanche Bowl is a nasty short and sweet drop and Busy Gully demands tight turns right under the chair. Chairs 4 and 8 access the far right, a mix of wilderness-type bowls at the top, narrowing into tree bashing in the East and West Ropes and at Fail Safe. **Intermediates and beginners** can handle everything else, particularly Chairs 2, 4 and 6. Snowboarders enjoy their own terrain park.

Child care starts at 12 months. Loveland offers a 3 Class Pass, where beginner skiers and riders (kids and adults) receive a free season pass after taking three lessons. Women in Motion clinics focus on ski and snowboard techniques and industry developments. Telemark Clinics are scheduled throughout the season.

Lift tickets (01/02): Adults, $42; children (6-14) $17; ages 5 and younger ski free. Lower rates early and late season. The Flex Ticket, valid any four consecutive hours during the day, is offered during the regular season only for $32.

Distance from Denver: 56 miles west via I-70 (about 80 miles from Denver airport).

Lodging information: (800) 225-LOVE (5683). Lodging can be found in Georgetown, Idaho Springs or Dillon, each within 15 miles.

Eldora Mountain Resort, Nederland, CO; (800) 444-0447, (303) 440-8700

Internet: www.eldora.com

12 lifts; 680 acres; 1,400 vertical feet

Eldora's stats are misleading: This skis and rides like a bigger mountain and draws significant crowds from Denver, Boulder and the Midwest states. Actually four mountains, the area lays out nicely according to ability level. In the back, experts and advanced skiers head for Corona Bowl's black- and double-black-diamond terrain. Runs like the West Ridge are definitely challenging, and the chutes and glades are for experienced skiers only. Indian Peaks and Challenge Mountain are laced with wide-open cruisers like everyone's favorite first run, Hornblower, while Little Hawk Mountain is the beginner and family skiing and riding zone. Snowboarders play in three terrain parks and what is claimed to be Colorado's steepest halfpipe.

Because this is the closest skiing to Denver, weekends can get crowded. But then, you won't have to drive the Interstate to get to Eldora—a fact that balances out the occasional lift lines. Excellent kids' and family programs and the most popular Nordic Trail system in the state. A new multi-story base lodge is scheduled to open for the 2001/02 season. The 16,000-square-foot lodge, built of logs and natural indigenous rock, is more centrally located and will house the rental shop, child care, ski school registration and dining services.

Lift tickets (00/01): Adult, $42; children/seniors, $17; kids 5 and younger & seniors 70 and older ski free.

Distance from Denver: 65 miles from DIA. 45 miles from Denver via U.S. highway 36 and state highway 119. 21 miles from Boulder. Eldora is the only ski resort with scheduled bus service seven days a week via the Regional Transportation District, (303) 299-6002.

Lodging information: (800) 444-0447 (Boulder Convention and Visitors Bureau). Accommodations are in the historic mining town of Nederland, plus Boulder and Denver.

Breckenridge

Colorado

Summit elevation: 12,146 feet
Vertical drop: 2,546 feet (lift-served)
Base elevation: 9,600 feet

Address: Box 1058
Breckenridge, CO 80424
✆ **Area code:** 970
Ski area phone: 453-5000 or
(800) 427-8308
Snow report: 453-6118
ⓘ **Toll-free reservations:**
(800) 221-1091; (888) 251-2399;
UK: (800) 289-7491
Toll-free foreign fax numbers:
UK: 0800-96-0055
Brazil: 000811-715-5559
Germany: 0130-82-7807
Netherlands: 06-022-6653
Fax: 453-7238
E-mail: breckguest@vailresorts.com (ski area)
cenres@gobreck.com (lodging)
Internet: www.breckenridge.com (ski area)
or www.gobreck.com (visitors' bureau)

Expert:★★★★
Advanced:★★★★★
Intermediate:★★★★
Beginner:★★★★
Never-ever:★★★★
Number and types of lifts: 25—1 six-pack chair,
5 high-speed quads, 1 triple, 7 doubles and 11
surface lifts
Skiable acreage: 2,043 acres
Snowmaking: 26 percent (516 acres)
Uphill capacity: 32,656 per hour
Snowboarding: Yes
Bed base: 23,000+
Nearest lodging: Slopeside
Resort child care: Yes, 2 months and older
Adult ticket, per day: $31–$57 (00/01 prices)

Dining:★★★
Apres-ski/nightlife:★★★★
Other activities:★★★

Breckenridge has become one of the snowsports industry's giants, attracting more than a million visits each season. A good number are Front Range skiers and riders, those who live in Denver and its suburbs. Another large portion is destination visitors from the U.S. And a third fast-growing group is visitors from Great Britain, Mexico and other countries.

Breckenridge has a split personality, but it's been that way from the beginning. It was named for a man who became a Confederate brigadier general, but its streets are named after past Presidents—Washington, Lincoln, Jefferson and Adams. The Victorian buildings lining the streets witnessed wild revelry during gold and silver booms and the discovery of Colorado's largest gold nugget—the 13-pound "Tom's Baby" in 1887—but they also stood silent over windswept, vacant streets when Breckenridge nearly joined the list of Colorado ghost towns after WWII.

Though the closest Breckenridge comes to being a ghost town these days is the mud season in May, it still displays its inherited division. Modern architecture around the base area is a contrast to the Victorian downtown, which houses hundreds of boutiques, scores of pubs and dozens of restaurants packed into brightly-colored, restored 19th-century buildings in Colorado's largest historic district.

You'll find your fellow skiers and snowboarders are a mixed bag. Though the general atmosphere is still more down-to-earth than at some other Colorado resorts, Breckenridge also attracts society's upper crust. New shops and restaurants tend to cater to the upscale crowd; now, with Vail's ownership, this trend probably will continue. Restaurant and ski-area workers remain as friendly as ever, and long-time Breckenridge locals still retain much of the devil-may-care attitude of their 19th-century predecessors, which helps balance out any stuffiness that the tourists may bring with them. For now, the Breckenridge crowd is not as free-spending as that of Aspen or Vail, nor as laid back as Crested Butte. It's middle-of-the-road and comfortable with plenty of great skiing.

 ## Mountain layout—Skiing

Breckenridge encompasses four interconnected mountains covering 2,043 acres. Skiers can load lifts from four base areas: the Quicksilver Super-Six high-speed double-loading chair from The Village at the bottom of Peak 9 (the high capacity of this new chair alleviates what used to be a crowded area); the Super Chair at Beaver Run, also on Peak 9; the Colorado SuperChair at Peak 8 (this was the original ski area that opened in 1961); and the Snowflake, a new double chair off Four O'Clock Road that accesses Peaks 9 and 10 on the left and Peaks 8 and 7 on the right. Free shuttles to these lifts run continuously from town. (Note: A close-in pay lot at Peak 8 fills by 9:30 a.m. most days.)

◆◆ **Expert:** Years ago, Breckenridge was known as an excellent beginner and intermediate resort, but the opening of the bowls of Peak 8, the North Face of Peak 9, and Peaks 7 and 10 added hundreds of acres of expert, steep terrain. Today Breckenridge boasts a very high percentage of black-diamond terrain (60 percent overall) and some of the highest inbounds skiing in North America, but still maintains its wide-open, well-groomed runs for beginners and intermediates.

Imperial Bowl, crowning Peak 8, tops out at nearly 13,000 feet, creating a total vertical that's only two feet shy of 3,400. If you noticed that our statistics show a much smaller vertical, it's because we list the highest *lift-served* terrain. Imperial Bowl is in bounds but not lift-served. If you want to ski it, you must hike first. Same with the highest bowls on Peak 7: You can ski from the 12,677-foot summit, but only if you hoof it to the top. Locals love it; visitors from sea level often pass up the opportunity to ski some of the best snow in the country (which is another reason why the locals love it). Peak 7, by the way, is entirely advanced and expert terrain—not a bunny slope in sight here.

The North Face on the back of Peak 9 is expert territory. Plenty of good skiers have begged for a rest after playing with Tom's Baby, and even prayers won't help lower intermediates who accidentally find themselves in Hades, Devil's Crotch or Inferno—once you drop down the face from Chair E, there is no escape.

◆ **Advanced:** Peak 10 is evenly split between black and blue runs. In the black-diamond category you'll find Mustang, Dark Rider and Blackhawk boasting monstrous bumps. Cimarron, marked black on the map, often is groomed. The Burn, dropping to the left of the high-speed lift, offers limited short-but-sweet tree skiing.

■ **Intermediate:** For the best cruising, head to Peak 10 and alternate between Centennial and Crystal. Runs here are slightly easier than those on Peak 9, but the pairing of a high-speed lift and mostly expert-marked terrain keeps crowds down.

On Peak 9, intermediates should take Lift B to the summit and ski down Cashier, Bonanza and Upper Columbia. More advanced intermediates enjoy American, Gold King and Peerless, which might be rated black at a smaller resort.

Peak 8 offers great intermediate terrain alongside the high-speed Colorado lift down Springmeier, Crescendo and Swinger; if those feel good, try the black-diamond slopes in this area, such as Callie's and Rounders.

●● **Beginner** ● **Never-ever:** Peak 9 has the best trails for beginners who have had a little experience (stick to the Quicksilver lift; the Beaver Run lift will take you higher to intermediate terrain). Peak 8 has the best terrain for a first ski day.

 ## Mountain layout—Snowboarding

Breckenridge encompasses four interconnected mountains covering 2,043 acres. Snowboarders can load lifts from four base areas: the Quicksilver Super-Six high-speed double-loading chair from The Village at the bottom of Peak 9 (the high capacity of this new chair alleviates what used to be a crowded area); the Super Chair at Beaver Run, also on Peak 9; the Colorado SuperChair at Peak 8 (this was the original ski area that opened in 1961); and the Snowflake, a new double chair off Four O'Clock Road that accesses Peaks 9 and 10 on the left and Peaks 8 and 7 on the right. Free shuttles to these lifts run continuously from town. (Note: A close-in pay lot at Peak 8 fills by 9:30 a.m. most days.) Now for the goods, read on.

Three words: Freeway Terrain Park. Peak 8's halfpipe and terrain park have become legendary among snowboarders. Breckenridge was the first mountain in the country to get a superpipe and it shows among the locals. On any given day, show up at the park and you'll quickly realize why you're *not* a pro snowboarder.

The superpipe is just that…enormous. Sometimes with walls over 14 feet (depending on the time of the season), it's definitely one of the factors that draw so many here. If you're planning a trip to Breck, it's good to know that the park and pipe are in full swing by the first weekend in December due to the Vans Triple Crown.

As for steeps and deeps, Breck's got a few secret spots, but they're under tight lip. Most of the locals get their steep on in the enormous backcountry surroundings of Summit County and only use the mountain for the park.

If you're not up to the fury of Freeway 8, Breckenridge has exactly what you need: Peak 9. Head to Peak 9 for a smaller terrain park suitable for all ages. They've even got small handrails and a pint-sized halfpipe (about 6 feet tall) for the first-time park experience. Peak 10's got a few high-speed cruisers that will let you open up your board, but all in all, Breck isn't known for it's steepness.

As for beginners, the whole mountain is your canvas. Stay away from the mogul runs and you'll be smiling ear to ear with the most beginner terrain in Summit County at your disposal. Peak 8 has the best terrain for a first snowboard day. Just stay out of the park.

Mountain rating

Breckenridge has many ingredients for the perfect winter vacation: good terrain for all levels, plenty of slopeside lodging and a charming town. It's urban enough to have a good variety of restaurants and shops, yet not so urban that you'll feel as if you never left home. Snowboarders will find that while Breckenridge might not be the steepest mountain out there, what it lacks in natural terrain it more than makes up for in the manmade department.

Cross-country and snowshoeing

The **Breckenridge Nordic Ski Center** (453-6855), near Peak 8 base on Ski Hill Road, has 28 km. of double-set trails for all abilities. Trail passes also are valid at the Frisco Nordic Center. Equipment rentals, lessons, and guided backcountry tours are available. You can also rent snowshoes.

Lessons (2000/01 prices)

Group lessons: Adults (13+) pay $60 for a full day, $50 a half day.
Never-ever package: Same as group lessons.
Private lessons: $115 per hour; multihour discounts available.

Special programs: Many, including daily programs and multiday programs offered a few times a season. Among the topics are women's clinics, racing, telemark lessons, bumps, Silver Skiing Seminars (50-plus age group), and lessons for disabled skiers.

Racing: NASTAR and self-timed courses are set up on Country Boy on Peak 9. NASTAR fees are $6 for two runs and $1 for additional runs. The self-timed course is $1 a run.

Child care (2000/01 prices)

Ages: 2 months to 5 years at the Peak 8 Children's Center; ages 3 to 5 years at the Peak 9 center.

Costs: $67 a full day, $55 a half day. Parents must provide diapers, formula, change of clothes, and so forth for infants. Child care for 3- to 5-year-olds includes a snow play program to build snowmen, go sledding and do other outdoor activities. Full-day programs include lunch.

Reservations: Required; call (800) 789-7669 well in advance.

Other options: Another possibility for child care and instruction is **Kinderhut** (800-541-8779 or 453-0379), a privately owned children's ski school and licensed day-care center. It accepts children 6 weeks to 6 years.

Children's lessons: These operate from two children's centers at the bases of Peak 8 and Peak 9. Ski instruction starts at age 3 with a special ski-school morning program and afternoon care for $75 (morning only lessons without care is $60). Ages 3–5 also have a combination of ski lessons and day care. Half day (no rentals) is $60; all day is $75 (with lunch, reservation required). Kids this age ride the lifts for free. Children 6–12 (skiing) and 7–12 (snowboarding) have their own classes for $75 a full day, and $60 a half day. Lift ticket is extra. Lift, lesson and lunch full day is $86; half day with lift and lesson is $71.

Lift tickets (2000/01 prices)

	Adult	Child (5-12)
One day	$57	$25
Three days	$171 ($57/day)	$75 ($25/day)
Five of six days	$245 ($49/day)	$125 ($25/day)

Note: These prices valid from December 23, 2000 to March 31, 2001.

Who skis free: Ages 4 and younger and 70 and older.

Who skis at a discount: Ages 65–69 pay $39 per day. Vail Resorts has a handful of different discounted prices based on time of the year, time of a skiers first visit, ski packages, Internet sales, supermarket sales, pre-purchasing and groups.

Interchangeability: Multiple-day lift tickets of three or more days purchased at Keystone or Breckenridge also are valid at sister resorts Vail and Beaver Creek (one day of a three-day lift ticket purchased at Keystone or Breckenridge is valid at Vail or Beaver Creek; two days of a four-day or five-day lift ticket; three days of a six-day or seven-day ticket). All lift tickets purchased at Keystone or Breckenridge also are valid at nearby Arapahoe Basin.

Accommodations

Breckenridge boasts extensive ski-in/ski-out lodging, and an assortment of B&Bs and private chalets, both in town and in the woods. Most lodging is moderately priced, but luxury and dorm rooms are available for those on both ends of the affordability spectrum. Early December, January and April-May are the most affordable times. Breckenridge's lifts have kept running into May some years, but one caveat: Many of the town's shops and restaurants start closing down at the end of April. Some restaurants that do stay open offer two-for-one meals. **Breckenridge Central Reservations** handles 98 percent of the resort's lodging. The resort Web site also handles reservations. (Phone numbers and e-mail addresses are in the stat box on this chapter's lead page.)

The Village at Breckenridge (800-800-7829; 453-2000; $$$–$$$$) surrounds the Peak 9 base area and is located next to the Quicksilver Super-Six chair (a double-loading six-person chair). Try to get into Plaza 1, 2 or 3, which are the most spacious units. The three-bedroom units here are giant. Many amenities are available: on-site health club facilities, indoor/outdoor pools, hot tubs, racquetball, steam, sauna and exercise room.

Beaver Run Resort and Conference Center (reservations and information: 800-525-2253; 453-6000; $$$–$$$$). This complex is slopeside on Peak 9. It has restaurants, outdoor hot tubs, indoor/outdoor swimming pools, a giant indoor miniature golf course and a great game room for kids. The Kinderhut child-care center, in the hotel, will take children from the ages of 1 to 3; kids 3 to 6 can take ski lessons.

You won't recognize the old Hilton, now called **The Great Divide Lodge** (800-321-8444; 453-4500). Vail Resorts poured $4 million into remodeling each guest room, the entire lobby and pool/spa area. But they kept one of its best amenities—it's only 50 yards from the slopes. **The River Mountain Lodge** (800-325-2342; UK direct 0800-897-497; local 453-4121; $239–$299 for a two-bedroom unit in January and February) is a group of studio to four-bedroom suites in the heart of town, only steps away from Main Street. The ski bus stops across the street. It's one of the town's most reasonable accommodations.

Distinctive inns have found an instant audience with guests who appreciate the genteel side of Breckenridge. Four such places—specifically built as B&B accommodations—are within walking distance of town, on the ski bus route, wheelchair accessible and do not permit smoking or pets.

The Wellington Inn (800-655-7557 or 453-9464; $$–$$$$) at 200 N. Main St. captures Victorian romance in its four spacious and beautifully decorated rooms. All have outside decks and bathrooms with spa-jet tubs. Poirrer's, a Cajun restaurant on the main floor, serves lunch and dinner during the summer months and dinner during the winter. One drawback: Its Main Street location is not for light sleepers.

Hunt Placer Inn (800-472-1430 or 453-7573; $$–$$$$) off Ski Hill Road near Peak 8 is named for the gold mining claim on the property. The decor in its eight rooms (all with balconies, three with fireplaces) evokes various times and places in history.

Little Mountain Lodge (800-468-7707 or 453-1969; $$$–$$$$) is anything but little. This white-washed log home has an intimate staying-at-a-friend's-home feeling. Innkeepers

Lynn and Truman Esmond add nice touches, such as placing a silver tray of coffee and tea at each guest-room door (there are 10) a half hour before breakfast.

Allaire Timbers Inn (800-624-4904 outside Colorado; 453-7530; $$$–$$$$) at 9511 Hwy. 9/South Main St. has great views. Hosts Jack and Kathy Gumph are very hospitable. Each of the eight guestrooms and two suites—all named after Colorado mountain passes—have private decks.

Several 19th-century homes in town have been converted into B&Bs, some of which are: **Evans House** (453-5509; request the Colorado Room; $$–$$$), **The Williams House** (453-2975; 800-795-2975; $$–$$$), **Fireside Inn** (453-6456; $–$$$$) and **Ridge Street Inn** (800-452-4680 or 453-4680; $$). The Fireside Inn also has gender-segregated dorm rooms for $20–$30 per night, with two sets of bunk beds per room and shared baths. A *Ski America* reader stayed there last season and found the accommodations plain but comfortable, and his roommates were "very pleasant and lotsa fun to go brewpubbing with."

The Lodge and Spa at Breckenridge (800-736-1607, 453-9300) underwent an extensive remodeling for its inclusion in the distinguished Small Luxury Hotels of the World by spring of 1998. The hotel—perched on a cliff at 10,200 feet with a magnificent view of the Breckenridge mountain range—houses Summit County's only full-service spa. The adjacent **Casey House** is a private home that offers the comforts and privacy of a mansion with five bedrooms and all the amenities of the Lodge and Spa available to guests.

 # Dining

In recent years, Breckenridge has gradually emerged from the dining doldrums. With the increase in upscale homes and vacationers from overseas, we expect the trend to continue.

For now, **Pierre's Riverwalk Cafe** (453-0989), 137 S. Main, stands alone in the field of excellent and expensive restaurants (entrées $18-$29). Owner/chef Pierre Luc prepares French dishes with a California twist, consisting mostly of fish and game delicacies such as ostrich, pheasant and rabbit. Desserts are deliciously French.

If you've enjoyed the fabulous meals at Top of the World Restaurant, you'll be disappointed to know it's now called **Overlook Pub & Grill** (453-9300) and it serves pub fare. It's located in the Lodge and Spa at Breckenridge.

Cafe Alpine (453-8218), 103 E. Adams St., has an eclectic mix of entrées, such as Italian arugula chicken, Moroccan lamb, Memphis rubbed pork, Colorado trout and Spanish tapas. This Victorian-home-turned-restaurant is a consistent winner in The Taste of Breckenridge annual contest. Prices are reasonable.

The Swiss Haven (453-6969), 325 S. Main, has melt-in-your-mouth cheese fondues, raclette, Fondue Chinois, and four types of rösti (a potato dish). Plan to spend the evening and linger over a cappuccino-and-kirsch (or two). As in Europe, they won't bring the bill until you ask for it, which can be pricey ($20+) if you order soup, salad and the homemade apple tart. **The Hearthstone** (453-7028), 130 S. Ridge Street, is in a stunning blue-and-white Victorian house that has undergone many facelifts over the years. The Old World ambiance, moderately priced selection of meat, chicken and seafood and the killer desserts make this a very popular spot with locals and visitors. The old **Brown Hotel** (453-0084), 208 S. Ridge, is another historic site that's heavy on atmosphere and light on the wallet.

Carnivores should check out the **Steak & Rib** (453-0063), 208 N. Main Street, where New Zealand rack of lamb and West Indian baby back ribs are served in an intimate, rustic atmosphere. Don't miss the Breckenridge Mudslides mixed in the Caribbean-themed bar.

Dining: $$$–Entrees $20+; $$–$10-20; $-less than $10.
Accommodations: (double room) $$$$–$200+; $$$–$141-$200; $$–$81-$140; $-$80 and less.

Other mid-priced recommendations on Main Street: **St. Bernard Inn** (453-2572); **Blue River Bistro** (453-6974); **Main Street Bistro** (453-0514) and **Pastini's** (453-1199), the latter two serving a variety of satisfying pasta dinners. For traditional Mexican and unforgettable margaritas, head for **Mi Casa** (453-2071) on Park Ave. Other ethnic dining options are **Poirrier's** for Cajun, now located in the Wellington Inn (453-1877); **Red Orchid** for Chinese (453-1881); and **Sushi Breck** for Japanese (453-8338).

Some suggestions for good cheap eats (less than $10):

Beer lovers should try the **Breckenridge Brewery** (453-1550), 600 S. Main St. The menu has mostly burgers, sandwiches and other brewhouse food, and the atmosphere is noisy; however, the micro-brewed beer is excellent. Or try **Rasta Pasta** (453-7467) for whimsical Jamaican-flavored pasta; **Angel's Hollow** (453-8585) for a big-as-your-head burrito; **Giampietro Pizzeria & Pasta** (453-3838); **Bubba's Bones BBQ** (547-9942) and **Fatty's Pizzeria** (453-9802), a town favorite since 1975. **Downstairs at Eric's,** 109 Main Street, expanded into the space across the hall that used to be known as The Underworld, naming it **Eric's II** and serving the same family-style menu so you should find plenty of seating. If you don't mind eating in a parking lot, **Windy City Pizza** (453-5570), next to City Market, has great deep-dish pizzas, a specialty. They also deliver.

Breakfast: The hands-down winner is **The Prospector** (453-6858) at 130 S. Main Street. The Huevos Rancheros will test your facial sweat glands. A pancake's width behind is **Columbine Café** (547-4474), 109 S. Main St., for its generous omelets and specialty coffees. For lighter fare and gourmet coffee, try **Mountain Java** (453-1874) upstairs at 118 Ridge St. or **Clint's** (453-1736), 131 S. Main St.

 ## Après-ski/nightlife

The liveliest après-ski bars are **Tiffany's** in Beaver Run, the **Breckenridge Brewery** for a great beer, **Park Avenue Pub** in the Village, and **Mi Casa**, with thirst-quenching margaritas by the liter. Tiffany's rocks until the wee hours, but after dinner most of the action moves into town.

Nightlife starts with a visit to **Crepes a la Carte,** a converted hot dog stand near Bubba Gump Shrimp Co. When every other restaurant in town is closed, you can still satisfy your sweet tooth with a chocolate coconut caramel crepe—or make up for that missed dinner with a cheese crepe. If you're having trouble adjusting to the altitude, head over to the **O2 Lounge** (453-6262), 500 S. Main Street, where you can enjoy an herbal martini and oxygen-enriched air in 10-, 20- and 30-minute increments.

Downstairs at Eric's, 109 Main Street, expanded into the space across the hall that used to be known as The Underworld, naming it **Eric's II**. Here you'll find a rowdy crowd on TV sports nights. A slightly older group with plenty of locals gathers at **Shamus O'Toole's,** 115 S. Ridge Street, a wide-open roadhouse with live music on most evenings and an eclectic crowd, ranging from absolute blue-collar to yuppies. Some nights the mix is intoxicating, and on others it's merely intoxicated, which often sets off fireworks.

Sherpa and Yeti's on Main Street is fairly new but has become the hot spot for live music and dancing, with a variety of bands playing blues, jazz, funk and reggae, plus local musicians' nights, all in an unfinished-sheet-rock atmosphere. This places really rocks, so if you packed your dancin' shoes, head here.

For a non-dancing, quieter time, try the **St. Bernard** on Main Street; a cozy bar in the back is often packed with business-class locals. **The Breckenridge Brewery & Pub** has live music specials, but in our experience, the atmosphere is pleasantly tame for chatting.

Salt Creek, 110 E. Lincoln, is the only Country & Western place in town, and a guaranteed good time. **The Dredge**, which is a replica of the dredge boats that churned the Blue River for gold in the early 1900s, has a classy bar. The old **Gold Pan**, 103 N. Main Street, is the oldest continuously operating bar west of the Mississippi and was one of the wildest places in the Wild West, with a miner or two known to be thrown through the saloon doors. A long, century-old, mahogany bar presides over a now worn, dimly lit room with a pinball machine tucked into the back corner and a couple of well-utilized pool tables frequented by a crowd of truckers, pool sharks sporting earrings, and the temporarily unemployed.

A slightly more mature clientele gathers at the **Big Easy Lounge** below Poirrier's at the Wellington Inn for brandy next to a roaring fire. If you don't mind the smoke, **Cecelia's Cigar Bar** makes great martinis. It recently expanded to add a dance floor and space for a DJ. A new attraction to the nightclub scene is the **Liquid Lounge**, near Cecilia's. You'll get great drinks and there's usually a DJ spinning tunes on the weekends. Saturday nights Tom Clancy plays guitar and leads a good ole Irish sing-along at **Clancy's Irish Pub** on the second floor of Towne Square Mall. It's a rollicking good time helped along by Irish beer on tap. They serve great potato soup and Irish stew, too.

Other activities

Exploring the old town of Breckenridge is great fun, either with a formal **historical tour** (435-9022) or on your own armed with a free guidesheet. **Good Times Adventure Tours** (453-7604) in nearby Frisco offers thrilling dogsled tours and snowmobile rides. Unlike other alpine sports operations, Good Times is very hands-on, letting customers run their own dogsled team or take their own snowmobile for a spin. Guides are professional and friendly and prices are reasonable.

Breckenridge Nordic Ski Center (453-6855) near Peak 8 base on Ski Hill Road, has evening **horse-drawn sleigh rides** (with dinner). The Breckenridge Recreation Center (547-3125) on Airport Road north of town offers an array of indoor activities, such as **swimming, tennis, racquetball, wall climbing, exercise machines** and **basketball.**

Downtown has scores of **boutiques.** Some of our favorites on Main Street: Adornments, Vintage West, LiftOff Sportswear, Alpen Collections, Tom Girl, The Sheepherder and Goods, all for clothing and accessories. Browse The Quiet Moose, 326 S. Main, even if you aren't furnishing a mountain home. Peek inside Creatures Great & Small if you're an animal lover. Collectors are discovering Breckenridge's **galleries,** six of them fine art. We recommend The Village Gallery; Paint Horse Gallery (western); and Skilled Hands for handcrafted goods by Colorado artisans. Quandry Antiques is another fun browsing spot.

Breckenridge has bloomed as a mecca for **weddings.** For a wedding and honeymoon guide, call 888-789-SNOW (7669). Also check the **Summit County** chapter for activities.

Getting there and getting around

By air: Breckenridge is 104 miles west of Denver International Airport. Resort Express has regular vans connecting the resort with the airport. Telephone: 468-7600 or (800) 334-7433.

By car: From Denver, take I-70 to Exit 203, then south on Highway 9.

Getting around: Nearly everything is within walking distance and buses cruise the streets regularly. The Summit Stage (668-0999) provides free transportation between Dillon, Silverthorne, Keystone, Frisco, Breckenridge and Copper Mountain. Keystone and Breckenridge also operate a free inter-resort shuttle, the Ski KAB Express (496-4200).

Copper Mountain

Colorado

Summit: 12,313 feet
Vertical: 2,601 feet
Base: 9,712 feet

Address: P.O. Box 3001,
Copper Mountain, CO 80443
✆ **Area code:** 970
Ski area phone: 968-2882
ⓘ **Toll-free information:** (800) 458-8386
Toll-free reservations: (888) 263-5302
Reservations outside U.S.: 968-2882
Fax: 968-3256
E-mail: contactcenter@ski-copper.com
Internet: www.coppercolorado.com

Lifts: 23–1 high-speed 6-passenger chair, 4 high-speed quads, 5 triples, 5 doubles, 8 surface lifts
Skiable Acreage: 2,450 acres
Snowmaking: 16 percent
Uphill capacity: 32,088 per hour
Snowboarding: Yes
Bed base: 3,300
Nearest lodging: Walking distance, condos
Child care: Yes, 6 weeks and older
Adult ticket, per day: $43–$55 (2000/01)

Expert: ★ ★ ★ ★
Advanced: ★ ★ ★ ★
Intermediate: ★ ★ ★ ★
Beginner: ★ ★ ★ ★
Never-ever: ★ ★ ★ ★

Dining: ★ ★
Apres-ski/nightlife: ★
Other activities: ★ ★

If ski resorts were people, Copper Mountain Resort would be the person who's easiest to figure out. He's straightforward, honest and organized, with a touch of wildness. His closet's neat and his attitude is contemporary. He knows where he's going—"the man with a plan." Copper's trail system works the way his brain does: logical, organized and laid out for maximum return on minimum effort.

Copper was lauded by the United States Forest Service as the "most nearly perfect ski mountain in the United States"—a commentary on the area's natural terrain features. As you face the mountain, the beginner slopes meander off on the right; the intermediate trails flow right down the center; and advanced runs drop off to the left. The most difficult stuff—chutes, cornices and double-diamond slits—beckons from the summit, where several lifts serve the wild child behind the man with the plan.

The base consists of corresponding areas: Union Creek for starters, Copper One Lodge for all of us and East Village for the adrenaline hogs. An efficient shuttle system connects the multiple personalities, and the map to the door couldn't be more straightforward: drive I-70 for an hour and a half, and you're at the door.

Copper's layout makes for a convenient vacation. Just as Mr. Obvious doesn't waste time or let things get too complicated, you won't waste precious minutes consulting the trail map or riding endless lifts to find your type of terrain.

The area is named after an old copper mine whose remnants remain in the Copper Bowl area (in summer the mine tailings are distinct). But, rather than attempt to honor days of old, Copper Mountain is a paean to modern-day master planning. Born in 1972, the base area has grown from a dowdy conglomeration of buildings with no focus or ambiance into adulthood at the hands of resort developer Intrawest. Now in its fifth year of intensive re-development, the recent improvements reflect commitment to an extensive plan to invest $500 million into Copper over a 10-year period. They're halfway to the finish line, and looking good.

The first phase began in 1998 in East Village with the construction of Copper Station, a day lodge and conference center, and Copper Springs Lodge, with 108 lodging units. At the same time the west side of the resort saw the Union Creek Base Lodge transformed into a dining, rental and retail area that connects via walkway to the Schoolhouse at Union Creek, a one-stop-shopping home for all beginner ski and snowboard school operations, especially convenient for families, with improved rental facilities, retail shops and restaurant. Four buildings that premiered in the 2000/01 season in The New Village at Copper—Copper One Lodge, Tucker Mountain Lodge, The Mill Club, and Taylor's Crossing—are joined by a fifth in 2001/02, Passage Point, completing Phase II of the development plan. Shops, restaurants, decks, open plazas for year-round festivities, and brand-new lodging accommodations sit just steps away from the slopes. Copper's nightlife and restaurants used to be limited, but no more. Molly B's leads the pack of a half-dozen new restaurants and bars that are determined to set new standards of après excellence.

Copper has come a long way toward enticing both families and dedicated singles to its village and ski hill—and it only took 30 years! Everything is gnarly, but we especially enjoy the hikes to the glades and chutes on Tucker and the bumps down the West Ridge.

 ## Mountain layout—Skiing

If you use lifts as meeting places, pay attention to the American *Eagle* and American *Flyer* chairs. If you're meeting someone at the top of one of those chairs, be very specific: They start in the same general area but unload on different peaks.

◆◆ **Expert:** Copper's mountain range tops out at 12,313 (Union Peak), 12,337 (Tucker Mountain) and 12,441 (Copper Peak), and there lie the double-diamond runs that slink through chutes, down steep ridges and into the woods. They are legitimate: Consequences of falling are real—whether in powder, bumps or crud. Resolution Bowl's steeps are short and swift; Spaulding bumps up nicely before it drops into glades. Extra added attraction: A no-charge (as in "free") 10-person snowcat makes laps to the top of Tucker Wednesdays through Sundays on a first-come, first-served basis.

◆ **Advanced:** The Super Bee six-person, high-speed chair accesses all terrain on the East Village side, including the relentless bumps on Far East, Too Much and Triple Treat under the Alpine lift. From the top of Super Bee you can slide down any of three short but sweet runs that parallel the Excelerator quad. Brennan's Grin will bring a smile to any serious bump skier's face.

Traversing to the right off Super Bee takes you to Storm King surface lift, the crown of Copper Peak and some of its toughest skiing. In Enchanted Forest to skier's left and Spaulding Bowl to skier's right, if you lose a ski here, you'd better have an uphill friend. If you survive Spaulding, you can choose from several very worthy expert runs to the bottom of Resolution Lift where there's seldom a wait.

The consistently good snow in Union Bowl under Sierra lift gets even better when you hike to the top of the cirque. Not always so with Copper Bowl on the backside of Union Peak. Its slopes are south-facing, so ask around before you dive in. It could be ugly or divine.

■ **Intermediate:** Exit to the right of the American Flyer quad and try the American Flyer, I-Beam and Windsong runs under the Timberline Express lift. Better yet, take the American Eagle quad chair from Village Center and dart down any of the runs under this lift. Off the Excelerator lift, you'll have the best intermediate runs of the resort at your feet. We learned of an event held recently that challenged skiers to log twice the vertical of Everest (that is, 66,000 feet) by doing laps off the Super Bee chair using either Collage or Andy's Encore. A friend hit 70,000 verts by 1:30 in the afternoon on these worthy intermediate highways that offer good grade without the heavy moguls or tight funnels that can turn a blue run black (and an unwary intermediate black and blue).

●● **Beginner:** Hop on the high-speed American Flyer or High Point lifts in the Union Creek area. Nearly the whole side of the mountain consists of sweeping runs lined by trees, perfect for the advanced beginner and lower intermediate.

For a long run to the bottom, beginners should bear left when getting off the high-speed American Flyer and take Coppertone for an easy cruise. From the High Point lift, head right down Woodwinds to the Timberline Express quad chair, ride to the top and ski the sweeping Soliloquy to Roundabout connection to the bottom.

● **Never-ever:** The Kokomo lift, at the far right border of the resort, serves a super gentle, isolated area. When you have these runs conquered, the next step is the nearby Lumberjack lift, another chair with only beginner runs beneath it.

Mountain layout—Snowboarding

Summit County's best-kept secret, Copper is a favorite of Colorado riders. Arrayed across the face of Copper Peak are more than 125 trails that progress from easy to thrilling to terrifying. This natural segregation of trails keeps rank beginners out of the way of overconfident intermediates and impatient experts.

For the showoff, there is a well-designed and maintained halfpipe on the Carefree trail that's viewable from The New Village at Copper. Tip: When you're using the American Eagle chair to get to the halfpipe near New Copper Village, *don't* take Easy Road or you'll be walking. Instead, cut to Sail Away for powder shots through the trees on your way to the Tsunami Pipe.

For those who dig solitude, there are the famed Copper Bowls, which feature treacherous steeps and plenty of fresh pow. Copper Bowl is a true backcountry experience that is now lift-served. Then there's the Spaulding Bowl at the top of the Storm King Poma ground lift—provided you can deal with a Poma. The chutes here funnel down to the quad-exhausting bumps of Resolution Bowl (or "Rezo," as locals refer to it). Three runs, and you'll be heading for the new Indian Motorcycle Café for a beer to chase away the lactic acid. Extra added attraction: A no-charge (as in "free") 10-person snowcat makes laps to the top of Tucker Wednesdays through Sundays on a first-come, first-served basis.

Mountain rating

The terrain keeps various skill levels separated naturally so that no one needs to feel intimidated or slowed down by fellow skiers or snowboarders. With the opening of Copper's upper bowls, this mountain is a contender, easy to navigate and long on choice.

Cross-country and snowshoeing

Head to the trails of the **White River National Forest** to play on your own. **Copper Mountain Cross-Country Center** is no more. However, you can still book overnight tours to Janet's Cabin, part of the 10th Mountain Division system and a gentle ski tour with a four-course progressive meal; women's clinics; the Backcountry Telemark Series and other telemark camps through the **activities center:** 968-2882 ext. 4INFO. The same network of trails can also be explored on snowshoes.

Lessons (2001/02 prices)

Group lessons: $50 for a half day.
Never-ever package: Half-day ski lesson, lift ticket and rentals costs $75; snowboarders, $84.

Private lessons: For one person, $180 for two hours, $110 for a one-hour bonus private on weekends and certain holidays, additional person $50; three- and six-hour private lessons also available.

Special programs: Early-Season "Tune Up" Clinics, Black Diamond Workshops, women's seminars (skiing/snowboarding), telemark clinics and Copper's Racing Fast Camps.

Child care (2001/02 prices)

Ages: 6 weeks to 4 years.
Costs: Full day with lunch costs $70; half day is $69 (morning only). Parents should provide diapers, a change of clothing, a blanket and a favorite toy. In-room babysitting services require 24-hour advance reservations or cancellations, and cost about $10 per hour, plus $1 for each additional child. Fun tip: In the "Belly Button" programs, the kids make chocolate chip cookies to give to mom and dad when they return at the end of the ski day. Yum.

Reservations: Required; call 968-2318, Ext. 38101; or (800) 458-8386. Copper Mountain long has received high marks for its children's care and learning programs.

Other options: Kids' Night Out, a "kids only" night filled with fun and games, videos and pizza for children up to age 10. Participation is free to parents who spend $30 or more while shopping or dining at Copper Mountain. Copper also offers **evening babysitting** in a guest's accommodations. **Baby's Away** (800-479-4030) rents and will deliver baby needs to your lodge, such as crib, stroller, car seat and toys.

Children's lessons: Full day (lunch, rentals, lesson, lifts), $89; without rentals, $84. Ages are 3–13 for skiing, 7–13 for snowboarding.

Lift tickets (2000/01 prices)

	Adult	Child (6-13)
One day	$55	$25
Three days	$147 ($49/day)	$54 ($18/day)
Five days	$215 ($43/day)	$85 ($17/day)

Who skis free: Ages 5 and younger, 70 and older ski free. Children always stay free. Children 13 and younger ski free at certain times. There is a Seniors Ski Free program for those 62 and older when they stay at Copper Mountain at certain times.

Who skis at a discount: Skiers aged 60–69 pay $39 per day.

Note: Multiday tickets are valid over a 14-day period (children's multiday tickets are valid the whole season). Also, discounted Copper lift tickets are sold at hundreds of ski shops, grocery stores and convenience stores in Denver and the rest of the Front Range. Call the resort to find out where to buy these tickets.

 ## Accommodations

Copper has been adding and renovating its accommodations rapidly, so most lodging is or seems brand new. Lodging through Copper Mountain Reservations (CMR) includes slopeside hotels, condos and homes. Hotel rooms go for $198-$252 per night; studios, $222-$282; one-bedrooms, $234-$324; two-bedrooms, $300-$390; three-bedrooms, $348-$456; and four-bedrooms, $432-$528. All guests who book their vacation through CMR can use the Copper Mountain Racquet and Athletic Club, which has an indoor pool, tennis, racquetball, massage facilities, weight room, spas, saunas and steam rooms. Call 800-263-5302 or go to www.coppercolorado.com.

The five buildings in **The New Village at Copper** include studios to five-bedroom condos. All units have jetted soaker tubs, gourmet kitchens and gas fireplaces; select buildings also provide outdoor spas, ski lockers and bike storage, and are steps away from the lifts. The **Copper Springs Lodge,** a classic mountain lodge in East Village, has 108 units. For 2001/02, there are new townhomes at **Trails' End** at the west side of Club Med near Union Creek. Larger units and upscale appointments add panache to this side of the village.

As with all ski areas that manage property, Copper offers lift/lodging packages that can save considerably, especially in early and late season. For example, from Nov. 1 through just before Christmas, premium studio units start at $109 per person, and again from April 6 through closing, when the area is blessed with some of the best snow of the season. This season if you book your complete vacation by Dec. 1, 2001, you'll get a 10-percent discount on lodging (includes Christmas reservations).

Two other companies book accommodations: **Carbonate Property Management** (800-526-7737) and **Copper Vacations** (800-525-3887).

Club Mediterranée is the first Club Med built in North America and one of its few U.S. winter clubs. Rooms are small. Programs and activities are nonstop, and everything is included in the price except drinks. There are ski lessons, dancing, and sumptuous spreads for breakfast, lunch and dinner. In fact, Club Med guests rarely venture outside the Club Med world except to ski—and even then they are still lesson-wrapped in the Club Med cocoon. For reservations, call (800) 258-2633 (CLUB MED).

Dining

Just as the new village has spiffed up its act, so has the food scene. **Molly B's Rocky Mountain Tavern** in East Village's Copper Station day lodge is the no-contest winner for both après ski and later in the evening. Named after the "Unsinkable" Molly Brown, a Colorado legend, it's reminiscent of an 1800s tavern and serves casual American fare; lunch, dinner and bar menus available.

Endo's Adrenaline Café in the Mountain Plaza building enjoys a strong following. **Jack's Slopeside Grill** at Copper One Lodge, a giant food court serving a wide variety of food from 7 a.m. to 6 p.m., also draws crowds. **Camp Hale Coffee** is there when you need it, serving bean brews and pastries at wake-up call.

In the Foxpine Inn, the **Double Diamond Bar and Grill** ($–$$) serves up the best burgers and soup around, and does a great job with pasta and its specialty, Colorado beef. A tip: Owner Dave Luthi hosts Friday Night Fish Frys all year long for only $5.95.

Restaurants near the Center Village include **Salsa Mountain Cantina** ($) for Mexican and **Imperial Palace** ($–$$) for Taiwanese and Szechwan Chinese. One local who used to live in Asia raves about the authentic deep-fried chicken wings and the great service at this family-owned eatery.

At **Creekside Pizza**, you can get single slices or the whole thing; their new management is doing a bang-up job. And, a secret: For under $20 you can partake in **Club Med's** (968-7000) famous breakfast and lunch bodacious buffets with unlimited wine and beer. For under $30, the same goes for a dinner that features an array of seafood, meats, salads and a huge dessert bar. Club Med is located in West Village just off Beeler Place. One caveat: You have to eat during specific dining hours. **Dinner sleigh rides** (968-2232; reservations required) cost $59 for adults; $35 for children aged 5-12 (2000/01 prices). A horse-drawn sleigh takes diners to a heated miner's tent for a gourmet meal.

Après-ski/nightlife

The old days are gone: Copper used to die at the end of the ski day. At 4:00, the base area was a ghost town as people retired to their condos. Things have changed. Under Intrawest's savvy eye, new spots that merit attention join old favorites. **Molly B's**, with its live entertainment and bar menu, is without question the hottest spot here. Moe Dixon, a longtime favorite entertainer, always gets people dancing on the tables. Recently, in fact, the owners had to reinforce the bar top, thanks to the hordes who refused to remove their ski boots when dancing on the bar. Ban dancing? *NEVER!*

A popular hangout is **Endo's Adrenaline Café** in the Mountain Plaza building, promising rocking music delivered by live d.j.'s and drink specials in a sport-oriented atmosphere; and **Jack's Slopeside** at Copper One Lodge, with live entertainment five nights a week thanks to headliner Jolly Dimas. The disco at **Club Med** is also open to the public. The **Indian Motorcycle Café** brings the term "unique" to Copper. This retail store, bar and restaurant is premised on the trendy 1901 Indian Motorcycles. Consider the flat screen TV, the red felt pool tables, chairs as soft as your leather jacket, and live music piped in from the only other Indian café—in Ontario—and you have something brand new in the west. We're told that Internet hookups also are available, and those of you at home can click onto the Web site and e-mail patrons at the bar. A new pick-up ploy?

A Russian bar and an Irish pub are scheduled to open on **West Lake at Copper One Lodge** just in time for Spring 2002.

Other activities

Other activities in and around the resort include **ice-skating, tubing, sleigh rides, snowmobiling, dogsled rides** and **hot air balloon floats. Copper Mountain Racquet and Athletic Club** (968-2826) has a lap pool, sauna, steam room and two indoor tennis courts. Spa services and massages are also available.

Opportunities abound in the **shops** at Copper Station, West Village and The New Village at Copper. Upper-end souvenirs, logo clothing and sports gear fill most of them. All American Goods sells USA- and Colorado-made products; 9600' specializes in outdoor clothing; and Rocky Mountain Chocolate Factory makes you-know-what. Stores on West Lake at Copper

One Lodge are scheduled to open just in time for Spring 2002. Here individual structures of between 800 square feet and 1,500 square feet will house boutique shops (think candles and jewelry).

For more activities see the Summit County or Vail chapters. Copper is about 20 miles from Vail and about 10 miles from the tri-town area of Dillon, Frisco and Silverthorne.

Getting there and getting around

By air: Copper Mountain is 90 miles west of Denver International Airport on I-70. **Resort Express** runs vans between the airport and your lodge, with many daily departures. You can make arrangements when you reserve lodging, or call Resort Express at 468-7600 or (800) 334-7433.

By car: Right off I-70 at Exit 195. You can see the trails from the freeway.

Getting around: Copper Mountain's updated, fairly new fleet of buses enhances an already superb (and free) shuttle service, running constantly between 8:00 a.m. and 11:00 p.m. Walking is also easy between the outlying condos and the village center. Free Summit Stage buses serve three nearby ski areas—Breckenridge, Keystone and Arapahoe Basin—as well as the towns of Dillon, Silverthorne and Frisco. Warning: The buses make lots of stops, and it can take up to an hour-and-a-half to make it down the road to the next resort. If you plan to head over to Vail or to the other Summit County areas frequently, you'll probably want a car, otherwise you don't need one. If you are not staying at Copper, one warning about parking: All parking lots cost money (about $10 per day), except the outlying Alpine lot near the highway.

Keystone

Colorado

Summit elevation: 11,980 feet
Vertical drop: 2,680 feet
Base elevation: 9,300 feet

Address: Box 38, Keystone, CO 80435
☎ **Area code:** 970
Ski area phone: 496-2316
Snow report: 496-4111
ⓘ **Toll-free reservations:** (800) 404-3535
Toll-free foreign numbers:
UK (fax): 0800-89-6868
Germany (fax): 0130 82 0958
Netherlands (fax): 060 22 3972
Mexico (fax): 95-800-936-5633
Brazil: (fax) 000811-712-0553
Fax: 496-4343
E-mail: keystoneinfo@vailresorts.com
Internet: www.keystoneresort.com
Bed base: 8,000
Nearest lodging: Slopeside, ski-in/ski-out
Resort child care: Yes, 2 months and older
Adult ticket, per day: $31-$57 (00/01 prices)

Number and types of lifts: 23–2 gondolas, 1 high-speed six-person chair, 5 high-speed quads, 1 quad, 1 triple, 5 doubles, 5 surface lifts, 3 magic carpets
Skiable acreage: 1,861 acres
Snowmaking: 49 percent
Uphill capacity: 32,175 skiers per hour
Snowboarding: Yes

Expert:★★★★
Advanced:★★★★
Intermediate:★★★★★
Beginner:★★★★★
Never-ever:★★★

Dining:★★★★★
Apres-ski/nightlife:★★
Other activities:★★★

Many winter vacationers associate Colorado skiing with 19th-century Victorian mining-town charm. You won't find that here, because Keystone was built to be a smoothly humming resort with buses shuttling to every corner, foot-of-the-mountain child care, one of the Rockies' largest snowmaking systems and one-number central reservations. The resort is perfect for families, couples or small groups of friends.

Keystone is a superb intermediate playground, but it has good terrain at either end of the ability scale, too. It has one of the nation's best summit-to-base beginner runs (Schoolmarm), and advanced skiing on North Peak and The Outback (known for bump runs, bowls and trees).

Keystone belongs to Vail Resorts, Inc., which has made many improvements in the past few seasons. Its newest lift is a high-speed six-person chair running skiers along the backside of Keystone Mountain. The resort is in the midst of one of the country's largest base area developments, creating a village that includes boutiques, coffee shops, restaurants and condominiums.

Mountain layout—Skiing

Unlike other areas that have peaks side by side, Keystone has three peaks one behind another. In front is Keystone Mountain, with beginner and intermediate terrain, and some new expert glades on its backside. In the middle is North Peak, and finally, the Outback. Other than one snaking green-circle trail, these latter peaks have just blue and black terrain. This unusual arrangement lends an exploratory quality to the day. As you get farther from the base area, the skiing feels a little wilder, a little more off-piste.

◆◆ **Expert:** Head to the farthest peak, the Outback. The 889-acre Outback is a mix of open-bowl skiing, natural chutes and tree-lined glades. The quartet of Timberwolf, Bushwacker, Badger and The Grizz are visible from North Peak and allow tree fans to pick how tight they want their forest to be. Two black-diamond bowls are accessible by a short uphill hike from the top of the Outback Express high-speed quad. (This in-bounds terrain tops out at 12,200 feet, giving Keystone a 2,900-foot vertical descent, slightly more than is listed in the stat box, where we list lift-served terrain.)

◆ **Advanced:** North Peak, the middle mountain, also has good advanced terrain, though it is generally tamer. From the top of Keystone Mountain, advanced skiers can reach the North Peak base down Mineshaft or Diamond Back. North Peak is a great spot for working on technique and steeps. Star Fire, rated blue, is a superb steep, groomed run, and a good warmup for this area. Black diamonds that plunge off this run are Ambush, Powder Cap or Bullet. On the other side of the lift, Cat Dancer and Geronimo offer a challenge, and experts can break their own tracks through the trees directly beneath the Santiago Express, a high-speed quad that serves this area.

On Keystone Mountain, there's only one section that develops pitch—Go Devil and The Last Hoot, which drop down the far-right edge of the area as you look at the map.

■ **Intermediate:** This level has the run of the three mountains, with appropriate terrain on each. Keystone Mountain has runs such as Paymaster, the Wild Irishman, Frenchman and Flying Dutchman that play with God-given terrain. The twists and natural steps on these cruisers represent trails at their best—they obviously did not have their character bulldozed out of them. Snowmaking covers 100 percent of the trails on Keystone Mountain, and the slope grooming ranks among the best in the country. The Mountain House base area has three chair lifts taking skiers up the mountain, and the other base area, River Run, is the lower station of the River Run Gondola. The gondola serves the night-skiing area until 8 p.m. The resort says it's the largest single-mountain night ski operation in the United States, covering 17 runs and 235 acres of terrain.

Intermediates also can head to North Peak down Mozart, a wide blue run. Its width is essential, because it's the main pathway to the two rear peaks. On North Peak, Prospector and Last Alamo are the easiest of the blues, with Star Fire a good test for the Outback. If you think Star Fire is fun, not scary, head down Anticipation or Spillway to the Outback and play on the intermediate runs under the Outback Express chair. The advanced-intermediate glades to the far right of the map—Wolverine, Wildfire and Pika—are not as tough as the glades of the Black Forest, but also not a spot for timid intermediates.

●● **Beginner:** Stay on Keystone Mountain. Trails cutting across the mountain are principally for beginners. You can take most of them traversing from the top of the Peru Chair, or take Schoolmarm along the ridge and drop down Silver Spoon or Last Chance. You can—and you should—ride the Outpost gondola to the gorgeous Outpost Lodge on North Peak. There, you can try Fox Trot, a gentle trail. If you're up for a blue, head down on Prospector and Mozart for the ride to the Keystone Mountain summit; otherwise, ride the Outpost gondola back to Keystone Mountain.

● **Never-ever:** Keystone has a learning center at the top of the Diamond Back trail on Keystone Mountain, with two learning runs and a triple chairlift. Keystone Mountain also has plenty of gentle terrain to practice on.

Mountain layout–Snowboarding

Ahhh…Keystone, the red-headed stepchild of Summit County. One of the last great holdouts to snowboarding, Keystone opened its doors to us only a few years ago, but like the father who wasn't there during our upbringing, is now showering us with presents.

That's right, Keystone has been progressively dropping down the cash to get us to go there, and so far it's been working. With a fine terrain park and halfpipe, various events, and the only legal night riding in Summit County, Keystone's been actively recruiting riders from its sister mountain Breckenridge. This season Keystone has committed to offering riders at least one hit from their opening day until they close for the season.

Experts are after one thing—that's powder—so head to the farthest peak, the Outback. The 889-acre Outback is a mix of open-bowl riding, natural chutes and tree-lined glades. The quartet of Timberwolf, Bushwacker, Badger and The Grizz are visible from North Peak and allow tree fans to pick how tight they want their forest to be. Two black-diamond bowls are accessible by a short uphill hike from the top of the Outback Express high-speed quad. (This in-bounds terrain tops out at 12,200 feet, giving Keystone a 2,900-foot vertical descent, slightly more than is listed in the stat box, where we list lift-served terrain.)

Other than the Outback, Keystone's steeps are mainly moguled, a major drawback for many advanced snowboarders. However, Keystone has been getting rather creative with their snowboard park. Last season we witnessed about five incarnations of the park, ranging from super beginner to Mt. Hood-sized, monster tabletop, loaded runs. Keystone ended up making a combination of the two extremes, but locals are secretly waiting for this year's inception to rival that of Breck's, but have maybe even longer runs (this season Keystone vows they'll have the *best* intermediate park). On the downside, they still do not have a superpipe, which really puts a damper on their progress with advanced riders.

For budding park riders and halfpipe tricksters, Keystone is perfect for you. The Area 51 halfpipe at its highest is around 9 to 10 feet, while Breckenridge's superpipe ranges in the 14-foot area, so it's much easier to learn in and less crowded. About 80 percent of the tabletops in the park are intermediate-friendly and there's an abundance of rails to conquer. However, this is where you'll spend most of your time, there aren't a ton of cruisers at Keystone, and the ones that are here are rather crowded. Remember, this is a mountain that's only been snowboarder-friendly for a short time, but they're learning.

Beginners should stay on Keystone Mountain. Trails cutting across the mountain are principally for you. You can take most of them traversing from the top of the Peru Chair, or take Schoolmarm along the ridge and drop down Silver Spoon or Last Chance. You can—and you should—ride the Outpost gondola to the gorgeous Outpost Lodge on North Peak. There, you can try Fox Trot, a gentle trail. If you're up for a blue, head down on Prospector and Mozart for the ride to the Keystone Mountain summit; otherwise, ride the Outpost gondola back to Keystone Mountain.

Keystone has a learning center at the top of the Diamond Back trail on Keystone Mountain, with two learning runs and a triple chairlift. There's another learning center at the base of the mountain in the Mountain House neighborhood/base area. Keystone Mountain also has plenty of gentle terrain to practice on.

Mountain rating

These mountains divide easily into categories, with some exceptions as noted above. Keystone has great beginner and cruising terrain. North Peak is for advanced skiers with expert tendencies. The Outback is for upper intermediates and experts. For snowboarders, Keystone's got some great potential. Hidden nuggets of fun exist throughout the mountain, but you've got to remember they're still pretty new to the game. Our guess is that we'll continue to see a lot of big changes over the next few seasons, and Keystone will eventually turn into a heavyweight contender.

Cross-country and snowshoeing

Keystone has an extensive cross-country touring area, with 18 km. of groomed trails around the resort, and an additional 57 km. of ungroomed backcountry skiing trails to ghost mining towns in the Montezuma area. The **Cross Country Center** (496-4275) moved last year to its new location at the River Course clubhouse off Hwy. 6. Lessons and rentals are available. Cross-country activities include moonlight tours and ecology tours. Snowshoe rentals also are available.

Lessons (2000/01 prices)

Group lessons: Meet daily at 10:30 a.m. and 1:30 p.m. for a 2.5-hour session. An intermediate instruction, called "Parallel Breakthrough," costs $96 for 2.5 hours with lifts and rentals. Advanced skiers can take "Mountain Masters" for a full day for $56 ($113 with lift and rentals). A series of ski and snowboard programs guarantee you'll "graduate" from class or you can return for a free lesson. "Guarantee to Green" is for beginner skiers, "Guarantee to Parallel" is for intermediate skiers, plus there's "Guarantee to Moguls." For snowboarders, there's "Get on Board" for beginners and "Get on the Mountain" for intermediates.

Never-ever package: A 2.5-hour lesson, lift ticket and equipment rental is $73 for skiing. An adult snowboard lesson-lift-rental package is $84.

Private lessons: $125 for 90 minutes, $165 for two hours, $245 for three hours, and $380 for six hours. Each additional skier pays $30.

Special programs: Clinics are held for women skiers, upper-intermediate to advanced skiers who want to crossover to snowboarding, snowboarders who want to learn halfpipe freestyle jumps, and more. Most are $50 for a 2.5-hour lesson. The Mahre Training Centers are held here exclusively. These are three- and five-day sessions conducted in part by either Phil or Steve Mahre, Olympic medal winners. The skiing, for all levels, teaches fundamentals. Evening classroom sessions review on-slope activities and techniques, and one of the Mahre brothers is available to answer questions. Both include six hours of instruction daily, video, races and time for fun. Lodging and lifts are not included. The Mahre courses run in December and January.

Racing: Nastar racing, clinics and a self-timed course are on Keystone Mountain.

Child care (2000/01 prices)

Ages: 2 months and older. (Keystone doesn't specify an upper age limit, but most kids older than 6 or 7 want to be on the mountain.)

Costs: Child care is $64 for a full day and $54 for a half day. Both include lunch. Children age 3 and older get outdoor snow play as part of the fun.

Reservations: Required; call 496-4182 or (800) 255-3715.

Other options: Baby's Away (800-979-9030) rents and will deliver baby needs to your lodge, such as crib, stroller, car seat and toys.

Children's lessons: 3-year-olds can take a learn-to-ski program that includes lesson, rentals, lunch and crafts, $76 for a full day, $66 half day. The programs for ages 4–14 include rental equipment, lift ticket, lesson and lunch for a full-day rate of $84.

Keystone puts a big emphasis on families and children's lessons. It has parts of the mountain that are designated Children Only, and they try to keep classes small, usually no more than five students.

Lift tickets (2000/01 prices)

	Adult	Child (5-12)
One day	$57	$25
Three days	$171 ($57/day)	$75 ($25/day)
Five of six days	$245 ($49/day)	$125 ($25/day)

Note: These prices valid from December 23, 2000 to March 31, 2001.

Who skis free: Ages 4 and younger and 70 and older.

Who skis at a discount: Ages 65–69 pay $39 per day. Vail Resorts has a handful of different discounted prices based on time of the year, time of a skiers first visit, ski packages, internet sales, supermarket sales, pre-purchasing and groups. Keystone also has one of the largest night-skiing operations in the country. If you buy a full day ticket, night skiing is also included. Night-skiing-only prices are available.

Interchangeability: Multiple-day lift tickets of three or more days purchased at Keystone or Breckenridge also are valid at sister resorts Vail and Beaver Creek (one day of a three-day lift ticket purchased at Keystone or Breckenridge is valid at Vail or Beaver Creek; two days of a four-day or five-day lift ticket; three days of a six-day or seven-day ticket). All lift tickets purchased at Keystone or Breckenridge also are valid at nearby Arapahoe Basin.

Nearby resorts

Arapahoe Basin, Arapahoe Basin, CO; 888-ARAPAHO (272-7246)

Internet: www.arapahoebasin.com

5 lifts; 490 acres; 2,270 vertical feet

A-Basin, as the locals call it, has the highest skiable terrain in North America, with a summit of 13,050 feet. The upper half of the mountain serves two above-timberline bowls that are sometimes subject to howling winds, plummeting temperatures and whiteout conditions. On a clear day, you have amazing views from the top of the Continental Divide. This is the closest thing Colorado has to skiing and riding the high Alps.

Dozens of expert runs drop from the top of the Pallavicini Lift. The "Pali" side of A-Basin is for the strong, hardy skier or snowboarder who braves bumps, weather, wind and super-steep terrain to push his or her envelope of experience. On the other side of the mountain, the entire east wall has chutes, gullies and steeps regularly searched out by experts. When all is said and done, the heart of A-Basin for experts is Pali, a steep stamped in nature.

For all its gnarly reputation, A-Basin has excellent beginner terrain. Sixty percent of the terrain is rated beginner and intermediate. Never-evers start on their own lift, Molly Hogan, and the flat, nearly separate terrain beneath it. You can buy a ticket to use only this lift for $5. Wrangler is a very wide flat trail on the far-left side of the map. Chisholm and Sundance are the next steps up the ability ladder. All three wind down from the top of the Exhibition chair lift. Intermediates can test themselves from the top of either the Lenawee (a triple replaces it for 2001/02) or Norway chairs and enjoy above-timberline bowl skiing. Thanks to its elevation, A-Basin doesn't hit its stride until late January when the east wall opens with sufficient snow cover. It's skiable until June, sometimes into early July. A-Basin is known for its spring skiing and "beach" scene with barbeques and volleyball games along the slope.

Here's our snowboarding advice: Those of you stuck on the idea of perpetually heading to Mexico for spring break, it's time to rethink your plans. There's nothing like A-Basin's spring corn snow, with a frequent overnight dose of powder. The riding here is *au natural*, with no manmade features, and no reason to regret this fact. The terrain varies from cornice jumps off the Norway Lift to sweeping beginner and intermediate runs. With a quick hike, the East Wall delivers treeless powder runs with an intermittent jump or two. Bigger air hits can be found in the Rock Garden off the Pallavicini Lift, along with some rowdy, tree-lined chutes. On the lower part of the mountain, North Fork's natural berms and bumps are also worth a diversion. There are no treacherous runouts to avoid, as every trail winds nicely back to the base. What really sets A-Basin apart, however, is its relaxed, no-frills attitude—oh, and it's unbelievably sunny base lodge deck.

Lift tickets (2000/01 prices): Adults, $44; children ages 6-14, $15; kids 5 and younger ski free. These are the prices mid-January to mid-April. Before and after, prices drop for adults; children's tickets stay the same. One child skis free with a full-price adult lift ticket. Though Vail Resorts doesn't own A-Basin, it has arranged for Keystone/Breckenridge lift tickets to be valid at A-Basin, too.

 Accommodations

Keystone Central Reservations (800-404-3535) can book lodging and arrange for air transportation, lift tickets and other needs. Keystone is mostly a condominium community, but it also has two hotels and a quaint bed and breakfast that formerly was a stagecoach stop in the 1800s. Unless you're booking very early or late in the season, room or condo rates start at about $200 per night. Midweek discounts bring the price down a bit too. Kids ages 12 and younger stay free with their parents, provided minimum occupancy is met and maximum occupancy not exceeded. All room reservations include free activities such as night skiing, ice skating, snowshoeing, cross-country skiing, yoga classes and Kids' Night Out.

The modern **Keystone Lodge** ($$$) also houses the main restaurants and conference rooms for business meetings. The Lodge underwent major renovation recently, including enlarged bathrooms with upscale fixtures, and telephones with dual data ports. **The Inn** ($) has 103 rooms within walking distance of Keystone Mountain.

The quaint **Ski Tip Lodge** ($–$$$$), which was a stagecoach stop in the late 1800s, is a near-perfect ski lodge. Rooms are rustic (in the best sense of the word) with true ski history, the dining room elegant and the sitting room warm and inviting. The Ski Tip Lodge rents rooms with breakfast included. Private rooms have baths, and the dorm rooms share one. The rooms are not huge but are comfortable and the food is very good.

Keystone divides its **rental condominiums** into seven "neighborhoods," with each group having a central swimming pool, shops and restaurants, and serviced by excellent shuttlebus access. Generally, the closer the condo group is to the lifts, the nicer it is and the more interior amenities it has.

The newest lodging at Keystone is in the attractive **River Run area**, which is walking distance from the River Run Gondola. The condos are spacious and convenient to the slopes and the best shopping in Keystone. The newest ski-in/ski-out condominiums in River Run are Lone Eagle and the Timbers.

Slopeside condominiums are virtually ski-in/ski-out—they are right across the street from the Keystone Mountain Base Area. The **Chateaux d'Mont** condos are spectacular, luxurious and worth every penny. We strongly recommend trying to get one of these units. Farther from the slopes, **The St. Johns** units have spectacular views and were built with just about every amenity. We also highly recommend the **Pines** condominiums.

This season Keystone has a new platinum collection of lodging properties. When guests stay at one of these upscale condos or townhomes, they receive free ski check, welcome gifts, fresh flowers, a complimentary bottle of wine, personal concierge and daily newspapers. Be sure to ask about it if you're in the mood for pampering.

Dining

Keystone is quietly gaining a reputation for fine dining, thanks to the Colorado Mountain College Culinary Institute based there. Qualified students apprentice for three years in the resort's restaurants under world-renowned chefs before receiving degrees in culinary arts from the American Culinary Federation. So, lucky Keystone visitors get to sample the fruits of their labors. Keystone has three dining experiences not to be missed—**The Keystone Ranch** ($$$), the **Ski Tip Lodge** ($$–$$$) and the **Alpenglow Stube** ($$$), the latter perched at 11,444 feet on North Peak and considered the highest gourmet restaurant in the country.

All are sophisticated gourmet restaurants in charming settings, perfect for romantic dinners or groups of adults (and not at all suitable for noisy young children). The chefs at each have a friendly rivalry, which helps to keep the standards high. Save room for dessert and appetizers. All require reservations, which you can make before leaving home by calling the activities/dining toll-free number, (800) 354-4386 (354-4FUN). If you're staying at a resort property, dial extension 4FUN (4386). If you're staying elsewhere in Summit County, call 496-4386. Use these numbers for all the restaurants we list here.

The **Alpenglow Stube** in The Outpost features rough-hewn timbers, massive fireplaces, vaulted ceilings and expansive windows. The Alpenglow Stube serves what we rate as the best mountain dinner available in the U.S.A. The adventure begins two valleys away with a ride on two separate gondolas suspended over the lighted slopes of Keystone Mountain. The restaurant, a large but cozy room that looks as if Martha Stewart's Swiss cousin was the decorator, features a six- to eight-course menu (for a fixed price of about $78 per person or a $90 degustation menu) of such non-traditional skiing fare as wood-grilled salmon, grilled wild game and slow-roasted duck. Figure about another $40 a bottle for wine. Patrons can sit at a counter with a view of chefs preparing the meal on open grills. Everything from the setting to cuisine is perfect—even more amazing considering that every bit of fresh food on your plate was transported via gondola or snowcat.

The **Keystone Ranch** ($$$) is a restored log ranch house, built in the 1930s as a wedding present to Bernardine Smith and Howard Reynolds. Reportedly, the only completely original part of the house is the fireplace, yet you feel as if you're dining at the

Dining: $$$-Entrees $20+; $$-$10-20; $-less than $10.
Accommodations: (double room) $$$$-$200+; $$$-$141-$200; $$-$81-$140; $-$80 and less.

home of an intimate friend. American regional cuisine is prepared with Rocky Mountain indigenous ingredients—such as piñon-encrusted lamb or elk with wild mushrooms.

The **Ski Tip Lodge** ($$$) exudes a homey, rustic flavor. It was an 1800s stagecoach stop turned private residence for Arapahoe Basin and Keystone founders Max and Edna Dercum. The restaurant follows its country inn theme with an elegant but down-home menu. It serves a prix-fixe, four-course meal for adults and a three-course meal for children 12 and younger. The famous Ski Tip Coffee, fortified with Irish cream, chocolate liqueur and Grand Marnier, restores your body heat after a chilling day on the slopes.

You say your kids want to ride the gondolas for dinner, too? Take the family to **Der Fondue Chessel** ($–$$), also at The Outpost at the top of North Peak. Enjoy fondue, raclette and wine by candlelight with music by a Bavarian band.

We like the Keystone Lodge's **Garden Room** ($$) overlooking the lake much better now that it's been refurbished to a more elegant contemporary setting. It's fun to watch the tableside preparations of the chef's specialties.

Keystone Village and River Run have several restaurants for more casual dining. In Keystone Village, try **The Bighorn** ($$) in Keystone Lodge or **RazzBerrys** ($$) in the Keystone Inn, which serves grilled items and pastas. The entertainment at **Out-of-Bounds Restaurant and Sports Bar** ($) begins with reading its unique menu with specialties such as Tree Hugger Linguine and Belt Buster Pub Steak. (We won't spoil the fun and tell you what they are.) Bring the kids. This place is really fun. For truly casual dining, we got a tasty individual-sized pizza and a draught beer sitting at the bar in the **Snake River Saloon.** Across Hwy. 6 in the Mountain View Plaza is **Mi Casa** (262-9185), serving the same high-quality Mexican dishes as its sister restaurant in Breckenridge.

At River Run, try **Kickapoo Tavern** ($) for appetizers or light fare. **The Great Northern Tavern** ($$), an elegant 1930s-style watering hole, features everything from pistachio encrusted walleye fillet to venison stew. **Paisano's** (pronounced pie-zano's; 468-0808, $$) features casual country-Italian dining. You can get a wide variety of pasta; also pizza for eating in or take-out.

Après-ski/nightlife

Keystone's nightlife is limited, at least in the categories of leaning on a bar, knocking back a few brews and dancing. The best bet for hanging out and meeting the other nightlife denizens is **Out-of-Bounds** with two bars and 29 television sets including one 60-incher with non-stop sports. The **Snake River Saloon**, one of Keystone's older establishments, rocks on weekends with live music for dancing.

For immediate après-ski activity, try the **Last Lift Bar** in the Mountain House at Keystone Mountain base or the **Snake River Saloon. Tenderfoot Lounge,** in Keystone Lodge, has piano entertainment and a 15-foot fireplace. **Gassy Thompson's Smokehouse Grill**, home of the generously spiked hot chocolate drink called the Jackwacker, serves up the best après-ski specials, at least in terms of price.

At River Run, **Kickapoo Tavern** draws a crowd on its patio on sunny days, and inside on snowy ones. Don't miss the Kickapoo Mountain Joy Juice, a surprisingly potent blend of rums and fruit juices. **The Great Northern** is Keystone's only brewery and chophouse, and its handcrafted brews make it a favorite après scene in River Run. The **Inxpot** brews specialty teas, gourmet coffees and offers a full-service bar.

A "don't miss" is the **Goat**—the true locals' hang out. This year the Goat opened a dining room and more upscale/sleek bar adjacent to the old, smoky dive that locals seem to still prefer. At the original Goat, catch a game of foosball, grab a Pabst Blue Ribbon and soak up the local scene. Warning: The décor is something you'd find in the basement of a fraternity house or at a garage sale in the 1970s.

Razzberry's, with live jazz music throughout the season and some of the valley's best martinis, is another great place to unwind after a day on the slopes.

 ## Other activities

All non-skiing activities are booked by calling the **Adventure Center** at 800-354-4FUN. **Adventure Point** on the summit of Keystone Mountain is similar to Vail's Adventure Ridge. It has what the resort claims to be the state's longest and steepest tubing runs and a snowbiking center.

Four different outfits lead **snowmobile tours,** which include guide, helmets, warm suits and boots. Keystone Lodge has a good **athletic club** across the street with two indoor tennis courts and a fitness center connected to the lodge featuring massages, a steam room, outdoor heated pool, weight rooms and a hot tub. **Sleigh rides** to the Soda Creek Homestead include a dinner with all the fixins. Call (800) 354-4386.

Ice skating in the middle of Keystone Village is open every day and night. The outdoor lake, reportedly the largest maintained outdoor skating lake in North America, is smoothed twice a day. Fees are $6.25 for adults, $5.25 for ages 13-17, $4 for children 5–12, and $1 for 4 and younger, not including skate rental.

You'll find a few of the standard souvenir and T-shirt **shops** in Keystone Village, but nothing memorable. River Run has some very good shops, mostly selling upscale costume jewelry, Native American pottery and crafts, and elegant clothing. Nearby good shopping is in Breckenridge or the Silverthorne Factory Stores.

Getting there and getting around

By air: Keystone is 90 miles from Denver International Airport via I-70. Transportation between the airport and the resort can be booked with the central reservations number, (800) 404-3535. Several ground transportation companies provide connections from the airport to the resort. Ask when you book your trip, or check in with one of the companies when you arrive in Denver.

By car: Take I-70 west from Denver, through the Eisenhower Tunnel, to Dillon at Exit 205. Head east for six miles on Hwy. 6.

Getting around: Within Keystone an excellent free shuttle system runs continuously from 7:30 a.m., passing every 15 minutes. In the evenings the shuttles run every 20 minutes until midnight on weeknights, and until 2 a.m. on Fridays and Saturdays. Bartenders and hotel doormen will call the shuttle for pickup in the evenings and late at night, 496-4200. If you're staying and skiing mostly at Keystone, you won't need a car.

The Summit Stage provides free transportation between Dillon, Silverthorne, Frisco, Breckenridge and Copper Mountain. Call 668-0999 for route information. Keystone and Breckenridge also operate a free inter-resort shuttle, the Ski KAB Express, at varying times according to demand. To check the schedule, call 496-4200. From Keystone you can catch a shuttle to Vail/Beaver Creek by making a reservation at the above number.

Beaver Creek

Colorado

Summit elevation: 11,440 feet
Vertical drop: 4,040 feet
Base elevation: 7,400 feet

Address: P.O. Box 7
Vail, CO 81658
✆ **Area code:** 970
Ski area phone: 476-5601 or (800) 427-8308
Snow report: 476-4888 or (800) 427-8308
ⓘ **Toll-free reservations:** (800) 427-8308
(see Vail chapter for foreign toll-free numbers)
Fax: 496-4980
E-mail: bcinfo@vailresorts.com
Internet: www.beavercreek.com
Expert:★★★
Advanced:★★★★
Intermediate:★★★★
Beginner:★★★★ **Never-ever:**★★★

Number and types of lifts:
13—6 high-speed quads, 3 triples, 4 doubles
Skiable Acreage: 1,625 acres
Snowmaking: 43 percent
Uphill capacity: 24,739 per hour
Snowboarding: Yes, unlimited
Bed Base: 3,341 in resort, 4,000 in Avon
Nearest lodging: Slopeside, hotels
Resort child care: Yes, 2 months and older
Adult ticket, per day: $57-$63

Dining:★★★
Apres-ski/nightlife:★
Other activities:★★

Beaver Creek over the past few years has become a village. What started out as a series of seemingly random hotels and condominiums has been knit together with a series of walkways and trails to create a true village atmosphere with a European flair. The concrete and stone complex of condominiums, hotels and shops now has a real soul and can rightfully take its place as one of the top luxury resorts in the country.

The center is pedestrian only, and shops and restaurants are scattered throughout. The Vilar Center for the Arts features top entertainment and forms the focus of the village along with the Black Family Ice Rink. Escalators whisk skiers and snowboarders from the shuttle drop-off point to the Centennial Express lift. More upscale than big sister Vail, the Beaver Creek experience is carefully scripted to appeal to the A-list guests and wannabes it draws. At the same time, those of more modest means won't feel out of place here anymore.

Those with a taste for being pampered are plopped squarely in the lap of luxury—at a price. Beaver Creek's unofficial motto used to be, "If you aren't worth a million dollars, don't even bother coming here." That pretentiousness is wearing off as the resort comes of age, but evidence of its ambitious youth remains. This isn't a place for penny-pinchers, or even the budget-conscious. The art galleries, gift shops and outfitters feature prices that are fitting for visitors with six-figure incomes.

Beaver Creek attracts much the same type of visitor as Deer Valley in Utah: The Fortune 500 crowd is right at home here and many of the condominiums are corporate-owned. The corporate owners have worked hard to create an exclusive air, with prices as upscale as its visitors. If you can afford it, the experience is enjoyable with all the bells and whistles.

But you don't *have* to go broke to truly enjoy the Beaver Creek experience, just don't stay in the village. Surprisingly, the regular resort amenities such as après-ski and dining are all very affordable and staying in a nearby town such as Avon, with a good shuttle system, makes this a resort for Everyman. It's fair to say that Beaver Creek is now in the same class as Deer Valley.

The rich and famous as well as the common folk will find very good skiing and snowboarding for all ability levels here. Visitors can ski or snowboard between Beaver Creek, Arrowhead and Bachelor Gulch. If you do this, be aware of the time it involves so you don't get stuck at Arrowhead after the lift closes when your car or lodge is at Beaver Creek (or vice versa). Complimentary Resort Transportation shuttles make the loop, but not as frequently as you might like.

Note: Beaver Creek is making a major effort to bring early-season and late-season skiers to the mountains. Pricing reflects that effort. Bargains abound if your want to ski before the end of January (excluding the holiday periods). Even bigger bargains can be found before December 13th, 2001 or after April 7th, 2002. However, the "high season" (Christmas/New Year and February 13 through April 6th) and its eye-popping prices are what most visitors will face. Those are the prices we use in this section.

Mountain layout—Skiing

If there's one characteristic that sets Beaver Creek apart from other mountain resorts, it's the extent to which its slopes are groomed. An enthusiastic fleet of snowcats patrols the mountainside 20 out of every 24 hours, looking for an opportunity to plow over a chunk of ice or a patch of powder. To ski at Beaver Creek is "to ski on corduroy." If you're an expert or advanced skier, don't let this scare you away. Beaver Creek leaves your terrain alone, so you'll find plenty of challenge. When the lines lengthen at Vail, they are nonexistent here.

◆◆ **Expert** ◆ **Advanced:** When Beaver Creek opened in 1980, its first runs were mostly beginner and intermediate. Some still think of it—mistakenly—as a cruiser mountain. Not so: Advanced skiers and experts should spend at least a day here, maybe more.

What's surprising is the amount of truly tough stuff. The Birds of Prey tops anything Vail offers—all long, steep and mogul-studded. If you want to feel like a world-class racer, the downhill course, one of the most difficult in the world, is groomed as often as possible (usually once a week) for a long and super-fast double-diamond cruiser. While somewhat shorter, Ripsaw and Cataract in Rose Bowl, and Loco in Larkspur Bowl, are equally challenging. Grouse Mountain is strictly for black-diamond types, no matter what the trail map may suggest. Only in spring, when slushier snow slows skiers down, should such runs as Screech Owl, Falcon Park and Royal Elk Glades be attempted by thrill-seeking advanced skiers.

■ **Intermediate:** Beaver Creek is an excellent resort for intermediates at every level. For those intermediates bordering on advanced, the runs under the Centennial Express lift are long and have a moderately steep pitch—enough to be exciting, but not the kind to scare you out of your bindings. If you can catch these runs after a grooming, the black-diamond-designated sections are definitely within the abilities of upper-intermediates. Centennial, the main run in this area, is not the best choice for a warm-up if the resort hasn't had snow in a while. It's in the shade early in the morning, and everyone uses it, so the surface can get skied off and a bit slick (but it's a super run under good conditions). Harrier, to the skier's left of Centennial, is a locals' favorite where you'll often find yourself skiing solo. Don't miss Harrier when it's been groomed. Another great intermediate route from Centennial Express is Redtail to the Larkspur Lift, then descend down Larkspur Bowl.

Early in the morning, the runs under the Strawberry Park lift are in the sun. We recommend Pitchfork for your warm-up, and a couple of the runs in the Bachelor Gulch area for a follow-up. Bachelor Gulch's runs are shorter and gentler than the ones above Beaver Creek Village—perfect for those in the middle of the intermediate ability range. Arrowhead is another good choice for intermediates, though its southerly exposure means thin snow at the tail end of dry spells. (By the way, Arrowhead's one black-diamond run, Real McCoy, is not that tough—unless the moguls have had a chance to build.)

If you're on the lower end of the intermediate scale, try the runs at the top of the Birds of Prey Express, explained further in the beginner section. Trails to avoid unless you have lots of confidence (or it's a soft-snow spring day) are the blue trails on Grouse Mountain.

●● **Beginner:** The easiest runs are at the top, accessed by the Centennial Express and Birds of Prey Express lifts. Once you reach the top, head over to Red Buffalo, Mystic Island and the other runs in the Slow Zone. Ride the Drink of Water lift again and again, because this area has no intermediate or expert runs where faster skiers will zip past you at high speeds. Flattops, Piney and Powell, to the other side of the Birds of Prey lift, are wide and gentle. A bonus is you get to see the same magnificent summit view that everyone else does. You get back to Beaver Creek Village on a long, clearly marked beginner run (it's really a catwalk) called Cinch. One thing beginners should watch out for: Beaver Creek has sudden shifts from beginner to expert terrain. The trails are well-marked, but when you're moving fast and trying to concentrate, the signs can fly by. The Arrowhead section also is good for beginners, with a winding run called Piece O' Cake.

● **Never-ever:** Beaver Creek's learning area is at the base, served by two lifts.

Mountain layout—Snowboarding

Riding at "The Beav" is an experience all its own. With so much grooming and round the clock snowmaking, the runs can have a consistency that's almost too perfect. Don't worry, though, because the natural deep powder can still be found almost all season—just look in the woods. The woods are actually Beaver Creek's No. 1 asset to snowboarders. Powder lines, world-class log slides that will make any skateboarder envious and cliff lines abound, making The Beav one of the favorites among Colorado locals in the know. Be sure to check the trail map for snowboard gladed zones.

◆◆ **Expert ◆ Advanced:** Beaver Creek has gotten a bad reputation as being too ritzy to be a serious mountain for riding. Some still think of it as a cruiser mountain, but ask any local and they'll claim an allegiance to the mountain for life. The Beav's got everything…and more…the best part is that while Vail's getting tracked up on a Saturday, most of The Beav's lines will remain untracked for days, so make it a point to head here instead.

What's surprising is the amount of expert riding here. Beaver Creek has an abundance of backcountry access gates that are perfect for any experienced rider. The best feature is that all the backcountry-accessible terrain funnels back to the lifts. So, in essence, you can ride up the lift with your family, run a line filled with drops and powder face shots while they're on a cruiser, and meet them back at the lift.

About 80 percent of the goods at Beaver Creek are found off Centennial and Birds of Prey. It's actually kind of funny, because the best beginner areas are at the top of the Birds of Prey lift, but it's also the access point for the Bald Spot, a favorite among powder hounds and locals.

Insider tip: If you're interested in logging, ask around, check the woods, but beware: Log slides are a favorite among the locals at The Beav and they take their locations very seriously. Last year, however, they brought the logs out of the woods and created an 18-hole logging golf course for the first annual logging Masters. Held in the area surrounding the

Moonshine Terrain Park, these logs reached epic proportions. Hopefully we'll all be lucky enough to have them out in the open again this season.

■ **Intermediate:** Intermediates should let it rip down one of America's best unheralded cruisers, Centennial, which dips and turns down the lower half of the mountain. Centennial will bring you right to the Moonshine Terrain Park, which has definitely stepped up to the plate in the past few years. Now sporting a superpipe, a yurt with foosball, cable TV and beverages, every type of rail imaginable and some nice-sized tabletops, Moonshine Terrain Park is great for everyone. From the expert who's working on his backside Rodeos, to the advanced-beginner in the pipe learning how to do frontside airs, it's the ideal park to perfect your style and to get away from the crowds that some of the other mountains draw.

All of the runs under the Strawberry Park lift, and just about every run under the Centennial Express, are great for intermediates. Bachelor Gulch and Arrowhead also offer solid intermediate riding, with just the right pitch and pockets for first-time powder hounds. Beginner park riders head to Zoom Room off the Birds of Prey lift.

●● **Beginner/Never-ever:** Stay away from Cinch! It's a beginner's nightmare: Intermediate and advanced riders should have no problem maintaining their speed on this catwalk, but to the first-time rider, it's literally a speed death-sentence.

The best place for the never-ever is the Haymeadow lift right at the base. It has the perfect pitch for learning to ride. Once you master the Haymeadow lift, move on to the easy carving family runs off Latigo. Remember: Just don't learn to jump on these runs, because ski patrol will not hesitate to pull your pass for airing in a family area.

Mountain rating

There's a bit of everything for everyone. Birds of Prey and Grouse Mountain are the spots for aggressive, bump-hungry experts. Intermediates will be happy with the cruising runs that are expertly groomed. Beginners can ski at the summit and see the view, a rare treat. Beaver Creak is a diamond in the rough for snowboarders. It may come off at first as being too glitzy and glamorous, but it has a reputation among riders for being the real deal once you get under its fur coat. That's one feature that a lot of high-profile resorts only wish they could claim.

 ## Cross-country and snowshoeing

For a truly different nordic experience at an alpine ski area, head to the **McCoy Park Cross-Country, Telemark and Snowshoe Center** at the top of the Strawberry Park Express Lift. Instead of skiing on the flats at the base of a ski area, you'll be on a 32-km. system at the summit, 9,840 feet, with views in every direction. Groomed and tracked for both skating and diagonal skate skiing, the trail system has one advanced (and exciting) loop, the Wild Side trail, but is basically beginner and intermediate. An ungroomed single track for snowshoers is called the Upper Atlas Traverse. Skiers and snowshoers can take one of several trails to the base, download on the Strawberry Park Express Lift or take the very gradual Home Comfort trail (6 km.) all the way down—fun with new snow to slow you down but speedy if there isn't.

Adult fees are $19 for all-day, $12 for a half day from noon; $9 for kids and $6 for seniors. Half-day track tours and half-day lessons for adults are $42 during regular season; $45 during peak season. The park also has snowshoe rentals and tours. One such full-day tour includes a gourmet lunch and costs $77. Snowshoe tours include rental equipment.

For more information on Nordic activities, call the Beaver Creek Cross-Country, Telemark and Snowshoe Center at 845-5313.

Lessons (2001/02 prices)

Lessons meet at the base area near the Centennial Express lift and at Spruce Saddle Lodge atop the Centennial Express lift. Instruction is available in nearly 30 languages. Call the Beaver Creek Ski and Snowboard School at 845-5300 or send a fax to 845-5321.

Group lessons: A day-long group is $100.

Never-ever package: Lesson and lifts for a half day cost $94; a full day costs $130(with rentals, $156). A better deal, available only during the value season (opening day through Dec. 13, 2001 and Jan. 5 through Feb. 14, 2002), is the Beginner Series (for ages 15 and older), which offers three consecutive full days of lessons for the price of one day: $149 for lessons, lifts and rentals. Skiers and snowboarders who complete the program are given a coupon good for three more lessons for the price of one at the next ability level.

Private lessons: $250 for two hours, $330 for a half day p.m., $360 for half day a.m., and $485 for a full day (for one to six people). One-hour lessons, when available, are $130. Call the Private Lesson Concierge at (800) 354-5630.

Special programs: Golden Gliders is the resort's new three-day program designed specifically for intermediate skiers ages 55 and up. Cost is $360 without lifts or $450 with lifts. Participants receive tailored instruction while sharing the mountain experience with their peers. Program runs Tuesdays through Thursdays weekly during the value season.

Racing: Two NASTAR courses and a coin-op course are next to the Centennial run.

 ## Child care (2001/02 prices)

Ages: 2 months to 5 years.

Cost: $76 per day during value season; $82 regular; $89 high season.

Reservations: Required; call 845-5325 or fax 845-5327.

Note: With one main base area, Beaver Creek is a good place to bring kids. The ski school and child-care center are right in the base village, although the Small World Play School is a bit hard to find. After crossing the Covered Bridge that leads into the village, turn left and walk down the stairs until you see the sign to your right. The Children's Ski and Snowboard School is in Village Hall. Hours are 8 a.m. to 4:30 p.m. Free pagers are available.

Other options: The Hyatt offers programs for children, as well as babysitting, days and evenings (949-1234). **Baby's Away** (800-369-9030; 926-5256) rents and delivers baby needs, such as crib, stroller, car seat and toys.

Lessons: Ski lessons are offered for kids 3 years (toilet-trained) to 14 years; snowboarding lessons are for ages 6-14. Cost is $87 per day off-peak; $99 peak. Prices include lesson, lift and lunch. Classes are divided by age and ability. Register at 8 a.m. or pre-register the day before. Reservations are not required. Call 845-5464 for information.

Skiing with your kids: Like Vail, Beaver Creek is sprinkled with Kids Adventure Zones. Kids can search out such haunts as the Tombstone Territory or the Hibernating Bear Cave.

 ## Lift tickets

	Adult	Child (5-12)
One day	$63	$39
Three days	$189 ($63/day)	$117 ($39/day)
Five of six days	$285 ($57/day)	$195 ($39/day)

Note: These prices valid from December 23, 2000 to March 31, 2001.

Who skis free: Ages 4 and younger.

Who skis at a discount: Ages 65–69 pay $55 per day, seniors 70+ pay $35. Vail Resorts has a handful of different discounted prices based on time of the year, time of a skier's first visit, ski packages, internet sales, supermarket sales, pre-purchasing and groups.

Interchangeability: All lift tickets purchased at Vail or Beaver Creek also are valid at sister resorts Keystone and Breckenridge, as well as at nearby Arapahoe Basin.

Accommodations

Beaver Creek lodging is expensive. It's tough to find a room for less than $200 per night, unless you want to vacation pre-Christmas or in April. **Hyatt Regency Beaver Creek** (800-233-1234; 949-1234; $$$$) has a health club, outdoor pool and spa and two excellent restaurants. Decor is elegant, and service is top-notch. The hotel has a program to match up singles so they can get double occupancy rates.

Chateau Residence Club (949-1616, fax 845-7710; $$$$) offers luxury condos with the amenities of a hotel. It echoes the castle-like elegance of the Banff Springs Hotel with suites starting at $750 per night with a three-night minimum. The staff is warm and welcoming no matter whether you're wearing a floor-length mink or fleece vest.

The Inn at Beaver Creek (800-859-8242; $$-$$$$), a ski-in/ski-out lodge on a smaller scale than the Hyatt, has 37 rooms and eight suites with a hot gourmet breakfast. Cocktails, cappuccinos and a light menu are offered après-ski. Guests also have a sauna and steam room.

The Beaver Creek Lodge (800-525-7280; 845-9800; $$-$$$$) is the only all-suite resort in the Vail Valley. The 71 units have living rooms, fireplaces, and TVs with VCRs. Once guests find the lobby to check in, the rest is easy.

The Centennial Lodge (800-845-7060; $$$$) claims to have the best prices on the mountain, but doesn't provide full hotel service. It has underground parking and a pool. This lodge has some condos and three hotel rooms. Both the Centennial Lodge and **Creekside Lodge** (949-7071; $$$$) are in the village. **The Poste Montane** (800-497-9238 or 845-7500; $$-$$$$) is located directly in Beaver Creek Resort Village as is **St. James Place** (800-859-8242 or 845-9300; $$$$). **The Pines Lodge** (800-859-8242; $$$$) is a condo-hotel near the Strawberry Park lift. Guests can enjoy a Jacuzzi, heated outdoor pool, fitness room and massage therapy. **The Borders Lodge** (800-846-0233; 926-2300; $$-$$$$) is a ski-in, ski-out condominium complex next to Chair 14, within easy walk of the village. Its condos range in size from one- to three-bedrooms and includes two outdoor hot tubs and year-round pool.

Many corporate- or privately owned condominiums are available for weekly rentals. Note that restrictions are more severe than for a hotel reservation. Hefty cancellation fees apply, so read the fine print before booking.

Elkhorn Lodge (888-833-5018; 845-2270; $$$$) has studios and one- to four-bedroom condos and penthouses with ski-in/ski-out convenience adjacent to the Elkhorn Lift (Chair 14). Amenities include fully equipped kitchens, fireplaces, balconies, spa tubs in the bathrooms, two outdoor hot tubs and a fitness area.

The Charter (800-525-6660 or 949-6660; $$-$$$$), which bills itself as having "all of the conveniences of a condominium with all of the luxuries of a world-class hotel," gives guests more of the typical Beaver Creek amenities—wonderful wood-paneled interiors, European decor, fireplaces and stunning mountain views. One- through five-bedroom units are available. Three restaurants offer menus to suit anyone's tastes.

If your budget won't support accommodations inside Beaver Creek's gates, head to the nearby town of Avon for the valley's best condo deals at the **Christie Lodge** (800-551-4320 or 949-7700; $$–$$$$). Or, you can stay in the town of Edwards, about two miles from Beaver Creek. One possibility there is **The Inn at Riverwalk** (888-926-0606 or 926-0606; $$–$$$). VailNet (www.vail.net) has a very good lodging search feature that will suggest lodging according to location, amenities and price.

Dining

Splendido at The Chateau (845-8808; $$$) is very popular for locals, especially for special occasions. Many regulars come for the piano player, Taylor Kundolf, but chef David Walford has a huge following for his succulent game and international finesse with offerings such as roasted Maine sea scallops and fried sweetbreads. The wine cellar is vast. It's one of the most elegant yet accessible properties in Vail/Beaver Creek.

Mirabelle (949-7728), a longtime local favorite at the bottom of the resort access road in an old farmhouse, serves well-prepared Belgian-influenced nouvelle cuisine.

SaddleRidge (845-5450; $$–$$$) is decorated with impressive Western antiques and artifacts the likes of which might only be found in a museum. It's open for dinner with a game-dominated a la carte menu. After dessert take a look at the saddle with Buffalo Bill's sketch impressed into the leather. The image is his own handiwork.

The **Golden Eagle** (949-1940; $$) is a less costly, though not less exotic, place to dine. With entrées such as medallions of Australian kangaroo and roast loin of elk on the menu, guests can take a culinary world tour without leaving their seats. Decorations are Bavarian and desert Southwest, exactly the unlikely mix you'd expect from a restaurant that serves a blue corn elk quesadilla and other odd but tasty treats.

The **Patina** (949-1234; $$–$$$), in the Hyatt, is a noteworthy Italian and seafood dining experience. The wine list is first-rate, the atmosphere is exciting, and the staff is helpful. Ask for a seat by the window and watch children roasting marshmallows over an enormous fire.

The **Grouse Mountain Grill** (949-0600; $$$), adjacent to the Pines Lodge, serves Rocky Mountain cuisine, featuring such dishes as Colorado Lamb and pretzel-crusted pork chops.

By Beaver Creek standards, **traMonti** (949-5552, $$–$$$) is one of the more inexpensive places to eat, with meat entrees between $20 and $30, and pastas less than that. In the Charter at Beaver Creek Hotel, traMonti serves pastas and risottos, and Northern Italian-prepared veal, steak, chicken and seafood. The restaurant is cozy, with upholstered highback chairs and white linen tablecloths, and has an outstanding view of the mountain through over-sized windows. Reservations are advised.

In Market Square, follow your nose to **Toscanini** (845-5590; $$–$$$), a busy Italian restaurant overlooking the outdoor ice rink and featuring basic seafood and pasta dishes. Special children's menu selections are available.

The **Swiss Stubli** (748-8618; $$–$$$) in Beaver Creek Plaza's Poste Montane Building lives up to its name, "Swiss living room." Its comfortable, cozy atmosphere combined with the authenticity of genuine Swiss cuisine from native Swiss chefs is perfect for both an intimate dinner for two and group get-togethers. Owners Christel and Roby Kuster, who are also native Swiss, recommend either the wiener schnitzel, veal bratwurst or rostizza lugano for lunch. Also try the veal Zurich style for dinner. Reservations are highly recommended. Open in the winter season from 3–9:30 p.m. (unofficially 10 p.m.) and in the summer season from 11:30 a.m.

In Avon try **The Vista Brasserie** (949-3366; $$) and **Cassidy's** (949-9449; $). **Masato's Sushi Bar** (949-0330; $$-$$$), in the Chapel Square complex, has great sushi chefs and other Japanese food. **Ti Amo** (845-8153; $$-$$$) is Avon's best for good-value Italian. Or try the town of Edwards, just west of Avon. In the Riverwalk Center, **Zino** (926-0444; $$) is the "in" place to be (same owners as Vail's Sweet Basil). Try the roasted mussels before diving into entrees that include pasta, risotto, and creative meat and fish dishes. The **Gore Range Brewery**, another hang-out, has outrageous salads, wood-fired thin-crust pizza, and peel-and-eat shrimp. There's also a very hip sushi restaurant called **Sato's** (926-7684).

Beaver Creek has a memorable dining experience, a night at **Beano's Cabin** (949-9090, book early; $$$). Groups are bundled onto a 40-person sleigh and pulled up the mountain under the stars by a snowcat. The cabin (a bit of a misnomer, since the building is fairly large) is upscale-rustic on the outside and elegant inside, with a roaring stone-hearth fire, log beams and well-prepared cuisine. The five-course meal concludes with remarkable desserts. The cost is per person, including the sleigh ride but not the wine, tax or gratuity.

Allie's Cabin (949-9090, book early; $$$) is a pine cabin with cathedral ceilings, river-rock fireplace and a romantic atmosphere. It's named for Allie Townsend, Beaver Creek's first female resident in the late 1800s. It's open to the public for dinner. A snowcat-drawn sleigh takes diners to the cabin, where you'll indulge in a five-course steakhouse meal. The cost is per person, including the sleigh ride but not the wine, tax or gratuity.

For breakfast, choices are fairly limited. **Patina** ($$) at the Hyatt has full breakfast buffet, featuring omelets made-to-order. You can get eggs, pancakes and waffles at **McCoy's**, a cafeteria set-up at the base of the mountain. **Beano's Rendezvous** ($) right by the Centennial Lift has good breakfast burritos. **On The Fly,** a tiny take-out place near the covered bridge and main bus stop, has egg wraps (scrambled eggs in tortillas) that are pretty tasty, but seating is limited to two small tables. For muffin-and-coffee breakfast fans, **Starbucks** is located one level down from the Centennial Express lift. **Beaver Creek Chophouse** in the Beaver Creek Lodge serves an American continental breakfast. **Pacific Ranch** in the Charter Lodge dishes out hot breakfasts daily.

Check out the Vail Dining section for dining in Vail Resort and Vail Valley.

Après-ski/nightlife

Asked what nightlife was worth a look, one worker first told us, "There isn't anything," then after a bit of thinking, amended her response to, "Well, there are some meeting places." The first place to stop on the way back to town from the Larkspur Bowl is **Red Tail Camp,** where revelers gather to begin après-ski. In the spring, the deck is packed and Sundays mean live entertainment al fresco.

The Coyote Cafe is popular among locals such as the Beaver Creek Ski Patrol, at the end of the day. This Mexican cantina/watering hole caters to locals, and with well drink and draught beer specials at the end of the day, its prices are reasonable. Bartenders can whip up a margarita to get you in the après-ski mood, and the staff is intentionally informal—in contrast with the rest of Beaver Creek. Don't plan on staying out late—it closes at 11 p.m. Coyote Café was very, very smoky. Ski clothes stink the next morning. It's too bad, because if you're young, a non-smoker and looking for après-ski, this is all that is available.

McCoy's is the place to go for live après-ski entertainment as soon as you leave the slopes. Also try the **Dusty Boot Saloon**, where you'll find mondo 46-ounce margaritas and a comprehensive tequila list. **Blue Moose Pizzeria** has great pizza and a fun atmosphere, and the lowest prices in Beaver Creek Village.

Dining: $$$-Entrees $20+; $$-$10-20; $-less than $10.
Accommodations: (double room) $$$$-$200+; $$$-$141-$200; $$-$81-$140; $-$80 and less.

The Hyatt Regency's **Antlers** bar, which stays open until 2 a.m., features entertainment from local musicians. At night, when the stars are out, it's a dazzling display for tired skiers and snowboarders.

Other activities

In 1998, the **Vilar Center for the Arts** opened. This 528-seat performing arts center is fashioned after a turn-of-the-century theater in Munich and no doubt is the premier cultural venue in the Colorado mountains. The year-round outdoor **Black Family Ice Rink** is in the heart of Beaver Creek. Ice skating exhibitions are held here in the winter every Monday night.

If you need to restore mind and body (like those sore skiing legs), visit one of Beaver Creek's spas. The **Allegria Spa** (748-7500), in the Hyatt, offers après-ski massages, ashiatsu, hot stone treatments, oil wraps and facials, just to name a few of its treatments. A 50-minute massage costs $90. The spa also has a fitness center and offers a number of classes including yoga, pilates, spinning and meditation.

Every Thursday night, level-five and above skiers are invited to join in on **Thursday Night Lights**, a ski-down with glow sticks followed by a huge fireworks show. Register at the Chidren's Ski and Snowboard School. The resort concierge (845-9090) can make reservations for other activities, such as **dogsledding, snowmobiling, snowshoeing, fly fishing, ice fishing,** and **sleigh rides.**

Beautiful **boutiques** line the pedestrian walkway in the heart of the resort. A special stop on your list should be The Golden Bear, just to the west of the skating rink in Beaver Creek. It's owned by local women whose logo is the golden bear, which you can find in all forms of jewelry and art. Great stylish clothes and other special gifts tempt the wallet.

Getting there and getting around

By air: Flights land at the Vail/Eagle County airport, about 35 miles west of Vail, and the Denver International Airport, 110 miles east. Eagle County airport is served by American, Northwest, Delta, America West and United.

Ground transportation between Denver and Vail is frequent and convenient. The trip to Vail takes about two-and-a-half hours. Contact Colorado Mountain Express at (800) 424-6363; Vail Valley Taxi (476-8294); or Airport Transportation Service (476-7576). Though flights into Denver may be a bit less expensive than Eagle, also consider the cost of round-trip ground transportation, where per person rates from Denver are about double those from Eagle.

By car: Beaver Creek and Vail are right on I-70, 100 miles west of Denver and 140 miles east of Grand Junction. Beaver Creek is 10 miles west of Vail and just 3 miles south of Avon.

Getting around: Beaver Creek is very self-contained. There is a complimentary shuttle that takes you anywhere within Beaver Creek between 6 a.m. and 2 a.m. daily. The shuttle is like a taxi, so ask your concierge or restaurant hostess to call (949-1938), and allow 10-15 minutes for pickup. Shuttles between Beaver Creek and Vail cost $3. If you plan to commute frequently between Vail and Beaver Creek, or if you are staying in one of the outlying towns such as Edwards or Minturn, you may want to rent a car. If you're not staying at Beaver Creek lodging, you can park in two different locations. In the village, at the base of the mountain, there are two lots that charge to park. Two free parking lots are located just outside the entrance to Beaver Creek, a free shuttle takes you the 2 miles to the base of the mountain. Allow extra time for this.

Crested Butte

Colorado

Summit elevation: 11,875 feet
Vertical drop: 2,775 feet
Base elevation: 9,100 feet

Address: P.O. Box A
Mt. Crested Butte, CO 81225
✆ **Area code:** 970
Ski area phone: 349-2333
Snow report: (888) 442-2333
ⓘ **Toll-free reservations:** (800) 544-8448
Toll-free foreign numbers:
U.K.: 0800 894085
Germany: 0800-101-0808
Mexico: 95-800-417-2772, ext. 2286
Australia: 0014-800-127-665, ext. 2286
Fax: 349-2397
E-mail: info@cbmr.com
Internet: www.CrestedButteResort.com (ski resort)
crestedbuttechamber.com (chamber of commerce)
Expert: ★★★★★
Advanced: ★★★★★ **Intermediate:** ★★★★
Beginner: ★★★ **Never-ever:** ★★★★

Number of lifts: 14–3 high-speed quads,
3 triples, 3 doubles, 5 surface lifts
Snowmaking: 37 percent
Skiable acreage: 1,058 acres
Uphill capacity: 18,160 per hour
Snowboarding: Yes
Bed Base: 5,750
Nearest lodging: Slopeside
Resort child care: Yes, 6 months and older
Adult ticket, per day: $49-53 (00/01)

Dining: ★★★★★
Apres-ski/nightlife: ★★★★
Other activities: ★★★

Great skiing and snowboarding—especially for advanced and expert levels—and down-home western friendliness make Crested Butte one of our favorite resorts. This season marks the 40th anniversary of the ski resort and they are celebrating with price rollbacks throughout the season.

Many Colorado resorts cater to the well-to-do celebrity or CEO visitor, and that's fine, but this is one place you can come if you want to avoid that scene. Crested Butte has a laid-back attitude and the locals have a way of looking at the better side of life.

The town is Colorado's largest National Historic District, with charm impossible to convey in words. More than 40 historic structures are tucked in and around the town. A walk down Elk Avenue, the main street, takes you past the old post office, built in 1900, and the Forest Queen, reputed to have once been a brothel. Buildings have been lovingly restored, and others have been built to look as though they've been there for 100 years. In contrast, the resort, about 3 miles away, is surrounded by modern condos and hotels.

Crested Butte has made a major commitment to snowmaking, which has ensured excellent coverage for early-season skiing; plus the resort has one of the highest average snowfalls of any ski town in Colorado. Crested Butte, with its world-renown steeps and gnarly terrain, has been home to the U.S. Extreme Freeskiing Championships for the last 11 years and the

U.S. Extreme Boarderfest for the last eight years. Also of interest, Crested Butte was the pioneering resort in the rediscovery and popularization of telemarking. It has long had more of these skiers per capita than any other big-time ski resort. The U.S. Telemark Championships are held here each February. Plus, in late March hundreds of free-heel skiers scramble up the North Face and drop 1,200 vertical feet through deep snow to compete in the Al Johnson Memorial Uphill/Downhill Race. Johnson used to deliver mail on Nordic skis to 1880s mining camps.

Guest services leads free "base to the face" tours meeting daily at 9:30 a.m. introducing the mountain to new visitors.

Mountain layout—Skiing

◆◆ **Expert:** The Crested Butte skier likes the terrain just as nature left it. You'll notice that named trails cover only about half the terrain. Looking at a trail map, on the left is a huge area called the Extreme Limits with a series of double diamonds punctuating the mountainside, and on the far right is another grouping of double diamonds hard against the area boundary. Both areas are tough, offering what experts claim is Colorado's best extreme terrain, comparable to Utah steeps. If you want to ski this terrain, plan to arrive mid-January or later, or you might find it closed.

A couple of random notes: The resort has free mountain tours for all levels, including the extensive expert terrain. Our stats reflect lift-served terrain—you can hike to the 12,162-foot level for a 3,062-foot vertical descent. (Also, our base elevation is at the point of the lowest lift. The base area where the facilities are is about 200 feet higher.)

◆ **Advanced:** Crested Butte's single blacks are long, bumpy and fun. Most are found under the Silver Queen and Twister lifts, but don't miss the Double-Top Glades served by the East River Lift.

■ **Intermediate:** Those in search of long cruising runs should go up Keystone or Silver Queen, and head down Treasury, Ruby Chief, Forest Queen, Bushwacker, Gallowich and variations of the same. Runs under the Paradise and Teocalli lifts are the best cruisers on the mountain—long and fast. The Paradise Bowl at the top of the Paradise lift gives intermediates a taste of powder on good days.

Advanced-intermediates can manage most of the runs down from the Silver Queen high-speed quad. The short and steep Twister and Crystal both have good bail-out routes about halfway down.

●● **Beginner:** Crested Butte has extensive green-circle terrain, served by the Keystone lift. However, this is not stuff you want to attempt with the skiing ability you learned from a book on the plane. Houston probably is the most gentle of the greens, but we'd color the rest turquoise—greens leaning into blues.

● **Never-ever:** Head to the Peachtree lift, take a couple of lessons and practice for a day or two before attempting the Keystone lift. When you're ready for Keystone, get off at the second stop and try Houston.

Mountain layout—Snowboarding

Advanced and expert riders can tackle true "extreme" terrain that includes 50-degree slopes, cliffs, chutes and untrammeled pow in any of five bowls that make up "Extreme Limits." These areas (often closed 'til mid season, awaiting deep snow conditions) are not for the weak or faint hearted; if you can't confidently negotiate the steepest double-blacks at other Colorado resorts, you don't belong in these lightly patrolled backcountry terrain that could justifiably be marked "triple-black diamond."

That said, the Headwall (just off the High Lift lift) is a good place to do a reality check: If this 40-degree steep and narrow chute gives you the heebie-jeebies, better stay on the groomed and patrolled runs within view of the Treasury, Teocalli and Paradise lifts.

Crested Butte's well-deserved reputation for extreme terrain masks the fact that this mountain is well suited to beginners and intermediates, too. Intermediates get their kicks in the Paradise Bowl, with its smattering of variably pitched slopes, easy glades, and mild, rolling mogul fields. The main Keystone Lift, which departs from the busy base area, accesses 145 acres of freeway-width beginner terrain.

The Crested Butte Academy snowboard team assisted with the redesign of the resort's halfpipe and terrain park last winter. The 370-foot halfpipe and a triple-air, three-rail, three-tabletop park is on Bushwacker under the Teocalli lift with easy shots into the trees.

Mountain rating

Crested Butte has terrain for every level of skier and rider. It needs it, because there are no alternatives in the near vicinity, with the notable exception of 2,200 acres of snowcat powder skiing at nearby Irwin Lodge, the largest such operation in North America.

 ## Cross-country and snowshoeing

Crested Butte is linked with one of the most extensive cross-country networks in Colorado. The **Crested Butte Nordic Center** (349-1707) is located at the edge of town, on 2nd Street between Sopris and Whiterock Streets. There are about 70 km. of Nordic tracks, which begin a few yards from the Nordic Center. The center also has an outdoor rink and sledding hill for après-Nordic activity. There are more than 100 miles of backcountry trails. Group lessons, half-day and all-day tours are scheduled several times each week, but private lessons and special tours must be requested two days in advance. Snowshoe activities are offered. Snowshoe and cross-country rentals are available. There are also hut-to-hut cross-country and snowshoe trips.

Snowshoe tours at Crested Butte Mountain Resort (349-2211 or 800-444-9236) depart from the Ski and Snowboard School at 9:45 a.m. and 1:15 p.m. daily. You'll ride the Keystone lift up the mountain, then make an easy loop that offers spectacular views. Tour takes about two-and-a-half hours with a snack break. The price of $45 includes Atlas snowshoe rentals, lifts, guides and snacks. Moonlight tours are offered December through February.

 ## Lessons (2001/02 prices)

Registration and reservations for all programs are at the ski school desk in the Gothic Center, 349-2252 or 800-444-9236.

Group lessons: Adult group lessons are $55 for a 2.5-hour lesson.

Never-ever package: A three-hour novice ski or snowboard lesson with lift ticket is $75. Check with the ski school for special 40th Anniversary pricing of only $25 during most of December, January and April.

Private lessons: $165 for two hours. Multihour and multiperson discounts available.

Special programs: Many, including workshops for extreme skiing and boarding plus clinics for seniors, halfpipe tricks, bumps, telemark, shaped skis, powder, and turning fundamentals cost $75 for 2.5 hours. There's a four-person maximum for these clinics.

Kim Reichhelm, a renowned extreme ski champion and former U.S. Ski Team member, teaches several four-day women's workshops here. We know Kim personally and can vouch for her ability to improve women's technique and confidence. These Women's Ski Adventures will be offered through Club Med and include clinics with video analysis, daily off-slope fun, gift bags, product demos, welcome and award dinners, breakfasts and lunches, lift tickets, lodging and more. Call (888) 444-8151 for more information on this program.

There are also daily North Face tours for extreme skiers for $20 a skier, leaving at 9:45 a.m., that guide skiers through Crested Butte's most challenging terrain.

Racing: NASTAR races cost $6 for two run, $1 for each additional run. Race workshops are offered. Register at the ski and snowboard school desk.

Child care (2001/02 prices)

Ages: 6 months to 7 years.

Costs: $70 for a full day, or $12 per hour. The program includes crafts, games, snow play and other activities, but no ski lessons, and toddlers have separate programs from the older children.

Reservations: Strongly recommended; registration and information are in the Kid's Ski & Snowboard World in the Whetstone Building at the base of the Silver Queen Lift; 349-2259 or (800) 600-7349.

Children's lessons: Programs for ages 3–7 include ski rental and supervised day care after the lesson; $80 for a full day (with lunch) or $70 for half-day (no lunch). More experienced kids have classes separate from beginners. For ages 8–12, half-day lessons in skiing and snowboarding are $70; a full day is $80 (includes lunch). These prices do not include lift tickets or rental equipment. The all-day Rip Session is for ages 8–15, Level 8 and 9 skiers and snowboarders; cost is $150. Race workshops also are offered for children. Register at the ski and snowboard school desk.

Lift tickets (2000/01 prices)

	Adult	Child (5-16)
One day	$53	Pay their age (see below)
Three days	$159 ($53/day)	
Five days	$245 ($49/day)	

Who skis free: Ages 4 and younger and 70 and older always ski free.

Who skis at a discount: Ages 65-69 ski for half the adult price. When children ages 5–16 ski with one full-paying adult, they pay their age to ski. This program has no blackout periods, nor any limits to the number of children, but proof of age may be required.

Irwin Lodge (2001/02 prices)

Irwin Lodge itself is worth the roughly one-hour snowcat ride 12 miles into the backcountry from Crested Butte ski resort. Nestled amidst the ever-greens on a ridge above a frozen lake in a picturesque valley, the long, wooden lodge consists of 25 rooms built around the perimeter of a massive lobby that runs the length of the structure. There is a large wood-burning fireplace in the middle of the spacious room, and lots of nooks and crannies with comfortable couches for reading, relaxing or eating. There is also a large hot tub on the porch with commanding views of the valley and lake. At one end of the lodge sits a small, woodsy bar for ski libations and socializing.

The very isolation of the lodge, which was built by an eccentric millionaire in 1974, has presented special challenges to past and present owners. Yet that same sense of being utterly removed from the rest of the world provides the special magic that has made Irwin Lodge legendary among an elite circle of skiers who have tasted its charms, and passed along its praises. Irwin Lodge runs may not offer as much vertical as some helicopter ascents, but on a good day you can get eight powder runs versus three or four for a typical day-long helicopter package, making this one of the great bargains for skiers who live to ski untracked powder. The weather may not always cooperate, and the valley is as dependent on snowfall as any other backcountry area. On a clear day with fresh snow, however, the Irwin Lodge experience is nothing short of epic.

Mornings begin with breakfast, then snowcats make their first climb to the ridge loaded with skiers and snowboarders, and cross-country skiers take off on organized tours. Skiing is available for every level of ability. We don't recommend this for a first-time ski experience, but we do recommend it for a first time in powder. Two groomed slopes serve the needs of intermediates. There are plenty of untracked, steep slopes for those with more experience.

The first impression as the snowcat trundles off down the mountain, leaving your small, guided ski group alone on a ridge 2,100 feet above the distant valley floor, is an overwhelming sense of quiet. It's a silence that pierces as much through your eyes as your ears. There are no ski-lift gears gnashing, no noisy lift-lines forming, none of the boisterous and colorful flotsam and jetsam that assaults the senses at the average ski area on any given day. Just your small group of adventurers, a pristine Rocky Mountain in its unadorned winter splendor, and the seductive whoosh of your skis as they chart a path through forests and glades of untracked powder. Welcome to the backcountry, snowcat ski experience.

Skiing normally starts at 9 a.m. and continues until 4 p.m. From noon to 1 p.m. everything stops for the lunch buffet while guests fuel up for the afternoon and the snowcats are serviced. In addition, Irwin offers snowmobiling, guided cross-country skiing, ice fishing and snowshoeing.

Packages combine lodging, three gourmet meals, activities and round-trip transportation from Crested Butte. Per-person, per-day prices in February are $480 for single occupancy, $430 double, or $405 triple or quad. Rates are for three days, from Sunday through Wednesday, and four days, from Wednesday through Sunday, only. Savings in January or March are about $100 per person, and there's a 5-percent savings for stays of seven days or longer. Contact Irwin Lodge, PO Box 457, Crested Butte, CO 81224; 349-9800 or (888) 464-7946 (888-GO-IRWIN); fax, 349-9801.

Accommodations

Most of the accommodations are clustered around the ski area in Mount Crested Butte. The historic town has a handful of lodges and quaint B&Bs, but they aren't as convenient to the slopes. However, they are less expensive and closer to the nightlife; and offer a taste of more rustic Western atmosphere. A free bus service takes you right to the slopes every 15 minutes, so the primary inconvenience of in-town lodging is the short bus ride.

Crested Butte Vacations (800-544-8448) can take care of everything from your plane tickets to hotel room, lift tickets and lessons. It also offers some of the best packages available. Before you make any arrangements, call and ask for the best possible deal.

Sheraton Crested Butte Resort ($$$–$$$$) is 225 yards from the Silver Queen high-speed quad. It has 252 rooms and suites with convenience that is hard to beat. **Club Med** (1-

Dining: $$$-Entrees $20+; $$-$10-20; $-less than $10.
Accommodations: (double room) $$$$-$200+; $$$-$141-$200; $$-$81-$140; $-$80 and less.

800-CLUBMED; $$$–$$$$), offers Club Med's second North American ski village and first dedicated to families. Club Med is all-inclusive with rooms, meals, lessons and entertainment included at one price.

The Plaza ($$$$), only 80 yards from the Silver Queen superchair, offers the most luxurious condos. There are two hot tubs, a sauna and covered parking. They give excellent value and are especially popular with groups because special functions can be arranged.

The Buttes ($$$–$$$$) are well-appointed condos close to the lifts. Rooms range in size from studios to three bedrooms. **The Gateway** ($$$–$$$$), across from the Peachtree lift and about a two-minute stroll from the Silver Queen, may be the best luxury of any condo on the slopes when you trade price for space and amenities.

Wood Creek and **Mountain Edge** ($$–$$$$) are convenient to the lifts, and the **Columbine** is a more moderate ski-in/ski-out property. These three, together with nine others within shuttlebus distance of the lifts, are managed by several agencies, so it's best to book through Crested Butte Vacations (800-544-8448).

Crested Butte Club (349-6655; $$–$$$$) on Second St. in town, is the upscale, old-world elegance champion of the area. Though the lifts are a bit far, this place is worth the inconvenience. Seven suites have been individually furnished with Victorian furnishings including double sinks and a copper-and-brass tub, as well as beautiful four-poster or canopied beds and a fireplace. The amenities include the fitness club, with heated swimming pool, two steam baths, three hot tubs, weight room, and massage and weight trainer. This is a No-Smoking property.

Claim Jumper (349-6471; $$–$$$), 704 Whiterock St., is a historic log-home B&B and another class act in town. It's filled with a collection of memorable antiques. Bedrooms have themes and are furnished with brass or old iron beds. There are only five rooms, four with private bath. Room rates include a full breakfast. Children are not encouraged. The Claim Jumper can arrange catered weddings and special-occasion receptions.

Christiana Guesthaus (800-824-7899; 349-5326; $–$$), 621 Maroon Ave., is only a block from the ski shuttle and a five-minute walk from downtown. This has a mountain inn atmosphere and most of the guests manage to get to know one another. The rooms are small, but guests spend a good deal of time in the hotel's living rooms so this doesn't really matter. Let the owners know if you need quiet, because some rooms get quite a bit of traffic from the owner's family and folk using the washers and dryers.

Forest Queen (349-5336; $), corner of Elk and 2nd, is inexpensive for a double with bath. **The Elk Mountain Lodge** (349-7533; $$–$$$) around the corner from the Forest Queen on 2nd Street has simple but comfortable rooms, all with private bath. Ask for Room 20 on the third floor with lots of space, a balcony and a great view.

Other B&Bs in town (which we have not inspected) are **Elizabeth Anne** (349-0147; 703 Maroon Ave.); **Purple Mountain Lodge** (349-5888; 714 Gothic Ave.) and the **Last Resort** (349-0445; 213 3rd St.).

PR Property Management (349-6281), at 214 6th Street, has rentals in private homes as well as condominiums. For something out of the ordinary, check with them for help.

Dining

Crested Butte is blessed with more excellent, affordable restaurants than any other resort in the West. One writer noted that the fine dining per capita is highest here of any resort in Colorado. You can dine on gourmet French cuisine in an intimate setting, or chow down on platters of family-style fried chicken and steaks.

WoodStone Grille (349-8030; $$$) at the Crested Butte Sheraton Resort is open for breakfast, lunch and dinner. It has wonderful Italian/American contemporary cuisine. For excellent fondue, raclette and other Swiss fare, head to the **Swiss Chalet** (349-5917; $$–$$$) across the street from the Sheraton. It is open only for dinner.

Timberline Restaurant (349-9831; $$$), at 201 Elk Ave., mixes a rustic Western bar downstairs with Mediterranean decor upstairs. Chef Tim Egelhoff combines seasonal products to create a Café French Cuisine, whose roots are classic French, with a pinch of California and a dash of the Rockies. The menu changes often. Open nightly, 5–10 p.m.

Near the four-way stop at 435 Sixth St. is **Buffalo Grille** (349-9699; $$–$$$), specializing in buffalo and beef steaks, free range and organic entrées served with a Western flair. Make reservations—the place is tiny.

Le Bosquet (349-5808; $$$) is in the Majestic Plaza at Sixth and Bellview. Signature dishes include Colorado roast rack of lamb, hazelnut chicken, and salmon with a ginger glaze. This is possibly Crested Butte's finest in formal French cuisine. There's also a bistro menu at its bar.

Soupçon Restaurant (349-5448; $$$) is hidden in the alley behind Kochevar's Bar. This log cabin started at half its current size in 1916 as a private residence to the Kochevars. Soupçon dates back almost a quarter of a century. This place is as romantic as it gets. Current owners Maura and Mac Bailey have created an innovative French cuisine, with menu items posted daily on a chalkboard. Reserve two to three days ahead for one of two seatings, 6 p.m. and 8:15 p.m.

The **Idle Spur Steakhouse and Crested Butte Brewery** (349-5026; $$–$$$) is always crowded and noisy. It offers the finest hand-cut steaks in town plus burgers (including vegetable and elk—sounds better than it is), Mexican entrées and a selection of fresh fish, all reasonably priced. Six beers are brewed in-house from the White Buffalo Peace Ale to the full-bodied Rodeo Stout. Brewery tours 2–5 p.m. daily during happy hour.

Powerhouse Bar Y Grill ($$–$$$), next to the Old Town Hall bus stop (130 Elk Ave.), is known for its unique Mexican specialties like cabrito, grilled trout, fajitas, tamales and tacos. Sip from dozens of types of Tequilas. Prices are quite reasonable and portions are huge. Be prepared for a wait though—this popular restaurant doesn't take reservations, and the line for tables can be more than an hour.

For hard-to-beat group and family dining, head to **Slogar** (349-5765; $$). It used to be the first bar the miners hit when returning from the mines and is decorated in old bordello decor. Slogar's offers a delicious skillet-fried chicken dinner with mashed potatoes, to-die-for biscuits, creamed corn, ice cream and even some other extras for a flat price. It also offers a family-style steak dinner. Reservations recommended.

For other substantial meals, head down Elk Ave. to **Donita's Cantina** (349-6674; $$), where the margaritas are giant and strong, and Mexican food comes in heaping portions. Be early or be ready to wait. No reservations. For a quick meal, try the **Last Steep** ($–$$) very popular with locals. The **Gourmet Noodle** (349-7401; $–$$) has many pasta dishes prepared fresh daily, espresso and cappuccino and tempting desserts, such as peanut butter pie and chocolate mousse.

The best breakfast is under debate by members of our staff. Some say it's **Paradise Cafe.** Others swear by the **Forest Queen.** Paradise Cafe hasn't been around quite as long as Forest Queen, where the atmosphere is authentic turn-of-the-century. Both are downtown and both serve hearty, traditional breakfasts (and lunch and dinner). New to the mix is the **Ruby**

Dining: $$$-Entrees $20+; $$-$10-20; $-less than $10.
Accommodations: (double room) $$$$-$200+; $$$-$141-$200; $$-$81-$140; $-$80 and less.

Mountain Bakery, across the street from the Paradise Café, which is more for the pastry-and-muffin crowd and can get very crowded.

For breakfast on the mountain, head to the **Avalanche** in the Treasury Center. Or make reservations for a **First Tracks Breakfast** (349-2378), where you'll meet at 8:15 a.m. at the Keystone Lift for first tracks on the mountain and an all-you-can-eat breakfast buffet.

For a good lunch, try **Bubba's on the Mountain** at the base of the Paradise lift or **the Avalanche** in the base area.

Crested Butte has several outdoor dining experiences, such as the **Twister Fondue Party,** every Sunday, Wednesday and Friday when at 4:30 p.m., diners board the Keystone Lift for a three-course on-mountain fondue dinner, followed by a gentle ski to the base by torchlight. **Paradise Sleigh Ride Dinners** are every Tuesday, Thursday and Saturday via snowcat-drawn sleigh. Call 349-2211 or 349-2378 for either of those.

Après-ski/nightlife

Here nightlife means wandering from bar to bar. The immediate après-ski action is centered in **Rafters** at the base of the lifts or **the Avalanche**. Then it begins to move downtown to the **Wooden Nickel**, with some wild drinks, and **the El Dorado**, known around town as "the Eldo" and, according to one local, has a "smokin' dance floor." **Talk of the Town** is a smoky locals' place with video games, shuffleboard and pool tables. **Kochevar's** is another local favorite where Butch Cassidy and the Sundance Kid used to saddle up to the bar. **The Idle Spur** is a microbrewery with live music and dancing on weekends. Cover charges are $5 to $10, depending on the talent.

Rafters has dancing and good singles action most nights in Mt. Crested Butte, and it's within stumbling distance of most of the lodging. Those staying in town can take an inexpensive town taxi service if they miss the last bus of the night.

The **Princess Wine Bar** at 218 Elk Ave. is the place to finish your night on the town. Serving a limited menu of appetizers, there are a few tempting desserts to enjoy with cappuccino or a fine dessert wine. With no doubt the best selection of quality wines by the glass, the Princess also carries a full list of cognacs, ports and single malts. Come relax by the fire. Open daily from 10 a.m. to "whenever."

Other activities

Crested Butte offers several winter activities. These include **snowmobiling, dog sledding, ice skating, sledding, winter horseback riding** with Powder Ranch, **sleigh rides** with and without dinners, and **ballooning**—weather permitting. Call Crested Butte Chamber of Commerce at 349-6438 for brochures and information. For resort activities, call 349-2211.

There are great **shops** at the resort and especially in town. Among them: Diamond Tanita Art Gallery, for jewelry, glass, ceramics, paper, forged iron and other functional art pieces; Cookworks, Inc., a gourmet kitchen shop; Book Worm Cellar, with local maps, Western art and collectibles; and the Milky Way for unique women's apparel and lacey things.

Getting there and getting around

By air: Despite its seemingly isolated location, Crested Butte is quite convenient to reach. The nearest airport is Gunnison, 30 miles from the resort. American Airlines has nonstop daily 757 jet service from Dallas/Ft. Worth, and United offers several daily jet and commuter flights.

Alpine Express (641-5074 or 800-822-4844) meets every arriving flight and takes you directly to your hotel or condo for about $41 round-trip ($26 for children 12 and under). For reservations, call Crested Butte Vacations or directly to the company.

By car: Crested Butte is at the end of Hwy. 135, about 30 miles north of Gunnison. It's about 230 miles from Denver via Hwys. 285, 50 and 135. Hertz, Budget and Avis operate at the Gunnison Airport.

Getting around: No need for a car. Crested Butte's free town-resort shuttle, running every 15 minutes, is reliable and fun to ride, thanks to some free-spirited and friendly drivers. Town taxi for after-hours travel is available at 349-5543.

Nearby resorts

Monarch, Monarch, CO; (888) 996-7669, (719) 539-3573

Internet: www.skimonarch.com

5 lifts; 670 acres; 1,170 vertical feet

Monarch, located on the Continental Divide, is known for powder and more powder. It gets about 350 inches of snow a year, but only about 170,000 skier visits (many Colorado destination resorts get that in just a couple of weeks). That means a lot more untracked snow to play in. Monarch installed a fixed-grip quad two seasons ago, its first chair larger than a double. The resort caters to families, and has groomed beginner and intermediate terrain for those who don't like the steep and deep. Experts can opt for snowcat skiing and riding on more than 900 acres of expert backcountry terrain. This area is fairly isolated and without many off-slope activities. Child care starts at 2 months.

Lift tickets (00/01 prices): Adults, $35; Children (7–12), $15; Seniors (62–69), $20. Children 6 and younger & seniors 70 and older ski free. Snowcat skiing/riding, $165 per person.

Distance from Denver: About 160 miles southwest via Hwys. 285 and 50. **Distance from Gunnison** (closest airport): About 35 miles east on Hwy. 50.

Lodging information: (800) 332-3668. Monarch has an overnight lodge 3 miles away; other lodging is in Salida, 18 miles east.

Purgatory at Durango Mountain Resort

Colorado

Summit elevation: 10,822 feet
Vertical drop: 2,029 feet
Base elevation: 8,793 feet

Address: One Skier Place, Durango, CO 81301
✆ **Area code:** 970
Ski area phone/Snow report: 247-9000
ⓘ **Toll-free reservations:** (800) 525-0892
E-mail: info@durangomountain.com
Internet:
www.durangomountainresort.com (ski area)
or www.durango.com (town)
Expert: ★
Advanced: ★★★
Intermediate: ★★★★★
Beginner: ★★★★★
Never-ever: ★★★★★

Number of lifts: 11–1 high-speed six-pack,
1 high-speed quad, 4 triples, 3 doubles,
2 surface lifts
Snowmaking: 34 percent
Skiable acreage: 1,200 acres
Uphill capacity: 15,600 per hour
Snowboarding: Yes
Bed base: 3,120 near resort; 7,000 in Durango
Nearest lodging: Slopeside
Resort child care: Yes, 2 months and older
Adult ticket, per day: $50-$53 (01/02)
Dining: ★★★ **Apres-ski/nightlife:** ★★★
Other activities: ★★★★

Purgatory at Durango Mountain Resort is a hidden gem. It's tucked away in Southwest Colorado, closer to Albuquerque than it is to Denver. It doesn't have the movie stars you'll find in Aspen or Telluride, nor does it draw the crowds you'll encounter at resorts west of Denver. What it offers is more bluebird days than any other resort in Colorado, plus snow that's usually good, and often great. And it's uncrowded. You'll seldom wait in lift lines except on holiday weekends.

Durango draws heavily from New Mexico, Arizona and Texas. You'll see plenty of Suburbans in the parking lot with Texas plates. Skiers wearing jeans and cowboy hats, whooping and hollering their way down beginner runs aren't uncommon. The preponderance of intermediate skiers means Purgatory's advanced trails are uncrowded, and fresh powder remains untracked even longer. Boarders will love the mountain's many terraced runs.

The ski area reaches back from the highway like a shoulder 2 miles up a glaciated valley—deceptively small from the main parking lot, but extensive in its choices once you start exploring. The mountain's only downside is that it's 25 miles north of town.

Durango's historic downtown is full of great restaurants, brew pubs and galleries. If you and your group can't have fun in Durango, well, you'd better just stay home. Inexpensive motels line Main Avenue, and rates for a single can dip as low as $29 a night during the ski season. Families, students, and others on a budget can enjoy a very low-cost ski vacation here.

Purgatory Mountain receives an average of 260 inches of snow per year. Early-season snowmaking efforts here focus on covering a few runs well rather than a large area. The best snow conditions are typically in February and March.

Mountain layout—Skiing

Thousands of years ago glaciers scraped out the Animas Valley, leaving behind terraced mountainsides. The terraces mean several of Purgatory Mountain's runs plunge downward for a bit, then level off, then plunge, then level off—all the way to the bottom, no matter what ability level you are. The effect is like a roller coaster ride. The roller coaster effect lures those who love to catch air (yes, there are warnings all over the place, but who can resist?), and those who need a breather will appreciate the flat rest stops. We counted, and you'll get about 10 to 15 turns in before the pancake, keeping terror to a minimum and forgiving the less athletic among us.

All the signs on the mountain refer to lifts by number, but the trail map provides names, and sometimes people use names too, so we'll give you both.

A heads up: In recent years Lift #5 (Grizzly) hasn't opened until later in the season, and has frequently been closed midweek. Most of the terrain it serves is accessible, with a little traversing, from either Lift #3 (Hermosa Park Express) or Lift #8 (Legends). When Lift #5 is up and running, always exit it beside the restaurant; everything above are cat tracks for traversing to other parts of the mountain.

◆◆ **Expert:** The toughest trail on the mountain is Bull Run, a double-black route that starts off rather gently beneath Dante's restaurant, next to Lift #5 (Grizzly). Once you're on the lower part of it, there's no getting off. It has a tough pitch as well as funnels and moguls. Bottom's Chute is a nasty surprise on your way to Lift #8 (Legends). Adventure skiers can try the powder stashes between Peace and Boogie. On the front side of the mountain, tree fans will like the aspens between Pandemonium and Lower Hades.

◆ **Advanced:** From the top of Lift #1 (Purgatory Village Express), what starts out as Paradise soon turns into Pandemonium, a black diamond that gets steeper and bumpier the further down you go. Likewise, Upper Hades also starts out mild, but turns hellacious once you drop over the headwall onto Lower Hades. Styx, next to the ski area boundary, can be heavenly after a fresh snowstorm. The short traverse to Styx created by the somewhat inconvenient placement of Lift #1's top station means you'll encounter fewer skiers than ever on this utterly fabulous run.

On the back side of the mountain, Snag, perhaps the most terraced run on the mountain, leads skiers to challenging chutes all leading back to Lift #3 (Hermosa Park). Bump fans should also consider Wapiti, a black run under Lift #5 (Grizzly) that grows igloo-sized bumps. Lift #8 (Legends) in the far back is the home of most of the black-diamond terrain. It's easy to do laps here, on mostly bumpy runs—without moguls, this would be strictly intermediate territory. Beware: The triple is a slow chair, so racking up vertical is an exercise in patience. Poet's Glade and Paul's Park offer nice glade skiing, Elliott's has a nice sustained pitch.

■ **Intermediate:** Intermediates seem to prefer the terrain served by Lift #3 (Hermosa Park Express). Regularly groomed runs include Peace, Boogie, Where, Zinfandel, and Airmail. On days with fresh snow Harris Hill can provide a fun cut-off. Want to ratchet it up a notch? From the top of Lift #3 continue down Legends toward Dead Spike. Dead Spike is frequently split groomed, with good intermediate "starter bumps" on the ungroomed side. Still not challenged enough? Continue further down Legends to the mid-loading station on Lift #8 (Legends). From the top of this lift, check out either Sally's Run or Chet's.

●● **Beginner:** After graduating from the bunny hill, beginning skiers should head for Lift #4 (Twilight). It serves terrain ideally suited for beginners and families with small children. You won't be endangered by a lot of advanced, fast skiers in this area. The easiest trail is Pinkerton Toll Road, a winding cat track. Divinity and Angel's Tread are wide runs. Columbine winds through several stands of trees, giving beginners the feeling of being deep in the woods. If this terrain is simply too easy, you may want to cut over from the top of Lift #4 over to Lift #3 (Hermosa Park) via Salvation, where you'll find groomed intermediate terrain.

● **Never-ever:** First-timers have their own learning area, Columbine Station, complete with its own lifts, ticket office and restaurant. It's directly across from the lower parking lots. After a couple of lessons on the terrain under the Columbine Lift, beginners can ride the Lift #7 (Graduate) back to the base area. The "Family Ski Zone" under Lift #4 (Twilight) would be the logical place for beginners to head next rather than taking Lift#1 (Purgatory Village Express) to the top of the mountain. A catwalk down to the Columbine beginner area will take intermediate and advanced skiers back to their cars at the end of the day, provided they parked in one of the two lower lots, but it's not recommended for use by beginners.

 ## Mountain layout—Snowboarding

The signature run is Snag, an exciting roller-coaster ride of steep, moderate, steep, moderate steps—all the way down! Advanced riders can catch air off each of the steps. Intermediates can use the flats above each headwall to catch their breath. Rider-constructed hits can often be found here and at various locations beneath Lift #8 (Legends).

On days with freshies, locals head for Lift #8. Powder hounds can head into the trees on Poet's Glade or Paul's Park. From Lift #5 (Grizzly), a delightful powder stash can often be found hidden away on Cathedral Tree Way (rider's left off Bull Run). On the front side try Styx—you'll most likely find waist-deep powder. Upper Hades transitions into Lower Hades, a major steep mogul field that, when covered with a foot or more of fresh powder, can be an absolutely amazing ride, along with Pandemonium and Catharsis.

Paradise offers wide-open corduroy for laying out sick carves. Sa's Psyche is equally good carving country. Pitchfork Terrain Park has a 450-foot halfpipe that transitions to a 15-foot quarterpipe, plus jibbing rails, a rainbow rail, two street rails, a balance beam and "The Serpentine," a 45-foot rail with kink to curve to kink to curve. There's also a 50-foot Big Air competition jump. Adjacent is Limbo, the slopestyle area, with back-to-back tables, multiple hits, line combinations and a "Hollywood Hit," visible from the lift, strictly for hot dogs.

You'll find way-too-flat traverses connecting the front and back side. Getting to the back side requires carrying a lot of speed on Hermosa Parkway. Reaching the maze at the bottom of Lift #3 (Hermosa Park) without having to unstrap and skate requires executing a kamikaze-style run. To return from the back side, avoid the much-too-flat BD&M Expressway. Instead, zigzag: Take Path to Peace, ride Lift #3 back up the mountain, Silver Tip it to either black-diamond Cool It or blue-square The Bank, then continue on past the bottom of Lift#2 (Engineer) to Demon. The right side of Demon is a gully that provides a natural halfpipe but be extremely careful of beginners finding their way home on Demon after lunch.

Beginners should take Lift #1 (Purgatory Village Express) and head for Sa's Psyche, beneath Lift #2 (Engineer). It's nicely groomed, gentle-pitched terrain, with only one flat spot. Snowboarders generally avoid Lift #4 (Twilight) because of lack of suitable terrain.

Mountain rating

Despite the mountain's name, this is Intermediate Paradise—such are the variety and plenitude of trails. Intermediates enjoy endless options for whoop-de-doing at high speeds. There are occasional frustrating flats—some folks call the resort "traversatory"—but for the most part you'll find plenty of fun. The Columbine area is devoted strictly to neophytes, with everything from a magic carpet to the Graduate triple when you're ready for the main mountain. Advanced skiers will have a great time, too, taking laps off the Legends Lift. Only experts looking for extremes will be disappointed.

Cross-country and snowshoeing

The **Nordic Center** (247-6000 Ext. 114 or 385-2114), maintained by the Durango Nordic Ski Club, is located just north of the Alpine ski area and across Highway 550. There are 16 km. of groomed trails for classic and skate skiing. Nordic skiers find the same undulating terrain as alpine skiers do, with appropriate terrain for various ability levels. The center offers clinics, races, group and private lessons, rentals, children's programs, daytime and moonlight tours. Daily trail fees are $8 for adults and $4 for children 12 and younger and seniors 65 and older. Rentals are $10 for adults, $6 for children and seniors. As part of Purgatory's Total Adventure Ticket™, one Alpine ski day can be exchanged for the Nordic package.

Lessons (2001/02 prices)

Group lessons: $30 for a 2-hour lesson. A three-lesson booklet is $79 (half-day lessons, use 'em when you want). Hint: Afternoon sessions tend to have far fewer students so you can receive more personalized instruction.

Never-ever package: Called First Things First, it offers first-time skiers and snowboarders half-day group lessons for $30; $60 includes lift ticket and rentals. This is a guaranteed lesson, with each instructor wearing a button: "Learn from me or learn for free." For people who have been on skis or a snowboard before who might not be ready to "go up the hill," a Second Things Second program is offered at the same rate.

Private lessons: $140 for two hours during peak hours (9 a.m.-1 p.m.); $110 for three hours during off peak hours (1- 4 p.m.). A full-day private lesson is $300. For a lesson with Purgatory's top snowboard instructor, ask for Nancy Vogel.

Special programs: Throughout the season, the resort offers clinics for snowboarding, racing, telemark skiing and mogul techniques. Call ahead for details, or check with the Resort Concierge desk. Clinics and daily events are announced on the daily snow report and posted with the list of groomed trails throughout the resort and on shuttles.

The Adaptive Sports Association (385-2163, Nov.-April; www.asadurango.org.) runs one of the nation's leading adaptive skiing programs here. Programs include lift ticket, adaptive equipment and lessons for the visually, physically or mentally impaired.

Racing: NASTAR racing occurs daily at the Paradise Events Arena. Runs are $2 or skiers can opt for self-timed race training gates.

Child care (2001/02 prices)

Ages: 2 months to 3 years.

Costs: $75 for a full day with lunch; $60 for half day. Toddlers (ages 2–3) get outdoor snow play, arts and crafts, games, movies and story time.

Reservations: Required; call 385-2144 or (800) 525-0892.

Note: Day-care staff also can recommend a babysitter who can watch your kids while you enjoy a night out. If you're not sure whether to put your child in day care or lessons, Durango Mountain's Kids Central, located on the second floor of the Village Center, will help assess your child's abilities and interests, then escort him or her to the appropriate spot.

Children's lessons: Ski lessons are available for kids 3-12 years old, snowboarding lessons are for kids 8-12. Full-day programs, including lift ticket and lunch, cost $75; half day with ticket, $60. Rentals are an additional $10. The program for ages 3–4 includes lunch, indoor activity, and an introduction-to-ski lesson with special skis that attach to snowboots (included in cost); ages 4-5 get the same only using full Alpine equipment (rental is additional $7). Reservations required for kids ages 3-5 (800-525-0892 or 385-2144).

 ## Lift tickets (2001/02 prices)

	Adult	Child (6-12)
One day	$50	$25
Multi-day (see below)		

Who skis free: Ages 5 and younger and 70 and older.
Who skis at a discount: Ages 62–69 ski for $35.
Note: There are early/late season discounts and higher holiday rates. The resort offers a Total Adventure Ticket™: Guests purchasing a four-day or more ticket can apply credit for a day of downhill skiing against a day of cross-country skiing or one of several vacation activities in southwest Colorado (examples include the Durango & Silverton Narrow Gauge Railroad train, a soak and massage at Trimble Hot Springs, or a sleigh ride). Call for details.

Accommodations

Durango Mountain Resort has three primary lodging areas. The condos at the base area are the most expensive. A limited number of resort hotels and condos within 10 miles of the ski area are slightly less. Motels in Durango can cost as little as $29 per night, but are 25 miles away. Except on holidays, motel reservations are seldom needed in town. All Durango and Durango Mountain Resort lodging can be booked through **Durango Central Reservations,** (800) 525-0892, or the **Durango Chamber of Commerce** (800) 525-8855. Online, check lodgings at www.durango.com. Several Durango properties are listed at **Vacation Rentals by Owner** www.vrbo.com.

Base-area lodging is available at the **Purgatory Village Condominium Hotel** (385-2100), **Best Western Lodge at Durango Mountain** (247-9669), which accepts pets, and the following condo complexes: **Angelhaus** (247-8090), **Brimstone** (259-1066), **East Rim** (385-2100), **Edelweiss, Graysill, Sitzmark** and **Twilight View**. Condos have full-service units (kitchens, fireplaces, common-area hot tubs and laundry facilities) and run from about $115 for a studio to $595 for larger suites. Hotel costs are about $105–$285.

Several other complexes are within 10 miles of the ski area. The prices at **Cascade Village, Needles, Silver Pick** and **Sheraton Tamarron Resort** range from $115–$445. Most of the outlying condo complexes offer free shuttles to and from the ski area.

Comfortable in-town lodging can be found at the **Hampton Inn** (247-0829), the **Doubletree** (259-6580), which accepts pets, and the **Marriott Residence Inn** (259-6200). A plethora of older, less-expensive motels line North Main Ave., including the **Day's End** (259-3311) and **Silver Spur** (247-5552), where the sign says John Wayne once slept. The **Spanish Trails Inn** (247-4173) offers kitchenettes, and is across the street from City Market. For fans of funky (but clean) little motels, consider the **Wapiti Lodge** (247-3961) which is walking distance to downtown.

Five historic lodging properties are worth mentioning. **The Strater Hotel** (800-247-4431; $$$) and the **General Palmer Hotel** (800-523-3358; $$–$$$) are multistory, brick hotels that date back over 100 years. Both are in the heart of the walkable downtown area. The Strater has a great Victorian-style hot tub area that would be the envy of many larger, more sophisticated properties and its Diamond Belle Saloon is a classic that's now non-smoking. **The Leland House Bed & Breakfast** and **The Rochester Hotel** (800-664-1920 for both; $$–$$$ for both), across the street from each other on East Second Ave., are historic lodges owned by the same family. The Rochester has two dog-friendly rooms. The Leland House has a Durango history theme. The Rochester Hotel has a Hollywood theme, with each room named for a film shot at least in part in Durango. "Butch Cassidy and the Sundance Kid," "Around The World in 80 Days" and "City Slickers" were all filmed in this region. **Jarvis Suites** (800-824-1024, 259-6190; $$-$$$) at 10th and Main are newly redecorated with a killer view of the action on Main St. Built in 1888, the hotel is on the National Register of Historic Places.

Two B&B's between town and the ski area are the **Apple Orchard Inn** (247-0751; $$), on CR203 near Trimble Hot Springs, and **Country Sunshine** (247-2853; $$) near where CR250 runs into 550N. Staying at either drastically reduces the amount of driving you do.

 Dining

There are several options at the base area. **Purgy's Pub** serves burgers, barbecue and pizza in a bar atmosphere. After a full morning of skiing you'll savor the hearty homemade soups and stews at the **Mountain Market Deli,** a local's favorite lunch spot. There's also the upscale **Joey's Italian Café**. The **Columbine Station** at the base of the beginner hill has lunch items and local brews along with "kid food."

Dante's, at the midway station of Lift #5 (Grizzly), serves lunch. Upstairs, **Café de los Pinos** has gourmet lunches with great views of the slopes and a nice bar. **The Powderhouse Restaurant** beneath Lift #2 (Hermosa Park) serves lunch fare along Italian themes.

For fresh fish and local game, try the **Cascade Grill** (259-3500; $$$), 2 miles north of the resort that offers elegant dining in a rustic setting. The new **Hamilton Chop House** (259-6636), north of the resort entrance, is excellent. **The Sow's Ear** (247-3527), at the SilverPick lodge, is famed for its large hand-cut steaks.

You'll find restaurants of almost every persuasion downtown. Most don't require, or accept, reservations. Entrées typically run $15–25 at the finer restaurants.

Seasons (382-9790, $$$), 764 Main Ave., features rotisserie-roasted dinners (sea bass, trout, chicken, lamb) and fine wines by the glass. Try the garlic mashed potatoes.

Ken & Sue's Place (259-2616, $$), 937 Main Ave., is a favorite among locals, as is **Ken & Sue's Place East** (385-1810, $$$) at 636 Main Ave. Continental fare with a homey twist make for memorable meals. Start with the field green salad with apples and gorgonzola, then order the pistachio-encrusted grouper served with a rum sauce on a bed of yams. At the East location try the lobster ravioli or the potato-encrusted trout.

Ariano's (247-8146, $$-$$$), 150 East College Dr., serves northern Italian cuisine. Swanky **Randy's** (247-9083, $$-$$$), next door at 152 East College Dr., serves just about the nicest prime rib in town and is one of the few restaurants in Durango that does accept reservations. Ask for a curtained booth for a romantic dinner.

The Ore House (247-5707, $$-$$$), 147 College Dr., is an Old West steak house, rustic and casual. **The Red Snapper** (259-3417, $$-$$$), 144 East 9th St., has fresh seafood, by far the nicest salad bar in town, along with an exotic saltwater-aquarium decor.

The Cyprus Café (385-6884, $$), 725 E. Second, offers delicious Mediterranean dishes at quite reasonable prices. Their lamb dishes are to die for. **Bayou Doc's** (259-6486, $$) cooks "Cajun With Attitude" and they aren't kidding.

Dining: $$$-Entrees $20+; $$-$10-20; $-less than $10.
Accommodations: (double room) $$$$-$200+; $$$-$141-$200; $$-$81-$140; $-$80 and less.

Francisco's Restaurante Y Cantina (247-4098, $$), 619 Main Ave., offers a Southwestern menu. Hidden-away **Gazpacho** (259-9494, $$), 431 E. Second Ave., has authentic New Mexican cuisine. **Tequilas** (259-7655, $$), 948 Main, where the waiters all pretend not to speak English, is the new local's favorite and serves the finest margarita in town, made with fresh-squeezed limes. Ask for an Especial.

Olde Tymer's Cafe (259-2990, $-$$), 1000 Main Ave., is tops for a good hamburger. Monday is burger night, Friday is the taco special. They recently went non-smoking. **Christina's Grille and Bar** (382-3844, $$), 3416 (North) Main Ave., offers very reasonably priced continental cuisine. The parking lot is always full, telling you something!

Carver's Bakery and Brew Pub (259-2545, $$), 1022 Main Ave., is the best place in Durango for breakfast; muffins and bagels are baked fresh daily. Carver's has a nice children's menu—their meals are served on a Frisbee they get to keep. **College Drive Café** (247-5322) bakes the best homemade cinnamon rolls (closed Monday/Tuesday). If you prefer the eggs-and-bacon-type breakfast, head for the **Durango Diner** (247-9889), 957 Main Ave. Sunday brunch at the **Doubletree Hotel** ($$) is outstanding and a good choice for visitors departing on Sunday, since the hotel is between the ski area and the airport. Or start the day off at the **Steamin' Bean** (385-7901, $) on Main Street, a great hangout for coffee, chess and chai.

Après-ski/nightlife

Skiers and riders congregate at **Purgy's Pub** after the lifts close. Purgy's sometimes has a band. **Shakers Martini Bar** on the 2nd floor at Purgy's, features top shelf liquors, jumbo shrimp and olive skewers. In general, however, apres-ski is found in town, not on the mountain.

Most ski areas have a "locals" spot, and here it's the **Schoolhouse Cafe**, a small and friendly hangout located 2 miles south of the resort. It's across the road from the Needles Country Store on U.S. Hwy. 550. This is where the lift ops, ski patrollers and other insiders fill up on beer and calzones the size of footballs. The music rocks, and the pool table is free.

A wa-aay popular après-ski spot that's available on trade with your Total Adventure Ticket™ is **Trimble Hot Springs**, 8 miles north of Durango on the way back from the ski area. Natural mineral springs bubble into two outdoor therapy pools, one heated to 90 degrees and the other to 105. A heated outdoor 50-meter pool awaits lap swimmers. Massages are available; call ahead (247-0111).

If you really want to party, go to downtown Durango—depending on the time of year, it's either jumping or mildly hopping. Spring Break, which goes on for several weeks in March, packs 'em in and the bars schedule lots of entertainment.

Carver's Bakery and Brew Pub offers several beers brewed on-site along with a full dinner menu. **Steamworks**, a brew pub on the corner of 8th Street and East Second Ave., pours award-winning beer and serves moderately priced food in a party atmosphere. **Lady Falconburgh's Barley Exchange** has 20 microbrews on tap and more than 80 different bottled beers. Its long picnic benches attract large groups of students from nearby Fort Lewis College. Their Philly Cheese Steak is excellent. **El Rancho** is Durango's old standby. You've got to stop and have at least one drink there, along with a bowl of free popcorn. Other bars have come and gone but "The Ranch" has served liquid refreshment since the days when Jack Dempsey fought his first fight there, although historians now say the fight actually occurred across the street. A mural on the side of the old Central Hotel depicts Dempsey's first TKO.

Durango has quite a variety of musical entertainment. Flyers posted around town will tell you who's playing where. The **San Juan Room** at College St. and Second Ave. has dancing and live music. **Solid Muldoon's** is primarily a dance and pool-shoot spot for the college crowd, but worth a visit for the decor. **Coloradaponga's** is a smokey pool hall. **Scoot'n Blues** dishes up soul, jazz, and, of course, blues, blues, blues. Over at the **Diamond Belle Saloon** in the Strater Hotel, a ragtime piano player plunks out hit tunes from the Gay '90s—1890s, that is. The Diamond Belle recently went non-smoking, and their waitresses wear vintage-era costumes that are worth the price of a drink to see! A new favorite is **The Office** at the Strater, where the three-martini après-ski is *de rigueur*. Check out the $11,000 chandelier.

Other activities

If you haven't had enough on-slope time, the resort has a **tubing** hill. **Star Safaris,** a real family affair, takes you on a ride to the Powderhouse for nighttime stargazing with Colorado's largest privately owned telescope. Book these and other activities, such as **snowmobiling** and **dinner sleigh rides,** through the Durango Mountain Resort Ski Concierge in the Purgatory Village Center.

Durango has two **snowcat operations.** The **San Juan Ski Company** (259-9671; www.sanjuanski.com; closed Tuesdays) takes skiers and boarders to 35,000 acres of powder for about $175 (including lunch, guide included, age 12+). Reservations strongly recommended. **El Diablo** (877-241-9643, 385-7288; www.snowcat-powder.com), provides tours in the San Juan Mountains, including Molas Pass, near Silverton, a quaint Victorian mining town. Cost is about $125 including lunch.

Durango has a couple of off-slope activities unique in the ski industry. One of America's finest national parks is nearby, **Mesa Verde.** Anasazi Indian (Ancestral Puebloans) cliff dwellings dating back more than 800 years have been preserved here. Plan an early start for a day trip to Mesa Verde; it's about an hour west of Durango but over a mountain pass.

Another unique activity is the **Durango & Silverton Narrow Gauge Railroad** (www.durangotrain.com). Durango was founded in 1880 by the Denver and Rio Grande Railroad when they extended their line to Silverton in order to haul ore to a smelter being built on the river in Durango, near local sources of coal. Today, the train hauls tourists. Until a few years ago, it ran only in the summer. Now, daily in winter, it goes halfway to Silverton then returns to Durango, a five-hour round trip. The winter fare is about $45 for adults, $22 for children ages 5-11. Though the cars are enclosed, warm clothing is highly recommended. If you purchase a Total Adventure Ticket, you can exchange a day of skiing for the train ride.

If you don't have time for the train ride, consider just visiting the **Railroad Museum.** There are antique photographs, memorabilia, locomotives, a galloping goose, handcars and putt-putts, rare W.H. Jackson photos, railroad art and more. Admission is $5. There are several other museums in Durango to consider. The **Animas Museum** (259-2402), 31st St. & W. 2nd Ave., shows exhibits on area history and Indian cultures. Winter hours are Wed.-Sat., 10 a.m.-4 p.m. **Children's Museum of Durango** (259-9234), 802 E. 2nd Ave. upstairs in the Durango Arts Center, has hands-on exhibits for kids ages 2-11. Open Wed.-Sun., 10 a.m.-2 p.m. **Grand Motorcar & Piano Collection** (247-1250), 586 Animas View Dr., displays a variety of antique and classic automobiles and grand pianos.

For families with kids of all ages, the **Melodrama** (247-3400) is a wonderful excursion back in time, to a bygone era of heroes and villains. Held in the Diamond Circle Theater at 7th and Main next to the Strater Hotel. Nightly performances except Sundays; tickets are $17 for adults, $12 for children younger than 12. Adults will appreciate the full bar.

The Sky Ute Lodge and Casino offers basic gambling and some 380 Vegas-style slots.

Durango's **shops** smack of shabby chic, Old West and unique custom designs. The art **galleries** are first rate, and clothing and knick-knack shops stock great finds. Among our favorites: New West Galleries on Main between 7th and 8th, and Toh Atin Gallery, 145 W. 9th Street, for Southwestern art; and The Bookcase, 601 E. Second Ave., offers a fine inventory of used and collector books. The O'Farrell Hat Company, on Main near the General Palmer Hotel offers what are acknowledged as the world's finest cowboy hats. You'll have to dig deep in your pocketbook to put one of their hats on your head, though. Real deep.

Getting there and getting around

By air: The Durango-La Plata County Airport is 40 miles south of Durango Mountain Resort and about 15 miles from downtown Durango.

By car: The resort is 25 miles from Durango, 350 miles southwest of Denver, 232 miles northwest of Albuquerque and 470 miles northeast of Phoenix. There are no major mountain passes from the south or west. In summary, Durango is an easy, 4-hour drive from Albuquerque. It is a 6-8+ hour drive from Denver in the winter over numerous mountain passes, which frequently close when it snows. Chains or 4WD are occasionally required on Highway 550N heading from Durango to the resort during and immediately after major snowstorms; however, 99 percent of the time a front-wheel drive vehicle is all that's needed.

If you don't need lessons or rentals, the bunny hill offers the fastest access onto the mountain. Either get off the shuttle at the bunny hill or park your car in one of the two lower lots. You can purchase your lift tickets here, and at the end of the day, ski back to your car. From the bunny hill ride Lift #7 (The Graduate) directly to Lift #1 (Purgatory Village Express). To access the upper parking lots requires either chains or 4WD, and you'll do a lot more schlepping in ski boots and waiting in line at the base village than if you park low.

Getting around: Visitors have several ground transportation options: (1) Rent a car. If possible, request a front-wheel-drive vehicle. The Durango airport has a number of rental agencies. Cars can also be rented at the Strater and Doubletree hotels. Ask about transportation when making a reservation. (2) Some of the larger hotels offer shuttle service to and from the slopes. Others offer free or low-cost airport shuttles. Some lodges on the north end of town offer free nightlife shuttles for guests. (3) **Mountain TranSport** shuttles between town and the slopes, nine round trips between 6 a.m. and 10 p.m. Call the resort for departure times and places. In-town pickup points with signs listing the current schedule include the 25th St. fairgrounds and a shuttle stop at 34th St., just north of Christina's restaurant. (4) **Durango Transportation** (259-4818) provides on-call taxi service as well as airport pick-ups. Round-trip fare from the airport to Purgatory at Durango Mountain Resort is $60 per person. From the airport to the town of Durango, the fare is $15 per person, one-way. (5) The **Durango Trolley**, a red minibus decorated to resemble an antique trolley, provides in-town service up and down Main Ave. year round, every 30 minutes. The fare is 50¢. Winter hours are 7 a.m. to 7 p.m. (6) **The Buzz Bus** takes intoxicated patrons home when the bars close. It only costs $2. (7) More than a few locals simply hitchhike from this point rather than waiting for the bus. Locals typically stop and pick up riders; ask if you can contribute $5 for gas.

Downtown Durango is delightfully walkable. Here's something to know when trying to find a Durango street address: Nearly all of Durango's streets have numbered names. The streets parallel to Main are "Avenues" and the numbers usually are spelled out (Second Avenue, for example). The streets that intersect Main all are "Streets" and the number is seldom spelled out. Most tourists hang out on Main between 5th and 11th, and occasionally venture onto Second Avenue. 6th Street is better known as "College Drive."

Nearby resorts

Wolf Creek Ski Area, Pagosa Springs, CO; 970-264-5639
Internet: www.wolfcreekski.com
6 lifts, 1600 acres, 1600 vertical feet

Wolf Creek is the "non-resort" where skiers and riders go to drown themselves in fresh powder, explore the trees and launch off cliffs. Most of the time, you're not on a marked trail and fresh tracks can be found days after storms. This isn't a destination resort with endless groomers, cute shops and activities for non-skiers. It's a gateway to the backcountry.

Because of the tremendous amounts of snow, avalanche control is a big issue. There are gates to access the ridgeline between Treasure Chair and Boundary Bowl, the Waterfall area, Montezuma Bowl, the Knife Ridge Chutes and Horseshoe Bowls. For 2001/02, Wolf Creek is looking into installing a natural gas cannon in Horseshoe Bowl to reduce the amount of explosives required to clear chutes. Unlike bigger resorts, Wolf Creek doesn't go out of its way to dynamite every rock, pull every stump, or remove every downed tree, all of which actually improve the stability of the snow pack. They just let the snow bury it all.

The facilities at the base of family-owned Wolf Creek are limited: the ticket office, a cafeteria and bar, a restaurant, restrooms, a tiny ski shop and an even tinier rental shop. But Wolf Creek has a wonderful feel to it. In the cafeteria you'll enjoy homemade soups served from crockpots, and fresh egg salad sandwiches rather than frozen production-line, hockey-puck burgers. On sunny days the patio is popular, and brown-bagging is welcome.

Holy Moses, visible from the lift, only begins to give advanced skiers and riders a taste of what's available. For an even bigger taste, try black-diamonds Prospector and Glory Hole. The Waterfall area is served by the new Alberta Lift (formerly served by snowcat). To access the gates leading here, ride Treasure Chair, then follow Navajo Trail or shortcut down lower Glory Hole. Stay slightly skier's right to get to Alberta Lift, which serves only expert terrain off Knife Ridge. The only other way to reach the intermediate Burn Area farther down the bowl is Park Avenue, an intermediate run that's available as an escape route. A bit of hiking will take extreme skiers and riders over to Horseshoe Bowl, the resort's eastern-most bowl.

Advanced-intermediates should head for Silver Streak, Treasure, Alberta and Tranquility off Treasure Chair. Lower-level intermediates will enjoy trails like Charisma, Powder Puff and Windjammer off Bonanza chair. Snowboarders: Don't bother looking for a halfpipe and terrain park, you won't find one. Take advantage of the natural terrain features instead. Beginners should stick to Dickey Chair and either Bunny Hop or Kelly Boyce trails. Never-evers have a magic carpet and beginner's lift in front of the lodge.

We suggest you stay in either South Fork or, preferably, Pagosa Springs. As in Pagosa Hot Springs. Once you get past the slight sulfur smell, Pagosa's 11 different pools, all at different temperatures, are about the finest apres-ski experience there is. They're on the river, suitable for an icy plunge to make your skin tingle. Pagosa Springs has an old-world charm that's hard to describe. And it's inexpensive compared to destination resorts.

Lift tickets (2001/02): Adults, $42; children younger than 12 and seniors 65 and older, $25.
Driving distances: From Durango, 72 miles east on Highway 160; from Pagosa Springs, 23 miles; from South Fork, 18 miles. You'll need a 4WD vehicle to get to the mountain.
Lodging information: The resort does not have lodging and it doesn't handle lodging reservations, but you'll find a complete listing of nearby accommodations on the resort Web site.
Other resources: Pagosa Springs Chamber, 800-252-2204 or www.pagosaspringschamber.com; South Fork Business Association, 800-571-0881 or www.southfork.org/lodging.

Steamboat

Colorado

Summit elevation:	10,568 feet
Vertical drop:	3,668 feet
Base elevation:	6,900 feet

Address: 2305 Mt. Werner Circle
Steamboat Springs, CO 80487
✆ **Area code:** 970
Ski area phone: 879-6111
Snow report: 879-7300
ⓘ **Toll-free reservations:** (800) 922-2722
Fax: 879-4757
E-mail: info@steamboat-ski.com
Internet: www.steamboat.com
Expert: ★★★
Advanced: ★★★★
Intermediate: ★★★★★
Beginner: ★★
Never-ever: ★★

Number and types of lifts: 20–1 gondola,
4 high-speed quads, 1 quad, 6 triples,
6 doubles, 2 surface lifts
Skiable acreage: 2,939 acres
Snowmaking: 15 percent
Uphill capacity: 34,658 per hour
Snowboarding: Yes
Bed base: 18,306
Nearest lodging: Slopeside
Resort child care: Yes, 6 months and older
Adult ticket, per day: $44-$59 (2000/01)
Dining: ★★★★
Apres-ski/nightlife: ★★★
Other activities: ★★★★★

Steamboat's ad campaign would have you believe that horses outnumber the cars in its parking lot, that cowboy hats and sheepskin jackets are the preferred ski wear and that you trip over Lone Star longnecks on the dance floors. In reality, this is a big, sleek, modern ski area with more microbrews and gourmet coffees than spittoons.

Steamboat Mountain Village, the cluster of condos, shops and restaurants next to the mountain, is unpretentiously upscale. Boutiques offer elegant high-priced goods intermixed with T-shirt shops; gourmet restaurants are within steps of ribs-and-hamburger eateries. An occasional socialite swathed in fur passes, but right behind her will be someone wearing a 15-year-old ski parka. Everyone looks right at home.

In the village, the only cowboy hats you're likely to see grace the heads of Steamboat's resident celebrity, Billy Kidd, and the ticket punchers in the gondola building. Venture into downtown Steamboat Springs, though, and you may see cowboys sauntering down Lincoln Avenue. Northwest Colorado still has cattle ranches, so they'll probably be the real thing.

The downtown area—about five minutes by car and 15 minutes by a free shuttlebus from the village—squeezes into its dozen blocks a hodgepodge of old Victorian buildings, 1950s storefronts and a gas station or hardware store here and there. Good restaurants and nightlife hideouts are at the village, downtown, and on the highway linking the two. The bus runs between slopes and town every 20 minutes, making it easy to enjoy the village, town and everything in between.

Steamboat is also a great place for non-skiers. In addition to great shopping, it has activities that go beyond the usual sleigh rides and snowmobile tours (see *Other Activities*).

Mountain layout—Skiing

◆◆ **Expert** ◆ **Advanced:** There's a handful of double-diamond stashes here, but they're short and, while a bit unnerving, totally do-able. Expert descents here mean trees, bumps in trees, and short and sweet bump runs. Steamboat has only a few extreme steeps, but the runs from the Sundown Express chair are tree skiing and riding developed to an art. These trails all have been expertly thinned, both by humans and Mother Nature. Some trees are only about 10 feet apart, so stay alert. Such trails—natural slalom courses where the poles aren't spring-loaded—produce gallons of adrenaline even for the best skiers.

Other tough areas are off The Ridge to the north of Storm Peak. After a short hike along Over Easy, the double-diamond challenges are provided by Chutes 1, 2 and 3, No Name Chutes, the Christmas Tree Bowl, and other descents. The top of Morningside lift opens up first-rate expert skiing, but the runs are frustratingly short and end up in a long runout to the lift. Nice for a first run rush, but an hors d'oeuvre compared to "real" ski runs.

Morningside Park consists of 179 acres of intermediate and advanced terrain on the backside of Storm Peak. The 260 acres that make up Pioneer Ridge, off the Pony Express lift below the mid-mountain chairs, have gained a local fan club with long, winding and pinball-machine-style runs. It's fun because Steamboat shied away from the straight-down cut and went with the terrain angles here. It's black-diamond territory, but easy black diamond.

In Steamboat, glades abound: Don't be shy about ducking into places like the space between Concentration and Vagabond on the lower part of the mountain, or the "Twisticane" trees between Twister and Hurricane. Once you start looking, you'll see that the entire mountain is one big skiable forest.

■ **Intermediate:** Among the great cruisers are the blue trails from the Sunshine Chair (locals call this area "Wally World"), Sunset and Rainbow off the Four Points lift and Vagabond and Heavenly Daze off Thunderhead Express. The Sunshine Chair blues also have spots where beginning tree skiers can practice. If crowds build in any of those areas, take laps on the intermediate runs reached by the often-deserted Bashor and Christie chairs.

Longhorn, off Pioneer Ridge, is a locals' favorite with unparalleled views of the Yampa Valley. Skiers and riders can duck in and out of the lodgepole pines that border both sides of this run as they cruise off the Pony Express lift to the base of the Storm Peak Express lift.

On many of the black-diamond runs, though the terrain has steep spots and the moguls get pretty high, the trails are generally wide, allowing ample room for mistakes and recoveries. Westside, a black trail below Rendezvous Saddle, is steep but usually groomed. It's a good starting point for intermediates who wonder if they can handle the other black runs. If you're learning to do moguls, head for Concentration, marked black on the map, or Surprise, marked blue. Often half of each is groomed, while the other half is left to build bumps.

●● **Beginner:** With the exception of some gentle terrain served by the Bashor and the two Christie chairs, most of the green trails above the base area are cat trails. Wally World's gentle runs often attract classes, though, and you have to forgive skiers and riders who can't turn and stop. Many of the green runs feel narrow at times. Some intersect higher-ability runs where bombers sometimes use the intersection as a launching pad for the next section, and a few have slightly intimidating drop-offs on the downhill side. If beginners are part of your group, encourage them to enroll in a clinic so they will have a pleasant experience.

● **Never-ever:** A successful first-time experience—especially for adults—depends on two things: great instruction and suitable, uncrowded terrain. In the past, we've said Steamboat rates highly on the former, but not on the latter. However, the resort tells us they've re-shaped the learn-to-ski terrain, improving the grade of the slope and fall line. The new terrain, located at the base of the mountain and separated from other traffic, lets novices totally concentrate on the fun.

Mountain layout—Snowboarding

Steamboat's renowned champagne powder, which seems to fall in well-timed weekly accumulations, makes this a tree-boarders paradise. Shad-ows, with its steady pitch and widely-spaced aspen trees, is arguably the most perfect tree run in Colorado. And the new Pioneer Ridge ex-pansion, located below Storm Peak, invites exploration, although the long run-out makes a little hiking likely. When the pow blows out (*as if*) ride "The Dude Ranch," Steamboat's terrain park, or enter The Twilight Zone, a difficult glade run studded with moguls. If you're lucky, you might run into Banana George Blair, Steamboat's 80-something snowboard am-bassador and barefoot water skier extraordinaire. Always clad in yellow, Banana was ex-treme before the term was coined, and he's cooler than you, so share the love.

The resort tells us they've re-shaped the learning terrain, improving the grade of the slope and fall line. The new terrain, located at the base of the mountain and separated from other traffic, lets novices totally concentrate on the fun.

Mountain rating

Excellent tree skiing for experts, nice mogul runs for advanced, great cruisers for intermedi-ates. Improvements to the learning area make it better for beginners and never-evers now.

Cross-country and snowshoeing

The **Steamboat Ski Touring Center** (879-8180) at 2000 Clubhouse Drive has about 30 km. of groomed set tracks winding along Fish Creek and the surrounding countryside. The touring center has group and private instruc-tion, rentals, a restaurant, and backcountry guided tours. Snowshoeing also is available on 8 km. of trails.

Steamboat offers on-mountain snowshoe tours that meet each Wednesday from the top of the Silver Bullet gondola and are guided by the Mountain Ambassadors. Bring your own shoes or rent from Steamboat Ski Rentals (879-6111).

Track skiing is available at **Howelsen Hill** in downtown Steamboat Springs (879-8499) and at **Vista Verde** (879-3858; 800-526-7433), **High Meadows Ranch** (736-8416; 800-457-4453) and **Home Ranch** (879-1780), all guest ranches 18–25 miles from Steamboat Springs. The latter trio cater to overnight guests, but day visitors also are welcome. Vista Verde's 30-km. system is especially good for beginners—most of the terrain is quite gentle. High Meadows grooms about 12 km., with additional trails groomed as needed. Home Ranch has 40 km. of groomed track, and it offers cross-country, backcountry and telemarking.

For a real thrill, take a tour to **Rabbit Ears Pass** (guided tours available through Steam-boat Touring Center and Ski Haus, 879-0385); you'll be skiing on the Continental Divide. The marked backcountry ski trails range from 1.7 to 7 miles, from relatively gentle slopes to steep and gnarly, but on a clear day you can see forever. Call or visit the U.S. Forest Service (29587 W. US 40 in Steamboat Springs, 879-1722) to get current ski conditions and safety tips. Other popular backcountry areas are **Buffalo Pass, Pearl Lake State Park, Stage-coach State Recreation Area** and **Steamboat Lake State Park.**

Lessons (2000/01 prices)

Group lessons: $42 for two hours; $73 for all day, with multiday discounts and lift-lesson packages available. Snowboard group lessons cost $52 for a half day and $73 for a full day with lunch.

Never-ever package: Steamboat has two Learn-to-Ski/Ride Weekend packages early in the season for $21 per day. The package includes a limited lift ticket, two-hour lesson and rentals. But from Christmas vacation on, novices sign up for a group or private lesson. The resort allows novices to repeat the first lesson at no charge until they've learned to descend from the Preview lift in a controlled manner.

Private lessons: $100 for one hour, $160 for two and $210 for three. Semi-private rates (2–5 people) are $140, $235 and $310 respectively. Reservations required.

Special programs: Many, including telemark skiing, bumps, powder, first tracks, skiers 65 and older, women, disabled skiers—even a style clinic to teach grace. Group clinics last from 1.5 to 3 hours and cost $35 to $72. A Ski Week package for adults is available Monday–Friday including five two-hour lessons, video analysis and racing for $172.

Racing: Steamboat is the home to 43 Olympic and world medalists, so it's a natural for racing and competition programs. Steamboat has a course open most days from 10:30 a.m. to 12:30 p.m. for $5, with each additional run $1. A dual "pro race" format course also is available 9:30 a.m. to 3:30 p.m. at $1 per run. Both courses are in the Bashor area.

Steamboat also has the Billy Kidd Performance Center, which offers two- and three-day camps for adults who are at least of intermediate ability. The camps refine technique in the bumps, through race gates and on tough terrain. The cost is $195 per day.

Child care (2000/01 prices)

Ages: 6 months to kindergarten (usually age 5).

Costs: $76 all day (lunch included) or $53 half day. Multiday discounts are available. Parents must provide lunch for kids younger than 18 months.

Reservations: Required for all care programs, and must be prepaid. Cancellations must be 24 hours in advance to avoid being charged. Call the Kids Vacation Center, 879-6111, or make reservations through Steamboat Central Reservations, (800) 922-2722.

Note: Steamboat's children's programs have been very highly rated over the years by various magazines. The resort offers numerous, supervised evening programs for children and teens, ranging in cost from $9 per hour to $35. Call or visit the Web site for details.

Other options: Baby's Away (800-978-9030; 879-2354) rents and will deliver baby needs to your lodge, such as crib, stroller, car seat and toys.

Children's lessons: $76 for an all-day lesson (including lunch), or $53 for a 2.5-hour afternoon lesson for ages 6–15. Classes are grouped according to age and ability. Ages 13–18 who are at the intermediate level or higher can join the "Steamboat Teens" program offered each day Dec. 16-31, and again from Feb. 17 to April 1, 2001. The cost is $73 per day, with lunch. Ages 2-5 can opt for a one-hour private lesson and all-day child care for $164, including lunch. Children and teens also have a Ski Week program for $345. Their lessons are all day and lunches are included. Kids stay with the same instructor the entire week. Lift tickets are extra. Steamboat also has the Billy Kidd Performance Center, which offers two- and three-day camps for teens and kids who are at least of intermediate ability. The camps refine technique in the bumps, through race gates and on tough terrain. The cost is $195 per day for ages 16 and up, $180 for kids 7–15.

Lift tickets (2000/01 prices)

	Adult	Child (6 to 12)
One day	$59	$34
Three days	$174 ($58/day)	$102 ($34/day)
Five days	$265 ($53/day)	$170 ($34/day)

Who skis free: Children under 5. One child up to age 12 skis free the same number of days as his or her parent when the parent buys a five-day or longer lift ticket. Two kids, two parents, both kids ski free. Three kids, two parents, the third kid buys a ticket at $34 a day. No blackout periods, even during Christmas. Children must bring proof of age. Ages 70 and older ski free; photo ID required.

Who skis at a discount: Teens 13–18 ride lifts for $52 a day for up to four days; when parents buy a five-day or longer ticket, teens pay $46 per day for the same number of days as their parents. Ages 65–69 pay $35 per day. Adult, teen and child tickets are less (adults $44–$56 per day, depending on number of days, teens $39-$49, child $29-$32) very early and very late in the season, usually before mid-December and after the first week in April.

Accommodations

In general, staying in Steamboat Mountain Village is more expensive than in town. Condos outnumber hotel and motel rooms. Rates vary throughout the season. Before mid-December and after March 31 are cheapest; January comes next, and Christmas and Presidents' Weekend are most expensive.

Steamboat Central Reservations (800-922-2722, 879-0740; fax, 879-4757) will make suggestions to match your needs and desires. Let the reservationist know the price range, location and room requirements (quiet location, good for families, laundry facilities, etc.).

The Sheraton Steamboat Resort and Conference Center (800-848-8878, 800-848-8877 in Colorado, 879-2220; $$-$$$) a luxury full-service hotel, sits 60 feet from the Silver Bullet Gondola. Rooms were recently renovated, with more to come, plus its Morningside tower condominiums opened a few seasons ago. You'll find two- to four-bedroom units. We love the views and open design of the main living areas. The newly built **Steamboat Grand Resort Hotel and Conference Center** (877-269-2628, 871-5500, fax 871-5501; $$$-$$$$) is across from Gondola Square. There are studios to three bedrooms and penthouses.

Nearly all the other lodging at the ski area is in condominiums—hundreds of them surrounding the base. **Torian Plum** (800-228-2458, 879-8811; $$$–$$$$) is one of the best, with spotless rooms and facilities, an extremely helpful staff, the ski area out one door and the top bars and restaurants out the other. These are among the nicest condos we've stayed in, anywhere. Torian Plum's sister properties, **Bronze Tree** and **Trappeur's Crossing,** have similar prices. Bronze Tree has two- and three-bedroom units. Trappeur's Crossing is about two blocks from the lifts, but offers a free private shuttle from 7 a.m. to 11 p.m. Two new condo properties opened last season: **Timberline** at Trappeur's Crossing and **Creekside** at Torian Plum (800-228-2458, 879-8811, fax 879-8485). We walked through the construction phase and first finishes and were knocked out by the mountain-facing views, mountain-style furnishings and the ski-in/ski-out location at Creekside. Ditto (except for views) at Timberline, two blocks from the gondola, with on-call shuttle service.

Generally, prices are based on how close the property is to the lifts. Among those in the expensive category are the **Best Western Ptarmigan Inn** (800-538-7519, 879-1730; $$$) at the base of the Silver Bullet gondola, **Storm Meadows Townhomes** (800-262-5150, 879-

5151; $$$), **Norwegian Log Condominiums** (800-525-2622, 879-3700; $$$) and **Thunder-head Lodge and Condominiums** (800-525-5502, 879-9000; $$$). Or consider **Timber Run Condominiums** (800-525-5502, 879-7000; $$$) with three outdoor hot tubs of varying sizes; **the Harbor Hotel** in downtown Steamboat (800-543-8888, 800-334-1012 in Colorado, 879-1522; $$$) that includes a free bus pass; **The Lodge at Steamboat** (800-525-5502, 879-6000; $$$); and **The Ranch at Steamboat** (800-525-2002, 879-3000; $$$), with great views of the ski hill and the broad Yampa Valley.

Economy lodging includes **Alpiner Lodge** (800-538-7519 or 879-1430; $$) downtown, **Shadow Run Condominiums** (800-525-2622 or 879-3700; $$) 500 yards from lifts, and **Alpine Meadows Townhomes** (800-525-2622 or 879-3700; $$), just a bit further.

The Steamboat Bed and Breakfast (879-5724; $$$), just a few years old, is located at 442 Pine St. This B&B has rooms filled with antiques. Rates include breakfast. No children or pets allowed. **Caroline's Bed and Breakfast** (870-1696; $$), 838 Merritt St., is another good choice for those who like B&Bs.

Travelers who enjoy remote rural elegance will be delighted by a stay at **The Home Ranch** (879-1780; $$$$) in the town of Clark, a 40-minute drive up the Elk River Valley north of Steamboat. This is one of a handful of Relais et Chateaux properties in the U.S. Eight wooden cabins are nestled in the aspens of the Elk River Valley, with views of Hahn's Peak and the surrounding mountains. Each is distinctly decorated and has a hot tub on the porch and a wood stove inside. The main lodge also has six guestrooms, and is where everyone is served three gourmet meals per day (the dining room is exclusive to ranch guests). Rates also include lift tickets and a shuttle to the ski area, though many people will be happy exploring the cross-country and snowshoe trails at the ranch.

Between town and the mountain is the pleasant **Iron Horse Inn** (879-6505, fax 879-6129; $$) offering recently renovated suites with kitchenettes (small but functional) and a two-story building of clean and comfortable hotel rooms.

Some chain motels have shown up in the last couple of years. They're generally scattered in a row along Hwy. 40 just before the turnoff to the mountain. The newest is the **Fairfield Inn & Suites** (870-9000, fax 870-9191; $$). Sixty-five no-frills rooms are located a half-mile from Gondola Square on the free bus route. You'll find the 20-year-old **Holiday Inn Hotel & Suites** (824-4000; $$), as well as the newer **Inn at Steamboat** (879-2600, fax 879-9270; $$), **Bunkhouse Lodge** (871-9121, fax 871-9072; $$) and the **Super 8 Motel** (879-5230, fax 879-3341; $$). You may even decide to say in the world-famous **Rabbit Ears Motel** (800-828-7702, 879-1150, fax 870-0483; $$) on Lincoln Ave. right downtown.

Another option out of town is **Strawberry Park Hot Springs Cabins** (879-0342; $), about 10 miles north of Steamboat at the hot mineral springs. Covered wagons and cabins are both available for overnight stays. Lodging price includes a hot springs pass—lovely soaking outdoors on a winter night. Also on the road to the hot springs, 6 miles from the ski area, are the **Steamboat Log Cabins** (879-1060; $$) at Perry-Mansfield, complete with kitchens and woodburning stoves.

Dining

Steamboat has a great variety of restaurants. The area has more than 70 restaurants, including Cajun, Chinese, French, Italian, and Scandinavian. Look for the Steamboat Dining Guide in your hotel or condo—it has menus and prices.

If you're looking for fine dining, our staff dining expert, Katy Keck, suggests these:

Dining: $$$-Entrees $20+; $$-$10-20; $-less than $10.
Accommodations: (double room) $$$$-$200+; $$$-$141-$200; $$-$81-$140; $-$80 and less.

Without a doubt, the most impressive evening in Steamboat starts at Gondola Square at the Silver Bullet terminal. Here, you set off on the journey into the stars on the Silver Bullet to **Hazie's** (879-6111; reservations required; $$$) at the top of Thunderhead. Hazie's serves exquisite nouvelle continental cuisine, with unbeatable views. You can also have lunch (reservations recommended) from 11:30 a.m. to 2:30 p.m., featuring an assortment of soups and salads, entrées and burgers.

Ragnar's (879-6111; reservations for lunch suggested; $$–$$$) at Rendezvous Saddle features Scandinavian and continental cuisine. Start with the baked Camembert tivoli or gravlax with mustard dill sauce. Entrées include daily specials. Three nights a week (Thursday through Saturday), Ragnar's offers a fixed-price Scandinavian menu at $69 for adults. This evening also starts at Gondola Square, but once off the Silver Bullet at the top of Thunderhead, you climb into a sleigh to continue your journey to Rendezvous Saddle. We recommend a mug of hot spiced glögg before relaxing to music and enjoying the meal. Reservations are required at night.

For Steamboat's pinnacle of French dining, try **L'Apogee** (911 Lincoln Avenue, 879-1919; $$$). While the food cannot be too highly praised, it is the wine list that is truly impressive. There are more than 500 wines, ranging from $12 to $1,000 a bottle, all maintained in three temperature-controlled cellars. L'Apogee also features Steamboat's only cruvinet system, serving over 30 wines and ports by the glass. This crew also services the more casual **Harwig's Grill** (same address, no reservations; $–$$). Here, the menu reflects a passion for Southeast Asian flavors. Accompanying the selection of appetizers and entrées is a list of 60 very affordable wines. Open daily from 5 p.m.

Another fine-dining choice is **Antares** (57-1/2 Eighth St., 879-9939; $$$). Not coincidentally, all the principals are alums from L'Apogee. Serving new American cuisine, this restaurant—named for a star in the Scorpio constellation—is housed in the historic Rehder building, built in the early 1900s. Open daily 5:30 p.m. to 10:30 p.m.

For more than Mex, don't miss **La Montaña,** (2500 Village Drive, 879-5800; $$–$$$). The inventive menu goes way beyond tacos and fajitas. Their guacamole sauce is the house special and, as the song says, simply irresistible.

Chef Michael Fragola (formerly of La Montaña) has started his own fine-dining restaurant, the **Cottonwood Grill** (701 Yampa Aveune, 879-2229; $$-$$$). Located downtown on the Yampa River, Fragola features vibrant Pacific Rim Cuisine blending American and Asian flavors with traditional favorites.

The **Steamboat Smokehouse** (912 Lincoln Ave.; $–$$) has a no-credit card, no-reservations, no-nonsense atmosphere, with some of Colorado's best Texas-style hickory-smoked barbecued anything—you name it—brisket, sausage, turkey, chicken, ham and more. We love that we can toss our peanut shells on the floor and the beer mugs are iced.

A popular seafood restaurant is the **Steamboat Yacht Club** (811 Yampa Ave., 879-4774; $$). The dining room overlooking the river is perfect for watching night skiing or Wednesday night ski jumping on Howelsen Hill. Its menu is designed to mix and match fish, cooking techniques and sauces to suit your tastes. The Yacht Club also serves meat and poultry, and is one of the best restaurants for the price in town.

Here are some that have moderate prices ($$ per meal, including drinks) and a casual atmosphere:

At the ski area or close by:

Dos Amigos (879-4270) serves Tex-Mex food and sandwiches and is part of the infamous "Steamboat Triangle" après-ski circuit along with **Tugboat Grill & Pub** and **Mattie**

Silks' bars, and **The Cathouse Cafe**. **Grubstake** (879-4448) serves hamburgers and steak sandwiches. **Café Diva** (871-0508) is a new wine bar in the Torian Plum Plaza that also serves light meals. They recently expanded so it's not quite so tiny and there's more seating; the policy on reservations is loose.

Downtown:

Swiss Haven (871-1761) serves all kinds of fondues, raclette and traditional Alpine fare. You'll find it next to the Harbor Hotel. **Old West Steakhouse** (879-1441) is somewhat expensive, but has packed the crowds in for years with its generous portions of steak and seafood. You easily could make a meal out of the appetizers.

Giovanni's (879-4141) has not only Brooklyn-style Italian fare, but also what may be the largest collection of Brooklyn memorabilia this side of the borough. For more moderate Italian, head to **Riggio's** (879-9010) on Lincoln. Seafood and veal are especially good, and be sure to leave room for their homemade desserts.

Ore House at the Pine Grove (879-1441) is a Steamboat tradition serving steaks, seafood, elk and buffalo for more than a quarter-century. **Yama-Chans** (879-8862) is Steamboat's first Japanese restaurant and sushi bar. It's always doing a booming business. **The Cantina** (879-0826), Steamboat's original Mexican food restaurant, has a fun bar and a decent restaurant. It is downtown's equivalent of Dos Amigos. **Cugino's** (879-5805) makes a fine pizza. If you're in town for breakfast or lunch, try the **Creekside Café and Grill** (879-4925). Homemade soup, sandwiches and salads are served along with soothing classical music. For some quiet-time and a light lunch (sandwiches, homemade pasta salads and soups) head to **Off The Beaten Path** bookstore and coffeehouse (879-6830) across from the Harbor Hotel. We like the bookstore (especially because it stocks *Ski America & Canada*), the great gourmet coffees and the linger-as-long-as-you-want attitude.

Good breakfast spots are **Winona's**, where the lines form early and often, or **The Shack Café**, both downtown, or **The Tugboat Grill & Pub** at the base area. Also try **Market on the Mountain**, in the same complex as La Montaña, for homemade muffins, cinnamon rolls and bagels for breakfast and deli sandwiches; or **Mocha Molly's**, serving muffins, bagels and designer coffees at both the ski area base and in town.

Avid skiers can board the gondola at 8 a.m. and have breakfast at **The Early Bird Breakfast Buffet** at the top of the gondola until the slopes open. Biscuits and gravy are a specialty, with other high-fuel fare also served, cafeteria-style.

Après-ski/nightlife

Dos Amigos, as already noted, is one leg of the "Steamboat Triangle." Have margaritas here, then head for the **Cathouse Cafe** and **The Tugboat Grill & Pub** for beer or mixed drinks. Friday is Zoo Night at the Cathouse, where any beer that has an animal on the label or in the name is $2.50. Downtown, the **Old Town Pub** and **The Steamboat Yacht Club** have great après ski. Quieter après-ski locations on the mountain include **Three Saddles** in the Sheraton or **The Slopeside Grill**. Three Saddles, the former HB's, had a makeover in 99/2000 and is a wide-open, great-view kind of place now.

Steamboat has a single brew pub—the **Steamboat Brewery & Tavern** downtown. **Dos Amigos, Levels** and the **Tugboat Grill & Pub** bring in the bands and the crowds. Downtown, the lively spots include **The Tap House**, the **Steamboat Smokehouse** and **The Old Town Pub**. You might also check out **The Cellar Lounge** (formerly Murphy's) for good times late at night.

Dining: $$$-Entrees $20+; $$-$10-20; $-less than $10.
Accommodations: (double room) $$$$-$200+; $$$-$141-$200; $$-$81-$140; $-$80 and less.

Other activities

Steamboat has so much to do off the mountain, it's tempting to skip the skiing. Here is a mere sampling:

Soak in the natural thermal waters at **Strawberry Park Hot Springs** (879-0342), about 10 miles north of the ski area. Admission to the hot springs is $8–$12; a tour (transportation and admission) is $30. Unless you have four-wheel drive, spend the extra for the tour—the road to the springs is narrow, slick and winding, and parking is extremely limited. It's open from 10 a.m. to 10 p.m. during the week and stays open a little later on weekends. Helpful info: After dark, many bathers go without suits (unless it's a moonlit night, you won't see much), and Wednesdays are often designated as "clothing optional" days/nights. The only place to change is an unheated teepee, so wear your swimsuit under your clothes. Many people bring a plastic bag to store their clothes; otherwise steam from the pools combined with the cold air may freeze them. Water shoes will protect your feet from the rocky entry. Beverages are OK as long as they aren't in a glass container.

Families might prefer the **Steamboat Health and Recreation Center** (879-1828), in downtown Steamboat, with lockers, workout rooms and hot springs pools, and a water slide that kids enjoy.

Learn to drive on slick roads at the **Bridgestone Winter Driving School** (879-6104 or 800-WHY-SKID). Half-day ($115), full-day ($225) and multiday lessons on a specially constructed course are a unique experience, one that could save your life. Three of our contributors have taken the course, and all give it their highest recommendation.

Other activities include weekend **theater** from the Steamboat Community Players (879-3254), **dogsled rides** (879-4662), **snowcat skiing/riding** (879-5188), **ice skating** at Howelsen Ice Arena (879-0341), **ice climbing** (879-4857), **indoor climbing** (879-5421), **indoor tennis** (879-8400), **horseback riding** and **hot-air balloons** (several businesses offer these two activities, ask when you get into town), and far too many more to list. **Shopping** opportunities are many and varied, both in the village and downtown. Steamboat's **movie theaters** are downtown and at the mountain.

You can make reservations for activities through **Steamboat Central Reservations** (879-0740 or 800-922-2722), or **Windwalker Premier Tours** (879-8065; 800-748-1642).

Getting there and getting around

By air: Yampa Valley Airport at Hayden, 22 miles away, handles jets. American, Continental, United, Northwest and Midway have direct or nonstop flights from more than 100 North American cities. Three ground transportation companies provide service from the airport and from Denver International Airport—(all 970 area codes) Alpine Taxi/Limo, 879-2800; Western Coach 4x4 Limo, 870-0771, and Mountain Luxury Limousine, 879-0077. Avis, Budget and Hertz have cars available at the Yampa Valley Airport.

By car: Steamboat is 157 miles northwest of Denver. Take I-70 west through the Eisenhower Tunnel to exit 205 at Silverthorne (allow extra time if you want to stop at Silverthorne's factory outlet mall), north on Hwy. 9 to Kremmling, then west on Hwy. 40 to the resort.

Getting around: A car is optional. Steamboat has an excellent free bus system between town and ski area running every 20 minutes. Call 879-5585 for information.

Telluride

Colorado

Summit elevation: 12,260 feet
Vertical drop: 3,535 feet
Base elevation: 8,725 feet

Address: 565 Mountain Village Boulevard, Telluride, CO 81435
✆ **Area code:** 970
Ski area phone: 728-6900
Snow report: 728-7425
ⓘ **Toll-free reservations:** (866) 287-5016
Fax: 728-6228
E-mail: skitelluride@telski.com
Internet:: www.telluride-ski.com (ski area)
www.telluride.com (visitors guide)

Number and types of lifts: 15–2 gondolas, 7 high-speed quads, 2 triples, 2 doubles, 1 surface lift, 1 magic carpet
Skiable Acreage: 1,700 acres
Snowmaking: 15 percent
Uphill capacity: 20,286 per hour
Snowboarding: Yes
Bed base: 5,300
Nearest lodging: Slopeside
Resort child care: Yes, 2 months and older
Adult ticket, per day: $58–$63 (00/01)

Expert:★★★★★
Advanced:★★★★★
Intermediate:★★★
Beginner:★★★★★
Never-ever:★★★★★

Dining:★★★★
Apres-ski/nightlife:★★★
Other activities:★★★

When Butch Cassidy robbed the Bank of Telluride more than 100 years ago during the town's celebrated mining heyday, he left the best treasure behind.

But then, it would be difficult to fit the town of Telluride and its slopes into a pair of saddle bags. Nestled in a box canyon 8,725 feet high in the jagged San Juan Mountains of southwestern Colorado, the town of Telluride is a neat pattern of streets eight blocks wide and 12 blocks long, miniaturized by massive 14,000-foot peaks tumbling into neighborhoods. On a sunny day, when those white-capped peaks and red-brick buildings pop out from the bluest sky you've ever seen, there are few places on earth more beautiful.

Telluride is in a delightful time warp—a nostalgic blend of the Old West captured in Victorian buildings you'd swear were a movie set, and all the civilized pleasures of a modern resort. When skiing replaced the mining industry in the early 1970s, it saved the tiny community from becoming a ghost town. It also paved the way for preservation of the entire town—a National Historic District—and an orderly development of a world-class ski resort.

Telluride also has a different face, built up on the mountain. This hamlet, called Mountain Village, offers excellent access to the mountain, but is quite different in look and feel. Mountain Village is a master-planned community anchored by what is considered the area's most luxurious hotel, The Wyndham Peaks at Telluride.

A 2.5-mile gondola links the town of Telluride with Mountain Village. This free "gondola transportation system"—as the resort calls it—operates seven days a week from 7 a.m.

to midnight and makes commuting between the two towns for shopping or dining a snap. It also is used as a lift to the slopes, but you need a lift ticket to ski.

Though Telluride's early reputation was a place dedicated to steeps, it has added terrain that has transformed it into one of the nation's best learning slopes. For winter 2001/02, the resort is installing three new high-speed lifts in Prospect Bowl. This will add 733 acres of above-treeline thrills and world-class views along with glades, bowls and trails. The new expansion unites Prospect Bowl and the Gold Hill area with the rest of the mountain and nearly doubles the resort's lift-served terrain.

 ## Mountain layout—Skiing

◆◆ **Expert:** Start with what put Telluride on the skiers' map—The Plunge and Spiral Stairs. This duo is as challenging a combination of steep bumps as you can find anywhere. The left half of The Plunge is now normally groomed. If you manage to get down without too many bruises or sore spots, you can savor a sense of accomplishment. Mammoth is an alternate trail but not any easier.

Another good area for experts is the 450 acres of glade and above-timberline skiing in the Gold Hill area. These double-diamond runs are now lift-served to the 12,260-foot mark, making Telluride's legal vertical drop 3,535 feet. If it's a clear day after a powder dump, take a nanosecond to admire the view from the summit before you plunge in. It is magnificent. And, of course, you'll want to check out the new lift-served areas of Prospect Bowl.

◆ **Advanced:** Telluride uses a winch cat to "split-groom" (meaning half is smooth and half is left to build bumps) some of the runs on the front face. The Plunge is normally split-groomed, creating one of the steepest and most daringly exciting snow highways we've seen. Bushwacker's normally monstrous bumps were merely huge, thanks to a grooming a few days earlier. While some highly accomplished skiers may mourn this development, the face still has plenty of terrain that mere advanced skiers won't touch, and at least now there are enough bodies riding Chair 9 to justify the electric bill.

■ **Intermediate:** Telluride is one of the few resorts that has an hourglass shape to its ability chart—lots to offer at either end, but comparatively slim in the middle. Intermediate trails here tend to be short. See Forever is the exception—nearly 3 miles top to bottom. True intermediate terrain is under Lift 5 (Palmyra) and Lift 4 (Misty Maiden), but the Telluride Face with its occasional grooming is now acceptable for strong intermediates looking to rise to the next level. The most fun for an intermediate would be repeated trips up Lift 4, and down Peek-a-Boo, Humboldt Draw, Pick and Gad and Tomboy. The black-diamond runs off Lift 6 are short and you can assess from the chair whether you can handle them. If not, just head toward See Forever. The new Prospect Lift in Prospect Bowl adds terrain that is ideal for intermediates, including open bowls and gladed runs.

Just learning moguls? Head for the top of Lifts 4 for split-grooming and Lift 5, where you can practice, practice, practice before trying out The Face.

●● **Beginner:** Lift 10 is a perfect spot to develop confidence because the runs are long and very gentle, and no high-ability speed demons come here. With the addition of Ute Park—the new beginner training area in Prospect Bowl—Telluride is one of the top spots on the continent for this ability level.

For those looking to improve: Telluride divides its runs into six categories instead of three or four. One green circle is easiest, then double greens, then single blues, then double blues, single black and double black. This allows an easier progression for those still developing their skills.

● **Never-ever:** The Meadows, served by a Chondola (a hybrid high-speed quad with gondola cars also on the cable), is as close to a perfect novice area as you will find.

 ## Mountain layout—Snowboarding

Turn Telluride's trail map over and, surprise, they've got a snowboard-specific trail map loaded with useful information. Here's where you'll find local riders' favorites listed. Different symbols and colors indicates not only the terrain parks but also too-flat runs for snowboarders to avoid, such as Bridges and Galloping Goose, along with regularly groomed "carving country." Telluride's trail map indicates six levels of trail difficulty, from green, double green, blue, double blue, black, and double black. This map, along with benches for strapping in at the tops of most lifts, makes Telluride exceedingly board-friendly.

Telluride's Surge Air Garden Terrain Park has more than 11 acres and 480 vertical feet of berms, banks, spines, rails, mailboxes, quarterpipes, tombstones and tabletops. Get there by riding Lift 4 or the Gondola. The Launch Pad hangout is at the top of the halfpipe and offers riders a crankin' stereo system and excellent views of the park while taking a break. If you want, you can skip the manmade and head to Lift 9. East and West Drains form two natural halfpipes that are 2,000-feet and 4,000-feet long respectively. In addition, there's a 1,200-foot natural quarterpipe on Bushwhacker. Lift 9 provides more vertical than any other lift on the mountain, serving runs including The Plunge, a sick run visible from town.

For big powder days intermediate boarders will enjoy short and steep runs off Lift 5 including Dew Drop (look for hits), Ophir Loop and Silver Tip. Avoid Cake Walk when you're done riding this lift. Instead, ride it back to the top then stay rider's right and pick up Lift 6. You can then ride See Forever back to Mountain Village or the Gondola. For advanced gladed areas, Lift 6 is your best bet. Check out the trees between Alais Alley and Silver Glade.

For riders addicted to bowl skiing and deep powder, Gold Hill offers the ultimate in big-board freeriding. Say *adios* to the 10- to 20-minute hike accessing Little Rose—it's now lift served. And so is the vast terrain in Prospect Bowl.

Mountain rating

Telluride is a rite of passage for experts. It's a chance to test oneself against consistent steeps and monstrous bumps. Telluride makes a serious effort to groom formerly expert slopes to make them advanced, and advanced slopes to put them within reach of intermediates trying to graduate to the advanced level. If you are an intermediate whose trademark trails are long, mellow cruising terrain, head elsewhere. For never-evers and beginners, there are few better places to be introduced to snow sports. Snowboarders should remember to refer to the back of the trail map, which gives you a rider's view of the mountain.

 ## Cross-country and snowshoeing

Here again the spectacular scenery makes cross-country a joy to experience. For high-mesa cross-country skiing this area is difficult to beat. The **Telluride Nordic Center** (728-1144) offers a 30-km. network of groomed trails around town and the ski area. Lessons are also available; group lessons meet daily at 11 a.m. at the center. If you'd like to ski the intermediate and advanced groomed trails at the top of Lift 10, buy a $12 ticket at the downhill ski area ticket windows. Adult and children's group lessons are priced at about $30; $38 with rentals. Full-day backcountry tours cost about $65. Equipment rentals—skis, boots and poles—for a full day are about $14 for adults and $9 for children.

Guided tours wind through the San Juan Mountains and a five-hut, 68-mile network of intermediate and advanced trails. Huts are approximately 6 miles apart and each is equipped with padded bunks, propane cooking appliances and a big potbelly stove. The same rates apply to all programs: about $22 per person cabin fee and $25 a day for provisions, which covers breakfast, lunch and dinner. Guides are available for groups, held to a maximum of eight skiers. Call the **San Juan Hut System** for rates: 728-6935.

Nearby is the **San Juan Guest Ranch** (626-5360; 800-331-3015), which accommodates overnight visitors. Day visitors also may use the trails. Usually, at least 12 km. are groomed, but sometimes additional kilometers are groomed if guests' needs warrant it. The ranch also offers ice climbing, backcountry touring and avalanche awareness training.

Lessons (2000/01 prices)

Telluride's school, run by Annie Vareille Savath for 20-some years, has a good reputation. A successful learning experience requires two things: good instruction and appropriate terrain. Telluride has both. Clinics operate out of the Mountain Village Activity Center, a one-stop facility that has lift tickets, lessons, rental shop, overnight equipment storage, children's ski school and child care. A computer system links Telluride Sports' six rental shops and stores client information permanently so future rentals can be paperwork-free and equipment can be returned to any shop.

Group lessons: Small-group lessons—four people or fewer—are offered in afternoons-only for advanced beginners through experts for $70. All-day group lessons cost $80 with more than four to a group; two-hour clinics are $38.

Never-ever package: $85 for skiers or snowboarders, includes a full day of lessons, lifts and rentals. Nordic and telemark are offered only on certain days; call for specifics.

Private lessons: $170 for two hours. An all-day lesson is $480.

Special programs: Many, including a highly acclaimed Women's Week program that offers lifts, races, video analysis, seminars, and wine and cheese parties. A five-day session is $575, while a four-day session is $500. A five-day program called Ski Forever teaches skiers ages 30 and older how to use biomechanics and equipment to increase their chances of being able to ski for life. That program, with both day and evening activities, costs $575.

Racing: NASTAR two-hour clinics cost $38 or run the course for $3 per run or $9 for five runs. The course is near the Smuggler Express lift. A self-timed course is $1 per run.

Race camps are geared toward the recreational racer, the NASTAR enthusiast or anyone looking to pick up the pace. Intended for all ages, race camps incorporate some of the latest in coaching techniques and are customized to fit the needs of an individual or group. Four-day clinics are offered at select times for $450.

Child care (2000/01 prices)

Ages: 2 months to 3 years.
Costs: $70 for a full day with lunch, $60 for a half day.
Reservations: Required; call 728-7533 or (800) 801-4832 at least 24 hours in advance. Children's ski and day-care programs are in the Village Nursery and Children's Center in the Mountain Village Activity Center. The activity center's most unique design is the glass kiosk atop the nursery's central playroom, which allows parents to peer down at their little ones without being seen.

Children's lessons: The Children's Ski & Snowboard School teaches kids ages 3–12 (snowboard lessons are offered for kids 6–12). Lessons, lift and lunch are $90 a full day, with multiday discounts. With lessons, rentals cost an additional $15. Half-day lessons are available. A one-hour, one-on-one lesson is $60 available from 8:45–9:45 a.m. A supervised program called Adventure Club is available before and after ski school programs; it's free for those enrolled in ski school.

 ## Lift Tickets (2000/01 prices)

	Adult	Child (6-12)
One day	$63	$35
Three days	$189 ($63/day)	$105 ($35/day)
Five days	$290 ($58/day)	$175 ($35/day)

Who skis free: Ages 5 and younger and 70 and older.

Who skis at a discount: Seniors ages 65–69 ski for $42. Prices are lower before mid-December. If you purchase multiday tickets 14 days in advance, you'll save up to $5 per day. Call the Telluride Skier Service Sales Department at (800) 801-4832 or 728-7533.

 ## Accommodations

In Telluride you can stay down in the historic town or in the Mountain Village. We start with some of our favorite spots in town; lodging in the mountain village is listed at the end of this section. Some lodging prices include lift tickets. For more information on these and other places to stay, call **Telluride Central Reservations,** (866) 287-5016.

The **Franklin Manor** (888-728-3351; $$$–$$$$) specializes in romantic getaways. Named for artist Richard Franklin, the manor showcases his neo-classical works in a gallery and all five uniquely decorated bedrooms. **The San Sophia Bed & Breakfast** (800-537-4781; $$$–$$$$) is near the gondola and Lift 8. This cozy B&B is considered one of Telluride's best, with exceptional service.

A luxury spot to stay is **The Hotel Columbia** (800-201-9505 or 728-0660; $$$–$$$$) right at the Telluride base of the new gondola. The hotel was built to look historic, but with the space and amenities of modern hotel rooms, such as fireplaces, big beds, a rooftop hot tub and luxurious bathrooms. The hotel has an office for guests' use, equipped with fax, copier and computer.

The historic **New Sheridan Hotel** (800-200-1891 or 728-4351; $–$$$$) is a step back in time. It's on Colorado Avenue close to everything, with a shuttle stop for the resort outside the front door. **The Johnstone Inn** (728-3316 or 800-752-1901; $$–$$$$) is a B&B with eight small quaint rooms with private bath and a full breakfast every morning. **Bear Creek Bed & Breakfast** (728-6681 or 800-338-7064; $–$$$), in a brick building on Colorado Avenue, has ten rooms with private bath and TV, roof deck, sauna and steam room.

The **Ice House Lodge** (800-544-3436 or 728-6300; $$$–$$$$)**,** a block from the gondola, has 6-foot tubs, comforters, balconies, custom furniture, a continental breakfast and après-ski goodies. The **Camel's Garden** (888-772-2635 or 728-9300; $$$$) was opened in 1998 in the gondola plaza. In stark contrast to the town's prevalent Victorian theme, this contemporary luxury property has underground parking and a small conference space.

Dining: $$$-Entrees $20+; $$-$10-20; $-less than $10.
Accommodations: (double room) $$$$-$200+; $$$-$141-$200; $$-$81-$140; $-$80 and less.

The **Manitou Bed & Breakfast** ($$$) is decorated with country fabrics and antiques. It is near the gondola and is a two-minute walk from the town center. Each room has a double bed. **The Riverside Condos** are perhaps the nicest in town and near the base of the gondola. **The Manitou Riverhouse** is just as close to the lifts, but be ready for lots of stairs if you rent here. Around the Coonskin Base check into **Viking Lodge**, **Etta Place** and **Cimarron Lodge**, where you can almost literally fall out of bed and onto the lifts. More moderately priced units are **West Willow** and **Coronet Creek**. All the properties in this paragraph (and others not listed) are managed by **Telluride Resort Accommodations,** (800) 538-7754 (LETS-SKI). The central check-in desk can get backed up at times—if you are traveling with young children, or need to get into your condo right away for other reasons, discuss that with the reservations agent at the time of booking.

In the Mountain Village
The most luxurious property is **The Wyndham Peaks at Telluride** (800-789-2220 or 728-6800; $$$$). This ski-in/ski-out resort hotel boasts one of the largest full-service spas in the country. Rates include daily spa access.

The highly praised slopeside **Inn at Lost Creek** (888-601-5678, 728-5678; www.innatlostcreek.com; $$$$) is a beautifully rustic, yet classic lodge with 32 uniquely decorated rooms that include fireplaces, jetted tubs and steam showers, plus two roof-top hot tubs, topnotch guest service and the 9545 restaurant. The great room, crafted of native stone and weathered timber, is warmly inviting. Choose from studios to two-bedroom suites. **Aspen Ridge Condominiums** (800-324-6388; 728-4217) is another of the Mountain Village's newest luxury properties, offering three-bedroom condos with saunas, steam showers, hot tubs and fireplaces.

Mountain Village has many condos, some of which start at $200 per night (double that for the ones closest to the lifts) and top out around $800. Call ResortQuest Telluride (800-538-7754) for more information.

Telluride has a **Regional Half-Price Program** with seven neighboring towns. If you stay in one of these spots, you can get half-price lift tickets throughout the season. The towns, their distance from Telluride and the number to call are: Cortez/Dolores/Rico/Mancos, four towns 25–70 miles away, (800) 253-1616; Montrose, 65 miles, (800) 348-3495; Ouray, 47 miles, (800) 228-1876; and Ridgeway, 37 miles, (800) 754-3103. Durango, which is nearer to Purgatory at Durango Mountain Resort, also is part of this program, (800) 228-1876. Durango is 125 miles from Telluride and just 25 miles from Durango Mountain Resort. If you want to do both resorts on one trip, it might be worth a call to this program.

 Dining

Telluride has about 30 restaurants in town and the Mountain Village. There are several fine restaurants.

La Marmotte (728-6232; $$–$$$) near the Ice House Lodge serves French cuisine. **221 S. Oak** (it's both the name and address; 728-9507; $$–$$$) is in a Victorian house with regional American dishes that vary in response to the freshest products available. **Appaloosa** (728-6800; $$–$$$) at Wyndham Peaks serves gourmet fare.

The **Powderhouse** (728-3622; $$) on Colorado Avenue is another good choice. **The Cosmopolitan** (728-1292; $$), in the Hotel Columbia at the gondola base, serves eclectic American fare. **Rustico** (728-4046; $$), on Telluride's main street, is run by Italian natives and has good food at good prices. In addition to pasta, it has homemade foccacia and a tiramisu worth the fat grams. **Campagna** (435 W. Pacific, 728-6190; $$) serves Italian specialties. It's directly behind The Alpine Inn.

Allred's, at the top of the gondola and 10,535 feet above sea level, made its debut last season. The timber-and-stone perch offers staggering views of the 13,000-foot peaks that frame Telluride and the twinkling lights of the historic town 1,800 feet below. The menu features regional American dishes with international overtones that change each night, along with a special tasting menu for guests who wish to pair a selection of fine wines with several signature dishes. Other on-mountain spots are **Gorrono Ranch**, mid-mountain on Misty Maiden, a rustic barn-like spot that offers American favorites and barbecue on a sunny deck; **Giuseppe's**, at the top of Lift 9, with quick Italian fare in a cozy setting; and **Big Billie's**, at the base of lifts 1 and 10, with southwestern and barbecue items and ideal for families.

In the Mountain Village, **Legends** at Wyndham Peaks (728-6800) is open for breakfast and lunch only, while **Appaloosa** serves Southwestern fare for dinner. Get pizza at **Pizza Chalet** (728-7499).

Back to town for more casual and moderate dining: **Leimgruber's** (728-4663) serves German cooking and beer imported from Munich. It's a hot spot when the lifts close, too. **The Floradora** (728-3888) claims the best burgers. **Excelsior Cafe** (728-4250) has good-value North Italian cuisine. For pizza, head to **Roma Bar and Grill** (728-3669). **Sofio's** (728-4882) serves good Mexican cuisine but be prepared for a wait. It's worth it—have a margarita. For a more holistic evening, take a dip in the Orvis Hotsprings, followed by dinner at **Bon Ton** in Ouray. Call Telluride Express, 728-6000, at least 24 hours ahead if you need a ride.Plan one evening for a magical sleigh ride dinner at **Skyline Guest Ranch**, even if you aren't staying there. Call (888) 754-1126 far in advance for reservations.

Coffee houses have hit Telluride, and visitors have several to choose from: **The Steaming Bean, Maggie's, Between the Covers, Café Vienna** and the **Coffee Cowboy.** All are on Colorado Avenue. **Skiers Union**, located at the bottom of Lift 4, has great juices and coffee. **Wildflour** is a gourmet bakery in Camel's Garden by the gondola, and **Baked in Telluride** is a 20-year-old bakery in a century-old warehouse. The locals call it by its acronym, BIT, and it's great for deli sandwiches, pizza and inexpensive dinners, washed down by its own brews.

 ## Après-ski/nightlife

For immediate après-ski, stop at **Leimgruber's Bierstube** near the Coonskin Lift (Lift 7) for a selection of great German beer, oom-pah-pah music and a sure shot at meeting folks. The new **Limeleaf** in the old Swede Finn Hall on Pacific Street is another locals' favorite. **Eagle's Bar and Grille** on Colorado Avenue has a huge bar, a No Smoking policy and great happy-hour prices.

For live music go to the **Fly Me to the Moon Saloon** with entertainment Thursday through Saturday. **The Last Dollar Saloon** has the best selection of imported beer in Telluride, plus pool tables and dart boards. It's a bit of a manly-man beer bar—not many women hang out. The old Victorian **New Sheridan Bar** is one of the "must sees" in Telluride to experience the essence of the Old West.

 ## Other activities

The mountain offers **snowbiking** daily. A lift ticket is required; one session includes a lesson and boot and bike rental. You can go on **sleigh rides** at Skyline Guest Ranch (888-754-1126); **gliding** with Telluride Soaring (728-

5424); **horseback riding** with Roudy, Telluride Horseback (728-9611); **hot-air ballooning** with San Juan Balloon Adventures, 626-5495; **snowmobile tours** with Telluride Outside (728-3895). There's a pond in Mountain Village for **ice skating**. It isn't every town that has a colorful past like Telluride's, so the **Historic Walking Tour** (728-9746) is well worth the time. **Helitrax** (728-4904, 800-831-6230) provides helicopter skiing for downhill and cross-country enthusiasts. **Telluride Outside** (728-3895, 800-831-6230) is a good source for almost any outdoor winter activity.

Non-skiers and those who need a break might enjoy stretching their creative muscles at the **Ah Haa School for the Arts** (728-3886), which offers weekly and daily classes on painting, silk dyeing and more. Telluride has great **shopping.** Some of our favorites, all on Colorado Avenue: Lizard Head Mining Co., for its extraordinary custom-made jewelry; At Home in Telluride, with distinctive housewares; and Picaya, with some nice and inexpensive jewelry and clothing. A nice souvenir is Kornbluh candles, locally made beeswax candles with an unusual scent, or a hat from Horny Toad Activewear, a national outdoor clothing company headquartered here. If you decide you'd like a Nordic wool-and-felt hat like a lot of locals wear, call Kim Chapin-Richard, a member of the ski patrol and hat maker, 728-3443. She'll need a few days' notice.

Getting there and getting around

By air: Telluride has a small, weather-plagued airport five miles from town, served by United Express from Denver and America West Express from Phoenix. Montrose, 65 miles away, is where most visitors arrive, either by plan or by a weather diversion from Telluride. Continental has daily nonstop jet service to Montrose from Houston, and nonstop service from Newark on Saturdays. American Airlines offers daily nonstop jet service to Montrose from Dallas/Forth Worth and Chicago. United has daily jet service from Denver and often, from other cities as well.

If you fly into the Telluride airport, no matter what the weather, pack a carry-on with enough essentials to get you through 24 hours. These small planes fill with people, then add as much luggage as they can safely transport. This is a sound policy, but it also means that your bags may be delayed. If you arrive without your bags, check with your airline to see if it will provide a voucher for rental clothing and gear at local sporting goods stores. Ways around the problem: 1) Fly to Montrose. The drive is farther, but you'll have your bags with you. 2) Send your bags early via UPS or Federal Express to Mail Boxes Etc. in Telluride. That business will arrange for your bags to be delivered to your lodging (inbound and outbound). Allow 10 business days for shipping. Call 728-8111 for complete details.

Ground transport is provided by Telluride Express (728-6000), Mountain Limo (728-9606) and Alpine Luxury Limo (728-8750). Call 24 hours in advance for Montrose pickups.

By car: Telluride is 335 miles from Denver via I-70 west, and Hwys. 50, 550, 62 and 145. From the southwest, it is 125 miles from Durango via Hwys. 160, 184 and 145. From the Montrose airport head south on Hwy. 550 to Ridgway, then take Hwys. 62 and 145 to Placerville and Telluride.

Getting around: A car is unnecessary. The town is just 12 blocks long—you can walk anywhere. If you have them, bring boots with at least an ankle-high cuff. During warm spells, the snow melt on the side streets can get quite deep. A free bus service runs in town, and the free gondola makes the commute between town and the Mountain Village a snap. Call Dial-A-Ride (728-8888) when you get to the base of the gondola in Mountain Village, and a van will ferry you without charge to destinations in the Mountain Village.

Vail

Colorado

Summit elevation: 11,570 feet
Vertical drop: 3,450 feet
Base elevation: 8,120 feet

Address: P.O. Box 7
Vail, CO 81658
✆ **Area code:** 970
Ski area phone: 476-5601
Snow report: 476-4888 or (800) 404-3535
ⓘ **Toll-free reservations:** (800) 404-3535
Toll-free foreign numbers:
U.K. (fax): 0800-891-675
New Zealand (fax): 0800-44-0415
Australia (fax): 0014-800-128-088
Mexico (fax): 95-800-010-1028
Brazil (fax): 000811-515-5557
Fax: 845-2609
E-mail: See Web site for e-mail addresses
Internet: www.vail.com (resort)
web.vail.net (Vail Valley)

Expert:★★★★ **Advanced:**★★★★★
Intermediate:★★★★★
Beginner:★★★ **Never-ever:**★★★
Number and types of lifts: 33–
14 high-speed quads, 1 12-person gondola,
1 quad chair, 3 triple chairs,
5 double chairs, 9 surface lifts
Skiable acreage: 5,289 acres
Snowmaking: 10 percent
Uphill capacity: 51,781 per hour
Snowboarding: Yes, unlimited
Bed base: 41,305 within 10 miles
Nearest lodging: Slopeside, condos & hotels
Resort child care: Yes, 2 months and older
Adult ticket, per day: $31-$63
Dining:★★★★★
Apres-ski/nightlife:★★★★
Other activities:★★★★★

Vail is a *complete* area, with all of the essential ingredients that form the magical stew of a world-class winter resort. Vail was conceived as a transplanted Austrian village with condominium convenience, raucous nightlife and quiet lounges, fine dining and pizzeria snacking. Its off-slope activities are unsurpassed—shopping, skating, movies, museums, sleigh riding and so much more—everything money can buy. Bring lots of money—temptations abound, and bargains are few.

But village and expenses aside, there is above all The Mountain. Vail Mountain is a single, stoop-shouldered behemoth with three distinct mountain experiences: There's a huge front face of long and very smooth cruisers, an enormous back-bowl experience of wide-open adventure unlike anything this side of the Atlantic, and now the Blue Sky Basin expansion providing lift access to a backcountry experience.

Vail's network of high-speed quads is also the largest in the country. Combined, the mountain and its system of 33 lifts let you do more skiing and less back-tracking than almost any other resort you can name. This is truly a skier's mountain.

As important as it is, skiing and riding only constitute part of the total winter-vacation experience. A true world-class resort has to have amenities and atmosphere, and Vail is one of a kind in both areas. You'll find city conveniences such as 24-hour pharmacies (which you don't appreciate until you need medication in a more rural resort), but you won't find the typical Colorado mining-town atmosphere because Vail never was a mining town. About 35 years ago, it was pasture. Developers who saw the potential of the mountain built a village styled after an Austrian ski town.

Vail is what we call "urban skiing." This city-town just doesn't feel rural. It bustles with traffic—and people—jams in peak periods. You won't see too many stars at night in the village—too many streetlights. But for many of the urban guests, Vail is just rural enough to let them feel they are getting away from it all. They find the well-lit streets comforting. They want the amenities of big-city life and they don't mind paying for it. Vail is their kind of place.

Fortunately, it is segmented: You can concentrate on separate bowls and faces for a morning or afternoon, always having the choice of a new path down the mountain.

The Lionshead area makes up the western end of the front side of Vail and is a good place to start if you're staying on that side of the village. The main access is the Eagle Bahn Gondola (lift 19), but three more chairlifts also serve the trails here. Chair 8, directly parallel to the gondola, is where the ski school and locals start off to dodge the occasional hordes.

At Blue Sky Basin, skiers and snowboarders will find an experience unlike anything else at Vail—from the rustic character of the buildings to the views, the snow, and the challenging glade skiing and steeps. When some of the trails are groomed, low-intermediates can ski this remote area, which is peaceful and secluded. If they are not groomed, you need to be a strong intermediate who can handle powder and dance through some trees. It's really quite exciting.

The two main areas of Blue Sky Basin, Vail's newest terrain expansion, were named for Vail founders Pete Seibert and Earl Eaton (Pete's Bowl and Earl's Bowl). The basin is to the south of Vail Mountain's Back Bowls, on the south side of Two Elk Creek. The first high-speed quad—the Skyline Express Lift—runs from the bottom of Tea Cup Bowl up the ridge between Pete's Bowl and Earl's Bowl, providing the main access to terrain in the area. The second high-speed quad—Earl's Express Lift (Chair #38)—is in the western part of Earl's Bowl and runs up the east face, where skiers and riders can access acres of gladed terrain. The third high-speed quad—Pete's Express Lift (Chair #39)—runs up the eastern-most point of Blue Sky Basin in Pete's Bowl to access more than 125 acres of intermediate terrain. A fourth high-speed quad—the Tea Cup Express Lift (Chair #36)—has been built in Tea Cup Bowl to provide better skier circulation to the west wall of China Bowl and access from the bottom of Blue Sky Basin back to the front side of Vail.

Note: Vail is making a major effort to bring early-season and late-season skiers to the mountains. Pricing reflects that effort. Bargains abound if your want to ski before the end of January (excluding the holiday periods). Even bigger bargains can be found before December 13th, 2001 or after April 7th, 2002. However, the "high season" (Christmas/New Year and February 13 through April 6th) and its eye-popping prices are what most visitors will face. Those are the prices we use in this section.

Mountain layout—Skiing

If you're skiing with a group, arrange a meeting place in case you get separated. This is one big, big mountain. After about a week here, you'll still be discovering new pitches and trails. By the way—locals call the lifts by their numbers rather than their names. If you want to play with them, do the same.

♦♦ **Expert** ♦ **Advanced:** While expert and advanced terrain is a relatively small portion of Vail's total offerings, we give it thumbs up because of the "sheer volume" quotient. Overall, nothing should scare the bejeebers out of you, but you *will* have to sweat.

On the front side, as you face the hill, check out the double-black diamonds named Blue Ox, Highline and Rogers Run. Don't let the double-diamonds fool you—this is advanced terrain, but nothing that's dangerous. The straight-down-the-lift, waist-high, mogul-masher Highline is the stiffest test of the three, its challenge upgraded by the fact that it spills right under Chair 10 (Highline lift) where other talented skiers are free with their vocal evaluations of your work. Nearby Prima, off Chair 11, is tougher still, and the best skiers like to make the Prima-Pronto run their endurance test. Pronto drops right down to Chair 11 (Northwoods Express) and gets its share of oglers in line. The only authentic gut-suckers on the front face are the tops of South and North Rim off the Northwoods lift, leading to a tight but nice Gandy Dancer, and even those are short and sweet.

Under the Vista Bahn, when there's enough snow, The Chutes beckon. It's a bit of work to get to them, and the payoff is short, straight timber bashing. Lionshead has only three very short sections of advanced terrain. Simba's short, steep stretch at the bottom often bumps up, as does Minnie's Mile, a short run that pops out onto the cruiser Born Free, and Lower Ledges.

Solid skiers, of course, will also want to explore Vail's famous Back Bowls. Stretching 7 miles across, they provide more than 2,734 acres of choose-your-own-path skiing. On a sunny day, these bowls are about as good as skiing gets.

■ **Intermediate:** These folks will run out of vacation time before they run out of trails to explore. Few other mountains offer an intermediate expansive terrain and seemingly countless trails. Especially worthy cruising areas include the long ride down the mountain under and to the right of the Eagle Bahn Gondola, almost any of the runs bordering the Avanti express chair, the Northwoods run, and the relatively short but sweet trio down to Game Creek Bowl. Our vote for best run on the mountain, and one available to advanced-intermediates (though parts are rated black), is the top-to-bottom swath named Riva Ridge.

Lionshead is all about intermediate skiing. The trails tend to roll from Eagle's Nest down to the valley like ribbon candy—each trail has a steeper section followed by an easier stretch, and steep is a relative term. Simba is a long swooping run, good anytime, and often chosen as the last run. Born Free is another classic intermediate run that leaves from Eagle's Nest and loops lazily to the valley floor.

Confident intermediates also can enjoy the Back Bowls, but stick close to groomed trails in China Bowl and Tea Cup Bowl. (Poppy Fields in China Bowl often is groomed during the day, too.) If you get tired or frustrated with the natural conditions, you can bail out easily.

In Blue Sky Basin, when some of the trails are groomed, low intermediates can ski this remote area, which is peaceful and secluded. If they are not groomed, you need to be a strong intermediate who can handle powder and some trees.

●● **Beginner:** Best areas are at Golden Peak and Eagle's Nest, and a group of short green runs under the Sourdough Lift on the top left of the trail map. Vail doesn't have a large area of concentrated green runs. Most lifts on the front face have one or two green-designated trails, a bunch of blue trails and one or two blacks. Take a trail map. Pay attention to the signs.

Vail is one of the few resorts that has beginner terrain at the top of the mountain. Take the Eagle Bahn Gondola to Eagle's Ridge. A group of short green runs are served by a chair lift to skier's right (east) of the gondola, and beginners can do laps on this chair. The best part is beginners are the only ones using the chair. Beginners can follow a series of cat tracks with names like Cub's Way and Bwanaloop that crisscross the mountain. On the trail map, they are denoted with dotted green lines.

A series of crisscrossing cat tracks, some of which are named Cub's Way, Gitalong and Skid Road, allow beginners to work their way down the mountain. If cat tracks make you nervous, Vail's trail map marks them with dotted lines. However, it's tough to avoid them here, unless you stay in the Eagle's Nest area and ride that gondola back down.

● **Never-ever:** There are small learning areas in the Golden Peak base area and the top of the Eagle Bahn Gondola at Eagle's Nest. From Eagle's Nest, never-evers can return to the valley via the gondola.

 ## Mountain layout—Snowboarding

If you're with a big group, set up a meeting place and make sure to give at least a 15-minute meeting window, this mountain is huge. A good meeting place is at the top of the Vista Bahn, or any of the Mid Vail restaurants because of their location at the middle of the mountain.

♦♦ **Expert** ♦ **Advanced:** Let's make it easy: If you're going to ride Vail, I mean really *ride* the mountain, it's time to throw the map out the window. You're not going to ride runs, you're going to ride chairs. If you tried to remember every little run at Vail, not only would you go mad, but you'd probably drop a few levels in I.Q.

For Vail's front side, experts are going to want to ride Northwoods lift a lot. On a powder day this is a great place to hit—rocks, steep lines and cliff gaps abound—but once it's tracked, get out of there. Head rider's right of the Vista Bahn (on a good snow day), or to The Riva Bahn and Vail's world-class terrain park and superpipe. Advanced riders also enjoy Sheer Terror Glade, Riva Glade, Hairbag Alley, and Bird Baths. All are tight trees. On Lionshead, you'll get a kick out of Cheetah Gully, a gladed run just to the rider's left of the gondola.

The back side of the mountain is where Vail really shines. A good place to start is at the top of Game Creek Express, where you can access the Cornice through a short five-minute walk. Drop in off the cornice, then head down to the motocross jumps, which are exactly that, three giant windlips form natural tabletops that are perfect for throwing down new tricks.

Make sure you check out Blue Sky Basin, it's not to be missed. You'll find an experience unlike anything else at Vail—from the rustic character of the buildings to the views, the snow, and the challenging glades and steeps. The new area is different from the rest of Vail in terms of terrain—in layman's terms, if it's a powder day get back here as soon as you can! This is lift-accessed backcountry riding like nothing you've ever found here.

Insider Tip: For experienced backcountry riders, find a guide, get your Pieps and shovel, and check out East Vail for some of the best resort-accessed backcountry in Colorado.

■ **Intermediate:** Again, there are just too many runs to go into specifics, especially since this mountain was really designed for intermediates. The Avanti Chair and the gondola will be equal to heaven for you. Everything can be found here: Long high-speed cruisers, woods runs, gaps, kickers, logs and even hot dog stands.

●● **Beginner** ● **Never-ever:** Gold Peak is it. Not only do you get to learn on variable pitches and cruise on a high-speed quad, but also Vail was nice enough to put their immense terrain park right next to the beginner runs. Sometimes seeing the best riders in the world destroying the park right next to you can be humiliating for never-evers, but it can also inspire a beginner to greatness. Vail makes sure that beginners absolutely know what they are getting involved in when they first start out.

Insider Tip: Vail has an excellent beginner's instruction program. It's highly recommended that beginners take lessons, not only for the valuable skills they can pick up, but also for the guide service that the instructors provide on the mountain.

Mountain rating

Vail is one of the best winter resorts in the world for all but the extreme fringes of the ability chart. Super experts will miss the extreme terrain of a Snowbird, Jackson Hole or Squaw

Valley, and frankly, Vail is a little overwhelming for a first-timer's adventure. But for ability levels 2-9 (on a scale 1-10), Vail offers everything you can dream of.

 ## Cross-country and snowshoeing

Two cross-country centers serve Nordic skiers and snowshoers, one at **Golden Peak** and one at the **Vail Golf Course**. Both offer lessons, tours and rentals. Call 845-5313. Last season Vail beefed up its Cross-Country and Snowshoe Adventure Center at Golden Peak. Here guided tours and instruction are available through the Vail Cross-Country Ski School, where instructors specialize in cross-country skiing, telemark skiing, snowshoeing and skate skiing. Guests can book snowshoeing tours, telemark lessons and cross-country ski lessons and tours.

 ## Lessons

The ski school has offices and meeting places at Vail Village near the base of the Vista Bahn Express, at Lionshead next to the gondola, at Golden Peak next to Chairs 6 and 12, at Mid-Vail next to Chairs 3 and 4, and at Eagle's Nest at the top of the gondola. Private lessons meet at Vail Village. Lessons are taught in more than 30 languages. Call the ski school at 476-3239.

Skiers and riders watch a video that displays nine levels of skills the school uses to form classes, then place themselves accordingly in classes ranging from never-evers to advanced.

Group lessons: $90 for a full day. Vail offers a wide variety of lesson-lift-and/or-rental packages too detailed for us to list here.

Never-ever package: Full day lesson and beginner lift cost $120; with rentals, $150. A great deal, available only during the value season (opening day through Dec. 18, 2001 and Jan. 5 through Feb. 12, 2002), is the Beginner Series (for ages 15 and older), which offers three consecutive full days of lessons for the price of one day: $139 for lessons, lifts and rentals. Skiers and snowboarders who complete the program will be given a coupon good for three more lessons for the price of one at the next ability level.

Private lessons: One to six people cost $130 per hour, $250 for two hours, $330 for a half day afternoon, $360 for a half day morning, and $485 for the day.

Special workshops: Focus on specific skills or snow conditions, such as parallel skiing or bumps. Most are afternoon three-hour sessions for around $76.

A free Ski Tips program meets at 11 a.m. daily at Mid-Vail. The session gives you a chance to ski down a gentle slope alongside an instructor who will provide a critique and suggestions on which lesson program will offer the best benefits.

Kenny's Double Diamond Ski Shop in Vail hosts one of the best women's ski programs in the country. Owner Heidi Friedman brings equipment guru Jeannie Thoren to Vail in December and January to teach women the importance of properly fitted equipment. Participants demo the latest brands that Thoren modifies and custom-fits to each woman's specific bio-mechanics. Then they go skiing—better than ever. We know Jeannie well, and can heartily recommend this program. Call (800) 466-2704 or 926-5936 for more information.

Pepi's Wedel Weeks were created in the European tradition, which allows skiers to start off the ski season with an inexpensive lesson package. These are held for three weeks only, in November and early December. It's a seven-day program with breakfast, lessons every morning and afternoon, races, a welcome reception, an evening party, a fashion show and a farewell dinner. Call (800) 445-8245.

We've had first-hand experience at the "Her Turn" Adventure Workshops for Women, and strongly recommend them. You'll arrive on Thursday, and ski or snowboard on Friday, Saturday, and half-day Sunday with other women of like ability. Breakthroughs are common in the supportive small-group atmosphere. Program includes demo alpine skis and boards, video feedback, on-mountain lunch, après social, discussion sessions and goodie bag.

The Telemark Workshop Series is also a personal fave. Scheduled on weekends, they focus on-snow for a single day, and come in unisex, kids, and women-only varieties.

Racing: Vail has quite a recreational racing complex near the bottom of the Avanti Express lift with two NASTAR courses, two coin-operated courses, two courses reserved for groups, a course for teaching clinics and a Sybervision area. A surface lift serves the courses.

Child Care (2000/01 prices)

Ages: 2 months to 6 years.
Costs: Supervised playroom and non-skiing programs, $66 per day off-peak; $77 peak.

Reservations: Required; call 479-3285 or fax 479-3290. Small World Play School is run by the ski school at the Golden Peak base area. Small World Play School is open 8 a.m. to 4:30 p.m. Free pagers are available. Of note, Vail's child-care programs are state of the art.

Other options: For **babysitters** call 479-2292 or 476-7400. **Baby's Away** (800-369-9030; 926-5256) rents and delivers baby needs, such as crib, stroller and toys to your lodge.

Lessons: Classes are divided by age and ability. Children ages 3 (toilet-trained) to 6 can sign up for lessons in the Mini Mice, Mogul Mice or SuperStars programs. Children ages 6-14 can spend their day on the mountain or be entertained with videos and have supervised meeting rooms. Ski lessons are offered for kids ages 3–14; snowboarding lessons are for ages 6-14. Cost is $80 per day off-peak; $93 peak. Prices include lesson, lift and lunch. Register at 8:30 a.m. or pre-register the day before. Reservations are not required. Call 479-3239 for information. Children's Ski and Snowboard Centers are at both Lionshead and at Golden Peak. Both centers offer "one-stop shopping" for lessons and rentals.

Skiing with your kids: The resort is sprinkled with Kids Adventure Zones, like Thunder Cat Cave, Fort Whippersnapper and Chaos Canyon. Here children enter a magical land and follow in the tracks of the little Indians Gitchee and Gumee, as they accompany Jackrabbit Joe and Sourdough Pete on a quest to find the treasure of the Lost Silver Mine. Your little ones can hunt for these zones on the trail map. Once they find them, they can dive through tunnels, into trees and over bumps. Kids even have their own restaurant at Mid-Vail.

Lift tickets

	Adult	Child (5-12)
One day	$63	$39
Three days	$189 ($63/day)	$117 ($39/day)
Five of six days	$285 ($57/day)	$195 ($39/day)

Note: These prices valid from December 23, 2000 to March 31, 2001.

Who skis free: Ages 4 and younger and 70 and older.

Who skis at a discount: Ages 65–69 pay $55 per day or $99 for a season pass. Vail Resorts has a handful of different discounted prices based on time of the year, time of a skier's first visit, ski packages, Internet sales, supermarket sales, pre-purchasing and groups.

Interchangeability: All lift tickets purchased at Vail or Beaver Creek also are valid at sister resorts Keystone and Breckenridge, as well as at nearby Arapahoe Basin.

 Accommodations

Vail's lodging choices are so vast we can't even begin to list them here. Before you call Central Reservations, know your price range, what amenities you need and which ones you want, how close you'd like to be to the lifts and how close you'll settle for if you find nothing in your budget within that distance. Prices dip from 25 to 40 percent before Christmas and in April. But at that time, be sure the bus system is in full operation or that you're within walking distance of necessities; otherwise rent a car.

Vail's premier properties are clustered in Vail Village at the base of the Vista Bahn Express. Selecting the best place in town is a virtual toss-up between four hotels.

The Lodge at Vail (476-5011 or 800-331-5634; $$$$) is the original hotel around which they built the rest of the resort. It is only steps away from the lifts, ski school and main street action. The Lodge serves a great buffet breakfast. **Gasthof Gramshammer** (476-5626; $$$$) is at the crossroads of Vail Village. Our favorite and the most economical within this group of hotels is the **Christiania** (476-5641 or 800-530-3999; $$$$). **Sonnenalp Resort** (476-5656 or 800-654-8312; $$$$) is a group of buildings that exude Alpine warmth and charm and their spa is the place to head for sore muscle relief.

At the Lionshead end of town, the **Marriott's Mountain Resort at Vail** (476-4444 or 800-648-0720; $$$–$$$$) is top of the line and has an excellent location only three minutes' walk from the gondola. **Lion Square Lodge** (476-2281; $$$–$$$$) is steps from the Eagle Bahn Gondola and Born Free Express lift.

The Vail Cascade Hotel (476-7111 or 800-420-2424; $$$–$$$$) in Cascade Village is luxurious and the service is outstanding. The hotel has a dedicated ski lift that makes getting to the slopes a pleasure. It also has an on-premises athletic club and movie theater, both of which are also open to non-guests. And finally, its restaurant, Chap's Grill, is one Vail's best.

Condominiums are plentiful in the Vail region. The most reasonable for those who want to be on the shuttlebus route are in Lionshead, clustered around the gondola, and in East Vail at **Vail Racquet Club** (476-4840 or 800-428-4840; $$-$$$).

The **Vailglo Lodge** (476-5506; $$-$$$), in Lionshead, is a 34-room Best Western hotel that operates like an elegant B&B. It has easy access to the slopes and town. For other relatively more affordable lodging, try **Antlers** (476-2471; $$-$$$$) in Lionshead; **Manor Vail** (476-5000 or 800-950-8245; $$-$$$$) in Gold Peak; the **Chateau Vail** (476-5631; $$$-$$$$); and **Vail Village Inn** (476-5622; $$-$$$$). A recommended B&B is the **Black Bear Inn** (476-1304; $$-$$$) in West Vail.

 Dining

Eating out in Vail is as much of a tradition as skiing the Back Bowls. Always make reservations. Walk-ins have a slim chance of being seated. More than 150 bars and restaurants offer the spectrum of options from pizza to fine gourmet dining.

In the expensive category, **La Tour** (476-4403; $$$) and **The Left Bank** (476-3696; $$-$$$), both French, have long been considered Vail's best. Another standby, **Sweet Basil** (476-0125; $$-$$$), is consistently good with creative dishes. **The Tyrolean Inn** (476-2204; $$$), one of Vail's oldest and best-known restaurants just east of the village (and the Transportation Center), serves exotic game dishes like wild game pasta jambalaya in a classic Austrian setting. **Terra Bistro** (476-6836; $$-$$$) is just down the road from the Tyrolean on the east end

Dining: $$$-Entrees $20+; $$-$10-20; $-less than $10.
Accommodations: (double room) $$$$-$200+; $$$-$141-$200; $$-$81-$140; $-$80 and less.

of the Vail Mountain Lodge. Although difficult to find (the sign is very small), this upscale, eclectic restaurant specializing in "fusion cuisine" is a local favorite. **Chap's Grill and Chophouse** (476-7014; $$-$$$), in the Vail Cascade Hotel, serves some of the best steaks, wild game and seafood in the area. We like **Lancelot** (476-5828; $$-$$$) for prime rib, **Montauk** (476-2601; $$$) for seafood, **Alpenrose** (476-3194; $$$) for German and its wonderful breads and pastries, and **Wildflower** (476-5011; $$-$$$) in The Lodge for contemporary American and an excellent wine list.

Less expensive but just as scrumptious is the legendary **Pepi's** (476-5626; $$) for the best goulash and white veal bratwursts; and **Campo de Fiore** (476-8994; $$), with fine Italian fare, an extensive wine list and a friendly staff. **Cucina Rustica** (476-5011; $$-$$$) serves Tuscan-style Italian in The Lodge. **Blu's** (476-3113; $) fixes great classics, and if you're willing to drive west to a local's favorite in Eagle Vail, **Ti Amo** (845-8153; $$-$$$) won't disappoint. The **Gore Creek Grille** (476-2828; $$) offers creative seafood, meat and fowl specialties. Its bar claims the town's longest martini menu.

Those on a budget should try **Pazzo's** (476-9026; $), for pasta and create-your-own-pizza. **Bart and Yeti's** (476-2754; $$) in Lionshead is great for lunch or light dinner.

On the mountain, we recommend lunch at the **Two Elk Restaurant** (479-4560; $-$$) above China Bowl. It was re-built after being burned to the ground in an arson fire. Go early or late, because finding a seat at prime time is tough. Or try the lunch at **Larkspur** (479-8050; $$-$$$) in the Golden Peak base lodge. This restaurant is also one of our top choices for dinner. **Mid-Vail's food court** has moderate (for Vail) prices—$10 buys a huge potato with toppings, a local beer and a piece of fruit, for example. Or try the Lunch For Less meal deal for $6.95 including bowl of pasta, salad and a drink. Hungry and frugal, skiers head to **Clark Market Deli** (476-1199; $) in Vail Village for an inexpensive lunch.

The **Game Creek Club** (479-4275; $$$) is extremely exclusive with only 350 members (Ross Perot, Charles Schwab and so on), and it is members-only for lunch. They do let non-members in for dinner, though, and it is just a snowcat ride from the top of the Eagle Bahn. For about $85 per person, sans alcohol and gratuity but including the transportation, you get a six-course gourmet meal—a choice of game, seafood, veal, steak and lamb—and a gorgeous view of the valley below. Make your reservation to coincide with sunset. Another memorable Vail dining experience is **Beano's Cabin** (949-9090; $$-$$$) at Beaver Creek Resort. See the Beaver Creek chapter for details.

For breakfast, the best deal in town is at **D.J. MacAdams** ($) in Lionshead's Concert Hall Plaza, a tiny diner where you'll watch cooks make heaping plates of omelettes, scrambletts (like an omelette only using scrambled eggs) and blintzes. Wash it down with a fruit smoothie. It's open 24 hours, except Mondays (reopening at 7 a.m. Tuesday). If you're looking for a buffet breakfast (continental or hot) in a fine-dining atmosphere, head to **Chap's Grill** in the Vail Cascade Hotel ($$) or the **Mountain Grille Restaurant** at the Marriott's Mountain Resort at Vail ($$). You can also get a la carte items at both.

Down valley dining

Visitors with a car should drive west to exit 171 and turn off at old town Minturn where the **Minturn Country Club** ($$$) lets you grill your own meat or fish steak. Just across the street, the area's best Mexican food is dished out at the raucous **Saloon** (827-5954; $-$$)—a favorite of World Cup racers—or **Chili Willy's** (827-5887; $-$$). Stop by **Bonjour Bakery** (827-5539; $) to pick up several loaves of to-die-for bread, but call in winter before you make the trip. The **Turntable Restaurant** (827-4268; $-$$) wins accolades for its green chili.

Further down valley, past the Beaver Creek exit about 4 miles, keep an eye out for the **Grille at Singletree** (926-3528; $$-$$$) on your right. You'll find a lovely high-end Continental cuisine restaurant where you can dress up and enjoy the fabulous sunsets behind the New York mountain range. Lots of rock and an intimate atmosphere.

At the Edwards exit, left off the highway, check out the valley's oldest restaurant and bar, the **Gashouse** (926-3613; $-$$). Seafood, homemade soups, steaks, wild game and award-winning chili are served in a rustic 50-year-old log cabin. Après is good for lobster tails, little neck clams and jumbo lump crab cakes. At the Edwards Riverwalk center, drop into **Zino** (926-0444; $-$$) for antipasti, salads, pizza and pasta. The grilled yellow fin tuna is a lip-smacker. The best sports bar and grill could be **Paddy's** (949-6093; $-$$) on Highway 6. The house specialty prime rib is big and fat.

At Edwards Plaza II, look for **Asia** (926-8862; $-$$). There's Chinese, Thai, Japanese and Vietnamese cuisine all over the place. Personal and family dinners at $29-$33 per person seem pricey, but your dollar buys more food than a human should be allowed to eat at one sitting. The margaritas at **Fiesta's Café & Cantina** (926-2121; $-$$) are yummy (20 tequilas to choose from) and the family-style meals are user-friendly. Chicken enchiladas in white jalapeno sauce are the house specialty.

At **Markos** (926-7003; $) in the Edwards Business Plaza, you'll find pastas, pizzas and Caesar salads at rock bottom prices.

 ## Après-ski/nightlife

Après-ski is centered in the Village or in Lionshead. The **Red Lion** has a deck, live music and great nachos. In the Village, try **Sarah's** in the Christiania for squeezebox music with Helmut Fricker on Tuesdays and Fridays; and **Vendetta's**, a locals' favorite. **Mickey's** at the Lodge at Vail has the top piano bar. Several restaurants have house entertainers who are long-time career musicians. In Lionshead, **Sundance Saloon** fills up with locals and probably has the best drink prices in town, especially at happy hour in the late afternoon.

In Lionshead, Oktoberfest happens daily at **Katlenberg Castle**, the latest brewhouse of the 700-year-old royal brewing family of Prince Luitpold of Bavaria. Its massive dining room, built in the likeness of an authentic Bavarian castle, serves traditional German food, but we preferred the sun-splashed porch for end-of-the-day relaxing. Three specialty beers on tap and oom-pah-pah music create post-slope fun fit for a (Bavarian) king.

For later nightlife, **Club Chelsea** on Bridge Street caters to the over-30 crowd with three rooms—a DJ dance area, a piano bar and a sealed-off cigar bar—while a few doors away, **Nick's** attracts a young crowd with loud rock'n'roll. Another cigar-and-cognac spot is **Palmos** in the Gateway Plaza. **The Club** normally offers acoustic guitar music. **8150** has live alternative music. On weekends the **Sundance Saloon** in Lionshead has music.

 ## Other activities

Adventure Ridge at Eagle's Nest is an on-mountain activity center, open from 2 p.m. to 10 p.m. Families and adrenaline junkies enjoy this addition in the Eagle's Nest area at the top of the gondola. It includes an ice-skating rink, kids' snowmobile track, a lift-served tubing hill, ski-biking, thrill sledding and other activities. If you haven't tried ski-biking, do so. It is a hoot to go careening down the mountain at night with a light strapped to your head; just be prepared for exhausted legs (and don't do it the night you arrive if you tend to suffer at high altitude). Something we didn't try, but we think sounds, well, thrilling, is thrill sledding. You'll sled headfirst down the mountain at night from Adventure Ridge to the bottom of the Eagle Bahn gondola. Sleds have a hand-activated hydraulic brake system and four independently suspended skis. Headlamps and clear goggles are provided; helmets are available (must be at least 14 years old). Some activities require reservations, so call in advance. A restaurant serves very affordable family dinners. The gondola cabins are heated and lighted.

Vail has a number of **athletic clubs** and **spas.** The Vail Cascade Resort and Spa (476-7400) has indoor tennis courts, squash and racquetball courts, weight room, indoor track, outdoor heated pool and spa facilities. Aria Spa & Club at the Vail Cascade Resort has undergone a $4-million renovation and expansion that incorporated a 10,000-square-foot luxury spa within the existing 78,000-square-foot spa and club facility. We only wish it had been open when we visited last season! The Spa at Vail Mountain Lodge (476-7960) also has fitness facilities in Vail Village and the only climbing wall in the Vail Valley. The Vail Racquet Club (476-3267) in East Vail has indoor tennis, squash and racquetball courts, swimming pool and weight room.

Take a ride on the Vail Golf Course with **Steve Jones Sleigh Rides** (476-8057). The **Colorado Ski Museum** in the Vail Transportation Center traces the history of skiing in the state. Admission is free. Vail also has several **movie theaters,** an indoor **ice-skating rink,** several **hot-air balloon companies** and many other things to do. Call the Vail Activity Desk at 476-9090 for the complete list.

Vail's unique **boutiques and shops,** mostly upscale, can keep your credit card active for days. Late March is the best time to find bargains in ski wear and winter clothes.

Getting there and getting around

By air: Flights land at the Vail/Eagle County airport, about 35 miles west of Vail, and the Denver International Airport, 110 miles east. Eagle County airport is served by American, Northwest, Delta, Continental, America West and United.

Ground transportation between Denver and Vail is frequent and convenient. Contact Vail Valley Transportation at (800) 882-8872; Colorado Mountain Express at (800) 525-6363; Airlink Shuttle at (800) 554-8245; or Vail Valley Taxi (Eagle airport only) at 476-8294. Though flights into Denver may be a bit less expensive than Eagle, also consider the cost of ground transportation, which is about $60 per person round trip from Eagle and about $115 from Denver.

By car: Vail is just off I-70, 100 miles west of Denver and 140 miles east of Grand Junction.

Getting around: Most parts of Vail are very self-contained, and the free, reliable bus service runs throughout town from East to West Vail. Visitors and locals ride the bus, because parking is very limited and expensive. Shuttles to Beaver Creek cost $3 one way and depart from the Transportation Center above the parking structure in Vail Village.

During most times of the season, you won't need (or want) a car if your lodging is in Vail Village or Lionshead. Be sure to ask when you make your lodging reservations how close you are to the free bus service. The buses go where cars are not allowed, so the bus often will get you closer to your destination than if you drive. If you come in early or late season (early December or April), be sure to ask the person making your reservations whether the bus schedule will be cut back during your visit. If so, rent a car.

Winter Park
Colorado

Summit elevation: 12,060 feet
Vertical drop: 3,060 feet
Base elevation: 9,000 feet

Address: P.O. Box 36,
Winter Park, CO 80482
✆ **Area code:** 970
Ski area phone: 726-5514
Denver line: (303) 892-0961
ⓘ **Toll-free reservations:** (800) 729-5813;
(970) 726-5587 outside the U.S. and Canada
Fax: (970) 726-5993
E-mail: wpinfo@mail.skiwinterpark.com
Internet: www.skiwinterpark.com (ski area) or
www.winterpark-info.com (town)
Expert:★★★★ **Advanced:**★★★★
Intermediate:★★★★
Beginner:★★★★
Never-ever:★★★★★

Number of lifts: 22–8 high-speed quads;
4 triple chairs, 7 double chairs, 3 magic carpets
Snowmaking: 15 percent
Skiable acreage: 2,886
Uphill capacity: 34,910 per hour
Snowboarding: Yes, unlimited
Bed Base: 12,500
Nearest lodging: Slopeside
Resort child care: Yes, 2 months and older
Adult ticket, per day: $42-$56 (01/02 prices)

Dining:★★★
Apres-ski/nightlife:★★
Other activities:★★

Early this century, when the Moffat Tunnel through the Rockies was completed, Denverites began to ride the train here. The shacks first built for the tunnel construction crews made perfect warming huts for hardy skiers who climbed the mountains and schussed down on seven-foot boards. The ski area now is part of the Denver public parks system, which explains its name. Today Winter Park ranks as one of the largest ski areas in Colorado.

This is a great mountain with a wonderfully easy-going atmosphere. The ski area and most of the lodging are tucked into the woods off the main highway, which retains this town's rural feel. Winter Park also has several traditional mountain inns—the kind with large common rooms where people can read, talk or play board games. They are tough to find these days. We like them, and you'll find descriptions in the Accommodations section.

But, the times are changing. Completion of the Zephyr Mountain Lodge, with shops and a restaurant on the ground floor and condos above, has moved upscale slopeside lodging to Winter Park. These one-, two- and three-bedroom condos are available for nightly rentals. Winter Park is still charmingly funky, affordable and low-key, with lodging designed with families in mind, plus one of Colorado's most respected ski schools. The children's and disabled-skier programs are among the biggest, most advanced and most respected in the nation.

Although Winter Park maintains a great family reputation, it is a surprisingly good destination for singles. The town benefits from having only a few, but good, nightlife centers. Meaning that you get to meet most of the other skiers in town if that's what you want; and the mountain inn lodging gives singles a great opportunity to meet other vacationers over dinner and drinks, or while enjoying the hot tubs. If you're looking for a solid good time without the fanfare, Winter Park presents you with one of the best opportunities.

Mountain layout—Skiing

Though the mountain is completely interconnected by lifts, it has separate base areas: Mary Jane and Winter Park. So in this section, "the Winter Park side" refers to the portion of the resort to the trail-map right of the Zephyr Express chair lift.

◆◆ **Expert:** Visitors who have read about Winter Park arrive expecting a good intermediate resort with plenty of lower-intermediate and beginner trails. Yes, that's all here—what is surprising is the amount of expert terrain. Vasquez Cirque has nearly 700 acres of steep chutes and gladed powder stashes accessed by a hike or a snowmobile rope-tow ride, along the ridge from the Timberline chair lift.

Mary Jane is where you'll find the famous bumps and super-steeps. Try the chutes accessible only through controlled gates: Hole in the Wall, Awe Chute, Baldy's Chute, Jeff's Chute and Runaway, all reached by the Challenger or Summit Express chairlifts.

◆ **Advanced:** For advanced skiers, the most popular lift on the Winter Park side is the Zephyr Express. It provides access to Mary Jane (via Outhouse), or the advanced runs on the Winter Park side—Bradley's Bash, Balch, Mulligan's Mile and Hughes. From the top of Zephyr, bump fanatics can bop down Outhouse and end up at the base of Mary Jane.

At Mary Jane, head for the black runs off the Iron Horse chair. If you're still standing, you're ready for the runs off the Challenger chair—all black diamond, all ungroomed with monstrous moguls, and all tough as a bag of nails.

Parsenn Bowl has more than 200 acres of open space. If you can hit Parsenn on a good day, you're in for a treat. The upper part is wide open and medium-steep, while the gladed bottom is a delight, especially if you're just learning to ski between trees. Though rated blue and blue-black on the trail map, wind and weather conditions can make the bowl a workout. Winds occasionally close the Timberline lift, which provides the only access.

■ **Intermediate:** Vasquez Ridge on the Winter Park side has an excellent collection of cruising runs. (The only drawback to Vasquez Ridge is a long runout down the Big Valley trail; the Buckaroo trail lets you avoid it.) To change mountains, green-circle Gunbarrel takes skiers to the High Lonesome Express quad and the Mary Jane area.

The Sunnyside lift on the Mary Jane side has excellent runs for intermediates. If you can handle these with no trouble, try Sleeper, one of Winter Park's "blue-black" designated runs that help intermediates improve to advanced.

●● **Beginner:** The Winter Park base area serves most of the beginner trails. Beginners can ride to the top of the mountain to Sunspot and then ski down Allan Phipps or March Hare, or they can ski all the way back to the base using the Cranmer Cutoff to Parkway. When these become easy, try Cranmer, Jabberwocky and White Rabbit.

● **Never-ever:** Winter Park is one of the best ski areas in the nation for novices. Groswold's Discovery Park is 25 acres of gentle, protected learning terrain for beginners, served by a double, triple and a high-speed chair lift, which slows down for loading and unloading. Three "magic carpets," gently sloped ramp escalators at the base of the resort, allow children *and* adults to make repeated runs without getting on and off a chair lift.

Mountain layout—Snowboarding

While Mary Jane is famous for its bumps, it also boasts smooth glades and chutes off of the Summit Express and Challenger Lifts. Catch them on a powder day and you'll feel like a hero. Overall, the Mary Jane terrain is ideal for experts and advanced-intermediates, plus it's easy to negotiate with no flat runouts. For those on the hunt for air, head to the Winter Park side for the Cheshire Cat terrain park, the halfpipe above Snoasis or The Rolls boardercross course.

A note of caution: While the Winter Park side is better suited for beginners, it can be a challenge for riders simply because it is riddled with flats and runouts. To minimize walking, the Zephyr Express lift is the safest bet. Once you figure out how to get there, the Pioneer Express lift also offers some interesting intermediate terrain. On the way back to the Winter Park base, just be sure to take Parkway Trail to avoid Turnpike at all costs—*ALL COSTS*—it's longer and flatter than Kansas.

Mountain rating

Winter Park is one of the few mountain resorts that can truly serve the needs of all ability and interest levels. Very few mountains have both the nearly flat, isolated terrain that never-evers need, and the precipitous plunges that experts adore. Winter Park is lucky enough to have both, plus plenty at every stage in between. Riders should be aware that there are some flats on the lower-ability-level terrain that can be frustrating.

Cross-country and snowshoeing

Devil's Thumb Cross-Country Center (726-8231) has great views of the mountains and 105 km. of trails groomed for both skating and gliding. National-level competitors race and train here. The center is near Tabernash on County Road 83. Trail fees are $12 a day for adults and $8 for children and seniors; those ages 6 and younger ski free. Private lessons are $30 an hour; group lessons are $15 for a two-hour session. A learn-to-ski package is $28 with rentals and trail fee; children and seniors, $23.

Snow Mountain Ranch (887-2152; www.ymcarockies.org), eight miles west of Winter Park on Highway 40, offers 100 km. of groomed trails through a variety of terrain—open, wooded, hilly and flat. The system includes a lighted 3-km. loop for night skiing. The instruction staff includes national-level coaches and racers. Ski lessons, rentals, lodging, dining and child care are available. Trail fees are less than $10 per day. Snow Mountain Ranch is also a YMCA with inexpensive dorm and cabin lodging.

Redfeather on-mountain snowshoe tours are offered several times daily from the base of **Winter Park Resort.** The two-hour guided tour includes a chairlift ride to the tour's starting point, rental snowshoes, and information about native plants and animals. Cost is $25.

Winter Park and the Fraser Valley's extensive mountain biking trails are used in winter for snowshoeing. The trails are easy to follow and often packed down by snowmobile riders. The **Winter Park/Fraser Chamber of Commerce** has maps and information.

Lessons (2001/02 prices)

The Skier & Rider Improvement Center desks are at the Balcony House at the Winter Park base and for privates only at the Mary Jane Center. Teaching is Winter Park's forte, so a large variety of clinics and lessons are offered.

Group lessons: $40, 2.5 hours, for intermediate and higher; $27 for beginner levels. Quick Tips Learning Lane is a 15-minute session for advanced beginners to experts for $5. This program is located at the Winter Park Video Arena above the Snoasis restaurant.

Private lessons (for one or two people): $115 for 90 minutes. A First Tracks private lesson gets you on the mountain 30 minutes before the lifts open to the public—lesson goes from 8-9:30 a.m., cost is $80. Last Tracks is from 2:30-4 p.m., cost is $80.

Special programs: Many. An example: The Family Private lesson allows them to learn together, even if they have different abilities. Up to six can be in the group, and the instructor tailors the lesson to meet their needs. The cost is $250 for three hours and $425 for six hours.

Winter Park's National Sports Center for the Disabled, the world's leader in disabled ski instruction, has a full-time race-training program for disabled skiers. Instruction is available for all levels, and the race program is open to advanced intermediates or above.

The resort also has special multiday clinics at various times during the season.

Racing: NASTAR, daily on the Cranmer Trail above Snoasis Restaurant. It costs $5 for the first run; $1 for each additional run. Drop-ins are welcome in the Masters (25 and older) race-training program.

 ## Child care (2001/02 prices)

Ages: 2 months to 5 years.

Costs: Including lunch, $65 a day; $50 half day. Parents can rent beepers for $5 per day. Half day does not include lunch.

Reservations: Reservation forms are required and may be obtained from Winter Park Central Reservations or the Winter Park Children's Center. A $5 non-refundable fee is charged. Call 726-1551, or make your child-care reservations when you book your lodging. In any case, reserve early, as Winter Park sometimes hits capacity in its day-care program.

Note: Winter Park has always been a leader in creative children's ski programs. Its multistory Children's Center handles more than 600 children on some days and does it very well. The center is open from 8 a.m. to 4 p.m.

Children's lessons: Tots aged 3 and 4 have a full-day program for $85 with rentals and lunch. All-day programs for older children, including lifts and lunch, cost $75 without rentals; $85 with rentals; $5 discounts for each additional day. Snowboard lessons start with third-graders (in American schools, that's usually age 7) to age 14 through the Children's Center. Snowboard and boots rental is $20 per day.

 ## Lift tickets (2000/01 prices)

	Adult	Child (6-13)
One day (non-holiday)	$54	$18
Three days	$129 ($43/day)	$45 ($15/day)
Five days	$210 ($42/day)	$75 ($15/day)

Who skis free: Kids 5 and younger; seniors 70 and older.

Who skis at a discount: Ages 62–69 ski for $30. Disabled skiers ski for about half of the adult one-day price. Winter Park also offers early- and late-season discounts, and has discounts through Denver businesses. Half-day tickets are offered for mornings or afternoons. Beginner lift tickets on the Galloping Goose lift at Mary Jane cost $5 per day. Try to ski here at least two consecutive days. The per-day cost drops for a two-day or longer ticket.

 ## Accommodations

Winter Park Central Reservations can book 150 different lodging properties, plus air transportation, lift tickets and special activities. Call (800) 729-5813. This resort has a group of mountain inns unique in Colorado. They are like small bed & breakfasts but many include dinner, as well. They all serve meals family-style so guests get a chance to meet one another easily. Most inns have transportation to and from the slopes. The food is usually fantastic and plentiful, and the inn owners go out of their way to please their guests. These inns are perfect for solo travelers who want to meet others. In fact, singles can book a four-night package that includes mountain inn lodging with its meals, three days of lift tickets, and a Skier/Rider Improvement workshop to improve your skills while meeting others of similar slope abilities. Prices begin at $600.

There are several mountain inns in Winter Park. Perhaps the most upscale is the **Gasthaus Eichler** (726-5133; $–$$$). The inn is very European and the rooms are well decorated with down comforters on the beds. Each bathroom is equipped with a jetted tub. It's perfect if you want quiet elegant lodging in the center of town within walking distance of restaurants and nightlife. Prices include breakfast and a massive dinner.

Arapahoe Ski Lodge (726-8222 or 800-338-2698; $–$$$) also downtown, is a pleasant, friendly, No-Smoking mountain inn. The rooms have private baths. It features a large spa and indoor swimming pool. Prices include dinner, breakfast and transport to the slopes.

The Woodspur Lodge (726-8417 or 800-626-6562; $–$$$) has a massive living room with a fireplace, soaring roof and plenty of space. This central area makes a perfect meeting place for the guests. The rooms here are of two types—newly restored and old style. Ask for one of the updated rooms if you are staying as a couple and one of the older rooms for larger groups. The lodge is served by local buses as well as lodge vans that shuttle skiers to the area and the town. Rates include breakfast and dinner.

The Timber House Ski Lodge (726-5477 or 800-843-3502; $–$$$) is tucked into the woods at the edge of the area. A private trail lets you ski directly back to the lodge. You'll meet other guests in the giant living room with its stone fireplace, at family-style meals, or soaking in the outdoor hot tub. Rates include breakfast and dinner.

The other mountain inns are outside of town toward Tabernash. **The Outpost Inn** (726-5346; $–$$$), a B&B, is the most comfortable and homey. Vans shuttle skiers to and from the ski area. A spa attached to the building becomes a social center in the evenings. A maximum of 20 guests at a time stay at the inn. Rates include breakfast, but no dinner.

The Pines Inn (726-5416; $–$$) is a B&B just around the corner from the Timber House with a personality of its own. It is accessible from the ski area by the Billy Woods Trail, which also ends at the Timber House.

High Mountain Lodge (726-5958 or 800-772-9987; $$$–$$$$) is located outside of town and serves two meals a day from their highly acclaimed chef. It has about 15 rooms, an indoor pool and hot tubs.

Winter Park also has many condo complexes. The most luxurious is the **Zephyr Mountain Lodge** (800-977-6197; $$$–$$$$), a new slopeside condo-style hotel at the Winter Park base, featuring retail and restaurants on the ground floor with one-, two- and three-bedroom units on the upper floors. The **Iron Horse Resort Retreat** (726-8851; $$–$$$$) has a swimming pool and a fitness center. Iron Horse is about two miles outside of the town center near the base of the slopes, but has excellent shuttle service if you want nightlife.

Winter Park Mountain Lodge (726-4211; $–$$$) is across from the ski resort and is part hotel, part ski lodge. It was completely remodeled and enlarged in 1999 and is an attractive and affordable choice for those who want to be close to the slopes. It has an indoor pool, hot tubs, brew pub and game room, and also has cable TV and phones in each room.

The Vintage (726-8801; $$–$$$$) is also slightly out of the center of town but right next to the ski area. It features a restaurant, fitness room, swimming pool and good shuttle service into the town. The owner admires Winston Churchill and has Churchillian memorabilia throughout the hotel. The beautiful wooden bar came from a London pub. One of the finer properties in Winter Park, the Vintage has studios and suites available.

For condominiums in town, try either the **Snowblaze** (726-5701; $$$–$$$$) or **Crestview Place** (726-9421; $$$–$$$$). Both are across the street from Cooper Creek Square. Snowblaze has a full athletic club with racquetball court, swimming pool and fitness center, which are included in the price of the condo. Studio units normally come with a Murphy bed, and two- and three-bedroom units have baths for each bedroom, private saunas and fireplaces. Crestview Place does not have an athletic club or private saunas, but has fireplaces and full kitchens.

One of the most popularly priced condominiums is the **Hi Country Haus** (726-9421; $$$–$$$$). These condos are spread out in a dozen buildings and share a recreation center with four hot tubs, sauna and heated swimming pool. They are within walking distance of town and are on the shuttlebus routes.

A couple of inexpensive places to stay a few miles from town are especially good for Nordic skiers. **Devil's Thumb Ranch** (800-933-4339; $-$$), which has done extensive re-modeling, is a rustic retreat at a cross-country area in Fraser. Also try the **Snow Mountain Ranch** (970-887-2152; Denver line, 303-443-4743), which has Nordic trails, plus dorm fa-cilities and cabins. It's owned by YMCA of the Rockies, and it conducts year-round recre-ational programs.

Dining

Winter Park isn't packed with high-priced restaurants; instead, the emphasis has always been on good solid cooking. Recently, local bistros have gotten away from homestyle, stodgy cooking and are leaning toward new, innova-tive cuisine.

For fine food *and* a great view, head to the **Lodge at Sunspot** (726-5514; reservations required) for dinner. The Zephyr Express converts to a gondola for a comfortable ride to this spectacular mountain restaurant. A five-course menu is $59 without alcohol and gratuity on Friday and Saturday nights during ski season. A family barbecue for quite a bit less also is offered in the evenings. A twilight snowmobile tour with dinner at the lodge also is available.

The **Gasthaus Eichler** (726-5133; $$–$$$) in the center of Winter Park has an Austrian/German-influenced menu. Locals all rave about **The Shed** (726-9912; $$) on Hwy. 40, which has one of the most imaginative menus with an emphasis on Southwestern cuisine; and **Fontenot's Cajun Cafe** (726-4021; $$), with fresh fish dishes prepared New Orleans style.

The **Divide Grill** (726-4900; $$–$$$) in the Cooper Creek Square serves fresh fish, game specialties and steaks as well as Northern Italian dishes and has a good salad bar. **Deno's** (726-5332), a locals' favorite, has excellent pasta dishes as well as chicken, steak and shrimp selections.

Fairly new is **Smokin' Moe's** (726-4600; $$) in Cooper Creek Square, where you can load up on spicy barbecued ribs, hot links, chicken and "Okie baloney." For family fare try the **Crooked Creek Saloon** ($$) in Fraser for basic steaks and down-home cooking. The Fat Boy burger is a local tradition.

Hernando's Pizza & Pasta Pub ($–$$) with its central fireplace is highly recommended by locals, but is often crowded—you can opt for free delivery though. Great thin-crust pizza and unusual combinations are their specialty. It's especially popular with families. Also try the **Winter Park Pub** ($$), located downtown on Hwy. 40, which offers traditional pub fare, 15 beers on tap, and "Mystery Beer Night." There are a lot of 20-somethings here.

For the best eggs-and-bacon breakfast in town head straight to **The Kitchen**, but only if you aren't pressed for time. **Carver's Bakery & Café** behind Cooper Creek Square serves hearty breakfasts, amazing cinnamon roles, superb sandwiches and healthy dinners.

On the slopes, the best lunch is in the smallish, cozy **Club Car** restaurant at the Mary Jane base area. Be sure to save room for dessert—particularly the mud pie. The **Lodge at Sunspot** atop the mountain is a spectacular setting for a gourmet lunch.

Après-ski/nightlife

For après-ski, the **Derailer Bar** in the West Portal of the Winter Park Base area is the place to be. **The Shed**, in downtown Winter Park, has happy hour deals on margaritas and appetizers, and is popular with locals and visitors alike.

For sports events, go to **Deno's Mountain Bistro** with half-a-dozen TVs, plus more than 100 types of beer and 200 wines. **Kickapoo's** is a tavern/restaurant on the ground level of Zephyr Mountain Lodge, and it has an outdoor deck for drinks and dining on sunny days.

The dancing nightlife centers in these spots: **The Slope,** which has live music most weekends; **The Hideaway Bistro**, with the best Ladies Night in town on Wednesdays; and the **Crooked Creek** in Fraser also attracts those who want to kick up their heels. For a quiet drink without the loud music, head to **Winston's** in the Vintage Hotel or **Eichler's. The Iron Horse** sometimes has a guitar player in the bar, and a Comedy Club every other Wednesday in ski season. **Higher Grounds** in downtown Winter Park has established its reputation on their excellent martini bar.

The Crooked Creek Saloon in downtown Fraser also has food and music. Diehards using public transportation, take note: After midnight, you're on your own.

Other activities

Holliday Outfitters (726-1099) and Dashing Through the Snow (726-5376) have old-fashioned **sleigh rides** with a stop for refreshments around a roaring campfire. Dinner at the Barn Sleigh Rides (726-4293) offers a ride to a 90-year-old ranch, gourmet dinner and old-time entertainment.

Grand Adventures (726-9247), with **dogsled rides** pulled by spirited Siberian huskies, go through miles of spectacular backcountry. Dog Sled Rides of Winter Park (726-8326) is another option.

Trailblazer (726-8452) or Grand Adventures (726-9247) offer **snowmobile tours.** Snowmobile tours run about $35 for one hour, with multi-hour discounts. The ski resort offers an evening dinner tour where riders go up the ski runs. **Snoscoots** are scaled-down snowmobiles that drivers aged 9 and older can operate around a marked, flat track next to the highway between Winter Park and Fraser. For **snow tubing,** go to the Fraser Valley Tubing Hill (726-5954). Cost is $11 per hour after 6 p.m. and $10 per hour before 6 p.m.

There are a few **shops,** especially for sports equipment and clothing, but this is not Winter Park's forté.

Getting there and around

By air: Denver International Airport is a hub for several major airlines. Home James vans take skiers from the airport to Winter Park. The fare each way is about $37. Reserve through central reservations, or contact the van lines directly. Home James: 726-5060 in Colorado; or (800) 729-5813.

Dining: $$$–Entrees $20+; $$–$10–20; $–less than $10.
Accommodations: (double room) $$$$–$200+; $$$–$141–$200; $$–$81–$140; $–$80 and less.

By car: Winter Park is 85 miles northwest of Denver International Airport on Hwy. 40. Take I-70 west to Exit 232, then head toward Winter Park and Fraser on Hwy. 40.

By train: Amtrak's California Zephyr, which runs between Chicago and San Francisco, makes a stop in Fraser, only a few miles from the ski area. Check with Amtrak on current schedules. Skiers from Chicago board the train in the afternoon and arrive in Winter Park the next morning. West Coast skiers board in the morning and arrive by the next afternoon. Sleeper cars are available, but sleeping in the coaches is not as bad as one might think. There's lots of leg room, and the seats recline nearly all the way. Special packages make the trains very affordable. Call Winter Park Central Reservations for details at (800) 729-5813. Call Amtrak for information and train-only reservations: (800) 872-7245 (USA-RAIL).

The Ski Train is an unusual treat. This special train leaves Denver's Union Station every Saturday and Sunday from mid-December to April, and adds a Friday departure from mid-February to early April. It also adds special trips on a holiday schedule. Operating for more than 60 years, it brings 750 passengers from Denver directly to the Winter Park base area, chugging along 56 miles and climbing 4,000 feet. The train snakes through 28 tunnels and across canyons, ravines, and ice-crusted rivers. The scenery is as gripping as any we have seen in the Swiss and Austrian Alps. The train leaves Denver at 7:15 a.m. and departs Winter Park at 4:15 p.m. Paid parking is available in surrounding lots for about $4, but it varies. Two classes of train service are available; club car includes a continental buffet. Round-trip rates are about $65 club and $40 coach. For Ski Train information and reservations, call (303) 296-4754

Getting around: Rent a car for any extensive restaurant or bar hopping. If you plan to stick close to your lodging at night and your lodge transports you to the slopes, you won't need a car. The Smart Shuttle runs between all bars and lodging on Friday and Saturday from 10:30 p.m. to 2 a.m. No need to book first, just wait for the shuttle at the bar's entrance.

Nearby resorts

SolVista Golf and Ski Ranch, Silver Creek, CO; (970) 887-3384; 888-757-7669
Internet: www.silvercreek-resort.com
5 lifts; 287 acres; 1,000 vertical feet
Silver Creek once advertised itself as "Colorado's Smallest Destination Resort." With nearly two-thirds of its business coming from out of state, the description is accurate. The resort caters to families, and indeed is well suited for them, with ski-in/ski-out condos, a hotel, child care starting at 6 months, various snow-sliding devices (ski bikes and such) and many off-slope activities. Silver Creek has two mountains. East is the easier terrain, while West has slopes rated for intermediate to advanced skiers. Silver Creek is home to the second-largest night-skiing operation in Colorado, with a top-to-bottom terrain park under the lights. The resort also has 40 km. of groomed Nordic track adjacent to the Sterling base lodge.
Lift tickets: Adults, $37-39; Juniors (6-12), $15-18; Seniors (61-69), $23-25; 70+ and younger than 6, free.
Distance from Denver: About 80 miles west via I-70 and Hwy. 40. It's 15 miles north of Winter Park.
Lodging information: (800) 754-7458. Silver Creek has a slopeside hotel and condos.

Sun Valley

Idaho

Summit elevation:	9,150 feet
Vertical drop:	3,400 feet
Base:	5,750 feet

Address: Sun Valley Resort,
1 Sun Valley Rd., Box 10, Sun Valley, ID 83353
Area code: 208
Toll-free reservations: (800) 786-8259
(for Sun Valley properties)
or (800) 634-3347 (Central Reservations)
Snow report: (800) 635-4150
Fax: 726-4533 or 622-3700
E-mail: ski@sunvalley.com (general info) or
reservations@visitsunvalley.com
Internet: www.sunvalley.com or
www.visitsunvalley.com
Expert:★★★★ **Advanced:**★★★★★
Intermediate:★★★★★
Beginner:★★★ **Never-ever:**★★★

Number of lifts: 18—7 high-speed quads,
5 triple chairs, 5 doubles, 1 surface lift
Snowmaking: 30 percent
Skiable acreage: 2,054 acres
Uphill capacity: 28,180 per hour
Snowboarding: Yes
Bed Base: 6,000
Nearest lodging: Walking distance, condos
Resort child care: Yes, 6 months and older
Adult ticket, per day: $59 (2000/01 price)

Dining:★★★★★
Apres-ski/nightlife:★★★★
Other activities:★★★★

Sun Valley may provide America's perfect ski vacation. It has a European accent mixed with the Wild West. It is isolated, yet comfortable; rough in texture, but also refined; Austrian in tone, cowboy in spirit.

Ageless would be the one word to describe Sun Valley Village, America's first ski resort, built in 1936 by Union Pacific tycoon Averell Harriman. It exudes restrained elegance with the traditional Sun Valley Lodge, village, steeple, horse-drawn sleighs and steaming pools. In contrast, the town of Ketchum is all-American West, a flash of red brick, a slab of prime rib, a rustic cluster of small restaurants, shops, homes, condos and lodges. It's the town of Ketchum that actually curls around the broad-shouldered evergreen rise of Bald Mountain, known as Baldy to locals. Each snow ribbon dropping from the summit into the valley leads to the streets of Ketchum.

This is Hemingway country. When he wasn't hobnobbing with the glitterati of the day, he wrote most of *For Whom The Bell Tolls* in the Sun Valley Lodge, where photos show Hollywood celebrities who first made the place famous. Sun Valley has developed many famous winter-sport athletes: the late Gretchen Fraser, who was the first American Olympic ski champion in 1948; Christin Cooper, a 1984 silver Olympic medalist; and Picabo Street, who won a silver at the 1994 Olympics and a gold in the 1998 Olympics.

The Sun Valley Company keeps the skiing as up-to-date as any in America: The resort has a large computerized snowmaking system and seven high-speed quads, including one that rises a whopping 3,144 vertical feet in 10 minutes. Its three lodges—Seattle Ridge, Warm Springs and River Run—have won raves from skiers and architectural awards from the ski industry.

And yet, it is the celebration of its history that makes Sun Valley stand out from the rest of America's ski areas. If you enjoy history, you must stay at the Sun Valley Lodge, a beautifully kept-up property with a pronounced mid-20th-century feel. The elegance of a bygone era is in the details: uniformed doormen; a formal dining room; a large second-floor "drawing room" with the piano in the center, overstuffed chairs and sofas in the middle, and fireplaces at either end; and an immense "hot tub" swimming pool that dates to the early days of the resort. Then there are the continual showings on the lodge's in-room televisions of "Sun Valley Serenade," a 1941 movie starring Sonja Henie and John Payne that is as corny as can be when you see it at home, but is lots of fun when you see it in Sun Valley, especially when you later try to track down the exact filming locations on the mountain and in the lodge.

America's oldest ski resort has managed to age gracefully without losing any of the magic it had in its youth. Sun Valley's magic is in its fresh powder and vacation ambiance. It's the American version of the European ski week.

Mountain layout—Skiing

The main drawback to Sun Valley is the split in the ski areas. Bald Mountain (called "Baldy") is best suited for intermediate and advanced skiers, while beginners and never-evers should stick to Dollar/Elkhorn.

◆◆ **Expert** ◆ **Advanced:** Baldy's terrain is best known for its long runs with a consistent pitch that keeps skiers concentrating on turns from top to bottom, rather than dozing off on a flat or bailing out on a cliff or wall. Mile-long ridge runs lead to a clutch of advanced and intermediate bowls.

Limelight is a long, excellent bump run for skiers with strong knees and elastic spinal columns. Of the other black-diamond descents, the Exhibition plunge is one of the best known. Fire Trail, on the ski area boundary, is a darting, tree-covered descent for those who can make quick, flowing turns. The Seattle Ridge trail with hypnotic views curves around the bowls. The bowl area below is a joy. The downhill skier's right is a little easier, skier's left a little tougher, and you can catch the sun throughout the day. There are sections where you can do 50-yard-wide turns, but there is no easy terrain where you can relax your quads. The only flats are on top.

■ **Intermediate:** Baldy is good for this level, too. Trails are not apt to be quite so wide as at other Rocky Mountain resorts, but they're a lot wider than the ones in New England, and these trails are—for the most part—long, very long.

The best warm-ups are either the Upper and Lower College runs leading to the River Run area, or the Warm Springs run. Both descend from the top and head to the base (College takes a little jog and joins with River Run near the bottom). Warm Springs is labeled blue-square, while College is labeled green. Frankly, we didn't observe that much of a difference. Both are long, moderately steep, very well groomed and loads of fun. Other good spots are Cozy, Hemingway and Greyhawk in the Warm Springs area, often less crowded because the trail map shows a black-diamond entry (there's an intermediate cat-track entrance a little farther down that isn't as obvious on the map), as well as the Seattle Ridge runs, marked green but definitely intermediate level.

If you want to follow the sun, start your day in the River Run area, then shift to the runs dropping off Seattle Ridge and finish up cruising the Warm Springs face.

●● **Beginner:** Do not be fooled by the green-circle markings on the Baldy trail map. Beginners should not ski Baldy. The runs are seriously underrated for difficulty. Yes, yes, we're well aware that the green-blue-black ratings system reflects the relative difficulty of the trails at each individual resort. Sun Valley followed the rules and marked the "easiest" runs on Baldy with green circles. Compared to other resorts, however, these runs are blue—royal blue. If you are at all tentative about your skills, start out at Dollar/Elkhorn. However, this means you'll be isolated for lunch and après-ski from family and friends who are skiing Baldy. When you feel you're ready for Baldy, try the Upper and Lower College run first.

● **Never-ever:** Skiing parents can enroll their children in ski school at the River Run Lodge and Skier Services building at the base of the River Run trail on Baldy. The ski school will transport children enrolled in novice lessons to Dollar. Adult never-evers should head directly to Dollar. The terrain here is perfect for learning and good for intermediates perfecting technique or starting out in powder. Skiing on the Dollar side of this mountain is shorter and more limited than on the Elkhorn face, which offers a small bowl with greater pitch and more challenging runs.

 ## Mountain layout—Snowboarding

Baldy's terrain is best known for its long runs with a consistent pitch, great for turning perfect arcs. Be prepared for the mile-long ridge runs that lead to several advanced and intermediate bowls, but don't avoid them or you'll miss out on some prime terrain. If you're an intermediate planning to sample the Warm Springs terrain, just be aware that the intermediate entrance is a cat track. Novices and beginners will want to head to Dollar/Elkhorn. Pay close attention to the advice we've given in the skiing section above.

Mountain rating

If your ski group is solid intermediate to expert, you will thoroughly enjoy skiing together on Baldy. If your group is entirely never-ever to intermediate, you also will enjoy skiing together on Dollar/Elkhorn. (When the intermediates are ready for Baldy, the lower-level skiers may be ready for a day off to explore town.) Mixed-ability groups may not be as thrilled, unless they truly don't mind being separated.

 ## Cross-country and snowshoeing

The Sun Valley/Ketchum area has about 210 km. of trails overall. The closest facilities are at the **Sun Valley Nordic Center** (622-2250 or 622-2251), near the Sun Valley Lodge, where 40 km. of cross-country ski trails are groomed and marked for difficulty. They range from easy two-way trails on the golf course to isolated forest escapes. There is a half-track width for children as well as a terrain garden. The daily trail fee is $12, with discounts for half-day, children and seniors. Group and private lessons are available. The Atlas snowshoe center has 6 km. of free designated snowshoe trails. Snowshoe rental is $15 a day or $12 for a half day.

The Blaine County Recreation District grooms the **North Valley Trails**, which have more than 100 km. of groomed trails in the Sawtooth National Recreation Area supported by set trail fees or donations. The largest center is **Galena Lodge** (726-4010; grooming report, 726-6662) with 56 km. of trails, a full restaurant and a ski shop. It also has a 15- km. snowshoe trail and snowshoe rentals. A popular event is dinner, followed by moonlit skiing. Rentals and lessons are available, and every Thursday you can full-moon ski with a ranger and learn about natural history or wildlife. These tours are free with a trail pass. Galena is 24 miles north of Ketchum on Hwy. 75.

Wood River Trails features 30 km. of trails stretching north of Ketchum to Hailey and Bellevue. **Lake Creek** has 15.5 km. of trails, and three other areas have less than 10 km. each. The **Boulder Mountain Trail** stretches 30 km. from the Sawtooth National Recreation Area headquarters 8 miles north of Ketchum to Easley Hot Springs and Galena, and is groomed all winter, snow conditions permitting.

Avalanche and snow condition reports are available 24 hours a day from the Ketchum Ranger District at 788-1200, ext. 8027. North Valley Trails maintains a **grooming hotline,** 726-6662.

For backcountry tours through the largest wilderness area outside Alaska, contact either **Sun Valley Trekking** (788-9585) or **Sawtooth Mountain Guides** (774-3324). Both feature hut-to-hut skiing and the opportunity to stay in yurts as well.

Lessons (2001/02 prices)

Call the Sun Valley Ski School (622-2248 or 622-2231) for more information on any of these programs.

Group lessons: $40 for two hours, with multiday discounts.

Never-ever package: None. Never-evers will need to sign up for lessons, rent equipment and buy lift tickets separately.

Private lessons: $90 per person for one hour. Discounts are available for multiple hours (cheaper in the afternoon). All-day private costs $415 per person.

Special programs: Racing clinics run three hours per day for $65. A multiday women's clinic for upper intermediates is held several times each season—call for exact dates.

Child care (2001/02 prices)

Ages: The Playschool on the Sun Valley Mall offers care for kids 6 months to 6 years, but the upper age limit is not strictly enforced, should you have a 7-year-old who doesn't ski or ride.

Costs: Ages 6–18 months, $88 full day, $62 for a four-hour morning or afternoon session. Toddlers in diapers: $67 all day, $52 half day. Toilet-trained and older: $57 full day, $47 half day.

Reservations: Required, and priority is given to guests in Sun Valley resort hotels and condos. Call 622-2288.

Other options: Super Sitters (788-5080) has screened sitters trained in CPR and first aid who do in-room babysitting. **Baby's Away** (800-327-9030; 726-0199) rents and will deliver baby needs to your lodge, such as crib, stroller, car seat and toys.

Children's lessons: A four-hour session, including lunch, is $75 for kids 4–12 years old; snowboard lessons are for kids 7–12. Tiny Tracks is a ski lesson, from noon to 1 p.m., for kids 3–4 years old is $40. Discounts are available for multiple days in all children's programs.

Lift tickets (2001/02 prices)

	Adult	Child (Up to 12)
One day	$63	$35
Three of four days	$183 ($58/day)	$99 ($31/day)
Five of six days	$300 ($57/day)	$160 ($30/day)

These are prices for tickets valid both at Baldy and Dollar Mountains.

Who skis free: Children 15 and younger ski and stay free when they are with a parent (one child per parent) in a Sun Valley Resort hotel or condo or any participating property in Ketchum, Elkhorn or Warm Springs. Blackout periods for this offer are the Christmas/New Year holiday, most of February and half of March; call 622-2231 for specific dates.

Who skis at a discount: Ages 65 and older ski for $43 per day. Prices for those who ski only at Dollar/Elkhorn are: adult $24, child $18. Sun Valley lowers ticket prices in early and late season.

Accommodations

For **information or reservations** for Sun Valley and Ketchum, call (800) 634-3347.

The **Sun Valley Lodge** (800-786-8259, spells SUN-VALY; $$–$$$$) is the heart of the resort, though it is not slopeside. You can relax on terraces and in grand sitting rooms beneath coppery chandeliers. Gleaming outside is a skating rink once ruled by ice queen Sonja Henie. The village is a 3,800-acre Alpine enclave of pedestrian walkways, wall paintings, snow sculptures and spruce foliage. Because the Lodge was built well before the time of group tourism, each room is unique: pricing depends on room size and added factors such as view and balcony. **The Sun Valley Inn** (800-786-8259, spells SUN-VALY; $$–$$$$), about a hundred yards from the Lodge, is a bit less expensive but shares most amenities. Condos and suites are available; ask about packages.

Sun Valley's Elkhorn Resort (800-355-4676 or 622-4511; $$–$$$$), near Dollar Mountain, provides its own resort-hotel world away from Ketchum and Sun Valley. Name performers play during the winter season and the health club is well outfitted.

Knob Hill Inn (800-526-8010 or 726-8010; $$$–$$$$) is one of the Ketchum area's most luxurious, recently accepted into the exclusive Relais et Chateaux group. The building is so Austrian you feel as if you've stepped out of your car into the Tyrol.

The Idaho Country Inn (800-635-4444 or 727-4000; $$$–$$$$) is on a knoll halfway between Ketchum and Sun Valley. Each of the 10 rooms is individually decorated to reflect the Idaho heritage, for example, the Shoshone Room, Wagon Days Room, and Whitewater Room. Breakfasts are fabulous. The hot tub sits on a hill behind the inn with a perfect view.

River Street Inn (800-746-3611 or 726-3611; $$$–$$$$), a charming and recently renovated B&B, is within walking distance of the center of town. Rooms feature Japanese soaking tubs, which are very deep, one-person tubs.

Pennay's at River Run (800-736-7503 or 726-9086; $$$–$$$$) is a cluster of family-perfect condos within walking distance of River Run lifts. There is a big outdoor hot tub, and units have VCRs.

Best Western Tyrolean Lodge (800-333-7912 or 726-5336; $–$$), only 400 yards from the River Run lift, has an Alpine atmosphere with wood-paneled ceilings and downy comforters dressing the beds. A champagne continental breakfast is served. **Best Western Kentwood Lodge** (800-805-1001 or 726-4114; $$) with an indoor pool is in the middle of town, convenient to everything.

Clarion Inn (800-262-4833 or 726-5900; $$–$$$$) is a hotel with a large outdoor Jacuzzi and continental breakfasts. Rooms open to outdoor walkways and the decor is simple. **Christophe CondoHotel** (800-521-2515 or 726-5601; $–$$$$) has roomy condos with underground parking and heated pool. A fire truck races guests back and forth to the lifts.

Tamarack Lodge (800-521-5379 or 726-3344; $$) is smack in the middle of town with a hot tub and indoor pool. Good for families, the lodge is equipped with microwaves, refrigerators and coffee makers. It doesn't get any more convenient than this for nightlife and dining. Rooms with fireplaces cost more.

Povey Pensione (128 W. Bullion St., Hailey; 800-370-4682 or 788-4682; $) is a 108-year-old residence maintaining the original character of its builder, John Povey, a British carpenter, who built and lived in the house when Hailey was a mining town. Pastel wall coverings and antique furnishings give the three bedrooms an Old West character. This Pensione is about 13 miles south of Ketchum and Sun Valley. Children under 12 are not allowed. **Ski View Lodge** (726-3441; $) near downtown Ketchum has eight rustic individual cabins with open space in front of them and woodland and Bald Mountain views behind. The cabins have kitchens and phones, pets are welcome and there is a senior citizen discount. Rates drop 40 percent during slow seasons.

Lift Tower Lodge (726-5163 or 800-462-8646; $) gets its name from a section of an old ski lift. All rooms have two beds, a refrigerator, TV and phone, and the lodge has a Jacuzzi. Complimentary breakfasts include bagels, coffee and orange juice. The free bus stops in front. During value season the price of a room can be halved.

If you have a large group and need to rent a private home, call **Base Mountain Properties** (800-521-2515, 726-5601; www.basemountain.com) or **Premier Resorts** (800-635-4444, 727-4000). They have rentals near the lifts, downtown Ketchum, out at Elkhorn Village near the Dollar Mountain lifts, and homes that offer privacy and isolation.

Dining

On the mountain: The Warm Springs, Seattle Ridge and River Run day lodges have excellent restaurants. Skiers can settle down to a lunch of prime rib, salmon, stone-fired pizza and many other delights, all while enjoying panoramic views. The deck at Seattle Ridge is gorgeous. Deli and gourmet cafeteria-style clusters are the latest in on-mountain dining, and Sun Valley has these, too.

In Sun Valley Village: The **Sun Valley Lodge** dining room has old-time elegance and is the only spot in the area with live music and dancing with meals. Specialties include Steak Diane, Chateaubriand Béarnaise Bouquetière, and fresh Idaho trout or poached salmon.

The Ram attached to the Sun Valley Inn serves basic fare ranging from pasta to chops and steaks. **Gretchen's** in the Lodge has a fine dinner menu, and serves breakfast and lunch. The **Konditorei** has an Austrian flavor and excellent lunches, such as hearty soups served in a bread bowl next to a mountain of fruit.

In Ketchum: Sun Valley has some of the best restaurants in any ski resort in America. Anyone with fine dining on his or her mind will not be disappointed. The region's real gourmet action takes place here. The price ranges we give here are a rough guide.

These restaurants all vie for "best of Ketchum." **Michel's Christiania** (726-3388; $$$) run by Michel Rodigoz, serves fine French cuisine. **Felix** (726-1166; $$$), which has moved to 380 1st Ave. North, has a continental menu in a very Austrian setting. **Evergreen Bistro** (726-3888; $$$) has an elegant setting of wood, crystal and glass and quite possibly the town's best wine list. **Chandler's** (726-1776; $$$) serves gourmet meals in a series of tiny rooms. Ask to be seated near the fireplace if you are with a group; couples should ask for the small alcove off the main fireplace room. The three-course "prix fixe" meal is one of Ketchum's best bargains.

The Sawtooth Club (726-5233; $$) has a long bar with couches in front of a fireplace and small dining rooms tucked above and behind the bar. The food is good and reasonable.

The **Pioneer Saloon** (726-3139; $$), a local hangout going back into Ketchum history, is known for its prime rib and baked potatoes. **Ketchum Grill** (726-4660; $$) has a daring, innovative menu with flavor mixtures that will keep your tastebuds tingling, and **China Pepper** (726-0959) is the place to head for spicy Thai and Chinese food, as well as sushi. They get rave reviews from visitors. **Sushi on Second** (726-5181; $$) also has Japanese fare. Locals say **Globus** (726-1301; $$) has good Chinese/Thai food. **Panda Chinese Restaurant** (726-3591; $) serves Chinese meals from several regions.

Smoky Mountain Pizza (622-5625; $) has great, very affordable Italian fare and massive salads. **Piccolo** (726-9251; $$) has slightly more expensive Italian cooking in a cozy dining room, with fine light homemade pastas. **The Wild Radish** (726-8468; $$) is housed in a turn-of-the-century log cabin and serves wild game, seafood and fresh pasta specialties.

Warm Springs Ranch Restaurant (726-2609; $$) serves a wide-ranging menu including children's specials, and mountain trout swim in pools near the cozy cabin.

The spots for excellent and inexpensive Mexican food are **Mama Inez** (726-4213; $), at the start of Warm Springs Road near downtown Ketchum, or **Desperado's** (726-3068; $), just behind the visitor's center on Fourth Street. **Grumpy's** (no phone, we're told; $) is the locals' favorite for great burgers and beer; it's across the street from Mama Inez (and next door to a laundromat, in case you need to wash a few clothes).

Breakfast is important with most skiers. At the Sun Valley Lodge **Gretchen's** (622-2144; $) has plentiful fare with moderate prices and **Konditorei** (622-2235; $) in the Sun Valley Village has good breakfasts. The **Lodge Dining Room** (726-2150; $) serves an excellent Sunday brunch. The best breakfasts, however, are downtown in Ketchum. The **Kneadery** (726-9462; $) on Leadville Street has a cozy woodsy atmosphere. It's open for lunch as well.

Directly across the street from the Warm Springs Lodge at the base of Baldy is a Ketchum institution, **Irving's Red Hot** stand, where you can get great hotdogs. "The Works" (a dog smothered in fixings and chips) for only $2 is a lunch bargain that can't be beat.

One evening dining adventure that should not be missed is the horse-drawn sleigh ride dinner at **Trail Creek Cabin**. The cozy rough-hewn cabin dates from 1937 and can be reached by sleigh, car or cross-country skis. For the sleigh ride, make reservations 72 hours in advance, but you can always check for open space; call 622-2135. The sleigh ride costs $17. Dinners are approximately $16–$24. **Galena Lodge** (726-4010) also offers moonlight dinners in the warmth of a rustic lodge.

Après-ski/nightlife

The **Boiler Room** at Sun Valley has the Mike Murphy comedy show every afternoon at 5 p.m. for a moderate cover charge. Check the schedule for "Sun Valley Serenade" and Warren Miller movies at the **Opera House** in Sun Valley starting at 5 p.m. And the **Duchin Room** in the Lodge has music starting at 4 p.m. On Thursdays, head to **River Run Lodge** for jazz. If you are staying in Warm Springs, wander over to **Apples** for good après-ski crowds.

At the western-bar-themed **Whiskey Jacques,** patrons can listen to live music and dance inside an authentic log building. **The Pioneer Saloon** is famous for its steaks, prime rib, and decorations (mounted elk and moose). The saloon gets very crowded very early on weekends.

Another popular spot is **The Casino**, so named because there used to be slot machines where the tables now stand (gambling is now illegal in this part of the country). It's something of a departure from the more intense nightclubs in the area, with the dance floor replaced by pool tables.

Dining: $$$-Entrees $20+; $$-$10-20; $-less than $10.
Accommodations: (double room) $$$$-$200+; $$$-$141-$200; $$-$81-$140; $-$80 and less.

For more sedate and elegant night action try the **Duchin Room** at the Lodge featuring the Joe Foss Trio until 1 a.m. **The Sun Valley Wine Company** has a wine cellar, reportedly the largest wine selection in Idaho, and offers a light lunch and dinner menu. It is above the Ketchum state liquor store on Leadville Street. Choose a bottle of wine from its large inventory, then enjoy it in a quiet, conversation-oriented environment next to a fireplace.

Remember—if you are staying in Sun Valley or Warm Springs and plan on partying in Ketchum, the KART bus system stops running at midnight, but A-1 Taxi (726-9351) and Bald Mountain Taxis (726-2650) are available until closing.

Other activities

Snowmobiling is available through Mulligan Adventure Center (726-9137). The Sun Valley Athletic Club (726-3664) with daily and weekly rates is open to visitors with **child care, massage, aerobics, weights and swimming.** Also try High Altitude Fitness (726-1956). **Ice skating** is available year-round on the Sun Valley Resort outdoor rink.

Sun Valley Heli-Ski (622-3108) offers **backcountry ski adventures** for all levels of skiers. **Soaring** or winter glider rides are available through Sun Valley Soaring (726-3054). **Ice fishing/fly fishing** is offered by Silver Creek Outfitters (726-5282) and Lost River Outfitters (726-1706).

Shopping opportunities are extensive. A few shops worth highlighting: The Toy Store, for unique and educational toys from around the globe; Barry J. Peterson Jewelers, for Limoges collectors' boxes, Lesäl ceramics and unique jewelry; The Country Cousin for low-priced accessories and gifts; and T. D. Bambino, where you can have fleece clothing custom-made. You can pick up some great bargains on secondhand items at the Gold Mine Thrift Shop, 331 Walnut Ave. Because this supports the The Community Library in Ketchum, residents give their (sometimes barely) used clothing and sporting goods to this store. By the way, the **library** is a gem. It has an amazing regional history section.

Sun Valley Center For Arts and Humanities has performances and showings during the ski season. Call 726-9491 for a schedule or the Chamber of Commerce, 726-3423. **Art galleries** are another center of Ketchum's cultural life. Twelve galleries are members of the Sun Valley Art Gallery Association (726-2602). They provide a beautiful brochure with a map and offer guided evening gallery walks about a dozen times during the year.

Getting there and getting around

By air: The closest airport is Friedman Memorial, 12 miles south in Hailey, served by Horizon Air and Delta's SkyWest Airlines. Weather sometimes closes it, and it cannot handle big jets. Most guests arrive by jet at Twin Falls, about 90 minutes away, or Boise, about 155 miles and 2.5 hours away.

Several properties provide transportation, or you can use one of the following companies, most of which will pick you up in Hailey, Twin Falls or Boise: Sun Valley Stages (800) 574-8661; Teton Stage Lines 529-8036; or Sun Valley Express (800) 622-8267 or 342-7795.

By car: Sun Valley/Ketchum is 82 miles north of Twin Falls on Hwy. 75, and 152 miles from Boise.

Getting around: You don't really need a car if you're staying near the KART bus routes, which link Sun Valley, Ketchum and Baldy, running about every 20 minutes. For schedule information, call 726-7140.

Idaho
regional resorts

Idaho

Bogus Basin, Boise ID; (208) 332-5100; (800) 367-4397

Internet: www.bogusbasin.com
8 lifts; 2,600 skiable acres; 1,800 vertical feet

Bogus Basin, 16 miles from Boise, is much more than a day hill you might expect so close to a city. Like Colorado's Winter Park, Bogus is a big, community-owned, full-service destination resort. The mountain also has two restaurants, Nordic skiing and the 70-unit, mid-mountain Pioneer Inn. Child care starts at 6 months.

Bogus has night skiing every day until 10 p.m. on 1,500 vertical feet. That's the most extensive night skiing in the Northwest. It also has 360-degree skiing around its highest peak. The Superior Lift services 7,590-foot Shafer Butte on the front side and the Pine Creek lift serves the back side. Don't miss the back side. It's like the front on steroids.

And the name? Legend says that "fool's gold"—iron pyrite—was mined there and marketed to gullible city folks as the real thing. Real gold also was mined in the area, however, and all the ski runs are named after legitimate mines.

Lift tickets (01/02 prices): Adults, $37; children (7–11), $10; ages 6 and younger and ages 70 and older ski free.

Distance from Boise: About 16 miles north. Coming east or west on I-84, take the City Center Connector to River Street exit, then 15th Street to Hill Road to Bogus Basin Road.

Lodging information: The number for the on-site Pioneer Inn is (800) 367-4397. In Boise, the Grove Hotel (a Westcoast 5-star hotel) is central to downtown: (800) 426-0670.

Brundage Mountain, McCall, ID; (800) 888-7544, (208) 634-7462

Internet: www.brundage.com
6 lifts; 1,300 acres; 1,800 foot vertical

Brundage is definitely one of those underrated resorts. Payette Lake, which Brundage overlooks, is beautiful and sparsely populated, with many outdoor activities including good intermediate downhill skiing. From the top of the mountain, you can see the Salmon River Mountains, Payette Lakes, Oregon's Eagle Cap Wilderness and the Seven Devils towering over Hells Canyon, America's deepest river gorge. The skiing is pleasant and uncrowded, with occasional challenging drops, but mostly cruisers.

Brundage has a reputation for some of the lightest powder in the Pacific Northwest, and the mountain offers guided skiing via snowcat in a permit area of over 19,000 acres in the Payette National Forest. Child care starts at 6 weeks.

Lift tickets (00/01): Adults, $32; junior (13-18) and senior (65+), $25; children (7–12), $18; younger than 7, free.

Distance from Boise: About 100 miles north via Hwy. 55. The drive is quite scenic.

Lodging information: (888) 844-3246.

Silver Mountain, Kellogg, ID; (208) 783-1111

Internet: wwwsilvermt.com

7 lifts; 1,500 acres; 2,200 vertical feet

Silver Mountain's original name was Jackass Ski Bowl. The name honored the discoverer of the metal that brought riches to the valley more than a century ago. Local legend says a donkey got away from its owner, scampered up a hill, and was standing on a rock with a silvery glint when the owner caught up with it. Bunker Hill Mine, which also took lead, zinc and copper from the hillsides, ran the ski area for employee recreation and changed the name to Silverhorn. But in the early 1980s silver prices plunged and Bunker Hill closed.

The town decided to build a four-season resort, serviced by an aerial gondola to take skiers from the valley floor to the slopes. Silver Mountain began ski operations in 1990. The gondola, which the ski area claims is the longest in the world, descends low over the houses and yards of the town of Wardner before climbing to Silver's "base area," called Mountain Haus, at 5,700 feet. (A hefty portion of Silver's terrain is below the Mountain Haus, which gives the area its 2,200-foot vertical drop.) The gondola is the only way in and out. Silver has two connected peaks, Kellogg and Wardner. The gondola deposits skiers and snowboarders at Mountain Haus on the Kellogg side. From here they can fan out in several directions.

Silver has a lot of serious terrain, including monster glade skiing. For advanced skiers, the run rating always depends on snow conditions. On fresh powder days, take Silver Belt to Rendezvous on the Kellogg side. For great thrills on the Wardner side, cut down anywhere from the early section of the Wardner Peak Traverse. The best skiing on powder days is off the slopes between the tops of Chairs 4 and 2.

Experts love Silver Mountain. They can take the Wardner Peak Traverse to an inspirational knob with a stupendous view of the Silver Valley below. Some nice black-diamond runs go back down to the Shaft and Chair 4.

Silver Belt, from the triple Chair 2, is a wide and terrific intermediate warmup run. At the Junction you can turn down Saddle Back for a bumpier ride, or take a hard left on the Cross Over Run to the Midway load station on Chair 4 for a ride to Wardner Peak. From the top there are several trails back to Midway. Only advanced skiers pass Midway and keep going down through the Shaft to the Chair 4 base.

As good as Silver is for experts, it also offers a lot for beginners. Chairs 1, 2, 3, and 5 at the Mountain Haus base area all serve beginner terrain. Below the lodge, Ross Run is a wide beginner favorite, allowing crossover to Noahs and back again, ending on Dawdler with a choice to return to Chair 5 or Chair 3.

Note: Most skiers ski the Kellogg side, so to avoid even a mirage of crowds, ski the Wardner side. Lift lines are rarely a problem, but the gondola queue can back up for downloading at closing time (remember, you can't ski to the gondola base). To avoid morning clog, ride up a half hour early for breakfast at Mountain Haus.

Silver has some nice surprises. One is the free ski wax, right by the free ski check at Mountain Haus. Another is the guarantee: If snow conditions don't please you, return your lift ticket to the gondola base within an hour and a half and get a pass for another day.

Lift tickets (00/01): Weekend: adults, $30; college/senior (18-23/62+), $25; junior (7-17), $23. Weekday: adults, $23; college/senior (18-23/ 62+), $23; junior (7-17), $23.

Distance from Coeur d'Alene: 30 miles. **Lodging information:** (800) 204-6428. The best lodging is at the Coeur d'Alene Resort; packages available, call (800) 688-5253. The most affordable place to stay is at the base of the gondola in Kellogg.

Schweitzer Mountain, Sandpoint, ID; (208) 263-9555

Internet: www.schweitzer.com

8 lifts; 2,500 skiable acres; 2,400 vertical feet

Schweitzer is one of Idaho's largest ski areas, but it's still very uncrowded. One skier per acre (2, 500 acres) is a good-sized crowd here. Its acreage is second biggest in Idaho (Bogus Basin is slightly larger), and its vertical drop is second only to Sun Valley's 3,400.

Schweitzer has one slopeside hotel and a bunch of condos. A European-style village with shops, restaurants and lodging is planned for the future. White Pine Lodge, with one- to three-bedroom condos, plus 6,000 square feet of commercial space, is under construction; it's supposed to be ready for the 2001/02 season. Many visitors stay in Sandpoint, 11 miles away on the shore of beautiful Lake Pend Oreille. This is the sort of place that people visit, then try to figure a way to move there.

Schweitzer gets plenty of snow from its position in the Selkirks. When the storms come from the north, the snow is dry and fluffy, but more often it is wet and dense. It's drier than the Cascade Concrete that falls on Washington and Oregon areas, but still wet enough to have earned the local term, Panhandle Premix. When the skies are clear, the vistas are outstanding: From the top of Schweitzer, skiers can look east into Montana's Cabinet Range and north to the Canadian Selkirks. The view of big Lake Pend Oreille is memorable. Stella The Six-Pack Chair, a high-speed six passenger lift, replaced Chair 5 for the 2000/01 season. It carries skiers and riders to the ridge of the new Northwest Territory, what the resort calls "the land of dreams and adventure" encompassing the lift and an additional 150 acres of gladed and groomed terrain.

Schweitzer's runs and chutes are steepest at the top of its two broad ski bowls, North and South. The bowls are separated by the Great Divide run, a long wide ridge that gives you a continuous option to drop into either bowl. Chutes await advanced skiers in the South Bowl, reached by either Chair 1 or The Great Escape Quad. They're lettered A Chute, B Chute, and so forth. Upper Stiles and the adjacent Headwall Chutes are gonzo favorites. There is some double-black skiing from the rim of South Bowl, but most experts will head up the Great Escape and turn right to North Bowl. Patient trekkers will be rewarded with the Siberia Chutes. Intermediate skiers can wend their way down from the South Bowl summit, but are advised to unload midway on the Snow Ghost chair heading toward the summit of North Bowl. The runs under the Timber Cruiser chair, Cathedral Aisle and Zip Down, are intermediate favorites.

Beginners won't be able to get to the top, but can get a view by unloading midway up Chair One and heading down Gypsy. The Enchanted Forest and Happy Trails are perfect for children. Both run the length of the Musical Chairs chair, which goes right by the windows of the 40,000-square-foot Headquarters Day Lodge. The Enchanted Forest, with kid-high, widely-spaced mounds that children can go over or around, is barred to adults and jealous snowboarders. Schweitzer has a wonderful learning area, served by a separate chair and completely isolated from other traffic. Better yet, it is below the base area, so that never-evers can start out skiing, rather than sidestepping up the hill or riding a lift.

Lift tickets (00/01): Adult, $37; seniors, $32; junior (7-17), $27; 6 and younger free.

Distance from Coeur d'Alene: 50 miles. **Lodging information:** (800) 831-8810. We suggest you stay on the mountain at the Selkirk Lodge or ask about the new White Pines Lodge. In Sandpoint lodging is inexpensive (many rooms less than $100 a night) and fairly basic, ranging in size from the four-room lakeside Coit House B&B (208-265-4035) to the 60 rooms of the Lakeside Inn (800-543-8126) and Super 8 Motel (800-800-8000).

Big Mountain

Montana

Summit elevation: 7,000 feet
Vertical drop: 2,500 feet
Base elevation: 4,500 feet

Address: P.O. Box 1400
Whitefish, MT 59937
☎ **Area code:** 406
Ski area phone: 862-1900; (800) 858-4152
Snow report: 862-7669
ⓘ **Toll-free reservations:** (800) 858-4157
E-mail: bigmtn@bigmtn.com
Internet: www.bigmtn.com
and www.skiwhitefish.com

Expert:★★★★
Advanced:★★★★
Intermediate:★★★★★
Beginner:★★
Never-ever:★★★★

Number and types of lifts: 11–2 high-speed quads, 1 quad, 5 triples, 1 double, 2 surface lifts
Skiable acreage: 3,020 acres
Snowmaking: 5 percent
Uphill capacity: 13,800 per hour
Snowboarding: Yes
Bed base: 1,500 on mountain
Nearest lodging: Slopeside, hotels and condos
Resort child care: Yes, infants and older
Adult ticket, per day: $47 (2000/01 prices)

Dining:★★★
Apres-ski/nightlife:★★★★
Other activities:★★★

True ski-resort discoveries are getting harder to find. If you live in a state or province along the U.S.-Canadian border west of the Great Lakes, you probably already know about this spot with skiing that stretches on forever. You probably don't want us to tell anyone in the rest of the country about it. We understand, and of course we'll keep your secret.

If you are a skier who wants lots of terrain to explore and a no-fluff off-slope atmosphere, you should head for this aptly named ski resort tucked into the far northwest corner of Montana. This is an area popular with Seattle, Calgary, west coast and northern midwest skiers. Many hop on Amtrak's Empire Builder, which on its run between Seattle and Chicago dumps a load of eager skiers in Whitefish within sight of Big Mountain's trails.

Though sometimes the resort and the community business leaders long to see their name in the various annual listings of top ski resorts (acreage-wise, it ranks in the top 10, maybe even top five, depending on how you count), most other times, they'd rather just keep it the Northwest's little secret. Many folks here are expatriates from other ski areas that were once as laid-back and unpretentious as Big Mountain is now.

Everything is clean and comfortable, but you won't find concierges or valet parking. This is a down-home place where a fur coat would look out of place except on a grizzly-bearded mountain man.

The ski area is 8 miles from the town of Whitefish, up a winding road that can be a bit scary in bad weather. At the ski area base is a cluster of hotels and condo properties and a few restaurants and bars. In Whitefish there are more hotels, the best restaurants, shopping and the biggest variety of nightlife.

The weather here is a mix of the Rockies and Pacific Northwest maritime, called "inland maritime." It creates spectacular "snow ghosts," trees encased in many layers of frost and snow, at the summit. It also produces plenty of fantastic light powder, but without the sunshine you'll find in the southern Rockies. If you forget your sunscreen, you'll probably survive, but don't forget your goggles. Pack your sunglasses too—sunny days do occur, and when they do, the skiing is spectacular. You'll want those sunglasses to see the seemingly endless view of the mountains of Glacier National Park as well as the Flathead Valley and the huge lake that dominates it.

Expanded beginner terrain for the 2001/02 season will include a new triple chair that replaces the "Platter" lift on the lower west mountain just above Big Mountain Village. Beginner skiers will enjoy enhanced lift access to Question Mark and Hope Slope.

Mountain layout—Skiing

◆◆ **Expert** ◆ **Advanced:** If you can see it, you can ski it! Within the boundaries are 3,000 acres of sprawling terrain; another 1,000 acres is in the U.S. Forest Service permit area. Big Mountain's ski school offers free tours of the mountain at 10 a.m. and 1 p.m. daily (open to intermediates, too).

The main access to Big Mountain is the Glacier Chaser, which moves skiers up 2,200 feet to the summit. If you ski straight ahead when you get off the chair you'll drop down the north slope, a mostly intermediate series of runs alternating with tree-studded steeps.

If you make a U-turn when you get off the Glacier Chaser you'll reach wide, well-groomed intermediate trails, surrounded by fields of powder and thousands of trees beckoning to advanced and expert skiers. Throughout this entire Good Medicine area skiers and boarders can choose how tight they want their trees, and they have plenty of opportunities to bail out onto the groomed trails. Locals also can direct you to Movie Land, which starts with dense trees and then opens for great steep tree skiing before ending on Russ's Street. The Bigfoot T-bar, added last year, provides access to north-facing expert terrain that includes gladed powder runs through a big timber forest.

For big-air fans, Big Mountain has a cornice next to the Summit House. Runs from this cornice, and almost all skiing to the left of the high-speed quad, end up on Russ's Street.

■ **Intermediate:** Go straight off The Glacier Chaser for the groomed runs under Chair 7, or make a U-turn to reach Toni Matt, The Big Ravine or MoeMentum (formerly North Bowl; named for Olympic downhill champ Tommy Moe), all perfect for power cruising with wide GS turns. Toni Matt, Inspiration and the Big Ravine provide top-to-bottom cruising.

Lower-intermediates should make a few runs off Chair 2 or the T-bar before they try The Glacier Chaser. Chair 2's runs are equivalent in pitch to the blue runs off the front of the summit, but much shorter. This lower-mountain area is also lighted for night skiing. The Bigfoot T-bar, going into its second winter, accesses three new low-intermediate trails covering about 20 acres that have been cut on the southern exposure above Russ's Street and the Evan's Heaven area. When you're ready to try the summit runs, try the ones down the North Slope first. The toughest part will be the upper part of MoeMentum, which can build formidable moguls by afternoon.

●● **Beginner:** Chair 3 is the best bet for beginners, though they may be frustrated at not being able to ski from the summit. There's a green trail from the summit called Russ's Street, but it has a few intermediate pitches. Look for the expanded beginner terrain for the 2001/02 season and a new triple chair that replaces the "Platter" lift on the lower west mountain just above the village.

●**Never-ever:** Never-evers have an excellent learning area, separate from other skiers, on the gentle trails under Chair 6 (which costs nothing to ride, by the way).

Mountain layout—Snowboarding

From the top of Glacier Chaser, the hardest choice is deciding on which wide-open, rolling, impeccably groomed trail you should lay out a string of razor sharp, horizontal-flying Euro carves. A hint: There's no wrong answer, but just be sure to keep your speed on the cat track at the bottom. After a few warm-ups, duck into the trees almost anywhere across the mountain for some smooth powder turns, or head to the expansive out-of-bounds areas.

It's no wonder why Big Mountain is consistently rated highly by snowboard magazines, as it makes an honorable attempt to cater to riders. It sponsors its own snowboard team and has a handful of seasonal events. It also has a boardercross course and terrain park on White-tail that serve up tabletops, hits, gap jumps and berms.

Mountain rating

The ski patrol's generous out-of-bounds policy and the abundance of tree skiing make this a delight for expert and advanced skiers. Intermediates will like the resort's superb grooming and long cruisers. The learning area is one of the best. The lower-intermediate trails added last year and this year's expansion of beginner terrain beef up the offerings for this level. There's now plenty to keep skiers and boarders of all abilities happy for four or more days.

Cross-country and snowshoeing

Big Mountain Nordic Center is adjacent to the Outpost Lodge (bottom of Chair 6) and has 15 km. of groomed trails (862-2900). There is no trail fee for children 6 and younger. All others pay $5. Downhill ski pass holders can use the cross-country trails for free. Trail passes, maps and rentals are available at the Outpost Lodge or the Big Mountain Ski Shop in the base village. There is also lighted night skiing and snowshoeing at the center.

Grouse Mountain Lodge (862-3000) in Whitefish has 15 km. of groomed cross-country trails and night skiing with 2.4 km. lighted. The **Izaak Walton Inn** (888-5700), 62 miles east on Highway 2 (also an Amtrak flag stop), has 30 km. of groomed trails as well as guides who take skiers into the Glacier National Park wilderness. Guides for groups of two to four or more cost $60–$95 per person.

Glacier National Park provides a natural cross-country paradise. Here the unplowed park roads and trails provide kilometer after kilometer of ungroomed passages. Check with the communications center (888-5441) or the park rangers for weather and snow conditions. Mountain Timbers, a lodge in West Glacier, a half-hour east of Whitefish, offers 15 km. groomed cross-country trails on 240 private acres. Located at the western terminus of the Going to the Sun Highway, the lodge is on the edge of Glacier National Park with spectacular views into the Park.

Lessons (2001/02 prices)

Group lessons: Half day, $30; full day, $48.
Never-ever package: Limited lift ticket and two-hour lesson (rentals extra) for skiing or snowboarding is $30.

Private lessons: One or two people, half day costs $155 ($50 for each additional person); full day costs $300 ($50 for each additional person). One-hour Quick Tips costs $72 (as available).

Special programs: Big Mountain has design-your-own clinics for groups of up to 11; plus afternoon lessons for bumps, steeps and powder at the same price as group lessons. Ask about them if you're interested. Telemark and Nordic lessons are by appointment only, $75 each for one or two people. Women's workshops and advanced skiing seminars are taught at select times. Call the ski school at 862-2909 for dates and prices.

Racing: A NASTAR course is open off Chair 3 Thursdays through Sundays 11 a.m.–2 p.m. Cost is $5 for two runs and $1 for each additional run.

Child care (2001/02 prices)

Ages: Newborns to 12 years.

Costs: Full day, 14 months and older, $40 including lunch. Full day for infants younger than 14 months is $60 ($30 for half day), not including lunch. The day-care facility, in the Alpine Lodge at the base of Chair 3, is open three nights a week until 10 p.m. for babysitting at $7 per hour for 14 months and older. The facility has room for just three infants at a time, so reserve far in advance. Discounts available for families with multiple children.

Reservations: Required for infants and recommended for toddlers, 862-1999.

Children's lessons: For skiers ages 3–4, and snowboarders ages 4–7, private lessons are required. Cost is $45 for a 45-minute lesson. Ages 5–6 have a one-hour lesson that costs $18. Rentals and lift tickets are extra in both cases. Full day for older children includes four hours of lessons (two sessions) for $48; half-day, $30. Lift tickets, rental gear and lunch are optional, but not included in the price. Learn to Ski (ages 7-14) and Learn to Snowboard (8-14) is a half-day lesson, limited lift ticket and rentals; skiers pay $42, snowboarders pay $46. Reservations are recommended for all children's lessons.

Lift tickets (2001/02 prices)

	Adult	Junior (7-18)
One day	$47	$34
Three days	$138 ($46/day)	$99 ($33/day)
Five days	$220 ($44/day)	$155 ($31/day)

Who skis free: Children ages 6 and younger. Night skiing costs $14, but is free with a day or multiday ticket.

Who skis at a discount: Skiers ages 62 and older and college students pay $39, with no multiday discounts. A ticket for lower-mountain lifts only is $26, and can be upgraded to a full-mountain pass by paying the difference. If you have a season pass or frequent skier card at *any North American resort,* you pay just $39 (no blackout dates). All skiers and riders pay just $20 between Nov. 22 and Dec. 16, 2001. Between April 1 and April 7, 2002, lift tickets are just $10.

Note: Day and multiday ticket holders may ride the Glacier Chaser to the Summit House for dinner without charge on select nights; The Glacier Chaser turns into a gondola for night riding. Other passengers headed for the summit at night pay $9.

Nearby resorts

Blacktail Mountain, a fairly new area in northern Montana, offers panoramic views of Glacier National Park and Flathead Lake. The parking lot is at the top of the mountain so you get to ski before you ever board a lift. If the facilities seem familiar, it's because Blacktail's three lifts were bought used from Crystal Mountain, WA; Steamboat Springs, CO; and Calgary's Olympic Park. The ski area is in Lakeside, about 45 minutes south of Kalispell, which itself is about half an hour from Whitefish.

Blacktail Mountain offers three lifts, 24 runs on 200 acres with a vertical drop of about 1,500 feet. Lift tickets are $25 for adults; $16 for junior ages 8–18; free for ages 7 and younger and 70 and older (01/02 prices). The 17,000-square-foot lodge at the "base" area houses everything—the ski shop, ski school, bar and restaurant all are located in the three-story building. Day care is only $15 for a full day. You can buy a hamburger, fries and a soda for less than $5. Really.

Accommodations

All accommodations, both in town and on-mountain, should be reserved by calling **Big Mountain Reservations** at (800) 858-4152. Lower rates are available before Christmas, in January and in April; higher rates apply in the last two weeks of December.

The **Alpinglow Inn** ($$) lies at the center of the village. This lodging has beautiful views from the restaurant and perhaps the most convenient location for skiers. Sauna, two outdoor hot tubs overlooking the valley, laundry facilities and gift shop on site. The American plan includes lodging, lifts and meals, and the Alpinglow is the only one on the mountain to offer such an all-inclusive plan that lets you know your vacation costs before you leave home. The **Edelweiss** ($$–$$$$) is centrally located in the base area and has studios, one- and two-bedroom condos. Complimentary ski waxing and bottle of wine.

Glacier Village Property Management (GVPM) offers a wide variety of slopeside condominiums, townhomes and single-family homes: from studios to four-bedroom condos, from ski-in/ski-out chalets to hostel lodging. Some to consider:

The **Hibernation House** ($$) is touted as the "friendliest lodge on the mountain." It is the least expensive and has rooms with a queen bed, twin bunks and a private bath. There is a large indoor Jacuzzi, laundry and a clean and inviting lobby. Full daily breakfast is included in the cost.

The **Kandahar Lodge** ($$–$$$$) at Big Mountain looks like a mountain lodge should— log decor, spacious public areas and a soaring stone fireplace. The rooms are large and the food outstanding. A free shuttle takes guests to the base area and at the end of the day skiers and riders can glide right to the door.

Kintla Lodge ($$$-$$$$) at the base of the mountain features outdoor hot tubs, sauna and underground parking. It is Big Mountain's newest facility and features all the luxuries of home in every unit.

Eight miles away in Whitefish is a variety of lodging. Many properties offer free transportation to and from the mountain, but be sure to ask when you make your reservation.

The **Pine Lodge** ($–$$$) boasts an indoor-outdoor pool with connecting swim channel, hot tub and free continental breakfast. **The Grouse Mountain Lodge** ($$–$$$) is the most comfortable and convenient hotel. Its rooms are spacious and a free shuttlebus takes guests to the mountain every morning. Cross-country skiing is right out the back door and downtown is within easy walking distance. **Good Medicine Lodge** ($$) is built of cedar timbers and has a rustic informal atmosphere. Rooms are decorated in a Western-Native American motif with fireplaces and solid wood furnishings. Rates include breakfast. The **Best Western-Rocky Mountain Lodge** ($) includes breakfast in its rates and features an outdoor pool and spa. For rock-bottom prices, try the clean and comfortable **Cheap Sleep Motel** ($).

 # Dining

The **Summit House** (862-1971) serves dinners on the top of the mountain on Wednesday and Saturday nights from 6 to 8 p.m. The high-speed Glacier Chaser quad chairs are replaced by gondola cars to whisk diners up the mountain.

At the base of the ski area, the best food and service is at **The Hellroaring Saloon** (862-6364). This 50-year-old, log-decor building served as the original base lodge. All food on the menu is homemade. It serves lunch and dinner.

Moguls Bar and Grill (862-1980) is at the base of Chair 2 and serves breakfast, lunch and dinner. For a special evening in the base village, try **Café Kandahar** (862-6098) where chef Andrew Topel serves fine French Provincial fare in an intimate setting. The restaurant has an extensive wine list.

The **Alpinglow Restaurant** (862-6966) has the best view of the Flathead Valley, while the **The 'Stube & Chuckwagon Grill** (862-1993) is inexpensive for lunch or dinner. You can't beat its outdoor deck on a sunny day.

Old West Adventures (862-2900) offers a 30-minute sleigh ride and dinner in an old roadhouse. Family-style dinners, live music and cowboy tales top off the evening.

The bulk of restaurants are in Whitefish. The finest dining in the area is at **Logan's** (862-3000) in the Grouse Mountain Lodge or across the street in the **Whitefish Lake Restaurant** (862-5285) at the golf course. The Szechuan shrimp pasta is marvelous. For local color, wood-fired pizza and great steaks try **Truby's** (862-4979). **Serrano's** (862-5600) has a Southwest menu. **Dos Amigos** (862-9994) is a basic Tex-Mex spot with a fine selection of imported beers. Microbrew fans can head for the new **Great Northern Brewing Company** on Main Street. It also serves food.

Locals and tourists sip espresso at the **Whitefish Times** or **The Buffalo Café.** If you can get a seat and listen a bit, you'll hear about everything happening in town. At the latter spot, try the Buffalo Pie—layers of hashbrowns, ham, cheese and poached eggs, or order the Cinnamon Swirl French Toast. It's open for lunch as well.

Après-ski/nightlife

If you enjoy a let-it-loose style of après-ski and nighttime fun, Big Mountain has one of the continent's best bars, **The 'Stube & Chuckwagon Grill** at the ski area base. Hundreds of ski-club T-shirts hang from the rafters; owner Gary Elliott has boxes of 'em and rotates them every so often. Among the various pranks and ceremonies is the Frabert Award, presented each week to the employee or visitor who commits the biggest goof-up. Other pranks are legendary, but why ruin the fun for those of you who are Bierstube virgins? Ask for your souvenir ring, in gold or silver. When ski clubs are in town and with a live band, the dancing goes full-blast until closing.

The **Hellroaring Saloon** serves some of the best après-ski nachos anywhere. Best deal: if you buy a Hellroaring baseball cap you get free beer every day you wear it to the bar. Also on the mountain, **Moguls Bar and Grille** has entertainment nightly.

Dining: $$$-Entrees $20+; $$-$10-20; $-less than $10.
Accommodations: (double room) $$$$-$200+; $$$-$141-$200; $$-$81-$140; $-$80 and less.

It's worth a visit to the **Palace Bar** on Central Avenue in Whitefish just to see its turn-of-the-century carved mahogany bar. **The Great Northern Bar and Grill** on Central Avenue offers live music from Thursday to Saturday and acoustic open-mike on Tuesday. Locals come for the burgers and wide selection of microbrewery beers and stay for the music.

Having all the Central Avenue bars lined up makes it easy to check out the scene and decide where you want to set up camp. Choose from **The Remington, Bulldog Saloon, Casey's** or **Truby's**, all notable in their own way.

For more mellow evenings try the drinks and the band at **Logans** in the Grouse Mountain Lodge. For a real cowboy evening, complete with live foot-stomping music and longneck beer bottles you can slip in your back pockets, head to the **Blue Moon Nite Club** in Columbia Falls at the intersection of Hwys. 2 and 40.

Other activities

For adrenaline junkies, the resort has **Thrill Sleds,** high-tech sleds featuring full suspension for a smooth ride, braking systems to keep you in control, and handlebars that steer the four small skis under the sled. Guided Thrill Sled tours are offered daily from the summit. New for 2001/02, try **snowbiking,** similar to mountain bikes but with skis on the bike and mini-skis on your feet. A real blast! **Snow tubing** is offered off Chair 6. **Snowcat skiing and riding** is offered in areas of the mountain not yet served by lifts. Snowcat tours are four hours and cost $60 per person (that's on top of the regular lift ticket) with four or more people; call 862-2909 for information.

Near the ski area, Horsepower Adventures (862-2900) has **sleigh rides** and **chuckwagon dinners.** Downtown in Whitefish sleigh rides leave the Grouse Mountain Lodge (862-3000) for a 20-minute ride to a camp near Lost Coon Lake. **Snowmobiling** is a favorite pastime of Montanans, so a variety of guide services are available. Canyon Creek Cat House (800-933-5133) is in nearby Columbia Falls, with more than 200 miles of groomed trails. Contact the Flathead Convention and Visitors Association at (800) 543-3105 for additional guide services. Snowmobile trails leave from Big Mountain's summit, where you can rent machines.

Shopping is limited at the base area although there are a variety of specialty shops along the Kintla shopping pavilion. Whitefish's Central Avenue has many art galleries and stores that stock Western clothing, jewelry and crafts. Montana Coffee Traders, on Hwy. 93 south of town, has many Montana food gift items, such as huckleberry syrup.

Big Mountain has a terrific **Guest Services and Information** center in the base village where you can find out more about other activities. Call 862-2900.

Getting there and getting around

By air: Glacier Park International Airport is in Kalispell, 19 miles south of the resort, served by Delta, Horizon Air and Northwest airlines. Call Flathead Glacier Transportation (892-3390) for ground transportation.

By car/train: Big Mountain is 8 miles from the town of Whitefish at the junction of Hwys. 2 and 93. Amtrak's Empire Builder, (800) USA-RAIL (872-7245), stops in Whitefish four times a week from Seattle, Portland, Chicago and Minneapolis. Kids ride free.

Getting around: If you stay and play at the mountain, you won't need a car. The S.N.O.W bus makes daily runs between Whitefish and the mountain. That works if you're staying in Whitefish and riding the bus to ski, but it's impossible for mountain lodgers who want to party late at night in town. The last run back up the mountain is at about 9 p.m. Taxi service is available. A car is essential if you plan to explore.

Big Sky

Montana

Summit elevation: 11,150 feet
Vertical drop: 4,180 feet
Base elevation: 6,970 feet

Address: P.O. Box 160001
Big Sky, MT 59716
✆ Area code: 406
Ski area phone (Hotel guest calls and switchboard): 995-5000
Snow report: 995-5900
ⓘ **Toll-free reservations:** (800) 548-4486
Fax: 995-5001
Internet: www.bigskyresort.com

Expert: ★★★★★
Advanced: ★★★★
Intermediate: ★★★★
Beginner: ★★
Never-ever: ★★

Number and types of lifts: 18–1 aerial tram, 1 four-passenger gondola, 3 high-speed quads, 1 quad, 4 triples, 4 doubles and 4 surface lifts
Acreage: 3,600 skiable acres
Snowmaking: 10 percent of trails
Uphill capacity: 18,000 per hour
Snowboarding: Yes, unlimited
Bed base: 4,250
Nearest lodging: Slopeside, hotel
Resort child care: Yes, infants and older
Adult ticket, per day: $52-$56 (01/02)

Dining: ★★★ **Apres-ski/nightlife:** ★★
Other activities: ★★

From the moment you land at Bozeman's Gallatin Field, which feels more like a private rancher's massive lodge than an airport, you know you're in for a different kind of vacation. Here you can expect lots of friendly employees in cowboy hats holding doors open for you, a genuine laid-back atmosphere, spectacular scenery and plenty of challenging terrain.

Big Sky, with its impressive Matterhorn-shaped peak scraping the heavens at 11,166 feet, is a serious skier's mountain near the summit, yet it has excellent cruisers closer to the base. In fact, the cruisers are such a delight that experts who wear themselves out on the tougher terrain will still have plenty to grin about as they swoop down the lower mountain, and adjacent Andesite Mountain, with friends and family.

An aerial tram with two 15-passenger cars whisks you up to the 11,150-foot mark on Lone Peak, giving a stomach-in-your-throat close-up of the craggy mountain just before coming in for a landing. If you get to the top and find that the chutes, couloirs and steeps are over your head, no problem—admire the views of the nearby Spanish Peaks Wilderness area and ride back down. Only 15 people per tram, so you'll have a marvelous feeling of privacy as you descend, either in the capsule or while attempting the steeps beneath it.

Big Sky is a true destination resort, far from large urban areas, yet just an hour from the nearest jet airport. It has a very European feel. Ski school director Hans Schernthaner is from Austria, and each year he brings in English-speaking Europeans to teach.

Mountain layout—Skiing

◆◆ **Expert** ◆ **Advanced:** The runs from the Lone Peak summit have become the test of who is an expert and who wants to be. Fortunately, if you decide once you're on top that you're in the latter category, you can ride back down. Every run from the top is rated double-black diamond, and justifiably so.

On a clear day, you'll get your first close-up view of the peak when you get off Gondola One. "Breathtaking" describes the magnificence of Lone Peak and the immense bowl beneath it. Above-treeline slopes beckon advanced skiers and snowboarders for untouched powder. You'll find steep pitches and wide-open terrain on the bowl's South Face.

The more adventurous can register with the ski patrol and test their skills in A-Z Chutes, the Pinnacles and Big Couloir, which are all out of bounds. (The latter run is 42-degrees steep and half-a-mile long). Out-of-bounds skiing is permitted, but only with the right rescue equipment. If you want to try this terrain, you have to take a transceiver, a shovel and a partner.

A fun mix of terrain from the summit is the steeps of Lenin to wide-open (and steep) Liberty Bowl to Dakota Gully to the delightful trees of Bavarian Forest. Hippy Highway then funnels you back from the boundary edge to the Shedhorn lift.

Experts also should head to the vast area on Lone Mountain's north side, where many locals ski. The Challenger chair climbs 1,750 steep vertical feet to open, hair-raising, in-bounds terrain. If you don't like chairs without safety bars, height makes this is a super-scary ride. Even scarier: Steep, long pitches drop down Big Rock Tongue, north-facing bowls greet skiers in Nashville Basin and trees pepper narrow chutes on Little Tree and Zucchini Patch.

Bump enthusiasts may be a little disappointed. Not enough traffic to build big bumps here, except maybe in the spring. Bad Dog, Moonlight and Midnight off Challenger chair, in The Bowl off Lone Peak Triple and on Upper Africa on Andesite Mountain bump up first.

■ **Intermediate:** Big Sky has two mountains that connect at the base, Lone Peak and Andesite. The blue-rated trails on both have a wide range in pitch and grooming. Some are kind and rolling, but others—such as the blues in the Shedhorn area—lean toward black. Not all the blue trails are groomed, and some have cat-track runouts or are simply too short.

On Lone Mountain, fine-tune your technique on the groomed cruisers under Gondola One and the Swift Current high-speed quad, such as Calamity Jane, Huntley Hollow and Lobo. For some bowl skiing, head to Upper Morningstar and the terrain off the Iron Horse Quad. Trails off Shedhorn lift are south-facing and get plenty of sun at times when the lower mountain is in the shade. Upper Sunlight to Sunlight is absolutely delightful. Views are of the backcountry and you'll feel a world away from the rest of the resort.

On Andesite, skis run fast and long on Big Horn, Elk Park Ridge, Elk Park Meadows and Ambush. Fine-tune your techniques on the manicured slopes of Tippy's Tumble or Silver Knife. During the spring, make sure to hit the trails off Thunder Wolf quad before the sun has turned them into heavy mashed potatoes.

●● **Beginner:** The south side of Andesite Mountain is great for beginners because of the wide, gentle slopes and because it gets a lot of sun. You can enjoy runs such as Sacajawea, El Dorado and Ponderosa from the Southern Comfort triple chair. Fewer hot shots ski on Andesite, a comfort if you get unnerved when someone passes by closely at high speed. On the way back to the base village, the winding Pacifier lets you admire awesome views.

On Lone Mountain, gentle rollers such as Mr. K, White Wing and Lone Wolf are reached via the gondola or the Explorer Lift. Mr. K gets high traffic as the lifts close down for the day, but it's nice and wide. If you're with people who are more accomplished than you, convince them to take a few runs on Mr. K and Lone Wolf, they'll enjoy it too.

● **Never-ever:** Big Sky has two surface lifts, a tow and a Poma lift, at Lone Mountain's base. Though not physically isolated from the rest of the terrain, the learning area is away from the high traffic pattern until the end of the day.

Mountain layout—Snowboarding

Big Sky has a nice halfpipe and terrain park on Andesite, by Ambush Meadows, reached by taking the Ramcharger quad and turning left. On Lone Mountain, there's a natural halfpipe on Lower Morningstar and another on Lower Buffalo Jump. A second terrain park is nearby on Crazy Horse. The park and pipes can be reached by taking either the Swift Current Express quad or Gondola One.

For some ridge riding and above-treeline faces, continue up from those chairs via the adjacent Lone Peak Triple and the Lone Peak Tram to the top of Lone Mountain at 11,150 feet (if you want to reach the 11,166 summit, you'll have to hike it, enjoy the view and hike back down). Under the Lone Peak Tram, you'll find some serious descents. The most extreme—and narrow—run on the mountain is Big Couloir, just to the right of the tram. If it's even open, watch some others pick their way down before you decide to try it. If you do, you are required to check in with the patrol and have a partner, beacon and shovel.

The South Face isn't as steep as the chutes under the tram, but you'll still find yourself leaning into the mountain when you're "taking a breather." Death slides are not uncommon here, so stay on the ball. If you like catching air time with the locals, there's often a group building jumps on Screaming Left, at the bottom of Liberty Bowl. If you prefer the woods, Bavarian Forest is a great romp. After the woods and runs below the face, try to stay central to avoid most of Cow Flats and Hippy Highway—end up as close to the Shedhorn lift as you can. Also try to avoid Middle Road when working your way back to the mountain village.

This mountain's great for laying out arcs too. Pick any groomer to your left off the Swift Current Express and Gondola One.

Mountain rating

Big Sky is excellent for most skiers and snowboarders; however, it doesn't have vast beginner terrain. The black-diamond runs here are solid black, so be careful not to get in over your head. If you don't like a combination of heights and chairs without safety bars, you may want to avoid the Lone Peak Triple and the Challenger lift (Shedhorn doesn't have safety bars but it's lower to the ground). Big Sky gets high marks for no lift lines, magnificent scenery and grooming that isn't overdone. This is a great mountain for groups with members of varying abilities, the lower-level trails are actually lots of fun for more accomplished skiers and riders too. Don't forget to bring your camera.

Cross-country and snowshoeing

Nationally acclaimed **Lone Mountain Guest Ranch** (995-4644; 800-514-4644) offers 75 km. of international-caliber Nordic skiing for all levels, with groomed and skating lanes. The trail system winds through open meadows and forested canyons.

Lone Mountain Ranch teams with **Alpenguide Tours of West Yellowstone** to offer a variety of backcountry skiing, including snowcat tours into the interior of Yellowstone, America's most beloved national park, to view its winter wonders. Tours also are available into the Spanish Peaks.

Deluxe, cozy cabins with fireplace and full bath can be rented for a week, with all meals, trail pass and evening programs for $1,250–$2,500, based on the group and cabin size. The Ranch has a Nordic shop with apparel, equipment and mementos. Trail pass is $10 for adults; children ages 12 and younger ski free. Half-day tickets are available, as are lessons.

You can rent **snowshoes** from the Lone Mountain Guest Ranch, Grizzly Outfitters (995-2939) and Big Sky Ski Rental (995-5841) in the Mountain Village Plaza's Snowcrest building for about $14 per day. Big Sky has a marked and separated snowshoe trail up a portion of Lone Mountain called Moose Tracks.

Lessons (2001/02 prices)

Group lessons: Half day, $36 for ski or snowboard lesson, with discounts for multiple half-day sessions.

Never-ever package: Half-day lesson with beginner lift ticket and rentals, $60. Those who wish to ski the whole day can upgrade to beginner chair ticket for additional $27.

Private lessons: Two hours (1-3 people) costs $170 in morning, $155 in afternoon, with multiple-hour discounts. A private one-hour telemark lesson is $75. Guide services (1-3 people) are $190 for half-day afternoon, $205 for half-day morning; $350 for a full day.

Special programs: Advanced clinics concentrate on Lone Peak's steeps and tackle moguls, powder or other conditions du jour, $39.

Racing: Check in with the ski school daily for details.

Child care (2001/02 prices)

Ages: 6 months and older.

Costs: $75 for a full day, ages 6-16 months; and $65 for a full day, $45 for a half day for 17 months–8 years.

Reservations: Call 995-2335. Hours are 8:30 a.m. to 4:30 p.m. Immunizations records are required. Reservations are required for all child care services and parents will need to bring some things, so call ahead. The bright, airy facility is at slopeside Snowcrest Lodge.

Children's lessons: Ages 3–4 can take a 45-minute introduction to skiing in the afternoon, $30 (day care and rentals extra). Mini Camp, ages 4–6, $92 includes lessons, activities and lunch. Ski Camp, ages 6–14, $86 includes lessons, activities and lunch. Prices do not include lift ticket and rentals for kids 11 and older. For information on lessons, call 995-5743.

Lift tickets (2001/02 prices)

	Adult	Juniors (11-17)
One day	$56	$44
Three days	$162 ($54/day)	$132 ($44/day)
Five days	$260 ($52/day)	$220 ($44/day)

Who skis free: Two children (up to age 10) ski free per paying adult.

Who skis at a discount: 70 and older ski for half price. College students with ID can ride lifts at the junior rate.

Lift tickets work just like the computerized systems in the Alps.

Accommodations

Big Sky is divided into four areas—the Mountain Village, Moonlight Basin Ranch, the Meadow Village and the Canyon. The farther you are from the lifts, the less you generally pay. These areas are serviced by a free shuttle system during the winter. A good starting point is **Big Sky Central Reservations**, (800) 548-4486, which can book most of the lodging listed here.

In the Mountain Village:

At the center of the Mountain Village are the new **Summit at Big Sky** ($$$$), the **Shoshone Condominium Hotel** ($$$$) and **Huntley Lodge** ($$$–$$$$). The Summit is a ski-in/ski-out condo-hotel with one- to three-bedroom units, plus eight penthouses. If watching television from the whirlpool in your living room while a fireplace warms you is a dream come true, then cough up the dough to stay here. You won't regret it. The Shoshone is a luxury ski-in/ski-out condo-hotel with spacious rooms, kitchens, fireplaces and jetted tubs, plus a lap pool, health club, steam bath and more. The Huntley has an outdoor pool, two Jacuzzis, sauna, workout room, game room and more.

Mountain Village has many condo complexes, some of which are only a few years old. **Lone Moose Meadows** ($$$$) is one of the newer slopeside complexes. If you want luxury, try **Snowcrest, Beaverhead** and **Arrowhead Condominiums** with two to four bedrooms ($$$$). You'll find two- and three-bedroom units at **Skycrest** ($$$$), which also has underground parking, or try the more moderately priced **Stillwater** ($$–$$$$), which has studios and two-bedroom units.

The slopeside **Mountain Inn** (1-800-HOLIDAY; $$$–$$$$), part of the Holiday Inn Express chain, is scheduled to open for the 2001/02 winter season. It has 90 suites that sleep up to six people. Continental breakfast, pool, two hot tubs and exercise room.

Condo and home rental agencies with Mountain Village and Meadow Village properties include **ResortQuest of Big Sky** (800-548-4488; 995-4800) and **Big Sky Chalet Rentals** (800-845-4428; 995-2665).

In Moonlight Basin Ranch (1 mile from the Mountain Village):

The new and very upscale **Moonlight Lodge and Spa** (800-845-4428; 995-2665; $$$$) has four ski-in/ski-out penthouse suites, and is home base to the two- and three-bedroom **Saddle Ridge Townhomes** and two-bedroom log cabins in **Cowboy Heaven.** Restaurant, bar, full-service spa and outdoor rink at the lodge. Everything you need and more. Managed by East West Resorts.

In the Meadow Village (6 miles away):

River Rock Lodge (800-548-4488; 995-4800; $$–$$$$) is a "boutique-style European hotel" built of stone and log with beautiful interior decor. Continental breakfast included.

East West Resorts (800-845-4428; 995-2665) manages several condo complexes here, including **Hidden Village** ($$$$), units set in the forest with in-house Jacuzzis and garage, and **Park** ($$$–$$$$), with head-on views of Lone Peak. **ResortQuest of Big Sky** (800-548-4488; 995-4800) has many condos on the cross-country trail system.

In the Canyon (3 miles from the Meadow Village, in the beautiful Gallatin River Canyon, 9 miles from the lifts, serviced by the shuttle):

Buck's T-4 Lodge (800-822-4484; 995-4111; $$$–$$$$), Big Sky's Best Western hotel, has two pool-size outdoor Jacuzzis, a large stone fireplace and a restaurant that specializes in wild game (see *Dining*). Lodging and lift packages (including continental breakfast and a newspaper) are priced *per room*, with lower rates for single guests—something rare and welcome in a world that penalizes solo travelers.

The **Rainbow Ranch Lodge** (800-937-4132; 995-4132; $$–$$$$) is on the Gallatin River. A luxurious lodge with a western-ranch style with an good bar and restaurant.

The **Comfort Inn** (800-228-5150; 995-2333; $–$$) is new and clean, though it has little charm. Budget accommodations include the **Corral Motel** (995-4249; $) and the **Cinnamon Lodge** (995-4253; $), the latter with RV hookups for $15–$20.

Dining

In the Mountain Village:

The best dining on the mountain is found at **Peaks** (995-8000; $$–$$$) in the Summit. The menu is new western cuisine, the atmosphere is elegant casual. **Huntley Lodge** (995-5783; $$–$$$) is fine dining in a rustic setting. The breakfast buffet is excellent and the mountain views are hard to beat. We weren't impressed with dinner, but the Chocolate Bomb dessert was simply yummy. The restaurant has one of Montana's largest wine selections. In the Mountain Mall, **Dante's Inferno** (995-3999) has tableside slope views and Italian cuisine, and **M.R. Hummers** (995-4560) is known for its baby back ribs. **Black Bear Bar 'n' Grill** (995-2845) is a casual spot for breakfast or dinner.

Other lunch spots: **Mountain Top** for pizza, **Scissorbills Bar and Grill** at the base of Silverknife ski run, or **The Dug Out**, on Andesite Mountain, which has super barbecue.

In Moonlight Basin Ranch:

The Timbers (995-7777; $$$) at Moonlight Lodge is a new slopeside spot on the north face of Lone Mountain. The food is average, but the rustic lodge atmosphere with stuffed mountain goats clambering up the 37-foot stone fireplace is magnificent. Lunch is served here also; on warm sunny days, eat on the large outdoor deck.

In the Meadow Village:

Most of the restaurants we liked best are here. Intimate candlelight and linen service await you at **First Place** (995-4244), featuring gourmet cuisine and famous desserts. **Edelweiss** (995-4665) has excellent Austrian and German food. **Rocco's** (995-4200) has Mexican and Italian food. **Gallatin Gourmet Deli** (995-2314) is a great choice for a casual but very tasty lunch or dinner. For breakfast, try the **Huckleberry Cafe** (995-3130), which has the best reputation in town, or the **Blue Moon Bakery** (995-2305), also great for lunch.

Lone Mountain Ranch Dining Room (995-2782; $$–$$$) serves excellent meals in a quiet, smoke-free environment in rustic elegance. Sleigh-ride dinners are offered; call ahead as space is limited. There's Guinness on tap and terrific pesto pizza at **Uncle Milkies Pizza and Subs** (995-2900). **Allgoods Bar and Grill** (995-2750) serves hickory-smoked ribs, chicken, pork, homemade stews and burgers. It also has a pool table, darts and poker (legal in Montana).

In the Gallatin Canyon:

Buck's T-4 Restaurant (995-4111; $$$) is the area's oldest and most popular dining establishment. Its specialties are wild game, Montana beef, veal and seafood. There's an extensive wine list and an original rustic bar built in 1946. If you're staying at the mountain or the meadow, ride the free shuttle. **The Rainbow Ranch Lodge** (995-4132; $$–$$$) may be the best restaurant in the area, with elegant dining overlooking the Gallatin River. An imaginative menu focuses on wild game, fresh seafood, vegetarian and terrific salads.

Aprèss-ski/nightlife

Check the local paper, *The Lone Peak Lookout* for entertainment listings.

The hub of night activity is the Mountain Village. Happy hour kicks off in **Chet's Bar** in the Huntley Lodge, with the Crazy Austrian show (just go see it). Chet's also has poker games (legal in Montana). The **Carabiner** in the Summit is a wonderful place to relax with a drink. Mellow live entertainment provides background music you can talk and hear over. Other places to check out in the Mountain Village are **Lolo's**, **Dante's** and **Roosters**. In Moonlight Basin Ranch, **Timbers** has a great outside deck and ice rink, inside you'll find a beautiful rustic setting. In the Meadow Village, it's quieter, but **Rocco's** and **Allgoods Bar and Grill** are likely to attract crowds at night.

In the canyon, check out the **Buck's T-4** game room, with pool tables, foosball and video games. Locals like the **Corral** and **The Half Moon Saloon**, with darts and pool. Both are roadhouse-style Western bars.

 ## Other activities

Poker is legal gambling in Montana, and nightly games are available. Ask around if this is your kind of fun. Just about all of the other activities are of the outdoor variety.

Snowmobiling in Yellowstone National Park is a major attraction. Most snowmobile shops offer a 10 percent discount with a Big Sky lift ticket and provide bus service from the resort and West Yellowstone. For information: Rendezvous Snowmobile Rentals, (800) 426-7669 or 646-9564; Snowmobile Yellowstone, (800) 221-1151; Yellowstone Adventures, (800) 231-5991 or 646-7735; West Yellowstone, (800) 541-7354 or 646-9695. To snowmobile closer to Big Sky call Canyon Rentals (995-4540) a half a mile south of the Big Sky entrance.

Dogsled rides are offered by Spirit of the North Dog Adventures (995-4644), Lone Mountain Ranch (995-2783) or 320 Ranch (995-4283). **Dinner sleigh rides** are also available.

Winter fishing on the Gallatin River is available through Gallatin Riverguides (995-2290) or East Slope Anglers (995-4369), who have licenses, equipment rentals and supplies. **Yellowstone National Park** is a big attraction, and yes, it's open in winter. The drive south along Hwy. 191 follows the Gallatin River, where much of the fly-fishing, coming-of-age movie, "A River Runs Through It," was filmed.

Tough day on the mountain? There are several **full-service spas** on the mountain: Solace Spa at Big Sky (995-5803), in the Huntley/Shoshone complex, and The Moonlight Spa (995-7704) in the Moonlight Lodge.

The Huntley Lodge shows free **movies** in the amphitheater at night. If you have the opportunity to attend an **avalanche search and rescue demo** by the ski patrol and their dogs, don't miss it. It's fascinating, and someday these dogs just might save your life.

The Mountain Mall has **shops and boutiques.** Plum Logo has Montana-made gifts and Big Sky T-shirts and souvenirs. The Lone Spur in the Shoshone Condo complex is a good spot for high-quality western clothing, jewelry and gifts. In the Meadow Village, shop at Grizzly Outfitters, Willow Boutique and By Word of Mouth (great wine selection and prices). Moose Rack Books has new, out-of-print and rare books in two locations. If you're into taste-testing local yummies, look for anything made with huckleberries.

 ## Getting there and getting around

By air: Several airlines serve Bozeman Gallatin Field Airport, an hour from the resort. The 4X4 Stage shuttles passengers between the airport, the resort and West Yellowstone. Call 388-6404.

By car: The resort is 45 miles south of Bozeman (and 50 miles north of West Yellowstone) on Hwy. 191 along the Gallatin River.

Getting around: If you stay at the Mountain Village, a car is unnecessary unless you plan to do a lot of sightseeing. A free shuttlebus runs between the Big Sky villages 7 a.m.–11 p.m., starting in mid-December through the winter.

Montana regional resorts

Bridger Bowl, Bozeman, MT; (406) 587-2111
Internet: www.bridgerbowl.com
7 lifts; 1,000 acres; 2,000 vertical feet

Bridger Bowl is a funky, friendly ski area that offers some of the best steeps, narrows and radical chutes in Montana. Its non-profit status means it can offer some great skiing and riding at a low price. Experts can enjoy the upper mountain and hike the perilous Ridge and Fingers. Skiing and riding the Ridge and Fingers requires expert ability, an avalanche transceiver, shovel, partner and knowledge of the terrain. Those of a lower ability level and families can ski groomed intermediate and beginner cruisers on the lower mountain.

Bridger has yet to install a high-speed quad, but the existing lift system adequately handles weekend traffic from the nearby Montana State University town of Bozeman. Child care starts at 18 months.

Distance from Bozeman: About 16 miles north by Hwy. 86.

Lodging information: Bridger Bowl Vacations, (800) 223-9609.

Red Lodge Mountain Resort, Red Lodge, MT; (406) 446-2610 or (800) 444-8977
Internet: www.redlodgemountain.com
8 lifts; 1,600 acres; 2,400 vertical feet

Tucked in a valley in the Beartooth Mountain Range lies the quaint old mining town of Red Lodge. Red Lodge Mountain's Grizzly Peak, located 4 miles west of town, caters to families and skiers and riders who are intermediates and above. The mountain recently added 700 acres of terrain in the Cole Creek area, two high-speed quads and snowmaking. There's a terrain park with tabletops, rail slides, spines, a quarterpipe and more; at least every two weeks features are upgraded or changed. Affordable lodging and lift packages can be arranged with the mountain's reservations office.

Distance from Billings: About 65 miles west on I-90 and south on Hwy. 212 (no passes).

Lodging information: (800) 444-8977.

Montana Snowbowl, Missoula, MT; (406) 549-9777
Internet: www.montanasnowbowl.com
4 lifts; 950 skiable acres; 2,600 vertical feet

This virtually unknown Montana hangout has been called The Un-resort—untamed, ungroomed, unpretentious and undiscovered. It also had a reputation of being unforgiving and not easily mastered by the faint of heart. Beginners and intermediates may find much of the terrain beyond their abilities. This unusual area is a local favorite and attracts the college crowd from the University of Montana.

Distance from Missoula: About 12 miles.

Lodging information: Gelandesprung Lodge is a slopeside, European-style lodge with shared and private baths, hot tub and kitchen; (800) 728-2695 or (406) 549-9777. The resort's Web site has a listing of nearby lodging. Missoula Chamber of Commerce, (406) 543-6623.

Ski Apache

Ruidoso, New Mexico

Summit elevation: 11,500 feet
Vertical drop: 1,900 feet
Base elevation: 9,600 feet

Address: P.O. Box 220
Ruidoso, NM 88355
✆ **Area code:** 505
Ski area phone: 336-4356
Snow report: 257-9001
ⓘ **Toll-free reservations:**
(800) 253-2255 (Ruidoso Chamber)
Fax: 336-8327
Internet: www.skiapache.com (resort)
or www.ruidoso.net (town information)
Expert:★★
Advanced:★★★★
Intermediate:★★★
Beginner:★
Never-ever:★★

Number and types of lifts: 11–1 gondola,
2 quads, 5 triples, 1 doubles, 2 surface lifts
Skiable acreage: 750 acres
Snowmaking: 35 percent
Uphill capacity: 16,500 per hour
Snowboarding: Yes
Bed Base: 2,200+ in Ruidoso; 4,000 in Ruidoso area
Nearest lodging: 12 miles away in Ruidoso
Resort child care: See child care
Adult ticket, per day: $40–$43 (2000/01)

Dining:★ (on mountain) ★★★ (in Ruidoso)
Apres-ski/nightlife:★★★
Other activities:★★★

Ski Apache, where trails cruise through the pines of the Mescalero Apache Indian reservation, sits at the end of a dramatic access road high above the cowboy town of Ruidoso in south-central New Mexico. This is the southernmost major destination ski area in North America, only 120 miles north of the Mexican border.

The region with the town and the resort occupies an oasis of pine-covered mountains surrounded by the sprawling New Mexican desert. From the Lookout Snack Bar, at the top of the gondola, the panorama is one of the most expansive to be found at any ski resort in North America. The view takes in the White Sands National Monument, the site of the first atom bomb explosion, the forest where Smokey Bear was rescued and the Old West towns where Billy The Kid roamed.

Trail names echo the Apache heritage—Geronimo, Screaming Eagle, Chino and Ambush. Skiers from Texas, Germans from nearby Holloman Air Force Base, and Mexican visitors all mix with the Mescalero Indians who make the resort work. You'll find no condo developments and no ski-in/ski-out hotels at the ski area—this is a pure ski resort. The elevation between 9,600 and 11,500 feet guarantees snow and the location in southern New Mexico tempers the weather and favors plenty of sunny days.

Twelve miles from the snowfields of Ski Apache and about 5,000 feet below the sacred Sierra Blanca peak (12,003 feet), the town of Ruidoso spreads along a valley floor surrounded by gentle pines. This town is mainly a summer resort with the focus on Ruidoso Downs—home of quarter-horse racing, five golf courses and a full May-to-October program of music and cultural events. This makes winter the bargain time for most B&Bs, motels and hotels here.

Mountain layout—Skiing

Bounded by two ridges, Ski Apache is divided roughly in half by a third ridge that runs parallel to the boundary ridges. The area's gondola runs along the center ridge from the base to the summit. At the top of the area on trail-map left, expansive Apache Bowl has wide-open skiing from 11,500 feet with about 650 feet of vertical. Most of the rest of the slopes are off the center ridge, which has a long intermediate trail running along the crest with expert and intermediate trails dropping to trail-map right. The rest of the skiing is near the bottom of the left boundary ridge. Again, a blue cruiser snakes along the crest and black-diamond pitches fall toward the base area.

◆◆ **Expert** ◆ **Advanced:** Experts won't find much in the way of truly extreme terrain, but there are plenty of steep pitches and hidden glades. Nearly half of this area's trails are black diamonds. Try to do a non-stopper down Caliente or Mescalero for great leg burners. For bumps head to The Terrible and Incredible. Plan to be challenged. Navigate the lightest snow in the north facing glades off Game Trail down into Deep Freeze.

Apache Bowl and The Face (which drops into the bowl from the center ridge) offer great powder skiing when the conditions cooperate. Those who want to stay in the bowl can upload using a triple chair that allows them to stay right in the bowl without working their way back down to the base.

■ **Intermediate:** This is a great resort for intermediates looking to improve. The blues are mellow and the blacks reach some excellent pitches. For cruising, stick to the ridges, or take your first runs on Ambush, Chino or Meadows, to the right as you unload from the gondola. For showoff time, take a few zips along Capitan, the blue-square run that drops right to the base area—it is a joy. If you're ready to put yourself to the test, try making powder turns in Apache Bowl.

●● **Beginner:** Beginners have their own area served by Chair 7. Those shifting from beginner to intermediate should try Deep Freeze, Snowpark and Smokey Bear. Novices can even ride the gondola to the top and wind their way down over 2° miles on Sierra Blanca Trail to the base.

● **Never-ever:** The learning area is off Chairs 3 and 5 at the base. This area is fenced off so those taking first-time lessons are not subjected to more advanced skiers and snowboarders zipping through their classes.

Mountain layout—Snowboarding

Apache Bowl is a favorite spot when powder falls or is blown over the ridge. Do laps off the lift that exclusively serves the bowl, then toss in some variety by riding up The Face and dropping off the ridge trails. The terrain forms natural halfpipes at the base of The Face. Yee-haw, as the Texans would say! The area has an excellent rental program with more than 150 boards from Burton and Gnu.

Mountain rating

This is an intermediate's playground, but advanced levels won't be disappointed. Beginners will be pushed for all they're worth—the shift from mellow terrain to more significant steeps is a big one. Sometimes it's hard to tell the blues from blacks. They're both tough.

Cross-country and snowshoeing

There is no cross-country skiing and snowshoeing at this resort.

Lessons (2001/02 prices)

Group lessons: Adult ski and snowboard lessons start daily at 10:30 a.m. and 2 p.m. Cost is $30 for a morning or afternoon session and an additional $15 for a full day.

Never-ever package: A full-day skiing or snowboarding lesson and ticket for the beginner lift is $43; a half day is $30 (add $3 during holidays). Two-day programs including lifts costs $108 for adults ($115 holidays).

Private lessons: $56 for one hour; $33 for each additional person.

Racing: Ski Apache has NASTAR races on Smokey Bear on Saturdays and Sundays.

Child care (2001/02 prices)

Ski Apache does not offer child care for non-skiing children younger than 4; however, day care is available through **Tender Tots** (257-5784) in Ruidoso.

Children's lessons: Kiddie Korral takes 4- to 6-year-olds in an all-day instruction program including lunch and snow play. Cost is $81 with rentals; $71 without rentals (holiday rates are $4 more). Ski and snowboard lessons for children ages 7 and older start daily at 10:30 a.m. and 2 p.m. Cost is $30 for a morning or afternoon session and an additional $15 for a full day (lift ticket not included). First-time skiers and snowboarders ages 7 and older can take an all-day lesson for $43. The best buy for first-timers is two days of lessons, a lift ticket and rentals. For kids ages 12 and under, it's $109 for skiers, $127 for snowboarders; for kids 13 and older, it's $126 for skiers, $142 for snowboarders. Reservations are recommended for all kids' lessons, call 336-4356 ext. 111.

Lift tickets (2001/02 prices)

	Adult	Child (12 and younger)
One day	$43	$28
Three day	$120 ($40/day)	$78 ($26/day)

Who skis free: Ages 75 and older.

Who skis at a discount: Half-day prices during regular season are $30 for adults and $20 for kids.

Note: Holiday prices are $3 more per day.

Accommodations

The Inn of the Mountain Gods (257-5141; 800-545-9011; $$) is set on a lake in the midst of the Mescalero Apache Indian Reservation, operated by the tribe. Rooms are basic motel with upscale touches.

For luxury amidst beautiful art, head to the **Hurd Gallery & Guest Homes** (800-658-6912; 653-4331; $$$$) in San Patricio near the junction of Rtes. 70 and 380 or around 30 miles from Ruidoso. Spectacular lodging starts at $200 a night.

Best Western Swiss Chalet Inn (258-3333; 800-477-9477; $), perched above town, is one of the last lodges before the turnoff to the resort. Views from the restaurant are beautiful. **Hawthorn Suites** (800-527-1133; 258-5500; $$$), Ruidoso's newest lodging, features a variety of upscale suites next to the Convention Center and the Links Golf Course. **Enchantment Inn** (378-4051; 800-435-0280; $) is a full-service hotel. **Shadow Mountain**

Dining: $$$–Entrees $20+; $$–$10-20; $–less than $10.
Accommodations: (double room) $$$$–$200+; $$$–$141-$200; $$–$81-$140; $–$80 and less.

Lodge (257-4886; 800-441-4331; $) is designed for couples with king-size beds, fireplaces and hot tubs. **Holiday Inn Express** (257-3736; 800-257-5477, $) includes breakfast.

Casa del Cocinero (336-7815; 800-360-3500) is very intimate with only three rooms—one with private hot tub—and a self-contained casita, or cabin. **Condotel** (800-545-9017; 258-5200; $$) has a large inventory of two- to six-bedroom condos and private homes that can be viewed on the Web at ww.ruidosoreservations.com.

Dining

The best meals in town seem to be found at **La Lorraine** (257-2954;$–$$) for French cuisine; the **Dan Li Ka** (257-5141; $–$$) at the Inn of the Mountain Gods for the finest in American cuisine; and **The Deck House** (257-3496; $–$$) for Mexican and American fare. **The Cattle Baron** (257-9355; $$) is the best place to head for steaks. **The Texas Club** (258-3325; $–$$) also serves great steaks and all-American fare.

Tinnies Silver Dollar (653-4425; $$) provides dining with a step back in time about 3 miles toward Roswell from the junction of Rtes. 70 and 380, or about 30 miles from Ruidoso. The yesteryear dining rooms are lined with paintings harking back to the Old West or showcasing the Hurd/Wyeth family art. **Spanky's** (354-2234; $$) in nearby Capitan, serves wonderful gourmet meals that belies it's name. Both are worth the drive.

Cafe Rio (257-7746; $–$$) on downtown's main drag serves a curious Mediterranean mixture (Italian, Portuguese, Greek) of pizza, pasta, soups and seafood in diner-like surroundings. **Chef Lupe's** (257-4687) has great Mexican food in a casual setting. **Ahna-Michelle's** (258-3333; $$) at the Best Western serves a Friday night Old Country German buffet and Saturday night prime rib in a Swiss atmosphere. **La Fuente** (257-0814) and **Casa Blanca** (257-2495; $) offers Tex-Mex and margaritas. **Farley's** (258-5676; $) has a good western family atmosphere with fajitas, burgers and pizzas. **Circle J Bar-B-Que** (257-4105; $) claims the best "homecooked BBQ." The **Inncredible Restaurant** (336-4312; $–$$) has been serving folk for three decades, so they must be doing something right. **Michelena's Italian Restaurant** (257-5753; $–$$) has good pasta and pizza with takeout.

For breakfast, we suggest **The Deck House Restaurant** (257-3496), **Denny's** (378-1389) and the **Log Cabin** (258-5029).

Après-ski/nightlife

Ruidoso is a great nightlife town. The Western flavor is strong and can't be beat at **W.P.S. (Win, Place and Show)** where you can dance the two-step and drink beer into the wee hours. This place is a blast.

Across the street from WPS is **Quarters**, a rock'n'roll and blues bar. Top up-and-coming southwestern talent plays here. It's a world of difference from WPS.

The Inn of the Mountain Gods has that age-old American pastime, gambling. You'll also find blackjack tables, roulette wheels and slot machines at **Casino Apache. The Billy the Kid Casino** is next door to the race track and has hundreds of slots, a grand bar and big buffet dinners.

Other activities

The added activities in the Ruidoso area make this far more than simply a ski vacation. Ruidoso has Western history, a fine museum, an extraordinary center for the performing arts and plenty of special events.

The **Hubbard Museum of the American West** (378-4142) encompasses the Museum of the Horse with horse art and thousands of artifacts from old carriages to wagons.

Spencer Theater for the Performing Arts (www.spencertheater.com; 336-0010; 888-818-7872) is stunning, rising dramatically from the plain. Examples of the ambitious world-class programs are singer Jack Jones, the Jimmy Dorsey Orchestra, and the Russian Ballet.

In nearby Capitan, visit the **Smokey Bear Historical State Park** where you'll see a display about forest fire prevention and pay a visit to Smokey Bear's grave.

The entire region is dotted with sites linked with **Billy the Kid and Pat Garrett**.

Getting there and getting around

By air: Fly into Albuquerque, about a three-hour drive away; or El Paso, about two hours. A shuttle service runs from El Paso (257-4948). Twice-daily air service is provided by Rio Grande Air (336-8111) from Albuquerque to Ruidoso.

By car: Ski Apache and Ruidoso are about halfway between Roswell and Socorro on U.S. Hwy. 380. The resort is 180 miles from Albuquerque and 130 miles from El Paso.

Getting around: You will need a car. A town shuttle takes skiers to the mountain once a day (early morning/late afternoon) or by reservation. Call 336-1683 or 877-903-7483.

Ski Santa Fe

New Mexico

Summit elevation: 12,000 feet
Vertical drop: 1,650 feet
Base elevation: 10,350 feet

Address: 2209 Brothers Road, #220
Santa Fe, NM 87505
☏ **Area code:** 505
Ski area phone: 982-4429
Snow report: 983-9155
ⓘ **Toll-free reservations:** (877) 737-7366
Within New Mexico:747-5557
Fax: 986-0645
E-mail: info@skisantafe.com
Internet: www.skisantafe.com
Expert: ★ ★
Advanced: ★ ★ ★
Intermediate: ★ ★ ★
Beginner: ★ ★ ★ ★
Never-ever: ★ ★ ★

Number and types of lifts: 7–1 high-speed
quad, 1 triple, 2 doubles, 3 surface lifts
Acreage: 550
Snowmaking: 50 percent
Uphill capacity: 7,800 skiers per hour
Snowboarding: Yes
Bed base: 5,500 in Santa Fe
Nearest lodging: About 15 miles away
Resort child care: Yes, 3 months and older
Adult ticket, per day: $38-$43 (2001/02)

Dining: ★ ★ ★ ★ ★
Apres-ski/nightlife: ★ ★
Other activities: ★ ★ ★ ★

At Ski Santa Fe, snow-covered trails curl through towering Ponderosa pines in the Sangre de Cristo mountains, only 16 miles from the city of Santa Fe, the very heart of Southwestern style. When you take the bright sunlight of the high desert, fresh powder snow and a skier-friendly mountain, then add pre-Columbian Indian Pueblos, Spanish architecture, art galleries and top it with a renowned regional cuisine, you have the savory mix that makes up a unique ski vacation.

Santa Fe (elevation 7,000 feet) offers interesting contradictions. It is old and new, high mountains and flat desert, with cool winters that surprise out-of-staters who think of New Mexico as hot and dry. Skiing in this state is unlike anywhere else on the continent. To get a more foreign-feeling ski vacation, you'd need a passport.

Some skiers think Taos Ski Valley is the only New Mexico ski area worth a long plane ride—not so. If your main interest is racking up vertical feet, then by all means head for Taos, but Santa Fe (just an hour north of Albuquerque) is a better destination for those who prefer a balanced ski-and-sightseeing vacation. Santa Fe is one of the most culturally fascinating cities in the United States. It is loaded with great restaurants, superior art galleries, a variety of activities, and the ski area is a lot bigger than most people imagine.

Founded by Spanish conquistadors in 1610, 10 years before the pilgrims landed in Plymouth, Santa Fe is North America's oldest capital city. It is rich in history and culture, but of a different kind from mining-town ski areas.

When the Spanish arrived, the area was already populated with 100,000 Native Americans, who spoke nine languages and lived in some 70 multi-storied adobe pueblos, some still inhabited today. For the next 150 years Santa Fe grew as a frontier military base and trading center, where Spanish soldiers and missionaries, Anglo mountain men and Native Americans mixed. In 1846, during the Mexican War, New Mexico was ceded to the United States. Santa Fe, at the end of the Santa Fe Trail, became a frontier town, hosting the likes of Billy the Kid and Kit Carson.

In the early part of this century, Santa Fe took on a new flavor. It became a magnet for men and women of the arts and literature. D.H. Lawrence, Ezra Pound, Willa Cather, Jack London and H.L. Mencken either lived or vacationed here. Artists Edward Hopper and Marsden Hartley spent time here, and Santa Fe was home to Robert Henri, George Bellows, Randall Davey and Aaron Copland. Today this city of 60,000 people is home to one of the world's premier art colonies.

 ## Mountain layout—Skiing

Ski Santa Fe sits 16 miles north of the city. Though the mountain is known as a day-area destination for Santa Fe and Albuquerque skiers, out-of-town visitors will find a surprising amount of terrain. All the mountain amenities such as restaurants, ski rentals, child care, ski school and ticket sales are at the base of the mountain just a few steps from the parking lot.

◆◆ **Expert** ◆ **Advanced:** For the most part, the mountain's expert terrain is to the left of the Tesuque Peak chair. With fresh snow, locals go first to Columbine, Big Rocks and Wizard. These runs all check in as very steep and are for advanced skiers only. Roadrunner is the expert bump run directly under the Tesuque chair. Tequila Sunrise and Easter Bowl have the best glade skiing. On the far side of the mountain, reached by the Santa Fe Super Chief quad, Muerte and Defasio have isolated trail skiing for advanced skiers.

While there are hopes to overcome environmental objections and put in a lift in the Big Tesuque Bowl, for the moment the intrepid ski into this area via Cornice. (Once skiers leave Cornice, they are outside the ski area's permitted boundary.) Big Tesuque skiers find natural powder, bowl skiing and trees. The bowls empty onto the area's entrance road, 3 miles below the base area, leaving you to hitchhike back up. First-timers should go with a local who knows this area: It's genuine backcountry, it's big and people occasionally get lost.

■ **Intermediate:** On a fresh powder day (once a week on average), local intermediates and advanced skiers head straight for the Tesuque Peak triple chair, up to 12,000 feet and the top of the mountain. To the right of the lift (as the trail map reads) is Gayway, a glorious, groomed pitch with several spicy turns that gives new meaning to the term "spectacular scenery." On a clear day, you almost get the feeling of flying, thanks to the 150-mile vista as the trail drops away. Parachute, which parallels Gayway, is a groomed black diamond with a somewhat steeper pitch. On the far side of the mountain, reached by the Santa Fe Super Chief quad, Middle and Lower Broadway have isolated trail skiing for intermediate skiers.

●● **Beginner:** This level will be happiest on the lower part of the mountain, on the wide boulevard of Easy Street. Advanced-beginners will find more challenges and a slightly steeper pitch on Open Slope and Upper and Lower Midland. If you're feeling adventurous, try Lower Burro for an exhilarating, winding trip through the trees on a mild pitch.

● **Never-ever:** Good terrain at the mountain's base served by Pine Flats lift is protected by snowfences. For children Chipmunk Corner lift provides a tucked-away learning area.

Mountain layout—Snowboarding

Generally speaking, the mountain's expert terrain is to the left of the Tesuque Peak chair. After a dump, locals go first to Columbine, Big Rocks and Wizard—all very steep and for advanced riders only. Tequila Sunrise and Easter Bowl have the best glades. Hike to the Big Tesuque Bowl via Cornice for freshies, bowl skiing and trees (once you leave Cornice, you're outside the ski area's permitted boundary). The bowls empty onto the area's entrance road, 3 miles below the base area, and you have to hitchhike back up. Go with a local who knows this area: It's genuine backcountry, it's big and it's easy to get lost.

On a fresh powder day (about once a week), local intermediates head straight for the Tesuque Peak triple chair and the top of the mountain. To the right of the lift (as the trail map reads) is Gayway, a glorious, groomed pitch with several spicy turns that gives new meaning to the term "spectacular scenery." On a clear day, you almost get the feeling of flying, thanks to the 150-mile vista as the trail drops away.

Beginners will be happiest on the lower part of the mountain, on the wide boulevard of Easy Street. Advanced-beginners will find more challenges and a slightly steeper pitch on Open Slope and Upper and Lower Midland. If you're feeling adventurous, try Lower Burro for an exhilarating, winding trip through the trees on a mild pitch.

Depending on conditions, Santa Fe opens an "alternative terrain" area for snowboarders.

Mountain rating

Many people think Ski Santa Fe is a small, gentle day area. It's not. It definitely has enough terrain to keep a skier of any level happy for two to three days. Its glades are great, though short; and Big Tesuque Bowl, when skiable, is an adventure. Santa Fe has a nice beginner area isolated by snowfences. Combined with Santa Fe's outstanding sightseeing opportunities, this is an excellent destination for skiers who don't want to be on the mountain every day (or all day). One warning: Ski Santa Fe has one of the highest lift-served elevations in the nation—12,000 feet on top, 10,350 feet at the base. If you're susceptible to altitude problems, take note.

Cross-country and snowshoeing

Santa Fe has no groomed or tracked trails. However, there are maintained backcountry trails in the **Santa Fe National Forest.** Aspen Vista Road, 2 miles below the ski area, is a popular and moderately difficult 7-mile trail. Black Canyon Campground, 8 miles up the ski road, is a popular area for beginners. Maps and information on conditions in the Santa Fe National Forest are available from the National Forest Service at 988-6940. For ski area information only, call 982-5300.

Lessons (2001/02 prices)

Group lessons: Adult lessons cost $30. A second session on the same day only costs an extra $18.

Never-ever package: Two group lessons, beginner lift and rentals is $58 for skiers, $75 for snowboarders.

Private lessons: $63 per hour; discounts for multiple hours.

Special programs: Among them are a women's program, classes for ages 50 and older, mogul clinics, telemark lessons and powder workshops. Call the ski school, 982-4429.

Racing: Coin-op and NASTAR Thursday through Sunday. Racing clinics available.

Child care (2001/02 prices)

Ages: 3 months to 3 years.

Costs: All-day program costs $56; $40 half day; $12 per hour.

Reservations: Required; call 988-9636. Only full-day packages for child care are sold during holiday periods. Ages 3 and 4 who are completely toilet-trained can register for Snowplay, a program that is "an introduction to the skiing environment." This program, which includes indoor and outdoor activities, is $62 all day and $46 half day.

Children's lessons: Ages 4–9, all day including lunch and lift ticket, $62 (add $12 for rental equipment). Half-day programs are $46. Four-year-olds have a morning lesson with play activities in the afternoon; others have lessons in both morning and afternoon.

Lift tickets (2001/02 prices)

	Adult	Teen (13-20)	Child (Up to 12)
One day	$43	$36	$31
Three days	$120 ($40+/day)	$100 ($33+/day)	$86 ($28+/day)
Five days	$191 ($38+/day)	$160 ($32/day)	$138 ($27+/day)

Who skis free: Skiers age 72 and older and kids shorter than 46 inches in ski boots.

Who skis at a discount: A ticket valid only on the beginner lift is $22. Ages 62–71 pay the child rate.

Accommodations

Ski Santa Fe has no base lodging, but even if it did, you'd want to be in Santa Fe for dining, shopping and the museums. More than 70 hotels, motels, inns, condominiums and B&Bs serve Santa Fe visitors. Winter is low season in this region, but the increase of visitors trying to take advantage of this have actually caused prices to rise from bargain to a moderate level during the past few years. Expect to pay about $75–$110 a day, per person, for a ski-stay package at one of the many hotels on Cerrillos Road and 25 to 50 percent more downtown.

Lift-and-lodging packages are the best deal; call **Santa Fe Central Reservations** at (800) 776-7669 or 983-8200 or the **Santa Fe Visitors Bureau** at (800) 777-2489 (777-CITY). Downtown is where the best restaurants, shopping and nightlife are concentrated, although we do recommend a few great dining options outside the Plaza area.

Hotel Loretto (800-727-5531; 988-5531; $$$) is Santa Fe's ultimate pueblo-style hotel. It was completely restored in 1998 and provides fabulous rooms only steps from the Plaza. Spacious rooms have traditional New Mexican decor with carved wood furnishings and authentic Native American art. **La Fonda Hotel** (800-523-5002; 982-5511; $$$–$$$$) is the historic place to stay. An inn of one sort or another has been on this site for 300 years (Billy the Kid worked in the kitchen here washing dishes). The current La Fonda incarnation was built in the 1920s. If you don't stay, at least stroll through and take a look—they don't make them like this anymore.

The way they make them now is across the Plaza from La Fonda. **The Inn of the Anasazi** (800-688-8100 or 988-3030; $$$–$$$$) is the politically correct place to stay. The hotel's restaurants use vegetables grown by local organic farmers. Leftovers are given to a homeless shelter and everything is recycled. The Southwestern decor and furnishings are immaculate. The dining room is very pleasant and the menu selections enjoyable; however, this is also a very expensive place to stay.

Next door, the **Hotel Plaza Real** (800-279-7325 or 988-4900; $$$) is convenient and comfortable. Of the 56 hotel units, 44 are suites with fireplaces. An ample continental breakfast is included. We also enjoyed the adobe **Inn on the Alameda** (800-506-9206 or 984-2121; $$$) which is handy to Canyon Road and offers a continental breakfast. In a village of adobe cottages, most featuring their own Indian kiva fireplaces, **La Posada de Santa Fe** (800-727-5276 or 986-0000; $$–$$$), just restored, is a short walk from the Plaza. On the grounds is the Staab House, a Victorian mansion serving as the restaurant.

Excellent B&Bs are **Adobe Abode** (983-3133; $$$–$$$$), **Alexander's Inn** (986-1431; $$–$$$), the spacious **Dancing Ground of the Sun** (800-645-5673 or 986-9797; $–$$$), the **Grant Corner Inn** (983-6678; $$), the intimate **Inn of the Animal Tracks** (988-1546; $$) and the classy **Water Street Inn** (984-1193; $$–$$$).

Other accommodations to consider are the historic **Hotel St. Francis** (800-529-5700 or 983-5700; $$), the **Hilton of Santa Fe** (800-336-3676 or 988-2811; $$$) and the **Hotel Santa Fe** (800-825-9876 or 982-1200; $–$$$), partly owned by the Picuris Pueblo. Families should try the **El Rey Inn** (800-521-1349 or 982-1931; $$–$$$), **Garrett's Desert Inn** (800-888-2145 or 982-1851; $$), the **Campanilla Compound** condominiums (800-828-9700 or 988-7585; $$$), and the **Otra Vez** condos (988-2244; $$–$$$). **El Dorado** (800-955-4455 or 988-4455; $$–$$$$) is the city's largest hotel with 219 rooms.

The closest lodging to the ski area is **Fort Marcy Hotel Suites** (800-745-9910; $–$$) just off the ski area road. They have 80 condominiums from one to three rooms and are only four blocks from the Plaza.

Many of the chain hotels, such as **Comfort Inn** ($$), **Days Inn** ($), **Holiday Inn** ($$) and **Hampton Inn** ($) have adopted the local adobe architectural style and are a little less expensive and conveniently located on Cerillos Road which makes them handy for getting to the ski area but out of walking range for downtown.

Dining

On the mountain, skiers have two choices. **La Casa Cafeteria** in the base lodge called La Casa Mall, and **Totemoff's Bar and Grill** at the base of the Tesuque Peak Chair. La Casa, with a French chef, offers a variety of options including a pasta bar and a daily special such as fresh salmon with lemon tarragon. Its breakfast burrito is wicked good, but only for brave palates. Totemoff's features burgers, salads, pasta, cocktails and a sun deck.

Back in the city, Santa Fe cooks and you're in for a treat. Including fast food, Santa Fe has nearly 200 places to strap on the feed bag. From traditional New Mexican cuisine to steaks and seafood, Santa Fe has more food variety than you could consume in a year and far more good restaurants than we have room to recommend.

Two main hotel restaurants shouldn't be missed. We recommend the spectacular dining room at **La Fonda, La Plazuela** (992-5511; $$$). Breakfast lets you enjoy the colorful dining room for more reasonable prices. We also highly recommend **Nellie's** (984-7915; $$) in the Hotel Loretto only steps from the Plaza. The food is surprisingly reasonable in price and delightfully inventive (such as bourbon- glazed veal chop or coriander-grilled sea bass).

Everyone recommends the **Coyote Cafe** (132 W. Water St.; 983-1615; $$$). The main dining room has a fixed-price menu and modern Southwestern cuisine; those in the bar can order à la carte. **Pasqual's** (121 Don Gaspar; 983-9340; $$$) is great for breakfast, but it's good anytime for delicious and beautifully presented New Mexican cuisine. Call for dinner reservations or expect to wait a long time. If you want to meet people, ask to be seated at the communal table. **La Casa Sena** (125 East Palace Ave.; 988-9232; $$$) is tastefully Continental. Don't miss the adjacent **Cantina** ($$), where waiters and bartenders sing cabaret between food and drinks. If you want to nibble tapas instead of dinner, this is the place to do it. **Julian's** (221 Shelby; 988-2355; $$$) is very upscale Italian, recommended by locals. **The Palace** (142 W. Palace Ave.; 982-9891; $$$) is a re-creation of a famous San Francisco eatery. This is Santa Fe's power lunch spot. It has been run for years by a trio of Italian brothers and offers respite from the pervasive Southwestern cooking. They also operate the more informal **Osteria d'Assissi** (58 S. Federal Pl.; 986-5858; $).

Some moderately priced restaurants are **Maria's New Mexican Kitchen** (555 W. Cordova Rd.; 983-7929; $), where you'll probably meet the affable owner Al Lucero, who wrote Maria's Real Margarita Book featuring history and recipes of the more than 50 "real" margaritas served in the restaurant. Robert Redford, a frequent customer when he's in town, wrote the foreword. The food is wonderful also, especially the posole and green chile stew.

The Pink Adobe (406 Old Santa Fe Trail; 983-7712; $$) is Santa Fe's oldest restaurant, a local favorite and sometimes difficult to even get reservations (which are necessary) for. They specialize in New Mexican and Creole foods. Prices are moderate to expensive. Next door, The Dragon Room is a favorite of locals and visitors alike for cocktails.

Cowgirl Hall of Fame (319 S. Guadalupe; 928-2565; $–$$) is what the name implies with authentic Texas-style barbecue, kid's menu and play area; plus fine dining at the attached Mustang Grill. Don't hestitate to join the tourists at **The Ore House** (upstairs at 50 Lincoln Ave.; 983-8687; $$) on the Plaza for free après-ski snacks. On Canyon Road, **Celebrations** (613 Canyon Rd.; 989-8904; $$) is in the heart of gallery row and is jammed at lunchtime. **Tomasita's Cafe** (500 S. Guadalupe; 983-5721; $) is fast food with a twist. Portions are large, service is friendly, and it's a favorite of Santa Fe families, so be prepared to wait. It is inexpensive, and has some of the best New Mexican fare in town.

The Plaza Restaurant (54 Lincoln; 982-1664; $) is a throwback to diner days; regulars swear everything is good and very affordable. **Zia Diner** (326 South Guadalupe; 988-7008; $) is an easy 15-minute walk from the Plaza and features All-American favorites (New Mexican style, of course) such as meat loaf stuffed with piñon nuts, basic pastas and soups. **Atomic Grill** (103 E. Water St.; 820-2866; $) serves wood-fired pizza, pastas and hamburgers together with about 80 bottled beers. There's take-out and delivery too.

 ## Après-ski/nightlife

Santa Fe has the usual live bands, bars and places to dance. But it has some unusual off-slope activities as well. To work out the kinks of a fresh powder day, stop at **Ten Thousand Waves** (988-1047, 982-9304) for a relaxing hot tub under the stars. About 3 miles from the Plaza and on the road from the ski area, it's a Japanese-style hot tub resort not to be missed.

For elegant après-ski (you can go in ski clothes), head for **Inn of the Anasazi** or **La Posada,** both close to the Plaza. In Santa Fe, a wonderful place to mix dinner with entertainment is at **La Cantina** (988-9232) in the historic Sena Plaza, a stately adobe built as a family home in the 1860s. The restaurant features New Mexican specialties and singing waiters and waitresses. For about $20, you can eat, drink and hear an exceptional dinner theater show, belted out between courses. Children are welcome, reservations a must.

Dining: $$$-Entrees $20+; $$-$10-20; $-less than $10.
Accommodations: (double room) $$$$-$200+; $$$-$141-$200; $$-$81-$140; $-$80 and less.

The **Catamount Bar & Grill** (125 E. Water St.; 988-7222) is a sports bar teeming with locals and tourists featuring big-screen TV, pool tables and specials like "Jägermeister Night."

Other activities

The **museums** in Santa Fe are first rate. Buy a three-day pass for $10, which will admit you to four of the best: the Museum of International Folk Art (strong in Spanish art of the area), the Palace of the Governors (for local history), the Museum of Indian Arts and Culture, and the Museum of Fine Arts. All are free on Fridays. The Georgia O'Keefe Museum has its on entry fees.

You should consider **touring** the eight Indian pueblos near Santa Fe. The San Ildefonso Pueblo, famous for its distinctive pottery style, is the most scenic. Its annual festival to honor its patron saint is in late January and features traditional clothing and dances. If you have a car, and especially if you are driving north on U.S. Hwy. 84/285 to Taos, be sure and take the Hwy. 503 turnoff at Pojoaque and drive east to Chimayo, site of the Santuario de Chimayo, famous for its dirt thought to have healing powers. At the end of the church parking lot, you'll find Leona's, a funky little walk-up where the tamale pie and burritos are exceptional. On the way to Taos you wind through foothills and into high mountain Hispanic villages like Truchas and Las Trampas. For beautiful woven blankets, stop at Ortega's in Chimayo, where family members still practice a craft brought to New Mexico in the 1600s by their ancestors.

An initial warning: It will be much cheaper to ski all day than venture into Santa Fe's many tempting **shops** and **galleries.** That warning given, more than 200 galleries feature Native American crafts and art, as well as fine art on a par with galleries in New York, Florence or Paris. On weekends, you can find bargains and excellent workmanship when local artisans sell their wares on blankets in front of the 390-year-old Palace of the Governors, a long-standing Santa Fe shopping tradition.

Canyon Road is the world-famous strip of galleries featuring wonderful art of all styles, for all tastes. The walk from the Plaza area is pleasant. The Waxlander Gallery features wonderful pastel still-life works of J. Alex Potter. Our favorite is Nedra Matteucci's Fenn Galleries, 1075 Paseo de Peralta, just south of Canyon Road. The day we visited, we counted four Zuniga sculptures starting at $80,000 each. Don't miss the garden.

For about $10 a day, the 19,000-square-foot **Santa Fe Spa,** 786 N. St. Francis Dr. (984-8727), has state-of-the-art exercise equipment, a heated indoor lap pool, massage staff, free child care and more. Also check out **Fitness Plus,** for women only, at 473-7315.

Call the **Santa Fe Visitors Bureau** (955-6200; 800-777-2489) for more information on these and other activities.

Getting there and getting around

By air: Albuquerque has the nearest major airport, 60 miles away. Private pilots can use the Santa Fe Regional Airport.

By car: Santa Fe is north of Albuquerque on I-25, an easy hour's drive. The ski area is 16 miles from town on Hwy. 475.

Getting around: Getting around Santa Fe and to and from the ski area is difficult without a car, though a shuttle service is available from the airport to major hotels and to the ski area. The airport in Albuquerque has the leading rental car agencies. For shuttles from the airport in Albuquerque to Santa Fe, call 982-4311. For information on the Santa Fe Ski Shuttle from the town to the ski area, call 820-7541.

Taos

with Red River and Angel Fire
New Mexico

Summit elevation: 11,819 feet
Vertical drop: 2,612 feet
Base elevation: 9,207 feet

Taos Ski Valley

Address: Box 90,
Taos Ski Valley, NM 87525
✆ Area code: 505
Ski area phone: 776-2291
Snow report: 776-2916 **Fax:** 776-8596
ⓘ **Toll-free reservations:** (800) 776-1111;
(800) 821-2437
E-mail: tsv@skitaos.org
Internet: http://skitaos.org/
Expert: ★★★★★
Advanced: ★★★★★
Intermediate: ★★★★
Beginner: ★★ **Never-ever:** ★

Number of lifts: 12–4 quad chairs,
1 triple chair, 5 double chairs, 2 surface lifts
Percent snowmaking: 46 percent
Uphill capacity: 15,000 per hour
Total acreage: 1,096 acres terrain, 687 acres trails
Snowboarding: No
Bed Base: 3,705 at base and in town **Nearest**
lodging: slopeside; hotels, condos
Resort child care: Yes, 6 weeks and older
Adult ticket, per day: $41-$45 (00/01 prices)
Dining (Including town): ★★★★
Apres-ski/nightlife: ★★
Other activities: ★★★

Northern New Mexico has some of the best skiing to be found in the United States. Taos has long been legendary for its steeps and deep powder, and nearby Red River and Angel Fire both offer excellent and different ski experiences. Most of the information in this chapter concentrates on Taos, which is a true destination resort, but we'll also give you a flavor of Red River and Angel Fire (see *Nearby Resorts* at end of chapter).

Taos Ski Valley is a little piece of the Alps, founded by a Swiss native and surrounded by hotels and restaurants built by Frenchmen and Austrians. It's near the town of Taos, which is a rich mix of Spanish and Indian cultures, blended over the centuries to produce the Southwestern style.

Taos Ski Valley holds another distinction: While many resorts walk a delicate marketing tightrope, touting whatever expert terrain they possess while trying not to scare anyone off, Taos enjoys its tough reputation. It wisely advises visitors to meet the challenge by enrolling in Ski-Better-Week, a package of lessons, accommodations, meals and lift tickets. Just about everybody staying at the mountain enrolls in ski school. If you aren't part of a class, you feel like the kid that didn't get chosen for the baseball team. Après-ski talk centers on Ski-Better-Week anecdotes, leaving independents to sit at the bar with little to add to the discussion.

The town of Taos is 18 miles from the Taos Ski Valley. Long a haven for artists, the town has galleries, shops, restaurants and hotels ranging from luxurious to pedestrian.

Mountain layout—Skiing

Taos has something for everyone in the intermediate, advanced and expert levels. Every good skier will be challenged every day.

◆◆ **Expert:** For tree skiers, Taos has a special challenge, the twin runs Castor and Pollux. They hardly look like runs, just steep wooded parts of the mountain, unskiable, where some joker put a sign that looks just like a trail marker. The trees are 2 to 15 feet apart, and advanced classes regularly train here.

Powder skiing lasts on Highline Ridge and Kachina Peak, for two reasons: They are double-black diamonds and Kachina Peak is reachable only after an hour-and-fifteen-minute hike from the top chair at 11,800 feet to the ridge at 12,500 feet. You can, however, ski off Highline Ridge and West Basin Ridge after only a 15-minute hike. Skiers are advised to go with an instructor or a patroller; at the very least, they must check in with the patrol at the top of Chair 6. The ski patrol will give you a rough screening to see if you can handle the double-diamond terrain. In any case you must ski the ridge with a partner.

◆ **Advanced:** An advanced skier won't be disappointed. All of the tree skiing is an effort and the black-diamond trails are as advertised. Hunziker, isolated by a short climb, provides good bumps that narrow about halfway down the trail. Otherwise test yourself on some of the off-trail skiing dropping from the ridges.

■ **Intermediate:** Taos has a lot of terrain at this level. Smooth bowls are found off the Kachina quad chair. Other good intermediate terrain is under Chairs 7 and 8. Anything marked as a blue trail is a blast, with plenty of length for cruising. Some at this level may feel pushed; if you're in that group, go ski the greens for a while and keep your head held high. Better yet, sign up for a class.

●● **Beginner:** Taos has some nice beginner terrain, such as Honeysuckle, which descends the skier's right side of the ridge. Bonanza and Bambi give beginners a way down on the other side of the ridge. The main problem is negotiating either White Feather or Rubezahl when they are crowded with skiers coming back into the village. Despite the slow-down efforts of ski hosts stationed every 20 feet or so, both runs resemble the Hollywood Freeway at rush hour, except that the faster skiers aren't stalled in traffic. They zip around the slower ones, who are gingerly wedging their way home. On busy days it's a mess. Timing is important: Come down early, or better yet, be one of the last to descend.

● **Never-ever:** Only athletic novices should attempt to learn here. Despite the highly regarded ski school, the jump from the tiny learning area to the mountain is enormous. Better learning terrain is at nearby Angel Fire or Red River.

Mountain layout—Snowboarding

Snowboarding is not permitted. Head to Angel Fire or Red River.

Mountain rating

Fifty-one percent of Taos' runs are rated expert, and half of the expert runs are double-black diamonds. True experts will be thrilled with the skiing off Highline Ridge and Kachina as well as the narrow chutes off West Basin Ridge. Intermediates will have a field day with great steep cruising. Beginners will be limited and never-evers terrified.

Rise up to meet Taos' challenge. If you normally ski blue runs at other resorts, you can ski Taos. It may be tough at first, but persist—you'll catch on. Taos can be an extremely rewarding ski experience *because* of its challenge. The runs demand you give it your best.

 ## Lessons (2001/02 prices)

Group lessons: Two hours, morning or afternoon, $37. Some lessons at Taos concentrate on specific skills, such as moguls or telemarking.

Never-ever package: Novice-lift ticket, 4.5-hour lesson and rentals for $60; two days cost $100.

Private lessons: For up to four skiers, costs are $95 for an hour, $140 for two hours, $215 for a half day, and $360 for a full day.

Special programs: Ski Better Weeks are the core of the Taos ski experience, developed by former French Junior Alpine champion and ski school technical director Jean Mayer. Participants are matched for five or six mornings of intensive lessons, and they ski with the same instructor all week. Sixty-five percent of the participants are intermediate or higher.

Ski Week costs $244 (low season) and $450 (high season) for six days. Many lodging properties offer the Ski Better Week as a package with meals and accommodations.

Super Ski Week is an intense course for adults who wish to focus seriously on improving their skills. Skiers are analyzed, videotaped and put through what amounts to a mini ski-racing camp every morning and afternoon for a total of five hours. This is not a program for the timid or late-night party types, but most will find their skills much improved by the end of the week. It's offered at selected times for $682–$692, depending on the season. There are Ski Week programs for women, teens and for ages 50 and older at select times during the season.

Taos Ski Valley also has shorter programs that concentrate on specifics, such as Moguls or Extreme Weekends, designed to aid advanced and expert skiers; and Women's Weekends.

Child care (2001/02 prices)

Ages: Ages 6 weeks to 2 years.
Costs: Full day including lunch and snacks is $59. Toddlers get indoor activities and snow play.

Reservations: Required; call 776-2291. There is one staffer for every two infants.

Children's lessons: The Kinderkäfig children's center is unfortunately an inconvenient distance from the main base area. A two-hour morning lesson, lunch and afternoon supervised skiing for ages 3–12 is $75 a day. (Ages 3–5 get a program that combines lessons, snow play and indoor activities.) Reservations are recommended; call 776-2291.

Lift tickets (2001/02 prices)

	Adult	Child (Up to 12)
One day	$47	$28
Three days	$129 ($43/day)	$78 ($26/day)
Five days	$215 ($43/day)	$130 ($26/day)

Who skis free: Ages 70 and older.

Who skis at a discount: Ages 65–69 ski for $31. Ages 13–17 ski for $37 a single day; $35 multiday. Taos reduces its ticket prices in the early and late seasons. Prior to Dec. 15 (except Thanksgiving weekend), tickets are $32 for adults, $27 for teens and $20 for children. Add $5 to all regular season rates between Dec. 27–31.

Cross-country and snowshoeing

Personal fitness trainer Bonnie Golden runs **Taos Fitness Adventures** (751-5977), with guided cross-country skiing and snowshoeing in the winter, plus hiking and custom programs in warmer weather. **Southwest Nordic Center** (758-4761) has cross-country lessons, tours and yurt trips. **Enchanted Forest Cross-Country Ski Area** (754-2374) is 40 miles northeast of Taos by Hwys. 522 and 38. It has 34 km. of backcountry trails, some groomed, and an elevation of 10,300 feet, from which you have great views of the Moreno and Red River valleys. Trail rates are $10 for adults, with discounts for teens, seniors and children. At the Miller's Crossing headquarters in downtown Red River, you can rent equipment (including pulks) and pick up trail maps.

Accommodations

Taos' **Ski-Better-Week** packages include up to seven nights lodging (Saturday to Saturday), six lift tickets and six morning lessons. In some cases, meals are included, too. Prices range from about $586 to about $1,600 per person, double occupancy. If price or specific amenities are concerns, call **Taos Valley Resort Association** (800-776-1111 or 776-2233) or **Taos Central Reservations** (800-821-2437).

The **Inn at Snakedance** (800-322-9815 or 776-2277; $$$$) has 60 ski-in/ski-out rooms. Amenities include a spa with hot tub, sauna, exercise and massage facility; a glass-walled bar; and a restaurant serving continental cuisine with a Southwest flair. Owners Mary Madden and Dan Ringeisen saved the fireplace from the old Hondo Inn, which used to occupy the space. The Inn offers the Ski-Better-Week packages with an optional meal plan.

The **Bavarian Lodge** (770-0450; $$$$) is about as good as it gets on the mountain when it comes to the German/Austrian good life. The interior art was created by Swiss artist Reto Messmer and the building features Bavarian antiques.

The **Hotel St. Bernard** (776-2251; $$$), managed by Taos ski school technical director Jean Mayer, offers the flavor of a European retreat. The cuisine and ambiance are both legendary and French. This hotel also offers the Ski-Better-Week packages with meals.

The **Hotel Edelweiss** (800-458-8754 or 776-2301; $$–$$$$) is right at the base of the village. The charming hotel has an outdoor hot tub and large sundeck. It offers the Ski Week.

The **Austing Haus** (800-748-2932 or 776-2649; $$) is 1.5 miles from the base of Taos Ski Valley and is an unusual structure. It is the tallest timber frame building in the United States and owner Paul Austing is justifiably proud of the 24-unit lodge he helped build. The food in the glass dining room is very good.

Between the ski area and town is a bed-and-breakfast inn, the **Salsa del Salto** (776-2422, $$–$$$). Formerly the residence of Hotel St. Bernard owner Jean Mayer, it's now run by Jean's brother, Dadou, a French-trained chef who cooks Salsa del Salto's gourmet breakfasts.

The town of Taos offers a wide range of accommodations. Prices are generally less expensive than staying at Taos Ski Valley. At the northern edge of town, **Quail Ridge Inn** (800-624-4448 or 776-2211; $$–$$$$) is a fully appointed condominium complex at a tennis ranch, including indoor and outdoor courts. Looking much like a pueblo, it exudes the Southwestern atmosphere. The **Fechin Inn** (800-911-2937 or 751-1000; $$–$$$$) is the most luxurious place to stay. **The Historic Taos Inn** (800-826-7466, spells TAOS-INN; $–$$$$) is the cultural center of Taos. The lobby, built around the old town well, is a gathering place for artists. Rooms feature adobe fireplaces, antiques and Taos-style furniture built by local artisans. The **Sagebrush Inn** (800-428-3626 or 758-2254; $$$–$$$$) is an historic inn with a priceless collection of Southwestern art in the lobby and some of the best nightlife in town. At the lower end of the price range are **El Pueblo Lodge** (800-433-9612; $–$$$), **Indian Hills Inn** (800-444-2346; $), and often, rooms in the chain hotels, such as **Holiday Inn** or **Ramada.** The least expensive is the skiers' hostel, **The Abominable Snowmansion** (776-8298; $) in Arroyo Seco, 9 miles from the Village, where the rates are about $25–$60.

We also enjoyed three other B&Bs in Taos, which seems to have an unusual number of fine choices: **Hacienda del Sol** (758-0287; $$), owned by John and Marcine Landon; the **Old Taos Guesthouse** (758-5448; $–$$), owned by Tim and Leslie Reeves (who are fun to ski with); and **Inn on La Loma Plaza** (758-1717; $$–$$$$), owned by Peggy Davis and her husband, Jerry (both former mayors in Vail and Avon, CO). B&Bs can be booked through the **Taos B&B Association,** (800) 876-7857.

The **Inger Jirby Guest Houses** (758-7333; $$$$), a creation of an artist from Sweden, are eclectically decorated, luxurious and only two blocks from the plaza.

Dining

Because so many properties here offer Ski-Better-Week packages, which include meals, most restaurants are operated by the lodges. The best independent eateries in the village are **Rhoda's Restaurant** (776-2005; $$), serving many New Mexican specialties, and **Tim's Stray Dog Cantina** (776-2894; $$).

The **Bavarian** (770-0450; $$–$$$), at the bottom of the Kachina Lift, may be the best lunch spot in the ski valley. If it is sunny, ask to sit on the deck. They serve wonderful spätzle, wienerschnitzel and strudel.

The **Hondo Restaurant** ($$–$$$) at The Inn at Snakedance is open to non-guests for breakfast, lunch and dinner and features winemaker dinners with California vintners. **Hotel Edelweiss** ($$–$$$) also serves three meals daily to the general public.

On the road into the valley, the **Casa Cordova** (776-2500; $$–$$$) specializes in American and Continental cuisine. **Tim's Chile Connection** (776-8787; $) is known for its chicken chimichanga and Pollo Borracho. **Renegade Cafe** at the Quail Ridge Inn (776-8319; $$) specializes in Mediterranean-style food.

The town of Taos has great variety when it comes to restaurants. **The Trading Post** (758-5089; $$) has a bit of everything—Cajun, New Mexican, Italian, steaks. **Jacquelina's** (751-0399; $$), on S. Santa Fe Road (also known as Paseo del Pueblo Sur), specializes in Southwestern cuisine. The pork loin, marinated in honey and chipotle chili, is outstanding. For the best burger in town, locals recommend the not-so-Southwest-sounding **Fred's Place** (758-0514; $–$$) on S. Santa Fe Road. The menu at the **Apple Tree Restaurant** (758-1900; $$–$$$) lists Southwestern dishes and continental cuisine. On the historic plaza, **The Garden Restaurant** (758-9483; $$-$$$) offers New Mexican as well as American, Italian and French entrées. **Doc Martin's** (758-1977; $$-$$$) in the Taos Inn has Southwestern cuisine.

Michael's Kitchen (758-4178; $) has phenomenally large and excellent breakfasts. Or head to **El Taoseño** (758-4142) for another great breakfast burrito.

Après-ski/nightlife

When lifts close at Taos Ski Valley, skiers head to the deck of the **Hotel St. Bernard,** the **Martini Tree Bar** at the Resort Center, or to drink German beer at **The Bavarian. The Inn at Snakedance** has entertainment nightly. Not much else happens here.

It's livelier in Taos town, but not wild (unless you hit the Alley Cantina on a good night). The **Alley Cantina** has a live band and wild dancing some nights. Check the schedule, you'll love it. **The Sagebrush Inn** has C&W dances. The Kachina Lodge's **Cabaret Room** has a dance floor and occasional acts such as Arlo Guthrie, and **Ogelvie's Bar and Grill** in Taos Plaza hops. For microbrew fans, **Eske's Brew Pub** off the Taos Plaza is the spot. Be sure to try the unique Green Chili Beer at least once. Skiers and local artists mix at the **Adobe Bar** of the Taos Inn, the living room for artsy locals. Order a margarita and watch the beautiful people. Up at the Taos Pueblo there is gambling at the **Taos Mountain Casino.** The *Taos News* has a weekly entertainment guide.

Other activities

Taos is quite historic. The **Martinez Hacienda,** built in 1804, is a monument to the Spanish Colonial era in Northern New Mexico. **Kit Carson** is buried in Taos and his home and museum are open to the public. The **Millicent Rogers Museum** has a fantastic collection of Indian jewelry and art. The **Fechin Institute** is worth a visit to see the Russian artist's art and architecture.

Adventure Tours in Taos (758-1167) has **sleigh rides** and **snowmobile tours. Taos Ice Arena** (758-8234) is open Thanksgiving through February. **Fly fishing** tours are offered in winter on the Red River by Los Rios Anglers (758-2798). For **snowmobiling** in Red River call BobCat Pass Adventures (754-2769), Sled Shed (754-6370) or Fast Eddie's (754-3103). Roadrunner Tours (377-6416) offers **horse-drawn sleigh rides** to a sheepherders' tent with a dinner cooked over an open fire.

In Red River there is a unique **Night Sky Adventure** (754-2941) that provides a powerful telescopic universe tour that takes advantage of the altitude and the clear winter skies.

Visit the **Taos Pueblo,** the 700-year-old home of the Tiwa Indians. Visitors are welcome to the pueblo, workshops, ceremonies and sacred dances, except for a four- to six-week period each winter when the pueblo is closed for religious reasons. For exact dates, call the Taos Chamber of Commerce (800-732-TAOS). The pueblo is open from 9 a.m. to 4:30 p.m.

Georgia O'Keeffe and R.C. Gorman have made Taos legendary with art lovers. You'll find about 80 **galleries** are here. Get a list from Taos Chamber of Commerce, 758-3873 or (800) 732-TAOS.

Getting there and getting around

By air: Albuquerque is the nearest major airport, 135 miles south. Rental car agencies are at the airport. For ground transportation, contact Faust's Transportation, 758-3410 in Taos or 843-9042 in Albuquerque; or Pride of Taos, 758-8340.

By car: I-25 north to Santa Fe, then Hwys. 285, 84 and 68 to Taos. Taos Ski Valley is 18 miles farther north on Hwy. 150. For Red River head north on Hwy. 522 and east on Hwy. 38. For Angel Fire go east on Hwy. 64.

Getting around: If you stay in Taos Ski Valley village and have no desire to go into the town of Taos 18 miles away, you won't need a car. If you want to visit the town, or aren't staying at the ski area, you'll need one. In Red River you won't need a car, but you'll need one to get there. The same goes for Angel Fire, where you can park your car and forget it.

Nearby Resorts

Angel Fire Resort, Angel Fire, NM; (505) 377-4207 or (800) 633-7463

Internet: www.angelfireresort.com
5 lifts; 445 skiable acres; 2,077 vertical feet

Angel Fire is a modern, purpose-built resort about a half-hour—22 miles—east of Taos. The accommodations are all very close to the slopes and the mountain has been created for families and mellow skiing with touches of challenge.

This resort is especially good for beginners and intermediates. You have to go out of your way to get into trouble. It's about as good as it gets for families and those who want to take it easy. The resort has added some expert terrain, but it's tucked away where no one will accidentally get into trouble. **Beginners** will want to take Headin' Home from the top of the high-speed Chile Express quad. Stay on the trail or drop down Bodacious and wend your way back to the base area. Beginners can also experience the back bowl by winding down Highway, then dropping off Hallelujah or La Bajada to end up at the base of the Southwest Flyer, another high-speed quad. **Intermediates** will have fun on Fat City, Fire Escape, Mother Lode and Arriba in the back bowl. We recommend staying in the back bowl. On the front side you can cruise down some good intermediate trails such as I-25, Prospector and Jasper's, but all end in a long runout to the base area. **Advanced/Expert** levels will find meager offerings but they can be fun. A cluster of black runs under Lift 6 provides a challenge. To the far skier's right of the back bowl, a new series of advanced runs were recently added to Detonator and Nitro.

Angel Fire has snapped up the opportunity to become New Mexico's premier snowboarding destination, thanks to Taos' steadfast refusal to allow snowboarding. The recently installed Chile Express high-speed quad whisks boarders to the top of the 10,622-foot mountain in a fraction of the time it took the two triples it replaced. Sound systems pump out great tunes underneath the lifts. Angel Fire has a young feel to it, unlike the conservative, staid atmosphere of some larger resorts.

There are three terrain parks with tabletops, rail slides and spines. One is near the top of the mountain, on Fat City, reached by Lift #3. The second park is off Exhibition near the base of the mountain, served by Lift #2. For 2001/02 Angel Fire acquired a Pipe Dragon and is constructing the only halfpipe in New Mexico, on Angel Food. The resort hosts world-famous shovel racing in February, after which the course is transformed for a slopestyle competition held each March.

Beginner boarders will appreciate both Dreamcatcher and Lift #2, servicing Exhibition and Valley. You get what is, in effect, a superb bunny hill with two distinct levels of difficulty. In addition there's beginner terrain at the top of the mountain, on either side of the Nastar race area, that's served by a short lift. The Summit Haus, a yurt-style restaurant with a full-service bar at the peak, adds a nice extra touch. Intermediate and advanced riders will prefer the back side of the mountain, serviced by yet another new, high-speed quad. Hell's Bells is a favorite run amongst advanced boarders. Intermediates will enjoy Fire Escape and Hully Gully, shifting to front-side runs like I-25 and Prospector on days when the sun is hidden and snow is powering down. Unfortunately, front-side runs all end in a long runout to the base area since the new lift eliminated midway loading. Expert snowboarders are not forgotten—hiking-accessed trails in the Back Basin including Nitro, Detonator and Baa-da-bing offer some of the steepest terrain on the mountain.

Angel Fire has an excellent ski school that focuses on beginner and intermediate skiers as well as children. Their snowboarding instruction is consistently highly rated too. Angel Fire Resort Day Care (800-633-7463), housed in a separate building, is open 8 a.m. to 5 p.m. Full-and half-day programs provide activities for children ages 6 weeks through 11 years. Costs range from $55 to $75 for day care and children's lesson programs. Angel Fire resort has recently expanded its children's ski and snowboard school with a 6,000-square-foot building designed specifically for kids.

Adventure Park, at the summit, has a day tubing hill and Nordic Center. Here you'll find 19 km. of cross-country and snowshoe trails with beautiful views of New Mexico's highest mountain, Wheeler Peak. Lessons and rentals are available.

Lift tickets (2001/02): Adult, $43; teen (13–17), $35; youth (7–12), $27; multiday discounts apply. Early and late season rates are lower. Ages 6 and younger and ages 70 and older ski free.

Accommodations: The Angel Fire Resort Hotel (800-633-7463; $$–$$$) has standard and deluxe rooms and suites. The resort has managed **condominiums** ($$-$$$) and has a full program of ski packages. The hotel is slopeside and the condos have a shuttlebus.

Dining/après-ski/nightlife: Dining is a resort affair. There aren't many choices outside of the base area. The top spot is **Aldo's Cafe and Cantina** (377-6401; $$), with southwestern cuisine, right next to the Chile Express lift. **Branding Iron** has breakfast and lunch in the resort hotel. **Zebadiah's** (377-8005; $–$$) is off the resort and has a good family restaurant. For pizza call **Beverly's** (377-2337; $). **Summit Haus,** at the summit, and **Village Haus,** on the base area deck, both have snacks, grilled items and full-service bars. Angel Fire snoozes in the evenings, but **Village Haus** has live entertainment, 3 p.m.-7 p.m. every weekend. There is also a bit of an après-ski buzz in **Jasper's.**

Red River Ski Area, Red River, NM; (505) 754-2223 or (800) 331-SNOW

Internet: www.redriverskiarea.com
7 lifts; 290 skiable acres; 1,600 vertical feet

Red River, about an hour drive—37 miles—north of Taos, has no pretensions about Indians or the Spanish. This once was a down-and-dirty goldmining town with saloons and bordellos lining the streets. Today, Red River is one of the prettiest ski towns and most convenient to be found in the U.S. Two main lifts drop right into town and most hotels and condos are within walking distance of them. If you don't want to walk, take the town trolley that makes its rounds every 15 minutes.

This is a fun mountain, a lot of fun. Red Chair and Copper Chair reach the summit from different spots in town. This is not high-speed quad territory; all these lifts are fixed-grip. There's a terrain park for those who like tricks and air. From the highest point, Ski Tip, **beginners** can drop to the other side of the peak to test about a dozen easy runs served by a double chair. Beginners can also ski all the way back to the base area along Cowpoke Cruise, which meanders down the entire 1,600 feet of vertical. **Intermediates** have the entire skier's right of the mountain for fun and games. These trails are the definition of cruiser delights. **Advanced and expert** skiers can head to skier's left from Ski Tip. Here, those seeking challenge will find a mix of trees and black-diamond trails.

Red River claims to be one of the great teaching mountains. It has an excellent ski school that focuses on beginner and intermediate skiers as well as children. Red River's Youth Center and Buckaroo Child Care is open from 8 a.m. to 4:30 p.m. Children from 6 months to 4 years are accepted for child care, ages 4–5 have lessons and indoor activities, while ages 6–10 are grouped in classes according to age and ability. Costs range from $30 to $73, depending on number of hours and whether lunch and rental equipment is included.

Lift tickets (2001/02): Adult, $43; teen (13–19), $38; juniors and seniors, $29; multiday discounts are available.

Accommodations: Almost all hotels are relatively close to the lifts and the town. For **lodging information,** call (800) 348-6444 or 754-2366. **Lifts West Condo/Hotel** (800-221-1859 or 754-2778; $–$$) has spacious rooms and a wild second-floor hot tub. **The Auslander Condominiums** (800-753-2311 or 754-2311; $$), **Black Mountain Lodge** (800-825-2469 or 754-2469; $$), **Copper King Lodge** (800-727-6210 or 754-6210; $–$$), **The Riverside** (800-432-9999 or 754-2252; $) and **Silver Spur Lodge** (800-545-8372 or 754-2378; $–$$) are all almost ski-in/ski-out.

Dining/après-ski/nightlife: Don't come here looking for fancy gourmet fare. This town is focused on good down-home meals with quantity. That said, **Brett's** (654-6136; $$) has an elegant dining room and a menu where everything from seafood to lamb is spiced with gourmet phrases. **Texas Reds Steakhouse and Saloon** (754-2922; $$) is everything a cowboy steakhouse should be. From the newsprint menu to the charbroiled beef, this is a carnivore's paradise. **The Lodge at Red River** (754-6280; $$) has a good family restaurant with plenty of steaks, but you can find trout and shrimp as well. **Timbers** (754-3090; $$) is another western-style steakhouse. For Tex-Mex head to **Sundance** (754-6271; $) or to **Angelina's** (754-2211; $). For N.Y.-style pizza and other Italian meals try **Pappa's** (754-2951; $). For breakfast head to **Colonel Js,** across from the Chamber of Commerce, for an "All U Can Eat" feast, to the **Alpine Lodge** for their breakfast burritos, or to **Shotgun Willie's** for the "Mountain Man Breakfast."

Red River is the nightlife capital of the region. If you want a rocking time, this is the spot to come. The town is normally packed with a young college crowd that loves to dance and sing. Head to the **Motherlode Saloon** for a chance to two-step and hear great live music. The **Mineshaft Theater** has concerts. **The Black Crow Coffeehouse** boasts top C&W and folk acts. **Texas Reds** often has singers in the bar. And the **Bull O'The Woods Saloon** has cowboy karaoke. **The Lonesome Pine Pub** serves eight New Mexico microbrews on tap. **Chubbies Tavern** rocks during après-ski with the college crowd. This is a good party town.

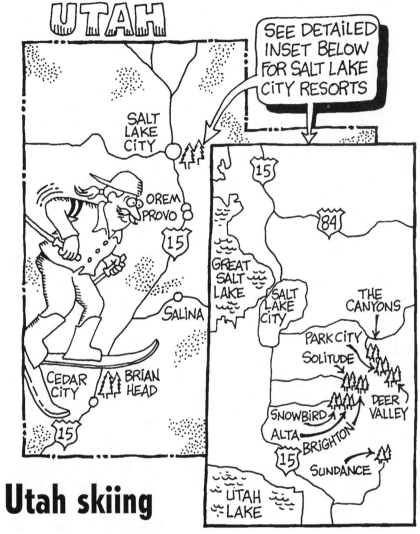

Utah skiing

and staying in Salt Lake City

If a corporation could build the perfect ski resort, it would have lots of feathery snow overnight and frequent sunny weather during the day, a nearby major airport yet no airplane noise, and a variety of lodging and nightlife to appeal to a broad section of the skiing public. No ski corporation built Salt Lake City, but it certainly fits that description.

Eleven downhill ski areas, three Nordic ski areas and the only North American facility with public ski-jumping instruction and bobsled rides are within an hour's drive of the Salt Lake City International Airport, one of the country's major air hubs. Utah's snow is legendary. It's light, fluffy and abundant. But that's not all. These resorts don't feel the need to be carbon copies of each other. Each of the 11 nearby resorts has a distinct personality. If you think variety is the spice of life, get ready for a well-seasoned feast. Seven of the 11 resorts are detailed in the next three chapters, plus we provide capsule descriptions of two others.

With the XIX Olympic Winter Games coming for 17 days in February 2002 (Feb. 8-24), followed by the VII Paralympic Games, March 7-16, public perception leans toward thinking Utah is out-of-bounds for regular skiing this winter. Not so. The Games will affect only 2 percent of Utah's skiable terrain, and that's at only three ski areas: Snowbasin, Park City Mountain Resort and Deer Valley Resort. All ski areas, including those hosting events, will be open for business as usual. All non-alpine events, and that's most of them, will be held at specialty venues in the area. It's true that some large sponsoring corporations have reserved entire hotels for themselves, but a lot of that lodging will be released about a month before the Games begin. Plenty of other lodging is still available, even during the Games. For lodging availability in Salt Lake City, call 800-847-5810. For Park City area lodging, call 800-453-1360.

If you still think you can't get a drink in Utah, you're way behind the times. In most places you won't notice any difference between buying a beer here and at home (we explain the liquor laws later in the chapter). But you can't have two drinks in front of you at the same time, and at some tables, only beer and wine are allowed. Salt Lake City claims more microbreweries per capita than any other western metropolitan city. Though we can't verify that claim, we can verify through firsthand experience that the breweries serve a very tasty product. Salt Lake City is unsurpassed in its variety of evening entertainment. Pro basketball, hockey, theater, comedy clubs and high-energy dance clubs are among the options.

Salt Lake City

Salt Lake City is a great spot to stay for several reasons. One, you're centrally located to sample all the major ski areas. Two, hotels are relatively inexpensive, perhaps a result of having more than 17,000 rooms available for nightly use. Three, Salt Lake City has lots of fun stuff to do at night.

The Utah Transit Authority (287-4636) has a very efficient ski bus system serving Brighton and Solitude in Big Cottonwood Canyon and Snowbird and Alta in Little Cottonwood Canyon. The buses are clean, pleasant and inexpensive, and go directly from downtown to the ski areas. This system incorporates the city's new TRAX light rail trains and specially equipped ski buses to the ski areas. UTA also has a free fare zone downtown, convenient for sightseeing and evening activities. Lewis Brothers Stages (800-826-5844 or 359-8677) has a SkiExpress service that picks up skiers and snowboarders from downtown hotels and takes them to one of seven ski areas. Many of the hotels include the service in their rates.

 ## Accommodations

Although rates are a little higher downtown than in outlying parts of the city, it is worth the extra few bucks to be close to Salt Lake City's major attractions.

The Grand America Hotel (258-6000 or 800-621-4505; $$$-$$$$) is Earl Holding's latest holding ,which include Sun Valley Resort, Snowbasin Ski Resort, Little America. It is in downtown Salt Lake City, the luxury hotel has 377 rooms and 398 suites.

Salt Lake Marriott (531-0800 or 800-345-4754; $$–$$$) is across from the Salt Palace Convention Center and is connected to the Crossroads Plaza shopping mall. **Howard Johnson Express Inn** (521-3450 or 800-541-7639; $–$$) is two blocks from Temple Square.

Doubletree Hotel (328-2000; $$–$$$) is a few blocks farther south on West Temple, but it's within stumbling distance of the Zephyr Club (see *Après-ski/nightlife*). Another choice in this area is the recently renovated **Peery Hotel** (521-4300; $$-$$$$), which is historic and nicely elegant, but subject to street noise.

The **Hotel Monaco** (595-0000; $$–$$$), Salt Lake's newest boutique downtown hotel, is in an historic renovated bank building. Definitely not a cookie-cutter property, the Monaco will deliver a pet goldfish to your room at your request and serves up free back and neck massages during the complimentary evening wine reception in the lobby. And don't be surprised if you see your favorite rock star or NBA team in the lobby. This is *the* place to stay for those hot groups. The lively Bambara, an award-winning bistro-type restaurant, is just off the lobby (see *Dining*).

Little America Hotel and Towers (363-6781; $–$$) has some of the largest rooms we've seen in a hotel—great for spreading out all the gear that skiers carry. Also recommended are **Embassy Suites Hotel** (359-7800; $–$$) and the **Sheraton Salt Lake City** (532-3344; $$$–$$$$). The **Marriott University Park Hotel** (801-581-1000; $–$$$) is near the University of Utah, farther from downtown but closer to the resorts. It is at a higher elevation than downtown, so it has a dandy view of the city from its glassed-in hot tub.

Salt Lake City Center Travelodge (531-7100; $–$$), **Travelodge Temple Square** (533-8200)**, Deseret Inn** (532-2900; $) or **Cavanaughs Olympus Hotel** (521-7373; 800-426-0722; $$–$$$$) all offer plenty of beds.

Those looking for the coziness of an inn can try **The Brigham Street Inn** (364-4461; $$–$$$), on East South Temple near the university. Three B&Bs in historic buildings are clustered about seven blocks from Temple Square, each with wonderfully decorated rooms: **The Anniversary Inn** (363-4900; 800-324-4152 ; $$–$$$$), **Anton Boxrud Bed & Breakfast** (363-8035; 800-524-5511; $–$$) and **The Armstrong Mansion B&B** (531-1333; 800-708-1333; $$–$$$$).

The **Salt Lake Convention & Visitors Bureau** offers a free consumer housing service at 800-847-5810 and local reservationists promise to get you the best rate at dozens of Salt Lake hotels.

Dining

Downtown Salt Lake City has many restaurants in nearly every food category you can name, including Peruvian and Thai. It leads the nation in per capita Jell-O consumption, but that must be due to the stay-at-homes—we've never seen Jell-O on a menu here. You may want to dress up a bit (meaning a buttoned shirt and khakis instead of a T-shirt and jeans) for the finer establishments. See our nightlife section for an explanation of "private clubs," which some of these restaurants are.

We're told **Metropolitan** (173 W. Broadway, 364-3472; $$$), voted "Salt Lake's Best Restaurant 1998-99," has world-class gourmet cuisine that rivals some of the best of any other major city. It also serves vegetarian entrees.

Bambara (363-5454, 202 S. Main St.), voted "Salt Lake's Best Restaurant 1999-00" and "Best Contemporary American" in 2001, specializes in fresh, seasonal foods in a nouveau bistro setting next to the lobby of the newly refurbished Hotel Monaco.

Dining: $$$-Entrees $20+; $$-$10-20; $-less than $10.
Accommodations: (double room) $$$$-$200+; $$$-$141-$200; $$-$81-$140; $-$80 and less.

Casually elegant Italian dining can be found at **Baci'Trattoria** (134 W. Pierpont Ave., 328-1500; $$). For Asian dining, **Xiao Li** (307 W. 200 South; 328-8688; $$) in the warehouse district has the most interesting atmosphere, but **Pagoda** (26 E St., 355-8155; $–$$) has been around the longest, since 1946. **Mikado** (67 W. 100 South, 328-0929; $$) has fresh fish and sushi, and has been in business for four decades. **The Golden Phoenix** (539-1122) in downtown Salt Lake has been recognized as one of the top Chinese restaurants.

Cafe Pierpont (122 W. Pierpont Ave., 364-1222, $–$$) and **Rio Grande Cafe** (270 S. Rio Grande, at the Amtrak Station, 364-3302; $) are downtown's best bets for Mexican.

Salt Lake's American and steak and seafood restaurants offer a wealth of choices. **New Yorker** (60 W. Market St., 363-0166, $$$) has an elegant atmosphere in the dining room. Its more casual neighbors, **Market Street Grill** (322-4668; $$) and **Oyster Bar** (531-6044; $$), emphasize seafood, but also serve steaks and chicken. (Market Street Grill has great breakfasts, by the way.) Big appetites will love the **Radizio Grill** (220-0500), an authentic Brazilian-style steakhouse. Free appetizers, gourmet salad bar, beef, chicken, pork and seafood served on skewers to your table. Kids younger than 9 eat free. **Lamb's** (169 S. Main, 364-7166; $$) is Utah's oldest restaurant, dating to 1919, and also features fine art photography by Utah artists.

At the base of Little Cottonwood Canyon is **La Caille** (942-1751; $$$), which gets rave reviews for its French cuisine, serving staff and setting. It was built the to look like a French chateau and surrounded by gardens filled with swans, peacocks, rabbits and other animals. Make reservations; this place is *tres chic.* There's a B&B on premises.

These are just a tiny portion of what's available in Salt Lake City. A great resource for finding restaurants—particularly if you like certain kinds of food—is the Web site www.citysearchutah.com, which has a searchable database.

 # Après-ski/nightlife/other activities

Utah's liquor laws: Baby-boomer skiers remember when getting a glass of wine meant a trip to the state liquor store before going to a restaurant, then paying a setup fee before you could consume your own brown-bagged bottle. Now it's much easier, but here are a few tips:

Restaurants that have liquor licenses (most do) can serve alcohol from noon to midnight "to customers intending to dine." However, you won't find the wine list at the table. Your server will ask if you'd like "a beverage," at which point you can ask for the alcohol menu. Some restaurants are designated as private clubs, which means you'll have to pay a temporary membership fee to get in.

Bars don't exist in Utah, at least not by that name. If you are planning just to drink, not eat, you'll have to do so at a **private club.** Don't be deterred by restaurant or nightclub advertising that has phrasing like this: "A private club for the benefit of its members." You, too, can become a member. Utah residents buy an annual membership costing up to $35 for each club. Visitors pay $5 for a membership, valid for two weeks for the visitor and five guests. Annual members can bring guests, too.

To avoid the charge, ask outside the facility if someone will agree to be your "sponsor." Once you're inside, thank your sponsor and split for separate tables. (Unless, of course, you think you might like to get to know him or her a little better, in which case, offer to buy the drinks.) Legally, you're supposed to leave with your sponsor, but no one watches that closely (and once inside, you can always find a new sponsor). If you lack such audacity, just think of the membership as a cover charge. But don't be shy about asking. Utahans are accustomed to this method of staying within the law; in fact, some single Utahans use "Need a sponsor?" as a handy pickup line.

Taverns may or may not serve food, depending on the establishment. The only alcohol served at taverns is 3.2-percent beer.

After a day of skiing at Alta and before you get back to Salt Lake, check out **River's Restaurant,** on your left at the southeast end of the Salt Lake Valley at the bottom of the mountains, for high-end brew, pub food and great après-ski atmosphere.

For an unusual happy hour, stop by the **Cotton Bottom Inn** (273-9830) at the base of Big and Little Cottonwood Canyons. This is a raucous, sawdust-on-the-floor tavern with great garlicburgers and an earthy crowd. The address is 2820 E. 6200 South, but it's a little hard to find. Ask a local to direct you.

For good blues, try the **Dead Goat Saloon** (Arrow Press Square, 165 S. West Temple). A quieter, pleasant location is **Green Street** (in Trolley Square), which Salt Lake City's career crowd seems to favor.

Salt Lake City has three brew pubs, **Squatter's Pub** (147 W. Broadway; 363-2739), **Desert Edge Brewery at the Pub** (Trolley Square; 521-8917) and **Red Rock Brewing Co.** (254 South 200 West; 521-7446). All brew their own beer and serve excellent pub fare.

If you like movies *and* microbrews, head to **Brewries** (677 South 200 West; 322-3891). This establishment combines second-run (movies that already have been shown but aren't yet in video stores), independent and classic films with a gourmet-pizza-and-beer restaurant. Many people come to eat or drink, then decide whether to hang around for the movies being shown on four screens. You must be 21 years old.

This isn't the typical ski-town nightlife activity, but classical music lovers shouldn't miss the free 8 p.m. Thursday night **rehearsals of the Mormon Tabernacle Choir** at Temple Square. You can drop in and leave as you wish.

One of our top five ski-town dance nightclubs is **Zephyr Club** (301 S. West Temple; 355-5646). It surpasses its billing as "Salt Lake City's premier showcase for local and national entertainment."

One place we're planning to try the next time we're here is **Club Manhattan** (5 E. 400 South; 364-7651). We're told it's in the "everything-old-is-new-again" genre, with cocktails, overstuffed chairs and a live piano-and-strings band for swing and ballroom dancing. We've been known to enjoy a little cheek-to-cheek dancing on our trips, but the right atmosphere and music is hard to find. The crowd here dresses up.

You can go shopping at **Trolley Square,** shops and boutiques in a restored trolley barn (you can buy Olympic souvenirs at the Olympic Spirit store); attend a **Utah Jazz** (355-DUNK) basketball game; or attend theater, symphony, dance or opera performances. You can even check out your ancestors at the **Family History Center** at the Mormon computer center located inside the restored historic Hotel Utah (15 ES Temple St.). Built in 1912, this was every U.S. president's elegant shelter. Be sure to bring a list of family ancestors, names and dates to make your free search worthwhile.

For a more complete list of restaurants, nightlife and other activities, pick up a free copy of *This Week Salt Lake.* This excellent guide tells you what is happening within a two-week period (sports, theater, etc.) and is a handy reference guide to the city's ongoing attractions. Another great guide is *Utah After Dark,* which rates the private clubs and taverns throughout most of the state, and tells which ones have live music, pool tables, sports TV and more.

The Interconnect Adventure Tour

Experienced skiers can ski to five different resorts via backcountry routes on this all-day tour. Six to 14 skiers are led by mountain guides. Some traversing and walking are necessary, so you need to be a confident skier and in good physical condition. The four-area tour (Solitude, Brighton, Alta and Snowbird) is offered three days a week, while the five-area tour (those four and Park City) goes the other four days. Each tour costs $150, including return transportation and lunch. Reservations required; call 534-1907.

Getting there and getting around

By air: Salt Lake City is one of the country's major airports. Northwest Airlines connects Minneapolis with Salt Lake and several other major airlines fly here. But Southwest Airlines provides the most flights at affordable fares with connections to every corner of the country. Fares from Southern California are particularly good, thanks to ongoing competition between Delta and Southwest Airlines.

By train: Amtrak's California Zephyr stops here, arriving at 4 a.m. for eastbound trains and midnight for westbound trains. Call (800) USA-RAIL (872-7245).

Getting around: Rent a car if you want to cover a lot of ground in the evening; otherwise, use public transportation. Getting to the resorts is a snap. Several ground transportation companies operate shuttles to the ski areas from Salt Lake City hotels. Lewis Brothers Stages (800-826-5844; 801-359-8677 in Salt Lake City) is very reliable. Round-trip from the airport to the Cottonwood Canyon or Park City resorts is about $22 per person; reservations required; minimum of three people. Don't worry too much about the minimum; in our experience, the vans are fairly full during winter.

Lewis Brothers also picks up at downtown hotels. Or take the Utah Transit Authority (UTA) Ski Bus, $4 each way (exact fare required) to the four Cottonwood Canyon resorts (Alta, Snowbird, Solitude, Brighton). We take the UTA bus whenever we're at a hotel that's near the bus stop. The buses are clean, convenient and best of all, cheap. UTA buses run at night downtown until about 11:30 p.m., but only about once per hour. Call 287-4636 for more info.

Nearby resorts

The next three chapters detail the skiing and amenities at Snowbird, Alta, Solitude and Brighton, and the three Park City resorts. Here is information about three other Utah resorts—two near Salt Lake City and one at the southern part of the state.

Snowbasin, Huntsville, UT; (801) 399-1135

Internet: www.snowbasin.com
9 lifts; 3,200 acres; 2,940 vertical feet
You haven't really lived until you've run the Men's Downhill course at Snowbasin before breakfast. The 2002 Olympic committee chose Snowbasin to host the men's and women's downhill, Super G and Alpine combined races because of its very long runs within sight of the day lodge.

Three new lifts, all high-speed quads, rise more than 2,300 vertical feet in one ride. All other lifts, except the one serving the beginner slope and the Tram, are triples that rise 1,100 vertical feet or more. That's a lot of skiing from one lift ride. The very top of the downhill course, Allen's Peak, is reached by the Olympic Tram, an 8-passenger gondola that loads just below the top of John Paul Express. Snowbasin is rimmed by jagged peaks. There is a gentle learning area, but the vast majority of the terrain is best suited for intermediate level and higher. Three day lodges ranging in size from 14,000 square feet to 24,000 square feet are being built on the mountain, scheduled to open for the 2001/02 winter season.

Right now, Snowbasin is visited mostly by skiers and boarders who have heard good things from their friends. Once the world sees it on television this coming February, the secret will be out.

Snowbasin is owned by the same company that owns the Sun Valley resort in Idaho.
Lift tickets: Adults cost $43; Children (up to 11), $25; Seniors (65+), $30.
Distance from Salt Lake City: About 40 miles from the airport north via I-15 to Farmington, north on US 89 to South Weber, east on I-84 to exit 92 and north on UT 167 to Trapper's Loop. The route is very well signed.
Lodging information: Most lodging is in Ogden City, about 17 miles west, or Ogden Valley, about nine miles west. (800) 554-2741.

Sundance, Sundance, UT; (801) 225-4107; (800) 892-1600

Internet: www.sundanceresort.com
4 lifts; 450 acres; 2,150 vertical feet
Though this ski area has been owned by actor-director Robert Redford for over 30 years, it has never been highly marketed—and that's on purpose. Skiing is not the resort's main event; rather Redford has achieved a balance between outdoor recreation of all kinds, the arts and an intimate environment. Located on the slopes of breathtaking 12,000-foot Mt. Timpanogos, Sundance is regarded as the most beautiful ski area in Utah. To experience the challenging and varied terrain, get there early because the ski area limits lift tickets to 1,200 per day. Locals comprise 80 percent of the skier/snowboarder visits. Even when the 105 guestrooms are full there is never a crowd on the mountain. Lodging packages offer many different possibilities like free lift tickets and full breakfasts in the Foundry Grill.

Snowboarding is allowed. The area has a full service Nordic Center featuring 40 km. of groomed cross-country trails and 10 km. of snowshoe trails. You'll also find two excellent restaurants, an eco-friendly gift shop, the historic Owl Bar, and the Sundance Art Shack offering a full schedule of classes, retreats and workshops throughout the year. Guests also enjoy screenings of award-winning films from past and present Sundance Film Festivals. (This annual event, held in larger Park City during late January, celebrates the achievements of independent filmmakers.)

Lift tickets: Adults, $32 ($27 midweek); Children (12 and younger), $16; Children (5 and younger), free; Seniors (65 and older), $10.

Distance from Salt Lake City: About 50 miles south via I-15, east on Hwy. 52, north on Hwy. 189, then a short hop west on Hwy. 92.

Lodging information: 225-4107or (800) 892-1600.

Brian Head, Brian Head, UT; (800) 27-BRIAN (2-7426); (435) 677-2035

Internet: www.brianhead.com
6 lifts; 500 acres; 1,320 vertical feet

Brian Head, in Utah's southwest corner, holds two distinctions among Utah resorts: It is one of very few *not* within an hour of Salt Lake City airport, and it draws virtually all its customers from Southern California and Southern Nevada. For these skiers, Brian Head is very accessible (all freeway until the last 12 miles) and has an excellent variety of mostly intermediate terrain covered by that famous dry Utah powder.

Brian Head has skiing on two peaks. Navajo Peak has some of the best beginner and lower intermediate terrain to be found anywhere, while Giant Steps Peak has solid intermediate terrain with a few advanced pitches. In midwinter, the resort offers double-black-diamond snowcat skiing from Brian Head Peak's summit (11,307 feet), which overlooks Giant Steps. Each snowcat ride costs $5 if you already have a lift ticket (must be age 16 or older). We like this pricing concept, some folks will discover that one time up is plenty.

Child care starts at 12 months, and the town has several condo complexes, restaurants and a hotel. A tubing hill is open daily, and also at night every Friday and Saturday, plus during holiday periods. Brian Head also has night skiing on weekends and holidays. However, this is a quiet area in the evenings.

Lift tickets: Adults, $38 ($40 holidays); Children (6-12) and Seniors (65+), $25 ($27 holidays); younger than 6, free.

Distance from Las Vegas: About 200 miles north by I-15 and Hwy. 143.

Lodging information: (888) 677-2810; www.brianheadutah.com.

Alta

Utah

Summit elevation: 10,550 feet
Vertical drop: 2,020 feet
Base elevation: 8,530 feet

Address: P.O. Box 8007
Alta, UT 84092-8007
✆ **Area code**: 801
Ski area phone: 799-2263
Snow report: 359-1078
ⓘ **Reservations**: 942-0404
or (888) STAY-ALTA (782-9258)
E-mail: info@alta.com
Internet: www.alta.com
Expert:★★★★★
Advanced:★★★★★
Intermediate:★★★★
Beginner:★★★★ **Never-ever**:★★★

Skiable Acreage: 2,200
Snowmaking: 3 percent (50 acres)
Number and types of lifts: 12–1 quad,
1 high-speed triple, 2 triples, 4 doubles, 4 surface lifts
Uphill capacity: 11,284 skiers per hour
Snowboarding: Not allowed
Bed Base: 1,136
Nearest lodging: Slopeside, inns
Resort child care: Yes, 2 months and older
Adult ticket, per day: $38 (2001/02)
Dining:★★
Apres-ski/nightlife:★
Other activities:★

At the top of Little Cottonwood Canyon lies the ski land where time stands still. Entering Alta is like stepping back into an earlier, less hurried era of skiing. Instead of sky-rise hotels and flashy new condos, visitors find a handful of rustic, comfortable lodges. No giant billboards scream advertising messages, no faux-Swiss ski villages house trendy restaurants and no high-speed quads hurry skiers to the summit. Snowboarders are prohibited from using the lifts, and even the all-day lift-passes costing only $38 are decidedly retro.

How first-time visitors feel about the dichotomy of an absolutely world-class ski area with unsurpassed snow and beauty but no hyper-speed lifts to whisk them up the mountain will prove crucial to how they view Alta. Those who long for a less hurried, more communal skiing experience, then swapping lies and stories around woodsy bars and roaring fires, will find kindred spirits in Alta.

It's not that Alta isn't feeling the pressure created by high-speed expectations or the popularity of snowboarding. Rather, Alta officials have opted for lines and occasional crowds at the bottom of the mountain instead of on the slopes. So during busy times you may have to wait in line, but the reward of uncrowded slopes is worth its weight in gold. And they choose to keep sacred their world-famous powder for skiers.

"In a sense Alta is old-fashioned, but a lot of people tell us they're tired of the corporate feel of many newer ski resorts," said Bill Levitt, long-time mayor of Alta and owner of the Alta Lodge. "Eighty percent of my customers at Alta Lodge are return customers, and they hunger for skiing as it used to be, with lodging in small inns where people eat together at the same table and share that camaraderie, and where there are a lot of little kids running around. That's our future. We call Alta the Last Resort." Talk about old-fashioned: In his position as mayor, Levitt makes an annual salary of $1. Note: There are no developers on Alta's planning commission.

Alta's low-key attitude is rooted in its history. In half a century of mining, Alta went from obscurity to boom, followed by outrageous scandal when the mines suddenly collapsed in the early 1900s. By the 1930s, when the new Sun Valley was courting glamorous international figures, Alta was born from the simple desire of Salt Lake residents to have a place where they could ski without having to climb uphill. Beginning in 1939 using its old ore tram, Alta has pulled nearly four generations of skiers up to its ridges (some guests at the Alta Lodge have kept returning since the mid-1940s). It still bears a modest name: Alta Ski Area, without the word "resort" anywhere in sight. One other thing: It's pronounced AL-ta, like the name Al, not AHL-ta.

Alta provides a fine contrast to its neighbor Snowbird, just a mile down the road in Little Cottonwood Canyon. Where Snowbird with its high-occupancy tram and multistory hotel is high-tech, Alta with its serviceable lifts and multitude of mountain inns is homey. Powder pigs will most certainly have good reason to rejoice this winter. Beginning in the 2001/02 season, skiers can purchase an Alta Snowbird ticket for $68 a day and enjoy the two resorts' combined terrain (don't be surprised if snowboarders start converting to skiing *en mass*, snowboarding is still banned at Alta). Snowbird added a second high-speed quad this summer in Mineral Basin, connecting the two resorts. The lift transports skiers to the Sugarloaf saddle area (elevation 10,600 feet), joining Alta's Albion Basin and Snowbird's Mineral Basin. Skiers access the area by beginner and intermediate trails from the Albion Basin side, and by intermediate trails from the Mineral Basin side. In addition, Utah Transit Authority will connect the resorts' base areas with an expanded daily bus service.

Also new for 2001/02, in efforts to improve the skiing experience in the Albion Basin, the Sugarloaf lift will be upgraded to a detachable and the Supreme lift will be upgraded to a fixed-grip triple (don't worry about crowded slopes, uphill capacity is marginally affected).

The common areas of Alta's lodges provide a great way to meet new buddies. You may find yourself returning the same week each season and seeing the same faces. Skiers seem to forgive Alta for not keeping up with the trends. Of the skiers we know who have been here, the vast majority plan to return. Must be that no-fuss, home-baked warmth.

Mountain layout—Skiing

The ski area has front and back sides, and two base stations. Wildcat Base is the first one you reach. It has basic facilities—ticket office, restaurants, restrooms and ski patrol. The Albion Base houses the Children's Center, Ski School, restaurant, and retail and rental operations. Albion is where you find the beginner slopes, but it has intermediate and expert terrain at higher elevations. Albion and Wildcat are connected by a long, horizontal, two-way transfer rope tow: Just grab the rope and let it pull you along to the other base.

From the top of Germania Pass the runs down the front side return you to the Wildcat base area; runs down the back return you to Albion, or give access to the Sugarloaf and Supreme lifts. Skiers wishing to cross back into the Germania/Wildcat area have two choices: a traverse from the top of the Sugarloaf lift or at the base on the transfer tow.

To follow the sun, start the morning on Sugarloaf, then move to Germania on the front side at midday, and finish on Supreme.

◆◆ **Expert** ◆ **Advanced:** Powder is what Alta is all about. Not just because it gets a lot, but because, with its terrain of trees and sheltered gullies, it tends to keep it longer. While most skiers are swishing down groomed runs a couple of days after a storm, the Alta cognoscenti are secretly diving into snow pockets in side canyons and upper elevations.

Alta, like Snowbird, is a what-you-see, you-can-ski resort, with many ways down that aren't named on the trail map. Be individual. Be creative. That's the spirit of Alta.

Wildcat and Collins lifts serve advanced runs on the right side of the trail map—narrow trails, bump runs and many glades—with intermediate and more advanced runs on the left. From the left of these two lifts, skiers can get to an entirely different ridge, West Rustler, by taking the Germania lift. That means more steep and deep at Eagle's Nest and High Rustler for experts. The line at Germania may appear daunting on powder days but rarely averages more than 10 minutes, although if there's powder on weekends, it can crank up to 20.

If you head down the back side under the Sugarloaf chair, you'll find expert bowls as far as the eye can see. Swooping down into a gully to the left of the lift as you descend usually gives you powder pockets. A day or two after a storm try Devils' Castle, the steeps under the rocks accessible from Sugarloaf.

To the far left of the trail map, experts can take Supreme lift to Point Supreme, the 10,550-foot summit, and from there have plenty of steep tree skiing to the left in an area near the boundary called Spiney Ridge. Some sections are known as Piney Glades and White Squaw. It's all known as steep, and tremendously popular with Salt Lake skiers. Up here you can ski all day without ever going the same way twice.

Experts in search of a unique Alta experience should reserve the last run of the day for Alf's High Rustler, named after one of Alta's founding fathers. Getting to the run is adventure enough for some. Ride the Germania lift and take the high traverse. Stay on the traverse as it crosses the ridge toward Greeley Bowl, and keep right on traversing. The height and width of the traverse at this stage are not for the faint of heart. Eventually the traverse spirals around the top mountain knoll to High Rustler, a beautiful, steep run that is little skied, enjoys breathtaking views of the valley, and spills right out into the lodges below.

■ **Intermediate:** This group can start at either Wildcat or Albion. From Wildcat, stay to the left as you leave the Collins chair, then head down to the base on Meadow or over to Germania, where you'll find Ballroom and Mambo to the right as you leave the chair. On the Albion side, intermediates also have appropriate terrain under Sugarloaf and Supreme chairs. Intermediates have wonderful slopes here, plus a few very gentle pitches off to one side in the Albion area that don't get groomed—a super place to take your first powder turns. Alta doesn't skimp on grooming—we found the intermediate and beginner runs quite negotiable.

●● **Beginner:** ● **Never-evers:** From the Albion base, Sunnyside and Albion lifts access gentle terrain, a wide rolling beginner playground. Sunnyside has been upgraded to a bit more advanced-beginner run. Given a choice between Snowbird and Alta, beginners should definitely start here. Kids are very safe here. Not only are the slopes less intimidating, but also the skiers (we're talking fashion and attitude here, not ability). The mile-long beginner run herecan make a newbie feel like a real skier—and that's what the sport is all about.

Mountain layout—Snowboarding

Snowboarding is not permitted. Head next door to Snowbird.

Mountain rating

Alta is a great place for any level of skier. Teamed with neighboring Snowbird, it's especially hard to beat. Snowbird has the edge in continuous vertical drop—the Snowbird tram opens almost 3,000 feet of continuous expert vertical, versus the maximum expert drop of about 1,000 at Alta. However, Alta is much better for groups of mixed abilities. Alta is one of the few resorts that still bans snowboarding.

Lessons (2001/02 prices)

Bearing the name of Alf Engen, the Norwegian ski jumper who came to Utah in 1930, the ski school is recognized in the industry for its contributions to the development of professional ski instruction. Lower-level ski lessons meet at the base of the Albion lift, while upper skill levels meet below the base of the Germania lift. For all ski school programs, call 359-1078.

Group lessons: Two hours, $35.

Never-ever package: All-day group lessons cost $55; includes the learning tow. Rentals are available.

Private lessons: $130 for two hours. Alta recommends a two-hour lesson as a minimum. Additional persons can join the lesson for $40 each.

Special programs: Afternoon workshops focus on specific skills and are $45 for two-and-a-half hours; meet at the blue and white signs below the base of Germania lift. A telemark workshop is offered Tuesdays, Thursdays and Sundays for $45. Diamond Challenge is a two-and-a-half-hour afternoon workshop for Level 9 (true expert) skiers for $45. The instructor gives pointers, but mostly acts as a guide to Alta's steep powder stashes.

Racing: Alta's race course is at the Sunnyside lift; Friday and Saturday from 11 a.m. to 3 p.m. Pay the $7 fee ($10 for unlimited runs) at the race arena or at the ticket office.

Child care (2001/02 prices)

Ages: 2 months to 12 years.

Cost: All-day infant care by reservation only is $75. All-day child care (3 and older) with lunch is $55. Multiday discounts available.

Reservations: Requested. Alta's child care center is a state-licensed facility owned and operated by Redwood Pre-School, Inc. (742-3042).

Children's lessons: For beginner and intermediate skiers (skill levels 1–6), ages 4–12: All Day Adventure for skill levels 1–2 is $80 (with lunch); for skill levels 3–6, it's $95 (including lunch and lift ticket). Half Day Adventure for levels 1–6 is $35. For advanced and expert skiers (skill levels 7–9), ages 7–teens: All Day Explorer costs $107 (with lunch and lift); Afternoon Explorer costs $45. All children's lessons meet at the Albion base. For ski school programs, call 359-1078.

Lift tickets (2001/02 prices)

	Adult	Child (Up to 12)
One day	$38	$38
Three days	$114 ($38/day)	$114 ($38/day)
Five days	$190 ($38/day)	$190 ($38/day)

Who skis free: Ages 80 and older.

Who skis at a discount: Skiers pay $22 to use the beginner lifts in the Albion area. If you aren't too sure about the conditions, buy a single-ride ticket for any lift for $5. Bonus: All surface lifts are free.

Note: Alta skips all the discount gimmicks, figures out what it will take to run the place, and charges everyone the same low price. A new Alta Snowbird ticket that allows you to access both resorts' terrain costs $68 a day.

Accommodations

Alta is one of the few ski areas that still has traditional ski lodges where breakfast and dinner are included in the cost. This is a super way to meet new people, particularly if you are traveling alone. Most of these lodges have either dorm rooms or single occupancy rates available. Some of Alta's lodges do not accept all major credit cards; some don't accept any. Ask whether your room has a private bath, since some rooms do not. Rates are lower in value season, which is prior to mid-December, most of January, and April to closing.

Rustler Lodge (742-2200, 888-532-2582; $$–$$$$) is recently remodeled, and is mid-way between the Albion and Rustler/Wildcat base areas. It has an outdoor pool, saunas and hot tubs. Don't miss the restaurant and bar with picture windows looking right out onto the mountain. Prices include breakfast and dinner. No credit cards are accepted here; pay by personal check, travelers checks or cash.

Alta Peruvian (800-453-8488, reservations only; 742-3000; $–$$$) has similar ameni-ties, features movies each night, and is a short walk from the Wildcat base (or you can take the lodge's free shuttle). The rates include breakfast, lunch, and dinner (food's great, by the way). Dorm rooms, single rooms, double rooms with private bath, one- or two-bedroom suites and multiday discounts also are available. Alta Peruvian accepts credit cards.

The Alta Lodge (800-707-2582, reservations only; 742-3500; $$–$$$) is a 57-room mountain inn with saunas, hot tubs, and several common areas, including a library. By guest preference over the years, the lodge has only one television. Skiers grab a rope tow at the end of the day to get back up a small hill to the lodge. The Alta Lodge has the homey feel of a pair of well-worn slippers, not surprising since many of the guests are repeat customers who return each year and know each other on a first-name basis. Alta Mayor Bill Levitt is the proprietor, and he will be happy to regale guests with tales from Alta's storied past (and present). Our favorite is how a comely ski instructor once caught the eye and changed the life of the East Coast boy who would become mayor of Alta. Breakfast and dinner are in-cluded in the price, and the food is excellent. Credit cards and personal checks accepted. The same chef has been in the kitchen for 30 years.

Goldminer's Daughter (800-453-4573, reservations only; 742-2300; $$–$$$), named after a huge mining claim, is closest to the Wildcat lift. You can step out your door into the lift line, and drop by your room between runs for a hat or neck gaiter. Visa and MasterCard accepted here. **Snowpine Lodge** (742-2000; $–$$$) is Alta's oldest and smallest. It was extensively renovated a few years ago, and has an outdoor hot tub, Scandinavian sauna and a warm and homey atmosphere. Visa and MasterCard accepted here.

Two large condominiums, **Hellgate** (801-742-2020; $$$–$$$$) and **Blackjack** (801-742-3200; $$$$) are between Alta and Snowbird, with Blackjack better situated for skiing between the two resorts and therefore slightly higher-priced. Both have van service to the ski areas. Studios, one-bedrooms sleeping four, two-bedrooms sleeping six and three-bed-rooms are offered. There is no service charge.

Canyon Services (800-862-2888) rents luxurious condos and homes with fully equipped kitchens, washers and dryers and cable TV.

Dining

At night, most skiers dine in their lodges, since the meals are included in the lodging cost. Those who stay in condos need to make a grocery stop in

Dining: $$$-Entrees $20+; $$-$10-20; $-less than $10.
Accommodations: (double room) $$$$-$200+; $$$-$141-$200; $$-$81-$140; $-$80 and less.

Salt Lake City, or dine in the lodge restaurants that also are open to the public. For a sit-down lunch on the mountain, head to the **Collins Grill,** upstairs in the Watson Shelter. **Shallow Shaft** (742-2177; $$–$$$), on Alta's main road, is open for dinner only and has salmon, steak, pasta and chicken entrées.

Après-ski/nightlife

Bring your own. There's nothing going on but what visitors cook up—either in their condo or the lodge's common rooms. That said, the best nightime gatherings we found were at the **bar at the Alta Peruvian Lodge,** where guests and locals gather (with a cover charge on weekends) for drinks at a lively bar or around the fire. The dog curled around the couch is the local mascot. The **Sitzmark Bar** at the Alta Lodge is also good for après-ski story swapping. Local lore has it that the bookshelves at the Alta Peruvian have been voted the best nightlife in Alta. If your ski vacation is not complete without a vigorous night of dancing, stay in Salt Lake City and take the ski bus here during the day.

Other activities

Weekends and holidays at 1:30 p.m., 45-minute **guided interpretive ski tours** are given by a Wasatch-Cache National Forest ranger. Meet at the sign at the bottom of Cecret lift. **Heli-skiing** with Wasatch Powderbird Guides (742-2800; www.heliskiwasatch.com) is available in Little Cottonwood Canyon. A few **shops** in the Little Cottonwood Canyon area have local handicrafts, artwork and books, but skiers don't come to Alta for the shopping. Note, however, that one of our staff writers found a replacement lens for his goggles in the general store at Alta Lodge—no other shops in the region carried them. This place attracts those who like to ski from morn-ing 'til the last lift shuts down. If you must, you can always take a bus or drive down to Salt Lake City for a day of heavy-duty shopping.

Getting there and getting around

By air: Salt Lake City is a major airline hub, so flights are numerous from every corner of the continent. See the Snowbird chapter for ground transportation information. An additional ground transportation option is Alta Ski Shuttle (800-742-3406), which has airport shuttles every 30 minutes between 8 a.m. and 11 p.m. for $40 per person, round trip. The company also will provide transport outside of those hours for $100 per van, one-way, for up to five people, with advance notice.

   By train: Amtrak's California Zephyr stops here, arriving at 4 a.m. for eastbound trains and midnight for westbound trains. Call (800) USA-RAIL (872-7245) or see the Web site at www.amtrak.com.

   By car: Alta is 25 miles southeast of Salt Lake City in Little Cottonwood Canyon on State Hwy. 210. Drive east on I-80, south on I-215, Exit 6 to Wasatch Blvd., then follow the signs to Alta and Snowbird.

   Getting around: If you fly in, don't bother renting a car. Ground transportation from the airport or the city is frequent and plentiful. Most of Alta's lodges have free shuttles to get you to the slopes or to visit neighboring restaurants. If you are staying in Salt Lake City, take the Utah Transit Authority bus ($4 from downtown, $1.50 from the bottom of the canyon; exact fare required) or a Lewis Brothers SkiExpress van to Alta (about $20 roundtrip from downtown; 800-826-5844, or 359-8677 from Salt Lake City). Bus service links Alta and Snowbird for $1.

Deer Valley
Park City, Utah

Summit elevation:	9,570 feet
Vertical drop:	3,000 feet
Base elevation:	6,570 feet

Address: P.O. Box 1525, Park City, UT 84060
✎ **Area code:** 435
Ski area phone: 649-1000
Snow report: 649-2000 **Fax:** 645-6939
ⓘ **Toll-free information:** (800) 424-3337
ⓘ **Toll-free reservations:** (800) 558-3337
Internet: www.deervalley.com

Expert: ★★★★
Advanced: ★★★★
Intermediate: ★★★★
Beginner: ★★
Never-ever: ★

Number of lifts: 19—1 gondola, 5 high-speed quads, 3 quads, 8 triples, 2 doubles
Snowmaking: 27 percent
Skiable acreage: 1,750 acres
Uphill capacity: 39,700 per hour
Snowboarding: None
Nearest lodging: Slopeside
Resort child care: Yes, 2 months and older
Adult ticket, per day: $58-$65 (01/02 price)

Dining: ★★★★★
Apres-ski/nightlife: ★
Other activities: ★★

Deer Valley is one of America's most exclusive resorts. Everything is top notch from the manicured snow conditions to the gleaming brass and glass cafeterias. Deer Valley is as upscale as it gets in America, but without the upscale snobbery that seems to infect other expensive places in the country. Here, even the common folk can relax and leave feeling like they have received great value for their dollar. The resort itself is just a couple miles from the historic town of Park City. Deer Valley is basically a cluster of condominiums and upscale hotels huddled around a spectacular ski area. You can lounge in luxury up on the mountainside or head downtown to have fun in one of America's best ski towns. *(See Park City chapter)*

Deer Valley is renowned for pampering its guests with top-flight gourmet meals, palatial accommodations, attentive service and impeccable slopes. Some of the many amenities include guest service attendants who help get skis off car racks as you pull up to unload, tissues at every lift, restaurants to make a gourmet salivate, a free ski corral service where you can safely leave the best equipment, and grooming crews who comb the snow so pool-table smooth that everyone moves up a notch in ability. Experts who sneer at the daily slope manicure can ditch the main drag. Do not pass "Go" on your way to the chutes and bowls off Empire Canyon or to cop some bumps off the Sultan and Mayflower chairs, and quit your complaining. Deer Valley fills a marvelous niche in the ski world, satisfying those who want to be pampered and are willing to pay a little more for the privilege, as well as those who need some juice along with their eggs and toast. Keep in mind that there are really four mountains here, ranging from Little Baldy at 7,950 feet to the top of Empire Canyon at 9,570 feet.

Here, 2002 Olympic preparations have resulted in improvements, like the Empire Lodge, a lavish day lodge and restaurant at the bottom of the Empire Express in Empire Canyon. A new race course for guests has been added on Silver Hill in the Deer Crest area of the resort. This race arena operates similarly to Race Course on Bald Mountain, with a designated race course, timing and announcement system. Snowmaking was added to Trump, Ontario, Lower Sunset, Sunset West and Last Chance ski runs as well as to Empire Canyon on Supreme, Solace and Orion ski runs.

Mountain layout—Skiing

◆◆ **Expert:** Request an Experts Only trail map, which points out the toughest runs and several gladed and chute areas. Empire Canyon, topping out at 9,570 feet, is not only the highest point at Deer Valley, but also the gnarliest. The double-diamond Daly Chutes, the Daly Bowl and the Anchor Trees are short, steep and superbly challenging. Single-diamond terrain at Lady Morgan Bowl in Empire adds some nice vertical. The Empire Express opens 500 acres with eight chutes and three bowls.

Flagstaff Mountain, with both bump and cruising runs, is easy to navigate and a good rendezvous when several members of your group ski at different ability levels. Experts take a short traverse to the left off the top of this lift to Ontario Bowl's double-diamond tree skiing.

◆ **Advanced:** The Mayflower Lift, to the far left on the trail map, supplies respectable single-diamond terrain on both sides of the lift. Moguls on Morning Star, Fortune Teller, Paradise and Narrow Gauge are a delight. The long trails are bordered by glades—great places to drop into and out of on a whim.

While Mayflower and its neighboring chair Sultan feature ungroomed runs, the bumps rarely grow too big. Orient Express and Stein's Way are advanced cruisers with good pitch, and Perseverance, coupled with the initial steeper sections of Thunderer, Blue Ledge and Grizzly, is good for those entering advanced status.

■ **Intermediate:** Deer Valley offers both intermediate and advanced-intermediate terrain, though we're hard-pressed to tell the two apart. If you want to have plenty of company and beautiful scenery, the best runs are Sunset, Birdseye (both on Bald Mountain) and Success (on Bald Eagle Mountain). Areas with the most intermediate runs are served by the Wasatch Express, Sterling and Northside Express chairs. Run after run down trails such as Legal Tender, Wizard, Nabob, Sidewinder and Hawkeye are a blast. We like the runs under the Northside Express, too, mainly because they're farther from the base areas, so they're not as crowded as the Wasatch Express area.

The Empire Canyon and Deer Crest areas, added during the 98/99 season, also have some fun slopes for this level—try the advanced intermediate bowls Conviction, Solace and Orion in particular. The view of the Jordanelle Reservoir from the Deer Crest area is fabulous; however, the Jordanelle run has one wicked narrow part that may intimidate newly intermediate skiers, and don't even think about taking a beginner down it, assuming it'll be easy to get to the gondola base parking lot. A fun place to test your intermediate tree- and bump-skiing legs is in the unnamed area on Flagstaff off the Ontario trail, or by sneaking through the trees at the top of the Quincy Lift. They're worth a giggle.

Other great areas are Flagstaff Mountain and Bald Eagle Mountain, known as the "lower mountain." Last Chance passes by a lot of spectacular homes, perfect for lookie-loos.

If you are a timid intermediate, stick to Deer Valley's green-circle runs at first. We find the greens here to be a bit turquoise, just a shade easier than the true blues.

●● **Beginner:** Deer Valley's offerings at this level have improved in past years. Best spots are the outside runs on Flagstaff Mountain, Ontario and Mountain Daisy/Banner. If you are a timid beginner, read the Never-Ever advice. If you're a brave soul who just needs some practice, we especially recommend Sunset, a gentle, scenic route that descends from the top of Bald Mountain—but head back to the base before day's end or you'll find yourself in the role of a human slalom pole, being passed at close range by more proficient skiers. There's also the Little Chief Family Ski Area in Empire Canyon, which is one run that hardly seems worth the traverse and chair lift experience to get there.

● **Never-ever:** The novice area is gentle enough, but it's a big step to the next level. Some of Deer Valley's green runs also access trails and runouts that better skiers use to reach the base area. A beginner might feel as though he or she is riding a scooter on a freeway, which can be intimidating in this land of speed and curve.

Mountain layout—Snowboarding

Snowboarding is not allowed. Head for The Canyons or Park City Mountain Resort.

Mountain rating

Deer Valley has built a reputation for pampering at a price, but its slopes include tougher trails than it gets credit for. Expert skiers on our staff were hugely surprised by the challenging terrain and found plenty of reasons to grin. On a scale of one to 10, one being a never-ever and 10 being a top-flight expert, we'd say that Deer Valley is best for levels three through eight (maybe a nine with the Empire Summit terrain). And that's no slam: The vast majority of skiers fit that profile.

Cross-country and snowshoeing

White Pine Touring (615-5858) offers 18 km. of track and skate skiing, plus track, skate and telemark lessons at the Park City golf course and an adjacent dairy farm. Rates are $10 daily for adults; $5 for kids 6-12; younger than 6 and older than 65 ski free. For those who want to get off the flats, half-day snowshoe (Wed. & Sun.) and ski (Tues. and Fri.) tours in the Uinta mountains are also available. To venture out on your own, this is a good stop for advice and maps of the local mountain bike trails that are accessible (many from downtown Park City) and perfect for snowshoeing.

The Homestead Resort (654-1102; 800-327-7220), 14 miles southeast of Park City in Midway, has 12 km. of skiing at Homestead Golf Course and 18 km. at Wasatch Mountain State Park. Snowshoeing and snowmobiling also are available. Trail fees are $6 for adults and $3 for children. Nearby, **Soldier Hollow** is a free community area that will be the site of the 2002 Olympic cross-country competitions.

Lessons (2001/02 prices)

Group lessons: In Deer Valley speak, "semi-private" lessons (levels 1-6) for adults 18 and older costs $95; choose from a three-hour a.m. or four-hour p.m. group (oops! we mean semi-private) lessons.

Never-ever package (lifts, lessons, rentals): None.

Private lessons: $85 for one hour (*very* private, for one or two skiers), $295 for three hours, $525 all day; reserve in advance.

Special programs: Women have occasional three-day clinics for $365 (lift ticket extra).

Racing: A race program called Medalist Challenge is held on the Race Course above Silver Lake Lodge, reachable by the Sterling or Wasatch Lifts. The cost is about $9 for two runs and the daily chance to earn a medal. About once a week, Deer Valley's Director of Skiing, Stein Eriksen, an Olympic gold medalist and World Champion, runs the course so you can compare your time to his. Heidi Voelker, a U.S. Ski Team veteran, also does this about once a week. A self-timed dual slalom is available, too.

Child care (2001/02 prices)

Ages: 2 months to 12 years.

Costs: Full day, with lunch, ages 2–12 years, $74. Full-day infant care, ages 2 months–2 years, including lunch if appropriate, $84. Half day is sold on space-available basis, cannot be reserved in advance.

Reservations: Recommended at all times but essential during holiday periods. Call 645-6648 or make reservations when you book lodging.

Other options: The Park City Chamber of Commerce can refer visitors to **child-care facilities** or **babysitting services.** Call (800) 453-1360 or locally, 649-6100. **Baby's Away** (800-379-9030; 435-645-8823) rents and will deliver baby needs to your lodge, such as crib, stroller, car seat and toys.

Children's lessons: Full day, ages 6 (first grade) to 12, is $115 for lessons, lift ticket and lunch. Ages 4–5 get a full-day program, also for $115. Three-year-olds have a program that is a combination of day care and ski lessons for $110. Advanced registration is recommended for these programs; definitely during holiday periods.

Lift tickets (2001/02 prices)

	Adult	Child (Up to 12)
One day	$65	$35
Three days	$183 ($61/day)	$90 ($30/day)
Five days	$290 ($58/day)	$140 ($28/day)

Who skis free: No one.

Who skis at a discount: Skiers 65 and older ski for $45 for a single day, $123 for three days and $195 for five days.

Note: For seven or eight days between Christmas and New Year's Deer Valley's multi-day discounts are suspended. However, ticket sales are limited, so on holidays the extra few bucks to ski Deer Valley are worth it. You can make advance ticket reservations when you book your lodging, and this is highly recommended during the Christmas period and February, Presidents' Day holiday week.

Park City interchangeable lift ticket

The Silver Passport gets you on the lifts at Deer Valley, Park City Mountain Resort and The Canyons. You must advance-book at least three nights of lodging to purchase the pass. You can use the pass at one resort each day that it is valid (meaning, you can't ski at Deer Valley in the morning and Park City in the afternoon). Snowboarders may not use Deer Valley's lifts, and the pass is not valid the week between Christmas and New Year. The cost, based on last season, for adults will be about $54 per day; children about $27. More information: Deer Valley Central Reservations, (800) 558-3337, Park City Mountain Reservations, (800) 222-7275 or The Canyons Reservations, (888) 226-9667.

Accommodations

At Deer Valley the lodging has a decidedly upscale flavor—and tariffs to match. All lodging in Deer Valley is costly. Even in the value season the least expensive starts at about $200 per night. Accommodations have the same high quality one finds at the resort itself, and much of it is slopeside. If it's in your budget, book it. If not, stay in Park City—only a short ride away on a frequent shuttlebus. There is plenty of other more reasonable lodging in and around the Park City area such as bed-and-breakfasts, country inns, chain hotels and condominiums.

Park City's lodging is roughly grouped either in the old town surrounding the Resort Center Complex or in the Prospector Square area. A wonderful new part of town is Lower Main (also called South Main), which surrounds the base of the Town Lift. All areas are served by the free shuttlebus system. See the Park City chapter for details on area lodging.

Top dog at Deer Valley is the **Stein Eriksen Lodge** (800-453-1302 or 649-3700; $$$$). Think of any luxury or service and you will probably find it—heated sidewalks between buildings, fireplaces in the rooms, fresh terrycloth robes, floor-to-ceiling windows. A $30-million expansion just added 11 lavish condominiums and a conference center.

After Stein's the places to stay on the mountain are the **Stag Lodge Condominiums** (800-453-3833 or 649-7444; $$$$) and the **Goldener Hirsch Inn** (800-252-3373 or 649-7770; $$$$), offering the elegance and service of a top Austrian hotel.

The **Pinnacle Condominiums** ($$$$) have spacious and well-appointed interiors, and they aren't too far from the bus stop. Ski-in/ski-out properties are the **Pine Inn** ($$$$) and **La Maçonnerie** ($$$$). All units have private spas.

The most economical Deer Valley condos are the **Snow Park** units, where a one-bedroom without hot tub is about $325 in the regular season.

For reservations in Deer Valley, call **Deer Valley Lodging**, which also manages numerous lodges, condominiums and private homes (800-453-3833 or 649-4040), or **Deer Valley Central Reservations** (800-558-3337 or 649-1000).

 ## Dining

The multi-level **Mariposa** (645-6715; $$$) at Silver Lake Lodge is the gourmets' top choice. To really get the full "taste" of Mariposa treats, try either the Chef's Vegetable Tasting or the Mariposa Tasting.

The **Glitretind Restaurant** (649-3700; $$$) at Stein Eriksen Lodge surprisingly offers creative, but very American fare. Glitretind's all-you-can-eat skier's lunch buffet with made-to-order pasta dishes, a carving table, various salads, cold meats and delectable desserts is a surprisingly affordable feast. The lodge's smaller, cozier **Valhalla** (645-6455; $$$) sticks with the American, too, but has more "exotic" main dish choices such as elk and buffalo.

The **Seafood Buffet** (645-6632; $$$) at Snow Park Lodge, spread out Mondays through Saturdays, is magnificent. Every type of seafood you can think of is here, and it's all you can eat—a real bargain. You won't want to miss the Dungeness crab and tiger shrimp. By the way, there's a gorgeous roast beef for landlubbers.

The **Goldener Hirsch Inn** (649-7770; $$$) in Silver Lake Village serves breakfast, lunch and dinner in an Austrian setting. Traditionalists will find weinerschnitzel, handmade bratwurst and raclette cheese, and others can enjoy the regional American specialties. The interior of the restaurant is a replica of one in Salzburg, while the inn is styled after an Austrian mansion.

Sai-Sommet (645-9909; $$$), pronounced say-so-may, in the Deer Valley Club is open to the public Wed.–Sun. Locals say make reservations early and save room for dessert.

McHenry's (645-6724; $$) in the Silver Lake Lodge serves moderately priced lunches and dinners in a casual atmosphere. The **Olive Barrel Food Co.** (647-7777; $$$), an Italian trattoria-style restaurant at Silver Lake Lodge, is overpriced in our opinion.

For a great breakfast value, head to the buffet at the **Snow Park Restaurant** and for lunch go to the **Silver Lake Restaurant**. These cafeteria-style restaurants glisten with shiny brass and sparkling glass. P.S. You gotta have the turkey chili. Then ask someone to direct you to the shop where you can buy the dry ingredients to take home and make your own huge pot of this delicious stuff.

  ## Après-ski/nightlife

Immediate aprés-ski centers at The Lounge right on the slopes where the deck gets packed on spring weekends when they have live entertainment. There are bars in the hotels for later on, but the real party animals head downtown to Park City where music plays and the fun really goes full steam.

 ## Other activities

Nearby Park City is packed with other activities to keep you busy after the skis are put away and Salt Lake City is only about a half hour away. See the *Park City chapter* and the *Salt Lake City chapter* for more details.

The **Sundance Film Festival** is in late January, showcasing new films from around the world.

Many companies offer **sleigh rides, snowmobile tours** and **hot-air balloon trips**. To reserve any or all of these activities and more, call one central number at ABC Reservations Central, (800) 820-2223 or (435) 649-2223. There is no fee and most adventures provide free shuttle service.

Getting there and getting around

By air: The drive from the Salt Lake City International Airport to Park City takes 45 minutes. Ground transportation makes frequent trips from the airport for $34-$46, round-trip (children's fares are $17-$35). Providers include Lewis Brothers Stages, (800) 826-5844 or (435) 649-2256; Park City Transportation, (800) 637-3803 or (435) 649-8567; and All Resort Express (800) 457-9457 or (435) 649-3999. If you arrive without reservations, go to the transportation counter at the airport and you'll ride on the next available van. Call 48 hours in advance for Park City-to-airport reservations.

By car: Park City is 32 miles east of Salt Lake City, by I-80 and Utah Hwy. 224.

Getting around: You will not need a car to get around Deer Valley. The condominiums all have shuttle systems as do the hotels. The Park City bus system has four routes with service every 20 minutes, if not more frequently, from 7 a.m. to 1 a.m. If you take a side trip to one of the Cottonwood Canyons ski resorts, Lewis Brothers Stages and Park City Transportation have shuttles for $22-$35 round-trip. Lewis Brothers offers a Canyon Jumper package to Solitude and Snowbird for $49 and $52, respectively, including transportation and lift ticket. Prepay the evening before you wish to ski.

Park City, Utah

Park City Mountain Resort

The Canyons

ⓘ Toll-free information:
(800) 453-1360 (Park City Chamber)
Fax: 649-0532 (lodging)
Internet: www.parkcityinfo.com (town)
Dining:★★★
Apres-ski/nightlife:★★★
Other activities:★★★

Walk outside the Alamo Saloon at dusk, just as the lights of Main Street begin to twinkle seductively and the sidewalks fill with après-ski traffic, and you can almost hear the clank of spurs. Squint your eyes and the strolling figures become the miners and cowboys who roamed this same street a hundred years ago, swaggering through 30-odd saloons in what was once one of the country's largest silver mining towns. Soon the vision is gone, and the people are once again modern-day funseekers. Yet the flamboyant atmosphere of the silver rush remains. Park City's mining heritage is quite evident at Park City Mountain Resort, where old mine ruins dot the slopes. The Park City Historical Society has put up signs describing each of the sites, so skiers and boarders can get a sense of history as they enjoy the day.

This town originally was founded by soldiers who had been sent west to discourage Brigham Young from ending the Utah Territory's association with the Union. Park City boomed during the mining era, then almost became a ghost town during the Depression and World War II. Now Park City can be counted among the world's top winter resorts.

This is the most accessible destination resort of its caliber in the country, just 30 miles from Salt Lake City via a major freeway. Accessibility was one of the key factors that helped Salt Lake City get the 2002 Olympic Winter Games. Park City, which is headquarters for the U.S. Ski and Snowboard Team, will host many of the Olympic events. Park City Mountain Resort and Deer Valley Resort (*see Deer Valley chapter*) will host the slalom, combined slalom, giant slalom, aerials, moguls and snowboarding, while bobsled, luge, Nordic combined and ski jumping will be at the nearby Utah Winter Sports Park. Even during the games, 96 percent of Park City Mountain Resort will be open for regular skiing and riding. The Games are set for February 8-24, 2002. Park City Mountain Resort and Deer Valley are ready to go.

The Canyons, another Park City area resort, has completed its fourth season under the ownership of the American Skiing Company. You may have heard of The Canyons under one of its previous names: ParkWest or Wolf Mountain. However, it looks a lot different now. Just about every lift and building has been replaced, rebuilt or otherwise improved. And every year, they open more terrain. Another peak with 325 acres was opened last season, putting The Canyons in the top five in the nation in skiable terrain.

NBC's Today Show has chosen to broadcast live from The Canyons for its Olympic coverage. The main broadcast center will be within The Grand Summit Resort Hotel, and there will be an outdoor set for audience participation. Live broadcasting will begin prior to the Opening Ceremonies and continue throughout the Olympic Games.

Park City Mountain Resort (PCMR) Facts

Summit elevation:	10,000 feet
Vertical drop:	3,100 feet
Base elevation:	6,900 feet

Address: P.O. Box 39, Park City, UT 84060
☎ **Area code:** 435
Ski area phone: 649-8111
Snow report: 647-5449
Toll-free reservations:
(800) 222-7275 (Park City Mountain Reservations)
Internet: www.parkcitymountain.com (PCMR)
Expert:★★★★
Advanced:★★★★
Intermediate:★★★★
Beginner:★★★ **Never-ever:**★★★

Number of lifts: 14–4 high-speed six-person chairs, 1 high-speed quad, 5 triple chairs, 4 double chairs
Snowmaking: 14 percent
Skiing acreage: 3,300
Uphill capacity: 27,200 per hour
Snowboarding: Yes
Bed base: 12,000
Nearest lodging: Slopeside, condos
Resort child care: None; lessons start at age 3
Adult ticket, per day: $49-$59+ (2000/01 prices)

Dining:★★★★
Apres-ski/nightlife:★★★★
Other activities:★★★

Park City internchangeable lift ticket

The Silver Passport gets you on the lifts at Deer Valley, Park City Mountain Resort and The Canyons. You must advance-book at least three nights of lodging to purchase the pass. You can use the pass at one resort each day that it is valid (meaning, you can't ski at Deer Valley in the morning and Park City in the afternoon). Snowboarders may not use Deer Valley's lifts, and the pass is not valid the week between Christmas and New Year. The cost, based on last season, for adults will be about $54 per day; children about $27. More information: Deer Valley Central Reservations, (800) 558-3337, Park City Mountain Reservations, (800) 222-7275 or The Canyons Reservations, (888) 226-9667.

Park City Mountain Resort

Completion of the Town Bridge that links Park City Mountain Resort to the heart of Park City is scheduled to open in time for the winter season, allowing skiers and riders direct on-snow access to the Main Street hub of Park City. This means that you can ski or ride straight to Main Street, have a choice of some 200 restaurants and shops to visit during lunch, and then ride back up the mountain on the existing Town Lift.

Mountain layout—Skiing

The Town Lift triple chair loads from the lower part of Park City's Main Street to the base of the Bonanza lift part-way up the mountain. Even on holidays or peak periods, the Town Lift is often empty, so you may want to take the free shuttle here and avoid the crowds. If Bonanza has a long line, ski down Sidewinder a tad, catch the Crescent chair, ski down King Con to the Silverlode chair and it'll take you to the Summit area. If Payday has a line, try the Eagle chair (to the far right of the base area) and head down blue-square Temptation to the King Con chair.

◆◆ **Expert:** Start off with a trip to the top of Blueslip Bowl off the Pioneer Lift. Reportedly, when this was the boundary of the ski area, resort workers regularly slipped under the ropes, made tracks down the bowl and then skied back into the resort. If you got caught, you were fired, or given your blue slip. If you can ski Blueslip with confidence, then try Jupiter Bowl and its neighboring bowls—McConkey's, Puma and Scott's. But if you decide Blueslip conditions aren't, uh, to your liking, never fear because Homerun is near—it begins at the top of the Pioneer lift and takes you gently down to the base area.

Jupiter Bowl has every type of steep expert terrain. To reach the Jupiter lift, take the Jupiter access road from the top of the Pioneer or Thaynes lifts. It's a long, flat traverse, so don't lose your speed. To the left as you get off the Jupiter lift are wide-open faces, especially on the West Face, which is the easiest way down (a relative term). The West Face is as far from the Jupiter Lift as you can ski. It can be covered with windblown crust, so you might want to ask about conditions before you board the lift. Narrow gullies and chutes, such as Silver Cliff, 6 Bells and Indicator, drop vertically between tightly packed evergreens. Head to the right as you get off the chair and try Portuguese Gap, a run more akin to having the floor open below you, or traverse to Scott's Bowl, which is just as steep. Main Bowl, closer to the lift, also offers some nice turns as it drops under the chair.

The adventurous (and those with parachutes) will find definite thrills in McConkey's Bowl and Puma Bowl. McConkey's is now served by McConkey's Hi-Speed Six-Pack. Puma still requires a long traverse across a ridge and some hiking from either the Jupiter or McConkey's lifts to reach its steep faces and chutes on the backside of Jupiter Peak.

◆ **Advanced:** If you're looking for steeps or moguls, try the blacks off the Motherlode triple or the neighboring Thaynes double. Glory Hole, Double Jack and the like offer a good challenge. Or, ski the front face of PCMR on the runs off the Ski Team Lift. Most of the deliciously long trails here are left *au naturel*, but Willy's is on the occasional grooming list. Hit it on the right day, and it's *fun*. For a groomed steep cruiser, try nearby Silver Queen.

■ **Intermediate:** Choices are mind-boggling. If you want to start with a worthy cruiser, take Payday from the top of the lift by the same name. The views are spectacular, and at night it becomes one of the longest lighted runs in the Rockies. This run also has a halfpipe.

Probably most popular are the 11 trails served by King Consolidated (called "King Con" by just about everyone). These runs have a steep, wide, smooth pitch.

Both intermediates and advanced skiers will enjoy the runs under the Silverlode chair. To avoid crowds, try the four blues under the Pioneer chair. Or, board McConkey's and take the intermediate ridge routes down from the top.

●● **Beginner:** Even those just getting into their snowplow turns can take the Payday and Bonanza chairs to the Summit House and descend a very long, easy, multi-named run. This trail starts as Claim Jumper, shifts to Bonanza, then finishes at the base area as Sidewinder. For an adventure and to see a different part of the mountain, take the Mid-Mountain Run to the Pioneer chair, where you can have lunch and watch experts head down Blueslip Bowl.

The only complaint about the beginner runs here is that everyone else uses them too. The upper parts of the green-circle trails are used as access routes, while the bottoms are the end runs for skiers coming off more advanced terrain. The greens here are wide and gentle, but they wind in and around tougher stuff. If you're just starting out and concerned about getting in above your head, carry a trail map and pay attention to the signage. And head to the bottom well before day's end if you like plenty of room.

● **Never-ever:** At the base area, the Three Kings and First Time lifts service good learning terrain

Mountain layout—Snowboarding

Park City Mountain Resort has some long, nearly flat runs that snowboarders will want to avoid. The two worst ones are Jupiter Access and Thaynes Canyon, both of which are used primarily to reach other parts of the mountain. In particular, Jupiter Access road from the top of the Pioneer or Thaynes lifts is a long, flat traverse, so don't lose your speed. You can avoid the worst traverses with advance planning. However, snowboarders have a bit of an advantage in Park City's hike-to powder bowls, because they get to hike to the best stuff in soft boots.

The best all-around freeriding area is below Home Run between the Claim Jumper and Parley's Park runs. Three lifts can get you there: Silverlode Hi-Speed Six-Pack, Motherlode Lift and Bonanza Hi-Speed Six-Pack. There are some good cuts through the trees, plenty of bumps and some wide smoothies good for kicking up the speed. At the opposite end of the ski area, both the Town Lift and the Payday Hi-Speed Six-Pack deposit you above the huge halfpipe on Payday.

Mountain rating

Most reviews of PCMR characterize it as a cruisers' paradise, which is true enough. While it may not have as many steeps as Snowbird or Alta, its bowl skiing and chutes are serious—even on the expert scale. PCMR doesn't have a huge amount of lower-end terrain, but beginners can get high enough to see the views—something they can't do at every resort. In our opinion, PCMR is the most predictable and most uninspired of the three resorts here.

Lessons (2001/02 prices)

Prices below are for peak periods, which covers most of the season.
Group lessons: $65 for three hours.
Never-ever package: $165 for a full day, includes lift ticket and rental equipment. For snowboarding lessons, PCMR is an authorized Burton Method Center, with a combination of Burton LTR (Learn To Ride) equipment and a proprietary teaching system that offers a 4-1 student to teacher ratio. The system is based on a two-board progression. Your first board has a lot of sidecut for easy turning and very soft flex. Once you start linking turns you move on to a board with even more sidecut for more advanced turning skills, and a more directional shape to ride more of the mountain.

Private lessons: $100 for one hour, $195 for two hours. The VIP Series, which teaches a skier or rider to move to the next skill level, is designed to assure that your learning experience will be glitch-free and effective. Choose from a six-hour private lesson for $495, or a three-hour private lesson for $270.

Racing: NASTAR is on the Blanche trail Wednesday through Saturday. Two runs cost $6; each additional run is $1. Park City Dual Challenge is set up on Clementine nearly every day. The cost is $1 per run; $5 for seven runs.

Child care (2001/02 prices)

PCMR does not have non-skiing child care. The Park City Chamber of Commerce can refer visitors to **child-care facilities** or **babysitting services.** Call (800) 453-1360 or locally, 649-6100. **Baby's Away** (800-379-9030; 435-645-8823) rents and will deliver baby needs to your lodge, such as crib, stroller, car seat and toys.

Children's lessons: Ages 3–12, $115 for a full day including two 90-minute lessons, hot lunch, snack. Children ages 3-5 also have some indoor recreation. Snowboard lessons, for ages 7-12, cost the same. PCMR requires reservations for all children's programs. Call (800) 227-7275.

Lift tickets

	Adult	Child (Up to 12)
One day	varies day to day*	varies day to day*
Three days	$165 ($55/day)*	$81 ($27/day)*
Five days	$245 ($49/day)*	$115 ($22/day)*

Who skis free: Ages 70 and older and 6 and younger.
Who skis at a discount: Ages 65–69 ski for $30.

*__Notes:__ PCMR charges slightly more during the two-week Christmas-New Year's period, Martin Luther King weekend in mid-January, and President's Weekend in mid-February. PCMR also does not announce its one- and two-day prices until the day you walk up to the window, basing those prices on "market demand." That "demand," a resort spokesperson told us, not only includes factors such as holiday periods, but also snow conditions—a "powder premium," as we termed it. PCMR even refuses to specify a high and low range for single-day tickets, though the 2000/01 price ranged from $41 to $59. The only way to guarantee a price is to buy a three-day or longer multiday ticket.

The Canyons

The first resort you pass on the way into Park City, The Canyons is a few miles away from the historic downtown area, though it is connected by a free shuttle service from many points. The new Grand Summit Resort Hotel is the focal point of the new base development. It appears as if ASC has finally tossed aside the cookie-cutter design used in their eastern Grand Summit hotels, and the hotel may actually be worthy of the adjective "grand." The circular base village with its arched entrance is warm and inviting, creating a cozy feel to an area that opens up to a humongous amount of terrain and awesome vistas.

There's good news for novices and beginners for the 2001/02 season. The Canyons has added a triple chair and expanded the terrain in the Dreamscape area, providing access to more beginner and intermediate trails. In addition, there's now snowmaking on Harmony, which connects the Dreamscape area to the Tombstone lift. There's also a new learning area behind Red Pine Lodge, separating novices from more accomplished skiers and riders.

The skiing and riding at The Canyons is spread across eight mountain peaks.

Mountain layout—Skiing

◆◆ **Expert** ◆ **Advanced:** Most of The Canyons' terrain is not visible from the base area. What you can't see are chutes and gullies as extreme as any in Utah. Most of the Canyons' real expert terrain is in the trees off the Ninety Nine 90 Express, Tombstone Express and the Super Condor Express. These lifts follow ridges, and the trees and snow drop away on either side. Ninety Nine 90 has heart-stopping chutes off to the right, like Red Pine and Charlie Brown. Peak 5 terrain is touted as intermediate tree skiing, but the trees—lots and lots of trees—make this area more of an expert's playground. The Condor chair takes you to terrain that is very steep, such as the South Side Chutes, or the dense glades of Canis Lupis. You can hike a few hundred feet to the top of Murdock Peak for ungroomed bowl descents. (Our stats reflect lift-served terrain; with the hike, the total vertical is 2,580 feet.)

■ **Intermediate:** There are blue runs from every chair, but sometimes only one or two descents per chair. The best trails for this level are in the center of the resort, under the Saddleback Express (Snow Dancer is quite nice), The Snow Canyon Express (wide paths here) and the lower mountain. The blue runs under the Condor and Tombstone chairs are nice intermediate challenges, especially the double-blues like Cloud 9 (running the length of the Tombstone Express) and Apex Ridge next to the Super Condor Express. Ski Aplande, which takes off from Apex Ridge, a few times and you may feel ready to move on to the black runs like Devil's Friend and Rendezvous Ridge.

●● **Beginner** ● **Never-ever:** There's a nice learning area at the top of the gondola, but The Canyons doesn't have a tremendous amount of gentle terrain. For 2001/02, the resort developed a new learning area behind Red Pine lodge—away from skier and snowboarder traffic—to help increase the comfort level of those just getting started. There's also new terrain in the Dreamscape area. We suggest this level enroll in lessons, in order to have a guide to keep them out of trouble.

Mountain layout—Snowboarding

The Canyons has six natural halfpipes and one constructed pipe. The naturals are spread throughout the area. Nearest the base area are two that can be reached via the Golden Eagle chair. The higher of the two, The Tube, runs off Broken Arrow next to Grizzly. The lower, The Black Hole, cuts off Super Fury and comes out on Flume, below the Snow Canyon Express. A long narrow creek bed/halfpipe runs next to Spider Monkey. It's a beginner's terror. Perhaps the most well-known natural pipe is adjacent to Upper Boa and called Canis Lupis. Two more natural halfpipes can be accessed via Saddleback Express: The first is part of Pine Draw, which is the beginner/intermediate terrain park, and the second is to rider's left of the trail CIA.

The main terrain park is CIA—a.k.a. Canyons International Airport—and it's been moved to the front face of the resort off of Red Hawk lift (don't confuse CIA the terrain park with

The Canyons

Summit elevation:	**9,990 feet**
Vertical drop:	**3,190 feet**
Base elevation:	**6,800 feet**

Address: 4000 The Canyons Resort Drive
Park City, UT 84060
☏ **Area code:** 435
Ski area phone: 649-5400
Snow report phone: 615-3456
ⓘ **Toll-free information:** (800) 754-1636
ⓘ **Toll-free reservations:** (888) 226-9667
Fax: 649-7374
Internet: www.thecanyons.com

Expert:★★★★★
Advanced:★★★★★
Intermediate:★★★★
Beginner:★★ **Never-ever:**★
Number of lifts: 14–1 gondola, 5 high-speed quads, 4 quads, 1 triple, 1 double, 2 surface lifts
Snowmaking: 4 percent
Skiable Acreage: 3,625 acres
Uphill capacity: 24,000+ per hour
Snowboarding: Yes
Bed base: 1,200 slopeside
Nearest lodging: Slopeside
Resort child care: Yes, 6 weeks to 4 years
Adult ticket, per day: $35–$58 (2000/01)

CIA the trail!). This improvement was made last year and received rave reviews from park-goers and mainstream skiers and riders alike. Now, those who want to "go big" can do so without interfering with general resort traffic. The park has at least three rails, five major hits and a halfpipe. Onlookers can watch riders in the park easily from the outside deck at Smokie's.

For riding in the trees, Peak 5 is a good option. Also try the steeps and chutes off the Ninety Nine 90 Express chair. A 20-minute hike from the top of Super Condor Express to Murdock Peaks' 9,602-foot summit will get you freshies in Murdock Bowl, Saddle Chutes or One-Hundred Turns. If you're looking for groomers with lots of space, the runs off Snow Canyon Express will get your board screaming and warm you up for trails off the Super Condor Express.

Mountain rating

The local motto is "If you can see it, you can ski it." Gates to out-of-bounds skiing have serious signs warning of avalanche danger. Lives have been lost in recent years by skiers who didn't heed the warnings. There is so much expert and advanced terrain within bounds at The Canyons that you can literally explore the mountain until you drop from exhaustion and still not get to everything during a weeklong vacation. Experts from the East Coast who prefer tree skiing and riding won't be disappointed—you'll find woods as tight as anything back home. Intermediates have plenty to choose from, and this is a great mountain if you want to improve to the next level. Beginners and never-evers now have increased terrain, though we haven't tried it yet. Hopefully, this rounds out the resort's terrain and ups the options for everyone.

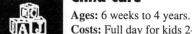

Lessons

Group lessons: Perfect Turn clinics are $47.

Never-ever package: Skiing or snowboarding, a three-day package with a four-hour lesson on day one, two-hour lessons on days two and three, equipment rental and limited lift access is $169. Reservations are recommended. A single-day package is $70 for day one, $80 each for days two and three.

Private lessons: $90 per hour for one or two skiers; $170 for two hours for one or two skiers and $185 for two hours for three to five skiers; all day lessons are $425 for one or two skiers and $475 for a private group of three or four skiers.

Special programs: Daily workshops offered include Intermediate Breakthrough, two hours, $45; Bumps and Diamonds, two hours, $45; Women's Turn, one- to three-day programs with U.S. Olympians Holly Flanders and Hillary Lindh, $129-$387.

Child care

Ages: 6 weeks to 4 years.

Costs: Full day for kids 2–4, with lunch, $67; half day, $47 with lunch. For kids, 3 months to 2 years, cost is $75 for a full day and $55 for a half day. Day care is offered 8:30 a.m.–4:30 p.m. No hourly rates available. Parents should supply a change of clothes and snow clothes. The Day Care Center keeps a list of independent babysitters.

Reservations: Recommended at all times but essential during holiday periods. For advance reservations, call 615-3402. For same-day reservations, call 615-8036.

Other options: The Park City Chamber of Commerce can refer visitors to **child-care facilities** or **babysitting services.** Call (800) 453-1360 or locally, 649-6100. **Baby's Away**

(800-379-9030; 435-645-8823) rents and will deliver baby needs to your lodge, such as crib, stroller, car seat and toys.

Children's lessons: The most requested program is a full day that includes lunch, lift ticket and equipment, plus indoor play time for younger children. It costs $110 for Canyon Cats, ages 4–6, skiing only, and Canyon Carvers, ages 7–12, skiing or riding. Morning clinics only, not including lunch, equipment or lift ticket, are $60. Canyon Cubs, ages 2–3, get full day care plus an hour-an-a-half private lesson for $160—reservations are required. It can be arranged in conjunction with the Grand Summit Resort Hotel Day Care Center or directly through Perfect Kids. Reservations are recommended: 615-3402 for Canyon Cubs; 615-3449 for Canyon Cats and Canyon Carvers.

 ## Lift tickets

	Adult	Child (6-12)
One day	$58	$29
Three days	$150 ($50/day)	$75 ($25/day)
Five days	$240 ($48/day)	$120 ($24/day)

Who skis free: Younger than 6.

Who skis at a discount: Skiers 65 and older ski for children's prices. Check out the American Skiing Company ticket Web site at www.meticket.com for other deals. Early- and late-season prices are lower, peak are higher.

 ## Cross-country and snowshoeing

White Pine Touring (615-5858) offers 18 km. of track and skate skiing, plus track, skate and telemark lessons at the Park City golf course and an adjacent dairy farm. Rates are $10 daily for adults; $5 for kids 6-12; younger than 6 and older than 65 ski free. For those who want to get off the flats, half-day snowshoe (Wed. & Sun.) and ski (Tues. and Fri.) tours in the Uinta mountains are also available. To venture out on your own, this is a good stop for advice and maps of the local mountain bike trails that are accessible (many from downtown Park City) and perfect for snowshoeing.

The Homestead Resort (654-1102; 800-327-7220), 14 miles southeast of Park City in Midway, has 12 km. of skiing at Homestead Golf Course and 18 km. at Wasatch Mountain State Park. Snowshoeing and snowmobiling also are available. Trail fees are $6 for adults and $3 for children. Nearby, **Soldier Hollow** is a free community area that will be the site of the 2002 Olympic cross-country competitions.

 ## Accommodations

In and around Park City are bed-and-breakfasts, country inns, chain hotels and condominiums. Park City's lodging is roughly grouped either in the old town surrounding the Resort Center Complex or in the Prospector Square area. A wonderful new part of town is Lower Main (also called South Main), which surrounds the base of the Town Lift. All areas are served by the free shuttlebus system.

In old Park City the best is the **Washington School Inn** (800-824-1672 or 649-3800; $$–$$$$). This is a very elegant 15-room (including three suites) country inn built in a former schoolhouse. Each room has a private bath and the name of each room honors a former Park City teacher. Everything is definitely first class. It has a hot tub and steam bath, and is steps away from the center of the old town. If you are on your honeymoon, ask for the Miss Urie Room. Room rates include breakfast and afternoon tea. No children under age 12.

The Blue Church Lodge & Townhouses (800-626-5467 or 649-8009; $$–$$$$) are constructed around an old church a block from Main Street. Listed on the National Register of Historic Places, it is a grouping of seven condominiums ranging from one to four bedrooms in the church, with four additional townhouses across the street. A continental breakfast is included, but it doesn't fit the category of B&B in the classic sense. It has indoor and outdoor spas and laundry facilities.

If the key to lodging, as in real estate, is location, location, location, then **Treasure Mountain Inn** (800-344-2460; $$–$$$$) at the top of Main Street is a winner. These are studio and one- and two-bedroom condos with kitchens. Each of the three buildings has a coin-operated laundry, and there is a hot tub in the courtyard. Rooms are quiet, but step outside and you are smack dab in the middle of the nighttime action. Another spot on Main Street is the **1904 Imperial Hotel** (800-669-8824 or 649-1904; $$$), a B&B in a historic old house. All rooms have their own bath, telephone and TV, and most accommodate couples. There's a big hot tub for everyone to use (guests also can reserve private hot-tub time). Lizzie is the hotel's ghost, who turns lights on and off and rings bells to get attention (she never appears in person). Legend is that Lizzie was killed in the Mayflower Room by a jealous lover. The hotel's sister property, **The Old Miners' Lodge** (800-648-8068 or 645-8068; $$–$$$) is two blocks from Main Street on Woodside Avenue. Intermediate skiers can ski to the back door, but it's a long walk down a hefty flight of stairs to get to the Town Lift. The lodge is historic and quiet (it's a member of Select Registry), with rooms that all have private baths but no TV or in-room phones.

The bargain spots are dormitory digs and rooms in the **Chateau Après Lodge,** "A Skier's Ski Lodge" (649-9372; $–$$). Another choice is **Budget Lodging** (649-2526 or 800-522-7669; $$–$$$$), with hotel rooms to four-bedroom. College students should head to the **Main Street Dorms** (managed by R&R Property Management, 800-348-6759, $) to save money and be close to all the best nightlife. You'll share bathrooms, a lounge and a kitchenette, but there are private ski lockers. A four-bed room is $80 during the regular winter season, so you and three friends will each pay $20 per night.

The **Marriott Summit Watch** (647-4100 or 800-223-8245) is smack in the middle of this pedestrian complex with restaurants, shops and the Town Lift right outside the door. A draw is the Marriott's Aquacade, a pool and activities center built under old trestles. Every evening there's something scheduled for kids, such as crafts, movies or an ice skating excursion, ranging in cost from $15 to $30.

Near the Resort Center you'll find another cluster of hotels and condos. These four are all upscale. **Silver King Hotel** (800-331-8652 or 649-5500; $$$–$$$$) is about 100 yards from the lifts and at the hub of the transportation system. Some units have private hot tubs. **The Lodge at the Mountain Village** (800-824-5331 or 649-0800; $$$–$$$$) surrounds the base area lifts for true ski-in/ski-out. Lots of amenities—spas, health club, pool, steamroom and concierge. **Shadow Ridge Resort Hotel & Conference Center** (800-451-3031 or 649-4300; $$–$$$$) has a sauna, hot tub and laundry, plus underground parking. Offers hotel rooms to three-bedroom condos. **Snow Flower Condominiums** (800-852-3101 or 649-6400; $$–$$$$) is 100 feet from the beginner area. Each unit has single-person jetted hot tubs and underground parking. Studios to five-bedroom units.

For more economical condos, try the **Edelweiss Haus** (800-245-6417 or 649-9342; $$–$$$$) across the street from the lifts and the Silver King Hotel. Extras are a heated outdoor pool and hot tub. Hotel rooms to two-bedroom condos available.

One bargain lodging worth mentioning is the **Park City International Hostel** (655-7244), a few doors from the Egyptian Theatre on Main Street. Staying in a shared room costs $25; private rooms cost $90.

Other locations in town:

The **Inn at Prospector Square** (888-870-4386 or 649-7100; $$–$$$$) is a group of condos that includes use of its athletic club in the rates. **The Yarrow Resort Hotel** (800-927-7694 or 649-7000; $$–$$$$) is considered good family lodging. Children under 12 stay free and the hotel sits amid shopping, movies and restaurants. It is on the shuttlebus route, about a five-minute ride from Park City's Main Street.

The 199-room **Park City Marriott** (800-754-3279 or 649-2900; $$–$$$$) is an absolutely gorgeous full-service resort hotel. There are refrigerators and coffee makers in every room, plus double phone lines and desks with built-in outlets for those who must combine work with pleasure. The bus stop is right outside the door.

For luxury condos and houses at affordable prices as well as a chance to get some last-minute or off-peak bargains in the entire Park City area, call **Accommodations Unlimited** (800-321-4754 or 649-1128). A friend of ours also recommended **High Mountain Properties** for assistance booking condos, private homes and other lodging (800-239-6144 or 655-8363; www.highmountainproperties.com).

Accommodations at The Canyons

A few steps from the Flight of The Canyons gondola, **The Grand Summit Resort Hotel** (1-888-CANYONS; $$$$) has luxurious penthouses, one- to three-bedroom suites, studios and hotel rooms. Most of the 360 rooms have balconies, fireplaces, whirlpool tubs and full kitchens. Also offers full-service health club, including a heated outdoor pool with whirlpools, steamroom, sauna and massage. On-site restaurant, bistro and lounges.

The 150-room **Sundial Lodge** (1-888-CANYONS; $$$$) is in the heart of The Canyons Resort Village. The condominium lodge offers guestrooms and one- and two-bedroom condominium-style accommodations with kitchens and jetted tubs. Most condominiums have fireplaces and balconies. Guests have access to a rooftop hot tub and plunge pool.

Dining – Park City Area

Park City's restaurants get better every year—and more expensive. Pick up one of the two free dining-guide magazines to get menus, but be aware that not all the restaurants are listed. Main Street is where you'll find many of the best restaurants in town: The top four are **Grappa, Chimayo, Zoom** and **Riverhorse.**

If you can pay the freight, the Northern Italian menu, wine list and ambiance are outstanding at **Grappa** (645-0636, $$$). It's in a 100-year-old building, try and get a table by the fireplace. Many locals recommend **Chimayo** (649-6222; $$–$$$), owned by chef Bill White, for its inventive Southwestern cuisine (don't miss the dark chocolate flan). **Zoom Roadhouse Grill** (649-9108; $$$) is housed in the old train depot. Owned by Robert Redford, whose Sundance Film Festival transforms the town each January, it serves "plain folks food." Finally, the **Riverhorse Café** (649-3536; $$$) is a can't-miss choice for anyone who enjoys Contemporary American food in a low-key, elegant atmosphere.

Lakota (658-3400; $$$) is another restaurant favored by the trend-setting crowd. For Italian, **Mileti's** (649-8211; $$$) is still going strong after 27 years, or try **Cisero's** (649-5044, $$) and **Café Terigo** (645-9555).

Asian restaurants are popular, with **Mikado** (655-7100; $$$) the choice for Japanese, **Bangkok Thai** (649-8424; $$$) for Thai, and **Taste of Saigon** (647-0688; $$) for Vietnamese food. Park City also has four Chinese restaurants. **The Dragon Garden** (655-0101; $) is the spot for a quick and cheap Chinese fix. Many Park City restaurants offer excellent take-out. After a wipe-out day on the slopes and a soak in the hot tub, we devoured a tender Moo Goo Gai Pan and a tasty mixed vegetable dish from **Szechwan** (649-0957; $). Take a free shuttle into town for pick up or have food delivered for an additional 20% of the total.

The restaurants on Lower Main are new, and most lean toward expensive. **Wahso** (615-0300), owned by the ubiquitous Bill White, serves Asian/European food. **Dynamite Dom's** (615-8457, $$–$$$) and **U. S. Prime Steakhouse** (655-9739, $$$) are upscale steakhouses. **Jambalaya** (658-1252, $$) serves Cajun fare, **Mulberry Street** (649-0888, $$) serves "American with an Italian flair," and **Mulligan's Pub** (658-0717, $$) has an Irish menu.

Off Main Street, one restaurant that vies for best-in-town honors is **Adolph's** (649-7177; $$$) next to the U.S. Ski and Snowboard Team office on Kearns Blvd. It serves Swiss and American cuisine. Hidden on Park Ave., **Chez Betty** (649-8181, $$$) in the Copperbottom Inn serves excellent American/French cuisine in a formal setting. Farther from the center of town is the **Juniper Restaurant** at the Snowed Inn (647-3311; $$$, reservations required), with gourmet food in an elegant old Victorian setting. You'll need your own transportation.

More recommendations are: **Nacho Mama's** (645-8226; $–$$) for tasty Southwestern/Mexican food and margaritas that go down far too smoothly; **Baja Cantina** (649-4440; $$) at the Resort Center; and the **Irish Camel** (649-6645; $$) on Main Street for good drinks and acceptable Tex-Mex food. The lowest-priced Mexican restaurant is **El Chubasco** (645-9114; $), in Prospector Square.

The Eating Establishment (649-8284; $) is a locals' cheap-eats favorite, as is the **Park City Pizza Company** (649-1591; $). **Texas Red's Pit Barbeque** (649-7337, $–$$) is the red-meat-eater's choice. **Grub Steak** (649-8060; $$–$$$) gets high marks.

For breakfast, **The Eating Establishment** on Main Street is the leader for hearty-meal fans (the menu includes some trendy selections, such as smoked salmon Eggs Benedict), while **Ziggy's** is the egg-and-pancake choice for those staying at the Park City Mountain Resort base. **Off Main Cafe and Bakery** does omelets and pancakes in the Prospector Square area. For a lighter breakfast, try **Einstein Brothers Bagel Bakery** in the Prospector Square area for a huge variety of bagels and spreads, as well as great coffee, or **Wasatch Bagels** on Kearns Boulevard next to Dan's Grocery Store. For funky local ambiance and a cheap breakfast special ($3.89 for egg, ham and cheese on a bagel), hit the **Main Street Deli.** The **Morning Ray Cafe** or **Mountain Air** are the places to share a java with the locals.

Deer Valley's dining mirrors its overall high quality (and cost), see Deer Valley chapter to see the dining options. It's easy to get there from Park City—if you don't have a car, take the free Park City Transit buses, which run until 10 p.m. To make advance dinner reservations (recommended) from anywhere in the United States, call (800) 424-3337 (424-DEER).

Dining at The Canyons

The Canyons has three on-mountain lodges for dining: **Red Pine Lodge,** at the top of the Flight of The Canyons gondola, serves healthy grilled food, pizza and deli sandwiches; **Sun Lodge at Snow Canyon** serves Asian and Mexican dishes; and **Lookout Cabin,** at the top of

Dining: $$$–Entrees $20+; $$–$10-20; $–less than $10.
Accommodations: (double room) $$$$–$200+; $$$–$141-$200; $$–$81-$140; $–$80 and less.

Lookout chairlift, has a table-served luncheon menu of grilled fish, meats and salads (not only is the food wonderful here, the mountain views are spectacular). **Doc's at the Gondola**, in the Grand Summit, is good for lunch and après ski. Also in the base area, **Smokie's Smokehouse** has family-style BBQ and Cajun fare. Yurt dining is available at 5 p.m. daily.

Après-ski/nightlife

Despite rumors of Utah party blahs, Park City has some of the best nightlife of any ski town. For the lowdown on Utah's liquor laws, including the "private club membership" you'll need for most of these places, see the Salt Lake City chapter.

Immediate slopeside après-ski centers are **Moose's** at Park City Mountain Resort base; and **The Forum** at The Canyons.

According to locals, **O'Shucks** is the place to be on Main Street for the younger folks (skiers and boarders) and **Lakota** is the hot spot for the more mature population. **Harry Os,** halfway down Main, is a giant warehouse of a bar, complete with six pool tables, a big-screen TV showing the game, and a boisterous younger crowd who need to be carded to get in. It is *the* place on Saturday nights. **The Alamo,** next door, is your basic saloon with pool tables, loud music and louder conversation.

Mother Urban's, named after a famous bordello madam is a cellar version of a knotty-pine mining shack that sells 55 beers (not bad for Mormon territory) and features live jazz Tuesdays, Thursdays and Fridays. Also try the **Wasatch Brew Pub** at the top of Main Street, where you can watch the brewing process even as you reap its yeasty rewards. **The Cozy** on Main Street has a large dance area with live bands every weekend and most other nights, too. **Mileti's** is casual, cozy and dark, making it a great place for the last drink of the night. **Adolph's**, in the newer section of town, with piano music, has been recommended for quieter evenings.

When the **Egyptian Theater** has plays, as it does often during the winter, it makes a nice evening's entertainment. **The Eccles Center** houses two live stages and is a year-round focal point for the performing arts in Park City. For weekly arts and entertainment events, call 647-9747 or 655-3114.

Other activities

Park City offers some rare sports treats: **ski jumping, luge and bobsled** at the Utah Winter Sports Park (649-5447). The park will host the 2002 Olympic competition in those events. Yes, you can fly off the end of a ramp just like the Olympians do (you'll be on much smaller ramps, but it will feel like the 120-meter jump, let us assure you). You can take jumping lessons (required rental helmets included), or ride on the Olympic luge/bobsled track in a neophyte-friendly luge "ice rocket" or as a passenger in a four-person bobsled. (They supply the driver and brakeman.) Schedules are different each day, and not every activity is offered every day, so call for specifics and prices. Definitely call in advance for a spot in the bobsled. The 48-second ride of your life, wild and rugged. You won't be disappointed. The park is closed Mondays and Tuesdays. It's worth a tour even if you don't participate in the sports.

Many companies offer **sleigh rides, snowmobile tours** and **hot-air balloon trips**. To reserve any or all of these activities and more, call one central number at ABC Reservations Central, (800) 820-2223 or 649-2223. There is no fee and most adventures provide free shuttle service.

In January 2000, the Mormon church opened a **Family History Center** at 531 Main Street. Computers are available for genealogy checks for anyone free of charge. **The Park**

In January 2000, the Mormon church opened a **Family History Center** at 531 Main Street. Computers are available for genealogy checks for anyone free of charge. **The Park City Museum** on Main Street details local history, and is excellent. Admission is by donation, and it is open every day, at varying times.

Park City's calendar has some unusual events. The **World Cup** ski racing tour kicks off each year at Park City Mountain Resort in mid-November. The **Sundance Film Festival** is in late January, showcasing new films from around the world.

Park City has two popular **shopping** areas: Historic Main Street in downtown Park City and a factory outlet center on the edge of town. The outlets include Eddie Bauer, Brooks Brothers, Gap, Nike and Polo among many others. You can jump on a shuttle or take a cab for $6 round trip per person. (Locals know to hop the Best Western hotel shuttle.) Take an hour or two and walk Main Street to find museums, art galleries and fine and funky shops. A must-see is Silver Junction Mercantile with every nook and cranny crammed full of old stuff, from rusty license plates and political buttons to Elvis and Beatles memorabilia. Nativo offers high-end young clothing and avant-garde jewelry. Tiff's owner buys amber directly from Poland which her partner polishes and sets in stunning silver for very reasonable prices. The Pendleton store in the Main Street Mall sells vintage Pendleton clothing at vintage prices.

Don't miss Changing Hands, a consignment shop way off the beaten track in the back of Galleria Mall. Great high-fashion ski clothes during the season and higher end labels for the rest of the inventory. Hard to find, but well worth it. If you are traveling with your pet or had to leave him at home, stop at the Love Your Pet Bakery to bring home a treat.

Getting there and getting around

By air: The drive from the Salt Lake City International Airport to Park City takes 45 minutes. Ground transportation makes frequent trips from the airport for $34-$46, round-trip (children's fares are $17-$35). Providers include Lewis Brothers Stages, (800) 826-5844 or 649-2256; Park City Transportation, (800) 637-3803 or 649-8567; and All Resort Express (800) 457-9457 or 649-3999. If you arrive without reservations, go to the transportation counter at the airport and you'll ride on the next available van. Call 48 hours in advance for Park City-to-airport reservations.

By car: Park City is 32 miles east of Salt Lake City, by I-80 and Utah Hwy. 224.

Getting around: If you're staying close to the town center or near a stop on the free bus line, you can do without a rental car. The town bus system has four routes with service every 20 minutes, if not more frequently, from 7 a.m. to 1 a.m. If you take a side trip to one of the Cottonwood Canyons ski resorts, Lewis Brothers Stages and Park City Transportation have shuttles for $22-$35 round-trip. Lewis Brothers offers a Canyon Jumper package to Solitude and Snowbird for $49 and $52, respectively, including transportation and lift ticket. Prepay the evening before you wish to ski.

Park City's calendar has some unusual events. The **World Cup** ski racing tour kicks off each year at Park City Mountain Resort in mid-November. The **Sundance Film Festival** is in late January, showcasing new films from around the world.

Many companies offer **sleigh rides**, **snowmobile tours** and **hot-air balloon trips**. To reserve any or all of these activities and more, call one central number at ABC Reservations Central, (800) 820-2223 or 649-2223. There is no fee and most adventures provide free shuttle service.

Dining: $$$-Entrees $20+; $$-$10-20; $-less than $10.
Accommodations: (double room) $$$$-$200+; $$$-$141-$200; $$-$81-$140; $-$80 and less.

Big Cottonwood Canyon

Utah

Solitude Mountain Resort
Brighton Ski Resort

Big Cottonwood Canyon's two resorts may only be a couple of miles apart, but they look like they're on different continents. Solitude is an emerging master-planned resort. Its blueprints call for a series of upscale, European-style condominiums, shops and restaurants. None of the 2002 Winter Olympic events will be staged in the Cottonwood Canyons, but Solitude's new village might be a big attraction to visitors who prefer to stay and ski away from the Olympic hoopla. Brighton, at the canyon's end, continues to court local snowboarders and skiers with no-frills facilities. It has no ambitious blueprints for future development to rival Solitude's (indeed, it's limited by local watershed restrictions).

Although Solitude resisted the snowboard movement for many years, Brighton was one of the first Utah resorts to embrace the sport. Snowboarders remain quite loyal to Brighton as a result. The combination of exciting terrain, lots of snow and low prices adds to Brighton's popularity with snowboarders.

While the two resorts look different, they remain similar in many ways. Ticket prices, at less than $45, are reasonable by Utah standards and a bargain by destination-visitor standards. Both have lots of intermediate slopes and comparable lift capacity, though Solitude has more diverse expert and advanced terrain.

Solitude has won awards for its trail and lift system. Six years ago, the resort's first overnight lodging opened. Its full-service hotel—The Inn at Solitude—includes a restaurant and shops. The opening of the Powderhorn Lodge last season added 83 condominiums in an elegant building, with more retail space for skier services, in Solitude's cozy pedestrian village. The luxurious Eagle Springs East is the newest lodging, completed in the summer of 2001. The legendary A-frame bar, The Thirsty Squirrel, has been torn down (a tragedy) and moved inside the Powderhorn Lodge. Solitude's new appearance is decidedly continental. A model of the new and improved village makes it look as if it were in Switzerland, not the Western United States.

Brighton refurbished many of its aging buildings and built a huge Brighton Center to house lift ticket sales, rental and retail shops and more restrooms and lockers. But it retained its cleanly utilitarian, Western appearance—a cross between log cabin and military barracks, that concerns itself more with substance than style. Last season, the Snake Creek Express high-speed quad replaced the Snake Creek triple, cutting travel time in half.

Cosmetic changes notwithstanding, both Brighton and Solitude continue to share a mountain ambiance that architecture and marketing can't alter. People come to ski or snowboard, period. Locals still mention both mountains in the same breath, and it will probably be decades before the resorts are thought of as separate—at least by Utahans.

Solitude Mountain Resort

Summit elevation:	10,035 feet
Vertical drop:	2,047 feet
Base elevation:	7,988 feet

Address: 12000 Big Cottonwood Canyon
Solitude, UT 84121
☏ **Area code:** 801
Ski area phone: 534-1400
Snow report: 536-5777
ⓘ **Toll-free reservations:** (800) 748-4754
Fax: (435) 649-5276
E-mail: info@skisolitude.com
Internet: www.skisolitude.com

Expert:★★★★ **Advanced:**★★★★
Intermediate:★★★★
Beginner:★★★★ **Never-ever:**★★★★
Number of lifts: 7–1 high-speed quad,
2 triple chairs, 4 double chairs
Snowmaking: 120 acres
Skiable acreage: 1,200
Uphill capacity: 11,200 per hour
Snowboarding: Yes
Bed base: 350; 12,000 in Salt Lake City
Resort child care: None
Nearest lodging: Slopeside, condos & hotel
Adult ticket, per day: $42-$44 (2001/02)
Dining:★★★
Apres-ski/nightlife:★
Other activities:★

Mountain layout—Skiing

Solitude's lift layout has a logical progression from beginner to expert areas. Skiers and snowboarders easily can progress here by a choice of terrain. If you are a novice, or hovering between two levels, be sure to read the section for the ability level you are now, and the one you want to be.

◆◆ **Expert:** Experts will like the routes off the Summit Chair. Test yourself first with the routes we describe in the Advanced section. If you think you're ready, head down the Back Door trail to Corner Chute, a steep black diamond clearly visible from the Summit chair. You might instead go into Headwall Forest, where you can pick your own line through the trees, or jump into a couple of long, steep, narrow chutes. You also can head over to Evergreen, rated a single-black diamond, but it looks mighty tough from the lift.

Another option will take you into Honeycomb Canyon, a wonderful playground for high-level skiers and boarders. Woodlawn is a marked run that follows the canyon floor. On the map it's rated black and blue. Check the grooming report before you head in: When groomed, it's a great advanced-intermediate run—otherwise, it's advanced all the way, with some gigantic mogul fields and a short but extremely steep section that looks like it might be a small waterfall in the summer.

The canyon sides are an expert's delight. From the top, traverse until you find a line you like, then go for it. You also can enter Honeycomb Canyon from the Eagle Ridge run in the main part of the ski area, but this entry is strictly double-diamond through trees. Speaking of trees, you'll find others to the left as you exit the Powderhorn chair and head down Milk Run, Middle Slope, Parachute or Cirque.

◆ **Advanced:** The Powderhorn chair has some single-black groomed screamers, such as Diamond Lane. Another lift that this ability level will like is the Summit chair. From its top, you can go one of three ways. The first takes you back down to the Summit chair base on upper-intermediate runs like Dynamite and Liberty. Eventually you'll meet the runs off the Sunrise chair, which head back to the base.

■ **Intermediate:** The Powderhorn and Eagle Express chairs have no green runs, just blue with a few black. If you're at the high end of the intermediate level, you'll like this terrain. If you're new to the intermediate level, try the Sunrise or Apex chairs.

●● **Beginner:** When skiers conquer Link, the next step is the Moonbeam II chair, where Little Dollie, Pokey Pine and Same Street will take them back down gently. Next is either the Apex or Sunrise chairs, where one green trail is surrounded by lots of blue.

● **Never-ever:** Novices start on the Link chair, a slow-moving lift that serves a nearly flat, very wide, isolated run, Easy Street.

Mountain layout—Snowboarding

Although Solitude resisted the snowboard movement for many years, riders are perfectly happy with the runs here. Solitude has more diverse expert and advanced terrain than Brighton. Snowboarders usually try to avoid Woodlawn/Honeycomb return because of the flats toward the bottom—they're just no fun as the terrain becomes travail. For that reason, riders may want to avoid Honeycomb Canyon off to the right of the Summit lift. They're fine runs, all single- or double-black, but it takes a traverse to get to them and then a runout to get to the Eagle Express lift. Any run toward the base from Eagle Ridge, above the Roundhouse, will satisfy. Take the Powder Horn chair to get there. Solitude's best collection of double-blacks is to left of the Powder Horn chair—Middle Slope, Parachute and Milk Run.

Mountain rating

Solitude is one of the few resorts in the United States that has excellent terrain for all levels; however, its green slopes tend to be crowded, which some novices will find very intimidating. One disadvantage to the trail layout for some groups: If your group has skiers or riders at the opposite ends of the ability scale, you'll likely spend your day on different parts of the mountain. Intermediates can ride lifts with beginners or experts, choose different trails and meet at the bottom, but not so for beginners and experts. At the same time, beginners may find this comforting, since they don't have to worry about hotshots on their trails.

Cross-country and snowshoeing

Located at 8,700 feet between Solitude and Brighton, the **Solitude Nordic Center's Silver Lake Day Lodge** is a spectacular setting for cross-country skiing and snowshoeing. It has 20 km. of prepared trails for both classic and skating styles, plus ski and snowshoe rentals, lessons (including telemark), light snacks and guided backcountry tours. During full moons, you can do moonlight cross-country skiing. Trail passes cost $10 for ages 11 to 69, and free for older or younger skiers. A half-day pass is $7; a two-day pass is $15. For more information, call 536-5774.

Lessons (2001/02 prices)

Group lessons: $40 for two hours. All-day lessons are $60.
Never-ever package: Rentals, lift ticket and a lesson is $70.
Private lessons: $75 per hour (1-3 people); $145 (4-6 people).

Special programs: For women, snowboarding, Nordic and racing, offered at various times. Call for details, (801) 536-5730.

Racing: Solitude has an electronically timed, side-by-side dual course on the Main Street trail, open every day, weather permitting, $1.50 per run.

Child care (2001/02 prices)

Solitude does not have non-skiing child care.
Children's lessons: Full day with lunch for ages 4-12 is $70; a half-day without lunch is $45. An all-day never-ever kids' package is $80.

Lift tickets (2001/02 prices)

	Adult (11-59)	Child (7-13)
One day	$44	$14
Additional days	see "Note" below	

Who skis free: Ages 6 and younger & 70 and older ski for free, but need to get a ticket at the ticket window.

Who skis at a discount: Seniors (60-69) pay $37. A beginner lift ticket, valid on the Link and Moonbeam II chairs, is $29.

Note: For multiday guests, it costs $44 for the first day and $42 for each additional day. Also, Solitude uses Ski Data Access, an electronic ticketing system that allows skiers to pay by the run, get future discounts or share a ticket with someone else. Basically, Access is geared towards locals who take a few runs a day, parents with young children (Mom and Dad share the ticket so they can switch babysitting duties), and destination guests who only want to ski or ride for a half day. The reuseable card allows you to pay for individual lift rides, sold in increments of 10. Ten rides cost $40. Radio-frequency beams deduct one ride from the card and you can use the remaining lift rides another day. Remember: Help keep ticket costs down be recycling your card when leaving the resort; drop it at any of the convenient locations resort-wide.

Accommodations

Solitude has beautiful base-area lodging—just enough to be a full-service destination resort without the sprawl or crowds. If you like to be first on the lifts, stay here. All lodging can be booked by calling (800) 748-4754.

The newest slopeside lodging, completed in July 2001, is **Eagle Springs East** ($$$–$$$$), featuring luxurious one- to three-bedroom condominiums with hand-finished furnishings, generous gourmet kitchens, comfortable living areas and balconies. Heated sidewalks surround a large outdoor heated swimming pool with a waterfall, plus a waterslide for kids of all ages. On each side of the pool are 18-person hot tubs. In addition, there's a kids' playroom with board games, a Playstation, foos-ball table, and computers with games. Just down the hall adults can play billiards or relax in the fireside lounge in the Club.

The Inn at Solitude ($$$$) has 46 rooms that are spacious, most with two queen beds (though kings and suites are available). All have terry-cloth robes to wear to the pool and spa, hair dryers, mini-refrigerators, TV with VCR (tape rentals are $5 a night), and daily newspaper delivery. Cost includes lift ticket, plus breakfast and dinner at St. Bernard's.

Solitude also has 18 condo units (one to three bedrooms) in a development called **Creekside at Solitude** ($$$–$$$$). The condos are spacious and well-appointed, and share an outdoor rooftop hot tub. Each unit has a private deck and fireplace, full kitchen and TV with VCR. The three-bedroom units have a jetted tub and four bathrooms, so the person sleeping on the living room sofa has a bathroom, too.

Dining: $$$-Entrees $20+; $$-$10-20; $-less than $10.
Accommodations: (double room) $$$$-$200+; $$$-$141-$200; $$-$81-$140; $-$80 and less.

Powderhorn Lodge ($$$–$$$$), completed during the summer of 2000, is slopeside with one-, two- and three-bedroom condos. Guests can enjoy an outdoor hot tub, pool table in the lobby and access to Club Solitude, located in Eagle Springs East.

Dining/après-ski/other activities

Dining: A very popular program is the **Solitude Yurt.** Twenty people cross-country ski or snowshoe to a yurt for a five-course gourmet meal and then ski or snowshoe back (it's a beginner trail both ways and the equipment is included in the cost). Reservations are a must for this, and don't be too disappointed if you can't get in. Salt Lake City residents really enjoy it and hog many of the available spaces. Coffee and water are the only provided beverages, but guests may bring their own corked wine and other beverages. The cost is $80, and no children younger than 8 are allowed. Call 536-5709 for reservations.

St. Bernard's is in the Inn and has a menu that leans toward Swiss and German entrées, such as wild boar stew and wienerschnitzle. The après-ski menu features an excellent cheese fondue, with generous portions of thick, European-style bread and warm cheese. Dinner for two at St. Bernard's will set you back about $100. **Creekside**, which is on the first floor of the Creekside condos, serves breakfast, lunch and dinner with much of the cooking done in the wood-burning oven. Pasta and pizza large enough for two to split are its specialties. Its entrees are less expensive than St. Bernard's—about $45 for two, including drinks.

Solitude's cafeteria, **Last Chance Mining Camp**, is on two levels and can seat about 400 skiers. **Sunshine Grill** is open for lunch and features a lively grill adjacent to the best people-watching on the mountain, affectionately called "the beach." Another place for a quick bite is the **Stone Haus** in the village or the **Thirsty Squirrel,** which serves items such as panini, nachos and pizza.

Après-ski: The "new" **Thirsty Squirrel** opened during the summer of 2001. Resort staff assures us its ambiance is much like its predecessor, right down to the pool table, wide-screen TV and local beer sold by the pitcher. There's also a beer bar at the **Last Chance Mining Camp** in the day lodge.

Other activities: The Inn at Solitude has a full-service **health and fitness spa** with a workout room, sauna, facials, massages and more.

Brighton Ski Resort

Mountain layout—Skiing

uu Expert u Advanced: Brighton regulars refer to the "Majestic" side, served by the Majestic and other chairs, and the "Millicent" side, served by the Millicent and Evergreen chairs. If avoiding lower-level skiers and boarders is your goal, stay on the Millicent side with fewer greens and blues than Majestic.

But don't miss the Majestic side, either. Experts should try a short but heart-stopping run called Hard Coin off the Snake Creek Express. The trees are so thick you can hardly pick a line, but it's a marked trail. Most of the advanced runs are under the Great Western quad. From its summit one can see the Great Salt Lake and Mt. Timpanogos, home of the Sundance Ski Resort. For moguls, try Rockin'R under Great Western, or Ziggy under Snake Creek. Clark's Roost and Rein's Run, off Great Western, are the toughest in-bounds descents.

Brighton has an open-boundaries policy, which means experts can head into the backcountry as they wish, just don't go alone.

Brighton Facts

Summit elevation:	**10,500 feet**
Vertical drop:	**1,745 feet**
Base elevation:	**8,755 feet**

Address: Star Route
Brighton, UT 84121
✆ Area code: 801
Ski area phone: 532-4731
Snow report: 532-4731
ⓘ **Toll-free information:** (800) 873-5512
Internet: www.skibrighton.com
Expert:★★ **Advanced:**★★★
Intermediate:★★★★
Beginner:★★★★
Never-ever:★★★★

Number of lifts: 7–3 high-speed quads,
1 triple chair, 3 double chairs
Snowmaking: 25 percent
Skiable acreage: 850
Uphill capacity: 11,500+ per hour
Snowboarding: Yes
Bed base: About 50; 12,000 in Salt Lake City
Resort child care: No
Nearest lodging: Walking distance
Adult ticket, per day: $37 (2000/01)

Dining:★★
Apres-ski/nightlife:★
Other Activities: ★

■ **Intermediate:** Intermediates have the run of practically the whole area. The Majestic side is more heavily wooded but with gentler pitches, while the Millicent side is a bit steeper, but with fewer trees. The Elk Park Ridge run descends 1,745 feet, summit to base, from the Great Western chair.

●● **Beginner:** Good beginner runs descend from the Majestic chair, and from the Snake Creek Express, which goes to the top of the mountain. Beginners should keep an eye out so they don't get onto an intermediate trail: Greens and blues do a lot of intertwining here.

● **Never-ever:** Brighton has a stellar reputation as the place where Utah skiers learn. The Explorer chair serves a gentle slope apart from general traffic.

 ## Mountain layout—Snowboarding

Even skilled snowboarders like to avoid runouts because they're tedius and tough to navigate when they flatten out. Thankfully Brighton doesn't have runouts below its excellent riding terrain, so there's no problem.

Expert and advanced riders can go for the Great Western quad, or for the trees off the Snake Creek Express. Clark's Roost and Rein's Run, off Great Western, are the toughest in-bounds descents. Brighton has an open-boundaries policy, which means experts can head into the backcountry as they wish, just don't go alone. The resort also has two halfpipes and a terrain park.

Brighton has a stellar reputation as the place where Utah boarders learn. The Explorer chair serves a gentle slope apart from general traffic. With Brighton's abundance of beginner and intermediate terrain, it's an excellent mountain for learning to link those turns. Start off the Explorer chair—busy speeders stay elsewhere on the mountain, so you can practice without looking over your shoulder all the time. Head next to the gentle runs off the Majestic chair. Once you have some confidence, go for the top of the Snake Creek Express. You'll be on top of the world. There are some nice green runs from both chairs.

Mountain rating

Good for beginners, excellent for intermediates and very good for advanced skiers and snowboarders. Brighton has a bit of true expert terrain, but it is not nearly as extensive as the other Cottonwood Canyons resorts. We recommend that out-of-state visitors head into the backcountry only if they are with a local guide.

Lift tickets (2000/01 prices)

Ages 11 to 69 pay $37. Brighton does not sell multiday tickets. Twilight tickets are available when lifts are running into the evening. Brighton also has about 200 acres of night skiing every day except Sunday.

Who skis free: Ages 10 and younger, two children per paying adult with no restrictions or blackout dates. Ages 70 and older also ski free.

Who skis at a discount: A beginner lift pass, good on two lifts, is $24. A single-ride ticket is $8. Night skiing and riding costs $20–$35, depending on the number of hours.

Lessons (2000/01 prices)

Group lessons: $26 for two hours, also offered at night (at night, the lift ticket is included). "The Works" package includes a group lesson, all-day ticket and all-day rentals for $57 for skiers and $67 for snowboarders.

Never-ever package: Includes a full day of rentals, beginner lift ticket and a group lesson—$44 for skiing and $54 for snowboarding.

Private lessons: $60 per hour, with each additional person $20.

Special programs: Includes clinics for women, seniors, telemark, adaptive and advanced technique. Inquire at the ski and snowboard school.

Child Care (2000/01 prices)

Brighton does not have non-skiing child care.

Children's lessons: Ages 4 to 7 get 1.75-hour lessons for $30 without equipment, $40 with equipment. A full day with lunch is $70.

Accommodations

The **Brighton Lodge** (800-873-5512 or 532-4731; $–$$) is small, cozy, has a Jacuzzi and is at the base of the lifts. **Das Alpen Haus** (649-0565; $$–$$$) is a charming B&B near the base of Brighton. Each of the four suites is named for a Swiss ski resort, and the atmosphere is Swiss Alpine.

Getting there and getting around

By air and train: Salt Lake City is a major transportation hub, so flights are numerous. Amtrak also serves the city.

By car: Solitude and Brighton are about 23 miles southeast of Salt Lake City in Big Cottonwood Canyon on State Hwy. 190. The most direct route from the airport is east on I-80, south on I-215, Exit 6 to Wasatch Blvd., then follow the signs to Solitude and Brighton.

Getting around: You can ride the Utah Transit Authority ski buses for $4 from downtown or $1.50 from the park-and-ride at the canyon's mouth (exact fare is required). Or, take a Lewis Brothers SkiExpress van ($22 roundtrip from downtown; call 359-8677). During the day, UTA buses run between Solitude and Brighton for $1. If you don't like to eat at the same place twice, or you like nightlife, we recommend staying in Salt Lake City.

Snowbird
Utah

Summit elevation: 11,000 feet
Vertical drop: 3,240 feet
Base elevation: 7,760 feet

Address: P.O. Box 929000
Snowbird, UT 84092-9000
✆ **Area code:** 801
Ski area phone: 742-2222
Snow report: 933-2100
ⓘ **Toll-free reservations:**
(800) 453-3000
Fax: 947-8227
Internet: www.snowbird.com
Expert:★★★★★
Advanced:★★★★
Intermediate:★★★★
Beginner:MMM **Never-ever:**MMMM

Number of lifts: 11–1 aerial tram,
3 high-speed quads, 7 double chairs
Snowmaking: Minimal
Skiable acreage: 2,500-plus
Uphill capacity: 16,800 per hour
Snowboarding: Yes
Bed Base: 1,800+
Nearest lodging: Slopeside, hotel
Resort child care: Yes, 6 weeks and older
Adult ticket, per day: $45–$57 (2001/02)
Dining:★★
Apres-ski/nightlife:★
Other activities:★★

Practically every devout skier or snowboarder has a mecca for annual pilgrimages to rekindle the flame and commune once again with the snow spirits. The choices for these meccas are deeply personal. When the winds of November bring the year's first snowfalls, however, many devoted skiers find themselves drawn almost irresistibly up the winding ascent to the brawny splendor of Snowbird Ski & Summer Resort.

The initial allure is the snow, but it is much more than that. Suffice it to say that Utah's little disputed claim to the "greatest snow on earth" is based largely on the slopes and bowls of Little Cottonwood, a canyon whose steep sides and craggy beauty are more reminiscent of the Alps than much of the Rockies. Snowbird itself receives an annual average of 500 inches of light, champagne powder that typically arrives early and stays around long enough for everyone to enjoy 200 days of skiing. Among powder aficionados, Snowbird is spoken of in the hushed tones of the truly reverent.

Snowbird's sleek, modern, high-rise hotel and condo complex that seems to spring out of the mountain's roots—the Iron Blosam Lodge, The Cliff Lodge, the Lodge at Snowbird and the Inn at Snowbird—also speak to the soul of the serious skier. Snowbird has luxurious accommodations and fine dining. The rock-solid but unobtrusive design of the resort takes nothing away from the looming mountains, leaving no doubt that their majestic appeal is what truly draws skiers back year after year.

Governed by strict laws regulating development, Snowbird has not been particularly aggressive in expanding its realm over the years. Recently, however, there have been subtle signs of promising change. A couple of seasons ago, Snowbird started guided snowcat tours on 500 acres in Mineral Basin, south of the Hidden Peak summit on the back side. Two seasons ago, this powder paradise became a reality for all skiers and riders when Snowbird installed a high-speed quad in Mineral Basin. The speedy, four-minute-long Mineral Basin

Express keeps powder hounds in their pleasure while the Basin's 1,429 vertical feet test the stamina. This new terrain includes intermediate, advanced and expert runs in a nearly tree-less setting.

Snowbird has been amending its reputation as a destination primarily for the steep-and-deep skiers and powder monkeys. Off the Baby Thunder lift, the resort has a largely protected area that has gentle slopes great for less experienced skiers. Two additional slopes are also being regularly groomed to the corduroy smoothness favored by cruisers. Snowbird is a resort where the whole family can find skiing to suit them. But Snowbird still has the tough stuff that put it on the map.

Powder pigs will most certainly have good reason to rejoice this winter. Beginning in the 2001/02 season, skiers can purchase an Alta Snowbird ticket for $68 a day and enjoy the two resorts' combined terrain (don't be surprised if snowboarders start converting to skiing *en mass*, snowboarding is still banned at Alta). Snowbird added a second high-speed quad this summer in Mineral Basin, connecting the two resorts. The lift transports skiers to the Sugarloaf saddle area (elevation 10,600 feet), joining Alta's Albion Basin and Snowbird's Mineral Basin. Skiers access the area by beginner and intermediate trails from the Albion Basin side, and by intermediate trails from the Mineral Basin side. In addition, Utah Transit Authority will connect the resorts' base areas with an expanded daily bus service.

Mountain layout—Skiing

With the addition of Mineral Basin, Snowbird is divided into three dis-tinct areas: Peruvian Gulch, Gad Valley and Mineral Basin. Thanks to a computer overhaul, the Tram now whisks skiers to Hidden Peak in six minutes, where a day at "The Bird" can begin. Warm up in Mineral Basin, where the sun shines and warms early in the day. After a couple runs in the bowls, head over to Gad Valley for a leisurely 3,000-vertical-foot drop down to the Gadzoom high-speed quad. A northeast exposure on the Peruvian Gulch side keeps The Cirque's steep runs good all day, a treat for the late morning or early afternoon once the legs are warmed up but not shot.

◆◆ **Expert:** No gut-wrenching decisions here. The most experienced skiers head for the tram. Hanging across a cirque and rising to the 11,000-foot summit, it brings 125 skiers at a time to Hidden Peak, unseen from the base lodge. When the first tram arrives on powder days there's a dash for the slopes. Skiers and snowboarders hurl their equipment and then themselves over the railings to make the first tracks. After this thrill, things calm down a bit, and you can decide whether to get equipment on quickly and be the first down The Cirque, or wait a bit, let others dash, and then go where they don't.

Drop under the tram into Peruvian Gulch, with intermediate, advanced and expert routes down, or head left into the Little Cloud area. Most tram riders opt for Peruvian because of its zigzag intermediate run, Chip's. Experts can go either way. On the Peruvian side, experts tackle The Cirque, a plunge that drops into almost 3,000 vertical feet of expert slopes. You can choose a run about as steep as you want, some with chutes that hold only enough powder to slow your virtual freefall. Anyone who has dropped down Upper Silver Fox, Great Scott or Upper Cirque deserves to be treated with reverence—they're using up the extra lives they were blessed with. From the tram ridge, Primrose Path is an unrelenting black diamond, normally the choice of those who think twice about tiptoeing around The Cirque. Here at Snowbird, what you can see, you can ski. So pick your own way.

Should you decide to drop over to the Little Cloud side of Hidden Peak, the skiing is somewhat tamer—by Snowbird standards. You reach the toughest stuff on this side—Gad

Chutes, Barry Barry Steep and others—by taking the Cirque Traverse from the tram.

◆ **Advanced:** Before you tackle the tram blacks at the top, take a test run on Chip's on the Peruvian side, or Regulator Johnson or Road to Provo on the Little Cloud side. Regulator Johnson, which is marked black on the map, now has a wide groomed swath down the center. Some of our staff think this descent is easier than Chip's sharp and crowded switchbacks, even though Chip's is rated blue.

Another good spot for advanced skiers is the Gad 2 chair. Gad 2 opens narrower trails through the trees and over megabumps. Gadzooks, Tiger Tail, Black Forest and Organ Grinder are equal challenges.

■ **Intermediate:** Do not board the tram without a test run elsewhere. A good tryout run is Big Emma from the top of Mid-Gad. Big Emma is rated green on the trail map, but its difficulty can vary with conditions. Many a beginner has halted along its upper rim, asking passing skiers and boarders, "Is there an easier way down?" On cold hardpacked days, Big Emma is a challenge even for intermediates.

If you can ski Emma with ease, you have several options for the next test. Any of the blue-square runs off the three Gad chairs will be fun, and if you can handle them, you should be ready to tackle the easiest runs off the tram.

The Baby Thunder area helps to bridge the steepness gap between Snowbird's novice slope and Big Emma. You can also work on technique on the greens under the Wilbere chair.

●● **Beginner:** The Baby Thunder area is great for lower-level skiers. It's gentle and isolated from faster traffic. Terrain between the runs is left ungroomed, great for practicing powder or tree skiing. Because it's a little off to one side, the initial access is a bit tricky to find. Ask a host at the base area to advise you, because directions may vary depending on the day's conditions. We recommend lessons for beginners, if only to have a guide to keep you out of trouble. Baby Thunder also includes a dedicated family area.

If it's a gorgeous day and you'd like to see the view, buy a tram ticket and ride back down. (And don't let any of the hot-shots shame you into skiing down—nothing from the top is easy by beginner standards. Oddly, the Mineral Basin Road run on the back side is an easy green, but there is no easy route down the front side to the base area.)

● **Never-ever:** Chickadee, out the door from the Cliff Lodge, is a near-ideal novice slope. (Our only gripe is the chair lift height is set for children, but we can work around that minor inconvenience.) At the very beginning of the day, skilled skiers use Chickadee to get to the other chairs, but aside from that, novices have it all to themselves.

 ## Mountain layout—Snowboarding

With the addition of Mineral Basin, Snowbird is now divided into three distinct areas: Peruvian Gulch, Gad Valley and Mineral Basin. Thanks to a computer overhaul, the Tram now whisks you to Hidden Peak in six minutes, where a day at "The Bird" can begin. Warm up in Mineral Basin, where the sun shines and warms early in the day. After a couple runs in the bowls, head over to Gad Valley for a leisurely 3,000-vertical-foot drop down to the Gadzoom high-speed quad. A northeast exposure on the Peruvian Gulch side keeps The Cirque's steep runs good all day, a treat for the late morning or early afternoon once the legs are warmed up but not shot.

Many Snowbird riders head straight to the wide-open, sometimes mogul filled Little Cloud Bowl or to the enticing trees off of Gad II. Follow a local for the best lines here, and if possible, take the tram to the Gad lifts to avoid a walk on the cat track. For hardcore riders, nothing beats the runs off either side of the Cirque. While the Cirque Traverse is long and filled with annoying dips, it's worth every bit of pain. The farther down the traverse you go on the Peruvian Gulch side, the easier it gets, though nothing off of here is for the faint of heart. A side note: Avoid the testosterone market on Great Scott Chute—within 100 yards there's others that are harder with better snow and more fluid fall lines. For some solitude, try the 10-minute hike to Baldy Mountain's chutes and powder fields. For air, head to the enormous halfpipe on Big Emma, or any number of cliffs and drop-offs. On most parts of the mountain there are intermittent flats; just anticipate, keep your speed, and you'll get through them. And at the end of the day, take the Traverse to the very end, and join the partyers atop Lone Pine, basking in the day's last rays of sun.

Mountain rating

Experts, you have arrived. A healthy half of Snowbird terrain is for you. These are not public-relations black diamonds, either—they really are tough. You will leave exhilarated or frustrated, depending on whether you attack them or they attack you.

Everyone else, expect to be pushed. Owner Dick Bass, who has climbed the highest mountain on every continent, affirms, "What we gain too easily, we esteem too lightly." Let that be your rallying cry. You will improve, a phenomenon you may not recognize until you ski those home slopes you thought were a challenge. If Snowbird exhausts you or you're here for a week and know all the routes in your comfort zone by heart, go next door to Alta, which has more mellow intermediate and beginner trails.

Lessons (2001/02 prices)

Snowbird Mountain School (933-2170) has four one-stop locations for ski and snowboard school registration and buying lift tickets. Tickets are not included in the lesson price. The offices are on Level 1 of the Cliff Lodge (you'll find two here, Camp Snowbird is for kids' programs), the Plaza Deck of the Snowbird Center and the Cottonwood Room on Level 2 of the Snowbird Center.

Group lessons: $72 for all day; $54 for half-day, afternoon-only classes.

Never-ever package: $59 includes ski or snowboard rentals, half-day lesson and access on the Chickadee lift.

Private lessons: For one to two people, $90 per hour ($80 between 9 and 10 a.m.) with multi-hour discounts; for three to six people, $125 per hour ($100 between 9 and 10 a.m.).

Special programs: Mountain Experience allows advanced or expert skiers to join a guide and launch an assault on the entire mountain for $85 for one day. Other 2.5-hour clinics teach style, bump skiing and snowboarding. A four-day women's camp is offered several times a season, and can be purchased with or without lifts and lodging. Skiing and snowboarding are separate women's seminars. Call for current prices.

Racing: A coin-operated course is open each day, weather permitting. The course is to one side of Big Emma, accessible by the Wilbere or Mid-Gad chairs.

Child care (2001/02 prices)

Ages: 6 weeks to 12 years.

Costs: $80 a day, with lunch, for ages 6 weeks to 3 years, and $70 for ages 3–12. Half-day and multiday discounts are available. Evening babysitting is $13 an hour, a little more for an additional child, but you must be staying in a Snowbird lodge to use this service.

Reservations: Required. Call Camp Snowbird at 933-2256, or reserve when you book your vacation. A non-refundable $25 registration fee is applied toward your final day.

Children's lessons: Full day (lunch and lessons) is $80. Half day for beginner and lower intermediate skiers is $54. Ability levels are separated. Ages 3 and 4 get 90-minute lessons for $55. Two children per instructor makes this very popular, so sign up in advance.

Lift tickets (2001/02 prices)

	Adult	Child (6-12)
One day	$57	Free (see below)
Three days	$147 ($49/day)	
Five days	$225 ($45/day)	

Who skis free: Two children younger than 12 ride the chairs free when an accompanying adult purchases a lift ticket. (Tram access costs $9.) Children of lodging guests ski the entire mountain free, and there's no limit on the number of children as long as they are Snowbird lodging guests.

Who skis at a discount: Ages 65 and older, $43. Chickadee chair-only ticket is $11.

Note: These are the prices with Tram access. For chairs only, the one-day prices are $47 for adults; $35 for seniors. Don't buy Tram access if you aren't skiing there; you can always upgrade a day's ticket to include the Tram for $9. A new Alta Snowbird ticket that allows you to access both resorts' terrain costs $68 a day.

Accommodations

All lodging at Snowbird is within walking distance of the base lifts, and can be reserved by calling Snowbird Central Reservations (800-453-3000; fax, 947-8227; www.snowbird.com). Winter season is mid-December through early April; value season is before and after those dates. Snowbird also has added a January value season, where rates are between the high and low seasons. Snowbird's season is a long one, lasting well into May most years. Lodging is plentiful in Salt Lake City.

The Cliff Lodge ($$$–$$$$) spreads like an eagle's wings at the base. Inside there's an 11-story atrium, a renowned spa, and a glassed-in rooftop with a heated pool that overlooks the slopes. The pool complex has a trio of hot tubs and an outdoor heated pool, and a nearby fruit-juice bar. Mountain-view rooms have picture windows from the shower that peer into the sleeping area and the view beyond (there's a shower curtain you can pull for modesty). The Cliff Lodge also has luxurious suites. Children younger than 12 stay and ski free with adults. The 27,000-square-foot Cliff Spa, on the top floor of the hotel, has 20 treatment rooms and a variety of treatments for body, face, hair and nails, as well as an exercise facility. Call 933-2225 for the spa, 933-2268 for the salon.

The Lodge at Snowbird ($$–$$$$), **The Inn** ($$–$$$$), and the **Iron Blosam Lodge** ($$–$$$$) are three condominium complexes with similar layouts. Not as elegant or as expensive as the Cliff Lodge, but they are well maintained, roomy and comfortable. Amenities include outdoor swimming pools, indoor hot tubs and saunas. Rates start at $119 for an efficiency or studio during value season, and top out at $519–$769 for a one-bedroom with loft during winter season.

Dining

The Aerie ($$$) on top of the Cliff Lodge is considered one of Utah's best restaurants, for good reason. The decor is elegant and tasteful, the views from the large picture windows spectacular, and the food and house piano player are excellent. **The Keyhole Junction** ($–$$) offers Mexican and Southwestern fare. The **Summit Sushi Bar** ($–$$) on Level 10 of the Cliff Lodge serves fresh hand-rolled sushi. At ground level of the Cliff Lodge's atrium, the **Atrium Restaurant** ($–$$) is fine for quick continental breakfasts, lunches and snacks. At the Iron Blosam Lodge, **Wildflower Ristorante & Lounge** ($$–$$$) serves outstanding Mediterranean cuisine. **The Lodge Bistro** ($$) in the Lodge at Snowbird has a cozy atmosphere with an eclectic bistro menu.

Other restaurants are in the Snowbird Center at the base of the mountain. **The Steak Pit** ($$) serves steak and seafood. There's usually a wait, but it's worth it. The rest of the eateries in the Snowbird Center cater to the ski crowd, serving breakfast and lunch. **The Forklift** has easy access to the slopes yet with a large fireplace that adds atmosphere. For cafeteria service, **The Rendezvous** has the usual, plus a well-stocked salad island. **Pier 49 San Francisco Sourdough Pizza** has pizza with lots of toppings, and **Birdfeeder** has gourmet coffees, including espressos, and light snacks.

Après-ski/nightlife

Snowbird's nightlife is very quiet. For the liveliest après-ski, try **Tram Club**, on the bottom floor of the Snowbird Center, with retro decor and a picture-window view of the tram's huge operating gears. It's your best bet if you want to dance. **Wildflower Lounge** is mellow. In the evening, **The Aerie** has a bar with live jazz several nights a week. **Keyhole Junction** has TVs showing sports events.

Remember: The nightspots are "private clubs" that charge a $5 two-week membership fee. If you are staying at a Snowbird lodge, the membership is included with your accommodations; however, the Tram Club is owned separately and so requires a separate membership. At night, you can take the free Snowbird shuttle to and from the Snowbird Center and the various restaurants and nightspots at the lodges. If you're staying at the Cliff Lodge, you can walk across the Chickadee novice slope to get to the Snowbird Center; however, we recommend the shuttle, which runs until 11 p.m. (sometimes later). The walking route is slippery, and you'll be dodging skiers and others who use that slope at night.

Other activities

Snowbird offers **guided backcountry tours** and **snowshoe tours**. All tours are dependent upon weather conditions, ability level and time availability. Call 933-2147 for more information. During the day, Snowbird operates a **tubing** hill. **Ice skating** is available during the day and in the evenings. You also can go **night skiing** on the Chickadee novice slope outside the Cliff Lodge.

Join Wasatch Powderbird Guides (742-2800, www.heliskiwasatch.com) for spectacular **helicopter skiing** in Little Cottonwood Canyon.

The **Snowbird Canyon Racquet Club,** at the mouth of the canyon, has indoor tennis, racquetball, squash courts, aerobics classes and a complete fitness center. The resort owns it; ask about rates.

Snowbird is not a good place for non-skiers and people who don't love the outdoors unless they plan to spend considerable time at the Cliff Spa (see *Accommodations*). The only other diversion is **shopping**, and a champion browser will finish off the dozen or so shops in half a day. However, the Salt Lake Valley, where you'll find more extensive shopping, is a short drive away. An actors' troupe stages a **Murder Mystery Dinner Theatre** once a month from January through March; call the resort for information on that and other entertainment special events.

 ## Getting there and getting around

By air: Salt Lake City is a major airline hub, so flights are numerous. Ground transportation is well organized—Lewis Brothers Stages charges $45 per person, round-trip, between the airport and Snowbird or Alta. Call (800) 826-5844 or head to the Lewis Brothers counter at the airport when you arrive.

By train: Amtrak's California Zephyr stops in Salt Lake City (at 4 a.m. coming from the West Coast, but the fare is cheap. From Chicago, the train arrives at midnight). Call (800) USA-RAIL or consult the Amtrak Web site, www.amtrak.com.

By car: Snowbird is 25 miles southeast of Salt Lake City in Little Cottonwood Canyon. The most direct route from the airport is east on I-80, south on I-215, Exit 6 to Wasatch Blvd., then follow the signs.

Getting around: If you fly in, don't bother renting a car—Snowbird is entirely walkable. If you plan to ski a lot of other Utah areas, stay in Salt Lake City (see Utah Skiing chapter). Utah's new light rail system makes getting to Snowbird quick and easy. Take the light rail from the downtown hotels for $1, for an additional 75 cents a bus will take you to Snowbird's doorstep. A Lewis Brothers SkiExpress van to Snowbird is about $15 roundtrip from downtown (call 359-8677 from Salt Lake City). Lewis Brothers also has the Canyon Jumper between Park City and Snowbird for $20. Bus service links Alta and Snowbird for $1.25. A free Snowbird shuttle will get you to various points within the resort complex.

Grand Targhee

Wyoming

Summit elevation: 11,477 feet
Vertical drop: 3,477 feet
Base elevation: 8,000 feet

Address: P.O. Box SKI, Alta, WY 83422
📞 **Area code:** 307
Ski area phone: 353-2300
Fax: 353-8148
Toll-free snow report:
(800) TARGHEE (827-4433)
ⓘ **Toll-free reservations:**
(800) TARGHEE (827-4433)
E-mail: info@grandtarghee.com
Internet: www.grandtarghee.com
Expert: ★★★★★
Advanced: ★★★★★
Intermediate: ★★★★
Beginner: ★★ **Never-ever:** ★★

Number of lifts: 5–2 high-speed quads,
1 quad, 1 double, 1 magic carpet
Snowmaking: None
Skiable acreage: 2,000 lift-served acres
Snowboarding: Yes
Bed Base: 432 pillows (96 lodging units)
Nearest lodging: Slopeside, hotel and condos
Resort child care: Yes, 2 months and older
Adult ticket, per day: $44–$47 (01/02)

Dining: ★★★
Apres-ski/nightlife: ★
Other activities: ★

If you like to ski or snowboard in powder but can't afford a heli-trip, Grand Targhee is the next best thing. About 500 inches of snow falls here each winter, and when it does, Targhee's groomers don't exactly work overtime. You gotta love a ski resort that designates beginner, intermediate and advanced *powder* areas on its trail map.

Did we scare away those of you who still flounder in fluff? Don't flip the page yet. This is one of the two best lift-served resorts in America for learning powder skiing (ironically, Alta, UT, is the other; Grand Targhee's address is Alta, WY). The trouble with powder at other resorts is you usually find it only on the steepest slopes, and it's tough to get a feel for loose snow when you're also struggling with the pitch. Grand Targhee leaves powder on some of its gentle rolling terrain, too, so anyone who wants to conquer powder will never have a better chance. If you are an intermediate, rent a pair of fat skis and cut loose. If you really don't want to deal with powder, Targhee grooms a few paths from the top of each lift.

For 2001/02, the new Sacajawea high-speed quad will take you to 500 acres of terrain on Peaked Mountain that could previously only be reached by snowcat. About a third of this new terrain will be groomed, the rest is pristine glade skiing and open bowls that will be left untouched for freshies. Better yet, on adverse weather days, Peaked Mountain provides protection from the wind and low clouds.

The best part of this powder paradise is you won't have to share their fresh pillowy snow with the masses, because this resort is grandly isolated. Grand Targhee is in Wyoming, but the only way to get here is through Idaho. Its huge bowls of snow are on the western slope of the Tetons, which hug the border between the two states.

Targhee was the name of a local peacekeeping Indian chief who lived in the area more than 100 years ago. (You'll see his portrait painted on one of the buildings.) Grand comes from the 13,770-foot Grand Teton Peak. From here, you see the peak's less photographed but equally impressive west face.

When Averell Harriman was scouting for his dream resort in the 1930s, he narrowed the search to Targhee and the site that became Sun Valley. Local ranchers and farmers opened Targhee as a ski resort about 30 years ago. Targhee is close to ranch country, and many of its employees herd cattle or grow potatoes in the snowless months. A good number have never lived anywhere else. Though not talkative, they are quite friendly.

No ski area is perfect for everyone, however. If you go stir-crazy without a variety of restaurants and other things to do, we suggest you stay in Jackson and spend one day of your vacation here. But if you'd like to completely unwind, ski during the day, read a good book at night and head home new and invigorated, this is the place.

Mountain layout—Skiing

◆◆ **Expert** ◆ **Advanced:** Targhee has two mountains: 1,500-acre Fred's Mountain, which is lift-served, and Peaked Mountain, which now has 500 acres of lift-served terrain and another 1,000 acres of snowcat skiing. Experienced powderhounds will want to exercise the latter option. Ten skiers per snowcat, with two guides, head out to enjoy this snowy playground. The longest run is 3.2 miles and covers slightly more than 2,800 vertical.

The new lift-served 500 acres on Peaked has glades, bowls and some groomed runs. While we haven't had a chance to check out the new area, we're sure you'll want to take the time to do it.

■ **Intermediate:** As we said earlier, your best bet is to rent fat skis and head to the intermediate or beginner powder areas marked on the trail map. On Fred's Mountain, three chair lifts serve high, broad descents mostly above treeline. Fred's has excellent cruiser runs and good bump slopes. Targhee doesn't have enough skiers per acre to make bumps, so the groomers make their own on the Big Thunder run. Widely spaced and perfectly symmetrical, they are excellent for beginning mogul skiers and those whose knees can't take the pounding of skier-made bumps. There is also tree skiing here and there. The resort grooms about one-third of the runs; the rest is left to accumulate powder. About 80 percent of the new lift-served 500 acres on Peaked is for intermediates, including some groomed runs, bowls and glades.

●● **Beginner** ● **Never-ever:** Targhee has a small area of groomed beginner runs at its base, served by a magic carpet. But because this resort grooms so little of its terrain, and because there isn't much to do in the base area, we recommend you learn elsewhere. This is not a difficult mountain, but it's definitely not for first-timers.

Mountain layout—Snowboarding

So you want to ride the deep stuff... I mean the really deep stuff, but you can't afford heli gas? No problem, head to Grand Targhee, the thrifty powder hound's choice. Powder, powder, powder…this place is all about powder. Where else can you ride where the grooming policy on a powder day is to plow three lanes down the mountain for people who get stuck to get out?

Targhee has two mountains: 1,500 acres of lift-served terrain on Fred's Mountain, and 500 acres of lift-served and another 1,000 acres of snowcat riding on Peaked Mountain. Experienced powder hounds will want to take advantage of the snowcat riding. Ten riders per snowcat, with two guides, head out to enjoy this snowy playground. The longest run is 3.2 miles and covers slightly more than 2,800 vertical.

If you can't do the snowcat trip, don't fret—it's all good! Check the access gate to Mary's Nipple and you'll be more than happy. Hike up to the top and drop in for some 40-degree madness, or pick from your choice of doable cliffs (10- to 100-foot-plus) off the back side of the mountain. You'll have to hike back in if you opt for the cliffs. The new lift-served 500 acres on Peaked has glades, bowls and some groomed runs. While we haven't had a chance to check out the new area, we're sure you'll want to take the time to do it.

Intermediates have 1,200 acres of powder for riding. What else do you want? And with a new high-speed quad opening this season you'll be getting even more runs in the pow. Targhee has a small area of groomed beginner runs at its base, served by a magic carpet. For first-time snowboarders, Grand Targhee is one of the best places to learn. Where else can you learn how to ride without getting a single bruise?

Mountain rating

Great for intermediates and above. Superb for learning powder skiing or snowboarding. While this isn't a good place for first-time skiers, it's perfect for first-time snowboarders, partly because loads of snow makes for soft landings and partly because snowboards are made to float. Targhee usually gets double their famous neighbor Jackson Hole's amount in snowfall. And with days where there are maybe 200 people on the mountain, and 2-plus feet of powder, it's worth every dime.

Cross-country and snowshoeing

Grand Targhee Nordic Center has 15 km. of track groomed for touring and skating. The trails wind through varied terrain, offering beautiful vistas of the Greater Yellowstone area as well as meadows and aspen glades. Trail passes are $8 a day, $5 for a senior or child; children 5 and younger ski free. The ski school teaches telemarking as well as touring and skating techniques. Group lessons are $34 and private lessons $58 an hour.

A snowshoe tour focuses on wildlife, with the guide pointing out tracks and explaining how animals survive the winter. This tour is $34, two-person minimum.

Lessons (2001/02 prices)

Many instructors have been with the Ski Training Center since its first season in 1969.

Group lessons: $35 for adults, at 10 a.m. and 1 p.m. If you buy three or more lessons in advance, the cost is $30 each.

Never-ever package: A lift-lesson-equipment package costs $59. If a friend brings a beginner to the Ski School for this package, the friend gets a full-day ticket free of charge.

Private lessons: $59 an hour, $30 for each additional person.

Special programs: The resort has several special clinics such as Extreme Skiing, Women Ski The Tetons, snowboarding and telemark.

Child care (2001/02 prices)

Ages: 2 months to 7 years.

Costs: Kids 2 months to 2 years cost $45 per day, $33 per half day. Ages 3 to 5, day care only, is $42 per day, $30 per half day. The program includes two snacks and lunch for the full day, a snack for half day.

Reservations: Required; call (800) TARGHEE (827-4433). Babysitting services are available outside of regular day care; ask at the lodge front desk.

Children's lessons: Ski programs for ages 3–5 are $48 for a half day, $69 for a full day, with lessons, lifts, lunch and day-care activities. Ages 6 and older are $35 for a half-day; $68 for a full day, with lessons and lunch, but not lift ticket.

Lift tickets (2001/02 prices)

	Adult	Child (6-14)
One day	$47	$29
Three days	$135 ($45/day)	$87 ($29/day)
Five days	$220 ($44/day)	$145 ($29/day)

Who skis free: Ages 5 and younger.

Who skis at a discount: Those who ski more than one day at Grand Targhee probably are staying here too. In those cases Targhee's lodging-lift packages are the most economical and practical. On all Targhee lodging packages, children ages 14 and younger stay and ski free, one child per paying adult. Ages 62 and older ski at children's prices.

Note: A full day of snowcat skiing, including lunch, snacks and beverages served in a Snowcat Skiing souvenir mug, is $264, half day is $199. Here's a great deal: Book a three-day or longer package stay from opening (mid-November) through Dec. 20, 2001, and get a free day of snowcat skiing; on a seven-day package, you'll get two days on the cat free.

If you are staying in Jackson and coming here for a day, buy your ticket in advance at Grand Targhee ticket outlets in Jackson or Teton Village. You'll save about $5. Call 733-3135 in Jackson to find the nearest ticket outlet. The Targhee Express is about $59 for bus and lift ticket from Jackson Hole.

Accommodations

The village sleeps about 450 people at **two hotel-type lodges and a 32-unit, multistory condo building.** All are within an easy walk to lifts and base facilities. Most units are packaged with lift tickets, though you can rent them without buying lift tickets (though frankly, we have no idea why you'd want to). Nightly rates per room at the lodges run $68 to $150, at the condos $217 to $293.

Packages that include ski tickets and two group lessons are offered for seven nights and six days, five nights and four days, and three nights and three days. Super-Saver Seasons for 2001/02 include November through mid-December and April, where you'll save 30 to 40 percent. If you book a package from opening day to mid-December, not only will you get 30 to 40 percent off, you'll also get the free snowcat skiing described in the Lift Ticket section. January is Value Season, where rates are 20 to 25 percent lower than what we quote here.

Dining: $$$-Entrees $20+; $$-$10-20; $-less than $10.
Accommodations: (double room) $$$$-$200+; $$$-$141-$200; $$-$81-$140; $-$80 and less.

For the hotel and motel rooms, regular season (February and March) packages per person for two people range from $302 to $361 for three days and three nights, $460 to $556 for five nights and four days, and $645 to $775 for seven nights and six days. For the Sioux 2-bedroom condos (there also are loft studio condos that sleep up to four), regular-season packages per person for four people are $409 for three days and three nights, $634 for five nights and four days, and $881 for seven nights and six days. Call (800) 827-4433 (800-TARGHEE) for information.

Dining

There's not much variety here, but there's a lot of quality.

Skadi's ($$–$$$) is Targhee's finest restaurant, with entrées such as rack of lamb, whiskey chicken, shrimp scampi and poached salmon. Skadi's also serves breakfast and lunch. **Snorkel's** ($) is the spot for great gourmet pizza and pasta with fun and games for the family. Breakfast here features sinful pastries and espressos. **Wild Bill's Grill** ($) in the Rendezvous Lodge has breakfast, pizza, a soup and salad bar, sandwiches and Mexican food. The **Trap Bar** ($) serves a fine Idaho potato with all the trimmings, basic grilled sandwiches, burgers and chicken, plus après-ski snacks.

Après ski/nightlife/other activities

This is not Targhee's strong point. **Snorkel's** has après-ski with varietal wines by the glass, microbrew beers and upscale appetizers in a relaxed atmosphere. The **Trap Bar** is livelier, with live music. Otherwise, outdoor activities include a **heated swimming pool** and **hot tubs,** a **tubing park** ($8 per hour) and an **ice skating rink** (rental skates are $5; use of the rink is free). You can take a **sleigh ride** or go **snowmobiling. Dinner sleigh rides** cost about $30 for adults and $15 for kids. **Shopping** is limited to one boutique, a small general store and a ski clothing shop. At the **Spa at Grand Targhee,** you can indulge in a massage, herbal or mud wrap, sauna or aromatherapy session. Or settle in to watch **complimentary movies.**

Getting there and getting around

By air: Targhee is served by airports in Jackson, Wyoming, and Idaho Falls, Idaho. Jets fly into both airports and resort shuttles pick up guests by reservation. You can rent cars at either airport.

By car: Targhee is just inside the Wyoming border on the west side of the Tetons, accessible only from Idaho. From Jackson, follow signs to Wilson on Hwy. 22, then go north on Hwy. 33 at Victor, Idaho. Turn east at Driggs (the sign is on the roof of a building), and drive 12 miles to the ski area. About 8 miles from Driggs, you'll start to suspect you're lost, but keep going—you can't make a wrong turn. Coming from Idaho Falls, take Hwy. 20 to Rexburg, and turn east on Hwy. 33 to Driggs. Grand Targhee is 42 miles northwest of Jackson, 87 miles northeast of Idaho Falls and 297 miles north of Salt Lake City.

Getting around: If you are spending your entire vacation at Grand Targhee, don't rent a car—there's nowhere to drive. If you stay in Jackson, we recommend you ride the Targhee Express bus that picks up in Jackson and at Teton Village. It's about $15 round trip; call 733-3135. The highway between Jackson and Grand Targhee is steep going over Teton Pass (up to 10-percent grade). We caution against staying at Targhee and driving to Jackson for the nightlife—if you want Jackson's nightlife, stay there.

Jackson Hole

Wyoming

Summit elevation: 10,450 feet
Vertical drop: 4,139 feet
Base elevation: 6,311 feet

Address: P.O. Box 290
Teton Village, WY 83025
☎ **Area code:** 307
Ski area phone: 733-2292
Toll-free snow report:
(888) 333-7766 (DEEP-SNO)
ⓘ **Toll-free reservations:**
(800) 443-6931 **Fax:** 733-2660
E-mail: info@jacksonhole.com
Internet: www.jacksonhole.com
www.jackson-hole.com
Expert:★★★★★ **Advanced:**★★★★★
Intermediate:★★★★
Beginner:★★
Never-ever:★★★★

Number and types of lifts: 10—1 aerial tram, 1
eight-person gondola, 2 high-speed quads, 4
quads, 1 triple, 1 double
Skiable acreage: 2,500 acres
Snowmaking: 11 percent
Uphill capacity: 12,000+ per hour
Snowboarding: Yes, unlimited
Bed base: 10,000 in valley, 2,500 at base
Nearest lodging: Slopeside
Resort child care: Yes, 2 months and older
Adult ticket, per day: $52–$59 (01/02 price)

Dining:★★★
Apres-ski/nightlife:★★★
Other activities:★★★★★

Take your average Western ski resort, put it on steroids, and you're at Jackson Hole. The slopes are steeper, with more than half the runs rating a well-deserved black- or double-black-diamond designation. The runs are longer, including the 4,139 vertical feet covered by its infamous aerial Tram. And the views are more astonishing. Where else can you see miles upon miles of Yellowstone National Park as you negotiate the chutes and bowls?

Any wonder then that the base area—called Teton Village—and the nearby town of Jackson, just 12 miles away, reflect the extremes that Jackson Hole offers? Here, hotels that pamper the destination skier stand next to modestly priced hostels; rustic après-ski hangouts share a kitchen with upscale restaurants, and aging four-by-fours are parked next to late-model SUVs in the resort parking lot.

Though sprinkled with more than its share of gift shops and art galleries, the wooden sidewalks, low buildings, town square with Elk antler arches and small shops create a beautiful small-town feel.

During the winter, the real attraction here—and the one worthy of all the positive superlatives—is the skiing and snowboarding. Despite the installation of the high-speed Bridger Gondola, which added access to a number of intermediate to advanced-intermediate runs without having to board the Tramway, Jackson Hole is one heckuva challenging mountain. Sure, there's some excellent learning terrain—gentle, groomed runs that are a pleasure to descend. But if you ever get bored of them, you could easily find yourself over your head on terrain so steep it defies description.

Mountain layout—Skiing

uu Expert: Fully half of Jackson Hole's 2,500 acres is marked with one or two black diamonds. It's no wonder the area has a reputation for steep, exciting skiing. Board the big red tram for the 12-minute rise to the top of Rendezvous Mountain. This is where the big boys and girls go to play.

Once at the top, you have two choices. In one direction is the infamous Corbet's Couloir, a narrow, rocky passage that requires a 10- to 20-foot airborne entry. No thanks? Take the "easier" way down—Rendezvous Bowl, a huge face littered with gigantic moguls. Well, the bowl had waist-high bumps when we skied it—other times it's deep powder, another time it could be wind-packed crust. Point is, it's not groomed, so be prepared for anything. The Hobacks is another face that offers great lift-served powder skiing.

Jackson Hole also opens its backcountry gates for the season. The terrain is not patrolled and requires know-how and the right equipment. The resort is offering backcountry camps to teach proper skiing in the area. Ski smart out here.

◆ **Advanced:** Advanced skiers and boarders can handle the tram runs. The dotted-blue-line runs in ungroomed Casper Bowl are shorter versions of the stuff you'll encounter off the tram. The Amphitheater Bowl is a steep, bumpy run that skiers tend to avoid. Try Rendez-vous' longest run, Mountain Road Trail, which starts out at Rendezvous Trail, winds around Cheyenne and Laramie bowls (called South Pass Traverse here), then mellows just enough the rest of the way down to earn a blue rating on the trail map.

■ **Intermediate:** Remember that 50 percent of that 2,500 acres is *not* black diamond. Even better, most of the tough stuff is completely separate from the easier runs—intermediates seldom have to worry about getting in over their heads. Intermediates will want to stay on Apres Vous Mountain, with 2,170 vertical feet of beginner and intermediate terrain, and Casper Bowl, with its wide intermediate runs, sprinkled with a few advanced. Follow the solid blue lines for groomed terrain and the broken blue lines for ungroomed powder or bumps. You'll run out of gas before you run out of terrain. A cautionary note for brave intermediates: The difference between single-blues and double-blues is that usually, the double-blue is ungroomed.

●● **Beginner:** It's a big step from those gently undulating green-circle slopes to Jackson Hole's blues. Although the upper parts of Apres Vous and all of Casper Bowl are wide and groomed, they have a much steeper pitch than blues at other resorts, enough to intimidate some lower-level skiers. If you're leaning toward the advanced beginner category, you'll grow bored of the beginner runs rather quickly.

● **Never-ever:** One surprise at Jackson Hole is its excellent learning terrain. The base of Apres Vous mountain has a fenced-in area, called Fort Wyoming, below the East's Rest Cut-off and the base area. It's served by a "Magic Carpet" moving sidewalk. Faster skiers can't get in, so those just learning won't get nervous. Parents should take note that Jackson Hole's "Rough Riders" kids offering combines day care and children's instruction in one of the most innovative programs for young "never-evers" we have seen.

Mountain layout—Snowboarding

If you've ever seen the surf movie, "The North Shore," where a kid who surfs in an Arizona wave pool moves to the North Shore of Waikiki to surf some of the hairiest waves in the world, then you're on your way to under-standing how gnarly Jackson Hole really is. If you've only ridden in the East, or even some of the tamer mountains in Colorado, and you show up in Jackson, you're in for a BIG surprise.

Fully half of Jackson Hole's 2,500 acres is marked with one or two black diamonds, and with the mountain's no-rope-out-of-bounds clause, you can add the sickest off-resort backcountry riding available anywhere in the continental U.S. The terrain out there is for real, and if you're not prepared, or experienced, there is an enormous probability of getting seriously hurt or killed, so be careful.

For a quick assessment of your skills, take the tram up the mountain for your first run. Within minutes you'll quickly discover how good you really are. For the Hollywood huckers, there's Corbet's Couloir, a narrow, rocky passage that requires a 5- to 20-foot airborne entry into a usually tracked, steep mogul field. No way? Then consider the even more infamous S & S Chute (check out the video, "Subjekt Haakenson," to see Terje drop this line) or take the "easier" way down—Rendezvous Bowl, a huge face littered with gigantic moguls, bushes, rocks and, if you're lucky, powder. Follow that down to the Sublette chair and continue on to Dick's Ditch, or go to The Hobacks for some seriously ill powder on your way back to the base. If you've made it down on your first run without any fear, burning legs or slough slides, then move here now. You'll never be happy riding anywhere else—except maybe Alaska.

Most of the tough stuff is completely separate from the easier runs—intermediates seldom have to worry about getting in over their heads, which in this case is a very, very good thing. You're going to want to ride Apre Vous. Apres Vous on it's own could hold itself as a very strong freeriding mountain, which is why you'll find the halfpipe over here, along with various hits and kickers built by the locals. We don't recommend building your own kickers, if you're busted, they'll pull your ticket. Luckily there are natural booters and kickers all over the place; try following some local riders around for the inside line. And don't miss Upper Dick's Ditch, where you'll find a natural quarterpipe and halfpipe.

One surprise at Jackson Hole is its excellent learning terrain. The base of Apres Vous has a fenced-in area, called Fort Wyoming, below the East's Rest Cutoff and the base area. It's served by a "Magic Carpet" moving sidewalk. Faster boarders can't get in, so those just learning won't get nervous.

Mountain rating

Color Rendezvous Mountain and the Hobacks jet black, with occasional slashes of navy-blue advanced-intermediate. Casper Bowl is for intermediates to experts, depending on the grooming. Casper's groomed runs (a solid blue line on the trail map) are a cruising delight. The ungroomed blues (a dotted line) are just plain hard work, worthy of advanced skiers. Apres Vous is fantastic for intermediates and advancing beginners but so-so for advanced skiers. Never-evers will do fine the first couple of days, but beginner terrain is quite limited.

 ### Cross-country and snowshoeing

Nordic skiers can strike out for marked trails in **Grand Teton or Yellowstone National Parks,** or try one of the five touring centers near Jackson and Grand Targhee. Trail passes generally are $10 or less for adults, except at Cowboy Village at Togwotee, where trail use is by donation and you must bring your own equipment unless you're a guest there.

The **Saddlehorn Center** (739-2629 or 800-443-6139) serves as the hub of the Nordic systems in Teton Village with 17 km. of groomed track. Because it is next to the downhill ski area, it has telemark lessons as an option. Rentals, full-day beginner group lessons, half-day lessons for other levels and private instruction are available, as are guided tours into the backcountry of Grand Teton National Park. Trail fees: $10 for adults, $5 for children and seniors.

Other touring centers are **Spring Creek**, 20 km. with some fairly steep hills (733-8833 or 800-443-6139); **Teton Pines**, on a gentle golf course (733-1005 or 800-238-2223); and **Cowboy Village at Togwotee** (543-2847 or 800-543-2847).

Lessons (2001/02 prices)

The ski/snowboard school is not only the place to get instruction (and that isn't a bad idea, given Jackson Hole's extreme terrain), but it is also the place to engage a knowledgeable mountain guide. Jackson Hole's nooks and crannies can best be enjoyed with someone who knows them. Make reservations for any ski school program including mountain guides by calling 739-2610 locally or (800) 450-0477.

Group lessons: $65 for a full day (morning and afternoon sessions) and $50 for a half day in the afternoon. Afternoon semi-private three-person groups only cost $70.

Never-ever package: Jackson Hole's Learn To Turn program is $70 and includes a guarantee that learners will be able to control speed and make turns after one day of lessons. Beginners can repeat these lessons for free until they "get it." For snowboarders, the resort offers Burton's innovative Learn-To-Ride program.

Private lessons: Given most commonly in a three-hour morning lesson. Three a.m. hours cost $280 and three p.m. hours are $245 for up to five skiers. Early "Tram Privates" start at 8:30 a.m. with four hours costing $330.

Special programs: There are many, such as instruction for the disabled, the Mountain Experience for advanced to expert skiers that shows them the best terrain and snow conditions, and various camps for women, racing and teens offered at specified times of the season.

Racing: There's a NASTAR course off the Casper Bowl Triple Chair. The resort offers race-training clinics for $220 for four-hour programs.

Child care (2001/02 prices)

Ages: 2 months to 6 years.

Costs: $80 for a full day and $55 a half day. Toddlers get lunch and a snack; parents must provide food for infants.

Reservations: Required, call 739-2691. Bring your child's immunization records.

Other options: For babysitting at your hotel or condo, call **Babysitting Service of Jackson Hole**, 733-0685 or (800) 253-9650; or **Childcare Services**, 733-5178. These services, members of the Jackson Hole Chamber of Commerce, have sitters trained in first aid and child CPR. **Baby's Away** (888-616-8495; 733-0387) rents and will deliver baby needs to your lodge, such as crib, stroller, car seat and toys.

Children's lessons: The Explorers program for ages 7–14 is $80 for all day including lunch, $55 for half day. The resort also has ski lessons and day care for ages 3–6 (Rough Riders) as part of its day-care program. This program costs $80 for all day and $55 for a half day (including lifts).

Lift tickets (2001/02 prices)

	Adult	Child (Up to 14)
One day	$59	$30
Three days	$165 ($55/day)	$83 ($27+/day)
Five days	$260 ($52/day)	$130 ($26/day)

Who skis free: No one.

Who skis at a discount: Ages 65 and older ski at children's prices. Beginners pay a minimal lift ticket fee for the beginner lifts.

Note: Jackson Hole's ticket includes all lifts—chairs, tram, gondola, and surface lifts, a policy that went into effect a few seasons ago.

Nearby resorts

The **Snow King Ski Area**—half the cost of Jackson Hole—is in downtown Jackson, about 12 miles from Jackson Hole Ski Resort. Sixty percent of its 400 acres is rated advanced, thanks to a north-facing slope that plunges 1,571 feet. It doesn't have a lot of green-rated terrain, primarily a catwalk that traverses the mountain from the summit to the base. Because it is so steep, always shaded and often icy, locals call it "Eastern skiing out West." This small town area is a great practice hill with a steep consistent pitch. Lift tickets for adults are $30; for kids ages 14 and younger and seniors 60 and older, $20. The hill is open for night skiing Tuesday through Saturday. You can buy an hour ticket for $8; 2 hours for $12; 3 hours for $15. Snow King's Web site is at www.snowking.com; e-mail is snowking@wyoming.com. SnowKing also has a multi-lane tubing park open weekdays from 4 to 8 p.m. and weekends noon to 8 p.m. The cost is $8 per hour for adults; $6 for kids.

 ## Accommodations

Choose from three locations: Teton Village at the base of the slopes, with fewer restaurants and nightlife options; the town of Jackson, with lots of eating, shopping and partying but 12 miles from skiing; or hotels, condos and two fine resorts between the two. Town-ski area bus transportation is readily available.

We haven't listed all of the available lodging, so call **Jackson Hole Central Reservations** (800-443-6931) for more information. This agency can book your entire trip, from airline tickets to activities. Other booking agencies are **Vacations Incorporated** (800-228-1025) or **Rocky Mountain Reservations** (800-322-5766).

Note: Too many hotels here have combined "Jackson Hole" with "Inn," "Lodge" or "Hotel." Three of the five are Best Westerns, but two are at the ski area and one is closer to town. Another popular name is "Teton," with four lodges in the area choosing to start their name with that word. If you book one, pay attention to the exact name and the location, or your ground transportation could easily drop you and your luggage in the wrong place.

Teton Village

The following properties are all within steps of the slopes and each other, so the choice is on facilities or price rather than location. Most of these properties have ski packages.

Alpenhof (733-3242; 800-732-3244; $$–$$$$) is the most luxurious of the hotels. Built in peaked-roof Alpine style with lots of exposed and carved wood, it has an excellent restaurant and a large lounge that is a center of relaxed après-ski activity. Some of the 43 guest rooms have fireplaces. The hotel has a heated outdoor pool, Jacuzzi, sauna and game room.

The Best Western Inn at Jackson Hole (733-2311 or 800-842-7666; $$–$$$) has a convenient location, but it's showing its age. Rooms are spacious and many have kitchenettes, fireplaces and/or lofts. It has two restaurants, a heated outdoor pool and hot tub. One possible drawback: every time you leave your room, you step outside. That means bundling up to go to the hot tub or restaurant.

Marriott Resort Hotel and Spa at Jackson Hole (733-3657 or 800-445-4655; $$–$$$$), formerly a Best Western (see, we told you this was confusing), was completely remodeled in 1997. This is about as full-service as it gets. The hotel has two restaurants, one on the fancy side; the other an Irish pub. Also new are a spa and sauna, plus a private health club.

The **Hostel X** (733-3415; $) has some of the most inexpensive slopeside lodging in the United States. Rooms are spartan, but have private baths and maid service; amenities include a large lounge and game area and laundry facilities.

Village Center Inn (733-3155 or 800-735-8342; $$), next to the tram, has 16 one- and two-bedroom units, some with lofts. **Crystal Springs Inn** (733-4423; $$) has 15 basic rooms.

Condominiums and private homes are available through Teton Village Property Management (800-443-6840; 733-4610) and Jackson Hole Property Management (800-443-8613; 733-7945). Rates are about $125–$850 per night.

Jackson

Many of these accommodations also offer ski packages. All listed here are within a block of the public bus service to Teton Village unless noted.

One of the best, just off the main square, is the **Wort Hotel** (800-322-2727; 733-2190; $$$–$$$$), an 1880s-style, four-diamond AAA-rated hotel just off the main square. Inside is the Silver Dollar Bar, with its curving bar inlaid with 2,032 uncirculated 1921 silver dollars.

Snow King Resort (800-522-5464; 733-5200; $$–$$$) is a large hotel with a pool, indoor ice rink, game and fitness rooms and more. It is several long blocks from downtown, but right next to the Snow King Ski Area, which has night skiing.

The Quality Inn 49er Inn and Suites (733-7550; $$-$$$) is a three-building complex conveniently located at the edge of town and a stone's throw from an express bus stop. Suites are spacious and feature a fireplace, large bathrooms, excellent fitness facilities and a hot tub. At the **Parkway Inn** (733-3143; $$-$$$) bed and breakfast, the decor is decidedly Victorian. Don't miss the granola and fresh-squeezed orange juice for breakfast, and check out the fitness center and pool, a great place to unwind after a long day of skiing.

Two excellent B&Bs are **Rusty Parrot Lodge** (733-2000 or 800-458-2004; www.rustyparrot.com; $$$$) and **Davy Jackson Inn** (739-2294 or 800-584-0532; www.davyjackson.com; $$-$$$). Both have inviting rooms (some with fireplaces) with down comforters. Rusty Parrot has country lodgepole pine decor, while Davy Jackson leans toward Victorian, but you can't go wrong at either. Rusty Parrot is about two blocks from downtown and half a block to the bus; Davy Jackson is three blocks to downtown and a block to the bus.

The Bunkhouse (733-3668; www.anvilmotel.com; $), a no-frills dorm located in the basement of a motel comprises one 25-bed room, a separate room with couches for lounging and a kitchen area with microwave and refrigerators. There are separate men's and women's lavatories, and a laundry is available. The rate is $22 per night, and reservations are not accepted—it's first-come/first-served.

Between downtown and the ski area

The **Red Lion Wyoming Inn of Jackson** (800-844-0035; 734-0035; $$–$$$$) and **The Best Western Lodge at Jackson Hole** (800-458-3866; 739-9703 $–$$$) are practically next door to each other on Broadway (Hwy. 89) heading toward Teton Village from downtown. Red Lion Wyoming Inn is decorated with antique reproduction furniture, but has no pool or hot tub (though some rooms have Jacuzzis). It serves a continental breakfast, but there is no restaurant. The Best Western Lodge at Jackson Hole (there also is a Jackson Hole Lodge, which is quite different) is a delight for children, because its exterior is decorated with carved, painted bears and raccoons that hang from poles and peek from behind benches. It has a swimming pool and hot tub, and the Gun Barrel Steak House is next door.

One of the best spots to see the rugged Grand Teton and its neighboring peaks is from the **Spring Creek Ranch** (733-8833 or 800-443-6139; $$$–$$$$), atop the East Gros Ventre Butte, which blocks the view of Grand Teton from most of Jackson. The resort has luxurious hotel rooms, condos and houses for rent, a marvelous gourmet restaurant and unsurpassed views of the Jackson Valley, Grand Teton and the ski area. Shuttles to town and skiing are provided.

On Teton Village Road a few miles from the ski area and town is **Teton Pines Resort** (733-1005 or 800-238-2223; $$$–$$$$). Better known for its summer activities, including a stunning 18-hole golf course, it is open in winter and has ski packages. The amenities list goes on and on: free pickup from the airport, free indoor tennis, use of a neighboring athletic club, continental breakfast, gourmet restaurant, 14 km. of cross-country trails, pool and hot tub.

Dining

We'll start with the selection at the ski area, and work our way toward town.

If you're staying in Teton Village, be sure to spend at least one evening in town, if only to see the lighted elk-horn arches in the town square.

Teton Village

At the elegant end of the spectrum is the **Alpenhof Hotel** (733-3462, $$), a quiet, genteel place that serves German and Austrian specialties. At the other extreme is the very funky **The Mangy Moose** (733-4913; $), beloved for its salad bar, down-home steak-and-seafood menu, and lively atmosphere (wash down a Giant Enchilada with the Moose Juice Stout local brew). Somewhere in the middle is the Best Western's **J. Hennessey Steak House** (734-4400, $$), slightly upscale with a Western motif.

Masa Sushi (733-2311) serves Japanese food that gets raves from locals, while **Mountain Skillet** and the **Out Of Bounds Bar and Grille** (both 739-0244) have more family-oriented menus. **Al Dente** is an Italian restaurant that took over the building occupied by Jenny Leigh's. All three are in the Best Western Inn at Jackson Hole.

For a truly unique dinner experience, check out the **Solitude Cabin Dinner Sleighrides** (739-2603; $$$) a four-course meal served in a remote log cabin. Menu items include prime rib, salmon, soup, salad, dessert and live musical entertainment. Drinks aren't part of the fixed price, but you can bring your own (as long as you can handle the $5 cork fee).

The locals' breakfast favorite is at "the gas station," which is actually part of **Teton Village Market**, where the tasty breakfast burrito or scrambled eggs is $3.19 "out the door."

Jackson

For casual inexpensive dining, it's **Bubba's** featuring heaping plates of "bubbacued" ribs, chicken, beef and pork. Try the Mexican for breakfast or sink your teeth into one of Bubba's oversized omelettes. No sense in giving you the phone number (it's at 515 W. Broadway), because Bubba's doesn't take reservations. Be prepared to wait, and while you do, send a member of your party down the street to the liquor store—Bubba's is BYOB.

Another casual place is **Mountain High Pizza Pie** (733-3646, $). **Joe's Pizza** (734-5637, $) is home of the "mean, green pesto pizza." **Nani's Genuine Pasta House** (733-3668; $$) and **Anthony's** (733-3717; $$) got raves from locals for their authentic Italian regional cooking. **Lame Duck** (733-4311; $–$$) has the best reputation for Chinese cooking.

A good selection on the elegant end is **The Range** (734-8435; $$), which gives classes on game cooking in addition to serving it. It serves a five-course, fixed-price, regional American cuisine dinner from an open-style kitchen, and also serves lunch and à la carte entrées. Other upper-scale choices are **Off Broadway Grille** (733-9777; $$) for pastas, fresh seafood and meats; and **The Blue Lion** (733-3912; $$–$$$), known for its roast rack of lamb.

The hearty-breakfast king is **Bubba's**. For tamer breakfast fare try **The Bunnery** (733-5474) with excellent omelets, whole-grain waffles and bakery items and **Jedediah's Original House of Sourdough** (733-5671) for superb sourjack pancakes.

Between town and the ski area

For excellent, elegant dining, **the Granary** (733-8833; $$$) at Spring Creek Resort is hard to beat. Another top choice is **The Grille at Teton Pines** (733-1005, $$–$$$) at the Teton Pines Resort, with a beautiful dining room and extensive wine list. **Stiegler's** (733-1071, $$) has specialties from owner Peter Stiegler's home in Austria.

The Mexican restaurant with the best reputation is **Vista Grande** (733-6964, $–$$). For casual dining, try the **Calico Italian Restaurant & Bar** (733-2460; $$), halfway between Jackson and Teton Village at a bus stop on Village Road.

If you're headed to Grand Targhee, **Nora's Fish Creek Inn** in Wilson (733-8288, $$ for dinner) is a local favorite for any meal, especially breakfast.

For more ideas, pick up a copy of the Jackson Hole Dining Guide or browse through the rack of business-card-sized menus at your hotel (an excellent idea other resorts might well use). **Mountain Express** (734-0123) will deliver to your hotel from a dozen fine eateries.

Après-ski/nightlife

In Teton Village the rowdiest spot by far for après-ski and nightlife is **The Mangy Moose**. **Out Of Bounds Bar and Grille** at the Inn at Jackson Hole is quieter than the Moose, with acoustic music most nights. It's a good spot to get a quick drink, because it's to one side of the resort. **The Alpenhof Bistro** attracts a sedate group, as does the lobby bar in the Best Western Resort Hotel. The latter is a good spot to get a glass of wine and relax on overstuffed couches.

In town, **The Million Dollar Cowboy Bar** attracts tourists who love saddle bar stools, the silver dollars in the bar surface, and live Country & Western bands. Try it, corny as it sounds. It's cash-only, so leave the credit card at home. **The Silver Dollar Bar** is similar, with more silver dollars in the bar. Plus it serves great buffalo burgers and Starbuck's coffee. **Sidewinders Tavern** on Broadway is a sports bar with 22 televisions, pool tables, foosball and more. It has live music several nights a week and attracts a youngish, blue-collar crowd. **The Shady Lady Saloon** at the Snow King Resort has live entertainment several nights a week. **Jackson Hole Pub & Brewery** has good microbrews and live entertainment.

Other activities

Several unusual activities center around Jackson's abundant wildlife. The **National Museum of Wildlife Art** (733-5771) houses the nation's premier collection of fine wildlife paintings, sculptures and other art, some dating back 170 years. The excellent cafe overlooks the **National Elk Refuge** (733-0277), where 7,000 to 9,000 elk winter. Horse-drawn sleigh rides through the refuge are offered by the museum. Combination admission and sleigh-ride tickets are available.

An outstanding educational tour is offered through the **Great Plains Wildlife Institute** (733-2623). On the institute's wildlife spotting tours, you ride with a biologist to help note the location and numbers of various birds and animals. A four-hour tour costs about $70 for adults and $40 for adult-accompanied children aged 3–12, with snacks provided. Full day and multiday tours also are offered. We spotted bison, elk, eagles, moose, deer, bighorn sheep, trumpeter swans and pronghorn. Everyone gets to use binoculars and a powerful spotting scope for up-close viewing.

Horse-drawn **dinner sleigh rides** are offered by Spring Creek Resort (733-8833) and Solitude Cabin (733-6657). Bar-T-Five (733-5386) has a **winter dinner show** with a barbecue dinner and "yarn-spinnin' " leading the entertainment.

The Jackson Hole Nordic Center (739-2629 or 800-443-6139) has **dogsled tours** lasting anywhere from an hour to a day. The tours cover some 400 miles of scenic trails from the Shoshoni and Teton National Forests. Interested in more dog mushing? Then look into the Brooks Lake tour, a half-day trip through some of the most spectacular country, which takes you to the historic Brooks Lake Lodge on the Continental Divide.

Other activities include **snowmobile excursions** to Granite Hot Springs, **helicopter touring and skiing** and, of course, nearby **Grand Teton** and **Yellowstone National Parks**.

Shopping here is what it should be at all resort towns—a selection of high-quality, moderately priced goods with friendly, helpful salespeople. Shopaholics should stay in town (the Wort Hotel is right at the center of the action). The covered wooden sidewalks encourage window shopping, even when it snows. There are far too many good shops to single out any of them, but you'll find art galleries, plenty of Western clothing and items made from elk antlers.

You can pick up a shopping, dining or vacation-planning guide at the Wyoming information center on the north edge of town, or call the Jackson Hole Chamber of Commerce (733-3316).

Getting there and getting around

By air: American, Delta, Delta/Skywest, United and United Express serve the Jackson Hole airport. American has daily 757 jet service from Chicago and from Dallas.United flies 3 daily jets from Denver and from Los Angeles on Saturdays. Skywest serves Jackson with turbo-prop planes (30-seaters). Check with the resort central reservations (phone number is in the stat box) for air bargains.

By car: Jackson is on Hwys. 89, 26 and 191 in western Wyoming. The town is 10 miles south of the airport, and Teton Village is 12 miles farther by Hwys. 89, 22 and 390.

Getting around: Rent a car. Unless you want to get stuck in town or at the village, you'll need wheels. While buses run regularly, they can add up to 45 minutes to your commuting time during the busy après-ski period. Unless you are used to driving steep Rocky Mountain passes, we recommend that you take the Targhee Express (733-3101) to Grand Targhee in snowy weather. It's $15 well spent.

Motorists, take note: Highway signs say little about the ski areas. From town, follow signs to Teton Village to get to Jackson Hole Mountain Resort, and to Wilson when driving to Grand Targhee.

Southern Teton Area Rapid Transit (START) buses run frequently between Jackson and Teton Village to 10 p.m. in ski season for a small fee. Study the bus schedule and get on an express bus if you want to minimize your commute. Another good deal: books of bus passes sold at most resorts. They can save you a few bucks off the published fare. Five companies provide taxi services and airport shuttles: Jackson Hole Transportation (733-3135), Gray Line (733-4325), Buckboard Cab (733-1112), All-Star Taxi (733-2888) and All Trans (733-1700).

CALIFORNIA

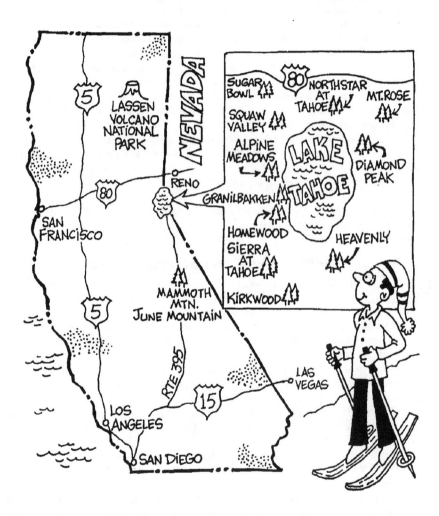

North Lake Tahoe Area

Alpine Meadows

Squaw Valley USA

Northstar-at-Tahoe

Diamond Peak

Sugar Bowl

with

Reno, Nevada

Toll-free reservations:
(888) 434-1262, North Lake Tahoe
(800) GO-TAHOE (468-2463), Incline Village/Crystal Bay
(800) FOR-RENO (367-7366), Reno
Internet: www.tahoefun.org (North Lake Tahoe)
www.reno.net (Reno)

Dining:★★★
Apres-ski/nightlife:★★(near the lake) ★★★★(Reno)
Other activities:★★★

Few regions on the North American continent have the ski-resort diversity of the Lake Tahoe region. When you consider the elements of a perfect ski vacation—variety of terrain, good snow, comfortable lodging, beautiful scenery, a wide choice of restaurants and nightlife, a myriad other activities, accessibility—Lake Tahoe would rank near the top in all but a couple of categories (and it would be above the median in those).

Lake Tahoe, one of the largest and most stunningly beautiful mountain lakes in the world, straddles the border of California and Nevada about 200 miles east of San Francisco. Tahoe has received accolades from travel writers for more than a century. Mark Twain was one of the first to note its beauty. In 1861, he wrote in *Roughing It*, Tahoe was "the fairest picture the whole earth affords." Because the lake is so deep and doesn't freeze, it retains its sapphire-blue color throughout the winter. Its name comes from a Washoe Indian word meaning "water in a high place"—the lake is about 6,200 feet above sea level.

Tahoe is best divided into two regions for vacation purposes. Though you can run your-self ragged by trying to visit every major area in a week, it's better to concentrate on the North Shore or the South Shore. The two regions provide different vacation experiences.

South Tahoe is densely developed, with high-rise casino-hotels hugging the California-Nevada state line, frequent big-name entertainment, and non-stop après-ski activity. It has three ski/snowboard resorts, one of which overlooks the twin towns of Stateline and South Lake Tahoe. Speaking in general terms, South Shore tends to attract first-time visitors who live outside California and Nevada, while the North Shore attracts fewer first-time visitors, but loads of Californians.

North Shore has history, is more spread out and a lot quieter, and has an amazing concentration of excellent skiing and snowboarding facilities. Resort skiing in California started in the North Lake Tahoe region in the late 1930s, when a group of investors, including Walt Disney, started Sugar Bowl. The 1960 Winter Olympics were staged at another North Tahoe resort, Squaw Valley. North Tahoe isn't as densely developed as the South Shore, but it covers a lot more miles of the lakeshore. Its Nevada side has casinos, but they are not as prominent as the ones at South Shore. The California side of North Tahoe is dominated by condos that are vacation homes for Northern Californians. There are restaurants and nightlife, but things get quiet once the sun goes down. If you like to collect ski pins, the North Tahoe region has 11

Alpine ski facilities (the lake is visible from five of them) and six cross-country areas. The five largest Alpine resorts are Squaw Valley USA, Alpine Meadows, Northstar-at-Tahoe, Diamond Peak and Sugar Bowl. The nearby resorts of Mt. Rose, Boreal and Homewood also are worth a visit if you're in the region. The remaining three—Granlibakken, Tahoe Donner and Soda Springs—are very tiny areas that destination visitors would be unlikely to visit.

Tahoe Interchangeable tickets (2000/01 prices)

The Ski Lake Tahoe interchangeable lift pass is good at Kirkwood, Heavenly, Sierra-at-Tahoe, Northstar, Alpine Meadows and Squaw Valley USA. Five of six consecutive days cost about $260 ($52 a day). The North Lake Tahoe Resort Association offers an interchangeable ticket that is valid anytime at Squaw Valley USA, Alpine Meadows, Northstar, Sugar Bowl, Mt. Rose, Homewood Mountain Resort and Diamond Peak, as well as four cross-country ski areas. This pass is good for savings of $10 to $19, depending on the resort. Call (888) 434-1262 or stop by the North Lake Tahoe Resort Association, 245 North Lake Blvd. in Tahoe City.

Squaw Valley USA

Squaw Valley USA is the best-known resort in the region, since it hosted the 1960 Winter Olympics. It offers some of the finest skiing in the United States. There aren't many trail-cut runs here, just wide-open snow fields—4,000 acres of them. Anything within the boundaries can be skied by anyone daring enough to challenge the mountain. All levels can be challenged here—experts and beginners alike ride side-by-side on the cable car to the top.

Access starts at the base with the 28-person Funitel. Or, board the 110-person cable car. Or, start with the Squaw One high-speed quad and then connect to other lifts. Six separate peaks, each with every conceivable exposure, overlook Lake Tahoe.

The Funitel, which carries 15 people seated and 13 standing, replaced Squaw Valley's gondola and follows its course from the base to the Gold Coast facility. The Pulse, a custom gondola, connects the resort's two mid-mountain complexes at High Camp and Gold Coast. It has five cabins that operate with the push of a button. These lifts enable guests to take a mountain tour without putting on skis or a snowboard (of course, skiers and boarders will use them, too). They can ride the cable car to High Camp, the pulse lift to Gold Coast, then download on the Funitel to the mountain's base.

For 2001/02, Phase I of Intrawest's new $250-million Village at Squaw Valley will open, with three buildings that house 139 condominiums, 19 shops and restaurants, and about 250 underground parking spaces. At full build-out, which is expected to take five to seven years, the European-style alpine village will have 11 distinct "neighborhoods" with 640 lodging units and 80 boutiques, restaurants and galleries. Basically, if you've been to Squaw before, you're not going to recognize it. On-mountain improvements include a new beginner area at the base of the mountain and a snowtubing zone.

Mountain layout—Skiing

◆◆ **Expert** ◆ **Advanced:** Extreme skiers will be in heaven at Squaw. Thirty percent of the runs are either single- or double-black diamond. Two popular spots are the Palisades above Siberia Bowl and Eagle's Nest at the top of KT-22. In fact, KT-22 has such a variety of terrain that some season-pass holders ski the peak exclusively. The Granite Chief, Headwall and Silverado lifts access

Squaw Valley USA

Summit elevation:	**9,050 feet**
Vertical drop:	**2,850 feet**
Base elevation:	**6,200 feet**

Address: Box 2007, Olympic Valley CA 96146
✆ **Area code:** 530
Ski area phone: 583-6985
Snow report: 583-6955
ⓘ **Toll-free reservations:** (888) 766-9321 or 800-545-4350
Fax: 581-7106
E-mail: squaw@squaw.com
Internet: www.squaw.com

Number of lifts: 30–1 cable car, 1 Funitel, 1 Pulse, 2 high-speed six passengers, 4 high-speed quads, 1 quad, 8 triples, 10 doubles, 3 surface lifts, 1 magic carpet
Snowmaking: 10 percent
Total acreage: 4,000 lift-served acres
Uphill capacity: 49,000 per hour
Snowboarding: Yes, unlimited
Bed Base: 3,500 within 3 miles
Nearest lodging: slopeside
Resort child care: Yes, 2 years and older
Adult ticket, per day: $41-$54

Expert:★★★★★
Advanced:★★★★★   **Intermediate:**★★★
Beginner:★★★   **Never-ever:**★★★

some of the most challenging terrain in the world. Locals will take you to terrain that resembles an elevator shaft.

■ **Intermediate:** Intermediate terrain has challenge and variety. Siberia Express accesses the largest intermediate bowl, advanced levels turn left getting off the lift, intermediates traverse to the right, which feeds into the Gold Coast terrain and other wide-open slopes. Newport, Gold Coast and Emigrant lifts offer acres of open-bowl intermediate terrain. Intermediates will like the Shirley Lake area served by a high-speed quad and a triple chair. For tougher runs, take the Headwall Lift, then opt for Chicken Bowl or drop over the back of the ridge to Sun Bowl, a beauty if conditions are right. Or, ride the KT-22 chair, head west on the Saddle Traverse, then drop into the Saddle, which is groomed. (And then you can say you skied off KT-22 at Squaw, a good pickup line in almost any North American après-ski bar.)

The Mountain Run is a crowded end-of-the-day cruise: top to bottom, it's a hefty three-mile run. Another great cruise is Home Run. Or give the Olympic High ski run a try. It follows the route of the original 1960 Olympic men's downhill. It begins above the bottom shack of Headwall and heads to the base, bypassing the Mountain Run entirely.

●● **Beginner** ● **Never-ever:** Though Squaw Valley's well publicized steep terrain has given it a menacing reputation, it has a little-known surprise: This is a great spot for never-evers to learn. Squaw has a gentle bowl at the top of the cable car known as Bailey's Beach, served by two slow-moving lifts. Though Bailey's Beach is not physically separated from the other terrain, better skiers rarely use it. Beginners usually long to head toward any summit just like the big boys and girls, and here they can. They just ride the cable car up to High Camp (where they'll also find restaurants, shelter and an outdoor ice rink), and at the end of the day, ride the cable car back down.

Mountain layout—Snowboarding

Let's just say that Squaw is monstrous, and so are its parks and pipes. In various locations you'll find a superpipe, two halfpipes, a quarterpipe, plus terrain features like table tops, rails, rollers and volcanoes. One of the parks is lit until 9 p.m. and has a pumping sound system. The pipe sessions can definitely get heated—prepare to be humbled by locals. There's a reason many pros call Tahoe home.

But, as much fun as the manmade features are, Mother Nature's features still can't be beat here. As too many riders say with a big sigh, this place is so-o-o sick. The in-bounds riding gets insane and, unfortunately, gets tracked up quickly by hordes of riders who know all the mountain's secrets. When you have Sierra Cement at the lower elevations, book it to Granite Chief, where you'll find pow instead. And when it's freshies all over, you just can't go wrong, especially since they can be accompanied by bluebird days that make you swear you've died and gone to heaven. On those days, make sure to hike Granite Chief or high-tail it to the cornice on Siberia or seek out the Hanging Gardens. Gotta huck cliffs? Head to Palisades. One of those sick bump riders? Then Headwall's for you.

There's also great terrain for beginners and never-evers, and it comes with a jaw-dropping view of Lake Tahoe and the surrounding mountains. Squaw has a gentle bowl at the top of the cable car known as Bailey's Beach, and it's served by two lifts.

Lessons

Group lessons: Lower-intermediate to intermediate skier levels get instruction through a "Ski Your Pro" format, where instructors are assigned to training areas on the mountain, and skiers can join in on the hour for as long as they want for $36. Higher-level skiers get two-hour workshops on specific skills, such as moguls, powder or gate training, also for $36. A book of five two-hour lessons is $150.

Never-ever package: A Fun in the Sun Adventure Package that includes a beginner lift ticket, equipment rental and a two-hour lesson is $62 for skiing or snowboarding.

Private lessons: $75 an hour; $25 for each additional person.

Special programs: Squaw Valley also has a full-service adaptive ski school.

Racing: A coin-op course is at the top of the Shirley Lake Express, $1 per run.

Child care

Ages: 2–3 years.

Costs: All-day care at the licensed Toddler Care center is $74 with lunch, activities and supervision, while half-day care is $54 (no lunch). A one-and-a-half-hour ski option for 3-year-olds is extra—call to get the price.

Reservations: Recommended; call (530) 581-7116. Parents must provide current immunization records. Children 4 and older enroll in ski school programs. The day care is in the Children's World center, which is a one-stop area for kids' ski school and day care.

Other options: Baby's Away (530-581-3930) rents and will deliver baby items (cribs, strollers, toys, etc.) to your hotel or condo. For **babysitting referrals,** call (530) 587-5960.

Children's lessons: Ages 4–12 can take an all-day lesson, with lunch, lift ticket, activities and instruction for $74. The half-day price is $54 and includes a snack instead of lunch.

Lift tickets

	Adult	Child (Up to 12)
One day	$54	$5
Three days	$144 ($48/day)	$15 ($5/day)
Five days	$230 ($46/day)	$25 ($5/day)

Who skis free: Ages 76 and older.

Who skis at a discount: Tickets for ages 65–75 and youth 13–15 are $27. Non-skiers can ride the cable car and gondolas for $14 for adults, $12 for seniors, and $5 for children younger than 13. Full-day lift tickets include night skiing until 9 p.m. (mid-December through mid-March). Night skiing only costs $20 for adults, $10 for seniors/youth and $5 for children.

 Accommodations at the resort

Olympic Valley (that's the name of the base-area town; Squaw Valley is the name of the resort) has several lodging choices. All lodges give easy access to the slopes, but evening activities are limited, though the opening of Phase I of the new pedestrian village promises some nightlife. If you're staying here, it is best to rent a car if you'd like to explore dining and nightlife in Truckee and Tahoe City.

For 2001/02, 139 new condominiums are available for rental in the **Village at Squaw Valley.** Call Squaw Valley's **central reservations** at (800) 403-0206.

Other lodging at the base of the mountain is listed below. Rates fluctuate quite a bit, depending on whether it's midweek or the weekend, early or late season, and whether there's a big group in residence. Generally, though, you can expect a range of $150 to $300 per night. We've listed the hotels more or less in order from most expensive to least.

The **PlumpJack Squaw Valley Inn** (800-323-7666 or 530-583-1576) opened a couple of years ago. This remodeled hotel, with 61 rooms, originally housed delegates to the 1960 Winter Olympics, and is right across from the cable car building. However, it's far from the dorm accommodations it used to be. The rooms now have down comforters, hooded bathrobes and VCRs. A lap pool and two hot tubs further pamper the guest experience.

The hotel and restaurant are operated by the same team that owns the highly successful PlumpJack Restaurant and Balboa Cafe in San Francisco (look for another Balboa Café in Squaw's new village). The new lodging blends intimate country charm with the style and service of a grand Continental hotel. Its name honors Sir John Falstaff, Shakespeare's swaggering, high-living character. Its restaurant is excellent—details in the Dining section.

Resort at Squaw Creek (800-327-3353 or 530-583-6300) is a multistory luxury hotel that blends well with the valley. It connects with the ski area by its own lift, and is a self-contained resort, with five restaurants and three pools (one of which is open in winter), several hot tubs and spa, cross-country skiing and an ice-skating rink. The resort recently expanded and remodeled the Health and Fitness Center.

Squaw Valley Lodge (800-992-9920; in California, 800-922-9970) is only a few yards' walk from the lifts. The lodge boasts a fully equipped health club, free covered parking and kitchenettes in the units.

The **Olympic Village Inn** (800-845-5243 or 530-583-1501) has five hot tubs, and all units have kitchens. Rates: About $195 a night on weekends, $165 Sunday–Thursday.

Red Wolf Lodge (800-791-0081) at the base of Red Dog Chair next to Children's World has studio, 1- and 2-bedroom units with full kitchenettes.

Alpine Meadows

It's hard not to like Alpine Meadows. For every level, particularly intermediate and advanced, Alpine Meadows has something to offer. It has expert terrain, sweeping intermediate bowls and scenic trails, and a good beginner area. The view from the base lodge suggests that Alpine is a relatively small area. Not so. You'll see just how big it is when you take the Summit Six (a six-seater) and see it unfold beneath you. In the Lake Tahoe area, Alpine Meadows has traditionally been the ski area with the earliest and longest season (it's open well into May and some years, until July 4).

Recently, the oldest chairlift at Alpine Meadows, 34-year-old Weasel Chair, was replaced with a new triple chair named Hot Wheels. Hot Wheels not only takes visitors to the beginner terrain, but it also is a major access chair to the back bowls. Scott Chair, which accesses expert terrain, was upgraded from a double to a triple. The added weight of the triple chairs will allow the Scott Chair to run more often in bad weather, good news to experts who want to get to this area during a snowfall. It also speeds you toward the Lakeview Chair, which has great views of Lake Tahoe from the top.

Mountain layout—Skiing

◆◆ **Expert:** This level has plenty of great bowl skiing and enough steeps to keep hearts in throats. Here's a route suggestion: Take the Summit Six and descend into the expert Wolverine Bowl, Beaver Bowl and Estelle Bowl (they're to the right as you ascend), then take the Summit Six again and cruise into the upper-blue territory of the Alpine Bowl. Finally, take the Alpine Bowl Chair and traverse to the Sherwood Bowls on the back side of the area or take the High Yellow Traverse to the Saddle Bowl. When you come up the Sherwood Chair, drop down Our Father—and you can say a few en route—then head to Scott Chair and try out Scott Chute for a direct plunge, or take it easy on tree-lined roundabouts. By then your knees will have earned a cruise. The Promised Land has great tree skiing for top skiers.

Alpine Meadows Facts

Summit elevation:	**8,637 feet**
Vertical drop:	**1,802 feet**
Base elevation:	**6,835 feet**

Expert:★★★★
Advanced:★★★★★
Intermediate:★★★★
Beginner:★★★
Never-ever:★★★
Address: Box 5279, Tahoe City CA 95730
✆ Area code: 530
Ski area phone: 583-4232
Snow report: 581-8374
ⓘ Toll-free information: (800) 441-4423
Fax: 583-0963

E-mail: info@skialpine.com
Internet: www.skialpine.com
Number of lifts: 12–1 high-speed six-person chair, 1 high-speed quad, 4 triples, 5 doubles, 1 surface lift
Snowmaking: 12 percent
Skiable acreage: 2,000 acres
Uphill capacity: 16,400 per hour
Snowboarding: Yes, unlimited
Bed base: 10,000 (N. Lake Tahoe Area)
Nearest lodging: Tahoe City, 6 miles
Resort child care: None
Adult ticket, per day: $54 (01/02 prices)

◆ **Advanced:** Take your warm-up in Alpine Bowl, staying to skier's right on Rock Garden and Yellow Trail as you cruise down to the Hot Wheels chair. Then head for the Back Bowls. If there's a line at Hot Wheels, you also can reach the bowls via the Scott Chair through the blue-square Lakeview area to Ray's Rut. Depending on your mood, you can stay on the groomed Sherwood run to check out the scene, or traverse to the steeper Sherwood Face or South Face. You may want to stay here all day—one of our staffers did.

■ **Intermediate:** Plenty of terrain for this level off these lifts: Alpine Bowl, Round-house and Lakeview. The terrain off the Kangaroo lift is a short intermediate run, but much of it is devoted to race programs and the terrain park. All this activity creates a narrow descent, something many intermediates are uncomfortable with.

●● **Beginner:** Good terrain under the Meadows and Subway chairs.

● **Never-ever:** This level has a small but sheltered area close to the base lodge. The terrain is quite gentle and seldom used by better skiers.

 ## Mountain layout—Snowboarding

For 2001/02, the halfpipe is being moved from the Roundhouse lift area to a new location near the terrain park, Roo's Ride, off the Kangaroo lift. The resort built a halfpipe mold through earth-shaping methods so less snow will be needed to maintain it during the winter. The pipe and terrain park also will be open for night riding 5-9 p.m. nightly, complete with an upgraded speaker system for tunes.

Even though Alpine Meadows is paying more attention to its manmade features, most riders agree that the natural terrain is the real reason to come here. If you like in-bounds hiking, this is the place for you. Unfortunately, you might be doing some hiking even if you're *not* looking for it: There are some flat spots and traverses that you might just find yourself cursing about. The biggest beware is traveling back from the Lakeview and especially the Sherwood lifts to the front side. It never hurts to ask one of the liftees, many of them snow-board and have helpful tips to make the trip less grueling.

The Bowls are great powder runs—with special kudos to Upper Beaver and Estelle Bowl—and there are plenty of steeps, gullies and nutty drops if you go looking for them. Mix it up with some of the tree runs such as Hot Wheels Gully, you'll be happy you did. If you're there after a fresh dump, look for the wind lips—you'll find yourself airborne for days—and see if you can find Munchkins and Outer Outer.

If you favor groomers, don't panic. Alpine does a real nice job and there's plenty to choose from all over the mountain. Beginners will find very gentle terrain and the learning area is sheltered from the rest of the trails.

 ## Lessons (2001/02 prices)

Group lessons: $34 for two hours, $20 for each additional two-hour session. Alpine also offers a coupon book of 10 two-hour lessons for $300 ($30 each). Anyone may use the coupons, so this is a good deal for families where everyone wants to take a refresher.

Never-ever package: A two-hour adult learn-to-ski or -snowboard program includes beginner lifts, equipment and instruction for $56. Two additional hours are $20. Same prices for lessons geared toward beginner-refresher and anyone still skiing and riding green runs.

Private lessons: For one person, $65 an hour, with discounts for multiple hours; all day is $340. For 2-4 people, one hour is $100, with discounts for multiple hours; all day is $420.

Special programs: Clinics for disabled skiers, women, or those who want to try shaped-ski techniques and various advanced skills such as powder, telemark, moguls and trees are also available. Most clinics cost $34. Five or more in a group can tailor their own program. Multi-day clinics on specific dates available also, call for details and prices. Telemark lessons are $34, including equipment rental, and are offered Saturdays and Sundays at noon and 1:45 p.m.

Racing: Daily race-training clinics are offered at $42, or you can buy a book of five sessions for $175. There is a race every Thursday, which costs $8 for two runs for all abilities with special prizes. Alpine Meadows also has coin-op racing.

Child care (2001/02 prices)

Alpine Meadows has no child care. Other options: **Baby's Away** (530-581-3930) rents and will deliver baby items (cribs, strollers, toys, etc.) to your hotel or condo. For **babysitting** referrals, call (530) 587-5960.

Children's lessons: Little Mountaineers for children ages 5–6 costs $79 for a full-day (including lunch, equipment, lift ticket and two 2-hour lessons); $52 a half-day. Half-day program is open to 4-year-olds, space permitting. Reservations are required, 581-8240. Private lessons for ages 4 and younger, $36 per half hour per person; lift ticket and equipment additional. Snowboard lessons for ages 4-6 are by private lesson only.

Junior Mountaineers is for children 7–12, skiing or snowboarding. A full-day program includes lunch, lift ticket and lessons, $79. Half-day cost is $52, includes a lift ticket. Never-ever packages cost the same. A 2_-hour intermediate or advanced group lesson is available for $34 (not including lift ticket), at 10 a.m. or 1:30 p.m.

Lift tickets (2001/02 prices)

	Adult	Child (7-12)
One day	$54	$10
Two days	$102 ($51/day)	$20 ($10/day)
Three days	$153 ($51/day)	$30 ($10/day)

Who skis free: No one.

Who skis at a discount: Ages 65–69 pay $30; seniors 70 and older pay $8; teens 13–18 pay $42; 6 and younger pay $6. Parents can get an interchangeable ticket that can be traded between them for $54 a day.

Accommodations at the resort

Alpine Meadows doesn't have accommodations at the base, but has lodging-lift packages with hotels and condos in the region. Call Alpine Meadows at (800) 949-3296. A bed-and-breakfast package includes some two-dozen North Shore lodges, some starting at $59 per person, double occupancy, for lodging and a lift ticket.

Northstar-at-Tahoe

Unlike Squaw and Alpine, Northstar is a planned resort area, designed to make ski vacationing easy. Condos line the lower slopes, and the runs are laid out for family skiing. Here an intermediate can feel like a World Cup racer. The grooming is impeccable—you'll have to look for bumps—and the entire area management and operations are squeaky clean.

You won't find bowls and cornices on Northstar's Mount Pluto, which makes the skiing here different than at Squaw or Alpine. The skiing is all trail-cut with a bunch of tree skiing. Last season Northstar opened Lookout Mountain, with 200 acres of terrain and a high-speed quad chairlift. There are five advanced/expert runs, named after the surrounding reservoirs Prosser, Stampede, Gooseneck, Boca and Martis. Here you'll find long steep runs, trees, and great views overlooking Truckee's Martis Valley and the surrounding mountain peaks.

Mountain layout—Skiing

◆◆ **Expert** ◆ **Advanced:** Lookout Mountain promises more terrain for high-level experts, but we haven't had a chance to test it. Advanced skiers or those aspiring to the upper levels of intermediate will find some challenge in the drops off the East Ridge (labeled as black diamonds, but the mapmaker was being generous). Normally most of the runs in this section are groomed and the others have moderate bumps. Tonini's is the longest, but The Plunge is the steepest. The only bad part is that it's over too soon. Chute, Crosscut and Powder Bowl are also fun—short but sweet. If you're an air skier, you'll be disappointed. These blacks would be blues at Squaw.

You'll find long rides with moderately steep and sustained pitch off the back side via Lookout Chair and the long traverse called Back Door. This run makes you feel as though you're in another mountain range, far away from any crowds. Nine stretched-out swaths provide some of the longest continuous pitches in the West, all served by the Backside Express

---

Northstar-at-Tahoe Facts

Summit elevation:	**8,610 feet**
Vertical drop:	**2,280 feet**
Base elevation:	**6,330 feet**

Expert:★
Advanced:★★★
Intermediate:★★★★
Beginner:★★★★★
Never-ever:★★★★
Address: Box 129, Truckee, CA 96160
✆ **Area code:** 530
Ski area phone: 562-1010
Snow report: 562-1330
ⓘ **Toll-free reservations:**
(800) GO-NORTH (466-6784)

Fax: 562-2215
E-mail: northstar@boothcreek.com
Internet: www.skinorthstar.com
Number of lifts: 15–1 gondola,
5 high-speed quads, 2 triples, 2 doubles,
3 surface lifts, magic carpets
Snowmaking: 50% of developed acres
Total acreage: 2,420 total acres,
500 developed acres
Uphill capacity: 21,800 per hour
Snowboarding: Yes
Bed Base: 5,500 at resort
Nearest lodging: Slopeside
Resort child care: Yes, 2 years and older
Adult ticket, per day: $52 (00/01)

quad lift. Though they're all labeled as advanced runs, a strong intermediate will have no difficulty in good conditions.

The gem of Northstar lies between these runs and through the trees. Start down Rail Splitter, then take off into the woods to the right or left. After a storm, Northstar is one of the prime areas where you can enjoy powder through the trees long after Squaw's powder has been skied off. Sawtooth Ridge, off Challenger on the back side, has steep off-piste terrain. It is open at select times during the season and only advanced skiers are allowed.

■ **Intermediate:** This group will enjoy most of the mountain, particularly the smooth blues that descend from the two ridges into Main Street, which is the intermediate run that nearly every other run on the mountain feeds into. Avoid Main Street except when you need to get to a lift. Strong intermediates should try some of the black runs here. While they are the toughest that Northstar has to offer and therefore labeled correctly, they are not the frightening steeps you'll find at Squaw or Alpine. They will provide a good challenge to an intermediate looking to improve.

●● **Beginner** ● **Never-ever:** Northstar is the best never-ever and beginner resort in this region because its gentlest terrain is below the gondola, while all the other runs are above it. Better skiers leave this area to the learners except at day's end, when some of them use it to practice tucks. Luckily for everyone, it is fairly flat here, so no one can keep up excessive speed.

Mountain layout—Snowboarding

If you like terrain parks and pipes, Northstar is right up your alley. You'll find seven terrain parks (not counting the kids' Paw Parks), a 17-foot superpipe and a halfpipe. Some of the parks have scaled-down features for beginners, Magic Moguls will remind you of a parking lot full of snow-covered VW bugs, and another is a snake-run with high walls. The Polaris Park pipe is lit for night riding on weekends and holidays. Northstar labels its parks on the trail map with happy faces, which makes them easy to find. As for Paw Parks, they're adventure zones for kids—pint-size terrain parks scattered across the mountain that include bumps, jumps, hideaways and snow play areas. Look for the paw prints on the trail map.

If you're craving serious steeps with sick air, you'll need to go somewhere else. Northstar is really geared more towards groomed cruising and woods riding. After a storm, this is one of the prime areas where you can enjoy powder through the trees long after it's been tracked out at other Tahoe areas. Start down Rail Splitter, then take off into the woods to the right or left. Sawtooth Ridge, off Challenger on the back side, has steep off-piste terrain. It's open at select times during the season and only advanced riders are allowed. We hear that the woods on Lookout Mountain are pretty sweet too, and the terrain is supposed to be the resort's steepest, but we haven't tested it ourselves yet. Jibboom and Powder Bowl are some other favorites.

Stay on the front side if you're like wide-open groomed runs for intermediates and beginners. The terrain here is mellow and will boost your ego. This is a good resort for learning to ride, too.

Lessons

Group lessons: Free, 1.75-hour skill improvement clinics are held at 10 a.m. and noon for advanced-intermediate and higher levels, skiing and snowboarding, ages 13 and older. Sign up at the summit, first-come/first-served. Other group lessons are $29 for ages 13 and older.

Never-ever package: First-time students ages 13 and older get a 1.75-hour lesson (skiing or snowboarding) with beginner lift access and rental equipment for $52; those at the next level have the same program but with expanded lifts for $69. First Timer Ultimate Package is a 4-hour lesson, equipment, beginner lift access, lunch and goodie bag for $89.

Private lessons: For ages 13 and older, $70 per hour with each additional person $29. Semi-private, with 2-4 people, $120.

Special programs: Three-day clinics are offered a few times per year from $289.

Racing: NASTAR races Thursday through Sunday and the coin-op course operates daily.

Child care

Ages: 2–6 years (toilet-trained).

Costs: All day, $56; $68 to include 90-minute ski lesson (ages 3-6). Half day costs $33. The program combines skiing with other activities, including art, snow play, science, drama and language development.

Reservations: Recommended; call (530) 562-2278. Located in Clocktower Building in Northstar's Village. Hours: 8 a.m. to 4:30 p.m.

Other options: Baby's Away (530-581-3930) rents and will deliver baby items (cribs, strollers, toys, etc.) to your hotel or condo. For babysitting referrals, call (530) 587-5960.

Children's lessons: All-day program for children ages 5–12 is $78 with lifts, lessons, equipment and lunch. An afternoon-only program is $67. A novice's package for skiing or snowboarding, similar to the adults' program, costs $45. Children 13 and older enroll in adult programs. Meet at Starkids Center at mid-mountain.

Lift tickets

	Adult	Child (5-12)
One day	$52	$15
Three days	$136 ($45/day)	$36 ($12/day)
Five days	$221 ($44/day)	$50 ($10/day)

Who skis free: Children under age 5 with a parent ski free.

Who skis at a discount: Ages 60–69 ski for $28 a day; 70 and older ski for $5. Unlimited gondola rides for non-skiers cost $10. Ages 13–22 ski for $42 a day, $112 for three days.

Note: Northstar's parking lot sometimes fills on busy days, and cars are turned away at the entrance.

Accommodations at the resort

This area was created for condo living. The village has a convenient lodge, with rooms from $174 a night, two-night minimum. The condo rates range from $159 a night for a studio to $289 for a two-bedroom, two-bath unit. Northstar also has full-sized homes for rent, accommodating five to eight people for $379 to $669 a night. Packages are totally flexible, and can be arranged for whatever resort amenities you need—airfare, lifts, rentals and lessons are just some of the choices. Reservations: (800) 466-6784.

Diamond Peak Facts

Summit elevation:	8,540 feet
Vertical drop:	1,840 feet
Base elevation:	6,700 feet

Expert:★ Advanced:★★★
Intermediate:★★★★
Beginner:★★★
Never-ever:★★★
Address: 1210 Ski Way
Incline Village, NV 89451
✆ Area code: 775
Ski area phone: 832-1177
Snow report: 831-3211

ⓘ Toll-free reservations: (800) 468-2463 or (800) GO-TAHOE
Fax: 832-1281 E-mail: info@diamondpeak.com
Internet: www.diamondpeak.com
Number of lifts: 6–3 quads, 3 doubles
Snowmaking: 75 percent
Skiable acreage: 655 acres
Uphill capacity: 9,800 per hour
Snowboarding: Yes, unlimited
Bed Base: 6,000
Nearest lodging: About 1/4 mile away
Resort child care: Yes, 3 years and older
Adult ticket, per day: $41 (2001/02 price)

Diamond Peak

Bigger is not always better, nor desirable. For skiers and snowboarders who don't want the expansive terrain of most Lake Tahoe resorts, let us recommend Diamond Peak, a medium-sized but exquisite jewel that destination vacationers too often overlook. Diamond Peak often is less crowded than the other large Tahoe areas and perfect for families. Visitors repeatedly remark about that this is a very friendly area. Take a camera—the view is beautiful.

Mountain layout—Skiing

Diamond Peak was the first U.S. resort to install a "launch pad" loading system, a conveyor belt covered with a skiable felt surface. All of its quad chairs have this family-friendly loading system.

◆◆ **Expert** ◆ **Advanced:** Solitude Canyon has the most advanced terrain. The rest of the resort's terrain falls from a single ridge that starts at the summit and ends at the octagonal Snowflake Lodge overlooking Lake Tahoe. The canyons and gullies off Crystal Ridge (a long blue run) are labeled advanced, but strong intermediates will have a blast on them.

■ **Intermediate:** This is a wonderful area for intermediates, especially families who don't want to worry about the kids taking a wrong turn and getting lost. The aforementioned Crystal Ridge is a 2.5-mile-long blue from the summit, with a stunning view of the lake. The lower-mountain runs off Red Fox also have a nice intermediate pitch.

●● **Beginner** ● **Never-ever:** This is a great learner's mountain more because of its friendly atmosphere and manageable size rather than its terrain (unfortunately, the amount of beginner terrain is a bit limited). Diamond Peak employs about 100 instructors—equal to much larger areas—another indication that it's a good place to learn.

Mountain layout—Snowboarding

The resort's terrain features attract boarders at every skill level, from first-timers to the most advanced. This is an excellent resort for riders who are ready to test themselves on the more adventurous terrain of canyons and gullies, since nothing here will give you the heebie-jeebies. Snowboarders also can find some alone time in the new "Glades," in the trees between The Great Flume and Thunder. Enjoy fantastic tree riding and untapped powder stashes. For boarders who like pulling some tricks, check out the new and improved terrain park. The park is located on Spillway (at the bottom of The Great Flume) and includes tabletops, spines, hits and jumps, all overlooking beautiful Lake Tahoe.

Lessons (2001/02 prices)

Group lessons: 105-minute clinics cost $23 (ski or snowboard); two sessions cost $36.

Never-ever package: Learn-to-Ski/Snowboard including beginner lifts, rentals and 105-minute lesson is $45.

Private lessons: $55-$65 an hour, depending on the time you take your lesson. Private adaptive lessons are available for disabled learners. Reservations required: (775) 832-1135.

Child care (2001/02 prices)

Ages: 3–6 years.

Costs: $30 for the morning or afternoon session; $48 for full day.

Reservations: Required; call 832-1130.

Note: Diamond Peak has the Bee Ferrato Child Ski Center, named for its director, a New Zealand native every kid will want to adopt as a grandmother. Bee's Snowplay is a program costing $15 per hour that lets children play in the snow under supervision.

Other options: Baby's Away (530-581-3930) rents and will deliver baby items (cribs, strollers, toys, etc.) to your hotel or condo. For **babysitting referrals,** call (530) 587-5960.

Children's lessons: All-day groups for ages 7–12 cost $69 for skiers; $79 for snowboarders. Ages 4–6 have full-day ski lessons with rentals and lunch for $79. Three-year-olds take private lessons. Reservations suggested for private children's lessons: 832-1130.

Lift tickets (2001/02 prices)

Adult tickets are $41 a day, $15 for children. Ages 5 and younger ski free.

Who skis at a discount: Ages 13–17 pay $33; ages 60 and older pay $15. Parents can buy an interchangeable adult ticket for $41 that either of them can use—a good deal for those with toddlers. Wednesdays are half-price days with a coupon, except holidays. Coupons are available in Incline Village at Porter's Ski & Sport and Village Ski Loft. Check out www.diamondpeak.com for the latest deals of the week. Last but not least, the ever-affordable Family Special Package starting at just $49 is one deal parents simply cannot pass up. The offer lets families customize a ticket package designed just for them. Packages available daily at any ticket window and valid for up to six persons with a maximum of two adults. Believe it or not, a family of four can hit the slopes for under $100.

Accommodations near the resort

Incline Village has several hotels and condo complexes. It also has private homes that can easily sleep 12–16 people. For **Incline Village** accommodations, call (800) 468-2463 (GO-TAHOE). The **Hyatt Regency Lake Tahoe Resort and Casino** (800-533-3288) is a four-star luxury hotel with rates from $135 to $705 a night. The **Inn at Incline Motor Lodge and Condominiums** (800-824-6391) has more modest facilities and rates starting around $70 a night. The **Tahoe Biltmore Casino** (800-BILTMOR) in Crystal Bay has midweek ski packages with Diamond Peak, including a lift ticket, lodging, a full breakfast and transportation to and from the slopes. Last season's price was $39 per night. The **Crystal Bay Motel** (702-831-0287) is an economy property from $35–$65 near casinos and **Haus Bavaria** (800-731-6222) is a European-style guest house with five rooms. The **Cal-Neva Lodge Hotel Spa Casino** (800-225-6382 or 800-CAL-NEVA) is split by the state line and once was owned by Frank Sinatra and visited by Marilyn Monroe. Rooms go for $85 to $289. Every room has a lake view, the best from the deluxe suites on the top three floors. There are also honeymoon bungalows with heart-shaped tubs, round beds and mirrored ceilings.

Sugar Bowl

Founded by Walt Disney, Sugar Bowl is one of the oldest resorts at Lake Tahoe and the oldest chair-lift-served resort in California. From the moment you step out of your car and board the Magic Carpet gondola to ride *down* across a pristine valley to the lifts, you feel you're stepping back in time. (You also can drive your car to the nearby base of Mt. Judah, but if you do, you're missing part of the fun.)

Sugar Bowl is another of Tahoe's overlooked ski areas, at least by destination skiers. That's a shame, because it has great variety. We recommend Sugar Bowl for a day's change of pace from the larger Tahoe resorts. However, remember that it's one of the first ski areas on the drive from San Francisco, Oakland and Sacramento and gets its big crowds on weekends so visit midweek if you can and take advantage of their $35 Tuesday through Thursday special ticket price.

Sugar Bowl has three peaks—Mt. Judah, with its own parking lot and base lodge; Mt. Lincoln and Mt. Disney, reached initially by the Magic Carpet gondola. The three peaks are connected. For 2001/02, Sugar Bowl is replacing the lift on Mt. Lincoln with a high-speed quad. The base of the new lift will be in the same location as the old one, but it will unload at the true summit of Mt. Lincoln (about 100 yards to the left of the old lift). New snowmaking will allow for good early-season conditions on 25 percent of the mountain. There also will be more seating available in the Mt. Judah base lodge.

Sugar Bowl Facts

Summit elevation:	8,383 feet
Vertical drop:	1,500 feet
Base elevation:	6,883 feet

Expert:★★
Advanced:★★★
Intermediate:★★★★
Beginner:★★★★
Never-ever:★★★
Address: P.O. Box 5, Norden, CA 95724
✆ Area code: 530
ⓘ Ski area phone/reservations: 426-9000
Snow report: 426-1111

E-mail: info@sugarbowl.com
Internet: www.sugarbowl.com
Number of lifts: 12–1 gondola, 4 high-speed quads, 4 quads, 3 double chairs, 1 surface lift
Snowmaking: 20 percent
Skiable acreage: 1,500 acres
Uphill capacity: 13,522 per hour
Snowboarding: Yes
Bed Base: 460
Nearest lodging: Slopeside
Resort child care: Yes, 3 years and older
Adult ticket, per day: $35-54 (01/02 price)

Mountain layout—Skiing

◆◆ **Expert ◆ Advanced:** Mt. Disney, one of three peaks at Sugar Bowl, has advanced runs off either side of a ridge. Mt. Lincoln also has advanced terrain. There's a very steep cliff area to the right of the Silver Belt chair that's double diamond, but the rest of the black diamonds are more advanced than expert.

■ **Intermediate:** Lower intermediates will find the best runs off the Christmas Tree chair. Stronger intermediates should progress to the Jerome Hill Express quad on 8,238-foot Mt. Judah and the Silver Belt lift to the top of 8,383-foot Mt. Lincoln. Crow's Nest lift on Mt. Disney also serves nice blue runs.

●● **Beginner ● Never-ever:** Beginners have beautiful long runs off the Christmas Tree and Mt. Judah chairs. A relatively new and expanded novice area at Mt. Judah is a big improvement over the previous one at the main base.

Mountain layout—Snowboarding

Sugar Bowl has incredible natural hits and quarterpipes—check out the 58's and Palisades off Mt. Lincoln, and the Sugar Bowl off the Disney Express. If that isn't enough there are two terrain parks and a halfpipe on Mt. Judah. The park for advanced riders has multiple tabletop and gap jumps, quarterpipes and spines. The second park is for less-advanced riders just learning to get their legs under them. Strawberry Fields and the steep chutes off Mt. Lincoln are not to be missed on powder days. The groomers off the Jerome Hill Express are great for high-speed arcs. Remember to keep your speed up for the flat between the Mid Mountain Lodge and Village Lodge.

Lessons (2001/02 prices)

Group lessons: $35 for two hours.
Never-ever package: The Fast Track package of lift ticket, two-hour lesson and rental (ski or snowboard) is $70 for adults, $60 for young adults (13–21).
Private lessons: $70 an hour, with each additional person $20.

Child care (2001/02 prices)

Ages: 3–6 years.
Costs: All day is $70, and half day (without lunch) is $50. Sugar Bears Child Care is a licensed center with educational and recreational activities as well as skiing and quiet time. The program includes snacks, lunch and ski equipment.

Reservations: Suggested. Call the ski area.

Other options: Baby's Away (530-581-3930) rents and will deliver baby items (cribs, strollers, toys, etc.) to your hotel or condo. For babysitting referrals, call (530) 587-5960.

Children's lessons: All-day program for ages 6–12 is $70, which includes lifts, equipment, lessons and lunch. The Fast Track package for never-evers includes lift ticket, two-hour lesson and rental (ski or snowboard) for $60 for teens, $50 for children.

Lift tickets (2001/02 prices)

	Adult	Child (5-12)
One day	$54	$12
Two days	$100 ($50/day)	$22 ($11/day)

Who skis at a discount: Ages 60–69 pay $30; ages 13–21 pay $40. Adults who turn in their all-day lift ticket by 12:30 p.m. receive a credit coupon for $16 off another day's ticket. There's a special on tickets, Tuesday through Thursday, $35.

Accommodations at the resort

Sugar Bowl has a lodge that is certainly unusual, and possibly unique at American ski resorts: a base lodge that also is a hotel. It is reached by the same four-passenger gondola that brings skiers to this part of the mountain. In addition to the usual services on the ground floor, Sugar Bowl's base lodge also has 27 rooms on the upper two levels. Though it was built in 1939, the rooms have been remodeled for a combination of historic charm and modern convenience. The dining room preserves the grace of a former era with its decor and jacket-required dress code. Room rates, based on double occupancy, start at $95 per night. Bed-breakfast-lift packages, available Sunday through Thursday, non-holiday, are $145 single occupancy, $195 double, $245 triple and $295 quad. Five-day ski weeks with two meals a day also are available; call for prices. Call (530) 426-9000 for reservations, well in advance.

Nearby resorts

Mt. Rose, Reno, NV; (775) 849-0704; (800) SKI-ROSE (754-7673)

Internet: www.skirose.com

5 lifts; 1,000 skiable acres; 1,440 vertical feet

Mt. Rose has the highest base elevation in the Tahoe area at 8,260 feet, which means it gets snow earlier than other areas (and gets snow when it's raining at lower elevations). It has two base areas, the result of Mt. Rose incorporating a neighboring ski area, Slide Mountain, several years ago. The Slide base area has primarily intermediate terrain with some advanced pitches, while the Rose side has very gentle beginner slopes, good intermediate trails and some long advanced runs.

Lift tickets: Adults, $45; Teens (13-19), $35; Children (12 and younger), $10.

Distance from Reno: About 22 miles on Hwy. 431.

Lodging information: (800) 367-7366 (FOR-RENO) or (800) 824-6348 (TAHOE-4-U).

Homewood Mountain Resort, Homewood, CA; (530) 525-2992

Internet: www.skihomewood.com

10 lifts; 1,260 skiable acres; 1,650 vertical feet

Homewood Mountain Resort, on the west shore of Lake Tahoe, is one of three Tahoe ski areas that can qualify for Best View Of The Lake honors. This area, though smallish by Tahoe standards, has more than 1,200 skiable acres accessible from either of two base areas called North Side and South Side. Child care starts at age 2 and is at the South Side Lodge.

Lift tickets: Adult, $42; Junior (11-18), $27; Senior (60+), $13. Kids 10 and younger ski free. Value days, Monday–Thursday (non-holiday) adults and juniors, $25; and seniors, $10.

Distance from Reno: About 50 miles from Reno via I-80 west and Hwy. 89 south.

Distance from Sacramento: About 120 miles via I-80 east and Hwy. 89 south.

Lodging information: (800) 824-6348 (TAHOE-4-U).

Boreal, Truckee, CA; (530) 426-3666
Internet: www.borealski.com
9 lifts; 380 skiable acres; 600 vertical feet
You can't miss Boreal when you're driving toward Tahoe from Sacramento. It is a wide ridge of fairly short ski trails right off I-80 on the Donner Pass. It's the closest resort to Sacramento and San Francisco. Boreal, purchased in 1995 by the company that owns Alpine Meadows, is very popular with riders, who like the short, straight runs off the summit and "Vans Snowboard Park," one of four terrain parks. Boreal also has runs down its back side.

Boreal has night skiing and a night halfpipe and terrain park. It is the home of the Western Ski Sport Museum, generally open during Boreal's ski hours.

Lift tickets (00/01 prices): Adults, $32; Adult night skiing, $20; Children (5–12), $10; Seniors (60–69), $15; Other ages, free.
Distance from Reno: About 45 miles west on I-80.
Distance from Sacramento: About 80 miles east on I-80.
Lodging information: (530) 426-1012.

Cross-country and snowshoeing

The Lake Tahoe region may have the greatest concentration of large cross-country ski areas in the U.S., with more than 800 km. of groomed trails. We have listed the bigger operations; local tourist offices can direct you to smaller and less expensive centers. Many of the ones we list here also have full-moon tours and snowshoe rentals and tours so call for information.

Six of these Nordic centers offer an **interchangeable trail pass.** They are Royal Gorge, Northstar, Spooner Lake, Squaw Creek, Tahoe Donner and Tahoe Cross-Country. The pass ranges from two days for $28 to six days for $66 and can be bought through the North Lake Tahoe Resort Association, (888) 434-1262 or (530) 583-3494. If you use the pass at Royal Gorge, there is a $4 surcharge.

Squaw Creek Cross-Country Ski Center (530-583-6300) is a small area at the Resort at Squaw Creek, which has rentals and lessons. Trails cover 18 km., are groomed daily, and range from beginner to expert. Trail fees are $12 for adults, $10 for children ages 12 and younger. Child care is available starting at age 4.

The largest private trail system in North America is in California at **Royal Gorge** (530-426-3871; 800-500-3871, nationwide; 800-666-3871, Northern California only; e-mail: info@royalgorge.com; Web site: www.royalgorge.com) just off I-80, west of Donner Summit at the Soda Springs exit. Royal Gorge has nearly 9,000 acres of terrain, and more than 300 km. of trails with a skating lane inside the tracks. They also make snow on some trails and use modern snowcats. Adult trail fees are $24.50, for teens (13–16), $11.50; with discounts for midweek, multiday tickets and skiers 65 and older. Ages 12 and younger ski free.

Royal Gorge has four surface lifts to help skiers up the tougher inclines. It is a full-service ski area, with rental equipment, ski school, ten warming huts, four cafes and a full-time ski patrol. Trailside lodging is at **Rainbow Lodge,** an historic 1920s B&B, or at **Wilderness Lodge,** a rustic retreat in the middle of the trail system. Book either through the ski area.

Northstar-at-Tahoe (530-562-2475) has 50 km. of groomed and marked trails. Trail fees: adults $20; children 5–12, $15; seniors 60-69, $10; seniors 70 and older, $5. Lessons (one-and-a-half hour) with equipment, $27. Rentals are available, as are snowshoe rentals.

All are near the day lodge and downhill slopes. This is one of the gentler trail systems in the area—very good for families and those just learning.

The **Tahoe Donner Cross-Country Area** (530-587-9484) also is off I-80 at Donner State Park exit. This area has 100 km. of trails, all double-tracked with wide skating lanes, and a day lodge with cafe. Tahoe Donner has California's only lighted night cross-country skiing, Wednesdays and Saturdays. Day trail fees are $18 for adults, $14 for teens ages 13–17 and seniors ages 60–69. Those younger than 12 and older than 69 ski free. Cross-country gear, snowshoes and pulk sleds are available for rental.

Tahoe Cross-Country Ski Area (530-583-5475; formerly Lakeview Cross-Country), two miles east of Tahoe City, is now a non-profit ski foundation. It has 65 km. of groomed skating lanes and tracks, a day lodge, cafe, lessons and rentals. Trail fees are $17 for adults, $12 for juniors 10–18 and seniors 60–69. Those older than 69 and younger than 10 ski free; call about bringing your dog. Snowshoes and pulk sleds also are available for rental.

Spooner Lake Cross-Country (775-887-8844, recording; 755-749-5349, live voice) on Hwy. 28, about a half-mile north of Hwy. 50, has more than 80 km. of trails, nearly all of which are machine groomed, with one 19-km. backcountry trail. Adult trail fees are $16.50; less for ages 7–15. Children younger than age 7 ski free. Lessons and cross-country gear, snowshoe and pulk sled rentals are available; you also can rent a backcountry cabin.

 ## Accommodations

The North Shore is relatively quiet. The accommodations below generally run less than $150; however, the more luxurious lodging will top out closer to $200. The North Shore has bed-and-breakfast inns, cabins on the lake, plush or spartan condominiums, and medium-sized casino hotels—a place for everyone. **North Lake Tahoe Resort Association Lodging Information & Reservations** is at (888) 434-1262 or (530) 583-3494. Its Web site is www.tahoefun.org (just a note: tahoefun.com gets you to the *Sacramento Bee* newspaper's guide to Tahoe). That agency is your best source for lodging-and-lift packages that include interchangeable lift tickets for several North Tahoe resorts. This agency also can suggest private homes and condos.

The most upscale bed-and-breakfast is the **Rockwood Lodge** (530-525-5273), originally built in the mid-1930s. There are five rooms, two with private bath. It has antique furnishings, plush carpet, brass-and-porcelain bath fixtures, and down comforters on the beds. The lodge is next to the Ski Homewood Ski Area, on the west shore of Tahoe about seven miles south of Tahoe City. **Note:** This is a No-Smoking inn and does not accept children.

The **Mayfield House** (530-583-1001), another B&B, was once a private residence in Tahoe City. The atmosphere is elegant and romantic, and full breakfasts come with the rate. Some rooms have a private bath.

Other B&Bs that are recommended are **The Cottage Inn** (530-581-4073; 800-581-4073) in Tahoe City; **The Shore House** (530-546-7270; 800-207-5160) in Tahoe Vista; or **Tahoma Meadows Bed & Breakfast** (530-525-1553) in Homewood.

Just south of Tahoe City is the **Sunnyside Lodge** (530-583-7200, or in California only, 800-822-2754), directly on the lake. There are 23 rooms, all with a lake view and a few rooms have fireplaces. No. 39 makes a great honeymoon suite, but reserve early because there is a four- to six-week waiting list. This is an excellent property with a lively après-ski bar and a good restaurant, the Chris Craft.

Perhaps the most luxury for the money on the North Shore can be found in the **Tahoe Vista Inn & Marina** (530-546-1515) in Tahoe Vista. The six units here are spectacular and sited directly on the lake. Rates range from about $160 a night for the smallest unit to $240 for a one-bedroom suite with a panoramic lake view.

The **Cal-Neva Lodge Hotel Spa Casino** (800-225-6382 or 800-CAL-NEVA) is split by the state line and once was owned by Frank Sinatra and visited by Marilyn Monroe. Every room has a lake view, the best from the deluxe suites on the top three floors. There are also honeymoon bungalows with heart-shaped tubs, round beds and mirrored ceilings.

The **Granlibakken Resort & Conference Center** (800-543-3221) in Tahoe City is a great place to stay. Lodging is in 160 privately owned suites and townhouses and some feature a kitchen and fireplace. Sizes start at one bedroom and top out at a six-bedroom, six-bath townhouse. Two saunas and an outdoor spa are on site. The lovely complex sits on a hill among towering pines and red firs, next to the site of a former ski jump used for the 1932 Olympic tryouts. Two cross-country ski trails and a beginner's Alpine hill also are on site. Ski packages are available with Squaw Valley and Alpine Meadows.

For families or anyone looking for a great deal, **North Lake Lodge** (530-546-2731), in Kings Beach only a few feet from the shore, is one of the oldest hotels but still in great shape. Continental breakfast is included and the shuttlebuses stop just across the street.

River Ranch (530-583-4264) on Hwy. 89 near Alpine Meadows is another moderately priced lodge. This historic ski lodge sits on the banks of the Truckee River and rooms are furnished with early American antiques. Continental breakfast is included, and the shuttles for Squaw Valley and Alpine Meadows are nearby. A rushing river lulls you to sleep.

Away from the lake in Truckee, but convenient to Northstar and Sugar Bowl, is the **Truckee Hotel** (530-587-4444), which has been welcoming guests since 1873. Mostly it housed timber and railroad workers, but one of the residents was a madam who reportedly ran a little business on the side. It has been renovated, but you'll still feel like you're sleeping in the Old West. Some rooms have baths—the old-fashioned, claw-footed kind. Some rooms have private baths, some don't. Some rooms are large enough to sleep six, and there is a restaurant, Coburn Station, that serves lunch and dinner.

The **Richardson House** (888-229-0365; 530-587-5388) is a B&B in Truckee that was built in the 1880s as a private residence. It has been fully restored. Six of the eight rooms have private baths. A full breakfast buffet is included, as well as 24-hour access to the "refreshment center." Beds and comforters are feather-filled.

Another recommended lodge is the **Best Western Truckee-Tahoe Inn** (530-587-4525) with 100 rooms and complimentary breakfast.

Accommodations—Nevada Northeast

Reno offers big-time casino atmosphere closer to the North Shore and at lower prices than you'll find surrounding the lake. Reno also has a planetarium and two major museums, and is 30–45 minutes by car from the North Shore resorts. This is a good place to stay if you want to save some serious money and have a big enough group to split a rental car cost. Some hotels have ski shuttles, but most visitors here probably will want a car. **Reno Central Reservations** is at (800) 367-7366 (FOR-RENO).

Dining (530 area code unless noted)

The opening of Phase I of the new Village at Squaw Valley brings with it several new restaurants, including **Balboa Café,** owned by the same team who own PlumpJack Squaw Valley (if you're familiar with San Francisco, you'll also be familiar with the fine reputation of their two restaurants there). After we've had a chance to visit some of the **new village restaurants,** we'll make sure to relay our recommendations. Until then, here are our suggestions. For those not concerned with price:

PlumpJack Squaw Valley (583-1576) is an extraordinary dining experience in a medieval style that is as unique as the cuisine is delicious. The wine list is carefully selected and prices are very reasonable, given the high quality. A bar menu features wood-fired-oven pizza, grilled chicken quesadillas and fine California wines by the glass. Reservations suggested.

Glissandi at the Resort at Squaw Creek (581-6621) brings New York and San Francisco style and service, all overlooking Squaw Valley. Reservations suggested. Try **Graham's** in Squaw Valley at the Christy Inn (581-0454).

Captain Jon's (546-4819) in Tahoe Vista serves seafood and French country specialties. Closed Mondays. **Le Petit Pier** (546-4464) in Tahoe Vista presents upscale French cuisine. Reservations needed. Open daily.

Swiss Lakewood Restaurant (525-5211), in Homewood, is Lake Tahoe's oldest and one of its finest dining experiences with impeccable service. Cuisine is French-Swiss and classic continental. Closed Mondays, except holidays.

Wolfdales (583-5700) in downtown Tahoe City is superb. Reservations are suggested.

Christy Hill in Tahoe City (115 Grove Street, reservations recommended, 583-8551) is a real find. Christy Hill offers superb lake views in an intimate, casually elegant atmosphere. The menu, which changes several times each week, is loaded with the freshest fish and specialty produce. The restaurant is open for dinner only from Tuesday through Sunday.

On the other side of the lake, in Incline Village, head for **The Lone Eagle Grill** at the Hyatt Regency (775-832-3250) for some of the best food on the Nevada lakeshore. The soaring stone and timber and the massive fireplace blend with magnificent views across the lake at sunset, and the cuisine and extensive wine list provide accomplished accompaniment.

Also in Incline Village, try **The Big Water Grille** (775-833-0606), at the bottom of the hill at Diamond Peak. A Native American name for Lake Tahoe, the Big Water features an eclectic menu and spectacular lake views—the perfect setting for romantic dinners, après-ski relaxation and group gatherings. The menu features American Contemporary cuisine with Mediterranean and Pacific-Rim influences.

For more moderate fare try:

Black Bear Tavern (583-8626) is in an historic A-frame log building with knotty-pine walls and a large stone fireplace. South of Tahoe City on Hwy. 89, it features top-rate dining at moderate prices—steak, chicken, and fresh salmon and swordfish when available. Portions are large, but save room for apple crisp, an old German recipe smothered in vanilla ice cream.

In Truckee: **Coburn Station** (587-7619) in the Truckee Hotel has good soups and interesting salads; the bar is cozy but the dining room is uninviting and small. **OB's** (587-4164) decorated with old farm antiques serves creative cuisine (example: potato-asparagus soup with nutmeg) at cheap prices.

Closer to Lake Tahoe: Try **River Ranch** (583-4264) at the access road to Alpine Meadows (ask for a table over the river or next to the river-rock fireplace; this is the best riverside dining in the mountains), **Sunsets** (546-3640) in Tahoe Vista for Northern Italian cuisine and beautiful lake views, **Jake's on the Lake** (583-0188) in Tahoe City, **Gar Woods** (546-3366) in Carnelian Bay, and **Za's** (583-1812) in Tahoe City for moderately priced Italian. **The Soule Domain** (546-7529) in Crystal Bay received consistent raves from people at both ends of the lake. For Mexican with a big dose of margaritas and a shoulder-to-shoulder crowd on weekends, a good choice is the **Hacienda del Lago** (583-0358) in Tahoe City in the Boatworks Mall. **Cafe 333** (775-832-7333) in Incline Village, written up in *Bon Appetit* several times, is favored by Incline locals. It has French country decor and a moderately priced menu.

For lots of good food at very reasonable prices: **Bacchi's** (583-3324) just outside Tahoe City or **Lanza's** (546-2434) in Kings Beach, both serving good Italian fare. **Bridgetender** (583-3342) has burgers and an extensive beer selection. **Mandarin Villa** (583-1188) in Tahoe City serves affordable Chinese food.

The casinos on the Nevada border serve inexpensive breakfasts, lunches and dinners.

For pizza, try **Pizza Junction** (587-7411) outside of Truckee, where they make Truckee River Beer; **Lake House Pizza** (583-2222) for a great lake view; **C.B's Pizza** (546-4738) in Kings Beach; or **Squaw Valley Pizza** (583-4787) at the entrance to Alpine Meadows resort.

Azzara's (775-831-0346) in Incline Village serves good, reasonable Italian food. **Austin's** (775-832-7778) gets raves for meatloaf and homemade soups. **Stanley's** (702-831-9944) is an Incline institution for Sunday breakfast and Friday night local entertainment in the bar. **Jack Rabbit Moon** (775-832-3007) gets the nod for dinner from knowledgeable locals.

The best breakfasts are at the **Squeeze In** (587-9814) in Truckee where the list of omelets requires a speed-reading course. The Squeeze In has all the atmosphere you could want in a breakfast joint, built in a former alley and only 10 feet wide. On weekends, expect to wait a while—this place is popular. Down the street is the **Coffee And**, which also serves up a good basic breakfast. Don't miss **The Fire Sign** (583-0871), about two miles south of Tahoe City, where many believe the best breakfasts and lunches in the region are served. If you're further to the north, try the **Old Post Office** (546-3205) at Carnelian Bay or the **Log Cabin** (546-7109) in Kings Beach. Near Alpine Meadows, try **The Alpine Riverside Cafe** (583-6896) for breakfast and lunch.

Après-ski/nightlife

At Squaw, local hangouts include the bar at **PlumpJack, Bullwackers** at the Resort at Squaw Creek, **Bar One, Plaza Bar** at the Olympic House and the **Red Dog Saloon** at the Opera House. The **new pedestrian village** will include several options, so make sure to ask around for suggestions. **River Ranch** on the Alpine Meadows access road was voted to have the top après-ski in North Lake Tahoe. Go before sunset to enjoy the winter wonderland scene across the Truckee River.

In Tahoe City, places to head include **Pete'n'Peter's, Rosie's Café, Pierce Street Annex** (behind Safeway near the Boatworks Mall) or **Jake's on the Lake**. **Sunnyside**, just a couple of miles south of Tahoe City on the lake, has a lively bar. **Hacienda del Lago** in the Boatworks has nachos 'till 6 p.m. For the best live music, try **Sierra Vista** adjacent to the Boatworks Mall. An offbeat après-ski spot is **Naughty Dawg** on the main road in Tahoe City, where you can get munchies and specialty drinks served in dog dishes. Watch out for "shotskis," a ritual of drinks served in an unusual way.

In Truckee, there is occasional music at the **Bar of America** and the **Pastime Club**, both at Commercial Row. The **Cottonwood Restaurant** overlooking Truckee on Hwy. 267 has jazz. The casinos on North Lake Tahoe have entertainment every night. Sure bets are the **Cal-**

Neva Lodge, The Crystal Bay Club, Hyatt Lake Tahoe and the Tahoe Biltmore. Incline locals hang at Hacienda de la Sierra, Rookie's Sports Grill and Legends.

Other activities

Squaw Valley's High Camp at the top of the cable car has ice skating, snowtubing, dining and more. There's also a new snowtubing zone at the base of the mountain. Polaris Park, located mid-mountain at Northstar, has lighted snow play areas for tubing, snow biking and other activities. It is open weekends and holidays, 3 to 9 p.m. Sleigh rides are available at Northstar-at-Tahoe, (530) 562-2480, and in the Squaw Valley meadow, (530) 583-6300. The region also has snowmobiling, scenic flights, hot-air balloon rides, horseback riding, bowling, movies and health clubs. Snowfest is North Tahoe's winter carnival, usually in late February/early March. Call (800) 824-6348 or (530) 583-3494 for a complete list of things to do.

For off-slope activity near Diamond Peak, check out the Incline Village Recreation Center, which has aerobics, basketball court, weight room and an indoor pool among its amenities. Visitors can use the facilities for $10 per day or $25 per week. Discounts are available for children, teens, seniors and families. Another spot for family fun is Bowl Incline with more than bowling. You'll find pool tables, other pinball gizmos, video poker built into the bar and a golf simulator where you can play seven world-class courses. Greens fees are $24 per hour and it takes about an hour to play 18 holes.

Getting there and getting around

By air: Reno-Tahoe International Airport has more than 100 nonstop flights a day from various parts of the country.

By train: Amtrak serves Truckee and Reno on the California Zephyr line, running from Oakland to Chicago. Call (800) 872-7245.

By bus: Shuttles run from almost every major hotel to each major ski resort. Check for schedules when you arrive. When you need to go from one end of the lake to the other, take the Lake Lapper (542-5900). Round-trip is $5. It's more for sightseeing and doesn't serve the ski areas. However, it does run at night.

Sierra Nevada Gray Lines (800-822-6009 or 702-329-1147) operates a daily ski shuttle between downtown Reno and Alpine Meadows as well as Northstar-at-Tahoe (except Saturdays) and Squaw Valley USA from mid-December through the end of March. Tahoe Casino Express (800-446-6128) runs between Reno airport and South Shore for about $17 each way.

By car: Driving time from Reno is about an hour to any major North Shore resort. San Francisco is about four hours away via I-80 to the North Shore. During storms, the California Highway Patrol doesn't let drivers come up the mountains without chains or a 4-wheel-drive vehicle, so be prepared.

Squaw Valley is on Hwy. 89 (runs between I-80 and Hwy. 28, which hugs the North Shore). Tip: If you are driving a rental car from Reno on I-80, headed west toward Northstar, Squaw or Alpine, you may pass through a California agricultural checkpoint. If you do, get off the freeway at the next stop and turn around. That checkpoint means you just missed the turnoff for Hwy. 89, just like one of our staffers did. The signs are dimly lit at night and tough to see a couple of hours before sunset.

Alpine Meadows is on Hwy. 89 (runs between I-80 and Hwy. 28, which hugs the North Shore). Tip: If you are driving a rental car from Reno on I-80, headed west toward Northstar,

Squaw or Alpine, you may pass through a California agricultural checkpoint. If you do, get off the freeway at the next stop and turn around. That checkpoint means you just missed the turnoff for Hwy. 89, just like one of our staffers did. The signs are dimly lit at night and tough to see a couple of hours before sunset.

Northstar-at-Tahoe is on Hwy. 267 (runs between I-80 and Hwy. 28, which hugs the North Shore). Tip: If you are driving a rental car from Reno on I-80, headed west toward Northstar, Squaw or Alpine, you may pass through a California agricultural checkpoint. If you do, get off the freeway at the next stop and turn around. That checkpoint means you just missed the turnoff for Hwy. 89, just like one of our staffers did. The signs are dimly lit at night and tough to see a couple of hours before sunset.

Diamond Peak is on Hwy. 28 in Nevada on the lake's east side. Tip: If you are driving a rental car from Reno on I-80, headed west toward Northstar, Squaw or Alpine, you may pass through a California agricultural checkpoint. If you do, get off the freeway at the next stop and turn around. That checkpoint means you just missed the turnoff for Hwy. 89, just like one of our staffers did. The signs are dimly lit at night and tough to see a couple of hours before sunset.

Sugar Bowl is off I-80 just west of Donner Lake. Tip: If you are driving a rental car from Reno on I-80, headed west toward Northstar, Squaw or Alpine, you may pass through a California agricultural checkpoint. If you do, get off the freeway at the next stop and turn around. That checkpoint means you just missed the turnoff for Hwy. 89, just like one of our staffers did. The signs are dimly lit at night and tough to see a couple of hours before sunset.

Getting around: As much as we hate to recommend adding more auto pollution to this pristine location, rent a car. Public transportation is getting better, but not yet to the point where we can honestly recommend using it exclusively. If you stay near one of the ski resorts, your dining and evening options would be limited. Squaw Valley, Alpine Meadows, Sugar Bowl, Diamond Peak, Northstar and Homewood all have shuttles from North Tahoe towns.

South Lake Tahoe Area

Kirkwood

Heavenly

Sierra-at-Tahoe

Toll-free reservations:
(800) AT-TAHOE (288-2463)
Internet: www.virtualtahoe.com
Dining:★★★
Apres-ski/nightlife:★★★★★
Other activities:★★★

Few regions on the North American continent have the ski-resort diversity of the Lake Tahoe region. Tahoe's south shore offers something unique—24-hour activity in its large casino-hotels that hug the California-Nevada state line. Here you'll find big-name musical entertainment (Willie Nelson, Tower of Power, Shaun Colvin, Hootie and the Blowfish, Chris Isaac, Brooks & Dunn, and Wynonna all passed through here in 2000) nearly every week during ski season, and you can stay up all night playing blackjack or feeding slot machines.

If you're in love and looking for a no-hassle way to get married, South Lake Tahoe's the spot. Especially around Valentine's Day, it is a common sight to see a wedding veil hanging from a car's back window, with the groom and best man in the front seats and the bride and maid of honor in back. We have more details in the *Other Activities* section.

Two of the largest Tahoe resorts, Heavenly and Kirkwood, are here. Heavenly is the most popular Tahoe resort with out-of-towners, probably because you can see its runs rising above town, almost close enough to touch from South Lake Tahoe Boulevard. Kirkwood has a well-deserved reputation for awesome terrain and massive amounts of snow, and the near completion of the mountain village at its base is metamorphosing it into a year-round resort. You also shouldn't miss Sierra-at-Tahoe, known for its tree skiing and a locals' favorite.

The lodging and general look of South Lake Tahoe takes many visitors by surprise. Instead of mountain-style luxury, it's a hodgepodge of '50s- and '60s- style budget motels, cabins and shopping-strip malls lining a very traffic-heavy main street. However, this is about to change. The South Shore is undergoing a major redevelopment. The new village will have luxurious lodging, shops, restaurants, a convention center, an outdoor skating rink, cinemas and other activities. If you've been here before, you won't recognize it even now, let alone by the time everything's ultimately completed in 2004 (most work will be completed in 2002, after which additional phases of development will take place at lodging facilities).

A word on phone numbers: Though the South Shore appears to be one big town, it's two towns in two states. If you're staying on the Nevada side, you'll need to dial the area code before all California phone numbers, and vice versa. Kirkwood is in another area code, 209.

Heavenly Resort

Heavenly is big. It ranks Number One at Lake Tahoe for highest elevation (10,040 feet), greatest vertical rise (3,500 feet) and longest run (5.5 miles). Heavenly has some good expert terrain—Mott Canyon on the Nevada side and its famous face run, Gunbarrel, on the California side. Other than that, however, the resort is most appropriate for intermediates and advanced skiers.

Heavenly is also the only two-state mountain resort—you can start out from either California or Nevada. Though the California base is better known because it's in clear view of

Tahoe Interchangeable tickets

The Ski Lake Tahoe interchangeable lift pass is good at Kirkwood, Heavenly, Sierra-at-Tahoe, Northstar, Alpine Meadows and Squaw Valley USA. Five of six consecutive days cost $260 ($52 a day).

South Lake Tahoe's casinos, skiers and snowboarders also can start from the Nevada side by driving on the Kingsbury Grade to either the Stagecoach or Boulder bases. Most visitors start from California, so beginning in Nevada is often a good way to avoid the crowds. A new gondola provides direct access from the center of the South Lake Tahoe/Stateline district to the resort. The almost-2-1/2-mile long ride takes just under 12 minutes.

But mostly, Heavenly is the view. The most spectacular view of Lake Tahoe—perhaps the most awesome view from a ski area summit anywhere—is at the top of the Sky Express. A photographer is stationed up there to take visitor photos, and often, there is a waiting line. From here on a sunny day just after a storm, the lake looks like a brilliant blue sapphire, nesting in soft folds of white velvet. As you traverse into Nevada, you'll see the muted browns, greens and yellows of the Nevada winter desert. Pack a camera. Heavenly is one of the most scenic resorts in North America, if not the world.

Mountain layout—Skiing

◆◆ **Expert:** The California base, on Ski Run Boulevard from Highway 50, strikes awe in all but the best skiers because the world seems to drop straight down into Lake Tahoe. Gunbarrel and East Bowl are 1,700-vertical-feet-high, straight ladders of bumps, often with dangerous-looking rocky protrusions in early winter or late spring.

On the Nevada side (see the advanced section for directions on crossing the state line), experts have their own playgrounds, Mott Canyon and Killebrew Canyon. These north-facing walls are peppered with pines and have half-a-dozen expert chutes. This lift-served area can only be entered through designated gates.

◆ **Advanced:** If the bumps on the California face look too menacing, leap over them by taking either the Gunbarrel Chair or the aerial tram. Then head down Patsy's (unfortunately a horrible bottleneck on weekends) to the Waterfall Chair, which gives access to superb advanced runs off Ridge, Canyon and Sky Express Chairs. From the top of the Sky Express, the best of the California side opens up. After you have admired the inspiring view of Lake Tahoe, drop down Ellie's if you are looking for bumps. Sometimes you can catch Ellie's when it's groomed, and then it's a screaming cruiser.

When you've had enough of California, strike out for Nevada, where 50 percent of the terrain is located. You get to the Nevada side from the top of Sky Express; go left along the Skyline Trail, which requires a bit of pushing. Here's a trick for advanced-intermediates who want the best of the Milky Way Bowl: The Skyline Trail dips a bit after you get off the Sky Express Chair. You then make a small climb and the trail starts down again. Just as you begin dropping, look to your right for tracks leading into the trees and follow them. After a short traverse you will end up at the top of the Milky Way Bowl, with about twice the vertical you would have found had you stayed on the trail. Those coming off the Dipper chair on the Nevada side can use the same traverse. From the top of Milky Way to the bottom of Mott Canyon is one long run that covers over 2,000 vertical feet through black and blacker terrain.

On the Nevada side, advanced skiers with moguls on their minds can bump down Big Dipper Bowl or traverse a bit further and try the Little Dipper.

■ **Intermediate:** If you want long smooth cruising, head to the right from the Sky Express when you get off the chair and steam down Liz's, Canyon, Betty's or Ridge Run.

The Nevada side has even better cruises. From the top of the Dipper Express are the Big Dipper and Orion. The Galaxy Chair is a good spot for low intermediates to gain confidence. For a cruise that seems to take forever, take Olympic Downhill to Stagecoach Base.

●● **Beginner ● Never-ever:** Though Heavenly is exactly that for intermediates and up, never-evers should pick another resort for their skiing baptism. Except for a tiny learning section at the California base, Heavenly's green terrain is smack in the middle of a place where four lifts have their boarding areas. People dart in every direction, making a most intimidating scene. However, everyone—non-skiers included—can ride the tram to admire the view of the lake. If you must take your first lesson here, go to the Boulder base area on the Nevada side, where there is a gentle slope and more room to spread out.

Note: If you've been skiing in Nevada, here's how to get back to the California base: Take the Dipper Express to the top and traverse right to the California Trail, or take Comet and then cruise the 49er run. The runs meander into a small depression where the 3-mile winding Roundabout trail down the face gets most of the intermediate traffic at the end of the day (beginners will want to ride the tram back down). Advanced sliders who want to descend The Face should board Patsy's or Groove, two short lifts that return you to the top. Tram riders should board Patsy's.

Mountain layout—Snowboarding

Riders don't come here for terrain parks and halfpipes, they come for the steeps, powder-filled canyons and powder stashes in the woods. The biggest bummer is the terrain layout isn't exactly snowboarder-friendly—the

---

Heavenly Resort Facts

California Side–	
Summit:	10,040 feet
Vertical drop:	3,500 feet
Base:	6,540 feet
Nevada Side–	
Summit:	10,040 feet
Vertical drop:	2,840 feet
Base:	7,200 feet

Expert:★★★★
Advanced:★★★★
Intermediate:★★★★
Beginner:★★ **Never-ever:**★
Address: Box 2180, Stateline, NV 89449
✆ Area code: 775
Ski area phone: 586-7000
Snow report: 586-7000

ⓘ **Toll-free reservations:**
(800) 243-2836 (2-HEAVEN)
E-mail: info@skiheavenly.com
Internet: www.skiheavenly.com
Number of lifts: 29–1 aerial tram, 1 gondola, 1 six-passenger high-speed chair, 5 high-speed quads, 8 triples, 5 doubles, 8 surface lifts
Snowmaking: 69 percent of trails
Total acreage: 4,800 patrolled acres
(1,084 skiable trail acres)
Uphill capacity: 37,845 per hour
Snowboarding: Yes, unlimited
Bed Base: 22,000 in S. Lake Tahoe
Nearest lodging: About a mile away
Resort child care: Yes, 6 weeks and older
Adult ticket, per day: $52-57 (01/02)

traverses are flat, flat, flat and you have to do a lot of strapping and unstrapping to move around the mountain. But, all that work is worth it, especially after a powder dump.

General consensus among riders is the California side is too bumped up (stay away from Gunbarrel and East Bowl if you hate bumps like most riders do), so the Nevada side is the place to play. Mott Canyon and Killebrew Canyon win hands-down as the favored spots: These north-facing walls are peppered with pines and half-a-dozen expert chutes. Both lift-served areas can only be entered through designated gates. For strictly trees, head to Dipper Knob Trees and the area known as the "western perimeter" (off Olympic Chair, ride the ridge to the trees, where you'll find natural hits, waves and lots of powder). On the California side, the best woods are Skiways and Maggie's Canyon (both are reached by the Sky Express lift).

Other playgrounds include the numerous hits in Sand Dunes, the waterfall in North Bowl trees and the natural pipe left of Sky chair. Stick to Stagecoach and Olympic lifts if you want to carve your brains out. And if you must head to the terrain park, ride the trees on the northeast side of it instead. By the way, there's a new halfpipe on California Trail. Never-evers should pick another resort for their snowboarding baptism.

Lessons (2001/02 prices)

Group lessons: For levels higher than advanced beginner, ski and snowboard clinics (called Mountain Adventure Clinics) cost $49. If you also need rentals and/or a lift ticket, ask about packages. You also can buy a three- to five-day clinic booklet at a discount. The booklet does not have to be used on consecutive days. Heavenly also packages lessons with lift tickets or rental equipment.

Never-ever package: A two-hour Perfect Turn clinic, rentals and access to the beginner lifts is $79, ski or snowboard. Ask about multiday savings.

Private lessons: $85 per hour. Discounts offered for multiple hours and for early-morning or late-afternoon lessons. Reservations suggested. Call (775) 586-7000, Ext. 6244.

Special programs: Heavenly has special theme clinics, such as Mott and Killebrew guided tours for experts, carving clinics, and clinics for women. Perhaps the most popular is Carver's Paradise, which gets you on the mountain a half-hour before the lifts open, clearly the best way to catch fresh powder and corduroy. Call for prices, dates and reservations on all these programs.

Racing: A coin-op course is on the Yahoo run on the California side, for $2 per run.

Child care (2001/02 prices)

Ages: 6 weeks to 6 years.

Costs: Full-day program costs $75; half-day, morning or afternoon, costs $55. Both include lunch. Ski instruction/day care combo programs also are available for ages 3 and older.

Reservations: Strongly recommended. Call the resort at (775) 586-7000.

Other options: Baby's Away (800-446-9030) rents and will deliver baby items (cribs, strollers, toys, etc.) to your hotel or condo anywhere in the Lake Tahoe area.

Children's lessons: Full day for ages 4–13 is $116, including instruction, equipment, lunch, snacks and lift access. Ages 7-13 can take snowboard lessons for the same price. The afternoon session costs $76, and does not include lunch. A Tag-A-Long private lesson allowing the parent to participate with their child is 75 minutes long and costs $85.

Lift tickets (2001/02 prices)

	Adult	Child (6-12)
One day	$57	$29
Three days (of 4)	$162 ($54/day)	$81 ($27/day)
Five days	$260 ($52/day)	$125 ($25/day)

Who skis free: Children ages 5 and younger ski free with a paying adult.

Who skis at a discount: Young adult (ages 13–18) ski for $47 a day; $132 for three days; $210 for five days. Ages 65 and older ski for child prices. A tram ride for nonskiers is $18 for adults and $12 for children. Heavenly's new gondola connects the resort to the town.

Kirkwood

The lovely drive through Hope Valley to Kirkwood from South Lake Tahoe takes only about 45 minutes, but it is light-years away in altitude and ambiance. There are no bright lights, no ringing jackpots, no wide blue lake, no high-rise buildings and no urban noise. Instead, you have the feeling that you are entering a special secret place, known to a select few.

Kirkwood is a superb area for skiing and snowboarding. In the past there's been few options for off-slope socializing and activities, but that's changing now that the resort is in the middle of building a mountain village with a pedestrian plaza including shops, restaurants and a skating rink. Terrain-wise, Kirkwood is the most balanced resort in the Tahoe region. It has one of the best learning areas in the country—several gentle runs that are off to one side, away from the main traffic and served by their own lift. Kirkwood will thrill any expert, even super-expert, with its steeps and dozens of chutes. And it offers great terrain for all ability levels between those extremes. Kirkwood's northeast exposure in a snow pocket gives light, dry conditions and produces storms that linger and dump more. Kirkwood frequently stays open into May with good late-season conditions.

For the past decade natural snow has often arrived late in the California mountains, so Kirkwood has added snowmaking on four of the most popular runs—Hay Flat, Buckboard, Race Course and Zachary—top to bottom, as well as the beginner tow, No. 8.

Kirkwood Facts

Summit elevation:	**9,800 feet**
Vertical drop:	**2,000 feet**
Base elevation:	**7,800 feet**

Expert:★★★★★
Advanced:★★★★★
Intermediate:★★★★★
Beginner:★★★★
Never-ever:★★★★★
Address: Box 1, Kirkwood, CA 95646
Area code: 209
✆ **Ski area phone:** 258-6000
Snow report: 877-KIRKWOOD (877-547-5966)

ⓘ **Toll-free reservations:** (800) 967-7500
Fax: 258-8899
Internet: www.skikirkwood.com
Number of lifts: 12–2 quad, 7 triples, 1 double, 2 surface lifts
Snowmaking: 2 percent
Skiable acreage: 2,300 acres
Uphill capacity: 17,905 per hour
Snowboarding: Yes
Bed Base: 10,500 in S. Lake Tahoe
Nearest lodging: Slopeside (400 units)
Resort child care: Yes, 2 years and older
Adult ticket, per day: $41-$52 (2001/02)

Mountain layout—Skiing

Kirkwood has both named and numbered its lifts. Locals and staff tend to use the numbers, so we list those in parentheses in the following terrain description.

◆◆ **Expert:** Wagonwheel/The Wall (Chair 10) and Cornice (Chair 6) rise from the base area to serve the toughest terrain. The resort cut an entry at the top of Wagonwheel to eliminate the leap formerly required to get into the double-black runs below the Sisters. Some of the best skiing is further west (right on the map), below False Peak through chutes and trees. Cornice serves single-diamond runs, including Palisades Bowl, to the far right on the trail map. Because getting here requires a bit of a traverse, you can find some good powder shots.

On the far left of the trail map, Sunrise (Chair 4) serves an area called The Wave because it gets a cornice that looks like a giant ocean breaker. On the right (west) side of the chair the half dozen runs of Thunder Saddle keep powder for three days after a snowfall because it takes three chairs to get there. Watch your step on the ridge. When you get near the bottom, after dropping down One Man Chute, Bogie's Slide or Corner Chute, tuck and keep your speed up for the flat run back to the Wagonwheel (Chair 10) or Cornice (Chair 6) lifts.

◆ **Advanced:** Both Sentinel Bowl and Zack's (Zachary on the trail map) are groomed every day, a draw for anyone looking for super-smooth steeps. If you want bumps, try Olympic, Look-Out Janek, or Monte Wolfe, on either side of the Cornice Chair. The Reut (Chair 11) has some great cruisers—black on the map, but a solid intermediate could handle them.

■ **Intermediate:** Intermediates can stay on the lower sections of the face, using Hole'n'Wall (Chair 7) and Solitude (Chair 5), or work their way over Caples Crest (Chair 2) to the Sunrise section, where there's plenty of groomed intermediate terrain. The entire lower mountain, with just a couple of exceptions, is perfectly suited for intermediates. When you're ready to test your black-diamond skills, try the runs off Chair 11. If you can handle those, you're probably ready for a groomed run in Sentinel Bowl.

●● **Beginner:** Beginners will find gentle trails served by Snowkirk Chair (Chair 1) to the east, and Bunny Chair (Chair 9) and Hole 'n' Wall (Chair 7) at the far west.

● **Never-ever:** Never-evers should head straight for the Timber Creek Lodge, a right-hand turn before you reach the main parking lot (there's a sign). Here novices will find a rental shop and ticket window, plus Chairs 9 and 7 (Bunny and Hole'n'Wall) that serve novice and low-intermediate terrain. Experienced skiers park in the main lot and get their tickets in the main lodge farther down the road, but if there's a novice in your group, you can get to the main area using Chair 7. Kirkwood has—by far—the best setup for novices in the South Tahoe region.

Mountain layout—Snowboarding

Kirkwood has the best pow in Tahoe—sick, dry and fluffy—and tons of gullies that are Mother Nature's very own halfpipes and quarterpipes. Kirkwood also gets high marks for its freestyle terrain park, reached by Caples Crest (Chair 2), and the halfpipe, reached by Solitude (Chair 5).

Besides the obvious double-black shots off Wagonwheel/The Wall (Chair 10) and the back side just waiting to be explored, experts will find some of the best riding is below False Peak through chutes and trees. The Cornice (Chair 6) serves single-diamond runs, including Palisades Bowl, to the far right on the trail map. Getting here requires a bit of a traverse and some hoofing, but you'll find great powder shots. Some favorite spots served by Sunrise (Chair 4) on the left side of the trail map: Drop the cornice at the spot called The Wave or float the river gully to the right of Thunder Saddle. Beware of the long flat back to the lifts after dropping off the ridge into the chutes that include One Man Chute and Bogie's Slide.

Chomping at the bit to carve some nice arcs? You'll find nice long, grooved runs here too. Stay on the lower sections of the face, using Hole'n'Wall (Chair 7) and Solitude (Chair 5), or work your way over Caples Crest (Chair 2) to the Sunrise section, where there's plenty of groomed intermediate terrain. Never-evers should head straight for the Timber Creek Lodge. Kirkwood has—by far—the best setup for novices in the South Tahoe region.

Lessons (2001/02 prices)

Group lessons: Kirkwood's Ski and Board School offers clinics for all levels. These are 110 minutes long, cost $30, and are designed to smooth out rough edges, rather than teach the basics from scratch. Packages including lifts and equipment are $85; young adults 13-22 pay $75.

Never-ever package: A First Time ski package including a two-hour lesson, beginner lift ticket and rental equipment costs $60. The first-time skier program uses the Elan PSX 133 cm. short carving skis that accelerate learning by adding stability and providing an early introduction to the sensation of "shaping" turns. Learn-To-Snowboard packages with a 2.5-hour lesson, beginner lift ticket and rental equipment are $60. Kirkwood offers novice snowboarders two follow-up lessons with the same benefits for $60 per day.

Private lessons: $70 for an hour, $25 each additional person.

Special programs: There are programs for women, all-mountain day camps, and Kirkwood Explorers that tackles non-groomed terrain. Call for dates and prices.

Child care (2001/02 prices)

Ages: 2–6 years, toilet-trained.
Costs: All day is $75 including lunch, a half day $55.

Reservations: Recommended; call (209) 258-7274. Licensed child care for infants can be arranged with an outside agency at (209) 258-8783.

Other options: Baby's Away (800-446-9030) rents and will deliver baby items (cribs, strollers, toys, etc.) to your hotel or condo anywhere in the Lake Tahoe area.

Children's lessons: Ski lessons for ages 4–12 and snowboard lessons for ages 7–12 include rental equipment, lunch, lessons and lifts for $80 for a full day and $65 for a half day. The package for those who have equipment is $70 for a full day, $55 for a half day. Ages 13 and older are considered young adults and enroll in the adult lessons. Kirkwood's children's center is located in the Timber Creek novice area, the first right-hand turn before you reach the main parking lot.

Lift tickets (2001/02 prices)

	Adult	Child (6-12) & Seniors (70+)
One day	$52	$12
Three days	$156 ($52/day)	$36 ($12/day)
Five days	$208 ($41+/day)	$48 ($9+/day)

Who skis free: Ages 5 and younger.
Who skis at a discount: Ages 60–69 ski for $25; young adults 13–24 ski for $42.

Sierra-at-Tahoe

Sierra-at-Tahoe often is overlooked by destination skiers to the South Shore. What a shame. If Heavenly gets a little crowded, or the previous night's partying has made the drive to Kirkwood unthinkable, point yourself west and drive 12 miles to this resort. Sierra-at-Tahoe has more than 2,000 vertical feet and 2,000 acres. That's not little. So let us rephrase: Drive 12 miles west to this fun, big resort with an intimate feel. Better yet, ride the free shuttles that stops at 43 locations in Stateline and the Highway 50 corridor.

The resort has opted to invest its money into on-mountain upgrades, consequently you won't find any lodging or even a mountain village at its base. You *will* find a compact base area that's easy to get around, fabulous terrain, an efficient lift network, and great customer service, thank you very much.

Mountain layout—Skiing

◆◆ **Expert** ◆ **Advanced:** Sierra-at-Tahoe has a good collection of bumped-up black-diamond trails under the Grand View Express and Tahoe King chairs. Castle, Preacher's Passion and Dynamite all cascade roughly 1,300 vertical feet. Roughly 1,500 of the 2,000 acres are tree skiing. Powder stashes often stay hidden in the old growth forest for days after a storm. Ride the Grand View Express to the top and just jump into the trees—anywhere. Five backcountry access gates were recently opened. Access is free with the purchase of a lift ticket and guided tours are available daily.

■ **Intermediate:** This is a wonderful area for intermediates. West Bowl will fast become the favorite area of the mountain for this level. Lower Main is a steep, groomed run that rises above the day lodge. It's gotta be the toughest blue run here. If you see this trail and gulp, don't worry. Fun awaits in West Bowl. The Backside is another good spot for intermediates.

●● **Beginner:** Sugar 'n' Spice is a 2.5-mile, easy cruise from the summit. Ride the Grand View Express chair and take a moment to look at the view of the lake (much better on the roof deck of the Grand View Grill). As you descend Sugar 'n' Spice, stay a good distance from the snowbank on the left edge of the run, especially when it gets to be head-high. Hot

Sierra-at-Tahoe Facts

Summit elevation:	8,852 feet
Vertical drop:	2,212 feet
Base elevation:	6,640 feet

Expert:★ ★
Advanced:★ ★ ★ ★
Intermediate:★ ★ ★ ★
Beginner:★ ★ ★ ★
Never-ever:★ ★ ★ ★
Address: 1111 Sierra-at-Tahoe Rd.
Twin Bridges, CA 95735
☎ **Area code:** 530
Ski area phone: 659-7453
Snow report: 659-7475

ⓘ **Toll-free reservations:** No lodging on site
Fax: 659-7749
E-mail: sierra@boothcreek.com
Internet: www.sierratahoe.com
Number of lifts: 9–3 high-speed quads, 1 triple, 5 doubles
Snowmaking: 22 percent
Skiable acreage: 2,000 acres
Uphill capacity: 14,921 per hour
Snowboarding: Yes, unlimited
Bed Base: In S. Lake Tahoe
Nearest lodging: About 12 miles away
Resort child care: Yes, 18 months and older
Adult ticket, per day: $48 (2000/01 prices)

shots like to shoot out of the trees between this run and Upper Snowshoe. Fortunately, Sugar 'n' Spice is plenty wide. Stay to the middle or the right and give the idiots some room.

Upper Snowshoe is another good beginner run, but be sure to turn right at Marten to meet up with Sugar 'n' Spice, or you'll be on Lower Snowshoe, a blue run. Another chair that serves good beginner terrain is Rock Garden.

● **Never-ever:** This is a great learner's mountain. Sierra-at-Tahoe has a super learning slope called Broadway, right at the day lodge and served by its own quad chair.

Mountain layout—Snowboarding

Sierra-at-Tahoe has three terrain parks, all marked with pink highlighting on the trail map. The advanced terrain park is on The Alley and has three rail slides, two hits, two tabletops (with multiple hits) and a 17-foot superpipe. Intermediates should head to the park on Upper Main, where you'll find four big tabletops. Beginners can try the berms and rollers in the park on Wagon Trail. Last season's big news was the new superpipe on Aspen/Aspen West. Like riding in the trees? About 1,500 of the 2,000 acres here are woods and powder stashes often stay hidden in the old-growth forest for days after a storm. Ride the Grand View Express to the top and just jump into the trees—anywhere. Five backcountry access gates were recently opened. Access is free with the purchase of a lift ticket and guided tours are available daily.

Lessons (2001/02 prices)

Group lessons: FREE lessons for strong intermediate through expert skiers or snowboarders are offered twice a day on a first-come basis for ages 13 and older. Breakthrough packages for advancing beginners through lowerintermediates, 1.5-hour lessons cost $32 for lessons only; $88 with lifts and equipment.

Never-ever package: A First Time package including beginner lifts, rentals and two-hour lesson is $65 for skiers or snowboarders. A two-day package is $105.

Private lessons: $70 an hour, with discounts for additional hours or early-bird lessons.

Child care (2001/02 prices)

Ages: 18 months–5 years.

Costs: $85 for full day (full day includes lunch); $85 for a program that includes an hour of ski instruction for ages 3–4. Call for half-day rates.

Reservations: Recommended; call (530) 659-7453.

Children's lessons: All-day ski or snowboard instruction (including lunch, rentals, lift ticket) is $85 for ages 4–12; $75 for afternoon half day (with no lunch).

Lift tickets (2001/02 prices)

	Adult	Child (6-12)
One day	$50	$10
Two of three days	$86 ($43/day)	$22 ($11/day)
Three of five days	$125 ($41+/day)	$33 ($11/day)

Who skis free: Younger than 6.

Who skis at a discount: Ages 70 and older pay $12; ages 60-69, $29; young adults ages 13-22, $40; multiday discounts available.

Cross-country and snowshoeing

The Lake Tahoe region may have the greatest concentration of large cross-country ski areas in the U.S., with more than 800 km. of groomed trails. Most of that is on the north end of the lake, but South Shore has a good network of trails, too. Most also allow snowshoes.

New for 2001/02, **Heavenly's Adventure Park** (775-586-7000) at the top of the gondola will include a cross-country skiing and snowshoeing center. You'll find 5 km. of groomed trails that meander through the forest and provide awesome views from nearly 3,000 feet above Lake Tahoe. Cross-country and snowshoe equipment is available; lessons daily.

Spooner Lake Cross-Country (775-887-8844, recording; 755-749-5349, live voice) on Hwy. 28, about a half-mile north of Hwy. 50, has more than 80 km. of trails, nearly all of which are machine groomed, with one 19-km. backcountry trail. Adult trail fees are $16.50; less for ages 7-15. Children younger than age 7 ski free. Lessons and cross-country gear, snowshoe and pulk sled rentals are available; you also can rent a backcountry cabin.

Kirkwood Cross-Country (209-258-7248) has 80 km. of machine-groomed tracks, skating lanes and three interconnected trail systems with three warming huts, including the 1864 Kirkwood Inn, a trappers' log cabin full of nostalgia. A professional ski patrol watches for injured skiers. Rental gear includes cross-country, telemark, snowshoes and pulk sleds. Lessons are also available. Adult trail fees are $16, ages 13-18 and 65+ are $12, children 7-12 are $5, children 5 and younger are free.

Hope Valley Cross-Country Ski Center (530-694-2337) is near the junction of Highways 89 and 88. It has about 100 km. of marked trails, a quarter of which are groomed. Trail fees are by donation. Lessons and rentals are available.

Camp Richardson Resort (530-542-6584) in South Lake Tahoe has a cross-country ski center with lessons, rentals and trails along the Lake Tahoe shoreline.

Sierra-at-Tahoe (659-7453) has more than 3 miles of groomed snowshoeing trails with daily rentals available.

 ## Accommodations

South Shore accommodations divide into four categories: the multistory casinos hugging the Nevada border for great views and nonstop nightlife; the top of Kingsbury Grade, near the base of Heavenly's Nevada side, for upscale condominiums and top-quality hotels; along the California lake shore for moderately priced motels; and at Kirkwood to escape the hustle and bustle. Here are our choices.

Central Reservations for South Lake Tahoe is at (800) 288-2463 (AT-TAHOE). If you plan to do all your skiing at Heavenly, **Heavenly Central Reservations** can arrange an entire ski vacation including airfare, transfers, lessons, rentals, non-ski activities, skiing and lodging. Call (800) 243-2836 (2-HEAVEN) or (775) 588-4584.

If you can stay here Sunday through Thursday nights, you can get extremely good deals. Lodging and lift packages can run as low as $69 per person, per night, double occupancy. If you're here Friday and Saturday, however, prices double or sometimes triple. South Shore has a wide variety of lodges and prices, however, tell the agent how much you want to spend.

The lodging and general look of South Lake Tahoe takes many visitors by surprise. They expect to see Rocky Mountain-style luxury. Instead, they find a lot of '50s- and '60s- style budget motels, cabins and shopping strip malls lining a very traffic-heavy main street. If we can be frank, much of South Shore is not very attractive.

However, this is about to change with the redevelopment project. Several beautiful hotels have been built in the past few years, and several more will be built in connection with Heavenly's new gondola, which is right at the state line and within walking distance of hundreds of hotel rooms. Among them is the Marriott Grand Residence Club (formerly Grand Summit) at the new Park Avenue base area. It will feature in-suite kitchens, laundry service, a ski-check room, as well as a number of retail shops when it is completed in November 2002.

Nevada allows casino gambling, California doesn't. Most of the visitors to this region come from Northern California's urban areas. Keep that in mind and you'll realize why the high-rise casino-hotels were built inches from the state line.

Many destination visitors like to be smack in the middle of the action. If you're in that group, try **Harvey's Casino Hotel** (800-648-3361 from outside Nevada or 775-588-2411 from Nevada; $$–$$$) and **Harrah's Casino Hotel** (800-648-3353 or 775-588-3515; $$–$$$$), which have everyone's highest ratings, from AAA to Mobil. Other casino-hotels within walking distance of the state line are **Caesar's Tahoe Casino Hotel** (800-648-3353 or 775-586-2000; $$–$$$$) and the **Horizon Casino Resort** (800-648-3322; $$–$$$$).

We like to be near the casinos, but don't want to hear that constant ringing of the slot machines when we come downstairs for breakfast. One of our favorite places to stay—in fact, our staff spent a few days together here a couple of seasons ago—is the **Embassy Suites Resort** (800-362-2779; 530-544-5400; www.embassytahoe.com; $$–$$$). Just 50 feet from the nearest casino, this property was chosen No. 1 in the 108-hotel Embassy Suites chain in a survey of 40,000 guests. It has an indoor atrium, indoor pool and spa, an exercise center, wedding chapel and on-site restaurants and nightclub. Cooked-to-order breakfast and a free happy hour is included in the rates, which start at about $95 for midweek packages.

For the Nevada side of Heavenly accommodations, there are scores of condos at Stagecoach Base and Boulder Base areas. At the base of Kingsbury Grade on Hwy. 50 you'll find the **Lakeside Inn & Casino** (800-624-7980; 775-588-7777; $–$$), which offers some of the best deals. The rooms are simple and motelish but access to the mountain is excellent.

The California side of South Lake Tahoe has many small motels lining Lake Tahoe Boulevard for miles. Among the best of the motel bunch are two Best Western properties— **The Timber Cove Lodge** (800-528-1234 or 530-541-6722; $–$$$), located on the beach; and **Station House Inn** (800-822-5953 or 530-542-1101; $$–$$$), within walking distance of the casino area, on the California side of the border.

For the rustic-minded, try the **Historic Camp Richardson Resort** (800-544-1801; $$–$$$), which offers cabin appeal with large fireplaces, spacious living rooms and full kitchens. Perfect for couples traveling together or families who enjoy various outdoor sports. Onsite sledding, snowshoeing, cross-country trails and wilderness sleigh rides complete this seasonal resort. The historic hotel and beachside inn provide more "civilized" accommodations within a 15-minute drive from Heavenly.

Inn By The Lake (800-877-1466; 530-542-0330; $–$$$) is less than 100 feet from the shore and two miles from the casinos. It has 100 guest rooms (including nine suites with kitchens), free continental breakfast, heated pool, bi-level spa, sauna and free shuttles to the slopes. Midweek and AAA rates available.

Lakeland Village (800-822-5969; 530-544-1685; $$–$$$$) has a hotel and condominiums on the lake with shuttlebus service to the bases of Heavenly and Kirkwood. The units range from studios to a lakefront four-bedroom, three-bath unit. For those who want a room just across from Heavenly's lifts on the California side, the **Tahoe Seasons Resort** has received good reviews from everyone locally (530-541-6700; $$–$$$$). Another possibility is the **Holiday Inn Express** (800-544-5288; 530-544-5900; $$–$$$$).

One for couples only: The **Fantasy Inn** (800-367-7736, 530-541-4200; $$$–$$$$) has about 60 rooms designed for romance. Tahoe had another Fantasy Inn a while back that was quite tacky, but this one is very tastefully done. Each room has one bed in a choice of several shapes (round, heart-shaped, water or regular mattress, king-size), a private spa for two, an in-room music system with 30 channels, adjustable peach-colored lighting and showers with double shower heads. Sixteen of the rooms are theme or theme deluxe suites, such as Rain Forest (plants and rattan decor), Caesar's Indulgence (a sexy black decor), and Romeo and Juliet (the honeymoon suite we didn't see because it was continually booked during our visit). A wedding chapel is on the premises. Theme suites are in the $245–$295 range. Ask about special ski and/or wedding package rates. If you are there with a special someone and you can swing it financially, rent a theme room—you won't forget it.

Accommodations at Kirkwood Resort

If you want big-mountain skiing and a get-away-from-it-all location, stay slopeside at Kirkwood. Kirkwood is working on a slopeside village with about 600 condos and many new shops and services such as an ice rink and recreation center/swim complex. Phase One is now complete and includes **Snowcrest Lodge, The Mountain Club** and the **Lodge at Kirkwood**. Perhaps the best part about the new village is that it's, well—new. All the rooms feature modern interiors, have a prime location on the slopes and make efficient use of space. Of the other condo-complexes on the Meadow Side, the top choice is **Sun Meadows**, which is across from the Solitude and Cornice chairs and about as centrally located as you can get in Kirkwood. The second choice is **The Meadows**, between Timber Creek and the Cornice Chair. Rates range from $110 for a studio to about $500 for a three-bedroom condo. Packages—particularly midweek stays—bring down the cost. Reservations: (209) 258-7000 or (800) 967-7500.

 # Dining

For the best restaurants in the higher priced category (all area codes are 530 unless noted):

Evan's American Gourmet Café (542-1990; $$$) on State Route 89 has become one of the best-liked restaurants on the South Shore. The chef prepares California Cuisine with an unusual flair. Expect to pay for his efforts, but they are reported to be well worth it. **Primavera Restaurant** (775-586-2000; $$–$$$) in Caesar's Tahoe Casino Hotel serves Italian poolside in an atmosphere reminiscent of quaint European cafés with excellent service, quality and wine list. For an excellent meal, great wine list and attentive service—with a beautiful view— head to **Friday's Station** (775-588-6611; $$$) at the top of Harrah's casino-hotel. Other recommendations are **Fresh Ketch** (541-5683; $$$) for fish; **Dory's Oar** (541-6603; $$$) for steaks and seafood; or **Zackary's Restaurant** (544-5400, $$–$$$) in the Embassy Suites hotel for its delicious blackened salmon, among other dishes. The mountainside **Summit Restaurant** ($$$) has quite a reputation, voted in the South Lake Tahoe's "Best" poll as serving the best desserts and providing the best romantic meal in the region. It also took the "best place to eat dinner when someone else is paying" award.

For good reasonable restaurants, try:

The Cantina Bar and Grill (544-1233; $) or **El Sol** (544-4954; $) for Mexican, **Scusa** (542-0100; $$) for Italian, **Sato Japanese Restaurant** (541-3769; $–$$) for surprisingly good sushi specials or **Dixon's Restaurant and Brewery** (542-3389; $) for microbrews and home-style cuisine. Of the casinos' affordable buffets (and there are many) we enjoyed **Harvey's** (775-588-2411; $) reasonably priced seafood buffet with large portions. Others to try are **Beacon** (541-0630; $$-$$$), on the lake, with blackened prime rib a specialty; and **Nephele's** (544-8130; $$), which serves California cuisine in a cozy setting and has private hot-tub rentals. Next door to Nephele's is an outstanding restaurant called **Café Fiori** (541-2908; $$). It doesn't seat many, so reservations are a must. The food and the wine iist are superb.

For great breakfasts head to **The Red Hut** (541-9024; $), where you can pack into a small room and listen to the talk of the town. Another branch is on Kingsbury Grade (775-588-7488, $), handy for skiers heading to the Nevada side of Heavenly. At **Heidi's** (544-8113, $), get anything from dozens of types of Belgian waffles to chocolate pancakes. If you're in over the weekend you must go to **Llewellyn's** (775-588-2411; $$) at Harvey's Resort Hotel for Sunday brunch, food is flavorful and the view breathtaking.

And just in case you crave a malt "so thick it holds the straw up," go to the **Zephyr Cove Resort**. Try the banana-chocolate shake. **Alpen Sierra Coffee Roasting Company** (544-7740), at Highway 50 and Pioneer, was voted "Best Coffee House in South Lake Tahoe" and offers locally roasted mountain coffee.

At Heavenly, table linen lunch service is offered at **Monument Peak Restaurant** ($–$$). Heavenly also has a gourmet picnic service, **Heavenly Mountain Caterers** (542-5153). Place your reservation by 10 a.m. the day prior and enjoy a steak or chicken picnic in a secluded outdoor location with great views. It's about $225 per couple.

If you're staying at Kirkwood, you'll probably discover the places to eat on your own— not a big selection, but all are pretty good. **Off the Wall Bar & Grille** in the Lodge at Kirkwood has California-style gourmet cuisine in a comfortable cozy atmosphere. The slopeside **Cornice Cafe Restaurant and Bar** is being revamped for the 2001/02 season into a sports bar/pub serving casual American fare with an extensive appetizer and happy hour menu. Also try **Kirkwood Inn**, built in 1864 by Zachary Kirkwood and in operation ever since, featuring hearty meals such as steaks and seafood; and **Caples Lake Resort**, fine dining overlooking scenic Caples Lake, a mile east of Kirkwood on Hwy. 88. At the **General Store** you can find inexpensive sandwiches and fresh cookies—great for a slope-side picnic.

Après-ski/nightlife

Head to **Chevy's** immediately after skiing or stop in the **California Bar** at Heavenly's Base Lodge. If you want quieter après-ski with a flickering fire-place, stop in at **Christiana Inn** across from the Heavenly ski area. Later in the evening, **Turtle's**, a Tahoe institution that relocated to the Embassy Suites, has good dancing. **Nero's 2000** in Caesar's Tahoe Casino Hotel has dancing seven nights a week, and live music on the weekends. They have reggae on Mondays and Alternative Night on Wednesdays. On our most recent visit here, we had a long list of places we were intending to check out. However, we ended up at **McP's**, a great Irish pub near the state line, on the first night and just kept going back. Great live music (listenable rather than danceable), a pool table in back, and packed every night. Other spots that had been recommended to us were **Mulligan's, Hoss Hogs, Bumper's, The Island** and **Dixon's**. The **Goalpost Restaurant & Bar** in Stateline is the hot spot for the late-late crowd.

And of course, the **casinos** have musical reviews that are extravaganzas of sight and sound. Some shows run through the season; others are top-name singers and comedians who do one or two shows.

Kirkwood's slopeside **Cornice Cafe Restaurant and Bar** is being revamped for the 2001/02 season into a sports bar/pub with an extensive appetizer and happy hour menu. The full bar will continue to offer a comprehensive wine list. You'll also find dart boards, a pool table, big-screen TVs and a stage for live music.

Other activities

South Tahoe has tons to do, but space doesn't permit us to list all the options. Ask your hotel concierge for suggestions.

New for 2001/02, **Heavenly's Adventure Park** (775-586-7000) at the top of the gondola will offer a variety of activities, including cross-country skiing, snowshoeing, lift-accessed snow tubing and snow play.

Ice skating is at the South Tahoe Ice Center, also called STIC (530-542-4700). Figure and hockey skates are available for rent, and the Tahoe Lakers pro hockey team plays on Friday and Saturday nights.

New at Kirkwood for 2001/02, there will be **ice skating** at the rink in the pedestrian village. Kirkwood also offers **dogsledding, sleigh rides, sauna and massage,** the **Swim Complex** with an Olympic-size pool and workout facilities, and a family **tubing hill.**

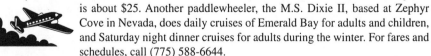

Weddings aren't your everyday optional ski activity, but if you're thinking of getting married with little fuss, this is one of the best spots to do it. As we said earlier in the chapter, Valentine's Day (Feb. 14) is the most popular winter day to be married, so plan well ahead if this is your intention. More than 20 wedding chapels dot the area, but probably the nicest ones are in the big hotels. These have features such as discreet video cameras that record the happy moment from several angles and lighting that changes with the music. Most have wedding concierges to plan every detail. You also can be married outdoors, either by the lake or on the slopes. California marriage licenses cost about $50; Nevada licenses are a bit less, plus no blood test is required. For more information, contact the Lake Tahoe Visitors Authority at (800) AT-TAHOE (288-2463).

Getting there and getting around

By air: Reno-Tahoe International Airport has more than 100 nonstop flights a day from various parts of the country. The airport is 55 miles from Heavenly. The Lake Tahoe Airport, near South Lake Tahoe and 10 minutes from Heavenly, has limited service from California. Buses and hotel shuttles take skiers to the resorts from both airports. Tahoe Casino Express (800-446-6128; www.tahoecasinoexpress.com) runs 18 times daily between the Reno airport and South Shore for $17 one way or $30 round-trip.

By boat: The Hornblower Tahoe Queen, an authentic Mississippi sternwheeler, double-decked and heated, takes South Shore skiers and snowboarders across Lake Tahoe to Squaw Valley (buses take skiers from the dock to the ski areas). Call (530) 541-3364. Round-trip fare is about $25. Another paddlewheeler, the M.S. Dixie II, based at Zephyr Cove in Nevada, does daily cruises of Emerald Bay for adults and children, and Saturday night dinner cruises for adults during the winter. For fares and schedules, call (775) 588-6644.

By bus: Shuttles run from almost every major hotel to the resort. Check for schedules when you arrive. Most of the shuttles that cruise around the North or South Shores are free, but when you need to go from one end of the lake to the other, take the Lake Lapper, which runs from 8 a.m. to 11 p.m. and costs about $5. The ski areas or hotels have more information.

By car: Driving time from Reno is about an hour. San Francisco is about four hours away (that's the way Californians describe driving distances), by Hwy. 50 to South Lake Tahoe. Sierra-at-Tahoe is 12 miles west of the lake on Hwy. 50. Kirkwood is on Hwy. 88 (follow signs from South Lake Tahoe). During storms, the California Highway Patrol doesn't let drivers come up the mountains without chains or a 4-wheel-drive vehicle, so be prepared.

Getting around: Bring a car if you intend to move frequently between the south and the north shores; otherwise, a car is optional. We'd say have one if you like to roam far afield at night. If not, you can walk to restaurants and nightspots near your hotel and use the ski shuttles during the day.

Mammoth Mountain

June Mountain

California

Summit elevation:	**11,053 feet**
Vertical drop:	**3,100 feet**
Base elevation:	**7,953 feet**

Address: Mammoth Mountain, Box 24; Mammoth Lakes Visitors Bureau, Box 48; both Mammoth Lakes, CA 93546

✆ **Area code:** 760
Ski area phone: 934-2571
& 800-MAMMOTH (626-6684)
ⓘ **Toll-free snow report/information:** (888) SNOW-RPT (766-9778)
Toll-free reservations: (888) GO-MAMMOTH (466-2666) **and** (888) MAMMOTH (626-6684)
Fax: 934-7066
E-mail: info@mammoth-mtn.com
Internet: www.visitmammoth.com (town); www.mammothmountain.com (ski area)

Dining:★★★
Apres-ski/nightlife:★★★
Other activities:★★★

Expert:★★★★★
Advanced:★★★★★
Intermediate:★★★★★
Beginner:★★★★
Never-ever:★★★★

Number and types of lifts: 30—2 gondolas, 1 six-pax chair. 8 high-speed quads, 1 quad, 8 triples, 6 doubles, 4 surface lifts
Skiable acreage: 3,500+ acres
Snowmaking: 25 percent
Uphill capacity: 56,600 per hour
Snowboarding: Yes, unlimited
Bed base: 30,000
Nearest lodging: slopeside
Resort child care: Yes, newborns and older
Adult ticket, per day: $48.80–$56 (01/02 prices)

June Mountain Facts
Summit elevation: 10,135 feet
Vertical drop: 2,590 feet
Base elevation: 7,545 feet
Number and types of lifts: 7—2 high-speed quads, 5 doubles
Skiable acreage: 500+ acres
Uphill capacity: 10,000 per hour
Bed base: 2,000 local

No mountain is better named than Mammoth. When you stand at the base lodge and scan the mountain, you can't even see a quarter of the ski terrain. The encircling ridge, all above treeline, promises dramatic skiing, but what you can't see is even better. Lower peaks such as Lincoln Mountain, Gold Hill and Hemlock Ridge, all with groomed swaths and moguled canyons, stretch six-and-a-half miles in width. Mammoth is one of the nation's largest winter resorts in size, and at times it's the nation's busiest, with more than 14,000 skiers and riders swooping over its slopes on an average weekend.

Its season runs from early November through June—legitimately. Mammoth often relies on its 430 acres of snowmaking to be open by Thanksgiving, but snow often falls by early November. Skiing and riding here on the Fourth of July is a well-loved tradition among the diehards who haven't had enough.

Mammoth attracts people who want one thing: to ski or snowboard. There isn't much at the top of the mountain road to distract you. There is a labyrinthine base lodge with ski school, lift ticket windows, rental shops and hundreds of lockers for locals and visitors. Across the parking lot is the Yodler chalet, brought piece by piece from the Alps and rebuilt to house a restaurant and bar. Slopeside is the Mammoth Mountain Inn.

At the bottom of the mountain road lies the small but spread-out town of Mammoth Lakes. There is just about all you need for a ski vacation short of luxury hotels—though those are being built. Mammoth is now owned in part by Intrawest, a ski and golf resort company based in Vancouver. Intrawest plans to build a large, slopeside pedestrian village with 1,000 residential units and 140,000 square feet of retail stores over the next 10 years.

Until that village is completed, being a pedestrian at Mammoth will continue to be tough. As the town grew to support the ski area's success, newcomers haphazardly transplanted Southern California sprawl and mini-malls to the mountains. Most visitors come by car from Southern California, but the few who don't will feel the need for wheels—not much is within easy walking distance. However, there is a free town bus that runs day and night.

If size intimidates you, Mammoth's little sister June Mountain, a half-hour drive from Mammoth Lakes, will appeal to you. Its Old World village atmosphere in a sheltered canyon is on a more human scale. That is not to say it's a puny resort: it has seven chair lifts and a 2,590-foot vertical rise (as opposed to 3,100 feet at Mammoth).

 Mountain layout—Skiing

This mountain is very, very large. Almost everything goes by number. The mountain is crisscrossed with a network of chair lifts numbered in the order they were built. It makes perfect sense to visitors who grew up with the mountain, but it's confusing to the first-time visitor who hears regulars planning their day football-quarterback style, "Take one to three, then back side to 23, down the ridge to 14, then to 13 and lateral to 19." Now that the resort has installed several high-speed lifts and given them names, regulars still refer to the lifts by their former number, which makes it even more confusing for the first-time visitor. For the record, Chairs 1, 2, 3, 4, 6, 11, 16 and 18 all have names now, and exist only in the memories and automatic brain-recall of Mammoth regulars.

If you come on a weekend, avoid the Main Lodge at the top of the mountain road (unless you're staying at the slopeside Mammoth Mountain Inn). Tickets are sold (in order as you come up the road) at Juniper Springs area, Canyon Lodge, The Roller Coaster lift, Stump Alley Express and the Main Lodge. Juniper Springs and the Canyon Lodge are actually off the main road to the ski area, so ask someone to direct you. To avoid weekend crowds, take Chairs 9, 25, 22, 21, 12, 13 and 14, listed from left to right on the trail map.

Never-evers should go to Canyon Lodge or Main Lodge. Those with a little experience also can start at Juniper Springs Lodge or the Eagle Express.

◆◆ **Expert:** Expert yaa-hoo skiers will strike out for the ridge, reachable by the gondola or a series of chairs. From the ridge, any chute or path will open into a wide bowl. Mammoth's signature run, a snarling lip of snow called Cornice Bowl, looms large in every expert's memory bank. Other runs dropping from the ridge are considered steeper and more treacherous. Reached from the gondola, Hangman's Hollow—Mammoth's toughest—is an hour-glass-shaped chute hanging from the summit and bordered by wicked rocks. At its narrow part there's space for only one turn—a perfect one. Other expert shots are off Chair 22, and on powder days you can often find untracked or less-tracked snow on the far east Dragon's Back off Chair 9, or the far west Hemlock Ridge above Chair 14.

◆ **Advanced:** One of the most popular advanced areas is the group of bowls available from Face Lift Express (formerly Chair 3). They're great warm-up runs for experts, but plan to get here early on weekends. This high-speed lift has helped lessen the formerly outrageous lines (that's our term; one of our favorite Mammoth employees describes it as "healthy"), but it is still busiest on weekend mornings around 9:30 a.m. Midweek, no problem.

A slightly less busy alternative is triple-Chair 5, the next chair to the left on the trail map, or Chair 14, to the far right on the map. At busy times, Chair 19 does not run. Chairs 22 and 25, which provide access to Lincoln Mountain and its intermediate runs and advanced chutes, rarely have lines.

When you feel like attacking the ridge, head to Dave's Run. Off the gondola, traverse the ridge to trail-map left, then drop down when the pitch isn't sheer vertical. Dave's is still pretty steep, but of the single-black options off the ridge, it's usually the least crowded. If you have any doubts, ride the gondola back down to Mid-Chalet, or take the upper-intermediate ridge trail to the Chair 14 area.

■ **Intermediate:** The middle part of the mountain is still above treeline, so those at this level have plenty of room to traverse on the single-black runs. Hidden canyons like Lower Dry Creek (off the Face Lift Express) are full of swoops and surprises, and require tighter turns. For long cruising, head to Eagle Express. Other intermediate playgrounds are served by the tree-lined runs from The Roller Coaster and Canyon express quads and Chairs 8, 20 and 21. At the other edge of the area is Chair 12 and the drop over to Chairs 13 and 14.

●● **Beginner:** If you aren't a first-timer, but still practicing turns, the runs near Canyon Lodge are best. Trails such as Hansel and Gretel weave gently through evergreens, providing sheltered slopes for learning, away from the speed demons. When you're ready for the next step, Christmas Tree, a long run under Eagle Express, is pretty gentle. This part of the mountain gets soupy in the afternoon on warm days, however. If you're intimidated by crowds, and you're trying to step up to the intermediate level, avoid Stump Alley and Broadway, both usually packed with speeders.

● **Never-ever:** The never-ever slopes are off the Discovery Chair at the Main Lodge and Chair 7 from the Canyon Lodge, separated from the hot shots.

June Mountain: June Mountain has none of the high broad bowls that make Mammoth Mountain famous. The steepest terrain at June, The Face, is as steep as anything at Mammoth. Because it is on the lower mountain, it unfortunately doesn't keep the snow as long as the upper runs. Since June is more sheltered than Mammoth and none of its slopes is above the tree line, June tends to hold powder longer than Mammoth's more exposed bowls and the snow doesn't crust up so quickly. There's a great view of June Lake from the upper runs.

Though June has a few expert drops, this level will be bored quickly. Intermediates will have a ball, however. Schatzi is a fantastic and long cruiser, and Matterhorn often is totally deserted. Beginners should stick to the mid-mountain, though Silverado is a gentle, long and uncrowded trail from the Rainbow Summit.

 ## Mountain layout—Snowboarding

So you're a leap-of-faith kind of rider? The plunge off the summit ridge offers a slew of descents with one thing in common: All are so sickeningly steep you can easily reach out and touch the snow while turning. Want to test Newton's theory of gravity? Drop into the steeps of Climax, pop the cornice into Dave's Run, dance between the rocks in The Wipeout Chutes or huck into Hangman's Hollow. If you really want to shake up your innards, dart through the rocks at the top of Phillipe's and straight-shoot it all the way to the bottom.

Mammoth is one of the carving capitals of the West. St. Anton, Stump Alley and Gremlin's Gulch are just three of the carving runs to hit. Make sure to get up early if you expect freshies or perfect corduroy. For long mellow cruisers with a view, explore the backside off the Face Lift Express, wander through Dry Creek's canyon and gullies, or ride Ricochet's open glades.

Main Park is arguably one of the best freestyle areas in North America. There's big air to be had off a slew of spines, gaps and tabletops. You'll find a superpipe and a halfpipe here too. Mammoth has two other parks: South Park, on Roller Coaster West, is geared for intermediates, and Canyon Lodge Park has a beginner pipe and smaller-scaled terrain features. No wonder riders are raving about this place! June Mountain also has a halfpipe and a snowboard park with jumps, a quarterpipe and tabletops.

Mountain rating

No matter what level you're at, you won't be shortchanged. First-time visitors should pack a trail map. (Seriously. One of our staff writers has skied here for two decades, but she still carries a trail map—and occasionally uses it.) If you're with a group, decide where to meet if you get separated. We usually pick a centrally located chair, rather than Mid-Chalet or the Main Lodge, which are usually loaded with bodies looking for other bodies. We just stay on the runs under that chair and watch from the lift until we all hook up.

June doesn't have Mammoth's range of terrain, but most skiers and boarders will enjoy it. The pace at June is slower and the crowds considerably fewer. It is a very good choice for midwinter Saturdays and holiday periods, as well as for families with young children who ski faster than their parents (it's difficult to get lost at June, but very easy at Mammoth).

Cross-country and snowshoeing

Twenty-five miles of groomed trails, actually summer roads, wind around four of the dozen or more high Alpine lakes for which the town of Mammoth Lakes is named. **Tamarack Lodge** (934-2442; 800-237-6879), a 75-year-old summer hunting and fishing lodge now owned by Mammoth Mountain, maintains these trails and charges $15 for access ($10 for those ages 11–17 and seniors; free younger than 11). The Lakes Basin includes many trail heads into the backcountry, where no fee is charged. Rentals and lessons are available. On weekends it's advisable to reserve.

Lessons (2000/01 prices)

Programs are the same at Mammoth or June unless otherwise noted. At Mammoth, lessons are available at both the Main Lodge and the Canyon Lodge. For reservations or questions call 934-0685 for the Main Lodge, 934-0787 for The Canyon Lodge. For June Mountain Ski School call 648-7733.

Group lessons: A three-hour lesson is $48 per person.

Never-ever package: Rentals, lift ticket and three hours of lessons are $74 for skiers and snowboarders.

Private lessons: For adults or children, $100 for one hour for one to five people; $10 for a sixth person. Discounts are offered early in the morning, but a 2 p.m. private costs $130.

Special programs: There are many, including three-day camps for various groups and skills that cost $220–$245. Call the ski school for dates.

Racing: Mammoth has a well-established racing heritage. It has hosted World Cup races, and several U.S. Ski Team coaches and executives call this resort home. Self-timed courses at Mammoth or June cost $1 per run. Racing clinics are available.

Child care (2000/01 prices)

Ages: Newborn to 12 years.

Costs: Care for newborn to 12-year-old children is $60 per day. Fees include snacks and lunch, except for infants.

Reservations: Strongly advised, six to eight weeks ahead. Day care is located at both The Small World Day Care Center at Mammoth Mountain Inn (934-0646), just across the street from the Main Lodge, and the child care center at June Mountain (648-7609).

Day care can be combined with ski and snowboard school for ages 4–12. They get supervised activities from 8 a.m. to 5 p.m., including a lesson from 10 a.m. until noon. Rate is $121, including lunch, lessons, day care and equipment rental. Mammoth has helmet rentals for the kids ($5), and pager rentals for the adults ($2).

Children's lessons: The Woollywood Ski School teaches kids 4–14. Full-day packages (lessons, lunch, rentals, lift ticket) for skiing or snowboarding (minimum age for the latter is 7) are $85 per child, if the child is aged 4–6 or is an older beginner. Full-day packages for children 7–12 who are not beginners cost $121. Lessons alone cost $35 for two hours, $48 for three hours, and supervised lunch and afternoon add-ons are also available.

Lift tickets (2001/02 prices)

	Adult (19+)	Child (7-12)
One day	$56	$28
Three days	$152 ($50+/day)	$76 ($25+/day)
Five days	$244 ($48+/day)	$122 ($24+/day)

Who skis free: Children ages 6 and younger ski free, as do never-evers taking a ski school lesson.

Who skis at a discount: Ages 65 and older ski for child prices. Ages 13–18 pay $42 for the day, $114 for three days; $183 for five days. A beginner lift ticket costs $25 and is valid on Chair 7 and the Discovery Chair.

Lift tickets may be used at either Mammoth or June; however, a June-only ticket (not valid at Mammoth) costs $40 for adults, $30 for ages 13–18, $20 for kids.

Ticket offices at Mammoth are at the Main Lodge, the Canyon Lodge and Juniper Springs areas. Additional satellite offices at two lifts—The Roller Coaster and Stump Alley Express—are open weekends and holidays.

Note: The multiday rates listed here are non-holiday. During holidays, regular per-day rates apply, though you still can buy a multiday ticket.

Accommodations

Mammoth Mountain Inn (934-2581; 800-MAMMOTH; $$–$$$$) is the most convenient. The inn includes a restaurant, two small sundries stores, and the resort's child-care facility. Lodging is deluxe to moderate and includes hotel rooms and condos. The better rooms are in the main building.

We list just a few of the places to stay. As a starting point, call **Mammoth Lakes Visitors Bureau** (888-466-2666) for a reservation referral. Generally, condos start at about $100 per night, while hotel accommodations—we use the term loosely, as Mammoth currently has more motels than true hotels—can be found for less than $80 per night. Sunday through Thursday stays are quite a bit cheaper than Friday and Saturday.

Mammoth Lakes has been called Condo City of the Sierras. Just beyond the central part of town, **Snowcreek** (934-3333; 800-544-6007; $$–$$$$) is huge and wooded with an athletic club that includes racquetball and basketball. It's actually a neighborhood. Units are spacious one-, two- and three-bedroom loft style.

Closer to the slopes, next to The Canyon Lodge, are many large condominium complexes with a range of units. Try **Mountainback** (934-5000; 800-468-6225) or **1849 Condominiums** (934-7525; 800-421-1849; $$$–$$$$).

In the middle of town, only a walk to restaurants and a shuttle to the lifts, you'll find **Sierra Nevada Rodeway Inn** (934-2515; 800-824-5132; $–$$$) has hotel rooms and chalet units. Check out **Alpenhof Lodge** (934-6330; $–$$$) and the **Snow Goose Inn** (934-2660; 800-874-7368; $–$$$), one of a few bed-and-breakfast inns in town, decorated with antiques, with breakfast served communally in a friendly atmosphere.

Mammoth has several inexpensive motels that offer rooms at $50 to $100 per night, including **Mammoth Thriftlodge** (934-2416; 800-525-9055), **Econo Lodge/Wildwood Inn** (934-6855; 845-8764) and **Swiss Chalet** (934-2403; 800-937-9477; $–$$). **Ullr Lodge** (934-2454; $) has rooms with private baths, rooms that share baths and dorm bunks.

June Mountain: The newest lodging in June Lake (the town where June Mountain is located) is among the nicest we've seen in this region. **Double Eagle Resort & Spa** (648-7004; $$$) has several two-bedroom cabins (all No Smoking), plus an on-site restaurant called Eagle's Landing that serves delicious meals and has a magnificent views.

June has two large condo complexes, with prices starting at less than $100 midweek and $135–$150 weekends. **Interlaken** has studios to three-bedroom units. **Edgewater** has only one size unit, suitable for six to nine people.Other lodgings at June are small and quaint, even funky. **The Haven** studios are about $70. Call **June Lake Properties Reservation** at (800) 648-5863 (648-JUNE) or **Century 21 Rainbow Ridge** at (800) 462-5589 for reservations.

Also try **Fern Creek Lodge** (800-621-9146; $–$$$), **Whispering Pines** (800-648-7762; $–$$), or **Boulder Lodge** (970-648-7533; $–$$).

Dining

Mammoth Lakes has scores of dining options, from gourmet French cuisine to deli sandwiches and quick takeout. The best gourmet food in town, according to locals, is at **Skadi** (934-3902; $$), with a romantic atmosphere. Another excellent choice for fine dining is **Cervino's** (934-4734; $$), with two recent *Wine Spectator* magazine Awards of Excellence on the wall and a menu that leans toward Northern Italian cuisine.

For the most romantic (and expensive) dining, head out to **Lakefront Restaurant at Tamarack Lodge** (934-3534; $$$) where the menu is basic but the presentation excellent. The atmosphere is Old World in a small dining room decorated with photos of movie stars who used to hang out here. Another top choice, with one of the best wine lists in town, is **The Restaurant at Convict Lake** (934-3803; $$$), four miles south of Mammoth Lakes on Hwy. 395. Look for the Convict Lake turnoff just south of the airport. The Restaurant at Convict Lake is under the same ownership as Cervino's, and it, too, has received two *Wine Spectator* Awards of Excellence.

Nevados (934-4466; $$) has been one of Mammoth's top restaurants for more than 20 years. For steaks, prime rib and seafood, head to **Whiskey Creek** (934-2555; $$), **The Mogul Restaurant** (934-3039; $$) or the **Chart House** (934-4526; $$). Although Mogul has built its long-time reputation as the best traditional family Mammoth steak house, our visit last season gave best marks to the expanded offerings of grilled seafood appetizers and entrees. Your friendly server doubles as your chef. The Mogul also has a children's menu. **Ocean Harvest** (934-8539; $$) is the prime seafood restaurant, offering fresh fish caught by the owner.

Families (or anyone with limited funds) will want to stop in at **Berger's** (934-6622; $-$$) for big, big portions. The tuna salad is massive and you can have not only burgers, but also chicken, salad or Canadian stew. Another family spot is **Angel's** (934-7427; $$) with great ribs, beans and barbecue.

Locals consider **Nik-N-Willie's Pizza** (934-2012; $) the best in town. Pizzas also are featured at **Giovanni's** (934-7563; $) or **Perry's Italian Cafe** (934-6521; $). The best Mexican food is at **Roberto's** (934-3667; $) with homemade tortillas and authentic big servings. Other Mexican-food choices are **La Sierra's** (934-8083; $-$$), **Gringo's** (934-8595; $-$$) with its "almost world famous Rotisserie Chicken," or **Gomez's** (924-2693; $).

Grumpy's (934-8587; $) holds the distinction of the town's best fried chicken, also the best cole slaw, all presented in a big-screen TV, No Smoking, sports-bar atmosphere.

Shogun (934-3970; $) has Japanese cuisine and a sushi bar. Try **Matsu** (934-8277; $) for inexpensive Chinese-American. **Austria Hof** (934-2764; $$) and **Alpenrose** (934-3077; $$) serve German and Austrian specialties.

The best breakfast in town is served at **Good Life Cafe** (934-1734; $), which has a very diverse early-morning menu, and also offers lunch-type meals. Locals also recommend **The Stove** (934-2821; $), with biscuits 3 or 4 inches high. Another restaurant with hearty breakfasts is **The Breakfast Club** (934-6944; $) at the intersection of Old Mammoth Road and Highway 203. Coffee lovers, your choices are **Looney Bean** (934-1345; $) on Main Street next to the Chevron station or **World Cup Coffee** (924-3629; $) on Old Mammoth Road across from the movie theater. Both have in-house bakers for rolls and muffins. For very good baked goodies and good gourmet coffee, try **Paul Schat's Bakery and Cafe** (934-6055; $) on Main Street, which serves breakfast on weekends; fresh-baked goodies daily.

For lunch or evening dining at the mountain, the best bet is the **Mountainside Grill** (934-0601) in the Mammoth Mountain Inn. Or head over to the more crowded **Yodler** (934-0636). Other on-mountain lunch best bets are the **Mill Cafe** at the base of Stump Alley Express and the **Canyon Lodge**. The Main Lodge has rather so-so cafeteria food.

In June Lake, the best dining is at the **Eagle's Landing Restaurant** (648-7897; $$) at the Double Eagle Resort and Spa. Other choices are **Fern Creek Grill** (648-7897) for breakfast, burgers, steaks and chicken; or The **Sierra Inn Restaurant** (648-7774) which has a slightly more upscale menu. The best dining is still in Mammoth Lakes.

Après-ski/nightlife

Après-ski gets under way at the **Yodler,** across the parking lot, or in the **Thunder Mountain Bar** in the Main Lodge, decorated with photos of early Mammoth days. At the Canyon Lodge base area, try **Grizzly's**. **Slocum's** in town is the après-ski hangout for ski patrol and instructors. At **Austria Hof**, there's usually live entertainment after the lifts close. Entertainment is also at the **Ocean Club** and Mammoth Mountain Inn's **Dry Creek Bar**.

Mammoth's longtime meet market (you may meet someone whose parents used to party hardy here in their younger days) is **Whiskey Creek,** which serves six microbrews. A much newer and hipper spot is the **High Sierra Rock 'N' Blues** on Old Mammoth Road.

There's plenty of nighttime hoopla at **Grumpy's**. Featured are five giant-screen TVs, pool, foosball, inexpensive chili and burgers. Visiting Brits like this place, and also hang out at the **Clock Tower Cellar** at the Alpenhof Lodge.

Dining: $$$-Entrees $20+; $$-$10-20; $-less than $10.

Accommodations: (double room) $$$$-$200+; $$$-$141-$200; $$-$81-$140; $-$80 and less.

Other activities

Snowmobiles can be rented from Mammoth Adventures (934-9645), DJs Snowmobile Adventures (935-4480; www.snowmobilemammoth.com); or Center Street Polaris (934-6888). The area has about 300 miles of snowmobile trails, some signed and groomed, others not. **Bobsledding or tubing** down a designated track is available through Sledz (934-7533). **Dogsled rides** are offered by Dog Sled Adventures (934-6270).

Hot-air balloon trips with High Sierra Ballooning Company (934-7188) take off from Mammoth Meadow. **Snowcreek Athletic Club** (934-8511) has a variety of indoor and outdoor facilities. **The Monkey Bar** (934-2776) offers an indoor climbing wall and **Golf 'n' Games** (924-1082) has indoor miniature golf and an arcade for kids of all ages.

Mammoth's **shopping** is oriented as much for the local population as for tourists. You won't find many trendy boutiques here, though there is a factory outlet center on Main Street, and many small shopping malls scattered throughout town. Mammoth Lakes also has two **movie theaters** (one with two screens), Minaret Cinemas and Plaza Theater (both at 934-3131). The Mammoth Times, the local weekly newspaper, is a good source for special events listings.

Getting there and getting around

By air: The nearest major airport is Reno, 165 miles away. Rent a car for the drive south, because ground transportation is spotty, and you probably will want a car in Mammoth. Mammoth's air service information changes frequently, so for the latest news, call the Mammoth Lakes Airport (760-934-3825), Mammoth Lakes Visitors Bureau, (888) 466-2666 or consult the MLVB Web site (www.visitmammoth.com).

By car: Mammoth is 325 miles north of Los Angeles on Hwy. 395, and 165 miles south of Reno on the same road. June Mountain is 20 miles north of Mammoth Lakes off Hwy. 395.

Getting around: The resort operates a free shuttle that runs throughout the town and to Mammoth's Main Lodge (four miles out) and to the Canyon Lodge and Juniper Springs. A nightly shuttle makes loops around town until midnight during the week, 1 a.m. on Friday and Saturday nights, or call Mammoth Shuttle (934-3030) or Sierra Express (924-TAXI; 924-8294). Most visitors have a car.

California regional resorts

Bear Valley, Bear Valley, CA; (209) 753-2301

Internet: www.bearvalley.com

11 lifts; 1,280 skiable acres; 1,900 vertical feet

Bear Valley is one of those word-of-mouth ski areas beloved by those who know it's at the winter terminus of Highway 4. This area has many things to like: 450 inches of snow annually; a town just big enough to provide lodging, food and alternate activities (cross-country skiing, ice skating and most snow sports); and an enticing advanced and expert area called Grizzly Bowl that makes up about 30 percent of the terrain. The Grizz is below the base area, and that's its drawback. With no snowmaking coverage and an elevation of 6,600–7,750 feet, Grizzly Bowl isn't always open. However, the upper mountain is covered by snowmaking and has a few black-diamond runs amid its great beginner and intermediate terrain. A good area for families, Bear Valley has child care starting at age 2 on weekends and holidays. It also sells an "Interchangeable Parent Ticket" for $40 that may be used by two parents who are taking turns caring for an infant.

Lift tickets (00/01 prices): Adults, $38; Young adult (13-23), $31; Children (7-12), $13; Seniors (65+) and children younger than 7, free.

Distance from San Francisco: About 190 miles east on I-580 and I-205, north on I-99, then east on Hwy. 4. Bear Valley is on the west slope of the Sierra Nevada and not accessible from Tahoe or Mammoth.

Lodging information: On the Web site, or press 5 after calling the recorded information line to get phone numbers for various hotels and condos. Two recommendations: The Lodge at Bear Valley (800-794-3866) is three miles from the slopes (as close as you can get) and smack in the center of the little town. About 25 miles down Hwy. 4 is The Dorrington Hotel & Restaurant (888-874-2164; 209-795-2164), a charming shared-bath B&B in a historic house. The restaurant is worth a stop.

Badger Pass, Yosemite National Park, CA; (209) 372-1000

Internet: www.yosemitepark.com/activities/badger/

5 lifts; 9 trails; 700 vertical feet

This is a tiny, 65-year-old ski area best suited for beginners, patient intermediates and families with young children. Though Badger Pass is charming (and the employees are wonderful), what makes it a great winter weekend destination is not the downhill skiing. It's special because it's inside Yosemite National Park. The park's legendary crowds disappear in the winter, so you'll share the majesty of the Yosemite Valley with a comfortable number of humans. Activities include ranger-naturalist snowshoe walks, ice skating, sightseeing tours and lots more.

Yosemite has a renowned cross-country ski center headquartered at Badger Pass with lessons, 40 km. of machine-groomed track and another 150 km. of marked trails, including a 17-km. skating lane on the rim of the Yosemite Valley to Glacier Point.

Lift tickets: Adults, $28 ($22 midweek); Children (12 and younger), $13.

Distance from San Francisco: About 230 miles east on I-580, I-205 and Hwy. 120.
Distance from Los Angeles: About 290 miles north on I-5 and I-99, then east on Hwy. 41.
Note: Hwy. 120 between Yosemite and Lee Vining is closed in winter, making Badger Pass inaccessible from Mammoth.
Lodging information: (209) 252-4848.

Snow Summit, Big Bear Lake, CA; (909) 866-5766
Internet: www.snowsummit.com
12 lifts; 230 skiable acres; 1,200 vertical feet
Big Bear Mountain, Big Bear Lake, CA; (909) 585-2519
Internet: www.bearmtn.com
12 lifts; 195 skiable acres; 1,665 vertical feet

Southern Californians just don't know how good they have it. On a sunny winter day, it is entirely possible to spend the morning skiing at Big Bear (as the locals call it) and the afternoon playing a round of golf in Palm Springs or surfing in the Pacific Ocean. These neighboring ski areas, in the mountain town of Big Bear Lake, are less than a two-hour drive from the fabled desert resort in one direction and the beach in the other.

The Big Bear areas, though at an altitude of between 7,000 and 8,800 feet, rely heavily on snowmaking to cover the runs. Both are snowmaking experts and have a reliable water supply from Big Bear Lake. Even if the season has been dry, you'll find surprisingly good snow on the runs. And if the winter has been a wet one, the conditions can be quite good.

The terrain is largely intermediate-level, with a couple of runs at each that qualify as advanced, not expert. Snowboarding is hugely popular here, with boarders constituting nearly half of the business. The town has many lodging and restaurant options and a charming, walkable downtown.

Neither area has child care; lessons start at age 4. Big Bear Mountain is one of many ski areas owned nationwide by Booth Creek.
Lift tickets (00/01 prices): Snow Summit: Adults, $38; Children (7-12), $10. Big Bear Mountain: Adults, $30; Children, $10. Note: Both resorts charge $45 for adults during Christmas, Martin Luther King and President's holidays; call for specific dates. Children's tickets during holidays are $20 at Snow Summit and $10 at Big Bear Mountain. Bear also gives a break to ages 13-22 during holidays with a $35 ticket.
Distance from Los Angeles: About 110 miles east on I-10, I-215, Hwy. 30, Hwy. 330 and Hwy. 18.
Distance from Ontario (nearest commercial airport): About 60 miles by I-10, I-215, Hwy. 30, Hwy. 330 and Hwy. 18.
Lodging information: Big Bear Lake Resort Association's Lodging Referral Service, (909) 866-7000.

Alyeska

Alaska

Summit elevation (lift-served):	**2,750 feet**
Vertical drop:	**2,500 feet**
Base elevation:	**250 feet**

Address: P.O. Box 249
Girdwood, AK 99587
✆ **Area code:** 907
Ski area phone: 754-1111 or (800) 775-6656
Snow report: 754-7669 (SKI-SNOW)
ⓘ **Toll-free reservations:** (800) 880-3880
Fax: 754-2200
E-mail: info@alyeskaresort.com
Internet: www.alyeskaresort.com

Expert:★★★
Advanced:★★
Intermediate:★★★★
Beginner:★★★★
Never-ever:★★★

Number and types of lifts: 9–1 60-passenger tram, 1 high-speed quad, 2 quads, 3 doubles, 2 surface lifts
Skiable acreage: 1,000 acres
Snowmaking: 42 percent
Uphill capacity: 10,355 per hour
Snowboarding: Yes
Bed Base: 533
Nearest lodging: slopeside, hotel
Resort child care: Babysitting services
Adult ticket, per day: $34-$45 (01/02)

Dining:★★★★
Apres-ski/nightlife:★★
Other activities:★★★

It's easy to miss the turn off Seward Highway to Alyeska. Chances are you'll be mesmerized by the jaw-dropping views over fjord-like Turnagain Arm, a tidal basin where the mountains literally plunge to the sea. What makes it even more unusual is that at this low elevation, the summits and often much more of these mountains are above treeline. If you cast your eyes eastward at just the right moment, you can detect a lift on Alyeska, looking like a neat surgical scar on the treeless peak. From the mountain, the view is even more spectacular, perhaps even hazardous.

With a location just 40 miles southeast of Anchorage, Alyeska offers convenient, big-mountain skiing without the threat of altitude sickness. A 60-passenger tram and the high-speed quad that services the summit mean lift lines are short on weekends, nonexistent midweek. At a time when fluky weather is wreaking havoc at snowsports areas in the Lower 48, Alyeska gladly suffers an embarrassment of riches: It averages more than 700 inches of snow each season, and had a high of 1,116 inches a couple years back.

The riches extend to the resort itself, where the Alyeska Prince Hotel provides luxurious accommodations at the tram base. The tram zips up 2,028 feet of Alyeska's 2,500 foot rise in just three-and-a-half minutes, rising over the forested lower half to the glaciers and open bowls near the summit and providing a birds-eye view of the mountain's two faces, the original main face and the newer North Face.

Contrary to popular opinion, the weather in this part of Alaska is quite tolerable in winter, with temperatures an average of 10 to 30 degrees Fahrenheit. What can make it seem colder here is the darkness that prevails during the heart of winter. By mid-February, however, Alyeska boasts more daylight hours than any other ski area in North America. And here's a real bonus for late-night revelers: Lifts don't even open until 10:30 a.m., meaning you can sleep in, have breakfast *and* get first tracks. Normal closing time is 5:30 p.m., but on Friday and Saturday from mid-December until mid-March, the lifts stay open to 9:30 p.m.

When Alyeska's skies are clear, the skiing is great. But the slopes sometimes are blanketed with severe whiteout or flat light conditions (we've checked with several ski journalists on this, and every one said this happened during part of their visit). Such conditions can be unnerving, especially above treeline, and can cause vertigo in susceptible skiers. Locals advise skiing at night (or late in the day) when visibility is better.

One of Alyeska's big pluses is its proximity to Anchorage, a bustling city with plenty to keep residents entertained through the long winter nights. Alaskans are particularly good at winter celebrations. We recommend visiting in late February during Fur Rendezvous, Anchorage's winter festival (see Other Activities), or early March, to coincide with the Anchorage start of The Iditarod dogsled race. By that time of year, the temperatures start to rise (average high is 30 degrees Fahrenheit; -1 degrees Centigrade) and daylight hours increase (almost 13 hours).

Alaska is one of the most spectacularly beautiful spots on Earth, winter or summer. The incentives for a winter visit are it's low season, so the price is right; crowds are light; and you can ski. Just keep in mind that Anchorage and Alyeska are one time zone beyond the West Coast of the United States. So if it's 9 a.m. in Los Angeles and noon in New York City, it's 8 a.m. at Alyeska.

Mountain layout—Skiing

uu **Expert u Advanced:** The high-speed quad Spirit of Alyeska carries skiers 1,411 vertical feet to the top of the lift-serviced terrain, which is at the base of the Alyeska Glacier. Up here it's wide-open, above-treeline skiing. The entire 2,500 feet of vertical is skiable in one continuous run, with intermediate to super-expert pitch depending on your choice of route.

You also can hike to the 3,939-foot summit of Mt. Alyeska, where expert-level Glacier Bowl and the Headwall await.

From the quad, experts can go right and drop down Gail's Gully or Prospector and take a gully left or right of Eagle Rock, then back to the quad. Experts willing to work can take the High Traverse from the quad, arcing through The Shadows between Mt. Alyeska and Max's Mountain, and dropping down through new snow and open steeps; or continue over the ridge to find good steeps and a short section of gladed skiing on Max's Mountain (when opened by the ski patrol).

The lower half of the steep North Face makes it possible to ski double-black terrain from the upper to the lower tram terminal. You can scout out this gnarly area while you ride up the tram. The upper part (called Tram Pocket) is above treeline; the lower part is heavily forested with two trails—Jim's Branch and Last Chance. Descend Tram Pocket, then cut over to the rest of Alyeska's runs to avoid the gladed area below. The North Face is open when conditions permit.

■ **Intermediate:** Alyeska also has an unusual combination of open bowl skiing and trails through the trees directly under Chairs 1 and 4. Intermediates can take the new quad chair, drop into the bowl and ski whatever they can see. It doesn't take much judgment to figure out whether you are getting in over your head, and this bowl gives you plenty of room to traverse out of trouble. The bowl funnels into Waterfall and ends on Cabbage Patch before reaching the base area.

For intermediates taking the Spirit quad chair to the top of the resort, swing left when you get off the chair and follow the Mighty Mite. This takes you past the Glacier Express restaurant in the Glacier Tram Terminal, and back to the quad by three intermediate routes, or tip down South Face (very steep and ungroomed).

●● **Beginner:** Beginners should stick to the area served by Chairs 3 and 7. The area is pretty big, but unfortunately used by everyone on their way home.

● **Never-ever:** Don't make the long trip to Alyeska solely to learn to ski. Not a huge amount of easy terrain, plus the flat light problem, could put a serious crimp in those plans. If "the Alaska experience" (scenery, dogsledding in Iditarod country, being able to brag you "survived" Alaska in winter) is your main goal, then definitely make the trip. You can find some great things to do off the slopes while everyone else skis.

 ## Mountain layout—Snowboarding

Alyeska's machine-built terrain park below Eagle Rock has several table-tops, rails and quarterpipes. It's the best bet on icy days. Throughout the season, the resort builds one or two halfpipes near the top of Chair 4 that are well maintained with a halfpipe groomer. Better yet, because of Mt. Alyeska's natural topography—with its steep vertical and rocky slopes—the entire mountain becomes a natural terrain park under a blanket of snow.

Cat trails cut across several sections of the upper part of the mountain, creating a series of awesome cat-track jumps. You can catch great air coming off the cat track just above Gun Mount 2. Jumps in "The Fridays" on North Face are a snowboarder's dream, as are hits on Half Moon and Horseshoe off the Silvertip Run. Many aren't on the trail map, so ask the locals and they'll gladly share some secret spots. Heading down the mountain is Lolo's Leap, with 10- to 30-foot drops into the trees.

Two spots to keep speed up or you'll be walking: Going into Ego Flats in the bowl area and on the Prince Run heading back to the tram base and the Alyeska Prince Hotel. In spring, wait until after noontime for the snow to soften for the best riding. The best-kept local's secret at Alyeska is anytime it's raining on the bottom, you can count on it dumping lots of fresh pow up top!

Mountain rating

Intermediates will have a field day, especially with the wide-open bowls and spectacular views from the top of the Spirit quad. Experts have some good drops but the real challenge of Alyeska is the tremendous variety of terrain and snow conditions from top to bottom. Snow may be groomed, cut up or untouched. Sometimes it's powder at the top, moistening to mashed potatoes at the bottom.

 ## Cross-country and snowshoeing

The 10-km. **Winner Creek trail** leaves from Alyeska's base and wanders through woods, across meadows and up and down gentle hills. The trail is not groomed, and locals recommend it for snowshoeing. Groomed and tracked trails are in the nearby **Moose Meadow** area—locals will point you there. It's groomed and tracked. Rental equipment is available at the Alyeska Prince Hotel's rental shop. In spring, you need to wait late enough into the morning for the ice cover to melt. Lessons are $40 an hour, $20 for extra students. Since they're not regularly scheduled, make advance reservations with the ski school by calling 754-2280.

If you are a serious cross-country enthusiast, Anchorage is the place to go. About 115 km. of groomed cross-country trails are in **Kincaid, Russian Jack** and **Far North Bicentennial parks.** Kincaid Park is the best developed, with more than 1,500 acres covered by trails for all abilities. The Nordic Skiing Association of Anchorage (561-0949; grooming report, 248-6667) maintains the trails, all supported by donations and volunteer labor (Hint: If you use the trails, please make a donation.). NSAA puts out a great map of the trails, printed on a water-resistant paper.

Lessons (2001/02 prices)

Group lessons: Alyeska packages its ski and snowboard lessons, a real benefit for those traveling from the Lower 48. For example, adult intermediate and advanced skiers can get a lesson, lift ticket and rentals for $60, or the lesson alone for $33. (The snowboard price is $63 for the package, $33 just for the lesson.)

Never-ever package: Never-evers pay $50 for a ski ticket-lesson-rental package, snowboard novices pay $55; for the lesson alone for both groups, it's $30. If you're not ready to ride Chairs 3 or 7 at the end of the lesson, the afternoon lesson is free.

Private lessons: Skiing, telemarking or snowboarding cost $50 an hour, $30 for extra students. Telemarking lessons are not regularly scheduled, so make advance reservations with the ski school, 754-2280. If you're enrolled in a private lesson, ask about discounted lift and rental prices.

Special programs: The Challenge Alaska Adaptive Ski School, a chapter of Disabled Sports USA, provides skiing for the disabled: all disabilities, all ages, by reservation only. A skier with a disability, and buddy, may buy discount lift tickets and rent adaptive ski equipment. Open daily, usually December 15 to April 15. The Alyeska Price Hotel and Tramway are fully wheelchair-accessible, and Challenge Alaska has material on other wheelchair-accessible accommodations and amenities. Challenge Alaska, Box 110065, Anchorage, AK 99511-0065; 563-2658; fax 561-6142.

Racing: A $1-per-run race course is open on selected dates.

Child care (2001/02 prices)

Ages: 6 months to 10 years.

Costs: For Little Bear's Playhouse: $35 full day, or $5 an hour, for all ages. For Alyeska Prince Hotel babysitting: $5 one-time fee, plus $8 an hour for one child; $10 an hour for two children; $12 an hour for three children.

Reservations: For Little Bear's, it's a good idea; call 783-2116 or ask when you reserve lodging. Little Bear's Playhouse, Inc. is a licensed child-care facility in Girdwood, the town where Alyeska is located. Girdwood's public transportation is virtually nonexistent. You may need to transport your child to and from the center; ask about that when you call. Little Bear's is open 7 a.m. to 6 p.m. weekdays, 10 a.m. to 6 p.m. on Saturdays, from Dec. 22, 2001 through April 20, 2002 (closed on Sundays). Babysitting service may be available by appointment, three days in advance, through the Alyeska Prince Hotel's guest service desk; call 800-880-3880 or 754-1111.

Children's lessons: Cubs and Super-Cubs caters to ages 3–4 learning to ski; Mini-Riders is for ages 5–7 learning to snowboard. Prices are $30 for skiing and $35 for snowboarding, includes lift ticket, one-hour lesson and rental; available only on weekends and Anchorage School District holidays. First Tracks is offered for ages 5–13 for skiing and 8-13 for snowboarding, offered daily and during Anchorage School District holidays. A two-hour lesson, all-day lift ticket and rental package ranges from $40–$45, depending on ability level; add $5 for snowboarding. If you don't need rentals, ask about discounted pricing. The children's programs are popular—try to make reservations (754-2280).

 ## Lift tickets (2001/02 prices)

	Adult	Child (8-13)	Senior (60-69)
One day	$45	$20	
Three days*	$102 ($34/day)	$52 ($17+/day)	

Who skis free: Children 7 and younger when skiing with a ticketed adult.

Who skis at a discount: Ages 70 and older ski for $7. Students (14–17) with ID pay $27 for day tickets. Beginner lift tickets (Chairs 3 and 7) cost $18. Adult guests of the Alyeska Prince Hotel pay $35 per day for all lifts and all hours. A family of four skis for $104 per day.

Note: Keep in mind that Alaskan winter days are shorter than they are farther south. The lifts don't start running until 10:30 a.m., but the "ski day" ends at 5:30 p.m. (Daylight lingers for about 90 minutes after the sun sets in early February, and you can see very well.) Night skiing on 27 trails covering 2,000 vertical feet runs Fridays and Saturdays 4:30–9:30 p.m. mid-December through mid-March: Adults $19, children and seniors $13. Late-night skiing (8-9:30 p.m.) is $10 and day tickets can be extended to 9:30 p.m. for just $10.

*The best deal on multiday tickets comes with lodging-lift packages.

 ## Accommodations

Because Alaska is quite a distance for most of *Ski America & Canada*'s readers, air-lodging-lift packages are a good idea. **Daman-Nelson Travel** has a great deal from the West Coast with round-trip air on Alaska Airlines, four nights at the Alyeska Prince Hotel, transfers and a three-day activity card good for lift tickets, cross-country ski rentals or snowshoe rentals. The 2001/02 per-person cost is $799 from California; about $100 less from the Pacific Northwest. Restrictions apply; call Daman-Nelson at (800) 343-2626 for details, or look at its Web site at www.d-n-travel.com.

The **Alyeska Prince Hotel** (800-880-3880, 754-1111; $$$–$$$$) is a self-contained resort. Packages are the way to go, and package rates begin at $199 per room per night, single or double occupancy. This package includes lodging, breakfast for two and two adult all-day lift tickets. That's an excellent deal for a hotel that has a $1,200-per-night Royal Suite. There is no charge for up to two children under age 18 who are staying in the same room in existing bedding with a maximum of two adults. The hotel is a Prince hotel, but its architecture is faintly reminiscent of the grand Fairmont hotels, such as the Fairmont Banff Springs Hotel and Fairmont Chateau Lake Louise. Though the hotel has 307 spacious rooms, several restaurants, shops and other guest facilities, it has a very intimate feel. The Alyeska Tramway is right outside the door, or you can ride Chair 7 to the lower-elevation terrain at the ski area's base.

Other than the hotel, lodging is in condos or bed-and-breakfast inns. The **Winner Creek Bed & Breakfast** (783-5501; $–$$) is a new log lodge owned by 30-year Alaska residents Victor and Kim Duncan. It's within walking distance of Alyeska. **Alyeska Accommodations** (783-2000) is a place to start, or you can get a list of B&Bs on the Girdwood community Web site, www.girdwoodalaska.com. B&B rates range from $45-$125 per night, based on double occupancy; condos range from $125-$250.

The larger bed base is in **Anchorage**, a 35- to 55-minute drive depending on weather. Major hotels include the **Millenium Hotel** (800-544-0553 or 243-2300; $$$–$$$$), which has served as Iditarod headquarters in recent years; **Anchorage Hilton** (800-HILTONS or 272-7411; $$$–$$$$), which is in the midst of renovations; **Holiday Inn** (800-HOLIDAY or 907-279-8671; $–$$); **Sheraton Anchorage** (276-8700; $$–$$$$); and **Westmark Anchorage**(272-7561 or fax, 272-3879; $–$$). The **Hotel Captain Cook** (276-6000 or fax, 258-4857; $$–$$$$) has a great downtown location, very convenient to the Fur Rendezvous festivities, shopping and restaurants. It also has one of the best hotel health clubs we've come across. Another place we liked downtown was the **Historic Anchorage Hotel** (800-544-0988 or 272-4553; $$–$$$$), very nice, quietly elegant, with 10 suites (each different), 16 standard rooms and complimentary continental breakfast.

We've listed a small portion of the lodging that's available. We expected lodging prices to be rock bottom in winter, but Anchorage does a steady convention business then. Prices aren't as high as they are in summer, but most are in the $100 to $200 per night range. More options are listed in the excellent free Visitors Guide, available by writing to the **Anchorage Convention & Visitors Bureau**, 524 W. Fourth Ave., Anchorage, AK 99501-2212. Phone: 276-4118, fax 278-5559, Web site: www.anchorage.net.

 # Dining

These are some of our favorite restaurants; see the Visitors Guide for more selections.

In the Alyeska Prince Hotel the **Pond Cafe** ($-$$) serves breakfast, lunch and dinner with a California-Alaskan menu—try the caribou stew with a big sourdough cheese roll and lots of vegetables. Elegant dinners are the Prince's forté. We heartily recommend the **Katsura Teppanyaki** ($$$), open for dinner five nights a week. It seats about 20 diners around a U-shaped table facing the chefs who prepare the meals in front of you. We also dined at the four-diamond **Seven Glaciers Restaurant and Lounge** ($$$) on the second level of the Glacier Terminal at 2,300 feet. The view is beyond belief and the gourmet meals are excellent. Call 754-2237 for reservations at all three. **The Bake Shop** (783-2831; $) in the ski area base lodge has superb soups, sandwiches, and energy-filled, buttered sticky buns. Lots of locals, ski instructors and patrollers here.

Alyeska vicinity: Perhaps the best restaurant in the area is the **Double Musky Inn** (783-2822, $$$), a mile from the lifts on Crow Creek Road. It's mind-boggling to find great Cajun food in Alaska (go for the French Pepper Steak). Service is great and the decor is a delight—Mardi Gras beads everywhere and posters on the ceiling. Dress is casual—some Alaskans wear muddy boots to dinner. Busy nights may require a two-hour wait, but it's worth it. (They served 340 dinners on Valentine's Day, 1997—many to lovers who made the drive from Anchorage.) No reservations, opens at 5 p.m.; closed Mondays.

Chair Five (783-2500; $-$$) is casual and big on burgers and pizza, but also offers prime rib, halibut and a tasty, very spicy chicken jalapeño. The Mediterranean pastas and sandwiches are good, too. It's in the Girdwood business district next to the Post Office.

Turnagain House (653-7500; $$-$$$), a white-tablecloth restaurant looking out on Turnagain Arm halfway to Anchorage, has a reputation for fine seafood and other dishes with excellent service.

Anchorage: A special-occasion restaurant for locals is **Simon & Seafort's Saloon & Grill** (274-3502; $$-$$$). It specializes in seafood and steak. Take a walk through the bar and try to find the on-purpose errors in the paintings. Ask for a table next to the large picture window, and get there before dark so you can admire the view across Knik Arm. Other choices for fine dining are the **Marx Brothers Cafe** (278-2133, reservations required; $$-$$$) for inventive continental cuisine and impeccable service in a cozy frame-house setting which reminds us of a small New England inn; or the **Corsair** (278-4502; $$-$$$), with continental cuisine offered by owner Hans Kruger. The style is elegant and the wine list is excellent. Expect to spend the whole evening.

For great views, especially at cocktail time, try the top-floor **Crow's Nest** (276-6000; $$$) at the Hotel Captain Cook, or **Top of the World** (265-7111; $$$) in the Hilton. **Josephine's** (276-8700; $$$) in the Sheraton also has a view, and is a good choice for Sunday brunch. Make reservations if dining at any of these restaurants.

Many Japanese have settled in Anchorage, and restaurants such as **Akaihana** (276-2215; $$) and **Tempura Kitchen** (277-2741; $$) are among the Asian eateries. They offer tempura, sukiyaki and other cooked dishes as well as sushi and sashimi. Anchorage also has Thai, Chinese and Korean restaurants.

For moderately priced, delicious food—and great beer—head to **The Glacier Brew House Restaurant** (274-2739; $$) on Fifth Avenue.

Families should head to **Sourdough Mining Co.** (563-2272; $) for great ribs and corn fritters; **Hogg Brothers Cafe** (276-9649; $) for wow omelets; the **Royal Fork Buffet** (276-0089, $) or **Lucky Wishbone** (272-3454; $) for the best fried chicken. **Gwennie's Old Alaska Restaurant's** (243-2090; $) costumed staff serves big breakfasts and sandwiches midst historic photos.

Après-ski/nightlife

The **Aurora Bar and Lounge** in the Alyeska Prince Hotel has a somewhat lively atmosphere in the bar, where skiers can watch sports on TV. Patrons may play the piano, sing and dance, and make the evening as lively as they want. The lounge is quieter, with a stone fireplace and comfortable sofas and chairs. For après-ski, head to the **Sitzmark Bar** at the base of Chair 3 for burgers and live bands on Friday and Saturday nights during ski season. The **Double Musky** and **Chair 5** also have taverns.

Anchorage has a highly developed nightlife and cultural scene, a legacy of pipeline days, long winter nights, and generous doses of oil patch money. The city reportedly had an orchestra before it had paved streets.

We love wacky watering holes that have unique character. Anchorage has two great ones, but one is closed most of the winter, unfortunately. For loud rock and dancing try **Chilkoot Charlie's**, 2435 Spenard Rd., "where we cheat the other guy and pass the savings on to you." (They sell T-shirts with that slogan—it's a great souvenir.) Chilkoot's is huge—six bars with about 30 beers on tap, two stages (the night we were there during Fur Rondy, one stage had a rockin' band and the other had the Fur Bikini contest), pool tables and games, and sports on TV (though it's impossible to hear the audio). Generally, the ratio of men to women is about seven to one, and any attire goes—one February night, we saw people dressed in gym shorts; others in business suits and cocktail dresses. The other unique nightclub is **Mr. Whitekeys' Fly By Night Club,** famed for its Spam appetizers and satirical, summertime Whale Fat Follies show. The club does a "Christmas in Spenard" show, but after that, it's closed for the winter, much to our disappointment. (We've seen the summer show; it's a hoot.)

Humpy's on Sixth Avenue has 36 beers on tap and occasional live entertainment. For quieter dancing and a slightly older clientele try **Legends** at the Sheraton or **Whale's Tail** at

Dining: $$$-Entrees $20+; $$-$10-20; $-less than $10.

Accommodations: (double room) $$$$-$200+; $$$-$141-$200; $$-$81-$140; $-$80 and less.

the Hotel Captain Cook, or the lounge at the **Golden Lion Best Western**. For country music, head to **Last Frontier Bar** or **Buckaroo Club**.

For theater, opera, drama and movies, buy the local newspaper (*Anchorage Daily News*). There's a Friday morning entertainment tabloid that's very helpful. You may be surprised at the visiting artists and productions at the **Alaska Center for the Performing Arts** downtown. For recorded information, call 263-2901.

Other activities

The variety of winter activities is staggering. We have room to list just a sampling. We encourage you to get the excellent free Visitors Guide from the **Anchorage Convention & Visitors Bureau**, 524 W. Fourth Ave., Anchorage, AK 99501-2212. Telephone: 276-4118; fax: 278-5559; Web site: www.anchorage.net.

Think of Alaska in winter and you think of **dogsleds**. Call Chugach Dog Sled Tours in Girdwood near the ski area (783-2266 for reservations, last-minute calls don't work; or make reservations through the guest services desk at the Alyeska Prince Hotel). If you're staying in Anchorage, drive about 20 minutes to the hamlet of Chugiak to Mush a Dog Team-Gold Rush Days (688-1391). As you travel the trail, you'll see a recreation of an Alaskan gold miner's camp. You'll be amazed at how cramped and cold those unheated tents must have been.

Dogsled races are a focal point of **Fur Rendezvous**, held annually in mid-February. The World Championship Sled Dog Race is the sprint (some sprint—25 miles a day for three days) counterpart to the more famous endurance race, **The Iditarod**, which follows Fur Rondy on the first Saturday in March. Fur Rondy also has fireworks, a snow sculpture contest, a small carnival, a snowshoe softball tournament (hilarious for spectators) and the World Championship Dog Weight Pull, a contest detailed in Jack London's book, *Call of the Wild*. Alaskan Natives come from all parts of the state for Fur Rondy, and many wear traditional fur parkas, stunning works of art with intricate patterns. By the way, if seeing people wearing fur offends you, don't come at this time. You'll only work yourself into a lather over something that has kept native Alaskans warm for centuries. If you're a dog lover, don't miss the start of The Iditarod, when about 1,500 sled dogs are parked on main street in downtown Anchorage. Early in the morning, you can visit with the dogs and the mushers.

Several companies offer **flightseeing tours** via helicopter or fixed-wing planes. It is the best way to see Alaska's spectacular mountains and glaciers and well worth the cost. We flew with Era Helicopters (800-478-1947, 248-4422; www.eraaviation.com) into the rugged Chugach Mountains that border Anchorage. On an overcast day, you'll gain an appreciation for the arduous conditions that 19th-century mushers endured to bring supplies over mountain passes from Seward to Anchorage. On a clear day, you'll see Mt. McKinley off in the distance, its broad hulk standing apart from surrounding mountains. Alpine Air (783-2360) operates airplane tours out of Girdwood. Prices begin at $49 for a one-hour tour and they will pick-up at the Alyeska Prince Hotel.

Alyeska offers **snowcat skiing and heliskiing** with more than 750 square miles of backcountry slopes. Chugach Powder Guides (783-4354) operates out of the Alyeska Prince Hotel. A full-day heli-skiing package is $575, with a guarantee of 16,000–20,000 vertical. A full-day snowcat package is $140 standby, $190 by advance reservation. **Tandem paragliding** with a certified pilot 2,300 feet above the ski area is another thrill for visitors. Available daily in summer and by appointment in winter. Call Alyeska for more details, 754-2275.

Backcountry skiers can explore the region with Alaska Off Piste (441-2249), an adventure skiing and alpine guiding company based in Girdwood. Per person rates are $175 for one, $125 for two and $100 for three or more for a day trip.

In Anchorage, the **Anchorage Museum of History and Art** (343-4326) is a must-see, with excellent displays that show 10,000 years of Alaskan civilization, from ancient days through the Gold Rush and the great earthquake of 1964. The **Alaska Native Heritage Center** (330-8000 or 800-315-6608) provides an introduction to Alaska's native population. Although it's not fully open in winter, special events such as cultural gatherings and art shows are reason enough to visit. If you're in law enforcement, don't miss the **Alaska State Trooper Museum** (800-770-5050), which tells the history of the state's law enforcement through exhibits, memorabilia and photographs.

In Seward, two hours' drive south of Alyeska Resort, you can visit the **Alaska Sea Life Center** (224-6300), funded by Exxon Valdez oil spill restoration funds and dedicated to understanding and maintaining the integrity of Alaska's marine ecosystem. It's a combination aquarium and museum, with interactive exhibits, displays and touch tanks for children. Renown Charters and Tours (800-655-3806 or 224-3806) offers an exciting **wildlife cruise** that circumnavigates Resurrection Bay and touches briefly into the Gulf of Alaska; transportation is available from the Alyeska Prince Hotel. The **Big Game Alaska Wildlife Center** (783-2025), just 10 miles south of Girdwood, is dedicated to the rehabilitation of orphaned and injured animals. Here you can get close enough to pet moose, Sitka deer, caribou and reindeer. Also on premises are birds of prey, buffalo and muskox. It's open daily, 10 a.m.–4 p.m. Admission is $5.

If you need another reason to visit Alaska in the winter, the **Northern Lights** might be it. If you've ever seen photos of the aurora borealis, with its green, blue and red streaks of light across an ink-black sky, you have an inkling of how magnificent this phenomenon is. For forecasts on when to plan your trip to maximize the chances of seeing the Northern Lights, go to this Internet site: www.geo.mtu.edu/weather/aurora. The Alyeska Prince Hotel has a unique Northern Lights wake-up service and a 7-minute electronic display of the aurora on the ceiling of the hotel's three-story lobby.

Getting there and getting around

By air: Anchorage International Airport is served by many major airlines. East Coast skiers who want to make the trek here would be well advised to find a travel agent who specializes in Alaska in order to find the best airfares and packages.

By car: Alyeska Resort is 45 miles south of downtown Anchorage. Get on Gambell Street south, which becomes the Seward Highway, Route 1, along Turnagain Arm, which has one of the highest tides in the world. The drive is quite scenic; try to alternate drivers so everyone can admire the view. Bring your camera and lots of film for the Dall sheep, moose, bald eagles, beluga whales and bore tides often seen along the way. Turn left at the Girdwood/Alyeska highway turn-off, the resort is 3 miles up the road.

Getting around: If you stay in downtown Anchorage or at the Alyeska Prince Hotel, you can get by without a car. Alaska Sightseeing or The Magic Bus (268-6311) can take you from the city to the resort with advance reservations. Ask at the hotel desk. Otherwise, you'll need a car. The Alyeska area (the town of Girdwood) doesn't have a local transportation system. However, the hotel runs a continuous free shuttle during mountain operations and in evenings by request. If you want to try some of the restaurants we listed, such as the Double Musky, make arrangements with the bell desk.

"Interior" British Columbia

Big White Ski Resort
Sun Peaks Resort
Silver Star Mountain Resort

From British Columbia's west coast, the mountain ranges roll east in ascending waves until they reach the Rocky Mountain peaks on the Continental Divide. The Divide forms the southern border between British Columbia and Alberta. British Columbia is the heli-skiing and Nordic touring center of the known ski universe, and that's in addition to the 35 or so alpine ski areas. There are a slew of heli-skiing outfitters and nearly 30 Nordic destinations. British Columbia covers 366,000 square miles, and more than 90 percent of that is provincial forests and parks. As Vancouver writer Steve Threndyle said, "B.C. is one of the few places in the world where people can still seek out an endless amount of recreational challenge in a vast, uncompromising wilderness setting."

The British Columbia highlands and plateaus take moisture from the Pacific storms that drop dryer snow in the Monashees, Selkirks, Kootenays and Purcells on their way to the Rockies. The skiing experience in western Canada has its own fingerprint, its own special flavor with an inviting appeal to skiers from eastern North American, Europe and Australia. It can be a bit like traveling to a foreign country. Distinctions range from snow to snacks, lodging to location. When you're in the West, informality is the rule, friendly folks the reason. After you've visited three of the up-and-coming resorts in this region—Big White Ski Resort, Sun Peaks Resort and Silver Star Mountain Resort—we think you'll agree that this is some of the most memorable skiing there is.

Big White Ski Resort

Big White, the fourth-largest ski area in Canada, overlooks the Okanagan Valley and its 100-mile-long Okanagan Lake. Though it's been around for nearly 40 years, it's been only in the last decade that it's grown into full resort status. The Okanagan Valley is the hot winter destination in the West, and many advise getting here soon while it's still relatively affordable.

Big White boasts, "We use only dry, natural Okanagan Powder." The village sits at 5,700 feet (B.C.'s highest base area) and lifts carry skiers up to 7,600 feet. That's about the same elevation as Whistler Blackcomb, but the air and snow are considerably dryer this far inland.

The resort has pumped in $100 million in the last five years. With more skiable terrain than Sun Valley, it's a good investment. For Australians, Big White is the second-biggest destination ski resort in B.C., behind Whistler Blackcomb. Last summer, the resort announced a $35.1 million expansion, adding an eight-passenger gondola, the Happy Valley Adventure Park with a tubing park and lodge, and $29.1 million of accommodations. For 2001/02, Big White has added four 3,000-foot runs in the area known as "Never-never Land," providing more intermediate and black-diamond terrain. Selective tree removal has added 100 acres of tree skiing, one of Big White's signature features. Big White also has slopeside village accommodations, Stonebridge Lodge Resort and Trappers' Crossing, scheduled for completion.

Big White Ski Resort Facts

Summit elevation: 7,606 feet
Vertical drop: 2,550 feet
Base elevation: 5,706 feet (Village base);
4,950 feet (Westridge base)

Address: Box 2039, Station R, Kelowna, B.C.,
Canada V1X 4K5
Area code: 250
Ski area phone: 765-3101
Snow report: 765-7669
Toll-free reservations: (800) 663-2772
Fax: 765-1822
E-mail: bigwhite@bigwhite.com or
cenres@bigwhite.com for reservations
Internet: www.bigwhite.com

Expert:★★★ **Advanced:**★★★★
Intermediate:★★★★
Beginner:★★★★ **Never-ever:**★★★
Number of lifts: 12–1 8-passenger high-speed gondola, 4 high-speed quads, 1 quad, 1 triple, 1 double, 1 T-bar, 2 surface lifts
Snowmaking: In the competition halfpipe only
Skiable acreage: 2,565 acres
Uphill capacity: 23,400 per hour
Snowboarding: Yes
Bed base: 10,200
Nearest lodging: Slopeside lodging, ski-in/ski-out
Resort child care: 18 months to 6 years
Adult ticket, per day: $48-$52 (2001/02, Cdn$)
Dining: ★★★ (resort), ★★★ (region)
Apres-ski/nightlife:★★★ (resort), ★★★ (region)
Other activities: ★★★

Mountain layout—Skiing

◆◆ **Expert:** Experts normally like the Gem Lake Express runs. Goat's Kick, left of the Ridge Rocket Express, is an especially fun challenge. Going to the right from the Alpine T-bar gets you into Parachute Bowl.

◆ **Advanced:** Natural hits and drops fall off the side of Perfection, Falcon Glades and around Westridge. For bumps, try Dragon's Tongue to the left of Ridge Rocket Express.

■ **Intermediate:** Good warm-up runs are the Sun Run from the top of the Alpine T-bar, Exhibition, Highway 33, Serwas and Sundance. There's also fine terrain off the Rocket and Powder chairs. Roller Coaster, Blue Sapphire and Kalinas Rainbow come recommended. International is an intermediate bump run. The blue ratings in the Black Forest are low-end.

●● **Beginner:** Millie's Mile, named after the owner's granddaughter, runs alongside the Black Forest Express. All lifts serve at least one green run.

● **Never-ever:** Hummingbird, served by the Plaza Chair, is designated for first-timers only. Woodcutter is also excellent, but mind the traffic.

Mountain layout—Snowboarding

The mountain has a world-class competition halfpipe and a quarterpipe for beginners that is lit for night moves. Freeriders have a good time most anywhere on the mountain. Particularly popular is the Sun-Rype Bowl and the adjacent Black Bear run, both reached by the Gem Lake Express. The bowl is a big gentle swoop of a run that can get you into some trees known as the Black Bear Glades. Also reached from Gem Lake Express is the single-black Blackjack, a good long fall-line run.

The only double-blacks are reached by the Alpine T-bar. There are some gentle ways down if you change your mind, but at least have a look on the way up to the right into Parachute Bowl. Easy Street has a permanent boardercross course. Big White has a boardercross training facility and was home of the 2001 Canadian Snowboard Championships.

Mountain rating

The mountain is big, with plenty of terrain to explore. Trails are mixed by ability level on almost every lift, so riders of all ability levels can take the same lift up together and meet again at the bottom. A few lifts serve primarily one ability level—the Power Chair serves mostly black runs, while Ridge Rocket Express has mostly blue runs under its airway. Big White has a separate learning area at its base. You'll find the toughest stuff off the Alpine T-bar at the summit. Grooming reports are posted at the top of each chair.

Cross-country and snowshoeing

Big White has 25 km. of trails, mostly groomed except for the backcountry double-black diamonds. The beginners' trail is a 4.3-km. loop from the Plaza Chair. Cross-country skiing is included with lift tickets. If skiers head down-mountain from the mid-mountain day lodge, the Plaza Quad Chairlift back up is free.

Lessons (2001/02; Cnd$ without GST)

Group lessons: A 2-hour lesson costs $35; multiday rates available.
Never-ever package: Includes Plaza lift ticket and gear rental, two-hour learn-to-ski lesson costs $47; learn-to-snowboard costs $56.
  Private lessons: All day, $330 (first three people), each additional person $50; half-day afternoon, $150 (first three people), each additional person $40; 2 hours, $140, each additional person $40; one hour, $75, each additional person $29.

Child care (2001/02; Cnd$ without GST)

Ages: 18 months to 6 years.
Costs: Hourly rate is $12; $55 for a full day (lunch included).
Reservations: Recommended. Call 765-3101.
  Children's lessons: Ages 4-12, full day is $63, half day is $42 (rentals are extra). Program for kids ages 4-6 includes indoor play time. For kids ages 4-12, a two-hour learn-to-ski lesson costs $45 (includes Plaza lift ticket and gear rental); learn-to-snowboard for kids 7-12 costs $53. A note about the kids' instruction center: It's recognized as a top program for kids. Security is tight. Parents are given pagers.

Lift tickets (2001/02; Cdn$ with GST)

	Adult	Youth (13-18)	Child (6-12)
One day	$52	$44	$27
Three days	$150	$126	$75
Five days	$240	$200	$115

Who skis free: Children 5 and younger; seniors 70 and older.
Who skis at a discount: Seniors 65–69 pay $36 for a one-day ticket.
  Note: Six-out-of-seven-days flex passes are available as of opening day: $300 for adults, $252 for youth, $150 for children, and $204 for seniors ages 65–69. Big White has night skiing, 5 p.m.–8 p.m., Tuesday to Saturday, from mid-December to end of March.

Accommodations

Big White has three hotels, a condo-hotel, 21 condo buildings, 150 private chalets, 21 RV hookups and two hostels, all ski-in/ski-out.

Stone Bridge Lodge ($$–$$$$), still under construction during the summer of 2001, is scheduled to open for the winter season. Centrally located in the village, these two-bedroom condo-hotel units feature a full kitchen, spacious living room, gas fireplace, two bathrooms and ski-in/ski-out convenience. **Chateau Big White** ($$–$$$$) is one of the newest lodgings. It's close to all amenities in the Village Plaza. Room types include deluxe rooms with two queen beds, loft suites with double and queen beds, and one- and two-bedroom suites. All rooms have gas fireplaces and kitchenettes with microwaves and fridges. The hotel has a lounge, four-star restaurant, underground parking and hot tub.

The **Inn at Big White** ($$–$$$$), formerly Coast Resort, is the most-requested property. This very centrally located hotel has 100 rooms and suites, an outdoor pool and hot tub, fitness room, restaurant and lounge. **White Crystal Inn** ($$–$$$$), a luxury inn, is recently renovated and includes cable TV and phones in the rooms, fine dining and a great lounge.

Located in the heart of the Village, the **Whitefoot Lodge** ($–$$) features a hot tub, sauna, cold plunge, elevator, and laundry. Some rooms have kitchenettes. It has an indoor hot tub, sauna, restaurant, lounge and grocery/liquor/video store.

Chateau On The Ridge ($$$–$$$$) has condos with kitchens, gas fireplaces and outdoor common hot tubs. **Das Hofbrauhaus** ($–$$$) is slopeside and has an indoor pool, hot tub and racquetball courts, plus a restaurant and lounge. **Eagles Resort** ($$$–$$$$) has 20 three-bedroom condos with gas fireplace and kitchens, plus a large hot tub on the property. **Graystokes Inn** ($$) has one- and two-bedroom condos, plus a common outdoor hot tub. **The Moguls** boasts fabulous views of the Monashee Mountains, an indoor hot tub and sauna.

The Legacy ($$–$$$$) consists of luxury one-, two- and three-bedroom condos with full kitchens and gas fireplaces, covered balconies and covered parking stalls. The **Monashee Inn** ($$–$$$) has an unsurpassed view of the Monashee Mountains. **Plaza On The Ridge** ($$–$$$$) is right on the ski run and features six outdoor hot tubs. Each unit has a fireplace and spacious kitchen. The **Ponderosa Inn** ($–$$$) is on the Easy Street ski run. It's family oriented with a hot tub and sauna. **Ptarmigan Inn** ($$–$$$) is next to the village and has hot tubs, a plunge pool and sauna. One- and two-bedroom units are available. **Snow Pines Estates** ($$–$$$$) has nice big chalets, either single-family or duplex, all with ski-in/ski-out access.

The **RV park** ($) provides easy access to the Black Forest Express lift. It has 32 full-service hookups with water, sewer, 30-amp electrical and cable TV. A chalet, hot tub and washroom with showers are on-site. Rates are $30 per night (Cdn$). The cheapest digs are at **Big White Hostels** (765-2100; $), a.k.a. **Bumps** and **Bumps Too**, where you get a dorm bunk for $15 per night (Cdn$), plus there's a common room with cooking facilities, Internet access ($4/hour, Cdn$) and a laundromat.

Dining

Unlike most other ski resorts, you don't have to drive or even walk more than a block or so to find a great meal. All restaurants are located in or near the village center and represent a swell variety of offerings. **Beano's** (765-3101 ext. 291; $), located smack in the middle of the main ticket/rental building, serves the best coffee, the best soup and the best sandwiches in the village. It's also an Internet cafe. Beano's owners are usually on site waiting on friendly Big White CEOs, managers and ski school directors enjoying their morning javas. Big White's owners and family live just across the street and like to check out what's happening with their guests and staff each morning. Drop by and say hello, lodge a complaint or give a suggestion. They'll be glad you did.

Snowshoe Sam's (765-1416; $$-$$$) is a legend at Big White. This multistoried establishment, up a flight of steps in the village, concentrates mainly on steaks and chops, although their seafood and pasta are quite good. You'll need dinner reservations, especially on the weekend. It's packed! Their claim to fame is their Gunbarrel Coffee. It's as much of a show as it is an after-dinner drink. Your waiter pulls up alongside your table with a 22-shotgun and pours flaming Grand Marnier down the barrel into a glass with brandy, cacao and whipped cream! The restaurant sells the most Grand Marnier in Canada.

The **Swiss Bear Dining Room** (491-7750; $$-$$$) in the Chateau Big White serves authentic Swiss cuisine, specializing in delicious fondues. Reservations recommended.

The **Powder Keg** (491-2009; $-$$), in the Inn at Big White, is a great family restaurant. The grill serves breakfast, lunch and dinner with an interesting menu (some good veggie choices). The bar offers typical pub food like wings, dips and sandwiches and a great view.

Grizzly Bear (765-4611; $$), in the White Crystal Inn, is a beehive at lunch serving a variety of tasty homemade soups. Dinners feature a European flair with specialties from award-winning chef Jari. An interesting wine list, mostly Canadian, Australian and Californian. **Coltino's Ristorante** (765-5611; $$), at Raakel's Hofbruahaus, serves Italian fare as well as Alberta beef. **Raakel's** next door has après-ski where they serve some mean salads, burgers and pizzas. They also offer the usual pub fare of wings, fries, even putine—that typical French Canadian dish of French fries topped with cheese curd and steaming hot gravy.

 ## Après-ski/nightlife

Big White has seven lounges and bars. Live bands perform regularly. **Snowshoe Sam's** is commonly thought of as the best ski bar in Canada, and we agree. It has DJ entertainment, live bands and games of chance. **The Powder Keg**, in the Inn at Big White, is a great après-ski spot. **Raakel's Ridge Pub,** in Das Hofbrauhaus, has dancing. In Whitefoot Lodge, there's a **market** (765-7666) with everything from liquor to video rentals.

 ## Other activities

Head to the Adventure Centre (765-8888) to find **Big White Dogsledding Adventures** for "mush your own dog team" tours, the **Mega Snow Coaster tube ride** with 10 lanes and lifts, **snowmobile tours, ice skating** and **snowshoeing. Whitefoot Medical Clinic** (765-0544) operates in the village from 3–6 p.m. for medical services and massages. Appointments are preferred, but not required.

 ## Getting there and getting around

By air: Kelowna Regional Airport is an hour's drive from Big White and less than an hour's flight from Vancouver, Calgary or Seattle. It's served daily by Air BC (Air Canada) and Horizon Air (5 daily flights) and WestJet (3 daily flights). U.S. Customs is right in Kelowna. There are even direct flights from Toronto. Airport shuttles serve the ski area, $29.91 adult and $20.56 junior (6–12) for one-way tickets, and $51.40 adult and $36.45 junior round-trip.

By car: Big White is 33 miles from Kelowna. It's 134 miles from Kamloops; 407 miles from Calgary; 278 miles from Vancouver; 346 miles from Seattle.

Getting around: Big White has a Budget rental agency on the mountain. One-way rentals to and from the airport can be booked through Central Reservations. No car is needed at Big White unless you plan to visit Kelowna (33 miles).

Sun Peaks Resort

Summit elevation:	6,824 feet
Vertical Drop:	2,891 feet
Base elevation:	3,933 feet

Address: #50-3150 Creekside Way,
Sun Peaks, B.C., Canada V0E 1Z1
Area code: 250
Ski area phone: 578-7842
Snow report: 578-7232
Toll-free reservations: 800-807-3257
Fax: 578-7843
E-mail: info@sunpeaksresort.com
Internet: www.sunpeaksresort.com
Expert: ★★★ **Advanced:** ★★★★
Intermediate: ★★★★ **Beginner:** ★★★
Never-ever: ★★★

Number of lifts: 6–2 high-speed quads, 1 quad, 1 triple, 2 carpet lifts
Skiable acreage: 2,418 acres
Snowmaking: 80 acres
Uphill capacity: 8,030 per hour
Snowboarding: Yes
Bed base: 3,000
Nearest lodging: Slopeside, ski-in/ski-out
Resort child care: 18 months-5 years
Adult ticket, per day: $49 (2001/02; Cdn$)
Dining: ★★★★ (resort), ★★★ (region)
Apres-ski/nightlife: ★★ (resort), ★★ (region)
Other activities: ★★★★

Sun Peaks Resort

As for Sun Peaks, skier word on the slope is, "Enjoy it before it gets too big." Its strides toward the future of skiing began with Nippon Cable's purchase of the former Tod Mountain in 1992. So far, more than $225 million has gone into the re-do, with $70 million more on the way. Al Raine and his Olympic ski-race-champion wife, Nancy Greene Raine, who helped build Whistler to the international destination it is today, call Sun Peaks home, and Nancy is the director of skiing. As a matter of fact, Sun Peaks is often called the next Whistler. That's stretching things a bit—a whole lot, in fact. But don't let that stop you. It's a very nice chunk of mountain village and resort, with nothing to apologize for. The huge bowls, wide runs, steep chutes and abundance of glades are enough to keep any skier or rider busy for a week or more.

The mountain has one of five North American detachable quads with a bubble, the 1.5-mile Sunburst Express. Off to its right are six single-diamond steeps, all in a row, plus one blue steep. Beginners have their own separate area near the Village Day Lodge in front of Nancy Greene's hotel. It's very much out of the way. Snowboarders have a couple of halfpipes and an obstacle course off to the side of the intermediate runs served by the Sundance Express. Just a warning: If you use lifts as meeting places, be aware that Sun*dance* and Sun*burst* chairs unload at different points.

"Friendly, chatty Kamloopsians will have you loading up the U-haul and moving west within one Sun Peaks chairlift conversation. They wrote the book on civic pride." This is how *Ski Canada Magazine* describes local Sun Peaks skiers and snowboarders in a recent "Best of Canadian Skiing" issue. Those locals began the ski area in 1961, with volunteers carving many of the runs that are skied today.

Mountain layout—Skiing

◆◆ **Expert:** The really advanced runs—the bowls, chutes and head walls—are up off the higher chairs and T-bar. Hat Trick, to the right of the Crystal triple chair, dumps you unceremoniously into the woods.

◆ **Advanced:** The six chutes to the right of the Sun*burst* Express are big favorites, but you'll have a fine ol' time in the Burfield Quad region. Off Juniper Ridge, to the left, are several challenging runs.

■ **Intermediate:** The Sun*dance* Express, to the right, gets you to the top of Sundance Ridge, where three blue runs (Grannie Greene's, Sun Catcher and Sunrise) begin. If you take the Sun*burst* Express, there are several good blue runs on the left. Higher up, even to the top of the West Bowl T-bar, there are lots of blue runs.

● **Beginner:** Except for the West Bowl T-bar and Crystal Chair, there are green runs descending from every lift. One of the most fun is the 5-miler that starts at the top of the Burfield Quad. If you want to do it again, be sure to take the Burfield Outrun under the Sunburst Express and back to the bottom of the Burfield.

● **Never-ever:** The area right in front of Nancy Greene's hotel is all for you. The three runs—Sunbeam, Gentle Giant and Cowabunga—cannot terrorize you, guaranteed.

Mountain layout—Snowboarding

Sun Peaks has two halfpipes and one terrain park. The terrain park is 2,500 feet long and is served by a high-speed quad. At 20 acres, it's one of North America's largest snowboard parks. Sun Peaks is a popular stop on the FIS Grundig Snowboard World Cup. The six single-blacks to the right of the Sunburst Express chair are a fair challenge and can keep a freerider busy all morning. Up higher, the Crystal Bowl, between the Crystal and Burfield chairs, is wide and single-black steep. If it's too much, and you want to avoid the Head Walls, blue-diamond Crystal Run is good for bailing.

Mountain rating

It's trite to say it, but this mountain has something for every skier and rider. It's a big mountain, but not hard to know after your first morning. Everyone who has skied before will benefit from a few warm-up runs off the Sun*dance* Express. That will be the comfort zone for most of us. The rest of you will want to hustle over to Tod Mountain across the way. Just stay out of the closed woods area at the bottom of the Crystal Chair.

Cross-country and snowshoeing

Sun Peaks has 40 km. of cross-country trails, half wilderness trails and half track-set trails and skating lanes. Renatls and lessons available. Snowshoeing, alone or with a guide, follows dedicated trails with bird feeding stations, wildlife viewing and a snow cave. Rentals include snowshoes, gaiters and an interpretive map. Tours include snowshoes, gaiters and headlamps for evening tours. Just 25 minutes from Kamloops is **Stake Lake Trails** (fax, 579-5653; snow phone, 372-5514), with 45 km. of well-groomed classic and skating tracks. Lovingly run by Kamloops Overlander Ski Club.

Lessons (Cnd$ without GST)

Group lessons: $29–$35 gets a 90-minute to 2-hour lesson.
Never-ever package: A 3-hour lesson plus lunch, $39.50. A 90-minute lesson, $29. Add $12 for ski rentals or $18.50 for snowboard rentals, plus $9 for a Sundance lift pass.

Private lessons: All-day lesson, $250 (up to 3 people); additional people, $40 each. Half-day lesson, $150 (up to 3 people); additional people, $40 each. For a 2-hour lesson, $96; 1-hour lesson, $60; additional people, $25 each.

Child care (Cnd$ without GST)

Ages: 18 months to 5 years.
Costs: Full day is $49 with lunch.
Reservations: Call 578-5430.
Children's lessons: Sun Kids is for ages 5-14. Full day with lunch, $58; half day, $35.
Sun Tots, for ages 3-5, is a 90-minute lesson that costs $25 (morning), $30 (afternoon).

Lift tickets (Cdn$ without GST)

	Adult	Youth (13-18)	Child (6-12)
One day	$49	$41	$26
Three days	$129	$114	$69

Who skis free: Children 5 and younger.
Who skis at a discount: Seniors 65 and older, $32.

Accommodations

Kids 12 and younger stay and ski free at Sun Peaks (one per adult). All hotels
are ski-in/ski-out; many other properties are as well.

Nancy Greene's Cahilty Lodge (578-7454; $$-$$$$) is practically on the
slopes. Nancy's gold and silver Olympic medals are displayed in the lobby. It's a condo-
minium lodge with hotel rooms, studio units and large family units. The lodge has a fitness
center, hot tubs and restaurant.

The deluxe, full-service **Sundance Lodge** (578-0200; $$-$$$$) sits right at the base of a
chair lift. Some of the units have kitchens, and all have coffee makers and microwaves. You'll
find a fitness center, restaurant and shops. A new 226-room **Delta Sun Peak Resort** is
scheduled to open by Christmas 2001. The **Woodlands Fireside Lodge** and **Woodlands
Hearthstone Lodge** (578-8588; $$-$$$) are both full-service hotels with deluxe studios and
suites. All suites have kitchens or kitchenettes and fireplaces. Plus there's a restaurant, fitness
center and whirlpools. **The Heffley Inn** (578-7878; $$) is a 26-room, European-style hotel
with a whirlpool, sauna and steam room. There's also a restaurant.

The **Sun Peaks International Hostel** (578-0057, www.sunpeakshostel.com; $) is a
large rustic lodge and offers slopeside accommodation from $20 per person (Cdn$). Amenities
include a fully equipped kitchen, commissary, large lounge area, Internet access, private and
semi-private rooms, and ski/snowboard storage lockers.

Dining

Bento's Daylodge, east of the Village Daylodge, is an OK quick cafeteria
stop in your busy ski day. The **Sunburst Daylodge**, mid-mountain, is a
cafeteria with great views. In the Sundance Lodge, you'll find the **Bolacco
Café** and **Bottom's Bar & Grill**. Bottom's is charmingly noisy.

High-country-style AAA Canadian beef is the specialty at the **Heffley Steakhouse**.
You quickly learn to trust the local McDonnell brothers' eclectic fusion menu at **Macker's
Bistro & Bar,** located in Nancy Greene's Cahilty Lodge. Imaginative continental cuisine is
served in the **Val Senales Dining Room.**

Après-ski/nightlife

Things are kind of quiet here at the end of the day, and that quiet is best experienced at the **Stube** in Sun Peaks Lodge. For a livelier time, head to **Bottom's Bar & Grill** or **Masa's Bar & Grill** in the Village Daylodge.

 ## Other activities

At Sun Peaks' **Annual Icewine Festival**, held in late January, participants stroll between village hotels and restaurants where 15 Okanagan Valley wineries are featured. Festival events included a wine tasting, a winemasters' dinner, a seminar and an awards presentation. Festival activities are scheduled for the late afternoon and evening to allow for skiing, dogsledding, snowshoeing and other winter fun.

Short **prayer services** are held every Sunday at the Sun Peaks chapel at 1 p.m. The chapel is located just southwest of the mid-mountain Sunburst Daylodge, at the top of the Sunburst Express Chairlift. Lift tickets are required to ride the chairlift.

Two outdoor **skating** rinks are located at the Sports Centre, which offers drop-in hockey, skate rentals, stick rentals, and more. When you're done skating, relax in the **outdoor pool** or **hot tub**. One-hour **dogsled rides** leave from the horse barn at the east end of the village. You can even mush your own team if you're age 14 or older. Tours are offered Tuesday to Sunday at 10 a.m., noon and 3 p.m. Visit the **Resort Activity & Information Centre** in the Village Day Lodge for tickets, or phone 578-5542. **Sleigh rides** leave from the Village Day Lodge; choose between valley tours or evening dessert rides.

Sun Peaks Snowmobile Tours supplies helmets with visors and all exterior clothing (except gloves). Drivers must have a driver's license; passengers need only be legal age, or have parental consent. Choose from a regular snow machine or high-performance.

 ## Getting there and getting around

By air: Kamloops Airport is served by two airlines, Air Canada via Central Mountain Air (888-247-2262 in Canada; 800-776-3000 in the U.S.) and Canadian Regional (800-665-1177 in Canada; 800-426-7000 in the U.S.). Both have connections into Kamloops Airport several times daily from Vancouver, Calgary and Edmonton. For shuttle service from the Kamloops Airport to Sun Peaks, call 319-3539. Cost is $27 one way. Children 12 and younger ride free.

By car: Sun Peaks is a 45-minute drive from Kamloops. From Vancouver it's 4 hours, from Seattle it's 5 hours, and from Banff it's 6 hours.

Getting around: There are regular shuttles (Wednesdays & Saturdays) to and from the resorts of Whistler (800-224-8424), Big White (800-807-3257) and Silver Star (800-807-3257). At Sun Peaks there is no need for a car.

Silver Star Mountain Resort

First-time visitors to Silver Star love the frontier ambience of the 1890s Victoria Gaslight village. With a street full of unique wooden buildings in surprising colors, and no cars, Silver Star has a compact touch of elegance, even with eight hotels, restaurants, plenty of shopping and an aquatic center. The mountain and its village are highly rated for family skiing and vie with Big White to be the second-largest downhill ski resort in British Columbia. The average snowpack here is 9 feet. Silver Star is usually the first British Columbia ski resort to open. The town of Vernon is at the mountain's base, 14 miles away.

Silver Star Mountain Resort

Summit elevation: 6,280 feet
Vertical Drop: 2,500 feet
Base elevation: 5,280 feet

Address: Box 3002,
Silver Star Mountain, B.C., Canada V1B 3M1
Area code: 250
Ski area phone: 542-0224
Snow report: 542-1745
Toll-free reservations: (800) 663-4431
Fax: 542-1236
E-mail: star@junction.net
Internet: www.skisilverstar.com
Expert:★★★★ Advanced:★★★
Intermediate:★★★★ Beginner:★★★
Never-ever:★★★★

Number of lifts: 10–2 high-speed quads,
1 quad, 2 doubles, 2 T-bars, 1 handle tow,
2 magic carpets
Snowmaking: No
Skiable acreage: 2,725 acres (+340 acres off-piste)
Uphill capacity: 13,800 per hour
Snowboarding: Yes
Bed base: 3,200 on mountain; nearby RV camping
Nearest lodging: Slopeside, all ski-in/ski-out
Resort child care: Newborn to 6 years
Adult ticket, per day: $45-$49 (2000/01 Cdn$)
Dining:★★★
Apr s-ski/nightlife: ★★
Other activities:★★★

Mountain layout—Skiing

From the top of the Summit Chair and the Vance Creek Express, you can see Sun Peaks and Big White. That's on a clear day, of course. From here, it's a 5-mile run to the bottom of Aunt Gladys at the Putnam Creek station.

◆◆ **Expert:** Don't delay—head straight to the Putnam Creek side and scout the Back Bowl. Look for Free Fall, Where's Bob, Black Pine and Kirkenheimer. Then work your way over to the other side of the Putnam Creek Express to 3 Wisemen, Headwall and Chute 5.

◆ **Advanced:** There are plenty of single-blacks on both sides of the mountain. Be sure to test yourself on Caliper Ridge, a trail that runs under the Putnam Creek Express.

■ **Intermediate:** Gypsy Queen, reached via Bergerstrasse from Paradise Camp, is the most popular blue run on the mountain. Another really great one, on the opposite side of the Putnam Creek Express, is Sunny Ridge. It takes off to the left just before Paradise Camp.

●● **Beginner:** You can't go wrong taking the Putnam Creek Express. From the top, Bergerstrasse/Aunt Gladys make a sweet 5-mile green run. You can also take the Main St. Skiway straight to the village.

● **Never-ever:** The area served by the Town T-bar is fenced to keep out the speedy interlopers, so it's a good place to make those initial turns.

Mountain layout—Snowboarding

Silver Star's halfpipe and terrain park are both located on Big Dipper, reached by riding down next to the Yellow Chair. The terrain park has a variety of manmade features for all skill levels. A second halfpipe is lit for night riding. It's served by the Summit Chair and located between Show Off and Milky Way. New for 2001/02 another, steeper, terrain park will be built; the entrance and exit to the freestyle aerial site will be widened and resloped; and the resort purchased new equipment for terrain park maintenance. The boardercross track is between Milky Way and Exhibition, near the Vance Creek Express.

On the Putnam side, watch out for the Bergerstrasse flats above Paradise Camp. Once beyond it though, there are plenty of single- and double-black runs that will keep your inner freerider happy. The runs all are served by the Putnam Creek Express. Just take Aunt Gladys to the left and pick your chute.

Mountain rating

Silver Star's two mountain faces ensure that skiers or boarders of all abilities will find what they need. The Vance Creek side offers long, rolling cruisers. The Putnam Creek side is a little wilder with groomed and ungroomed double-blacks, glades and bumps.

Cross-country and snowshoeing

Part of the **National High Altitude Training Center**, Silver Star's cross-country trails attract skiers from around the world. Many of them are Olympic athletes in training. For 2001/02, there are two fully certified biathalon ranges (one with 22 lanes). The network of trails includes the adjoining **Sovereign Lakes Cross Country** system, for a total of more than 105 km. of groomed and track-set skiing heaven, with several warming huts along the way. Adult one-day trail tickets cost $14 (including seniors) and children ages 6-12 pay $9. The trails at the resort are skating groomed, and 4 miles are lit for night skiing. Lessons and guided snowshoe tours also are available.

Lessons (2001/02; Cnd$ without GST)

Group lessons: A two-hour lesson, beginning at 10 a.m., $39.
Never-ever package: Discover Skiing includes lift, 90-minute lesson and rental, $35; Discover Snowboarding, $55.

Private lessons: 90-minute lesson, $89; two-hour lesson, $119; full day, $289. Discounts for additional person.

Special programs: Ski Weeks include five two-hour group lessons, social events, a fun race and video analysis for $159 (all age categories).

Child care (2001/02; Cnd$ without GST)

Ages: Newborn to 10 years.
Costs: $39 half day, $59 full day, $9 lunch option.
Reservations: Mandatory; call 558-6028.

Children's lessons: Children ages 3-10, full day (includes a four-hour group lesson), $59. Half-day (includes a two-hour group lesson), $39. A full-day package for Adventure Week includes five four-hour lessons and lunches, $249; a half-day package includes five two-hour lessons, $159. Youth ages 11-18 have lessons tailored after adult programs: two-hour group lesson, $39; Discover Skiing includes lift, 90-minute lesson and rental, $35; Discover Snowboarding, $55; Ski Weeks include five two-hour group lessons, social events, a fun race and video analysis for $159.

Lift tickets (2001/02; Cnd$ without GST)

	Adult	Youth (13-18)	Child (6-12)
One day	$49	$39.50	$24.50
Four days	$180 ($45/day)	$142 ($35+/day)	$88 ($22/day)
Five days	$225 ($45/day)	$177.50 ($35+/day)	$110 ($22/day)

Who skis free: Children 5 and under.
Who skis at a discount: Seniors 65-69 pay youth rates, 70 and older pay child rates.
Note: Multi-day rates include night skiing (when applicable), Nordic skiing and skating.

Accommodations

All Silver Star hotels are centered around the conference center, no more than a 45-second walk to anywhere in the village. Call **Central Reservations** at (800) 663-4431.

Creekside condominiums (877-630-7827; 558-7825; $$$-$$$$) have one- and two-bedroom units, a fireside lounge and an outdoor hut tub patio. The **Grandview** (877-630-7827; 558-7825; $$$) condominium complex has 33 two-bedroom units, each with a view of the Monashee Mountains. **Mountain Vacation Homes** (800-489-0599; 542-2459; $$$$) rents private homes located in residential areas on-mountain with easy access to lifts and village. There also is a 47-site **RV park** in the ski area.

The **Silver Lode Inn** (800-554-4881; 549-5105; $$-$$$) is a Swiss-style hotel with 32 rooms, some with kitchenettes, fireplaces and Jacuzzis. The **Lord Aberdeen Apartment Hotel** (800-553-5885; 542-1992; $$$-$$$$) has private-entrance, one- and two-bedroom apartments, each with a full kitchen. The hotel has a sauna and shops downstairs.

The **Silver Star Club Resort** (800-610-0805; $$-$$$$) has outdoor rooftop hot tubs on its three buildings. The Vance Creek Building has hotel rooms only, but most units in the Chilcoot and Silver Creek buildings have full kitchens.

The **Pinnacles Suite Hotel** (800-551-7477; $$$$) sits on the edge of the ski runs and has units with up to four bedrooms. **Putnam Station Inn Hotel & Restaurant** (800-489-0599; 542-2459; $$-$$$) features a unique railroad atmosphere, plus an outdoor hot tub under the water tower, Craigellachie Dining Room, Cellar Lounge wine bar, and access to the pool and weight room.

Samesun Ski Hostel (877-56CARVE; $-$$) offers ski-in/ski-out accommodations with hot tubs, free breakfast and linen service. Private or family rooms available; there's also the option of dormitory rooms.

Dining

Bugaboos Bakery Café, (545-3208; $-$$) noted for its award-winning strudels and coffee, is a European-style café. **Paradise Camp** ($), at the Putnam Creek mid-station, is good for an informal lunch or snacks. Some ski writers think it's the best place on the continent to enjoy a beer in the spring. In the Townhall day lodge, the **Town Hall Eatery** ($-$$) and the **BX Express Snack Bar** (558-6024; $) are just what their names suggest.

In the Silver Star Club Resort you'll find the full-menu/lounge **Clementine's Dining Room** (549-5191; $-$$), **The Italian Garden** (549-5191; $-$$) and the **Vance Creek Saloon** ($-$$), serving light meals and snacks until midnight. Don't miss the **Aberdeen Deli Company** (260-4904; $). Soups are a specialty and there's a wide variety of homemade fare.

Dining: $$$-Entrees $20+; $$-$10-20; $-less than $10.
Accommodations: (double room) $$$$-$200+; $$$-$141-$200; $$-$81-$140; $-$80 and less.

More upscale is the **Craigellachie Dining Room** (542-2459; $$) in the Putnam Station Inn. It has a full Okanagan wine list and a full menu selection. Uh-oh…*Ski Canada* magazine voted the Craigellachie the "Best Kids' Restaurant." Also in the Putnam, **The Okanagan Wine Cellar** ($$) is an intimate wine bar with light meals. It's open until 11 p.m. The **Silver Lode Inn Dining Room** (549-5105; $$-$$$) features Swiss and international cuisine and a buffet diner on Thursday evenings.

Après-ski/nightlife

Be sure to check out the *Entertainment Weekly* when you check in. It lists the special après-ski activities that vary from week to week. Meanwhile, head over to the **Vance Creek Saloon** where there's entertainment to be had Wednesday to Saturday. **Charlie's Bar** is quieter and more cozy. It's off the Silver Lode Inn Dining Room.

Other activities

Silver Star's **Adventure Park** has a lift-served Tubetown, skating pond, Mini-Z snowmobile park for kids, horse-drawn sleigh rides, snowmobile tours and snowshoe excursions. The **National Altitude Training Center** has a climbing wall (lessons available) and swimming pool; there's also either a feature activity or a movie in the auditorium almost every night. The **village** has a teen center, western saloon, bars, cafés, delicatessens, liquor store, ski & snowboard shop, clothing & gifts shop and a grocery store. Guided **snowmobile tours** are available. You can also take a ride through the village in a **horse-drawn carriage**.

Getting there and getting around

By air: Kelowna Regional Airport is about an hour's drive from Silver Star and a short flight from Vancouver, Calgary or Seattle. It's served daily by Air BC (Air Canada). Horizon has five non-stop flights daily from Seattle—a 50-minute flight. Airport shuttles serve the resort from the Kelowna airport (prices in Cdn$, including GST): Adult/youth round trip, $60; child round trip; $43; children 5 and younger ride free; there also is a return family package for $217. Reservations required, call Central Reservations at 800-663-4431.

By car: Silver Star is 40 miles northeast of the Kelowna airport. The resort is 6 hours from Vancouver and 7 hours from Seattle.

Getting around: Silver Star's village is complete, so there is no need to have a car. A free shuttle bus loops continuously throughout the resort until 10 p.m. daily; with two daily trips to the Sovereign Lakes Cross Country Area and weekly shopping trips to Vernon.

Panorama Mountain Resort

British Columbia, Canada
in the Canadian Rockies Region

Summit elevation: 7,800 feet
Vertical drop: 4,000 feet
Base elevation: 3,800 feet

Address: Panorama Mountain Village,
Panorama, B.C., Canada V0A 1T0
a Area code: 250
Ski area phone: 342-6941
Snow report: 342-6941
h Toll-free reservations:
(800) 663-2929 (North America)
Fax: 362-5833
E-mail: paninfo@panoramaresort.com
Internet: www.panoramaresort.com
Expert:★★★
Advanced:★★★
Intermediate:★★★★
Beginner:★★★ **Never-ever:**★★★

Number and types of lifts: 9-1 8-person
village gondola, 1 high-speed quad, 1 triple,
2 doubles, 4 surface lifts
Skiable acreage: 2,847
Snowmaking: 40 percent
Uphill capacity: 7,000+ per hour
Snowboarding: Yes
Bed base: 2,000 at the base
Nearest lodging: slopeside, ski-in/ski-out
Resort child care: Yes, 18 months and older
Adult ticket, per day: $42-$50 (2001/02 Cdn$)
Dining:★★★ (resort), ★★ (region)
Apres-ski/nightlife:★★★ (resort), ★★ (region)
Other activities:★★★

Panorama Mountain Resort is two hours south of Banff on the west side of the Continental Divide, which separates Alberta from British Columbia. Just think about the massive snowfall from clouds trying to rise over the Divide. Yum. British Columbians figure they get the best of the winter deal.

Since purchased by Intrawest Corporation in 1993, Panorama Mountain Resort has been a-building. The village, known as Panorama Mountain Village, is fast becoming one of the Canadian Rockies' premier winter vacation destinations. With the addition of ski terrain, high-speed lifts, restaurants, giant slopeside hot pools, accommodations and a village gondola, life is looking pretty good on the western slope of the Rockies.

With almost 3,000 acres, including bowls, the Extreme Zone, terrain parks and the FIS-regulation halfpipe, Panorama is definitely on the Canadian ski map. Panorama is known for its high percentage of intermediate, advanced and expert runs and, since everything is below treeline, its abundance of glade skiing. One of the lifts travels nearly a mile from the base area. Continue nearly another mile up the Horizon chair to get to most of the black-diamond runs. Two T-bar rides will get you to the very top, where a new summit hut café allows you to enjoy the "view of a 1,000 peaks." Oddly, Panorama seems to have more snowbladers than anywhere else we've ever been. First-time visitors can learn their way around with a free guide service.

Mountain layout—Skiing

Last season's addition of the 700 acres of "Outback" in Taynton Bowl has upped the fun meter here, and it was already almost off the scale. The bowl used to be strictly heli-skiing terrain, providing a backcountry experience for the intermediate and advanced skier, with loads of wide-open and naturally gladed runs. The main chutes are more than 1,700 vertical feet. Access to Taynton Bowl is off the Summit lift. Other good expansions have included Millennium run (a fall-line run between the top of the Horizon Chair and the Sunbird Chair), the Extreme Zone and the Sun Bowl. Experts will enjoy the Glades Summit, Schober's Glades, Hideaway and the double-black-diamond Extreme Dream Zone. Intermediates favor the Alive glades and Sunbowl. The secluded beginner area, with a platter and a chair, is in the lowlands, away from the hubbub.

Mountain layout—Snowboarding

The Showzone Terrain Park has an FIS-regulation halfpipe, and the mountain offers night riding to piped-in DMX music. But while most riders give the manmade stuff a thumbs up, they really come here for the natural terrain. This resort rocks for intermediate, advanced and expert riders. Last season the resort added "Outback" with 700 acres of backcountry terrain. You'll find chutes, glades and wide-open runs here. The only bummer for riders is T-bars take you to the summit, which can literally be a drag if you're not adept on them while on a board.

Cross-country and snowshoeing

The **Beckie Scott Nordic Centre** (342-6941 ext. 3840) offers 20.5 km. of groomed cross-country trails for classic and skating. The Nordic clubhouse (the Greywolf Golf Course Clubhouse in another season) has rental equipment, waxing service, lessons and refreshments, plus changing rooms, lockers and showers. Trail fees are $7 adults, $6 teens, $5 juniors. The Hale Hut warming cabin, on the Delphine Loop, has bathrooms and a firepit with firewood for those who need to take a break.

Lessons (2001/02; Cdn$ without GST)

The Bilodeau School of Skiing and Snowboarding is highly regarded. **Group lessons:** Powder, Bumps and Stumps is a one-day clinic (four hours) for intermediate and advanced skiers that teaches route selection and advanced skills. Cost is $89. Parallel Skier Clinics are for intermediate to advanced skiers who want to gain skill and confidence as all-mountain skiers. These 1 1/2-hour clinics meet at 1:15 p.m. and cost $39. The Free Ride Camp is for novice to intermediate snowboarders who are ready for long, cruising slopes, trees and powder. It includes skill development and guiding from an expert pro. The Freestyle and Half Pipe Camp teaches halfpipe tricks, jumping and hits. Both camps meet at 10 a.m. for four hours; cost is $69.

Never-ever package: First-time skiers can take a MagicTrax Group Lesson with specially trained MagicTrax instructors and "shortcut" shaped skis. A two-hour lesson and gear rental cost $49. First Run Snowboard (or Second Run for novices) is a three-hour group introduction to snowboarding. Cost is $89, including rentals.

Private lessons: One-hour lessons cost $69, 1 1/2 hours cost $89.

Special programs: Confidence Club for skiers is a three-day group clinic designed to help you master the blue runs. Cost is $129 for 10 1/2 hours of instruction.

Child care (2001/02; Cdn$ without GST)

Ages: 19 months through 5 years old.
Costs: $40 for all day (9 a.m. to 4:30 p.m.); $25 half day. Lunch is an additional $5.

Reservations: Call 342-6941 ext. 3260. Telus Mobility call-in stations are on the mountain for parents to check in on their wee ones. Evening babysitters available by arrangement.

Children's lessons: There are extensive lesson offerings for children. Register in advance with the ski school for all children's lessons, 888-SOS-7799 or 342-6941. The Snowbirds program is an introduction to skiing for kids ages 3-5 years old. Lessons are at 9:15 a.m. or 3:15 p.m. and cost $19; most children spend the rest of day in child care. The all-day Adventure Club (10:30 a.m. to 3 p.m.) is for kids ages 5-14 and costs $59 including lunch. First-time skiers ages 14 and older can take a MagicTrax Group Lesson with specially trained MagicTrax instructors and "shortcut" shaped skis. A two-hour lesson costs $49; includes gear rentals. First Run Snowboard for kids age 8 and older teaches the basic skills of sliding, turning on an easy slope and lift riding. The four-hour lesson starts at 10 a.m. and costs $89; includes rentals. The Free Ride Camp for kids 8 years and older is for novice to intermediate snowboarders who are ready for long, cruising slopes, trees and powder. It includes skill development and guiding with an expert pro. The Freestyle and Half Pipe Camp for kids 8 years and older teaches halfpipe tricks, jumping and hits. Both camps meet at 10 a.m. for four hours; cost is $59.

Lift tickets (2001/02; Cdn$ without GST)

	Adult	Child (7-12)
One day	$50	$27
Three days	$129 ($/day)	$69 ($/day)
Five days	$209 ($/day)	$109 ($/day)

Who skis free: No one.

Who skis at a discount: Teens (13-18) and seniors (65 and older) pay $39; three days, $99; five days, $164. Children ages 6 and younger pay $9 per day. Full-time students ages 19-25 with ID get 10 percent off adult rates.

Accommodations

Panorama has more than 400 slopeside condos and townhomes, plus a 102-unit hotel. All lodging is packaged with lift tickets. The best deal is $179 (Cdn$) per person for three nights and four days of skiing. Call 800-663-2929 for all slopeside lodging reservations, or book online at www.skipanorama.com.

Ski Tip Lodge, Tamarack Lodge, Panorama Springs Condo/Hotel, Taynton Lodge, Riverbend Townhomes and **Hearthstone Townhomes** ($$–$$$) are studio to three-bedroom condos and townhomes with a full kitchen, fireplace, VCR and television. All were recently built as Intrawest's signature lodging in the heart of the upper village surrounding the slopeside hot pools.

Horsethief Lodge and **Toby Creek Lodge** ($$) are family-style studio condos with one to three bedrooms, some with lofts, in the lower village. Units have a full kitchen, fireplace, television, VCR and underground parking. New Village Gondola and Toby chair provide easy ski and upper village access.

The **Pine Inn** ($–$$), located at the base of the ski lifts and close to Greywolf Golf course, has hotel rooms designed for budget-oriented guests. Rooms have full bath, television and coffeemaker

The **Elkhorn Cabin Bed & Breakfast** (888-767-7799) sits on Panorama Mountain overlooking Toby Creek Valley and across to Mount Nelson. It's rustic, romantic and very com-

Dining: $$$-Entrees $20+; $$-$10-20; $-less than $10.
Accommodations: (double room) $$$$-$200+; $$$-$141-$200; $$-$81-$140; $-$80 and less.

fortable. The package includes a fireplace, bed quilts, big pillows, washbasin, soap and towels, plus dinner and breakfast prepared in advance. Price per couple is $239 plus tax (Cdn$); for second couple add $139 plus tax (Cdn$).

Dining

With eight restaurants in the village, plus more down-mountain in Invermere, the dining options are plentiful, though we only had the opportunity to sample two. The **Starbird Steakhouse** ($–$$), behind the quad chair and gondola, serves good hearty breakfasts; light fare, sandwiches and pizza for lunch; and pasta, seafood, oven-baked pizza, beef and pork for dinner. The **Toby Creek Dining Room** ($$–$$$) serves tasty seafood, Alberta beef, wild game and pastas.

Aprèss-ski/nightlife

Outdoor hot tubs are available, plus the **Panorama Springs** giant slopeside hot pools. Inside fun is available at the **Jackpine Pub**, **Kicking Horse Bar & Grill**, **Heli-Plex Bar & Grill** and the **Glacier Nite Club**.

Other activities

In Ski Tip Lodge, the Mountain Adventure Centre (342-6941 ext. 3440) is a complete information and booking service for activities and events, including **hot springs tours, dinner shuttle to Invermere restaurants, day trip to Lake Louise, games arcade, sleigh rides, snowmobile tours, massage therapist** and more.

The nearby town of Invermere on the Lake has **shopping** and **working art studios.** Taxi and shuttle service are available. Toby Creek Adventures (342-5047 or 888-357-4449) offers **guided snowmobile tours,** specializing in hourly and multiday guided tours in the Columbia Valley between Fairmont Hot Springs and Radium Hot Springs.

Getting there and getting around

By air: Calgary International Airport is the gateway to Panorama. The airport is 185 miles from Panorama and is served by all major airlines. There is daily shuttle service from both Calgary International Airport and Banff. Transfers must be pre-booked with accommodations. Cranbrook Airport, 75 miles north of Panorama, is served by regional air carriers.

By car: From Calgary, take TransCanada Highway 1 west through Banff to the Highway 93 junction with Kootenay Parkway (about 12 miles past Banff). Take Highway 93 south to Radium, BC (63 miles). From Radium, drive south about 8 miles on Highway 95 to the town of Invermere, then continue 11 miles from Invermere directly to Panorama Mountain Village.

Getting around: While a car is certainly not needed at Panorama, the reality is that most visitors arrive by car, and they're handy for getting to Invermere on your own schedule.

Red Mountain

British Columbia, Canada

Summit elevation: 6,800 feet
Vertical drop: 2,900 feet
Base elevation: 3,900 feet

Address: P.O. Box 670
Rossland, B.C., Canada V0G 1Y0
✆ Area code: 250
Ski area phone: 362-7384
Snow report: 362-5500; (509) 459-6000 (U.S.)
ⓘ **Toll-free information:** (800) 663-0105
Toll-free reservations: (877) 969-SNOW (7669)
Fax: 362-5833
E-mail: redmtn@ski-red.com
Internet: www.ski-red.com
Expert:★★★★★
Advanced:★★★★★
Intermediate:★★★
Beginner:★★ **Never-ever:**★

Number and types of lifts: 5–3 triple chairs, 1 double chair, 1 T-bar
Skiable acreage:1,200-plus
Snowmaking: None
Uphill capacity: 6,150 skiers per hour
Snowboarding: Yes
Bed base: 300 rooms within 6 miles
Nearest lodging: slopeside, mountain inn
Resort child care: Yes, 18 months and older
Adult ticket, per day: $36–$43 + tax
(2001/02 Cdn$)
Dining:★★★★
Apres-ski/nightlife:★
Other activities: ★★

The charming town of Rossland and its surrounding mountains were settled by goldminers in 1897. Today it still has a gold-mine feel thanks to an unpretentious, friendly ski resort called Red Mountain. This resort epitomizes how skiing used to be—inexpensive, with friendly locals, low-frills, surprisingly excellent restaurants and a pure adrenaline rush from top to bottom.

Nancy Greene trained on Red, and won Olympic gold in 1968. Kerrin Lee-Gartner, also from Rossland, did the same in 1992. In fact, Red Mountain has contributed more skiers (27) to Olympic and World Cup competition than any other mountain in North America.

Red Mountain's casualness is appealing. Even today, maps don't show boundaries. This is the kind of place you come to if you want to ski or board all day long, have something to eat, wash it down with a cold beer, flop into bed at night, then do it all again the next day.

Mountain layout—Skiing

◆◆ **Expert** ◆ **Advanced:** Red Mountain consists of two distinct mountains, Red and Granite. Red has a few short and steep runs at the tippy top. But the real experts will want to head to Granite for fabulous tree skiing, chutes, glades, steeps and cliff bands. The Orchards, Chutes of Pale Face, Cambodia, Needles, Short Squaw, Beer Belly and the Slides are just some of the runs where experts will shine and many advanced skiers may be humbled. Bump enthusiasts can test their skills on Gambler Towers and Centre Star, while powder hounds will find secret stashes in Papoose Bowl, Sara's Chute and Beer Belly.

Tree skiing is a big draw here. No point in choosing a favorite run through the woods, because you may never find it again—skiers who have worked here for years still find new routes. Some locals come up in the summer and cut their own trails to open up secret stashes they discovered earlier. Skiers are advised to double up in the woods.

A free Snow Host service is available to newcomers, and it's smart to take the tour. The Snow Hosts will take you around the mountain, but are forbidden to take skiers down the extreme steeps and tight trees. Hire a guide for access to the best spots. A Michigan skier leaving after his first visit to Red summed it up, "What you see is not what you ski. Get a local or a guide to show you the way into the best runs."

■ **Intermediate:** On Granite, head to the Paradise Triple chair. Groomed runs such as Southern Belle, Southern Comfort, Gambler and Ruby Tuesday—among others—let you cruise and take a dip into the trees where you feel comfortable.

● **Beginner:** The beginner area is nicely separated from the rest of the mountain. Stick to the T-bar or the Silverload triple chair for a good spot to learn the basics. Terrain for those shifting from beginner to intermediate is limited.

●● **Never-ever:** Plenty of skiers learn here. Stay with the T-bar and Silverload triple.

Mountain layout—Snowboarding

The woods here are what appeal to freeriders. Caution: Many trails through the woods are unmarked, ungroomed and unpatrolled. Don't ride alone.

Red is one mountain where hiring a local guide can make a big difference in your vertical day. For starters, try Meadows, Mini Bowls, and Inagadadavida. Check the day's grooming report before tackling Main Run and Schuss. Maggie's Farm is considered advanced-intermediate because of the tricky tree riding.

Beginners should stay on the open slopes or practice off the T-bar. Of course, riding a T-bar on a snowboard is one of the toughest things you can do, so once you're up top the rest is easy. Strong-legged beginners like Long Squaw, a 5-mile cruiser that wraps around Granite Mountain.

Mountain rating

Red Mountain is exceptional for advanced-intermediate to expert skiers. Skiers and riders will find plenty of trees and very steep terrain. Solid intermediates will be pushed to their limits. Lower-intermediates and beginners may be discouraged by the lack of gentle slopes.

Cross-country and snowshoeing

Blackjack Cross Country Ski Club across the road (362-9465), has 40 km. of trails. About 25 km. are groomed, both double-tracked and for skating. Trails wind past hemlock stands and frozen beaver ponds. Day passes cost Cdn$7 or five days for Cdn$30.

Free cross-country skiing on tracks set after every snowfall is available 28 km. north of Rossland (on Hwy. 3B) in the **Nancy Greene Provincial Park.** The 45 km. of trails are maintained by the Castlegar Nordic Ski Club. There are also tracks set after snowfalls on the **Centennial Trail,** which runs from the upper part of Rossland to Red Mountain, for free cross-country skiing.

Lessons (2001/02; Cdn$ with GST)

For lessons or guides call 362-7115.

Group lessons: $30 for two hours on skis or snowboard; $100 for a four-pack of lessons.

Never-ever package (lifts, lesson and rentals): $45 for the first and second day skiing or snowboarding (T-bar and Silverlode only).

Private lessons: One hour, $50; three hours, $125. Guiding costs $125 for three hours (1-2 persons), $20 for each additional person. Guiding is for expert skiers and riders only.

Special programs: Every Sunday and Wednesday is Women's Day, with a two-hour lesson, discounted lift tickets and an après-ski party. The ski school also conducts weekly ski and snowboard camps, adult weekend camps, powder seminars and telemark lessons.

Child care (2001/02; Cdn$ with GST)

Ages: 18 months to 6 years.

Costs: Full day (4+ hours), $35; half day (less than 4 hours), $16.50; $5 per hour. Most bring lunch.

Reservations: Recommended. Call 362-7114. The child-care center also can provide a list of babysitters.

Children's lessons: For ages 3–6, a two-hour afternoon lesson with hot cocoa break is $30; an all-day program with lessons and day care is $45 per day (lunch $3 extra). Kids 7–15 get full-day group ski lessons for $60. Reservations are required.

Lift tickets (2001/02; Cdn$ without GST)

	Adult	Child (7-12)
One day	$43	$23
Three days	$111 ($37/day)	$57 ($19/day)
Five days	$180 ($36/day)	$93 ($18.50/day)

Who skis free: Children ages 6 and younger and seniors ages 75 and older.

Who skis at a discount: Skiers age 65–74 pay $28. Teens 13–18 ski for $35 a day, $93 for three days and $153 for five days. A beginner-lifts-only ticket is $10 (for T-bar and Silverload lifts).

Note: The five-day price we list is for a book of five non-transferable tickets that must be used within seven consecutive days.

Accommodations

Red Mountain Central Reservations can book all travel, lodging and ski packages. Its toll-free number is (877) 969-7669, or call 362-5666 if you are calling from another continent and can't access the toll-free number. We list a few choices, but there are others. Prices at Red Mountain are very reasonable, generally less than $100 per night (Cdn$).

The **Ram's Head Inn** (362-9577; $$) is only a short walk from the base area. This comfortable country inn is No Smoking with 14 units, hot tub, sauna, bountiful breakfast, recreation and a ski wax room in a cozy setting. The tiny, six-room, **Red Shutter Inn** (362-5131; $–$$) is right in the ski area parking lot with hot tub and sauna. The inn doesn't have a shuttle to the airport per se, but they will pick guests upon request.

The 67-room **Uplander Hotel** (362-7375; $–$$) in town has sizeable rooms and great dining. The **Swiss Alps Inn** (362-7364; $–$$$) is a bit out of the center of town, but has some No-Smoking rooms, large outdoor hot tub and a good restaurant with Swiss specialties. The **Rossland Motel** (362-7218) has rooms with kitchens; perfect for families.

Dining: $$$-Entrees $20+; $$-$10-20; $-less than $10.
Accommodations: (double room) $$$$-$200+; $$$-$141-$200; $$-$81-$140; $-$80 and less.

Rossland also has a series of B&Bs. Try **Angela's Place** (362-7790; $–$$), **Heron's Nest** (362-7365;$–$$), **Mountain Comfort** (362-9004; $–$$) or **Sleeping Bear** (362-7646).

The **Mountain Shadow Youth Hostel** (362-7160 or 888-393-7160; $) has rooms for $17 a night. Most bunks are shared with five others but there are a couple of private rooms. Kitchen facilities are open to all.

 ## Dining

This town is a major surprise when it comes to dining. At least three of the restaurants—Olive Oyl's, Mountain Gypsy and Louis Blue Room—serve diverse, upscale and contemporary cuisine that seems out of sync with the rustic mountain, mining town. Call for reservations.

Perhaps the finest cooking is found at **Olive Oyl's** (362-5322; $$–$$$). Next try **Mountain Gypsy** (362-3342; $$–$$$). Then head to the **Louis Blue Room** in the Uplander Hotel (362-7375; $$–$$$). These eateries offer excellent wines and dinner entreés such as salmon, prawns, sirloin steaks and tender lamb chops. Leave room for desserts at each.

We're told that in true Rossland tradition, the new **Idgies Restaurant** (362-0078; $$) serves wonderful wine and creative food with a "world flavor." The **Flying Steamshovel** (362-7323) is a lively pub and Mexican restaurant with great views. **Sunshine Café** (362-7630) has basic burgers and pasta in major portions.

For a full breakfast head to **Amelia's** in the Uplander Hotel, the **Sunshine Café**, or **Sourdough Alley** in the base lodge. **Clansey's** has baked goods and coffee. **Alpine Grind Coffee Shop** serves hot and cold breakfasts (and awesome Belgian waffles on weekends).

 ## Après-ski/nightlife

For immediate après-ski, head to the **Rafter's Lounge** upstairs in the base lodge. By 5 p.m., the action has headed to Rossland. The Uplander Hotel's **Powder Keg Pub** has terrific jazz every Wednesday and live music on most weekends. The **Flying Steamshovel** is another gathering spot, but the action is mostly where you and your friends get together. The biggest party of the year is the **Winter Carnival** for three days in January with a snow sculpture contest, dances and other festivities. Call 362-5399.

 ## Other activities

The Rossland Arena has **hockey games, curling matches** and public **ice skating.** High Mountain Adventures (362-5342) has **snowmobile tours** and rentals. There's a small collection of **shops.** Browse through Mainstage Gallery for local art, GoldRush Books and Espresso for you know what, the Cellar for Canadian-made gifts, and the Legacy Gift Room and Feather Your Nest for unique home décor.

 ## Getting there and getting around

By air: The airport in Castlegar, 20 miles north, is served by Air B.C. or Canadian Regional Airlines from Vancouver, Edmonton and Calgary. Hotel pickup and rental cars are available, or call Castlegar Taxi, 365-7222. The nearest airport with U.S.-carrier service is Spokane, 125 miles south. **By car:** Red Mountain is 10 miles from the Canada-U.S. border on Hwy. 3B. From Spokane, take Hwys. 395 and 25 north to Rossland. **Getting around:** We recommend a car for off-slope exploring. The town bus and hotel shuttles only go to the mountain in the morning around 8:30–9:30 a.m. and have pickups in the afternoon when the lifts close around 3:30 p.m.

Whistler Blackcomb
British Columbia, Canada

Whistler Resort Facts

Address: 4545 Blackcomb Way, Whistler, BC, Canada V0N 1B4 (resort)
4010 Whistler Way, Whistler, BC, Canada V0N 1B4 (Tourism Whistler)

✆ **Area code:** 604 **Ski area phone:** 932-3434 **Snow report:** 932-4211 **Fax:** 938-5758

ⓘ **Toll-free reservations:** (800) 944-7853 (800-WHISTLER)

Internet: www.whistler-blackcomb.com (resort) or www.tourismwhistler.com (Tourism Whistler)

Bed Base: 5,000+ **Nearest lodging:** Slopeside, hotel and condos

Resort child care: Yes, 3 months and older **Snowboarding:** Yes

Adult ticket, per day: $61-$62 (01/02 Cdn$ prices; including G.S.T. tax)

Dining:★★★★ **Apres-ski/nightlife:**★★★★★ **Other activities:**★★★★★

Whistler Mountain Facts

Base elevation: 2,140 feet (Creekside)
Summit elevation: 7,160 feet
Vertical drop: 5,020 feet
Number of lifts: 16–1 10-person gondola,
1 6-person gondola, 6 high-speed quads,
2 triples, 1 double, 5 surface lifts
Snowmaking: 4 percent
Skiable acreage: 3,657 acres
Uphill capacity: 29,895 per hour
Expert:★★★★★
Advanced:★★★★★
Intermediate:★★★★★
Beginner:★★★
Never-ever:★★★

Blackcomb Mountain Facts

Base elevation: 2,214 feet (Village)
Summit elevation: 7,494 feet
Vertical drop: 5,280 feet
Number of lifts: 17–1 eight-person gondola,
6 high-speed quads, 3 triples, 7 surface lifts
Snowmaking: 11 percent
Acreage: 3,414 skiable trail acres
Uphill capacity: 29,112 per hour
Expert:★★★★★
Advanced:★★★★★
Intermediate:★★★★★
Beginner:★★★★
Never-ever:★★

Whistler Blackcomb has consistently been rated as the most popular ski resort in North America, according to most ski and travel magazine surveys. There are several reasons for this: two mountains with the largest vertical drop on the continent (over 5,000 feet for each), tremendous bowl skiing, runs that wind down the mountain seemingly forever—the longest run is 7 miles—and to top it off, a marvelous five-village base area with lodging, restaurants and nightclubs, all within walking distance (cars are banned from Whistler Village center).

Both mountains are operated by Intrawest Corporation, which developed the beautiful pedestrian village at its base. Now, both mountains belong to the same family, and are the one great resort that most tourists always knew they were. Their recent name change reflects that merge: Intrawest at Whistler Blackcomb.

Generally, Whistler (the name most folks use for this two-mountain resort) gets rave reviews, but two drawbacks that come up most often by word of mouth sound worse than they really are. One is Whistler's weather. Located close to the Pacific Ocean at a low base altitude at just over 2,000 feet, Whistler can get heavy rain or dense fog at times. But, the weather at the bottom isn't always what's at the top—it may be raining in Whistler Village, but snowing (or even sunny) on the summit. Crystal-clear, sunny days are a frequent surprise, especially later in the season, and on those days skiing conditions are just awesome. Skiers will sometimes cite horrendous lift lines (primarily at base areas early in the morning) as the other problem, but in reality the few lines that develop look longer than the actual wait, thanks to high-speed lifts at the five base areas.

This is one of the most international ski resorts, attracting skiers from Australia, Asia, Europe and Latin America as well as North America. Whistler Village is European-style, built to house, feed and amuse tourists. It's huge. Whistler has more than 100 restaurants and bars, over 200 shops, plus more than 100 condos, B&Bs, lodges and hotels offer upwards of 5,000 units, with more being built.

There are five villages in the valley: Whistler Village, Village North, Marketplace (formerly known as Whistler North), Upper Village (the Blackcomb base) and Creekside (the original Whistler base), which has just undergone a major renovation. Town Plaza connects Whistler Village and Marketplace, and is lined with hotels, restaurants and shops. Each of these villages is about a five-minute walk from the others while Creekside is a five-minute taxi ride south.

Major improvements in recent seasons include an express lift at Whistler, The Peak chair, plus some beginner and intermediate runs underneath; and the Roundhouse Lodge on Whistler, with four restaurants and a conference facility with an adjacent Telus Guest Communications Centre for those who mix business with pleasure. There's now a restaurant, appropriately named Chickpea, at the top of the Garbonzo Express. A World Cup halfpipe also was recently built on Blackcomb.

Whistler Mountain has one high-speed quad starting at the Whistler Village base area. The Village quad (with a bubble), which alleviates congestion, ends at mid-station near the Children's Learning Center and connects to the second, the Garbonzo Express, which replaced the triple Black Chair. Four gladed runs off the Tokum and Bear Paw areas were cut in the north-facing Garbonzo Basin. This provides a third point of access to the alpine via Franz's chair and also opens more mid-mountain terrain that can be skied when the high alpine is shut down due to bad weather. Also now open is the Westin Resort & Spa, a 419-room, four-star hotel that wraps around the Whistler and Blackcomb gondola bases in the central Whistler Village base area (see Accommodations).

New for 2001/02, Intrawest continues the $50-million revamp of the Whistler Creek base that includes three condo-hotels and a pedestrian stroll with restaurants, shops and a grocery store. The first phase centers on a new retail/rental shop, expanded kids' ski school facility and a new Dusty's Bar and Grill, a long-needed update for the original apres-ski watering hole at Whistler (it opened for the 2000/01 season).

Mountain layout—Skiing

Ski both mountains. Part of the appeal is to stand on one mountain and look across the steep Fitzsimmons Valley at the runs of the other—to chart out where to go or gloat over where you've been. Both mountains offer complimentary tours for all abilities, which may be the best way for those new to this resort to learn their way around. Tours meet outside the Roundhouse Lodge on Whistler and the Rendezvous on Blackcomb at 10:30 a.m. and 1 p.m. The tour guides are seasoned skiers at both mountains so you'll get some history with your adventure.

uu **Expert u Advanced:** At Whistler, start at the Whistler Village Gondola and take a speedy ride up 3,800 vertical feet to the Roundhouse Lodge. Ascending over so much terrain, you'll think you're at the summit, but one glance out the gondola building reveals a series of five giant bowls above the treeline. These spread out from left to right: Symphony Bowl, Harmony Bowl, Glacier Bowl, Whistler Bowl and West Bowl (plus the unseen Bagel Bowl, far to the right edge of the ski boundary), all served by the Harmony Express and Peak Chair. Experts will pause just long enough to enjoy the view and then take the Peak Chair to the 7,160-foot summit, turning left along the ridge to drop into Glacier Bowl. Or they'll do the wide mogul apron, Shale Slope, in upper Whistler Bowl, rest awhile at the ridge and then have another go below Whistler Glacier. There are no marked runs here—it's wide open. Be creative and let fly. Double-diamond skiing off this summit is in West Bowl.

Though most of the expert playground is above treeline, the lower mountain has a few advanced challenges, most notably the Dave Murray Downhill, which starts at the top of the Orange Chair and drops more than 2,000 feet to the Whistler Creekside base.

There's another whole mountain. Blackcomb's gondola, Excalibur, is just to the left of Whistler Mountain's base. A high-speed quad, Excelerator, at the top of the gondola, connects skiers to another high-speed quad, Glacier Express, going to the glacier at the summit.

Another fast way up Blackcomb Mountain is on the speedy Wizard Express, a sleek quad with an aerodynamic Plexiglas windscreen that also keeps out the rain, which can be a menace at the 2,200-foot base area. At the top of the lift, 2,230 feet higher, you're still not halfway up the mountain. Hop on Solar Coaster, next to Wizard Express unloading area, for another 2,000 feet. Here at Rendezvous Restaurant are routes for all abilities.

To get into the wide-open territory from Rendezvous, take Expressway, a lazy beginner's traverse, to 7th Heaven Express. That lift takes you to Mile High summit, where a daily, free guided exploration of this upper terrain for intermediate and advanced skiers leaves at 11 a.m. From the Mile High summit, the routes off the back side into Horstman and Blackcomb Glaciers give the feeling of being hundreds of miles into the wilderness. You can also reach these glaciers by taking the Glacier Express, which you reach from Rendezvous by heading to the bottom of the Jersey Cream Express chair.

While going down the spine off the back of Horstman, keep to the left and peer over the cornice into the double-black-diamond chutes. Just seeing the abyss—or seeing someone hurl himself into it—gives quite a rush.

The best known of these severe, narrow chutes is Couloir Extreme. The entry requires a leap of faith and skill. Nearby is Cougar Chute, also a double black. One of the most difficult chutes on the mountain is Pakalolo, which is very narrow and steep with rock walls on either side. "You don't want to miss a turn," a local says. Another, called Blowhole, drops from the trail leading to the Blackcomb Glacier from the Horstman Glacier.

■ **Intermediate:** With the installation of the Peak Chair at Whistler, crews also cut some easier beginner and intermediate runs down from the top of the Peak. Frontier Pass, a blue run, and Matthew's Traverse, a green, give easier access to Whistler Bowl, West Bowl, Bagel Bowl and over to the Harmony Chair. There are two other intermediate ways down. One, Highway 86, is to the right of West Bowl, keeping to the ridge around Bagel Bowl instead of dropping in. The other is Burnt Stew, arguably the most scenic on the mountain. It goes high and wide off to the left of Harmony Bowl, sometimes flattening into a bit of a trudge. Reached by a long cat track that loops behind the bowls, its views are dominated by the imposing Black Tusk peak. Of the bowls at the top, Symphony is the by far mildest.

If you want to know what skiing a distance of 5 miles feels like, take the Alpine T-bar near Roundhouse Lodge and turn right to find the bronze plaque identifying Franz's Run, one of the longest ski trails in North America. It turns and pitches and rolls and goes forever, ending up at the Whistler Creek base. Any intermediate will enjoy this one.

At Blackcomb, intermediates will especially love the trails off the Jersey Cream Express. They are wide and as smooth as the name implies. The runs under the Solar Coaster Chair also are good blues.

Don't let the summit intimidate, especially in sunny weather. Intermediates can easily handle runs in the 7th Heaven area and on the two glaciers. In fact, the long run down the Blackcomb Glacier on a bluebird day is a memory you will cherish.

●● **Beginner:** At Whistler, beginners won't be able to experience the upper bowls, but will find green-circle routes down from the Roundhouse, which is, after all, more than 3,800 feet above the village. Pay attention to signs. Once you're on an intermediate trail, there's usually no escape.

A surprise for Blackcomb beginners is a sinuous run called Green Line. This takes off from the upper terminal of 7th Heaven Express and follows the natural contours of the mountain from top to bottom on trails that are groomed daily. It's a thrilling way for beginners to do big-mountain skiing, but getting down, down, down may take all day. Another easy descent from the Hut is Crystal Traverse. It winds below the glaciers, becomes the Crystal Road and passes the Glacier Creek Lodge before joining Green Line two-thirds of the way down.

● **Never-ever:** At Blackcomb, the learning areas are at the base. At Whistler, the never-ever area is at the gondola's midstation, about 1,000 feet higher than the base (the Children's Learning Center also is there). Both mountains' learning areas are covered by snowmaking and are fairly isolated from high skier traffic (Blackcomb's is sectioned off).

 ## Mountain layout—Snowboarding

Most riders, especially freeriders, prefer the Blackcomb side because of the preponderance of fall-line runs. The Whistler side was originally designed with the mountain's contours in mind, but a lot of fall-line runs have been added in recent years to even the score.

Blackcomb Mountain, which boasts a snowboard Camp of Champions, features a World Cup halfpipe near the bottom of the Catskinner Chair, just below the immense terrain park on Catskinner. Some flats to avoid, unless you just have to go across to the 7th Heaven Express, are 7th Avenue and Expressway to the right of the Catskinner Chair. Blackcomb cruisers like the runs around the Jersey Cream Express chair and the Jersey Cream Wall have some nice little jumps when the snow is fresh.

Whistler Mountain grooms its competition-grade halfpipe nightly. It's accessible from the top of the Emerald Express, and just below it is the terrain park on the Green Acres trail. Ridge riding and plenty of bowls can be reached from the top of the Harmony Express chair.

Mountain rating

When you ask locals which mountain they prefer, you get mixed responses. Even super experts have reasons for enjoying both, and intermediates will have a field day on either set of slopes. Beginners can have a good time, especially because they can get down from the summit (and it's always fun to get to the top). This is one of the best resorts for non-skiers, because of the many enjoyable activities off the mountain, and because non-skiers can ride the gondolas to admire the views.

 ## Cross-country and snowshoeing

Nordic skiing is available on the municipal **Lost Lake Trails,** 28 km. of double-tracked trails with a skating lane. Trails are well marked, and start a quarter-mile from the village. Trail passes are Cdn$10, $4 after 6 p.m. and free for kids after dark. At night, a 4-km. stretch of trail is lit until 10 p.m. The Chateau Whistler Clubhouse, on the golf course, is a great rest stop, as is the log hut at Lost Lake. Call 932-6436 for conditions or information.

Most avid cross-country skiers take **BC Rail** to the Cariboo region and the 100 Mile House, with more than 150 km. of groomed tracks. For information, contact BC Rail Passenger Services, Box 8770, Vancouver, B.C. V6B 4X6, or call 984-5426 or Great Escape Vacations at (800) 663-2515. **Snowshoe** treks are offered by Canadian Snowshoeing Adventures (932-0647) at the midstation of the Whistler Village Gondola.

 ## Lessons (2000/01 prices; Cdn$ not including GST)

Prices provided are for regular season, and are higher for peak periods and lower for value periods. It's best to call ahead for information and to reserve a space in a class, (800) 766-0449, or locally, 932-3434.

Group lessons: There are full-day and afternoon adult workshops in parallel skiing, bumps, powder and steeps. Snowboarders can choose from freeriding, carving or freestyle workshops. Prices vary, call for information.

Never-ever package: The new MagicTrax program is a full-day ski class. One day costs $109, three days cost $299 (includes novice ticket and rental). One-day and three-day snowboarding camps for adult beginners (average age is getting closer to 40) are $99 and $273, respectively. Camps include lessons, lift ticket and rental equipment.

Private lessons: $345 for a half day; $525 for a full day.

Special programs: Multi-day camps aim at women, advanced skiers wanting to reach a higher level, and other topics. Call for details and prices.

Racing: Whistler has a NASTAR course under the Green Express chair. Blackcomb has two NASTAR courses, one on Springboard under the Solar Coaster Express, and the other on Cougar Milk in the Jersey Cream area.

Child care (2000/01 prices, Cdn$ not including GST)

Ages: 3 months to 3 years.
Cost: Full day is $84, includes lunch and snacks.
Reservations: Required; call (800) 766-0449 or 932-3434. This program includes quiet play, story time and other activities designed specifically for each age group. Whistler/Blackcomb's child-care centers are at the Whistler Village Gondola base building, the Creekside Gondola and the base of the Wizard Express (Upper Village Blackcomb base).

Other options: The Fairmont Chateau Whistler suggests the **Nanny Network** (938-2823), which comes highly recommended for babysitting. Another babysitter service in the village is **Whistler Kids** (938-7316). The **Whistler Activity Center** (932-2394) can also refer you to babysitting services. **Babies on the Go** (905-0002) and **Fun for Kids** (932-2115) rent and will deliver baby needs to your lodge, such as crib, stroller, car seat and toys.

Children's lessons: Full-day lessons for ages 3–12 years (in various programs separated by age and ability) cost $79. Lunch is included, but rental equipment and lift tickets are extra. One popular program for ages 3–12 is a five-day camp at $365 that starts each Monday. Children's rental package includes a helmet. Teen programs are offered daily for $79 for a full day including lunch. Three-day teen camps cost $237.

Lift tickets (2001/02; Cdn$ including GST)

	Adult	Child (7–12)
One day	$62	$31
Three days	$186 ($62/day)	$93 ($30/day)
Five days	$305 ($61/day)	$153 ($30+/day)

Who skis free: Children ages 6 and younger.
Who skis at a discount: Teens (13–18) and seniors 65 and older ski for $158 for three days, $259 for five. Super seniors (75+) can purchase a $99 season pass with unlimited use, a great buy even for destination visitors planning to make one multiday trip for the season.
Note: Prices are rounded to the nearest dollar, and include Canada's Goods and Services Tax (G.S.T.). For more on G.S.T., see the Canada introductory chapter. Tickets are good at either mountain, and prices are a little higher during the week between Christmas and New Year's Day. Those who drive to Whistler can save about $5 (U.S.) per lift ticket by purchasing them at 7-Eleven stores in Squamish, a town about 25 miles south of the resort. This promotion is for B.C. and Washington State residents; ID will be requested.

Accommodations

Lodging varies from dorm bunks to European-style B&Bs to luxury hotels. Most guests stay in the village condominiums. Lodging has become quite expensive at Whistler, though you may be able to find some bargains off-season or with lift-and-lodging packages. The best starting point is **Whistler Central Reservations**, (800) WHISTLER (944-7853). Taxes of 17 percent will be added to lodging bills—10 percent hotel and the 7 percent Canadian Goods and Services Tax (GST). During holiday periods (generally late December), seven-night minimum stays are given priority, as a general guideline.

The 419-unit, all-suite **Westin Resort & Spa** (888-634-5577, 905-5000; $$$-$$$$) opened in April 2000. It's conveniently located mountainside in Whistler Village with ski-in/ski-out access to both mountains, a world-class spa and health club, an indoor-outdoor restaurant with a West Coast menu and a cozy lounge for après-ski.

The **Fairmont Chateau Whistler** (800-606-8244; $$$–$$$$) is part of what used to be Canadian Pacific Hotels. It has 558 rooms in 12 stories, an expansive sun deck stretching below the high turrets, two restaurants, an expanded lounge off the lobby for great après-ski, an extensive health club and a renovated world-class spa. Another full-service property is **Delta Whistler Resort** (800-268-1133 from the U.S. and Canada;932-1982; $$$–$$$$) with 292 rooms, 30 percent of which are kitchen-equipped suites.

The **Summit Lodge** (888-913-8811; 932-2778; $$$–$$$$), nestled in the heart of Whistler's Marketplace, is a quiet, luxurious boutique retreat with 81 fireplace suites, covered balconies, soaker tubs, kitchenettes, down duvets and dataport telephones. The **Pan Pacific Lodge** (888-905-9995; 905-2999; www.panpac.com/hotels; $$$–$$$$) is a high-end hotel just a few paces from the Blackcomb Excalibur and Whistler Village gondola bases. It has suites with gas fireplaces, kitchens, floor-to-ceiling windows and soaker tubs.

The **Residence Inn by Marriott-Whistler/Blackcomb** (800-777-0185; 905-3400; $$$–$$$$), with 186 units, is secluded, up at the end of Painted Cliff Road on the Blackcomb side beside the Wizard Express lift and alongside the Lower Cruiser run. Good bear sightings in this neighborhood. **Pinnacle International Resort** (888-999-8986; 938-3218; $$$–$$$$), on Main Street in Village Centre, bills itself as Whistler's first "boutique/romance hotel." It has suites with queen beds and double Jacuzzis close to the fireplace. The **Glacier Lodge** (800-777-0185; 938-3455; $$$–$$$$) is decorated in pale plush. The **Crystal Lodge** (800-667-3363; 932-2221; $$$–$$$$) has 137 rooms. Cozy common areas around the fireplaces give a European atmosphere. Families who don't mind a longer walk to the village center may find the **Tantalus Lodge** (800-268-1133 from the U.S. and Canada, or 604-932-4146; $$$–$$$$) suitable (it's a Delta Property). All 76 units have two bedrooms, two baths, full kitchen, fireplace and balcony.

The **Hearthstone Lodge** (800-663-7711; 932-6699; $$–$$$$), the **Listel Whistler Hotel** (800-663-5472; 932-1133; $$$–$$$$), and the **Blackcomb Lodge** (800-667-2855; 932-4155) all have good accommodations.The **Holiday Inn SunSpree Resort** (800-229-3188; 938-0878; $$$–$$$$) is in Whistler Village Centre. Its suite design is very imaginative, and maids are not allowed to use sprays in certain "allergy-free" rooms.

The **Coast Whistler** (800-663-5644; 932-2522) is well placed, just off the hubbub of the central core, with nice views of the Whistler Golf Course. The **Edgewater Lodge** (888-870-9065; 932-0688; $$$–$$$$) is on a peninsula of Green Lake, bordering a golf course and the River of Golden Dreams. Great for those who want luxury and no village bustle. The least expensive accommodations are outside the village at **Shoestring Lodge** (932-3338; $$) offering dorm beds for $28-$32 per night and twin or queen rooms at $95. **Whistler Resort and Club** (932-2343; $$–$$$) has rooms from $85 a night, depending on the season.

Two dormitory lodges and a youth hostel have beds at about $28 a night—**Fireside Lodge** (932-4545), **UBC Lodge** (604-932-6604; $) and **Whistler Hostel** (932-5492).

Whistler also has upscale B&Bs. These are located in residential areas and usually have no more than eight rooms. Most have private baths. Rates start at about $125 and include breakfast. Ask for those with BC Accommodations approval.

Durlacher Hof (932-1924; $$$–$$$$) is the genuine B&B article for skiers wanting an Austrian lodging experience. At the door, you swap your boots for boiled-wool slippers. Each of the eight rooms has its own bath and extra-long beds. On occasion, visiting celebrity chefs prepare dinner on the weekends.

Dining: $$$-Entrees $20+; $$-$10-20; $-less than $10.
Accommodations: (double room) $$$$-$200+; $$$-$141-$200; $$-$81-$140; $-$80 and less.

Dining

For years locals have recommended the **Rimrock Cafe and Oyster Bar** (932-5565) in Highland Lodge as the best restaurant in town. It is located at Whistler Creek, about a half-mile from the village. Well-prepared seafood is complemented by an extensive wine list. **Les Deux Gros** (932-4611) is another local favorite for the best in French fare. It's about a mile south in Twin Lakes Village.

Bearfoot Bistro (932-1133; $$$–$$$$) in the Listel Whistler Hotel has come a long way since it opened in 1996. Once a simple French bistro, the main restaurant is now a high-end French restaurant offering a fixed-price accomplished gourmet chef's menu that begins with 1,600 wines and a French tradition called "sabering." Guests can "saber" a bottle of champagne in a celebratory ceremony by running a sword along the seam of a champagne bottle and blow the cork against a distant wall to cheers of other diners. There is no menu per se but trust the chef with a multi-course dinner of oysters with Nashi pear, bronzed sea scallops, black cod, Ontario squab, loin of wild Arctic caribou, sorbet and soups, petit fours, all courses accompanied by friendly wines from the huge cellar. Where else could you get Dom Perignon by the glass? There's a less formal (and less expensive) bar with the same kitchen adjacent.

Aubergine (905-5000; $$-$$$) at The Westin features magnificent views and specialty seafood menus from their executive chef. Next door enjoy simpler fare from the **Firerock Lounge** (935-4338). If you're into beef, don't miss the classic **Hy's Steakhouse** (905-5555, $$-$$$) on the corner of Village Gate Blvd. and Northlands Blvd.

Val d'Isère (932-4666; $$-$$$), now in the Town Plaza, features fine French cuisine. Umberto Menghi, a flamboyant Italian chef whose TV cooking show is popular in Canada, is well known for his restaurants in Vancouver and two in Whistler—**Trattoria Di Umberto** (932-5858), more casual, and **Il Caminetto Di Umberto** (932-4442; $$–$$$), more formal, where Italian Tuscan cuisine is featured. You can also take home his private-label olive oil and Bambolo wines from Tuscanny. Locals call Umberto "their Emeril." Umberto's main man for 16 years, Mario Enero, owns **La Rua** (932-5011). **Araxi** (932-4540; $$–$$$), on the village square, serves Mediterranean dinners, imaginative pastas and pizza. A great place to people-watch.**Quattro's** (905-4844; $$–$$$), in the Pinnacle Hotel, is one of the most popular (and well-deservedly so) Italian/Mediterranean restaurants in the development north of the main village. It has an innovative kitchen and a 600-plus wine list.

The Old Spaghetti Factory (932-1081; $–$$) in the Crystal Lodge has moderate prices as does **Evergreens** (932-7346; $–$$) in the Delta Whistler Resort. Evergreens has a fine weekday buffet breakfast for $18.95; Sunday, $26. Right next door along the same promenade, the **Cinnamon Bear Sports Bar** (932-1982; $) serves typical bar fare, burgers, pizzas and salads from 11 a.m. to 11 p.m. **The Keg** (932-5151; $–$$) has good steaks and basic American-type food.**Auntie Em's Kitchen** (932-1163; $), in the Village North Market Place, is a way-above-average deli with a deep menu featuring monster vegetarian sandwiches, matzo-ball soup, breakfast all day, and good breads and sweets, especially the cranberry-date bar. **Ingrid's Village Café** (932-7000; $) on Skier's Approach near Village Square, is a local legend in Whistler. In business since 1986, meet the whole family as you enjoy a huge breakfast for cheap in their cozy deli.

Caramba (938-1879; $-$$), in Town Plaza, is a favorite of our staff Whistler experts. It is "Mediterreaneanish," with a great putanesca pasta, wood-fired pizzas, and a Caramba salad (chicken, butter lettuce, peanut sauce), all at very reasonable prices.

On the Blackcomb side, top dining spots are the **Wildflower** (938-2031; $$–$$$) in the Fairmont Chateau Whistler for fresh seafood and Pacific Northwest cuisine, and **Portobello** (938-2040; $$), which has a la carte dining at tables where you order from a menu but also has an extensive deli counter where you can order out. **Monk's Grill** (932-9677; $$–$$$), just down the way from the Chateau, features USDA steaks.

At the streetside entrance to the Le Chamois building is a local's favorite Thai restaurant, **Thai One On** (932-4822; $$), featuring nicely priced dishes for eat-in or take-out. **Zeuski's Taverna** (932-6009; $$), in the Whistler Town Plaza, has moderately priced Greek food. Lots of visiting Japanese tourists means excellent Japanese restaurants. **Sushi Village** (932-3330; $$–$$$) is legion. For steaks cooked Japanese steakhouse-style, it's **Teppan Village** (932-2223) or the very popular **Sushi Ya** (905-0155; $$–$$$) in the Marketplace area. They also do take out.

Moderate-priced dining is also available. **The Crab Shack** (932-4451; $$) across from the conference center has affordable steaks, chicken and pasta. Moe's Deli and Bar is now **Milestones** (938-4648; $–$$) but has the same huge family and casual-style menu and the Palomino Bar. A number of restaurants with international themes have recently opened in Whistler. In the Pan Pacific Lodge, **Dubh Linn Gate Old Irish Pub** (905-4047; $$), an authentic Irish pub, has a country feel with offerings of stews, steak & kidney pie, fish & chips and the best draft beer selection in Whistler. **Crepe Montagne** (905-4444; $$) serves up French everything: music, language and savory crepes. Fondue and raclette are also available. Great pancakes and waffles for breakfast.

Get a taste of Spain at **Fogata** (932-7518; $–$$$) where the campfire (fogata in Spanish) is a rotisserie which spins game, chicken and lamb for a Mediterranean menu. **Las Margaritas** (938-6274) offers healthy Mexican fare, heavy on vegetarian options (not only do our readers recommend it,it was voted the best Mexican restaurant in Whistler by Ski Canada magazine). **The Amsterdam Cafe** and **La Bocca** (932-2112) are primo people-watching spots, facing Whistler Village Square, the heartbeat of Whistler.

There's good food on the mountains, too. For fine dining, stop for lunch at **Christine's** (938-7353) in the back of Rendezvous Lodge on Blackcomb. Reservations are a real good idea here. The Roundhouse Lodge at the almost-top of Whistler boasts four restaurants (all 932-3434) including **Pika's**, still perfect for families craving burgers and fries or gourmet baked potatoes and home-made soup. Try **Steeps Grill** for a simple menu of barbecue, soups, stews, salads and the only place in the lodge where you can buy spirits. **Mountain Market** offers open cafeteria-style dining with your pick of pastas, paninis, fish & fries, salads and deli sandwiches by the inch! **The Hot Stove** features a variety of Asian dishes depending on your mood: Thai, Japanese, Chinese, Indian and Indonesian.

Eager skiers can board the Whistler Village Gondola at 7:15 a.m. for a first tracks $14.95 buffet breakfast (lift ticket extra; through mid-April) and first rights to the runs. Locals hail this as the best breakfast in town. On the Blackcomb side, the Glacier Creek Lodge has the **River Rock Grill** with potato bar, oriental noodle bar and a great array of pastas and pizzas. In the same lodge, the **Glacier Bite** offers hearty soups and salads, with bistro-style counter service.

Condo renters: **The Grocery Store** in the village will deliver groceries to your condo for your arrival. Prices are higher than your local grocery store, but reasonable. Call 932-3628 to get a grocery list. Other options for **groceries:** Food Plus (932-6193), open 24 hours, is lo-

Dining: $$$–Entrees $20+; $$–$10-20; $–less than $10.
Accommodations: (double room) $$$$–$200+; $$$–$141-$200; $$–$81-$140; $–$80 and less.

cated in Creekside; IGA Plus (938-2850) in the Marketplace; and Nester's Market (932-3545) 1 km north of the village—"Where the locals shop."

 Après-ski/nightlife

Après-ski spills out onto the snow from **Garibaldi Lift Co. Bar and Grill** at Whistler Village Gondola base and **Merlin's** at Blackcomb. Both are beer-and-nachos spots with lively music. **Citta** in the center of Whistler Village is also a good après-ski site. **Dubh Linn Gate Old Irish Pub**, an Irish pub in the Pan Pacific Lodge, is catching on for immediate fun when the lifts close. Enjoy a rousing atmosphere with Celtic music and 28 beers on tap.

Things don't slow down when the lifts close. Whistler/Blackcomb has happening nightlife, from hot and heavy to sweet and subdued. Among the 100+ bars and restaurants, some of the most popular include **Maxx Fish,** a dance club with a wild interior paint job to match the gyrations and sense of abandon, next to the new Amsterdam Cafe in Village Square. It's Whistler's funkiest local hangout for nighttime mingling. Drop into a deep couch or pull up a bar stool beside a famous local athlete. **Tommy Africa's** is located in Whistler Village behind the zebra poles. It's a hunt to find, but the music and atmosphere makes the search worth it. If keeping in step with the go-go girls is too tough, belly up to one of the five bars for fuel.

The **Savage Beagle,** near the Village Center, has been recently renovated. This doggie dancing heaven favors funk and acid jazz in a double-decker, double-loud lounge right in the middle of downtown Whistler. More people watch than dance, but it's the dancers who have all the fun. Open until 2 a.m. **Moe Joe's**, across from **Buffalo Bill's** (also a big bar scene), is near the conference center just off the main Village Square. Search out the legendary **Garfinkel's** featuring music for the younger crowd in its new location in the Delta Whistler Village Suites. See and be seen at this trendy spot located next door to Lush, the natural soap and fragrance store in Middle Village. Just breathe deeply and follow your nose.

On site at one of the less expensive lodges in Whistler, The Shoestring Lodge, is the oldest pub in Whistler, **The Boot Pub**, where many locals hang out. Located a kilometer north of the village, it has great live entertainment and an adjacent restaurant, Gaitors, with a lively Mexican twist. For a more civilized après-ski or evening drink, snuggle in at the Fairmont Chateau Whistler's expanded **Mallard Bar** just off the hotel lobby with a view of Blackcomb Mountain. Or check out the **Cinnamon Bear Bar** in the Delta Whistler Resort. The **Firerock Lounge** at the new Westin Resort & Spa is centrally located in the heart of Whistler Village.

 Other activities

The resort puts on a **Fire & Ice Show** each Sunday during the winter months at 6:30 p.m. to welcome guests. Entertainment includes an outdoor fashion show, free massages, snowmobile and carriage rides, games and activities for kids, and pros from the Ski & Snowboard School performing tricks off the Big Air Kicker and through a 10-foot flaming hoop.

Heli-skiing is offered by Whistler Heli-Skiing (932-4105). This company also features **scenic flights.** Hundreds of miles of logging roads are accessible for **snowmobiling**. Cougar Mountain Wilderness Adventures (932-4086) and Blackcomb Snowmobiles Ltd. (932-8484) have tours several times a day, and evening rides. Canadian Snowmobile Adventures (938-1616) offers luxury evening tours up Blackcomb Mountain.

Covered **tennis** courts are located at the Delta Mountain Inn. **Ice skating, swimming** and drop-in **hockey** take place at Meadow Park Sports Centre (938-PLAY) a few miles north of the village. **Sleigh rides** are offered by Blackcomb Sleighrides (932-7631).

If the weather's bad, or for apres ski, **Alpen Rock House** (938-0082) is a great stop for families with alternative activities such as bowling, pool, video games and food. It's located in the Whistler Village Courtyard under the Holiday Inn. Also visit the **Mountain Climbing Centre** (905-7625) where you can literally climb the wall, also underground behind the Westbrook Hotel. The **Whistler Activity and Information Centre** (932-2394) provides information and reservations for these or other activities. **Intrawest Activity Centre** (935-3360) can book activities as well.

Shopping is plentiful and we could write an entire chapter! But just enjoy the thrill of discovery. There are the usual offerings. We don't mention T-shirt shops as a general rule, but Shirtprint, 1030 Miller Creek Rd. near Village Square, stocks shirts of high quality and the prints can be personalized. Canadian-made gifts are at Skitch Knicknacks and Paddywacks, 4222 Village Square. Expressions provides a great rainy day activity: You Paint It Ceramics. You pick a pattern, or do a freehand paint job, and pick up your mug, bowl or whatever after the glaze is fired. It's in the Stone Lodge, unit 125 at 4338 Main St., Marketplace. If you're into authentic Northwest Coast art, the Black Tusk Gallery at the Summit Lodge in Whistler North on Main Street is a must. Experience the works of leading native artists in the forms of totem poles, bowls, jewelry and sculptures.

The local **medical clinic** (905-7089) is open 7 days a week. For emergencies (8am-10pm) call the **Whistler Health Care Centre** (932-4911).

Getting there and getting around

By air: Most major airlines fly to Vancouver. Allow plenty of time in the Vancouver Airport, both arriving and leaving, for customs declarations and currency exchange. Perimeter Transportation (266-5386) connects the Vancouver Airport to Whistler 12 times a day, with the last bus leaving at 12:30 a.m. Fare is about $53 one way. Reservations are required by noon, one day prior. Whistler Star Express (685-5600, 905-7688) also shuttles between the airport, Vancouver and Whistler for $55 one way, reservations required.

Note on ground transportation: The Perimeter bus pickup is only at certain hotels. If you are staying somewhere that isn't on the list, you must get yourself and your bags to a pickup point on time. So keep that in mind as you make lodging reservations.

By train: The most scenic way to travel is to board BC Rail's passenger trains. Trains leave North Vancouver at 7 a.m. daily, arriving at 9:45 a.m. They depart Whistler at 6:40 p.m. and arrive at North Vancouver at 9:15 p.m. Advance reservations are required, one day prior. Roundtrip fare is about $69 for adults, $44 for children ages 2–12. Taxis go from the airport to the train station and a bus picks up train passengers at several downtown locations. Call (800) 663-8238.

By bus: Greyhound Canada operates from the Vancouver bus depot at Main and Terminal, and charges about $21 one way; $42 round trip (call 800-661-8747, 932-5031). You can also check www.greyhound.ca.

Getting around: For local cabs, call Whistler Taxi (932-3333). There's a free Village Shuttle and a local transit bus as well (932-4020).

Oregon regional resorts

Timberline Lodge, Timberline,   OR; (503) 622-7979
Internet: www.timberlinelodge.com
6lifts—4 high-speed quads, 1 triples, 1 double; 1,430 lift-served acres; 3,590 feet vertical

Timberline is known for its summer skiing and beautiful, historic lodge (For more detail, see *Accommodations*). Timberline was the continent's first ski area to offer lift-served summer skiing, and now more than 50,000 skiers come each summer. The Palmer Snowfield has a steady pitch at the advanced-intermediate level. It's challenging enough that you'll find World Cup ski racers from several countries practicing technique. A high-speed quad, Palmer Express, allows Timberline to keep the terrain open nearly the entire year, and gives the area the greatest vertical drop in the Northwest—3,590 feet. The deep snows of winter sometimes require cat drivers to dig out the lift, the upper terminal of which is inside the mountain. Spring skiing is incredible off this lift. Palmer runs through Labor Day every year, conditions permitting (and they usually do).

Half of Timberline skiing is still below tree line and the main lodge, but few experiences in the skiing world match a ride up the Magic Mile Super Express and the Palmer Express to the top of the Palmer Snowfield. The original Magic Mile lift was the second ski lift in the country, after Sun Valley's. Silcox Hut, which served as the original top terminus and warming hut, has been restored and is open to overnight groups. Below the Timberline Lodge are many blues and greens, with a few short blacks. The trail system between the trees makes each run feel like a wilderness excursion.

Timberline has two terrain gardens to challenge the best riders. The base of Paint Brush Glade has a halfpipe. One terrain park is half way down Conway's Corner, reached by the quad express chairlift next to Stormin' Norman. The other is on Walt's Baby, reached by the triple chair blow the lodge. The main fun for cruising takes place up on the Palmer Snowfield above the Silcox Hut. Timberline is known for its summer snowboard camps on the snowfield. The U.S. Snowboard Training Center is there during the summer. Call (800) 325-4430.

Lift tickets (00/01): Adult day tickets, $37 weekends/holidays, $31 midweek.
Distance from Portland: 68 miles.
Lodging information: (800) 547-1406

Mount Hood Meadows, OR (503) 287-5438 in Portland or (503) 337-2222 at the mountain
Internet: www.skihood.com
12 lifts—4 high-speed quads, 6 doubles, 3 surface; 2,150 lift-served acres; 2,777 feet vertical

Mt. Hood Meadows has by far the most varied terrain of the Mt. Hood ski areas and is as big as many Western destination resorts. Heather Canyon has always been the favorite for experts, when it is open. Now three of its entry runs—Twilight, Pluto and Moon Bowl—are winchcat-groomed, which means advanced and upper-intermediate skiers can go where they before had feared to tread. Snowcat skiing adds another 1,020 feet of vertical drop.

A favorite intermediate area is under the Hood River Express chair, called "Hurry" (for its initials—HRE). The entire HRE pod will be designated slow speed for families and novice skiers and snowboarders. Beginners have the runs under the Daisy, Buttercup and Red chairs. Mitchell Creek Boulevard, reached from the Red chair, is particularly great for kids. Night skiers are served by four chairlifts near the lodge, one of them a high-speed quad.

For snowboarders, Meadows has a lot of what you'd have to call "free range" terrain. Most anywhere is good for riding and most of the mountain rides big. The east-facing runs between the Cascade Express and the boundary—more of a face actually—are all smoothies, good for working on the turns and swooping back and forth. Between the Cascade Express and the Mt. Hood Express are six little bowls and patches of trees—all single-black runs. For the real deal, head to the experts-only Heather Canyon, the bulk of it reachable from the Morning Star Express. Absolute Magnitude is the best to jump into from the Shooting Star Ridge. For the upper canyon, you have to take Cascade Express and turn right. Things are steeper up here, starting with A-Zone and 7151. To start way high with the runs into Super Bowl, you must take the Super Bowl Snow Cat up 1,700 feet of vertical from the top of Cascade Express. The ride costs $10 per trip. Meadows also has a groomed halfpipe, a natural halfpipe and three terrain parks. There's nice terrain for beginners too.

Lift tickets (00/01): Adult day tickets, $43; children, $25 pre shift (Shifts are 9 a.m.–4 p.m., 11 a.m.–7 p.m., and 1–10 p.m.)

Distance from Hood River: 35 miles.

Lodging information: (800) 754-4663

Mount Hood SkiBowl,OR; (503) 272-3206

Internet: www.skibowl.com

9 lifts—4 high-speed quads, 4 doubles, 5 surface; 960 lift-served acres; 1,500 feet vertical

Mt. Hood SkiBowl is gaining a reputation for challenging ski runs with the addition of its Outback area and 1,500 feet of vertical reached from Upper Bowl. The mountain is now rated at 60 percent expert, but the 65 runs have enough variety for all skills. Beginners have some nice terrain, although the unloading ramps on the Multorpor side can be steep and intimidating for those at this level.

Mt. Hood SkiBowl claims to be America's largest night-skiing area by virtue of the number of lights. It illuminates 34 runs, including some truly steep black-diamond runs. It also emphasizes ski racing, with programs for a variety of age groups.

For snowboarders, the Multorpor side and the Outback are favorites. The Terrain Park, which runs the full length of the Multorpor chair, features a halfpipe, table tops, an Air Zone, and every table located under night lights. The Stump Garden is a boarder-cross course, accessible from the Cascade chair. Both areas are open to skiers and boarders.

Lift tickets (00/01): Adult day tickets, $35 all day, $30 9 a.m. to 4 p.m.

Distance from Portland: 68 miles.

Lodging information: no central reservations

Mount Bachelor,Bend, OR; (541) 382-2442

Internet: www.mtbachelor.com

12 lifts—7 high-speed quads, 3 triples, 2 surface; 3,686 lift-served acres; 3,365 feet vertical

Mt. Bachelor is not your typical mountain. At other resorts, the highest point often is difficult to distinguish from neighboring summits, which may be just a few feet higher or lower. But Mt. Bachelor, a stately volcanic cone that is part of the Cascades mountain range, rises from Oregon's high desert and is visible for miles in every direction.

On the eastern side of the Cascades, where snow falls lighter and drier than at other northwestern resorts, Mt. Bachelor has become a popular destination for western skiers and snowboarders. Despite no on-mountain lodging and little nightlife, Mt. Bachelor attracts visitors with its dependable snowpack, clear dry air, average daytime winter temperatures of 26 degrees, and fine skiing and snowboarding from early November to July.

Visitors should keep in mind that all that snow results from a lot of storms, and winds often close the Summit Express chair, a high-speed quad to the 9,065-foot treeless summit. When the weather is clear and you're standing on top, you can see California's Mt. Shasta 180 miles to the south. That view, most commonly seen in spring, is fantastic.

Between the Outback and Red chairs is an unusual geologic feature, a lone cinder cone. It's not lift-served, so powder lasts there until it's wind-packed. By getting up a head of steam from Leeway, skiers can swoop up nearly two-thirds of the way and climb the rest.

Mt. Bachelor's Northwest Express Quad serves 400 acres of tree skiing and open-bowl terrain in an area called the Northwest Territory. When the Summit Express is open, experts should head for it. The steepest descent is through The Pinnacles, a jagged rock formation reached by a 150-foot hike from the top of the lift, then across the broad ungroomed expanse of Cirque Bowl. Next might be Cow's Face, far to the left of Summit Chair, steep but smooth. Because it's unknown to many skiers, it doesn't get carved into moguls, but wind packs it hard. You usually can find moguls on Grotto, Canyon and Coffee Run, all off the Pine Marten chair.

This mountain is best suited to intermediates. The Outback Express, with a 1,780-foot vertical rise, serves excellent intermediate runs. From this chair, Boomerang is the only run rated black, and it parallels the lift. One blue run, Down Under, often is left ungroomed for mogul enthusiasts. Other popular chairs for intermediates are the Pine Marten Express and the Skyliner Express. Old Skyliner, off the Pine Marten chair, has marvelous dips and rolls. Most of the lower mountain is sheltered by trees, but some runs, such as Flying Dutchman and Tippytoe, give the exuberance of upper-mountain skiing.

For beginners green-circle trails descend from every lift except the Summit and Outback chairs. More difficult trails are on either side, funneling the faster skiers away from those still learning to control their turns. Never-evers have their own high-speed quad chair at Mt. Bachelor, Sunshine Accelerator. High-speed quads move very slowly for loading and unloading, which makes them ideal to learn the tricks of riding chair lifts.

Mt. Bachelor has an excellent and extensive program for snowboarders at all levels, including the High Cascade Snowboard Camp, an adult seven-day camp offered before Christmas and twice in April.

The halfpipe is located under the short Yellow Chair near the West Village Day Lodge. It has 8-foot sidewalls running for 200 feet, and it's 35 feet wide. The terrain park is reached by the Skyliner Express and is just before Pat's Way. It has quarterpipes, tabletops, spines and whatever the groomer fancied the night before.

Most freeriding takes place in the Outback, which is loaded with trees and fall-line runs. For your final run in the Outback, try to take the Outback Express back up to Pine Marten Lodge. If you take the Northwest Express Quad up, you have to traverse the Northwest Crossover, and it's a bit flat. The New Summit Express gets you to the Peak of Mt. Bachelor, well above treeline. There are some good steeps in The Cirque. Everything else up there to the left of the Express is gentle terrain.

Distance from Portland: 162 miles. **Distance from Bend:** 17 miles.

Lodging information: (800) 800-8334

Mt. Baker

Washington

Summit elevation: 5,250 feet
Vertical drop: 1,500 feet
Base elevation: 3,500 feet

Address: 1017 Iowa St.
Bellingham, WA 98226
✆ **Area code:** 360
Ski area phone: 734-6771 (This is the number of the Bellingham office. Mt. Baker has only cellular service, used primarily for emergencies.)
Snow report: 671-0211 (Bellingham); (604) 688-1515 (Vancouver)
ⓘ **Toll-free reservations:**
(800) 487-2032 (Bellingham-Whatcom Convention and Visitors Bureau) or (888) 261-7795 (Bellingham's Best Buys Discount Hotline)
Fax: 734-5332
Internet: www.mtbakerskiarea.com

Expert:★★★★★ **Advanced:**★★★★★
Intermediate:★★★ **Beginner:**★★
Never-ever:★★★
Number and types of lifts: 10 – 2 fixed-grip quads, 6 double chairs, 2 rope tows
Skiable acreage: 1,000 acres
Snowmaking: None
Uphill capacity: 6,000 per hour
Snowboarding: Yes
Bed Base: 300 in Glacier
Nearest lodging: 17 miles away in Glacier
Resort child care: None
Adult ticket, per day: $23-$33 (2000/01)
Dining:★ (on mountain), ★★★ (in Glacier)
Apres-ski/nightlife:★
Other activities:★

Mountain resorts need snow, and this resort in the northwest corner of Washington State gets more of it than any other. This is not hype. During the 98/99 season, Mt. Baker set a new world record, certified by the National Oceanic and Atmospheric Administration, for a winter season's snowfall of 1,140 inches. So if you're looking in your atlas to find this wonder of white, we should tell you that the ski area is not actually located on the 10,778-foot volcano of the same name. It's on an arm of 9,127-foot Mt. Shuksan, one of the world's most photographed mountains. It's also one of the most listened to, since its careening chunks of steep glacial avalanche can be seen and heard for miles around (they're well out of the ski area, so no worries, mate). But imagine the thrill of witnessing a slide from a distant lift.

In an era when smaller ski hills and non-destination resort ski areas are disappearing, Mt. Baker's success is an exception. Location, location and location, between Seattle and Vancouver, B.C., has a lot to do with it, but the main ingredients are the average annual 615-inch snowfall and its "non-corporate" style of management. It's just funky.

Mt. Baker added an award-winning day lodge, two quad lifts and expanded intermediate terrain a few years ago. Now, even on record days lift lines never top five minutes.

Its terrain helps, too. This is truly snowboarder heaven, where the hardcore insist "snowboarding was born." The mountain offers all-day possibilities to skiers and snowboarders alike, with plenty of faces and woods that bring out the pioneer spirit. The slopeside White Salmon Day Lodge has spectacular views of Mt. Shuksan. It's 3 miles closer to the nearest town of Glacier, with full food service and espresso, beer and wine. The Cascadian architecture of the building is full of pleasant surprises, from the paw prints in the restrooms to salmon sculptures in the railings to hand-carved animal newel posts. Performance rental equipment is available here; you can find regular gear and instruction at the upper Heather Meadows Base Area.

One drawback to the low elevation of the ski area is that the freezing level can yo–yo, and marginally cold days can turn snow to rain without notice. Ski patrollers keep a few sets of dry clothes in their hut for themselves. Bring a change of clothes, it's good insurance.

Mountain layout—Skiing

Newcomers sometimes have a tough time figuring how to get back to the Heather Meadows Base Area, because everywhere they go takes them farther away. With 1,000 acres to play with, that doesn't sound likely, but the ski area is laid out over two mountains, the Pan Dome side and the Shuksan (pronounced SHUCK-sun) side. Four chairs serve each side, but Shuksan is by far the more popular. It has the heaviest-duty terrain for snowboarders under the double Shuksan Chairs and the gentlest groomed slopes for beginners and intermediates.

◆◆ **Expert** ◆ **Advanced:** The Pan Dome side, served by Chairs 1, 2, 3 and 6, is for the mogul bashers and chute shooters. Hot skiers can play here endlessly challenging the steep and deep. Every time experts take one run, they are sure to find another just as hairy. Shuksan has more wide-open, powder bowl type of terrain.

The out-of-bounds areas are extremely attractive at Mt. Baker and many pass the signs and do the hikes. But avalanches are a problem out of bounds, and sometimes people die. In recent years, quite a few people have lost their lives when they left the ski area's boundaries and got caught in snow slides. Before you head out of bounds (and you'd better know exactly what you're doing if you choose to do this), check with the ski patrol. You'll need a location device, a shovel, knowledge of the conditions and a companion with the same equipment. Do not go alone.

■ **Intermediate** ●● **Beginner:** Nearly 70 percent of Mt. Baker's terrain is labeled blue or green. Chairs 7 and 8 expand the Shuksan possibilities, but beginners may want to avoid Chair 8 for the time being—its terrain is mostly intermediate. The ride, however, rivals Blackcomb's Jersey Cream Express Chair for the majestic view of the mountain ridges past the area boundary at Rumble Gully.

On the Pan Dome side, beginners can easily get back to the lodge on the Austin and Blueberry runs. The signage is good, but don't follow tracks or other skiers if you don't know where they're going. You may end up on steep Pan Face or unmapped places called Rattrap and Gunbarrel. The ski patrol performs rescues on icy crags that are best avoided.

● **Never-ever:** The learning area is near the Heather Meadows base lodge (the only one of the two base lodges where you can get lessons and rentals at this point), served by Chair 2. The slope is long and gentle, not sectioned off, but not used by more accomplished sliders. Snowboard novices—some of whom feel immortal rather than timid—use this slope. Timid novices probably are better off learning elsewhere.

Mountain layout—Snowboarding

Mt. Baker has long been popular with snowboarders, even in the early days of the sport. In the old snowboarding days, snowboarders were carving turns here even where the ski patrol would rather not go. They opened new terrain within the boundaries and so helped skiers improve their skills. There were only a few boarders then; now they're up to 70 percent of the mountain's business, at least.

World champion snowboarders practice regularly at Mt. Baker and live nearby. Aside from the abundant snow, a main attraction for snowboarders is the natural halfpipe. Starting from the top of the Shuksan Chairs, it follows a creek bed for a few hundred yards and is normally buried under 20 feet of snow. The halfpipe is the site of the annual Mt. Baker Legendary Banked Slalom snowboard competition. In its 17-year history, the January event has earned a national reputation, attracting riders from all over the U.S., Canada and Europe. Baker also has opened a groomed permanent halfpipe, 600 feet long, 80 feet wide and 10-12 feet high, just to rider's right of Chair 7 on the White Salmon Side.

Mountain rating

"Of my 100 deepest powder days in the last 20 years, 80 of them have been at Mt. Baker Ski Area," a local powderhound and heli-skier recently said. The challenge is to pick your days carefully and finish your skiing by 10:30 in the morning, when the runs are packed out. And take note: About 70 percent of bodies at Baker are on boards.

Cross-country and snowshoeing

Mt. Baker grooms a short, gentle Nordic loop to the north and west of the main upper parking lot, at about 4,000 feet. There's a nominal fee. The road ends at the ski area, so touring opportunities are all down-mountain on logging roads. The rental shop has snowshoes for "deep stuff" days.

Lessons

Lessons are offered at the Heather Meadows base lodge on weekends and holidays; midweek and non-holidays, go to the White Salmon Day Lodge.

Group lessons: Ski and snowboard lessons start daily at 10:30 a.m. and 1 p.m. and cost $20 per person ages 7 and up.

Never-ever package: A 90-minute lesson, beginner lift ticket and equipment is $40 for skiers ages 7 and up; $43 for snowboarders ages 7 and up.

Private lessons: $50 for 90 minutes, each additional person costs $15.

Special programs: Mt. Baker's clinics focus on women, shaped ski techniques and the disabled (a SKIable Adaptive Program serves skiers who require adaptive equipment). Beginner telemark lessons are given on Sundays. Inquire about monthly telemark clinics with some of the best telemark instructors in the Pacific Northwest.

Child care

The resort does not offer non-skiing child care.

Children's lessons: For first-timers ages 4-6, an hour of getting used to being on snow, including some time on gentle slopes, cost $14; $25 with rentals. One-hour lessons for kids ages 4-6 who have on-mountain experience cost $16; $25 with rentals. Kids 7 and older take lessons through adult programs.

Lift tickets

	Adult	Youth (7-15)
Weekend/holiday	$33	$25.50
Monday-Wednesday	$23	$19
Thursday & Friday	$25	$20

Dining: $$$-Entrees $20+; $$-$10-20; $-less than $10.
Accommodations: (double room) $$$$-$200+; $$$-$141-$200; $$-$81-$140; $-$80 and less.

Who skis free: Ages 6 and younger. The beginner rope tow is always free.

Who skis at a discount: Ages 60–69 pay the youth price. Ages 70 and older pay $10.

Note: Midweek prices do not apply during holiday periods. Mt. Baker is open Fridays and weekends only during the month of April.

Accommodations

Self-contained campers are welcome to spend the night in the parking lot (no hook–ups, no charge), but the nearest accommodations are 17 miles away in Glacier.

Mt. Baker Lodging (800-709-7669 or 599-1000; $$–$$$$), in Glacier, rents vacation houses, from cedar cabins to large chalets, all with kitchens and fireplaces. The **Mt. Baker Chalet** (800-258–2405 or 599-2405; $–$$$$), at Mile Post 33 on the Mt. Baker Hwy. at the west end of Glacier, has 20 cabins and condos. The **Snowline Inn** (800-228-0119 or 599-2788; $–$$) rents studio units for up to four people and condo loft units for two to 10 people.

Bellingham, 56 miles from the ski area on I-5, has a wider range of accommodations, including Best Westerns and B&Bs. **The Hampton Inn** (800-426-7866 or 676-7700; $–$$) near the Bellingham Airport has fitness and business centers, free shuttles anywhere in Bellingham and tasteful rooms. Those older than 50 pay about $65 for a room for up to four people (only the person signing for the room needs to be older than 50). Continental breakfast included. They also offer ski packages with Mt. Baker. The **Bellingham-Whatcom Convention & Visitors Bureau** can be reached at (800) 487-2032 or www.bellingham.org.

Dining/après-ski/nightlife

The White Salmon Day Lodge offers food service with a beer and wine license. The Heather Meadows day lodge has a brown-bag room, a cafeteria-style restaurant and taproom. Restaurant-quality Mexican fare, soups, espresso and daily specials are available in the **Raven Hot Café** at the foot of the Shuksan Chairs and Chairs 6 and 3, the hangout for lunch. On your way home, for dinner you can't beat **Milano's Cafe & Deli** (599-2863; $–$$) at 9990 Mt. Baker Hwy. in Glacier, 17 miles away. Milano's specialty is fresh-made pasta at very reasonable prices. The salmon ravioli and tomato sauces regularly draw raves, and the Caesar salad may be the region's best. There's an excellent selection of Italian wines and regional microbrews. The atmosphere is excitedly après-ski, but most of the staff are snowboarders. The nearest evening activities also are in Glacier.

Other activities

Anything you can do in a national forest you can do here, but you have to bring your own gear—snowmobiles, for example. Groomed trails leave Glacier in all directions, but no place rents the equipment. Ice skaters even hike up to Alpine lakes, and backcountry tourers go everywhere.

Getting there and getting around

By air: Bellingham International Airport is served by Horizon and United Express. Rental cars are availablehere. Seattle's airport is about 160 miles south of the ski area. Vancouver, British Columbia's airport is about 100 miles away.

By car: The Mt. Baker Ski Area is at the end of the Mt. Baker Hwy., 56 miles east of Bellingham, I-5, Exit 255. The drive from Bellingham takes about 90 minutes; from Seattle, allow three hours; and from Vancouver, B.C., two hours.

Crystal Mountain

Washington

Summit elevation: **7,012 feet**
Vertical drop: **3,100 feet**
Base elevation: **4,400 feet**

Address: 33914 Crystal Mountain Blvd., Crystal Mountain WA 98022
Area code: 360
Ski area phone: 663-2265
ⓘ **Reservations:** 663-2558, 663-2262 or (888) 754-6400
Snow report: (888) SKI-6199 (754-6199)
Road conditions: (800) 695-7623
Fax: 663-3001
E-mail: comments@skicrystal.com
Internet: www.skicrystal.com
Expert: ★★★★
Advanced: ★★★★
Intermediate: ★★★★★
Beginner: ★★★
Never-ever: ★★★★★

Number and types of lifts: 10—2 six-passenger high-speed chairs, 2 high-speed quads, 2 triples, 3 doubles, 1 surface lift
Skiable Acreage: 2,300 (including 1,000 backcountry)
Snowmaking: 1.3 percent
Uphill capacity: 19,110 per hour
Snowboarding: Yes
Bed Base: About 350 (176 rooms)
Nearest lodging: Slopeside, cabins
Resort child care: None
Adult ticket, per day: $40 (2000/01)

Dining: ★★★★
Apres-ski/nightlife: ★★
Other activities: ★

When the weather is right and the snow is deep, hardcore skiers from all over the West Coast beam themselves to Crystal for unparalleled skiing. The terrain is steep and thrilling, and there's enough of it to keep the adrenaline rushing all day. There's enough snow too, often 12 feet deep at the top. It snowed 65 inches one day during a recent season—and the average annual snowfall is 380 inches.

It's Washington's only destination Alpine ski resort, just a 90-minute drive from Seattle. The on-mountain condos, lodges and restaurants delight local skiers who would otherwise have to leave the state for a ski vacation. It is now owned by Boyne USA, owners of Big Sky, MT; Brighton, UT; two resorts in Michigan; and Cypress Mountain near Vancouver, British Columbia. Boyne installed the Forest Queen Express at Crystal, Washington's first high-speed six-passenger lift, which replaced the old Chair 9.

In its second year of long-term ambitious plans, Crystal added a second "six-pack," The Chinook Express, which replaced the Midway Shuttle chairlift. Visitors ride the Chinook Express, connect with the Rainier Express and travel from base to summit in less time than it took to take the Midway Shuttle alone. Last season, the Green Valley high-speed quad up to Grubstake Point was installed, making this the third high-speed lift at Crystal in four years. The day lodge restrooms were renovated with "40 new bowls" and two winch-cat groomers now lay down corduroy on steep slopes.

With two high-speed, six-person lifts and two high-speed quads, skiers and snowboarders can now really exhaust themselves on Crystal's nearly 2,600-foot vertical—the best in the state. Future plans—subject to many approvals—call for an all-season 80-passenger tram, midmountain restaurant, and the conversion of many of the fixed-grip chairs to high-speeds.

Mountain layout—Skiing

Experts may only see one-third of the trails designated for them, but they'll find their real thrills in the backcountry terrain here. And there's something to be said for skiing and riding a mountain dwarfed by nearby 14,410-foot Mt. Rainier.

◆◆ **Expert** ◆ **Advanced:** Black-diamond runs are a whopping 43 percent of the terrain. That high percentage is because of the 1,000 skiable acres in the inbounds backcountry areas, most of which is not lift-served. It's the kind of terrain that is out of bounds at most ski areas—woods, chutes and steep bowls. With the new winch-cat groomers, expect to see corduroy on runs like Iceberg Gulch, Green Valley and Deer Fly.

■ **Intermediate:** Blue runs make up another 37 percent of Crystal's 2,300 acres. However, runs are fairly short, such as Lucky Shot, Little Shot and Gandy's Run, all from Summit House. For a longer run, ski Green Valley from the right of Summit House to the base of the Green Valley chair and continue to the base area on Kelly's Gap Road.

●● **Beginner** ● **Never-ever:** Beginners can have fun on Broadway and Skid Road, both served by the new base-area lift, The Chinook Express. Queens is a 3.5-mile run. Never-evers have their own Meadow and Fairway runs served by Discovery chair. Child novices now have a "moving carpet" lift called the Kid Conveyor instead of a handle tow.

Mountain layout—Snowboarding

Crystal has woods, ridges and carving slopes that keep freeriders coming back. Many intermediate and advanced riders enjoy the up-mountain area off Green Valley Chair, reached by taking Chinook and Rainier Express.

Both the Rainier Express to Summit House and the Green Valley Chair to Grubstake Point will get you to the Northway Ridge and Northway Notch. From those you turn right to the double-black-diamond bowls of North Country, which is only open if the Ski Patrol says it is. This is legal backcountry boarding at its best, with the added bonus of a shuttle ride from the bottom of Lower Northway back to the main lift area. It operates daily.

For the acrobatically inclined, the terrain park and halfpipe are next to the Quicksilver Chair. The Quicksilver beginner run is also right next to the chair.

Lessons

Group lessons: $35 for a two-hour session, $45 for four hours; with lift ticket and gear rental, it's $75 for a two-hour lesson for skiing and $85 for snowboarding.

Never-ever package: Two-hour lesson, lift ticket and rental gear, $39, skiing or snowboarding. The four-hour version is $10 more.

Private lessons: For one or two people, one hour, $65; two hours, $120; three hours; $175; full day, $300. Add $10 per hour for each extra person.

Racing: Crystal has a coin-operated course for $1 per run.

Child care

The resort has no non-skiing child care.

Children's lessons: Ages 4-11. Includes lift, lesson and supervision. Full day $65 (with lunch); half day $45. Rental equipment costs $10.

Lift tickets

	Adult	Youth (11-17)
Single day	$40	$35

Who skis free: Ages 10 and younger (limit of two kids per paying adult; after that, $20 per child). **Who skis at a discount:** Seniors 70 and over, $10. Beginner-only lift tickets (Discovery Chair) are $20. Crystal Mountain does not sell multiday tickets, but a book of five adult all-day vouchers saves about $3 per day. The vouchers may be used by anyone and are sold at the mountain during the afternoons or at Costco.

Accommodations

Lodging is walking distance from the slopes. Three hotels and 96 condominiums vary widely in styles and prices, from about $50 for two with a shower down the hall in the **Alpine Inn** ($–$$$) to around $363 for a **Crystal Chalet** ($$–$$$$) condo on the weekends. The parking lot has 21 **RV hookups,** $20 per night each; more on holidays. For hotels, call (888) SKI-6400 or (360) 663-2262; www.CrystalHotels.com. For condos, call Alta Crystal Resort at (800) 277-6475 or (360) 663-2500, www.AltaCrystalResort.com; or Crystal Mountain Lodging at (888) 668-4368, (360) 663-2558, www.CrystalMtLodging-wa.com.

Dining/après-ski/nightlife/other activities

Restaurants cater to both the white-linen and take-out crowds, with rustic dining, a cafeteria and après-ski lounges in between. **Sourdough Sal's** has live entertainment most Friday and Saturday evenings. The **Snorting Elk Cellar** in the Alpine Inn is always the place to gather after a great day on the slopes. The Elk has a terrific selection of microbrews, full cocktail service and expanded food service to the bar from its own deli. **Summit House**, a rustic dining lodge at the top of the Rainier Express lift (6,872 feet), serves gourmet pizzas and pastas along with soups and salads, but the main attraction is the view of Mount Rainier, so close it looks as if you can touch it. **Alpine Inn Restaurant,** open for breakfast and dinner daily, has fine foods and wines. It's across the wooden footbridge tucked into the woods. You can find all your essential grocery, bakery, beer and wine needs at **The Market at Crystal Mountain.** You'll find a hot tub, sauna, showers and game room at **East Peak Massage and Fitness** (663-2505), located next to Silverskis condominiums above parking lot "C."

Getting there and getting around

By air: Seattle-Tacoma airport is served by most major airlines.

By car: Crystal is 76 miles southeast of Seattle and a 64-mile drive from Sea-Tac Airport. Drive south on I-5 from Seattle, take Exit 142 east to Auburn, Hwy. 164 to Enumclaw, and Hwy. 410 east to Crystal Mountain Boulevard.

By bus: Service from Puget Sound is available on the Crystal Mountain Express. Call (800) 665-2122, 8 a.m. to 5 p.m.

Dining: $$$–Entrees $20+; $$–$10-20; $–less than $10.
Accommodations: (double room) $$$$–$200+; $$$–$141-$200; $$–$81-$140; $–$80 and less.

Other Washington State Resorts

The Summit, Snoqualmie Pass, WA; (425) 434-7669; (206) 236-1600 (info line)

Internet: www.summit-at-snoqualmie.com

22 lifts; 1,916 acres; 2,200 vertical feet

The Summit comprises four separate ski areas, all within a mile of each other on Snoqualmie Pass. Three are connected by trails, and the fourth, Alpental, is a mile away on another face. The four areas—Alpental, Summit West, Summit Central and Summit East—share an interchangeable lift ticket and offer a free shuttle so skiers can get from one to the others. Our stats reflect the combined lifts and acreage, while the vertical listed is for Alpental. The vertical drop at the other three areas varies from 900 to 1,080 feet. Alpental has the most rugged reputation, Summit West features gentle green and blue runs, Summit Central has mostly gentle terrain with a few serious black-diamond drops off the ridge, and Summit East has some great tree runs and a snowboard halfpipe among its attractions. At least one of the areas (sometimes two) is closed every weekday, but the entire complex is open weekends and holidays. (If you want the specific schedule, call or visit the Web site.) A Nordic ski area offers 55 km. of trails. Child care starts at 12 months and is offered at Summit West and Summit Central. Night skiing operates until 10:30 p.m. (9 p.m. Sundays) on any mountain open that day. Night child care is available by reservation.

Lift tickets (01/02 prices): Weekend/Holiday: adults, $37; youth (7-12)/senior (62-69), $24; children 6 and younger, always $7. Weekday: adults, $29; youth/senior, $20.

Distance from Seattle: About 50 miles east on I-90.

Lodging information: Summit Inn, (800) 557-7829.

Stevens Pass, Skykomish, WA; (206) 812-4510

Internet: www.stevenspass.com

10 lifts; 1,125 acres; 1,800 vertical feet

The geographical elevation combined with dry wind from the east make the snow conditions nearly perfect throughout the operating season. The annual average snowfall is 450 inches and snowpack is 105 inches. The upper-front of Big Chief Mountain is steep and dense with Alpine conifers and a few skinny runs, providing the most challenging terrain at Stevens. The lower-front of Big Chief has one open intermediate run. The backside of Big Chief, called Mill Valley, faces south and has lots of very open runs and is popular among Stevens die-hards. On the front of Cowboy Mountain lies the most intermediate runs and lighted night-skiing terrain. From the top of Cowboy, amazing scenery and backcountry access is possible, as well as more challenging experts terrain. In the heart of the base area is the beginner terrain and tube city. The night terrain offers something for everyone—two lighted high-speed quads combined with four additional lifts access 12 major runs through 400 acres. Night operations run seven nights a week, 4–10 p.m. Tube City is lit until 9 p.m. The Kid Zone Childcare is for kids ages 3 months to 12 years old. The Stevens Pass Nordic Center has 30 km. of groomed cross-country and snowshoe trails.

Lift tickets (01/02 prices): Weekend/Holiday: adults, $43; children (7-12), $27; senior (62-69), $30; ages 6 and under & 70 and over ski for $5.

Distance from Seattle: About 78 miles northeast on Hwy. 2. **Lodging information:** SkyRiver Inn in Skykomish, (360) 677-2261. Leavenworth, with its Alpine Bavarian theme, is 35 miles east of Stevens Pass. For Leavenworth lodging, call Bavarian Bedfinders at (800) 323-2920, or the Leavenworth Chamber Of Commerce at (509) 548-5807.

Hotel Legend

- 🚐   Airport Shuttle
- ⛷   Ski-in /ski-out
- 🏊   Indoor heated pool
- 🏊   Outdoor heated pool
- 🏋   fitness center
- 🍴   restaurant
- 🐾   Pets OK
- 🚭   No Smoking
- 💨   In-room Hairdryers
- 🅿   Parking

visit us online at
www.resortspace.com

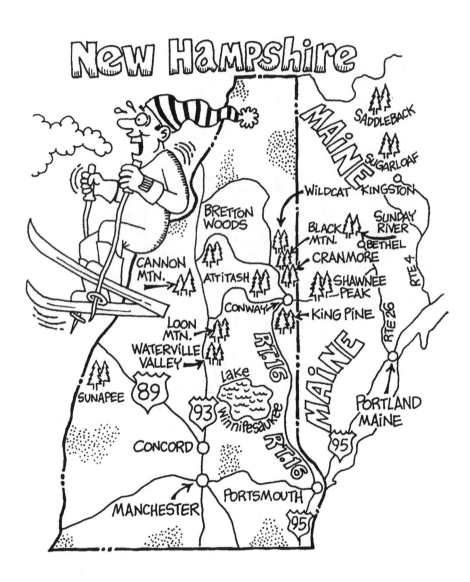

Sugarloaf/USA

Maine

Summit elevation: 4,237 feet
Vertical drop: 2,837 feet
Base elevation: 1,400 feet

Address: RR 1 Box 500, Carrabassett Valley, ME 04947
Area code: 207
Ski area phone: 237-2000
Snow report: 237-6808
ⓘ **Toll-free reservations:** (800) 843-5623 (THE-LOAF) or (800) 843-2732 (THE-AREA).
Fax: 237-2718
E-mail: info@sugarloaf.com
World Wide Web: http://www.sugarloaf.com/
Expert:★★★★★
Advanced:★★★★★ **Intermediate:**★★★★
Beginner:★★
Never-ever:★★

Number and types of lifts: 14—2 high-speed quads, 2 quads,1 triple, 8 doubles, 1 surface lift
Skiable acreage: 1,400 acres
Snowmaking: 92 percent
Uphill capacity: 21,805 per hour
Snowboarding: Yes, unlimited
Bed base: 5,400
Nearest lodging: Slopeside, condos and hotel
Resort child care: Yes, 10 weeks - 5 years
Adult ticket, per day: $49-$51

Dining:★★★★
Apres-ski/nightlife:★★
Other activities:★★

If you approach Sugarloaf by daylight, the first view is a jaw-dropper. As you round Omigosh! corner on Route 27, the mountain looms with runs snaking down from the crown in every direction. Sugarloaf is a major mountain, with more than 2,800 feet of continuous skiable vertical and the only above-treeline lift-serviced skiing in the East and the legendary Snowfields. The variety of skiing goes beyond its already impressive size: Each of the mountain's many runs has its own unique twists and turns, and the skiing is "boundary to boundary" skiing (off trail between the trees). As one guide put it, "Sugarloaf not only has good uphill capacity, it has exceptional downhill capacity, too." Sugarloaf is a skiers' and riders' mountain, with plenty of challenge for those who seek it.

Because it faces north toward the nearby Canadian border, Sugarloaf does not have an overabundance of sunshine. This, combined with its high latitude and elevation, means big natural snowfalls that come early and stay late. It's not unusual for the season to begin in early November and last into May. When the sun peeks over the north side in March and April, Sugarloaf is a favorite spring skiing and partying spot.

Terrain is just one of the reasons many loyal skiers don't hesitate to drive an extra hour or so to get here. Sugarloaf skiers are a different breed, with more in common with those who ski Vermont's Jay Peak than with sibling Sunday River, two hours south. Another plus: Most of the employees are Maine natives who love the mountain and want others to love it, too.

Make no mistake about it, Sugarloaf is in the boondocks, but its compact base village provides a choice of restaurants and bars, a handful of shops, an arcade, health club, two hotels and plenty of condos, all of which are either on the shuttle route or lift serviced. Indeed, this is one mountain where it's easy for family members to separate for the day and regroup for lunch or after skiing or riding. Late last season, the new Anti-gravity Center opened at the base of the access road, providing a place to work off any energy not burned on the slopes.

This center boasts one of the highest indoor climbing walls in New England as well as an indoor skating part, basketball court, weight room and more.

Mountain layout—skiing

◆◆ **Expert:** This is a good all-around mountain for any level of skier, but what sets it apart is that it has enough steep and challenging runs to keep experts happily banging the boards all day. In addition to more than 500 acres of classic wooded New England ski trails, Sugarloaf also has 80 to 100 acres of treeless snowfields at the summit, where experts can experience Western-style, open-bowl skiing. Powder collects on the Backside, but the front face has some of the steepest terrain in New England; White Nitro literally falls away beneath you. The only downside is that only one lift, a fixed-grip quad, services the summit. Although it is much more reliable than the gondola it replaced, it still shuts down on occasion due to high winds.

Experts can easily figure out where to ski. Double-diamond on the trail map is the honest truth. Steep black runs beckon from the summit, and most also can be accessed from the East Spillway double chair. In general, the runs get more difficult the farther east you venture. Given the boundary-to-boundary policy, Sugarloaf has quite a few sweet glades, too. For a challenge, try Rookie River, Cant Hook or Max Headroom.

◆ **Advanced:** The blacks down to the King Pine quad are all sweet and steep, if a little short. Bump monkeys should head for Choker, a natural snow trail on this side of the mountain, or to Skidder on the west side; groomers are under orders not to touch these trails. Ripsaw, Bubblecuffer and Upper Winter's Way, all natural snow trails, are also off limits to groomers. Narrow Gauge is perhaps the 'loaf's most famous trail. It's the only one in the East that the FIS has homologated for all Alpine disciplines.

■ **Intermediate:** Advanced intermediates will find that they can handle most of the single-diamond blacks on this mountain. With a few exceptions, the western half of the mountain is an intermediate playground. Tote Road and Timberwind are both long (Tote Road is 3.5 miles), wide cruisers that wind from the summit to the base—skiers can be on these trails for a half hour, notes one regular. Hayburner and King's Landing both swoop down a continuous fall line, making them ideal for cruising.

●● **Beginner:** At the base of the mountain, beginners will find the very broad and very gentle Boardwalk run. Those looking for a little more challenge graduate to the paths from the top of the Double Runner chairs and from there to the Wiffletree quad. Terrain off the Bucksaw chair offers even more challenge: a steeper pitch or narrower trails. To escape crowds, head to West Mountain, suitable for advanced beginners and lower intermediates.

● **Never-ever:** First-timers start on the long, gentle Birches slope, served by two chair lifts, Snubber and Sawduster. This is a great learning slope with only one caveat: It also is the access slope for a lot of slopeside lodging, so first-timers should quit a little early.

Mountain layout— Snowboarding

SuperQuad area: Double Bitter or Wedge are winding and narrow, with natural bank turns and drop-offs. Skidder has a natural quarterpipe, rider's right. King's Landing and Hayburner have natural knolls. Sugarloaf's competition Superpipe is supposedly the biggest, longest and most consistent in the East. It's followed by the Stomping Grounds, a double-black diamond terrain park. At the right-hand cutoff to Candyside is a super kicker onto a steep, smooth landing.

West Mountain is ideal for novices and lower intermeidates, with long, gentle cruising trails that incorporate some steeps at the beginning. West Mountain trail also has some nice banks on the rider's left, but beware of the clearance underneath the double chair and be sure to cut right toward Windrow near the end of the steeps to avoid the flats. Scoot, located below Bullwinkle's, has a BorderX course, with bank turns, lips and a practice park with 15-foot hip jumps, then successive tabletops.

King Pine area: Misery Whip is at most nine feet wide and usually ungroomed and full of huge whales. Take Boomauger to open up speed and lay down huge carves. Rip Saw and the Rip Saw Glades have nice drop-offs on rider's left at the beginning. Exit the King Pine Bowl from the top, heading left toward Spillway. From bottom, the only way out is Crosshaul, which is long, flat and torturous.

Locals can be found almost anywhere in the woods in glades that they have spent the summers working on with their own chainsaws. Unbeknownst to the rest of the world, these glades include some of the biggest cliff drops on the East Coast, but don't waste your time looking for them on a map. If you're lucky you may follow a pack of riders into the woods at exactly the right moment, but be ready to keep up.

Mountain rating:

A giant in terms of vertical (a continuous 2,820 feet), Sugarloaf/USA is a favorite for Eastern experts and advanced skiers, with great tree, mogul and open-bowl skiing. Traditional New England skiers will find those classic narrow winding trails they love, while intermediates and beginners will find plenty of wide open cruising. Though just one (albeit impressive) peak, Sugarloaf/USA offers as much variety as its once rival and now fellow American Skiing Co. resort, Sunday River.

Beginners and never-evers might be upset by the better skiers schussing through their learning area, which also serves as the trail back to the condos. However, on a good day, the more advanced skiers usually stay on the upper trails until long past lesson time.

Cross-country

The **Sugarloaf/USA Outdoor Center** (237-6830) is the largest and most complete in Maine, with 105 km. of trails groomed with double tracks and lanes for skating. Most of the trails are well suited for beginners and inter-mediates. The center is off Rte. 27, south of the resort access road. Three trails reach it from the resort's lodging facilities and the village area. The center also has a lighted Olympic-sized outdoor skating rink and a 6,000-square-foot lodge with a giant fireplace, a south-facing deck, and food and drink at the Klister Kitchen, a locals' favorite.

Group and private lessons are available, as are equipment rentals. The all-day trail fee is $16 for adults, $10 for ages 13–18 and $10 for ages 6–12 and 65 and older. Multiday ticket holders may exchange a day of downhill for a day of cross-country including trail fee, lesson and equipment. Exchange tickets at the guest services desk in the base lodge.

Lessons

Group lessons: The ski school uses the Perfect Turn® program. It combines state-of-the-art ski technique and educational theory (see Skiing for Every-one chapter). Perfect Turn has 10 levels of clinics. For lower intermediates and above, the clinics normally last 90 minutes with a maximum of 11 clients. Enrollees watch a short video that demonstrates various ability levels. This eliminates the "ski-off," which can take up 40 minutes of a two-hour lesson. Clinics meet three times each morning and cost $25. The ski school uses the Perfect Turn® program.

Never-ever package: Perfect Turn levels for never-evers to beginners are 90 minutes to two hours. The $65 Level-1 package includes the clinic, shaped skis, boots and poles, and a lift ticket for learning lifts. The resort guarantees Level 1 skiers that they will be able to ride a lift, turn and stop by the end of the clinic, or they can repeat it free or get their money back. Levels 2–3 cost $70 per clinic. New skiers start on shorter shaped skis on learning terrain, then "graduate" to longer skis on more challenging terrain.

Learn-to-Ride programs start at $65 and include coaching, equipment and a lift ticket.

Private lessons: $62 an hour.

Special programs: The Women's Turn program offers three- and five-day programs with at least five instruction hours on the snow and after-ski activities. The cost is $380 for three days and $670 for five, which includes clinics, lift tickets, lunch and activities. Special 90-minute Women's Turn clinics are $25.

Child care

Sugarloaf's spacious child center is staffed by caring and nurturing workers. Some vacationers come here specifically because it is so good.

Ages: 10 weeks to 5 years.

Costs: Full-day, $46; half day, $30; additional day, $40; additional half days, $30.

Reservations: Required; call (207) 237-6959.

Note: There are children's activities every night except Sunday in the Mountain Magic Room in the base lodge. Ages 5–12 have one type of activity, while teens do something else. Examples include games and movies for the young set, and skating, dances, Wallyball games (a volleyball-type game played on a racquetball court) and PG-13 movies for the teens.

Children's lessons: Perfect Kids programs are available for those ages 3-17 and range in price from $36 for half day to $62 for full day with lunch. Register at the Perfect Turn desk or in the Magic Mountain room in the base lodge. Moose Alley is a special kids-and-instructors-only section of the mountain where kids can do some controlled tree skiing.

Lift tickets (2001/02 prices)

	Adult	Junior (6-12)
One day	$52	$33
Three days	$150 ($50/day)	$99 ($33/day)
Five days	$250 ($50/day)	$165 ($33/day)

Who skis free: Children ages 5 and younger; however, they must have a lift ticket, which can be obtained at a ticket window.

Who skis at a discount: Teen (ages 13–18. called "young adult" here) ski or board for $47 for one day, $138 for three days and $230 for five. Ages 65 and older ski or ride for the junior price. College students can ski or ride for just $26, with and ID card, from Dec. 17-21, 2001, and Jan. 7-8, 2002.

Accommodations

Sugarloaf is a planned condominium community in the mold of Keystone or Copper Mountain. That said, it is one of the more tasteful layouts we've seen, the central village blending in well with the overall environment. Make reservations using the toll-free numbers listed in the stat box at the beginning of this chapter.

The **Grand Summit Resort Hotel** ($$$$ ✕⚐⬆️🅿️🍴✳️💤) is the centerpiece of the Alpine village. The slightly more modest **Sugarloaf Inn** ($$$$ ✕⚐⬆️🅿️✳️💤) has a New England inn ambiance. The Sugarloaf Inn offers packages that include ski lessons and use of the Sugarloaf Sports & Fitness Club, with pool, spas, massage therapy, tanning beds, exercise equipment and indoor racquetball and squash courts.

More than 900 condo units are spread throughout the resort, all designed so skiers can ski back to their lodging. (Not all have lift access, but a shuttle runs from the lodging to the lifts.) Families like the **Gondola Village** units because they are close to the state-licensed child-care facility. The **Bigelow, Snowflower** and **Commons** units are more luxurious, and the **Sugartree** units offer easy access to the health club.

The resort has an RV parking area serviced by lifts.

Kingfield, 15 miles from the mountain, offers more affordable lodging. **Three Stanley Avenue** (265-5541; $ 🅿️✳️⊝) is a Victorian-style B&B that has rooms with either a private or shared bath. The **Herbert Hotel** (265-2000; $–$$ 🅿️🐾) is an old-fashioned country inn that welcomes dogs as well as their owners.

In Stratton, seven miles north, the **Spillover Motel** (246-6571; $) has clean rooms at reasonable rates. For budget accommodations, call The **Widow's Walk** (800-943-6995 or 246-6901; $), a no-frills bed and breakfast, also in Stratton.

Dining

Sugarloaf is compact, but it has 18 eateries that range from pizza and burgers to fine dining. The best part is many offer ski-in/ski-out lunches, a big plus for those who dislike crowded base lodges. For dinner, reservations are normally essential.

In the base village, you can't miss with **Gepetto's** (237-2192; $–$$). This family-friendly restaurant has been one of the region's most popular for more than 20 years, and it offers an express lunch soup-and-salad bar. For pizza or burgers in a homey, noisy atmosphere, try The **Bag and Kettle** (237-2451; $–$$), locals call it The Bag. You can rate the local talent on Blues Monday while eating a Bag-burger and get the lore of Sugarloaf from the locals. For seafood, head to **Shucks**, (237-2040; $$). **D'Ellie's** (237-2490; $), a small, mostly take-out restaurant underneath Shucks, has excellent homemade soups, sandwiches and salads. There's an express line for soups and drinks, but get sandwiches early and stash them away to avoid a long wait during peak lunch hours or order in the morning for later pickup. It also serves a hearty breakfast. If your idea of breakfast is a cuppa Joe and a bagel or muffin, head to **Java Joes**. For fine dining and atmosphere, make reservations at The **Seasons** (237-6834; $$–$$$) at the Sugarloaf Inn. The lobster stew at the **Shipyard Brewhaus** is memorable.

For an English pub experience, take the shuttle to **Theo's Microbrewery & Pub** (237-2211; $–$$), where the Sugarloaf Brewing Company peddles its wares. On Wednesdays, Saturdays and other nights during vacation weeks, take a snowcat to **Bullwinkle's** (237-6939; $$$$), Sugarloaf's on-mountain restaurant, for a five-course, fixed-price candlelight dinner.

Hug's (237-2392; $–$$), about two miles from the mountain's access road, is a good choice for traditional Italian food served family style at reasonable prices. Even more kid-friendly is **Tufulio's** (235-2010; $–$$), located in Carrabassett Valley.

Dining: $$$-Entrees $20+; $$-$10-20; $-less than $10.
Accommodations: (double room) $$$$-$200+; $$$-$141-$200; $$-$81-$140; $-$80 and less.

In Kingfield: No trip to a Northeast ski area is complete without a visit to an authentic New England inn, and The **Inn on Winter's Hill** is worth the 15-mile drive. Sitting on the hill named after Sugarloaf's founder, Amos Winter, the inn has an excellent restaurant, **Julia's** (265-5421; $$-$$$). **One Stanley Avenue** (265-5541; $$-$$$) is the best and most expensive restaurant in town. Chef Dan Davis serves a creative menu of regional cuisine prepared in classic ways. The **Herbert Hotel** (265-2000) is also worth a visit.

In Eustis, 11 minutes north of Sugarloaf, the **Porter House** (246-7932; $$) draws diners from Canada, Sugarloaf and Rangeley and with good reasons: Excellent food, an award-winning wine list, a homey atmosphere and choices for every appetite.

Après-ski/nightlife

On sunny days après-skiers crowd the decks of The **Beach** or The **Bag.** The hot spot for live music and dancing at night is the **Widowmaker Lounge**. For a more subdued atmosphere, try the **Sugarloaf Inn,** home of the **Shipyard Brewhouse** or The **Double Diamond Steakhouse and Pub** in the Grand Summit Resort Hotel.

Judson's Motel, on Rte. 27, is a favorite with UMaine and Colby College students. Pre-teens have **Pinocchio's,** with video games, pinball and board games.

Other activities

Sugarloaf has a **Turbo Tubing** park with its own lift and four 1,000-foot chutes. The park is open Wednesday–Saturday for two sessions daily, 3–5:15 p.m. and 6–8:15 p.m. The fee is $10 per session. The new **Anti-gravity Center**, at the base of the access road has an indoor climbing wall, skating park and track as well as trampolines, a weight room and multi-use basketball court.

Dogsledding, horse-drawn sleigh rides, snowmobiling, snowshoeing, ice fishing and **skating** are among the activities that Sugarloaf Guest Services can arrange (237-2000). The resort also has a health club with an **indoor pool** and **outdoor hot tubs.**

Special events: Sugarloaf rolls back prices during **White White World Week**, held in late January. The annual **Reggae Weekend**, usually in mid-April, is a two-day bash with indoor and outdoor reggae bands. Book well in advance, as it usually sells out.

Shopping: The village has several shops, including Pat Buck's Emporium, that features handcrafted items by Maine artisans; and Goldsmith Gallery, with gold and silver jewelry, photo frames, and similar items. In Kingfield you'll find Scent-sations, where you choose your favorite scent and the store will put it into lotions, shampoos and body oils.

Getting there and getting around

By air: The closest commercial airport is the Portland International Jetport. The Augusta airport is serviced by U.S. Air/Business Express. Bangor International Airport also is serviced by major airlines. Guests who fly into Bangor or Portland and who reserve lodging & lift stays through Sugarloaf/USA reservations can reserve transportation at the time of booking.

By car: Take I-95 north to Augusta, Rte. 27 through Farmington and Kingfield. Or take the Maine Turnpike to the Auburn exit, Rte. 4 to Farmington and Rte. 27 through Kingfield. The drive is about two-and-a-half hours from Portland.

Getting around: A car is optional—nearly everything in the resort is within walking distance. A free on-mountain shuttle runs on weekends and during holiday periods and is on call during the week. To do anything away from the resort complex, you will need a car.

Sunday River

Maine

Summit elevation: 3,140 feet
Vertical drop: 2,340 feet
Base elevation: 800 feet

Address: P.O. Box 450
Bethel, ME 04217
✆ **Area code:** 207
Ski area phone: 824-3000
Fax: 824-5110
Snow report: (207) 824-5200;
ⓘ **Toll-free reservations:** (800) 543-2754
E-mail: snowtalk@sundayriver.com
Internet: www.sundayriver.com
Expert:★★
Advanced:★★★
Intermediate:★★★★
Beginner:★★★★★

Number of lifts: 18–4 high-speed quads,
5 quads, 4 triples, 2 doubles, 3 surface lifts
Snowmaking: 92 percent
Skiable acreage: 654 acres
Uphill capacity: 32,000 per hour
Snowboarding: Yes, unlimited
Bed base: 6,000 on mountain; 2,000 nearby
Nearest lodging: Slopeside
Resort child care: Yes, 6 weeks to 6 years
Adult ticket, per day: $47-$52,
$54 holidays (01/02 prices)
Dining:★★
Apres-ski/nightlife:★★
Other activities:★★

Sunday River, just outside of Bethel and tucked against the Sunday River, is maturing and that's a good thing. Baby Boomers who came for the guaranteed snow and the extensive terrain and who bought the mountain's many condos, thus helping to launch the American Skiing Co., are still coming. But now they're bringing their grown children and even grandchildren. Sunday River is ready for them with a wide variety of steeps, intermediate cruisers, learning slopes, glades and terrain features for every level.

In Maine (just six miles from the picturesque New England village of Bethel) with a spectacular view of New Hampshire's White Mountains, Sunday River, for all its vertical, is very horizontal (it is more than three-and-a-half miles across its eight separate peaks. Veterans of the mountain can readily recite the trails that move skiers from one peak to the next, but those new to Sunday River might want to study the trail map extensively before venturing out. This is especially true if the desire is to ski or board from one end (White Cap) to the other (Jordan Bowl).

The resort lacks a true center. There are three separate base lodges: South Ridge, Barker Mountain and White Cap, with South Ridge being the hub, housing the ski school, the corporate offices and a grocery store. The North Peak Lodge is a great mid-morning or luncheon meeting place, being reasonably accessible from all but White Cap peak.

Skiing/riding is definitely the emphasis at Sunday River, so plan to get good and tired doing it because Sunday River, with its spread-out base and separate ski-in, ski-out condo complexes, tends to be rather quiet at night, especially during midweek.

Known for its impressive snowmaking and lift system, Sunday River can suffer from its own popularity (while lift lines are seldom long, its trails do get full. To avoid crowds, the recommendation is to start your day at Jordan Bowl and make your way back across the general flow of traffic (an ideal scenario for those staying at the Jordan Grand Hotel).

Mountain layout—Skiing

♦♦ Expert ♦ Advanced: Oz is a playground for high-level sliders. Served by a fixed-grip quad, it features a 500-yard-wide steep swath with tree islands and glades. You won't find the trails zigzagging across the fall-line; Oz is a collection of straight fall-line tree-studded drops.

Aurora Peak, served by a fixed quad chair and a triple chair, is still the spot to find tough skiing. Northern Lights, rated blue on the map, provides an easier way down the mountain, though it's no stroll through the park. Celestial, reached from Lights Out, is one of the nicest gladed trails. It starts out steep and wide, but mellows and narrows as you descend.

From the top of Barker Mountain a steep trio—Right Stuff, Top Gun and Agony—provide advanced skiers long sustained pitches. Agony and Top Gun are premier bump runs. Right Stuff is a cruiser early in the day after it's been groomed, but normally develops moguls by afternoon. Tree-skiing fans will find the Last Tango glade between Right Stuff and Risky Business. This black-diamond natural slalom area is the gentlest and most spacious of the resort's seven mapped glades. Though it's not particularly steep, it's tight. A work road about two-thirds of the way down allows skiers to bail out onto Right Stuff. Those who continue through the trees will find the terrain getting steeper and narrower. If you're less than an expert, you won't have much fun on Last Tango's lower third.

From the top of Locke Mountain, T2 plunges down the tracks of an old T-bar providing a spectacular view of Bethel, the valley and Mt. Washington.

The White Heat run is a wide swath straight down the mountain from the peak of White Cap. Double-diamond Shockwave, considered by many locals as tougher than White Heat, offers 975 vertical feet of big bumps and steep pitches. Two gladed areas, Hardball (skier right) and Chutzpah (skier left), start out deceptively mellow and open-spaced, but watch out. Technically, they are the most demanding on the mountain.

■ Intermediate: Advanced intermediates are at home at Sunday River. The top of North Peak has the largest concentration of blue runs, though there's an intermediate way down from the top of every peak, and for the most part, these are wide, undulating trails, such as Obsession off White Cap. Jordan Bowl provides some of the best blue-square cruising in New England down Excalibur and Rogue Angel, with the wide-open Blind Ambition glade accessed by the mellow cruiser Lollapalooza. An advanced intermediate trail is Monday Mourning, which starts out steep and wide but mellows near the end, where the race arena is located. Lower intermediates can head to the White Cap quad (far left on the map) and enjoy the relatively mellow Moonstruck, Starburst and Starlight runs. Off Barker Mountain, Lazy River is narrow by Sunday River standards and a fun cruise, but it can be strewn with people during busy times as it's the main route to adjoining Spruce Peak.

●● Beginner: Once a skier is past the basic snowplow and into stem Christies, much of Sunday River beckons. The North Peak triple chair opens long practice runs like Dream Maker. Lollapalooza, the green-circle trail in Jordan Bowl, is "like Dream Maker on steroids," as one frequent visitor said. It's long and wide with great views, but not a trail that beginners should start out on; the upper part can get bumped up on busy days, and probably should have a blue rating. Farther down it's quite mellow.

● Never-ever: First-timers start on Sundance and then have the entire South Ridge area to practice linking their turns. Twelve beginner runs in the South Ridge area are serviced by a high-speed quad, a triple, a double and a surface lift. This area can be crazy, though, as it is the resort's hub.

Mountain layout—Snowboarding

Sunday River is good for riders of all ability levels. Beginners should park at the South Ridge area, which has a large selection of beginner terrain. The double-barrel mini halfpipes (two back-to-back mini halfpipes with a spine in between where they meet) here are a good place to practice balancing in the pipe and making turns at the top of the 3.5-foot walls. Intermediates should head to American Express, which has gentle, winding terrain accented with natural rollers and drop-offs. Risky Business, off the Spruce Peak triple is ideal for carving. It's wide and steep, and there's a natural halfpipe, riders' left, just after it crosses under the chairlift. Keep left at the base, for two consecutive drop-offs, created by cross-cuts. The landings are fairly long, steep, and smooth. Take note: The only trail on the mountain that is definitely not intended for snowboarders is Kansas, which is infamous for its long and almost uphill traverse.

Sunday River's **terrain parks** are groomed and engineered by snowboarding director Josh Lempert, an avid rider and BorderX racer who tests the jumps and halfpipes daily. The five terrain parks feature a variety of man-made obstacles such as table tops, spines, rollers, step-up jumps and the previously mentioned double-barrel halfpipe. Beginners have their own park, **Whoville**, at South Ridge, created solely for the purpose of giving beginner riders a chance to get their first air on some friendly, gentle jumps that promote confidence and balance. **The Park**, located on White Cap, is geared towards intermediate riders. Also good for intermediate-to-advanced riders is **RiderX** on Barker Peak, which will be beefed-up this year as another park, Nebula will be removed.

The new **Superpipe**, on Barker Mountain, has 16-foot walls. It is built on top of an 18-degree pitch that allows riders to continue gaining speed as they catch air repeatedly. There's also a mini-pipe at South Ridge and a quarter pipe on Starlight.

Mountain rating

Sunday River offers a vast amount of terrain for all skiing levels. Beginners can start on the lower mountain area, then work their way up onto the intermediate trails in the North Peak area. Intermediates and advanced skiers have lots of options on every one of eight peaks. Experts will find super steeps, glades and monster bumps on Oz, Jordan Bowl, Aurora Peak, Barker Mountain and White Cap. The resort's snowmaking system is one of the best and biggest anywhere, and its lift system moves skiers and riders quickly and efficiently. It's important to keep a trail map handy to navigate from one side of the resort to the other. It can feel as if you're spending more time getting from one place to another rather than skiing.

 ## Cross-country and snowshoeing

Sunday River does not have a dedicated cross-country center, but this part of Maine is known for some of the best Nordic skiing and snowshoeing options in New England within an hour's drive (see also the Mt. Washington Valley chapter and The Balsams listing under regional New Hampshire resorts). Golf course skiing, with some wooded trails, is available at the **Bethel Inn Cross-Country Ski Center** (824-2175). The center has 40 km. of marked and groomed trials, 30 of which are groomed for both diagonal and skate skiing. It has rentals, lessons and evening sleigh rides. The Bethel Inn also has instruction in telemark. If you're a novice Nordic skier, this is a great place to learn as many of the trails are quite gentle. Midweek, the trail fee is also good for entrance to the outdoor heated pool, sauna and fitness center, until 4 p.m.

Closest to the slopes, the **Sunday River Ski Touring Center** (824-2410) is run by the Sunday River Inn, located on the Sunday River access road. It has 40 km. of groomed and tracked trails, as well as 2 km. lit for night skiing. It's family oriented, with warming shelters, an overnight yurt, a groomed dog trail, a downhill practice area and instruction. Ice skating, snowshoeing, sleigh rides and an outdoor hot tub and sauna round out the amenities.

Owned by a former cross-country ski racer, **Carter's Cross-Country Ski Center** (539-4848) has two locations. One, on Intervale Road, is just five miles from Sunday River, and has great views of the downhill area. It has 60 km. of trails for all levels (half groomed) and has a back-country experience with rustic get-away cabins. Carter's Cross-country Center in Oxford, off Rte. 26, provides another alternative for skinny skis, with 25 km. of tracks.

Telemark Inn (836-2703) has wilderness cross-country skiing with unlimited backcountry skiing into the White Mountain National Forest. The inn also has 20 km. of groomed trails.

Guided fireworks showshoe treks depart from the Snow Cap Lodge at **Sunday River** on Thursdays and Sundays.

Lessons (2001/02 prices)

Group lessons: The Sunday River Ski School created the innovative teaching program called Perfect Turn®. It combines state-of-the-art ski technique with state-of-the-art educational theory. The Sprint Perfect Turn Discovery Center offers one-stop shopping: lift tickets, lessons and rental equipment are all in one spot.

Perfect Turn has 10 levels. For lower intermediates and higher, the clinics normally last 90 minutes with a maximum of six skiers. Skiers watch a short video that demonstrates various levels of skiing ability. The video eliminates the "ski-off," which usually takes up about 40 minutes of a two-hour lesson. Clinics run about every half hour and cost $30.

Never-ever package: The package includes the clinic, shaped skis, boots and poles, a lift ticket for the South Ridge and North Peak. It costs $65 for Level 1. Sunday River guarantees Level 1 skiers that they will be able to ride a lift, turn and stop by the end of the clinic, or they can repeat it free or get their money back. The second and third lessons cost $85 apiece.

Private lessons: $65 per hour, additional person is $40; all day costs $350, additional person is $165.

Racing: A course is on Race Arena, adjacent to the Monday Mourning trail. It is available for private groups by appointment and open to the public on a limited basis.

Children's lessons: Sunday River's children's programs are among the best-organized and smoothest-running at any resort. The flow from equipment rental to classes is outstanding and all facilities are separate, which makes dealing with youngsters much easier.

Age 3 starts with Tiny Turns, an hour of private instruction with a half- or full-day session in day care. The private clinic is $30 if the child is registered in day care; otherwise, the clinic cost is the regular private rate.

Mogul Munchkins is for ages 4–6; Mogul Meisters is for those 7–12 years of age.

Perfect Kids clinics cost $55 for a full day, $65 with rental equipment, $88 with rental and lift ticket. Half-day clinics are $28, $40 with rental equipment.

Child care (2001/02 prices)

Ages: 6 weeks to 6 years.

Costs: All-day programs are $45 including lunch, and half-day programs are $25 for older toddlers. Discounts apply for siblings. Bring diapers, formula and food for infants.

Reservations: Advised midweek, required weekends. Call 824-3000. The main child care facility is at South Ridge. Child care, day and evening, also is available at the Grand Summit Resort Hotel and the Jordan Grand Resort Hotel.

Children's lessons: Sunday River's children's programs are among the best-organized and smoothest-running at any resort. The flow from equipment rental to classes is outstanding and all facilities are separate, which makes dealing with youngsters much easier.

Age 3 starts with Tiny Turns, an hour of private instruction with a half- or full-day session in day care. The private clinic is $30 if the child is registered in day care; otherwise, the clinic cost is the regular private rate.

Mogul Munchkins is for ages 4–6; Mogul Meisters is for those 7–12 years of age.

Perfect Kids clinics cost $56 for a full day, $65 with rental equipment, $89 with rental and lift ticket. Half-day clinics are $28, $40 with rental equipment.

Lift tickets (2001/02)

	Adult	Young adult (13-18)	Child (6-12)
One day*	$49	$44	$32
Three days	$140 ($47/day)	$126 ($42/day)	$91 ($30/day)
Five days	$228 ($46/day)	$206 ($41/day)	$148 ($30/day)

*Midweek tickets are $1 to $2 less; holiday tickets are $1 to $2 more.

Who skis free: Children ages 5 and younger with parent.

Who skis at a discount: Ages 65 and older ski for child rates.

Multi-resort discounts: Sunday River is one of the American Skiing Company (ASC) resorts. ASC has set up a Web-based discount lift ticket site at www.meticket.com.

Accommodations

The Summit hotels and condominiums are the most convenient to the slopes. But Bethel also has a group of excellent B&Bs and old country inns. Call **central reservations** (800-543-2754).

The **Jordan Grand Resort Hotel and Conference Center** ($$-$$$$ ☝ ✕ ⌾ P ⎙ ⚫ ▓) is slopeside to Jordan Bowl, but miles by car or shuttle to the rest of the resort. Enjoy whirl-pool spa, indoor/outdoor pool, full-service health club, restaurants, child care. Be forewarned, the walls are not well soundproofed.

The **Grand Summit Resort Hotel and Conference Center** ($$-$$$$ ☝ ✕ ⌾ P ⎙ ⚫ ▓) is trailside with a 25-meter heated outdoor pool, athletic club and fine dining. The **Snow Cap Inn** is a short walk from the slopes and the **Snow Cap Ski Dorm** next door offers affordable digs. All but the dorm offer packages with lift tickets.

Locke Mountain Townhouses are the most upscale, but hard to get, with the ideally located **Merrill Brook** condominiums not far behind. Sunday River has nine condominium complexes throughout the resort; all are convenient to the slopes and have trolley service.

In Bethel, the **Bethel Inn and Country Club** (824-2175; $-$$$ ✕ ⌾ P ▓) has old-style atmosphere and first-rate rooms. The rates include breakfast and dinner. The inn also has a cross-country center and health club (see *Cross-country*) and a shuttle to the ski area.

The **Four Seasons** is in an old elegant building with excellent French cuisine (824-2755 or 800-227-7458; $$-$$$). The **Sudbury Inn** (824-2174; $$-$$$) has one of the best restaurants in town and is a favorite watering hole. The **Holidae House** (824-3400; $-$$ P ⚫ ◉) in Bethel is filled with Victorian-era antiques and elaborate decorating touches.

Dining: $$$-Entrees $20+; $$-$10-20; $-less than $10.
Accommodations: (double room) $$$$-$200+; $$$-$141-$200; $$-$81-$140; $-$80 and less.

The **Chapman House** (824-2657; $–$$ 🅿⊰🅜😊) is a B&B in the heart of Bethel offering rooms in the rambling main house as well as a ski dorm in the attached barn. There is a bountiful hot buffet breakfast. Guests have use of a kitchen, laundry, saunas and game room.

The **Victoria Inn** (824-8060 or 888-774-1235; $$–$$$$✕⊰😊⊰🅿) is an ornate country inn/B&B in a magnificent Queen Anne-style house. The bedroom-with-loft suites in the attached carriage house are ideal for families. The excellent restaurant is also open for dinner.

The **Briar Lea** (877-311-1299 or 824-4714; $$) has six rooms with private baths, two of which can be connected as suites for families. The inn also has a good restaurant, and inn guests can order whatever they want from the menu for breakfast.

Less than a mile from the area, the **Sunday River Inn** (824-2410; $–$$$ ✕🅿⊰😊) is a traditional lodge with large fireplaced living room. Family-style breakfast and dinner are included. There is cross-country skiing (see *Cross-country*), ice skating, snowshoeing, skijouring (harnessed dogs pull a person on skinny skis), plus a wood-fired hot tub and sauna. Choose from dorm rooms, rooms with shared or private baths. Shuttles take guests to ski.

Information about **other lodging** is available through Sunday River's central reservation line (800-543-2754) or the Bethel Area Chamber of Commerce (824-3585).

Dining

Sunday River is striving to improve its dining and recently split its restaurants into a separate operation from its cafeterias and food courts. This is a welcome sign from a resort where the food is often described as expensive and awful. One budding dining adventure is an evening **dinner snowcat ride** to the North Peak Lodge for dinner, followed by fireworks. It is offered most weekends and holidays.

Legends (824-3500, ext. 5858; $$$) in the Summit Hotel has a great menu and wine list. **Walsh and Hill Trading Company** (824-5067; $$–$$$) in the Fall Line Condominiums serves steaks and seafood. **Rosetto's Italian Restaurant** (824-6224; $$–$$$) in the White Cap Lodge is open for dinner daily and for lunch on weekends and holidays.

Foggy Goggle ($–$$) in the South Ridge base is packed for lunch, with good reason. The **Peak Lodge and Skiing Center** ($–$$) at the summit of North Peak, is a popular lunch spot with a giant deck. **BUMPS!** ($–$$) in the White Cap Lodge serves a pub menu which should be avoided unless you're starving.

In Bethel try the **Sudbury Inn** (824-6558; $$–$$$) and the **Bethel Inn** (824-2175; $$–$$$). Downstairs, **Sud's Pub** ($–$$) is popular for après-ski and pub food. The **Victoria Inn** (824-8060; $$–$$$) offers fine dining in an elegant setting. The **Moose's Tale** (824-3541; $–$$) in the **Sunday River Brewing Company**, according to locals, now serves food worthy of its excellent on-premise-brewed ales. The **Briar Lea** (877-311-1299 or 824-4714; $–$$) is a good choice for when you want a nice meal in an unfussy setting. It also has a children's menu. Back in business again, but under new ownership, is **Mother's** (824-2589; $–$$), which serves a wide-ranging menu of soups, salads, sandwiches and dinner specialties.

The **Matterhorn** (824-6836) serves brick-oven-baked pizza and fresh pasta and the **Great Grizzly American Steakhouse** are in the same location in a large barn on the access road. The former serves brick-oven-baked pizza and fresh pasta and the latter serves, of course, steak, plus seafood and nightly specials. Get there before 6 p.m. and your dessert is free

Après-ski/nightlife

If you strike it rich you may find midweek action at Sunday River and in Bethel, but the real fun heats up on weekends.

Immediate après-ski is at the base of the slopes. **Foggy Goggle** in the South Ridge base area is the liveliest of the mountain spots. Try the **Barker Brew Haus** in the Barker Mountain base area or **BUMPS!** at the White Cap Base Lodge. Off mountain, head to the **Sunday River Brewery** or **Sud's Pub**, in town. On the access road, the **Matterhorn** is an all-ages bar with 48-ounce Glacier Big Bowl drinks and extensive beer choices, including Guinness

At night, **BUMPS!** has bands on weekends and comedy on Tuesdays. The crowd leans toward young. The **Sunday River Brewery** has live music and excellent homemade brew. Downtown, the **Backstage** usually has karaoke during the week, with Country & Western and rock'n'roll bands on weekends. It also has the only pool tables in town. **Sud's Pub** has bands ranging from blues to bluegrass. For local flavor, come on a Thursday for Hoot Nite, an open-mike forum that has been running for 16 years. A more sedate crowd fills **Legends** at the Summit Hotel for its acoustic music. It has family entertainment every Saturday.

 ## Other activities

Shopping: Bethel has unusual shops—Bonnema Potters, with pottery depicting the Maine landscape; Mt. Mann, a native gemstone shop; and Samuel Timberlake making fine reproductions of Shaker furniture.

Swimming pools and saunas are in virtually every resort condominium complex. Guests staying at the few condos that don't have them get privileges at nearby complexes. The ski dorm has video games and pool tables.

You can take **BMW test drives** from the Grand Summit and Jordan Grand hotels and even sign out a vehicle to go into Bethel for dinner.

The White Cap Base Lodge houses the **Nite Cap Fun Center** for families. Activities here include an arcade; lighted tubing park, halfpipe and skating rink; and guided snowshoe tours. Tube, ice skates and snowshoe rentals are available. Fireworks take place here every Thursday and Saturday evening.

Bethel Station, about four miles from Sunday River, has a four-screen **movie theater**.

Arrange **snowmobile** rentals and tours through Sun Valley Sports (824-7533) or Bethel Outdoor Adventures (824-4224), which also offers **snowshoeing** tours.

Indoor laser tag, miniature golf and rock climbing are available at B.I.G. Adventure Center (824-0929).

For one-day or multiday, fully-outfitted **dog-sledding** trips, call Mahoosuc Guide Service (824-2073), located in Grafton Notch.

 ## Getting there and getting around

By air: Portland International Jetport is 75 miles from Sunday River. Private pilots can land in Bethel. Bethel Express Corporation will pick up from either airport by reservation (824-4646).

By car: Sunday River is in western Maine an hour and a half from Portland and three-and-a-half hours (with no traffic) from Boston. From I-95, take Exit 11 in Maine to Rte. 26 north, continue to Bethel, then take Rte. 2 six miles north to Sunday River.

RV parking, no hookups, is allowed in designated parking areas at the resort. An RV park is also at White Birch Camping, in Shelburne on Rte. 2.

Getting around: Public transportation is planned between the resort and Bethel. During the regular season, on-mountain transportation between the base areas is quite good on old trolley cars. The shuttle loop expands to include the condos at night. In shoulder season, the mountain shuttles are by request only. A car makes everything more convenient.

Maine regional resorts

Maine Saddleback, Rangeley, ME; (207) 864-5671

Internet: none available
5 lifts; 41 trails; 110 acres; 1,830 vertical feet

Underdeveloped, uncrowded, untamed are the words most often used to describe this area located in prime snowmobiling territory, just 45 minutes from Sugarloaf. Saddleback's wide-open, gentle learning slope with its own chairlift, Gold Rush, attracts those wishing to learn the sport far from prying eyes. This is an old fashioned, family area, where it seems everyone knows just about everyone else. The sun-soaked base lodge is always filled with brown-bags at lunch, and this isn't discouraged. Purchase a chocolate chip cookie in the cafeteria, and the workers may even offer to warm it up for you so the chips are all melty.

Saddleback is known for its rugged upper-mountain terrain. An old double chair reaches about two-thirds of the way up the mountain, the only lift to the summit is a T-bar, and the track is often rated black-diamond. Experts can have fun in the Nightmare Glades, on Bronco Buster or on Mule Skinner, consistently picked as one of the East's Top 10 extreme ski trails.

Saddleback settled its long-running dispute with the Appalachian Mountain Trail last season, which means its now free to develop. The ski area has the potential to be one of the biggest in the East. Stay tuned to see what develops here.

The resort has on-mountain condominium lodging, but you'll have to make your own entertainment here when the lifts shut down. Rangeley, seven miles from the base, is a good-sized town with at least a dozen restaurants.

Lift tickets: Adults, $42; Children (7-13), $28.

Distance from Boston: About 5+ hours. Take 95 North to the Maine Turnpike, get off at Exit 12 and follow Route 4 north through Farmington to Rangeley.

Lodging information: For the limited number of condos on the mountain (400 trailside), call the ski area number, (207) 864-5671. To reach the Rangeley Chamber of Commerce, call (800) 685-2537.

Big Squaw, Greenville, ME; (207) 695-1000

Internet: none available
4 lifts; 18 trails; 1,750 vertical feet

Big Squaw offers a taste of skiing the way it used to be, right down to the 30¢ Cokes in the cafeteria line and the $25 weekend lift tickets. A family of four can ski and stay here for less than they can ski at most other resorts. Trails vary from skinny, New England-style bump runs to broad cruisers. The views from the summit extend across Moosehead Lake to Mt. Katahdin. A motel attached to the base lodge provides convenient, though Spartan, accommodations. While rooms here are downright cheap, you'll have to go to Greenville for meals or time your dining to when the base lodge is open. Greenville has a handful of pleasant inns, including the posh Lodge at Moosehead Lake. Be forewarned, though, Big Squaw is remote, and Greenville offers little in the way of nightlife.

Lift tickets: Adults, $25; Children (7-13), $15.

Distance from Boston: About 5+ hours. Take 95 North to Newport (Exit 39), then Rte. 23 to Guilford, then Rtes. 6 and 15 north to Greenville then Greenville Junction. Watch for ski area signage on your left.

Mt. Washington Valley

New Hampshire

Attitash, Cranmore, Wildcat, Black Mountain, and five touring centers
Also: King Pine and Shawnee Peak

Mt. Washington Valley Facts

Address: Chamber of Commerce
P.O. Box 2300, N. Conway, NH 03860
ⓘ **Toll-free information:**
(800) 367-3364
Dining:★★★★★
Apres-ski/nightlife:★★★★
Other activities:★★★★★

✆ **Area code:** 603
Phone: 356-5701
Fax: 356-7069
E-mail: info@mtwashingtonvalley.org
World Wide Web:
www.mtwashingtonvalley.org
Bed base: 7,500+

If anyone wants skiing and a whole lot more, Mt. Washington Valley is the place. Here, the craggy White Mountains form a valley dominated by the imposing Mt. Washington, the East's highest peak at 6,288 feet and world renowned for its wicked weather. Seven downhill ski areas are within easy driving distance, offering a variety of terrain and skiing experiences. Add the Jackson Ski Touring Foundation (one of the world's best cross-country trail systems), the Great Glen Trails Outdoor Center, the Mt. Washington Valley Ski Touring and Snowshoe Center and a myriad indoor and outdoor activities, and you've got a vacation that shouldn't be missed.

This was a destination resort long before anyone came here to ski. A quarter century before the Civil War, fashionable Northeasterners started coming here, first by stage line and then by railroad and carriage, for the summer to beat the heat, to meet Hawthorne and Emerson, watch Bierstadt paint his mountain landscapes and find suitable husbands for their daughters. Today, the few remaining grand old hotels they visited have been brought up to date to add their charm to the mix of condos, motels, country inns and B&Bs. The Valley, as locals call it, is still busier in the summer months than in the winter.

Legends of the early days of skiing, the late '30s, surround you. Ride up the Wildcat summit quad and look back at the fantastic bulk of Mt. Washington with its huge, scooped-out ravines. This is hallowed ground, where Toni Matt on his wooden boards schussed over the Tuckerman headwall in one long arc to win the 1939 Inferno race, summit to base in six and a half minutes; a record that still stands.

Most of all, what made this area one of the pioneers of downhill skiing in America is the Eastern Slope Ski School, founded by Carroll Reed. This is where the Arlberg method of ski instruction was introduced to North America by Benno Rybizka and his Austrian teacher, the great Hannes Schneider, who was released by the Nazis in return for banking concessions.

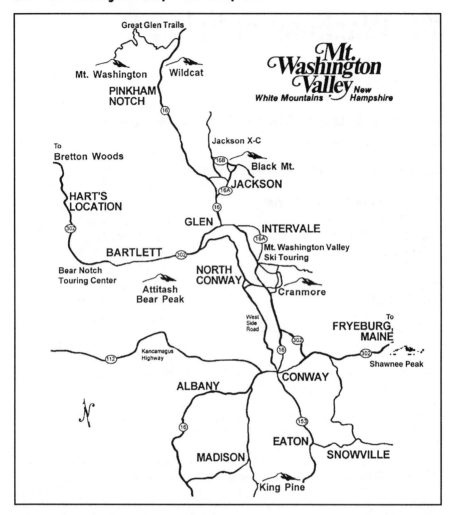

Restaurants, many of them tucked into the tiny country inns or restored barns in the Valley, are world class and have acknowledged gourmet reputations. Besides the skiing, picturesque inns and tempting restaurants, there are scores of tax-free factory outlet stores in Conway and North Conway, making the region a top shopping destination.

One thing that would make it a bit more enticing would be some cooperation between the ski areas, hoteliers and merchants to make this valley a true regional resort. No single ski resort in the Valley is a worthy winter destination by itself, but as a group of resorts, combined with the Valley towns and the surrounding cross-country trails, Mt. Washington Valley becomes a formidable vacation force. Other winter resorts across the United States and Canada would struggle to offer as complete and varied an experience. This is a wonderful place to come and ski, snowboard or cross-country. Wouldn't it be nice if a shuttlebus connected the resorts with the picturesque towns and if the Valley offered a lift pass that would allow visitors to ski a different area each day? Unfortunately, rather than making it easier for visitors to discover the benefits of the Valley, the locals seem to march to different drums in different directions. Visitors are left to scramble for themselves to squeeze the essence from what is surely the most-blessed ski region in the Northeast.

Attitash Bear Peak
Mountain layout—Skiing

Just west of Glen on Rte. 302 in Bartlett, Attitash Bear Peak is an all-around, two-mountain resort with a few expert touches. The Attitash side still features a warren of narrow New England trails filled with history, and the newer Bear Peak trails provide wider and longer, rolling and cruising terrain plus some glades.

Ptarmigan, on Attitash, is supposed to be one of the steepest trails in New England, but it is manageable for good intermediates because of the elbow room on the run. The rest of the mountain is enough to keep 80 percent of skiers perfectly satisfied, with Northwest Passage to Cathedral and Saco to Ammonoosuc providing inspired cruising, while Idiot's Option and Grandstand are favorites for those seeking a knee workout. The problem with the Attitash side of the mountain is the lack of a high-speed, base-to-summit lift.

Not so on the Bear Peak side, where there's a high-speed quad backed by several other chairlifts. Bear Peak features Illusion, Avenger, Kachina and Myth Maker: a foursome of cruising delight (the diamonds shouldn't scare any strong intermediate away, unless the trails haven't been groomed). Seeking more challenge? Jump into the peak's ever-expanding glades.

The Attitash base is the primary one. Here you'll find the massive Adventure Center that houses all of the Learn to Ski and Ride programs and children's programs. Lessons, rentals and child-care are all under one roof, and just outside, beginners have a new "Snowbelt" lift. First-timers graduate from that to the adjacent, protected learning slope served by a triple chair. From there, they move on to beginner trails around the neighboring Double-Double lifts. Attitash has created a family fun zone in this area.

If you're parked at Bear Peak or staying in the Grand Summit at its base, the quickest way back is to take the base-to-base shuttle.

Mountain layout—Snowboarding

Bear Peak is best for free riding, carving and glades. Attitash has a terrain park; elements and the halfpipe; and a Palmer-X course on Thad's Choice that is designed like a boardercross course, complete with starting gates. All the elements flow, so most ride from start to finish. It's easy to avoid anything you don't want to hit, and the landing areas have plenty of room. The inground halfipe on Lower Ptarmigan is 500-feet long with 12- to 14-foot walls. It is one of the largest in New Hampshire. At the end of the pipe is a huge terrain element with a giant landing area. Attitash employs a full-time park and halfpipe groomer as well as park rangers who patrol these areas. The transitions between Attitash and Bear Peak are the only flat areas. When riding from Attitash to Bear Peak, avoid Bearback and ride the quad instead. When riding from Bear Peak to Attitash, avoid Bear Right to Stonybrook. Instead, when you see the bridge, take Bear Notch Pass to Stonybrook Bypass. Here, it's worth it to unstrap and walk the 50 feet to the top of the bypass. From there on, it's all downhill. The shuttle is another way of moving between the two areas.

Attitash Bear Peak Facts

Summit elevation:	**2,300 feet**
Vertical drop:	**1,750 feet**
Base elevation:	**550 feet**

Expert:★★
Advanced:★★★
Intermediate:★★★★
Beginner:★★★★
Never-ever:★★★★★
Address: P.O. Box 308, Barlett, NH 03812
✆ **Ski area phone:** 374-2368
Snow report: 374-0946
ⓘ **Toll-free reservations:** (800) 223-7669
E-mail: info@attitash.com
Internet: www.attitash.com
Number and types of lifts: 12–2 high-speed quads,1 quad, 3 triples, 3 doubles, 3 surface lifts
Skiable acreage: 280 acres
Snowmaking: 98 percent
Uphill capacity: 14,385 per hour
Snowboarding: Yes
Bed base: 1,600 **Nearest lodging:** slopeside
Resort child care: Yes, 6 months and older
Adult ticket, per day: $42-$53 (2001/02)

Wildcat Facts

Summit elevation:	**4,062 feet**
Vertical drop:	**2,112 feet**
Base elevation:	**1,950 feet**

Expert:★★★ Advanced:★★★
Intermediate:★★★★
Beginner:★★★
Never-ever:★★★
Address: Rt. 16, Pinkham Notch, Jackson, NH 03846
✆ **Ski area phone:** 466-3326
Snow report: 1-888-SKI WILD
ⓘ **Toll-free reservations:** 1-800-255-6439
E-mail: thecat@skiwildcat.com
Internet:www.skiwildcat.com
Number and types of lifts: 4–1 high-speed quad, 3 triples
Skiable acreage: 225 acres
Snowmaking: 90 percent
Uphill capacity: 7,200 per hour
Snowboarding: Yes, unlimited
Bed Base: None at the area
Nearest lodging: AMC, about a quarter-mile
Resort child care: Yes, 6 months and older
Adult ticket, per day: $39-49(00/01)

Lessons (2001/02 prices)

Group lessons: $30 per session.
Never-ever packages: $70, including rentals, lifts and lessons.
Private lessons: $65 per hour for one student.

Child care (2001/02 prices)

Ages: 6 months to 6 years.
Cost: $45 per day, including lunch. Tiny Turns designed for kids ages 3-5 costs $60 an hour, $40 for children in child care.
Reservations: Recommended, call 374-2368.
Children's lessons: $75 full day, $55 half day; includes lessons, lift ticket and rentals.

Lift tickets (2001/02 prices)

	Adult	Young adult (13-18)	Child (6-12)
One day (weekend/midweek)	$49/$42	$44/$37	$32/$27
Three days (weekend)	$129	$119	$79
Five days (weekend)	$209	$189	$119

Note: There is a $4 premium for adult holiday tickets.

Cranmore Facts

Summit elevation:	**1,700 feet**
Vertical drop:	**1,200 feet**
Base elevation:	**500 feet**

Expert: ★ **Advanced:** ★ ★
Intermediate: ★ ★ ★ ★
Beginner: ★ ★ ★ ★
Never-ever: ★ ★ ★
Address: Skimobile Road,
N. Conway, NH 03860
☎ Ski area phone: 356-5544
Snow report: 356-7070

Toll-free reservations: 800-SUN N SKI (786-6754)
Internet: www.cranmore.com
Number and types of lifts: 7–1 high-speed quad, 1 triple, 3 doubles, 2 surface lifts
Skiable acreage: 185 acres
Snowmaking: 100 percent
Uphill capacity: 7,500 skiers per hour
Snowboarding: Yes, unlimited
Bed base: 250
Nearest lodging: slopeside
Resort child care: Yes, 6 months and older
Adult ticket, per day: $32 (2001/02)

Who skis at a discount: Students with college ID ski for same price as Young Adults. Seniors ages 65-69 ski for $36 weekend/holiday, $32 midweek; 70 and older pay $36 weekend/holiday, $15 midweek. On Sundays, children ages 6-12 pay their age for a lift ticket. Multiday Etickets purchased online at www.attitash.com at least 14 days in advance offer an additional 10 percent off the already discounted multi-day price.

Cranmore Mountain Resort

Mountain layout—Skiing

Cranmore is one of the oldest ski resorts in the nation. Its good balanced terrain, modest size (yet with an extensive trail system) and convenient location practically in the center of North Conway also makes it an ideal family mountain. As part of the family of Booth Creek Resorts (Loon Mountain, an hour away, and Waterville Valley, an hour-and-a-half, are sister resorts), Cranmore now calls itself a "snowplay" resort rather than just a ski resort. In addition to the standard skiing and snowboarding, Cranmore offers tubing and snowtoys such as snowbikes, snowscoots and ski foxes that give its clientele an alternate way to get down the mountain. Cranmore offers interchangeable tickets with Loon and Waterville, and night skiing on Saturday nights and throughout holiday periods. It also has lift-serviced tubing on eight groomed lanes Fridays, Saturdays and during holiday weeks.

Mountain layout—Snowboarding

The Palmer X Park, located off the South Slope, has been designed with the entry level or intermediate skier or rider in mind. It's filled with gentle rolls, banked corners and manageable terrain features. There's also a halfpipe directly in front of the base lodge.

Lessons (2001/02 prices)

Group lessons: Quick Tip lesson is $25. A package including lift ticket plus rental equipment or Quick Tip lesson is $52, with both, it's $62.

Never-ever packages: Adult two-hour Getting Started lesson, $35; with lift ticket and rental equipment, it's $62.

Private lessons: $55 per hour for one student.

Child care (2001/02 prices)

Ages: 6 months to 5 years.
Cost: $50 for a full day or $8 per hour. The second child in the same family pays half price.
Reservations: Recommended, call 800-SUN-N-SKI (800-786-6754), ext. 8541 or 8542.

Children's lessons: $55 half day, $60 full day. A child's all-day lift ticket with rental equipment and full-day lesson is $78, with half-day lesson it's $68.

Lift tickets (2001/02 prices)

Adults tickets cost $32 and ticket for children ages 6–12 cost $18, any day. Children ages 5 and younger ski free.

Wildcat Mountain

Wildcat Mountain has no condominiums or trophy ski houses lining its trails, no fancy base village with shops and restaurants, therefore giving a taste of what skiing used to be like. What you'll find is back-to-basics skiing with old-style trails that ebb and flow with the mountain's contours. It's a true skiers' mountain. When you sink your teeth into Wildcat, it often bites back.

Wildcat sits across a narrow ribbon of highway from Mt. Washington, home to some of the highest recorded winds in the world. While Mt. Washington's summit, at 6,288 feet, is higher than Wildcat's, at 4,062, the stunted evergreens coated with rime ice on both give testament to the harshness of the environment. Wildcat can be brutally cold, but the location and elevation does have a silver lining: Snow is plentiful — an average year yields at least 15 feet — and it comes early and stays late, often well into May.

Wildcat has made major progress in the past few years. Investments in snowmaking and grooming equipment have helped tame the conditions. Trees have been thinned to create glades. Trails have been widened, making them easier for lower-level skiers to navigate. Even the once wild and woolly Wildcat Trail is less menacing. It's been widened, but it's seldom groomed, so it still growls. The base lodge has been rebuilt. Best of all, a high-speed quad, installed in 1997, now zips skiers and riders from base to summit in a little over six minutes.

Mountain layout—Skiing

Wildcat deserves its reputation as an experts' mountain, but it's much more than that. The Snowcat area, with its own triple chair and trails, is an ideal place for first-timers and shaky beginners, and the 2.75-mile cruise down Polecat from the summit gives advanced beginners an authentic alpine experience.

Intermediates have plenty to play on here, too. The Tomcat triple reaches about two-thirds of the way up the mountain and are a good retreat when the wind blows hard and cold, perhaps shutting the summit quad. The Bobcat triple reaches a little below midmountain and provides access to the narrow trails at Wildcat's core, two glades and the Bobcat slope, which is often used for races.

From the summit, experienced back-country enthusiasts can take the plunge to the village of Jackson. The Wildcat Valley Trail, cut in 1972, descends 3,245 vertical feet over 17.8 km. Be sure to check conditions first with the Jackson Ski Touring Foundation (383-9355), and never ski this trail alone: it is not patrolled and has natural hazards (the first corner alone is enough to make you religious).

Confirming that religious experience is Lynx: It might just convince you that Wildcat is God's chosen mountain. For decades, Lynx has been the 'Cat's most popular trail. It's easy to see why. Lynx plays with you, dropping quickly at the summit, then rolling around a few bends before dropping and rolling again. A different view, changed terrain or a trail split hover around every bend. When taken from summit to base, there are few trails in New England that can compare for range of terrain and the sheer joy of skiing.

Mountain layout—Snowboarding

Wildcat has a new halfpipe on the lower portion of the Bobcat Trail, where the terrain park is located. The best trail is the Lynx due to its contours and fall-line riding. Keep your speed up at the bottom of Wild Kitten to get back to the lift without hoofing it.

Lessons (2001/02 prices)

Group lessons: $28 per session.
Never-ever packages: $54, including rentals, lifts and lessons.
Private lessons: $54 per hour for one student.

Child care (2001/02 prices)

Ages: 2 months to 6 years.
Cost: $44 for a full day, $34 for a half day. Full-day program include lunch.

Reservations: Recommended, required for children younger than 18 months; call (800) 255-6439.

Children's lessons: $79 full day, includes lunch, $69 half day; includes lessons, lift ticket and rentals.

Lift tickets

	Adult	Teen (13-17)	Junior (6-12)
One day (weekend/midweek)	$49/$39	$39/$34	$29/$27
Two-day (weekend)	$91	$74	$56
Two-day (midweek)	$69	$64	$49

Who skis free: Children age 5 and younger with a ticket-holding parent.
Who skis at a discount: Seniors (65 and older) ski for Teen prices.

Mt. Washington

A trip to Tuckerman Ravine on the east side of Mt. Washington is a rite of spring for New England's skier and riders. Called the birthplace of extreme skiing, skiers have hiked into this snow-filled glacial cirque since 1914, and in the 1930s, races were even held here. The first giant slalom in the U.S. was held in Tuckerman's, as well as a truly sick event called the American Inferno, which started at the very summit of Mt. Washington and ended 4,200 feet lower at Pinkham Notch. The only trick is that you get to Tuckerman's the old-fashioned way: You climb it. From the Pinkham Notch Visitor's Center, a wide trail climbs 2 miles to a hut called HoJo's. Although visitors are no longer allowed to sleep (or even warm up) in the hut, it has camping and outhouse facilities. From here, the floor of the Ravine is reached via a steep hike.

Although skiing Tuck's is only for experts as it ranges anywhere from 40-55 degrees in pitch, less experienced folks still make the trek either to watch or ski the shallower terrain close to the ravine floor. Most people head straight for Lunch Rocks, an outcropping on the right as you hike in. From here, you can kick steps into the snow and hike up any of the gullies or the famous headwall. The aerobically ambitious can hike all the way to Mt. Washington's summit and ski the more gentle snow fields above the Ravine. But remember, the only way back down is via the Ravine's precipitously steep terrain. At day's end, you either ski down the Sherburne Trail or, if snow is thin, hike down the way you came. For weather and trail information, call 466-2721.

Cross-country and snowshoeing

Jackson Ski Touring Foundation (383-9355 or 800-927-6697; Box 216, Jackson, N.H. 03846), on Rte. 16A, is a Mecca for Nordic skiers. It has more than 150 km. of trails (87 km. are groomed), suitable for all ability levels. Country inns are spaced throughout the region. The base lodge is located around the corner in Jackson Village, directly across from the Red Fox Pub.

Mt. Washington Valley Ski Touring and Snowshoe Center (356-3042; Box 130, Intervale, N.H. 03845) has more than 65 km. of inn-to-inn trails, plus ski school and rentals. It also offers guided start-gazing tours and animal-tracking clinics.

The Appalachian Mountain Club (466-2721) maintains a network of touring trails radiating from the AMC Camp at Pinkham Notch. About 7 km. are rated Easiest or More Difficult (requiring skills up to a strong snowplow and step-turn), but about 40 km. are rated Most Difficult, with long challenging hills and narrow trails. AMC also has unusual dining; see that section for more details.

Great Glen Trails (466-2333) has 40 km. of cross-country skiing and snowshoeing trails at the base of Mt. Washington, which translates into jaw-dropping scenery all around you. Great Glen Trails will operate in the 2001-2002 season from The Mt. Washington Auto Road's Glen House. Here you'll find an outfitter shop, rentals, excellent cafeteria and instruction. One loop and the learning area have snowmaking. Telemarkers, cross-country skiers and snowshoers can take a snowcat partly up the Mt. Washington Auto Road, then ski down; sightseers also are welcome. The resort recently added a snowtubing park.

Bear Notch Ski Touring Center (374-2277) is one of the valley's best kept secrets. With a truly beautiful setting just north of Bartlett Village (Rte. 302), the 60 km. of Bear Notch trails offer uncrowded wooded scenery and a $9 weekend pass.

The Nestlenook Recreation Center (383-9443), also in Jackson, has 35 km. of touring tracks that wind through its 65-acre farm. **Purity Spring Resort** (800-373-3754 or 367-8896), near Madison, has 15 km. of groomed and tracked trails. Rentals and lessons are available.

Accommodations

Accommodations in the Mt. Washington Valley are among the most extensive in skidom if you like romantic, tiny country inns and bed-and-breakfast establishments. You won't find high-rises, but great old historic inns accommodate those who prefer the atmosphere of a large resort hotel. The Valley also has moderately priced motels suitable for families

For condominiums, chalets and motel suites, call **Top Notch Vacation Rentals** (383-4133, 800-762-6636; $-$$$$), which works with properties all up and down the valley. **Luxury**

Mountain Getaways (603-383-9101, 800-472-5207; $$ - $$$$) has everything from 1-bedroom condos to luxury villas. **Attitash Mountain Village** (603-374-6500; 800-862-2600;$-$$$$), across the road from the area, has inexpensive motel packages to upscale 3-bedroom condos.

For lodging information (but no reservations), call the **Mt. Washington Valley Chamber of Commerce** at (800) 367-3364 or visit its Web site. Lodgings are listed by region:

Bartlett (Attitash/Bear Peak Resort)

Right at the base of Bear Peak, the ski-in/ski-out **Grand Summit Resort Hotel** (364-1900 or 800-223-7669;$$-$$$$) provides all amenities for skiers from saunas and hot tubs to fitness rooms and restaurants. **The Bartlett Inn** (374-2353, 800-292-2353;$-$$) is informal and comfortable with family cabin units and cross-country trails out the back door.

Gorham

If you are skiing at Wildcat, this town, just to the north of The Valley, is where to stay. The modern **Royalty Inn** (466-3312 or 800-437-3529; $-$$) has 90 rooms of varying sizes that are all very spacious and well kept. Kitchenettes are available, but have a stovetop without an oven. The family-owned **Town & Country Motor Inn** (466-3315 or 800-325-4386; $) is a bit older and simpler, with 70s decor and smaller rooms. Families will want to stay in the same building that houses the pool, video games, sauna and Jacuzzi. Children age 15 and younger stay free. The inn also has dorm-style accommodations starting at $15 per person.

Pinkham Notch

To be really close to Mt. Washington, and to get a head start if you're climbing, skiing, or using its cross-country trails, there's the **Joe Dodge Lodge** (466-2727; $) at Pinkham Notch, run by the Appalachian Mountain Club, with room for 104. The two-, four- and five-bunk rooms are simple, and rates include either one or two meals. Three public rooms have fireplaces; one has a well-used piano, another is stocked with games and activities for children and the third has a library.

Jackson Village

This town is the home to a collection of old-time mansions, hotels, farms and houses that have grown into upscale B&Bs. Most ooze country touches, are filled with antiques and charm and offer dining on premises.

The Inn at Thorn Hill (800-289-8990 or 383-4242; $$$–$$$$), with views of Mt. Washington, is elegant without being stuffy. Rates include breakfast and a three-course dinner.

Eagle Mountain Resort (383-9111; for reservations, 800-966-5779; $-$$$) is one of those lovingly restored classic 19th-century resort hotels. Children age 15 and younger stay free if sleeping in existing beds.

The Wentworth Resort Hotel (383-9700 or 800-637-0013; $$$–$$$$) has spacious rooms with period baths. Ask about the three- and five-day midweek cross-country packages that include lodging, breakfast and dinner.

The Christmas Farm Inn (383-4313 or 800-443-5837; $$–$$$) is a cluster of buildings around a larger house, each as quaint as the next. All rates include breakfast and dinner. A 15-percent service charge and taxes will be added to your bill.

The Inn at Jackson (383-4321 or 800-289-8600; $-$$), is right through the covered bridge. The country breakfast will get you up in the morning and keep you going all day.

Dining: $$$-Entrees $20+; $$-$10-20; $-less than $10.

Accommodations: (double room) $$$$-$200+; $$$-$141-$200; $$-$81-$140; $-$80 and less.

Whitneys' Inn (383-8916 or 800-677-5737; $$-$$$), is a restored, 1840s farmhouse that sits at the base of Black Mountain, allowing Alpine and cross-country skiing from the door. Children may eat early at the kid's table with supervised activities following, allowing the adults the opportunity to enjoy their meal and relax.

The Crowes' Nest (603-383-8913; 800-511-8383, $-$$) is a more recent addition to the Jackson B&B scene, a stone's throw from the Jackson Ski Touring Foundation's trails.

Intervale

The 1785 Inn (800-421-1785 or 356-9025; $-$$$) is a country inn with what has been called the best view of the valley. It also boasts an excellent dining room that is open to the public for dinner, and one of the most extensive wine lists in New England.

The Langley House (356-9060; $-$$) has five recently redecorated rooms as well as a restaurant and bar. It's on Rte. 16A in Intervale. You can cross-country ski or snowshoe right out the back door of **The Forest Inn** (356-9772; 800-448-3534; $$), a cozy B&B also located on 16A, and **The New England Inn** (603-356-5541; 800-826-3466; $$-$$$$), also in the same vicinity, has everything from inn rooms to romantic cabins and its new deluxe lodge.

North Conway

With a few exceptions, North Conway's lodging is more motels and hotels with national chains being recently added to the lodging mix.

Stonehurst Manor (356-3113 or 800-525-9100; $-$$) was created from a turn-of-the-century mansion that belonged to the Bigelow family of carpet fame. It is still manorial. The setting, rooms and restaurant are absolutely elegant. Breakfast and dinner meal plans are optional. **The Buttonwood Inn**, North Conway (356-2625 or 800-258-2625; $$-$$$), is tucked in the woods with cross-country skiing from the back door. The **Eastman Inn** (356-6707 or 800-626-5855; $-$$) is a B&B with 14 rooms in one of the oldest houses in town, newly restored with antique charm. Breakfast with waffle irons almost at your table is superb.

North Conway Grand Hotel (800-648-4397; in New Hampshire 356-9300; $-$$$$) at Settlers' Green in North Conway, handy to all the best outlet stores, children younger than 17 stay free. **White Mountain Hotel and Resort** (356-7100 or 800-533-6301; $-$$) at the foot of these ledges (the enormous, sculptured, granite cliffs you see from all North Conway). The views back across the Valley toward Cranmore are unmatched. Don't miss the lavish Friday seafood buffet. **The Eastern Slope Inn Resort** (356-6321 or 800-862-1600; $$), in the heart of North Conway, is a classic New England inn. The **Green Granite Inn** (356-6901 or 800-468-3666; $-$$) is on Rte. 16 on the mile-and-a-half shopping strip. It has an indoor pool and a hot tub, and evening movies and children's programs are offered during weekends and vacation periods. **The Holiday Inn Express Hotel & Suites** (356-2551, 800-465-4329; $$-$$$) is on the strip but in a quiet spot behind one of the town's oldest cemeteries. Kids younger than 18 stay free. **Red Jacket Mountain View** (356-5411 or 800-752-2538; $$-$$$$), is a rambling building and some loft rooms and townhouses, both good for families. It has a panoramic view of the Moat Range and an indoor pool and hot tub. **The Briarcliff** (356-5584, 800-338-4291; $-$$), updated from a classic 1950s motel is affordable and convenient.

For rock-bottom prices, head to **Hostelling International-White Mountains** in Conway (447-1001;$) or the **Ski Dorm** (800-356-3596 or 356-2044;$) at the Cranmore Mountain Lodge with bunk and breakfast.

Dining

Mt. Washington Valley has a number of excellent restaurants. Those noted in the next three paragraphs serve meals worth a special trip. The **Rare Bear**, at The Bernerhof (383-4414; $$-$$$), in Bartlett on Rte. 302, has its own nationally famous cooking school. **Stonehurst** (356-3113; $$) and **The 1785 Inn**, in North Conway (356-9025; $$-$$$), have excellent cuisine. In Jackson, **The Christmas Farm Inn** (383-4313; $$-$$$), **The Inn at Thorn Hill** (383-4242; $$$), **Wentworth Resort Hotel** (383-9700; $$-$$$), and **Wildcat Inn and Tavern** (383-4245; $$) are all fairly expensive and serve gourmet meals.

If you're willing to travel to the outskirts of the valley, you can get fine gourmet dining with great winter views at the **Notchland Inn** (374-6131; $$-$$$), in Hart's Location; the **Snowvillage Inn** (447-2818; $$$), in Snowville; and the **Oxford House Inn** (207-935-3442; $$-$$$), over the border in Fryeburg, Maine.

For more down-to-earth meals, try the **Red Parka Pub** (383-4344; $$) for great barbecued spare ribs and prime rib. It doesn't take reservations; expect up to an hour wait on Saturday nights. **Moat Mountain Smoke House & Brewing Co.** (356-6381, $$) ,at the northern edge of North Conway, lists wood-grilled or smoked entrées, such as salmon, brisket, port and ribs, as well as lighter fare such as pizza and quesadillas. **Bellini's** (356-7000; $-$$) serves massive portions of southern Italian cooking while **Marcello's** (356-2313; $$) is more northern Italian.

The **Red Jacket Mountain View** (356-5411; $-$$), which looks like any other giant hotel from the outside, serves very good food. **Horsefeathers** (356-6862; $-$$), in North Conway, is perhaps the most popular spot in town. For a good time and plenty to eat, it's hard to beat, but it you're looking for gourmet, pass this one up, the menu promises more than it can deliver. **Delaney's Hole-in-the-Wall** (356-7776; $-$$), a big locals' haunt, inexplicably has a southwestern flair. Head to the **Shannon Door Pub** (383-4211; $) for Irish entertainment and good thin-crust pizzas. Pizza, from thin-crust to deep-dish, is found at **Elvio's** (356-3307; $) on Main Street.

For casual meals, **Brandli's Pizza Pasta Grill** (356-7878; $-$$), in Settlers Green, meets the test of good and cheap and lots to eat. For Mexican, locals head to **Margarita Grille** (383-6556; $-$$), formerly Margaritaville, just beyond the Red Parka, on Rte. 302, in Bartlett, or to **Cafe Noche** (447-5050; $), in a brightly colored building on Main Street, Conway.

The **Muddy Moose** (356-7696; $$) has affordable prices as well as some exotic choices, such as Wild Boar Marsala or Venison Pasta. On particularly crowded weekends in the Valley, head to **the Red Fox Pub & Restaurant** (383-6659; $$), in Jackson. With seating for 200, chances are you won't have to wait. Look for a great choice of microbrews. The Sunday Jazz Brunch here is a locals' favorite and a bargain at $5.95 per person.

For breakfast, head to **Gunther's** (356-5860; $), for giant waffles and pancakes (356-5200; $), or the **Sugar House Eatery** (356-6295; $), both on the main drag in North Conway. An all-day breakfast spot, **Guldie's** ($), is on the Rte. 16 strip. In Jackson, we recommend **Yesterday's** (383-4457; $) or the **Wentworth Resort Hotel** (383-9700), which serves an exceptionally good breakfast for $8.

If you're staying in Gorham, try **Welsh's** (466-2206; $), a family restaurant that serves hearty breakfasts and lunches. The oversized muffins and charbroiled burgers are delicious. **Libby's Bistro** (466-5330; $$), on Exchange Street, serves an ever-changing menu of creative entrees such as duck au poivre with a balsamic rhubarb sauce and strawberry rhubarb chutney. At the Appalachian Mountain Club (466-2727; $$), meals are served family-style: a great way to meet some new friends.

Après-ski/nightlife

One of the best ski bars in the country is the **Red Parka Pub**, which offers lively après-ski and then nightlife activity into the wee hours. Something is happening every night, and its informal style runs to beer served in Mason jars to vintage skis and creative license plates covering the walls. On nights when there is no live music, live comedy or a movie is featured.

The place to be in Jackson is the **Wildcat Tavern**, where folk rock is served on weekends. On Friday and Saturday nights, **Horsefeathers**, in North Conway, hops, and the **Up Country Saloon** has live dance music. Locals hang out in **Hooligans**, **Horsefeathers** and **Delaney's Hole-in-the-Wall**, all in North Conway.

 Other activities

Shopping: For bargain hunters, Mt. Washington Valley may have the best shopping of any ski resort in the nation, with more than 100 factory outlets and no sales tax. The area also has many unusual boutiques with creative gift items. Stop by the Chamber of Commerce in North Conway and pick up a Visitor Guide or a shopping guide; there are far too many stores to list here.

The **Cranmore Sports Center** (356-6301), at Cranmore base, is a huge all-season facility, with indoor and outdoor tennis courts, pool, aerobics classes, steamroom and sauna. It is also home to a huge (30 by 40 feet) indoor climbing wall. Classes are available through **International Mountain Climbing School** (356-6316). The owner, Rick Wilcox, has climbed Mt. Everest. **Eastern Mountain Sports** (356-5433) is in the Eastern Slope Inn. Both schools offer a range of winter climbing and hiking programs, including ice-climbing instruction, ascents of Mt. Washington and traverses of the Presidential Range.

The **Appalachian Mountain Club** (466-2721) has an active schedule of courses and workshops on ski touring, snowshoeing, avalanches and more.

Take a **sleigh ride** in the Valley, try Nestlenook's horse-drawn sleigh (383-0845) or The Stables at the Farm off West Side Road (356-4855).

Cranmore, Black Mountain, King Pine and Shawnee Peak have very active **tubing** hills.

In Conway, visit the Ham Arena (447-5886) for indoor **ice skating**. It has open skating, rentals and concessions. Two-hour skating lessons start at $4 for children and $5 for adults. Call ahead for public skating hours. You can also ice skate in Jackson, North Conway and at King Pine's covered ice arena (free with a lift ticket).

Getting there and getting around

By air: The closest airport is Portland, Maine, with major airline service from all over the country. It is about a 90-minute drive from North Conway. Manchester Airport, in New Hampshire, is served by Southwest, US Air, MetroJet, United, Continental Express, ComAir and Business Express/Delta Connection, and is about a two-hour drive.

By car: The Mt. Washington Valley is 140 miles north of Boston. Take I-95 to Rte. 16, then north on 16/302. An alternate route is I-93 north to Rte. 104 to Rte. 25 to Rte. 16 and on to North Conway. From Portland, follow Rte. 302.

North Conway has been notorious for its weekend traffic jams going through town. The new North-South connector road is scheduled to be complete to North Conway Village by December 2001, offering a good alternate route for those coming from the south. Even so, be patient if you're behind the wheel at 4 p.m., when the lifts close. Or, if you are driving from the Jackson/Wildcat/Attitash Bear Peak end of town to the south, take West Side Road to avoid most of the shopping traffic and the North Conway crowds.

Getting around: Bring a car.

Other Mount Washington Valley Resorts

Purity Spring Resort/King Pine Ski Area, East Madison, NH

(800) 373-3754 or 603-367-8896; Internet: www.kingpine.com

6 lifts; 17 trails; 350 vertical feet; 35 skiable acres

This small area, part of family-run Purity Spring Resort, has a modest vertical drop, but for those just starting out and parents who want to keep an eye on young children, it is an ideal resort. On-mountain lodging, a health club with indoor pool and packages that include lodging, skiing, meals and full use of the resort's facilities make this a good value for young families. King Pine does have one short, steep trail, reportedly one of the steepest in the state, but top-level skiers are better off somewhere else. Night skiing is available Tuesdays, Fridays, Saturdays and holidays, and the resort also has 15 km. of groomed and tracked cross-country trails. Other activities include snow tubing, snowshoeing and ice skating.

Lift tickets (00/01 pricing): $29 for adults weekends, $21 weekdays. Kids (6–12) ski for $19 weekends, $12 midweek. Night skiing: $15 adults, $10 children. Kids 5 and younger ski free.

Distance from Boston: About 2.5 hours via I-95, Rte. 16, Rte. 25 and Rte. 153.

Lodging information: (800) 373-3754.

Shawnee Peak, Bridgton, ME

(207) 647-8444; Internet: www.shawneepeak.com

5 lifts; 35 trails; 225 acres; 1,300 vertical feet

About a 35- to 45-minute drive from North Conway in Bridgton, Maine, this family resort offers fantastic views across Maine flatlands and lakes to the White Mountains. It has excellent snowmaking and a twice-a-day grooming program that allows for "first tracks" twice daily, if you're lucky. The mountain is primarily a day trip for Portland-area residents, but its terrain offers a bit of something for everyone. It is perfect for families, with the toughest runs at the top and left side of the mountain as you look at the trail map, and wide-open beginner slopes to the right (or west). Excellent, tight gladed areas are nestled between the two sides of the mountain. Most of the trails to the left are New England-narrow. Upper/Lower Appalachian is a great steep cruiser with fantastic views that uses almost all the mountain's vertical. Shawnee features the most extensive night-skiing facilities in New England with a lighted vertical drop of 1,300 feet covered by 17 trails.

Lift tickets (00/01 prices): $39 weekends/holidays and $29 midweek for adults; $25 on weekends/holidays and $21 weekdays for ages 6–12 and 65 and older. Children age 5 and younger ski free when accompanied by a paying adult. Night skiing (daily, except Sunday, 4–10 p.m.) is $21 for adults and $19 for juniors/seniors. Other tickets available include Twilight (12:30-10 p.m.) and day/night (9:30 a.m.-10 p.m.) The beginner lift is free during the week and every night.

Distance from Boston: About 3 hours. Take 95 North to 295 to the Forest Ave./Route 302 West exit and follow Rte. 302 through Bridgton. The access road is approximately 6 miles beyond downtown.

Lodging information: For the limited number of condos on the mountain, call the ski area number, (207) 647-8444. For lodging in North Conway, call the Mt. Washington Valley Chamber of Commerce, (800) 367-3364.

Black Mountain, Jackson, NH

800-698-4490; Internet: www.blackmt.com

4 lifts–1 triple, 1 double, 2 surface lifts; 140 trail acres; 1,100 vertical feet

Black Mountain, a compact ski area at the top of Jackson Village on Rte. 16B, may be the best place in the valley for beginner lessons and family skiing. Wide open Whitneys' Hill was the site of the first ski lessons in the Valley, in 1936, and it's still an ideal place to take your first turns or have your children take theirs. The best beginner trails down the mountain are Sugarbush and Black Beauty, while Upper Galloping Goose and Mr. Rew offer some short expert fun. Upper intermediate or expert skiers can play in the glades. Located on the Jackson Ski Touring trail system, Black has more than its share of telemark skiers, both beginner and experts; its top-to-bottom Skinny Ski Inferno is a classic event. Finally, Black Mountain's southern exposure provides a warmer place to ski when it's just too cold at other valley areas.

Lift tickets: (00/01 prices) $32 adults weekends, $20 weekdays, $20 Juniors (18 and younger) weekends, $15 weekdays. Children 5 and younger ski free. The Passport, a day ticket valid for two adults and two juniors on a weekend, costs $89.

Lessons: Group lessons: $25 per 90-minute session. Never-ever packages: $40, including rentals, lifts and lessons. Private lessons: $40 per hour for one student.

Lodging information: 800-698-4490.

Bretton Woods

New Hampshire

Summit elevation:	**3,100 feet**
Vertical drop:	**1,500 feet**
Base elevation:	**1,600 feet**

Address: Route 302,
Bretton Woods, NH 03575
☎ **Area code:** 603
Ski area phone: 278-3320
Snow report: 278-3333
ⓘ **Toll-free reservations:** (800) 258-0330
E-mail: skibw@brettonwoods.com
Internet: www.brettonwoods.com
Expert: ★
Advanced: ★
Intermediate: ★★★
Beginner: ★★★★★
Never-ever: ★★★★★

Number and types of lifts: 8–2 high-speed quad,
1 quad, 1 triple, 2 doubles, 2 surface lifts
Acreage: 375 trail acres
Snowmaking: 95 percent
Uphill capacity: 8,000 per hour
Snowboarding: Yes, unlimited
Bed base: 3,400+
Nearest lodging: slopeside
Resort child care: Yes, 2 months and older
Adult ticket, per day: $40-$53 (01/02 prices)
Dining: ★★★★
Apres-ski/nightlife: ★★
Other activities: ★★★

Bretton Woods is a well-known name in the history of the United States. The grand Mount Washington Hotel, a National Historic Landmark, first opened to summer guests in 1902. It was the setting for the 1944 International Monetary Conference, where the gold standard was set at $35 an ounce, and the American dollar was established as the backbone of the international exchange system. In 1999, the resort completely winterized the hotel to welcome cold-weather guests and initiated one of the largest expansions of any ski area in New Hampshire.

Long known for its laid-back terrain and no-stress atmosphere, those who haven't visited Bretton Woods are in for a surprise. It now has the most skiable acres of any area in New Hampshire, and although it retains the laid-back, family-friendly atmosphere, development of West Mountain added some much needed steeps, although these are woefully short, and some fun glades. This year the mountain has developed 30 acres of steep, wooded terrain in Rosebrook Canyon with 10 tree chutes. This is the first step in the development of Mt. Stickney, slated for 2003.

Given its remote location and its two high-speed quads, liftlines are rare. Perhaps the area's biggest attribute, though, is the view. From the slopes, the Presidential Range of the White Mountains dominates the skyline, with the majestic Mt. Washington Hotel lying below its namesake peak.

Mountain layout—Skiing

This is a mountain that was designed for beginners and intermediates but now has a growing assortment of glades and short steeps to provide a thrills. The traditional Bretton Woods trails such as Sawyer's Swoop, Big Ben and Range View have been joined with an excellent series of expert glades in the newly developed West Mountain and Rosebrook Canyon. The trail names sound more sinister than they really are, however they do offer a quantum leap in difficulty over previous Bretton Woods trails.

With the new terrain, virtually everyone can enjoy skiing this area without feeling like they've done it all. Only extreme skiing junkies will be out of place, and probably won't be found here unless they are skiing the trees out of bounds.

Mountain layout–Snowboarding

Riders will find a combination half-pipe and terrain park on Bretton's Wood. This park has been evolving and expanding each season. West Mountain is popular with riders for the natural hits here both on the trails and in the glades. When making your way back from West to the main base area along Crawford Ridge, it's important to get your speed up and maintain it. Another place to maintain enough speed to get you across the flats is near the bottom of Two Miles Home.

Mountain rating

This is a perfect place for beginners and a wonderful place for intermediates to cruise and feel great about their skiing. Advanced skiers will find challenge in the glades. This is an ideal area for families or those traveling in groups of mixed abilities or varying age groups.

Cross-country and snowshoeing

The 100 km. of cross-country and snowshoeing trails, located on the grounds of the Mount Washington Hotel, offer 1,700 acres of spectacular scenery. The trail system is dotted with a series of restaurants and lounges. Intrepid cross-country skiers can glide from the top of the Bretton Woods ski area back to the hotel. This area averages 170 inches of snow every year.

Trail fees are $15 for adults (ages 13-64) and $9 for juniors (ages 6-12) and seniors (ages 65 and over). Children (5 and under) ski free. Snowshoers can use the skate lanes of the cross-country trails with a trail pass. Complimentary guided hour-and-a-half ski tours through the Ammonoosuc Valley available. They leave from the Nordic Center daily.

There is a cross-country ski school and a telemark ski school as well. Atlas snowshoes are available for sale or rent. The variety and extent of trails rivals that of the nearby Jackson Ski Touring and Vermont's Stowe system.

Lessons (2001/02 prices)

Group lessons: $29 for 90 minutes.
Never-ever package: This includes equipment, all-day lessons and a limited lift ticket for $55 per day.
Private lessons are $59 an hour.
Special programs: Intermediate programs include equipment, lessons and lifts for $79.

Child care (2001/02 prices)

Ages: 2 months to 5 years.
Costs: The Babes in the Woods program with stories, crafts and games is $55 for a full day (8 a.m.–4:30 p.m.) with lunch and $45 for a half day, a.m. or p.m.

Snow Play and Ski Readiness all-day care with a gentle introduction to skiing, for children ages 5 and younger, is $75 for a full day (8 a.m.–4:30 p.m.) with lunch or $65 for the morning only.

Reservations: Required; call 278-3325.

Children's lessons: The Hobbit Ski and Snowboard School (ages 4–12) has ski and snowboard lessons including lunch and rentals for $79. Snowboard programs are for ages 8–12. Reservations are required for snowboard programs: call 800-278-3345.

Lift tickets (2001/02 prices)

	Adult	Teen (13-18)	Junior (6-112)
One day (weekend)	$53	$43	$33
Three days (weekend)	$135	$109	$84
Five days (weekend)	$199	$159	$124

Who skis free and at discount: Younger than 6 ski free; Seniors 65 and older ski for $15 midweek, non-holiday. On non-holiday Wednesdays, two ski or ride for $44. A ticket for the Crawford Beginner double chair is $15. The $199 Bold and the Beautiful Midweek Season Pass is an interchangeable pass good at Bretton Woods or Cannon Mountain (on sale at the Bretton Woods ticket offices throughout the season). Midweek non-holiday tickets are $42 for adults, $35 for teens and $29 for juniors for one day; $94, $79 and $69 respectively for three days; $149, $124 and $105 respectively for five days.

Note: Night skiing is offered Friday and Saturday and nightly during holiday weeks. A twilight ticket, valid 2-9 p.m., is $35; a night ticket, valid 4-9 p.m. is $19.

Accommodations at the resort

Be sure to ask about packages, as Bretton Woods offers plenty, including themed weekends such as ballroom dancing and more. The **Mount Washington Hotel** ($$$-$$$$) is one of the most breathtaking hotels in the country. The grand dining room and period decor add to the magic. Staying here is a step back in time with excellent service and a touch of elegance.

The restored 1896 **Bretton Arms Country Inn** ($-$$), a National Historic Landmark, has spacious rooms, old fashioned charm and an excellent dining room.

The **Bretton Woods Motor Inn** ($-$$) features less expensive accommodations between the downhill and cross-country areas.

Bretton Woods also has a grouping of townhouses. All Bretton Woods properties can be reached through (800) 258-0330 or 278-1000. In winter the ski area provides complimentary shuttle buses to and from the slopes.

Other area accommodations

Built of granite, the **Notchland Inn** (374-6131 or 800-866-6131; $$-$$$$), in Bartlett, has 13 rooms, all with fireplaces. It has a hot tub, skating and cross-country skiing from the door.

The Inn at Forest Hills (823-9550, fax 823-5555; $-$$) is a beautifully restored, English Tudor-style B&B built into a house which was once part of the grand Forest Hills Hotel. It's just about a mile from the village of Franconia, on Rte. 142, heading toward Bethlehem.

The Mulburn Inn (869-3389; $) is another B&B in a great Tudor-style setting with oak staircase and stained glass windows. It's located in Bethlehem, once considered one of the fresh-air centers of New England, only about 10 minutes from Bretton Woods.

Dining: $$$-Entrees $20+; $$-$10-20; $-less than $10.
Accommodations: (double room) $$$$-$200+; $$$-$141-$200; $$-$81-$140; $-$80 and less.

Six miles north of the region at the crest of Sugar Hill, you'll find the **Sunset Hill House** (800-786-4455 or 823-5522; $–$$), a restored turn-of-the century inn built in 1882 in the era of Grand Hotels and Resorts. You can still stay in luxury and elegance, with wonderful views of the Presidentials. This mountain resort also has 30 km. of cross-country tracks (free for guests, $6 trail fee for others). Call for ski-and-stay programs.

Dining

The opulent **Main Dining Room at the Mount Washington Hotel** (278-1000; $$-$$$) provides a unique and grand setting for any meal complete with serenading orchestra, daily menus and an extensive wine list. Proper attire is required. For gourmet cuisine in a more intimate, fireplaced century-old atmosphere, try the **Bretton Arms Restaurant** (278-1000; $$-$$$). Many locals say it's the best restaurant at the resort.

Other spots recommended by locals for fine dining are **Sunset Hill House** (823-5522; $$–$$$) and **Notchland Inn** (374-6131 or 800-866-6131; $$–$$$) in Hart's Location.

At Bretton Woods, the **Top o' the Quad Restaurant** ($$) serves casual lunches daily, with views of Mount Washington's summit. Back down the mountain, only a quarter-mile from the slopes, try **Darby's Diner** ($-$$) for traditional diner fare. **Fabyans Station** ($-$$) is a good eatery in an old railroad station. In Franconia head to **Hillwinds** ($$).

Après-ski/nightlife

The après-ski centers around the Mount Washington Hotel where guests dance to a dinner orchestra or head into the stone foundation of the hotel to the Cave Lounge which offers an intimate dancing atmosphere.

Other activities

Shopping: The factory outlet bonanza of North Conway is 30 miles southeast of Bretton Woods. No sales tax makes buying all the sweeter.

The Mount Washington Hotel has plenty of non-skiing activities including **horse-drawn sleigh rides**, a **skating rink** and an indoor pool. The resort also has tubing area and a separate sports center with pool, racquetball courts, exercise and weight rooms, Jacuzzi and sauna. Nearby Cannon is home to the **New England Ski Museum,** a collection of ski memorabilia well worth a brief visit. **Cannon's tram** is open for non-skiing sightseers for $9 a ride.

The Rocks Estate in Bethlehem has **sleigh rides** and offers some **forestry-related activities**, being owned by the Society For The Protection of New Hampshire Forests. Call (800) 639-5373. The Sunset Hill House, about six miles north of Cannon and the Old Man of the Mountain, has **sleigh rides** and **ice skating**. Call (800) 786-4455 or 823-5522.

Nearby Twin Mountain is one of New England's top **snowmobiling** areas.

Getting there and getting around

By air: Boston's Logan Airport is 150 miles away from the area. Manchester Airport, 100 miles south, is serviced by Southwest, MetroJet, Comair, Continental Express, Delta's Business Express, USAir, and United. The airport phone number is 624-6556; its Internet address is www.flymanchester.com.

By car: From I-93 heading north, Bretton Woods is on Rte. 302: take Exit 35 to Rte. 3, which meets Rte. 302 at Twin Mountain.

Getting around: A car is a necessity to reach the resort conveniently, but a shuttle bus operates throughout the resort.

Cannon Mountain

New Hampshire

Summit elevation: 4,180 feet
Vertical drop: 2,146 feet
Base elevation: 2,000 feet

Address: Franconia Notch State Park
Franconia, NH 03580
☏ **Area code:** 603
Ski area phone: 823-8800
Snow report: 823-7771
Fax: 823-8088
ⓘ **Toll-free reservations:**
(800) 227-4191
E-mail: info@cannonmt.com
Internet: www.cannonmt.com
Expert:★★
Advanced:★★
Intermediate:★★★★
Beginner:★★★
Never-ever:★★★

Number and types of lifts: 7–1 70-person aerial
tram, 2 high-speed quads, 3 triples, 1 surface lift
Acreage: 163 skiable acres
Snowmaking: 95 percent
Uphill capacity: 11,000 per hour
Snowboarding: Yes, unlimited
Bed base: 13,000 nearby
Nearest lodging: about 1/2 mile
Resort child care: Yes, 6 weeks and older
Adult ticket, per day: $33–$44 (01/02)

Dining:★★
Apres-ski/nightlife:★
Other activities:★★

State-owned Cannon Mountain, located in breathtaking Franconia Notch, is the farthest north of the three resorts lining I-93. It's also the most historic. The first racing trail in North America, now called the Taft Slalom, was cut into Cannon in 1933 and brought several major races to Cannon, including the National Alpine Championships. The aerial tramway was also the first in North America and opened for business in 1938. In 1980, the tram was updated to the current 70-person model, but the old tram houses still remain at the base and summit, and the resort still enjoys the charm of the early skiing days. Not as popular as Loon or Waterville, Cannon has a devoted following that appreciates its historic significance. An added plus is the New England Ski Museum, located adjacent to the tram base.

Besides the Tramway Base Station—the first base area you come to after exiting I-93 at Exit 2—Cannon's main base lodge, the Peabody Base Area, is off Exit 3. In 1999, Cannon underwent the largest ski resort expansion in New Hampshire, including a major renovation to the Peabody Base Lodge. But the resort is still recognizable. Long known by experts as one of the most challenging mountains in the East, Cannon enlarged its beginner and intermediate terrain. The Brookside novice slope, served by its own triple chair, was added below the Peabody Base Lodge, as well as a new building to house children's programs. Parkway and Lower Cannon, both beginner runs, were widened, and Lower Cannon was divided by netting, with one side designated for lower-level skiers (unfortunately, it is difficult to tell which side is which). The state also blasted 35,000 cubic yards of granite to widen Middle Ravine and Middle Cannon, both mid-mountain intermediate trails, and Big Link, which brings skiers and riders back to the Cannonball Express Quad (serving the summit), was also widened.

But experts, do not despair. With a 2,146-foot vertical served by the 70-passenger tram, the challenge is still there. The summit is also accessible via a new high-speed quad that takes intermediates and experts from the Peabody Base Area over halfway up the mountain to access the expanded terrain or the summit trails via the Cannonball Express Quad. A new triple chair also takes experts up from the Peabody Base Area to the famous Front Five trails. Beginners can also use this triple to access the gentler terrain nearer the base.

Though that three-letter word "ice" has been sometimes associated with the mountain, Cannon takes mountain preparation very seriously and added four groomers to its squadron last year. Of Cannon's 163 acres, 95 percent are covered by snowmaking, and its higher base altitude in Franconia Notch often finds it enjoying snow while other nearby mountains have rain. The trails are narrower in legend than they are in reality, and the mountain can actually be skied by most intermediates. This is still a place for advanced skiers to play and intermediates to push themselves.

When the weather is good, skiers and riders also flock to Cannon for the sheer scenic beauty. From the summit, you can see all the way to New Hampshire's Presidential Range. You also see no signs of civilization except for the highway and base lodges. Lodging is available 15 minutes south in Lincoln or Woodstock or about 5 minutes north in Franconia.

Mountain layout—Skiing

◆◆ **Expert** ◆ **Advanced:** Experts can either take the tram or the Peabody Express Quad. From the quad, skiers and riders can reach the summit via the Cannonball Express Quad. The Profile Trail right under the summit express quad is a wide, straight trail that takes you down almost to mid-mountain. Or experience New England skiing the way it used to be by winding down Skylight or Upper Ravine. From the tram's summit station, you can take Upper Cannon, Tramway or Vista Way, all intermediate trails that are challenging but certainly negotiable. The steepest is Upper Cannon which offers New England-style steeps and whoop-dee-do turns—almost too many to count— through the high-elevation scrubby pines.

The Front Five, as known to locals, are the intimidating-looking trails seen from the highway; they are accessed via Paulie's Extension or Lower Cannon. Three of them, Avalanche, Paulie's Folly and Zoomer, are marked black and rightfully so, especially Zoomer's bumps, and all five look as if they plunge straight into Echo Lake. But the other two, Rocket and Gary's, have less pitch and no bumps. None is as frighteningly steep as it appears, and they each present the best routes back to the tram.

■ **Intermediate:** Although touted as an expert's mountain, intermediates will find plenty of terrain to suit their skills. From the summit, you can take either Vista Way, Tramway (the widest of the three) or Upper Cannon. These feed into a collection of intermediate runs, including Middle Cannon and Middle Ravine. Or from the top of the Cannonball Express Quad, treat yourself to Upper Ravine, which swoops its way through the subalpine forest. Intermediates wishing to return to the tram without scaring themselves on the Front Five can follow the Tram Cutback from Gary's, the easiest of the Front Five.

●● **Beginner:** The bottom half of Cannon has five long runs that will suit beginners: Toss-Up, Lower Cannon (now divided into two halves to, in theory, keep faster skiers segregated from beginners), Parkway, Gremlin and Turnpike. The Eagle Triple Chair from the Peabody Base Area is the best way to access this terrain. More daring beginners can take the Peabody Express Quad. A slew of intermediate runs feed into the beginner trails.

● **Never-ever:** The Brookside learning area adjacent to the Peabody Base Area opened last year and is ideal for never-evers. The area is segregated from the rest of the mountain (so experts won't zoom through), and it is serviced by its own triple chair lift as well as a surface lift. Never-evers can rent equipment and sign up for lessons at the Brookside Learning Center to the right of the Peabody Base Lodge parking area.

Mountain layout–Snowboarding

Snowboarding is allowed on the entire mountain, but the resort lacks a halfpipe and terrain park.

Cross-country

The Franconia Village X-C Ski Center (800-473-5299) has 105 km. of trails, 65km of which are groomed and tracked. Ski, stay and sleigh packages are available through the Franconia Inn at the same telephone number.

Lessons (2001/02 prices)

Group lessons: $25 per session; $100 for book of five lessons.
Never-ever package: Introduction to Skiing or Snowboarding is $49 and includes a lesson, shaped ski or snowboard rental and Brookside lift ticket. A follow-up Refresher course is also $49.

Private lessons: $45 for one hour, $70 for two hours, plus $25 for each additional hour and $10 for each additional person per hour. An Early Bird discount of $35 per hour applies to lessons at 8:45 a.m. A half-day lesson is $95; a full-day lesson is $160. Best deal: 3-person private lesson for $75, plus $25 for each additional person. A half-day private lesson is $95 and a half-day semi-private lesson for two is $125.

Other: All-day ski guides are available for $275 for up to six people.

Racing: Recreational racing is offered weekends and holidays at 1 p.m. at $1 per run. Training sessions are at 10 a.m. and cost $20.

Child care (2001/02 prices)

Ages: 6 weeks and older.
Costs: For children 6 weeks to 1 year: $9 per hour; $25 per half day; $50 per full day. For children older than 1 year: $8 per hour; $23 for a half day, $48 for a half day with private lesson; $45 for full day with lunch, $65 for full day with lunch and private lesson.

Reservations: Advised; call 823-8800.

Children's lessons: Cannon Tykes, for ages 3-4: $30 private lesson with rentals. Cannon Kids (for skiers ages 4-8) and Mountain Explorers (for skiers and riders ages 8-12) have morning and afternoon sessions with all-day ticket is $60; morning or afternoon session with all-day tickets is $50; afternoon session with afternoon ticket is $40. Five-day program with two sessions daily and lift ticket is $250. Five-day program one session daily and lift ticket is $225. Rental equipment for all programs is $10.

Lift tickets (2001/02 prices)

	Adult	Teen (13-19)	Child (6–12)
One day, weekend/midweek	$44/$33	$36/$22	$28/$22

Who skis free: Ages 5 and younger when with a ticketed adult.
Who skis at a discount: Ages 65 and older ski at child rates. On Tuesdays and Thursdays, two people can ski for the price of one (excluding Dec. 25, 27 and Jan. 1).

Accommodations

Cannon has no slopeside lodging, but nearby Lincoln and Woodstock (about 15 minutes south) and Franconia (about 5 minutes north) have accommodations to suit just about any needs. Please consult the chapter on Loon for recommended accommodations in the Lincoln/Woodstock area, or call Lincoln/Woodstock Central Reservations at (800) 227-4191.

Long known as a ski town, Franconia has several quaint New England Inns, the nicest being the **Sunset Hill House** (800-786-4455 or 823-5522; $–$$ ♿ ✕ P ✖) and the **Franconia Inn** (800-473-5299 or 823-5542; $$-$$$). Located just outside Franconia on historic Sugar Hill (the site of the first ski school in North America), the Sunset Hill House is a restored farmhouse built in 1789 that has wonderful views of the Presidentials and the Green Mountains. The Franconia Inn is a lovely turn-of-the-century inn with hand-hewn beams in the cozy lobby and a sunny dining room. Some of the rooms have been renovated recently; others still have quaint old bathrooms with claw-foot tubs. Both the Sunset Hill House and Franconia Inn offer cross-country skiing (free for guests, $8 trail fee for others). Of note, the Franconia Inn is located on Rte. 116 2.5 miles south of Franconia. Unless your car has good suspension, we recommend you take I-93 to Franconia, then follow signs for Rte. 116. There is a short-cut from Cannon off Rte. 18, but the road gives new meaning to the term "frost heave."

The Inn at Forest Hills (800-280-9550 or 823-9550; $–$$ P ✖ ☺) has been beautifully restored by Joanne and Gordon Haym. The English Tudor-style B&B is built into a house which was once part of the grand Forest Hills Hotel. We hear the full New England breakfast with a gourmet twist is not to be missed. The Inn is located just about a mile from the village of Franconia, on Rte. 142, heading toward Bethlehem.

Among the least expensive places to stay are the **Hillwinds Lodge** (800-906-5292 or 823-5551; $-$$), which is owned by the same people who own the Franconia Inn; **Parker's Motel** (800-766-6835 or 745-8341; $ P ☜), which is about five miles from Cannon Mountain, the **Riverbank Motel** (800-633-5624 or 745-3374; $ ☜ P ✖☰) or the **Cannon Mountain View Inn** (800-823-9577 or 823-9577; $), right off Exit 37 in Franconia. We also hear that the **Kinsman Lodge** (823-5685, fax 823-9512; $) is a casual and affordable B&B located on Easton Road in Franconia.

Dining

For elegant dining experiences, locals recommend the **Sunset Hill House** (823-5522; $$), which also has great views of the Franconia Range, and the **Franconia Inn** (823-5542; $$-$$$), which has a bright, sunny dining room. Both establishments require reservations, even if you are staying there.

For more traditional fare, head to the **Village House** ($–$$) in downtown Franconia or **Hillwinds** ($$), which specializes in grilled steaks and seafood.

For breakfast, head up Sugar Hill outside Franconia to **Polly's Pancake Parlor** (823-5575; $). Or drive a few miles up I-93 to Littleton and the **Littleton Diner** (444-3994; $), a traditional old diner car where you can get a great breakfast.

If you are staying in the Lincoln/Woodstock area, please see our chapter on Loon for dining recommendations in the area.

Après-ski/nightlife

With no restaurants nearby, Cannon is not exactly bustling with après-ski activities. But down the road in Franconia, try Village House, a comfortable lounge with a lot of classic ski history and an evening entertainer who plays après-ski at the mountain's lounge. Or try Hillwinds, a large bar and lounge with live entertainment and a huge crowd on weekends.

Other activities

The **New England Ski Museum** sits adjacent to Cannon's Tramway Base Station and has a collection of ski memorabilia well worth a visit. The museum is open noon-5 p.m. Friday-Monday, and admission is free. **Cannon's tram** is open for non-skiing sightseers for $9 a ride.

The **Rocks Estate** in Bethlehem, on a hilltop about 10 miles from Cannon, has **sleigh rides** and offers some forestry-related activities, since it's owned by the Society For The Protection of New Hampshire Forests. Call (800) 639-5373.

The Sunset House in Sugar Hill outside Franconia on Rte. 117 has **sleigh rides** and **ice skating**. Call (800) 786-4455 or 823-5522.

Getting there and getting around

By air: Boston's Logan Airport is about 145 miles away from Cannon and the Franconia area. Manchester Airport, 85 miles south, is serviced by Southwest, MetroJet, Comair, Continental Express, Delta's Business Express, USAir, and United. The airport phone number is 624-6556; its Internet address is www.flymanchester.com.

By car: From I-93 heading north, Cannon is visible from I-93 just north of Franconia Notch State Park. Take Exit 2 for the Tramway Base Station, Exit 3 for the Peabody Base Area.

Getting around: As there is no on-mountain lodging, a car is a necessity.

Hotel Legend	
🚐	Airport Shuttle
🎿	Ski-in /ski-out
🌊	Indoor heated pool
🌊	Outdoor heated pool
💪	fitness center
✕	restaurant
🐾	Pets OK
🚭	No Smoking
💨	In-room Hairdryers
Ⓟ	Parking

Dining: $$$-Entrees $20+; $$-$10-20; $-less than $10.
Accommodations: (double room) $$$$-$200+; $$$-$141-$200; $$-$81-$140; $-$80 and less.

Loon Mountain

New Hampshire

Summit elevation: 3,050 feet
Vertical drop: 2,100 feet
Base elevation: 950 feet

Address: RR1, Box 41
Lincoln, NH 03251
✆ **Area code:** 603
Ski area phone: 745-8111
Snow report: 745-8100
Fax: 745-8214
ⓘ **Toll-free reservations:**
(800) 229-7829
E-mail: info@loonmtn.com
Internet: www.loonmtn.com
Expert: ★ **Advanced:** ★★
Intermediate: ★★★★
Beginner: ★★★★
Never-ever: ★★★

Number and types of lifts: 9–1 gondola,
1 high-speed quad, 2 triples, 3 doubles,
2 surface lifts
Acreage: 275 skiable acres
Snowmaking: 98 percent
Uphill capacity: 10,550 per hour
Snowboarding: Yes, unlimited
Bed base: 13,000
Nearest lodging: slopeside
Resort child care: Yes, 6 weeks - 8 years
Adult ticket, per day: $40-$51
Dining: ★★★
Apres-ski/nightlife: ★★★
Other activities: ★★★

Easy accessibility, good terrain and a beautiful natural setting combined with the nearby resort town of Lincoln, with its shops, restaurants, inns and motels, have contributed to Loon Mountain's popularity. Like many of the other ski resorts in the White Mountains, Loon has decent vertical, and many of the runs maintain their pitch from top to bottom (unlike some resorts where most of the runs wash out to beginner terrain near the base). Although the mountain's black diamond terrain will keep experts entertained, overall Loon is an intermediate's mountain. The blue runs are true intermediate runs, and beginners who have ventured into intermediate terrain may find that Loon's blue squares test their limits. Loon has two base areas, separated by parking lots but connected by a steam train that shuttles skiers and riders back and forth, a real hit with children.

The resort enjoys some of the friendliest staff around, which keeps skiers and riders coming back. It also offers plenty of family-friendly activities, including snow-tubing, both day and night (with a new separate area for younger children this winter), snow toys, a climbing wall, an expanded ice skating rink and horseback riding year-round.

When it comes to lodging, the resort is a behemoth. It's one of the few resorts where the bed base, 16,000 pillows, is larger than the lift capacity. This has created crowded conditions at times. Fortunately, Loon has made a number of improvements during the past few years. Among these were trail improvements to relieve congestion in high-traffic stretches, new lifts to get people up the mountain faster, more snowmaking coverage and the creation of a dedicated learning area. Loon has also extended tubing to daytime hours on the Little Sister trail near the gondola.

Another plus: Loon Mountain limits lift ticket sales to keep the mountain experience positive. Continued improvements have meant the sold-out signs quit coming out every weekend; now it's about four days per season, with perhaps 10 near-sellout days. To ensure that you'll get a lift ticket on those busy days, you can reserve tickets with a major credit card ahead of time; call (800) 229-LOON (5666) or log onto www.loonmtn.com. The Unconditional Satisfaction Guarantee also ensures you'll like the conditions or you'll ski or ride free on your next visit.

Loon is owned by Booth Creek Ski Holdings, which owns nearby Waterville Valley, Mt. Cranmore in the Mt. Washington Valley as well as resorts in the West. The three New Hampshire areas have interchangeable lift tickets and season's passes.

Mountain layout–Skiing

◆◆ **Expert** ◆ **Advanced:** North Peak runs are challenging and well removed from lower-intermediate traffic. The steeps are there, but half the bumps are groomed out. To reach North Peak, take the gondola, then ski down Big Dipper, Triple Trouble or Angel Street to the North Peak Triple Chair. In fresh snow, experts will like the three tree skiing areas: One is accessed off Upper Flying Fox, another off Angel Street and the third off Haulback between Lower Flume and Lower Walking Boss.

■ **Intermediate:** Loon is loaded with intermediate terrain, and the intermediate runs are good and solid, with no expert surprises around the next clump of trees. The upper trails are a bit twisted, narrow and seemingly undirected, but they open onto a series of wide intermediate pistes. A favorite is Flying Fox, a delightful cruise with old-fashioned twists and turns through the trees and granite boulders. Depending on snow conditions, skiers can link up with the west side trails via Upper Speakeasy, or they can drop down to the parking lot on any of the wide cruising runs (Rumrunner is a good choice, if there isn't a race on it), and take the 100-yard-long steam train ride to the adjacent base area and the gondola. If you want to sample trees, try Misgiving Link and Scaler off Grand Junction.

ll **Beginner:** The center of the mountain, serviced by the Seven Brothers triple chair, has good intermediate trails that advanced beginners can handle. The east side of the chair has beginner runs such as Grand Junction, The Link, Brookway, and Lower Bear Claw.

● **Never-ever:** Never-evers have an improved learning area to the right of the Governor Adams Base Lodge.

Mountain layout–Snowboarding

Loon has a snowboard park called Loon Mountain Park adjacent to the gondola. It includes a 400-foot-long halfpipe and other terrain features. Riders can get easy access to the Loon Mountain Park by taking the Kanc Quad or the Seven Brothers lift. The gondola is also an option if riders don't mind the long run from the summit to the top of the park.

Cross-country and snowshoeing

The **Loon Mountain Cross-Country Center** (745-8111, ext. 5568) has 35 km. of groomed and tracked trails that wind along the scenic Pemigewasset River. Children ages 5 and younger and seniors 70 and older ski free.

Lessons

Group lessons: $27 for 2 hours.
Never-ever package: For skiers or riders, this includes equipment, all-day lessons and a limited lift ticket for $63 per day. Enroll at either rental shop.

Private lessons: $60 an hour; $35 for additional hours, $35 for each additional person.
Racing: A race course is served by the Seven Brothers lift.
Children's lessons: Full day for ages 3–4 including lunch and lifts is $69, half days $49.
Full day for children ages 5–6 costs $69; $49 half day. An Adventure Ski Camp for ages 7–12
groups children by ability level. Price is $79 a day, including lunch. All children's lessons are
run out of the new Children's Center, which also houses a rental shop for skiers and boarders
to age 6. Reservations are required in all programs; call 745-6281, ext. 5160 or 5162.

Child care

Ages: 6 weeks to 8 years.
Costs: Half day, $45; full day, $59.
Reservations: Required; call 745-8111. Hours: 8 a.m. to 4:30 p.m. Loon
has a spacious Children's Center near the Governor Adams Lodge, which replaced the center
at Mountain Club.

Lift tickets

Weekend Prices	Adult	Young Adult	Child (6-12)
One day	$49	$44	$31
Three days	$121 ($40+/day)	$107	$77
Five days (midweek)	$154 ($30+/day)	$125	$99

Who skis free: Children ages 5 and younger.
Who skis at a discount: Ages 70 and older pay $10 midweek (non-Holiday), but the
regular adult price on Saturday, Sunday and Holidays.
Midweek prices are $41 for adults, $34 for young adults, $26 for children.
Note: Ticket sales are cut off after approximately 6,000 have been sold. To reserve tickets, parking or ski rentals in advance by major credit card, call (800)-229-LOON (5666) or
visit www.loonmtn.com.

Accommodations

The Mountain Club on Loon (800-229-7829 or 745-2244) is a ski-in/ski-
out property with everything under one roof, from parking to swimming
pool, fitness club to restaurants. One problem: Many of its rooms have a
double Murphy bed with two small day beds along the windows. This arrangement is fine for
couples, or for a family with young children, but it is awkward for two adults who don't want
to sleep in the same bed. Instead, request two rooms that, when adjoined, make a suite. Loon
also has condominiums. Make reservations through the Mountain Club.

Reservations and information for many of the properties in Lincoln and Woodstock can
be obtained through the **Lincoln/Woodstock Central Reservations** at (800) 227-4191.

The newest hotel in town is the **Comfort Inn** (800-228-5150 or 745-6700; $$) right off
I-93 at Hobo Railroad. It opened in January 2000 and offers regular hotel rooms and one-
bedroom suites with kitchenettes. Two prominent properties right on the Kancamagus High-
way (Main Street) in Lincoln are **The Mill House Inn** (800-654-6183 or 745-6261; $-$$$) at
The Mill and the **Nordic Inn** (800-536-1038; $-$$), which offers condominiums (studios-3
bedrooms). The **Rivergreen Resort Hotel** (800-654-6183 or 745-2450; $$-$$$), owned by
the same group that owns The Mill House Inn, is also a condominium hotel. The last in a trio
of "Mill" properties is **The Lodge at Lincoln Station** (800-654-6188 or 745-3441; $$-$$$),

a hotel situated on the Pemigewasset River. Accommodations are studios to one-bedroom suites. All of these properties are about one mile west of Loon.

Another couple miles away from Loon is **The Woodstock Inn B&B** (800-321-3985, 745-3951; $–$$ ✕⌂≋🐾🍴), a typical quaint New England lodge. The main building is more than 100 years old with no two rooms alike. You'll find the rooms tucked under the rafters, some with private bath, or shared bath, all with casual charm. The restaurant in the front of the inn is one of North Woodstock's most elegant; the one in the station at the rear is one of the town's liveliest. Some rooms have hot tubs.

Wilderness Inn B&B (745-3890; $–$$ Ⓟ🐾☺) is run by the Yarnells, a couple with small children, who make other families with youngsters welcome in their house. Parents note: This place has laundry facilities! The B&B is only steps from the center of North Woodstock, which is filled with shops and restaurants.

Three motelish properties along Rte. 3 in Lincoln, one exit up I-93 from Loon, join for advertising and have similar accommodations with mostly identical prices, but each has slightly different amenities. **Indian Head Motel Resort** (800-343-8000, 745-8000; $$ ✕⌂Ⓟ🐾🍴) is one of the centers of après-ski action with live bands and a great ice-skating pond and cross-country trails. **The Beacon** (800-258-8934, 745-8118; $–$$$ ✕⌂Ⓟ🐾⌐) has indoor tennis and large indoor pools but attracts the bus-tour crowd. **Woodward's Motor Inn** (800-635-8968, 745-8141; $–$$ ✕⌂Ⓟ🎾🐾) is the most family oriented. It has the area's only racquetball court and the best steaks in the region. Another reasonably priced motel along this stretch of Rte. 3 is the **Drummer Boy Motor Inn** (800-762-7275 or 745-3661; $–$$$). All are located off I-93's Exit 33.

🍴☕🔪 Dining

The most elegant dining experience in the Lincoln/Woodstock area can be found at the **Woodstock Inn's Clement Room** (745-3951; $$–$$$), which gets high ratings from locals for its informal dining with style. The Woodstock Inn also serves great daily breakfasts as well as a fabulous weekend brunch.

At Loon Mountain, try **Seasons on Loon** (745-8111; $$) or **The Black Diamond Bar** (**$–$$**), both at the Mountain Club. Locals claim the **Open Hearth Steak House** (745-8141; $$) at Woodward's Motor Inn has the best steaks. **Gordi's Fish and Steak House** (745-6635; $–$$) is family-oriented and features Maine lobster and steaks. The **Olde Timbermill** (745-3603; $$) in The Mill is set in a modernesque, barn-like building that is also one of the nightlife centers in Lincoln.

Truant's Tavern (745-2239; $–$$) serves clever dinner entrées in a mock schoolhouse atmosphere; drinking in class was never so much fun. The bar hops on weekends. **Woodstock Station** (745-3951; $–$$), in an old train station on Main Street, offers a creative menu of reasonable meals, from meatloaf to Mexican, makes its own beer, and is a local favorite. **G.H. Pizza** (745-6885; $) serves traditional and gourmet pizza, as well as hot and cold subs. But locals agree that the best pizza in town is found at **Elvio's Pizzeria** (745-8817; $). We're also told **Chieng Gardens** (745-8612; $–$$) in Lincoln Square offers decent Chinese food.

For breakfast try **Sunny Day Diner** (745-4833; $) or **Peg's Place** (745-2740; $), both in North Woodstock. The best coffee in town can be found at either **Java Joe's** ($) in The Depot or the **Pycolog Bakery Café** (745-4395; $) which opened last winter and is on the Kancamagus Highway right across the street from The Mill. Both coffee places have excellent pastries, too.

Aprèss-ski/nightlife

After skiing at Loon, head to the **Black Diamond Bar in the Mountain Club** for good weekend entertainment and a quiet après-ski spot. The **Paul Bunyan Lounge** at the Octagon base has a young, rowdy crowd and really rocks. Or head to **Babe's** at the Governor Adams Lodge.

North Woodstock-area locals set up party camp at **Truant's Tavern** and the **Woodstock Station**. **Gordi's Fish and Steak**, in Lincoln, has great munchies. **Indian Head Resort,** in Lincoln, offers good après-ski. From Wednesday through Sunday, live bands rock the joint. The **Tavern Sports Bar** is a low-key darts, video game and pool hall. Downstairs, the **Olde Timbermill** has the area's best singles action, with bands on weekends.

 ## Other activities

Shopping: The town of Lincoln has several specialty shops worth a look, including some factory outlets, along the Kancamagus Highway in town. The factory outlet bonanza of North Conway is 35 miles east of town, but the drive takes about one hour in winter. No sales tax makes buying all the sweeter.

Loon Mountain has **skating, day and night tubing** and après-ski **entertainment** for families.

Profile Mountaineering, in Lincoln, offers introductory **ice climbing** and **winter mountaineering**. Alpine Village has a **rock-climbing wall**, as does the Pemi Valley Rock Gym (745-9800) in Woodstock. Alpine Adventures (745-9911) in Lincoln offers guided **snowmobile tours**. Creations in The Depot has **make-your-own pottery**. Lincoln also has four **movie theaters**.

 ## Getting there and getting around

By air: Boston's Logan Airport is 140 miles away from Loon. Manchester Airport, 80 miles south, is serviced by Southwest, MetroJet, Comair, Continental Express, Delta's Business Express, USAir, and United. The airport phone number is 624-6556; its Internet address is www.flymanchester.com.

By car: From I-93 heading north, Loon Mountain is about 2 miles up the Kancamagus Highway (Route 112) from Exit 32 in Lincoln.

Getting around: A car is a necessity unless you stay in the Lincoln-Woodstock area. Lincoln-Woodstock has a shuttle service and taxi, available anytime.

Waterville Valley

New Hampshire

Summit elevation: 4,006 feet
Vertical drop: 2,020 feet
Base elevation: 1,984 feet

Address: One Ski Area Rd.,
Waterville Valley, NH 03215
✆ **Area code:** 603
Ski area phone: 236-8311
Snow report: 236-4144
Fax: 236-4344
ⓘ **Toll-free reservations:**
(800) GO-VALLEY (468-2553)
E-mail: info@waterville.com
Internet: www.waterville.com
E x p e r t : ★
Advanced: ★ ★
Intermediate: ★ ★ ★
Beginner: ★ ★ ★
Never-ever: ★ ★ ★

Number and types of lifts: 11–2 high-speed quads, 2
triples, 3 doubles, 4 surface lifts
Skiable acreage: 225 acres
Snowmaking: 100 percent
Uphill capacity: 15,187 per hour
Snowboarding: Yes, unlimited
Bed base: 2,500
Nearest lodging: quarter mile
Resort child care: Yes, 6 months - 4 years
Adult ticket, per day: $37-$44 (99/2000 prices)

Dining: ★ ★ ★ ★
Apres-ski/nightlife: ★ ★
Other activities: ★ ★

Waterville Valley is the first "big" resort you come to as you drive north on I-93 from southern New Hampshire or Massachusetts, making it one of the most popular ski resorts in New Hampshire. Besides its location, the resort gained its reputation from staging more than 10 World Cup ski races over the past quarter century (Waterville founder Tom Corcoran finished fourth in the 1960 Olympic giant slalom). Though many of the trails are well suited for racing, in truth, the resort is better known as an intermediate's mountain, and in recent years, its reputation has changed to that of a family resort. Still, it enjoys significant vertical for an eastern resort, and it uses it well. Almost all the trails follow the fall line, and they maintain their pitch almost from top to bottom.

Waterville Valley is sufficiently self-contained so that most visitors, once they enter, do not venture any farther than the slopes, just a short shuttlebus ride away from the lodging in Town Center. Here you'll find shops, restaurants and bars. Most of the off-slope activities are centered here, such as cross-country skiing, sleigh rides, and a huge sports complex with indoor and outdoor swimming pools, tennis, squash and racquetball courts and indoor track. There is an indoor skating rink, and a handful of shops in the village center.

On the mountain, Waterville has one fairly large base area, making it ideal for families who don't want to get separated amidst multiple base lodges. Two high-speed quads start right outside the base lodge, one being the Quadzilla. Despite its scary name, the lift is decorated like a happy dog wearing a whirly-bird beanie. You can tell how windy it is by how fast the propeller turns! The other quad, the White Peak Express, takes skiers and riders *almost* to the summit (it was shortened recently to prevent repeated shut-downs by high winds at the summit). The High Country Double services these intermediate upper slopes when weather (and snow) conditions are right.

The Kids Fun Zone has on-snow activities such as tubing, Snowblades and snowbikes, all free with the purchase of a lift ticket. Intermediate and advanced skiers can take advantage of free From-the-Summit one-hour clinics.

Waterville Valley belongs to the Booth Creek resort family, which means it offers a wide variety of snow toys and tubing as do its sister New Hampshire resorts, Cranmore and Loon Mountain. Lift tickets are interchangeable at these three resorts.

Mountain layout—Skiing

◆◆ **Expert** ◆ **Advanced:** One of the toughest runs, True Grit, develops big moguls and drops down the Sunnyside face. With several tough rollers and steep pitches, the World Cup Slalom Hill is a good place for experts to test their carving skills. There's also a tree skiing area off Lower Bobby's Run; it starts about halfway down the trail on the left. An interesting note—Bobby's Run (both Upper and Lower) was named after the late Senator Robert Kennedy who frequented the resort after it opened in 1966.

■ **Intermediate:** Waterville's trails are not New England's typical steep and narrow pistes. Most are wide swaths through the trees, and there's elbow room and a chance to check out the slope before committing to the fall line again.

Two former tough mogul runs, Ciao and Gema, now are groomed daily. Such trails as White Caps, Sel's Choice, Old Tecumseh and Tippecanoe are intermediate and advanced playthings. Upper Bobby's Run is a great intermediate trail, but if you don't want to find yourself on a black diamond or double-diamond mogul trail (Lower Bobby's), make sure you take a strong left to Terry's Trail or Old Tecumseh.

Something more resorts should do: Waterville has a designated "easier mogul field." For those wanting to move to the next level, this is great practice.

●● **Beginner:** Beginner terrain at Waterville is limited, and beginners who have skied blue runs at other resorts might find Waterville's intermediate terrain challenging. But the Valley Run is a beginner/lower intermediate heaven with enough width to allow skiing for a couple of days down different sections. This run is now served by Quadzilla, a high-speed quad that takes skiers to the top of the run in 4.5 minutes.

● **Never-ever:** Never-evers have a small area with a separate lift.

Mountain layout—Snowboarding

Waterville's lift-served Exhibition Terrain Park & Halfpipe, located right above the base area, has two halfpipes and two terrain parks open to riders and skiers. The resort boasts that the Wicked Ditch of the East halfpipe is the longest in the state. The park has jumps, tabletops, rails, hips, trannies and launchers. A second terrain park, The Boneyard, was the first terrain park in the East. Kids have their own terrain park, Little Slammer, where they can train for the big stuff. Oblivion, a winding trail with banked sides, is the trail of choice for riders. Also popular are the glades, off True Grit. Alpine riders carve up World Cup. WV has plenty of events for riders of all abilities, and in late March, the pros come for the World Quarterpipe Championships, a wild weekend.

Mountain rating

Unless you have young children, you might find Waterville a bit limiting for a week's vacation, but it can be a lot of fun for an extended weekend. There is a little bit of something for everyone, but the emphasis is on little bit if you are an accomplished skier. Though the area made its name in the race arena, there is little more that those good courses. That said, the black diamonds are really black diamonds, and the blue squares are true intermediate runs, making them challenging for beginners. This makes Waterville Valley feel like a bigger mountain than it really is.

Cross-country and snowshoeing

Waterville has 105 km. of trails, 70 of which are groomed and tracked for skating and classic skiing through the White Mountain National Forest. This cross-country center and the trail system is considered one of the best in New England by Nordic aficionados.

Rentals and lessons are available, as are guided cross-country and snowshoe tours for all levels and ages. Call 236-4666 for more information. Cross-country trail fees are included as part of the Winter Unlimited lodging package. Otherwise, daily tickets cost $14 for a full day, $10 for a half day. Rentals cost $18 for classic equipment, $22 for skate ski equipment.

Lessons

Group lessons: $28 for 2 hours. This year Waterville will also offer free from-the-summit clinics for upper-intermediate and advanced skiers. The one-hour clinics will meet twice daily in the afternoon.

Never-ever package: Skiing or snowboarding, $62 for lower mountain lift ticket (includes J-bar, Lower Meadows and Valley Run J-lift), two lessons and equipment. A special Passport provides two follow-up days for $XX.

Private lessons: $65 an hour plus $35 for each added hour and $35 for each added skier.

Racing: A recreational course on Utter Abandon has races Wednesdays, Fridays, Saturdays and Sundays.

Child care

Ages: 6 months to 4 years.

Costs: All day is $42, with multiday discounts. Half day is $32, hourly is $10 (2-hour minimum). Lunch is $5, or children may bring their own.

Note: Women's Wednesdays include free child care (max. two kids per ticket), 50-percent of half-day or full-day kids camps, 50-percent off group lessons, free use of the athletic club and more with the purchase of non-holiday Wednesday ticket.

Reservations: Required if you want to ensure a space. Call 236-8311, Ext. 3196. Waterville has two nurseries at the base area.

Children's lessons: Kids Camps lessons costs $63 a day for ages 3–5. Rental equipment is $15 extra; lunch is also extra. Programs for ages 6–8 and 9–12 cost $51 a day, not including lift ticket. Rentals cost an additional $16, and lunch is extra. Call for half-day prices.

Lift tickets

Weekend Prices	Adult	Teen (13-18)	Child (6-12)
One day	$47	$41	$15
Three days	$115 ($38+/day)	$102 ($34/day)	$45 ($15/day)
Five days	$168 ($33+/day)	$142 ($28+/day)	$75 ($15/day)

Holiday prices are higher. Lift tickets may be used at Loon and Mt. Cranmore.

Child ticket includes use of snowtoys and tubing in Exhibition Park from 9 a.m. to noon.

Who skis free: Kids 5 and younger ski free anytime. Waterville often runs a Kids Ski Free promotion (for ages up to 12) when parents buy multiday lodging packages; ask about it.

Who skis at a discount: Ages 65 and older ski at children's rates Monday-Friday and non-Holidays. Midweek one-day prices are $40 for adults, $33 for teens, and $15 for children. Midweek three-day prices are $105 for adults, $86 for teens and $45 for children. Midweek five-day rates are $149 for adults, $120 for teens and $75 for children.

Accommodations

Waterville Valley has 2,500 beds in its Village, located about 1.5 miles from the slopes. To make reservations at any of the Waterville Valley accommodations listed below, call (800) GO-VALLEY (468-2553) or 236-8311. The "Winter Unlimited" package is all inclusive, offering all of Waterville's winter activities plus lodging for one price. With one call, you can book lift-and-lodging packages, kids' snowsports lessons and child care.

The **Golden Eagle Lodge** with condominium suites features a distinctive design reminiscent of the turn-of-the-century grand hotels at the White Mountain resorts.

Additionally, Waterville has three hotel properties and four groups of condominiums all located in the valley. The **Valley Inn and Tavern** operates as a country inn with rates that can include meals, and the **Black Bear Lodge** is more hotel-like. All are in the same price range with two-day lodging and lift weekend packages starting at around $80 for rooms in January (per person, double occupancy) and averaging around $150 during the regular season (February and March, excluding President's Day week). The **Best Western/Silver Fox** offers continental breakfast and is the most economical place to stay. **Condominiums** are also available.

Dining

The most elegant dining experience in Waterville Valley can be found at the **William Tell** (726-3618; $$-$$$) on Rte. 49 just down the valley from the resort. The William Tell has a strong Swiss-German accent with excellent wines.

On Saturday nights, take a 30-minute snowcat ride up the slopes to the **Schwendi Hutte** (236-8311, ext. 3000). The food is some of the best in the valley, as is the ambiance. Reservations are required, and the snowcat ride and meal cost $65/person.

The **Wild Coyote Grill** (236-4919; $-$$) in the White Mountain Athletic Club is the best restaurant in Waterville Valley Village. The menu offers nouveau cuisine with a Southwestern flair, and the calimari is a specialty. Or head to **Latitudes** (236-4646; $) for moderately priced family fare. For pizza, call **Olde Waterville Valley Pizza Co.** (236-3663; $). **Valley Inn** (236-8336; $$) and **Diamond Edge North** (236-2006; $$) are also located in Town Square, but we have yet to eat at either.

Lunch can be purchased at any of the four on-mountain restaurants. The **Schwendi Hutte,** at the top of the White Peak Express Quad, is the best of the lot: Don't miss the lobster bisque. On sunny spring days, head for BBQ on the deck of **Sunnyside Up** on Valley Run. The base area has a cafeteria, pizza corner and **T-Bars**. The food at T-Bars is nothing to write home about, but the ski memorabilia lining the walls is interesting.

For breakfast, pick up coffee and pastries at the **Waterville Coffee Emporium** (236-4021; $) or the **Jugtown Sandwich Shop** (236-3669; $). The Coffee Emporium also cooks up omelets, eggs, French toast and waffles. Both are located in Town Square.

Après-ski/nightlife

Waterville now has a collection of bars in Town Square, each with slightly different après-ski. They are all within a few steps of each other. **Legends 1291 Latitudes** and **Diamond's Edge** serve a good time, and later in the evening they stand in the same order, ranging from loud disco and rock to quieter music. **T-Bars**, at the mountain, has the normal collection of skiers for après-ski until 5:30 p.m.

Just down the road from Waterville, on the way back to the interstate, try the **William Tell**, for a cozy quiet après-ski, or the **Mad River Tavern**, for a more raucous setting. Both have popular dinner menus.

Other activities

Shopping: Waterville Valley's Town Square has several specialty shops selling books, souvenirs, gifts, clothing and jewelry.

Waterville Valley has **sleigh rides** and an **indoor fitness center** with pool, track, weight rooms and more, as well as a covered ice arena for **skating.** The resort also offers a full recreation program that includes activities for toddlers, youngsters and teens such as ice cream socials, basketball and dances.

Getting there and getting around

By air: Boston's Logan Airport is 130 miles south of Waterville Valley.

Manchester Airport, 70 miles south, is serviced by Southwest, MetroJet, Comair, Continental Express, Delta's Business Express, USAir, and United. The airport phone number is 624-6556; its Internet address is www.flymanchester.com.

By car: From I-93 heading north, Waterville Valley is 11 miles up Rte. 49 at Exit 28.

Getting around: Waterville Valley is self-contained and offers a shuttle from the Village to the slopes. It's wise to take the shuttle, since parking at the ski area can be a nightmare, although valet parking is available for $15. If you plan to venture away from the Village or want to try to Loon, Cannon and Bretton Woods farther north, a car is a necessity.

Nearby resorts

Tenney Mountain, Plymouth, NH; (603) 536-4125

Internet: www.tenneymtn.com
45 trails, 4 lifts, 1,400 vertical feet, 110 skiable acres
Tenney is an intermediate skier's playground, with 25 of its 45 trails for the mid-level skier. It's known for narrow, winding trails, such as Edelweiss, the 1-3/4-mile trail skiers would descend after climbing to the summit even before Plymouth residents Sam Hall and John French opened Tenney for skiing in the mid-1950s. Trails are tight and rugged and the experience is old-fashioned skiing, before the age of broad, open slopes. The mountain closed in the early 1990s and was re-opened in 1996 by the Wilkinson Corporation, which renovated and expanded the base lodge, rebuilt the snowmaking system and added snow tubing.
Lift tickets (00/01): Adults $36 weekends/holidays, $25 midweek/Sun. p.m.; Teens (13-19)/students/military $25 weekends/holidays, $20 midweek/Sun. p.m., Juniors (6-12) $20 weekends/holidays, $15 midweek/Sun. p.m.; 5 and younger or 70 and older always ski or ride free.
Distance from Boston: About 130 miles via I-93 to exit 26, Tenney Mt. Highway.
Lodging information: (800) 237-2307

Dining: $$$-Entrees $20+; $$-$10-20; $-less than $10.
Accommodations: (double room) $$$$-$200+; $$$-$141-$200; $$-$81-$140; $-$80 and less.

New Hampshire Regional Resorts

The Balsams Wilderness, Dixville Notch, NH; (603) 255-3400; (800) 255-0800, NH; (800) 255-0600 U.S. and Canada
Internet: www.thebalsams.com
3 lifts; 13 trails; 87 acres; 1,000 vertical feet

When you need to be pampered, owe your loved one a romantic weekend or want a family vacation without hassle, The Balsams Wilderness delivers. This remote resort, situated on a private, 15,000-acre estate located in far northern New Hampshire, easily earns its four-star rating. This is not, however, a ski resort. Rather, it's a resort where skiing is just one of many amenities. The mountain is small, but crowds are rare here. A good thing, given the old fashioned, slow lifts.

But who cares! The Balsams Wilderness is one of New Hampshire's surviving Grand Resort Hotels. It resembles a Disney Castle, with huge public rooms rambling from one to another. It's also the site of the first-in-the-nation primary, and the Ballot Room is a history lesson in itself. Guest rooms are mostly understated with an old fashioned charm complemented with some amenities. Only a few rooms have televisions, but there is a big screen in the TV room.

Almost everything is included in one daily, per person rate: meals, skiing, entertainment and more. Guests are pampered with attentive service. Award-winning chefs prepare a full breakfast buffet (or you can order from the menu) and five-course dinner daily. You can put your car keys away once you check in, and you don't even need to carry your wallet. Children's programs, which even include mealtimes as well as skiing, keep the youngsters occupied so the parents can relax or take part in other planned activities. And when the kids are in bed, the hotel offers movies in a full-size theater, dancing and entertainment nightly in two lounges and often the ballroom, too.

Oh, yeah, we shouldn't forget the skiing. The terrain is primarily intermediate, but these long winding trails just invite leisurely cruising. A separate beginner's practice hill is served by its own T-bar and is bathed in sun most of the day. Expert skiers will not be tested here, but will enjoy the narrow twisting Notch and the glades off of it. The alpine trails are varied, the people are very friendly (they are really up in the woods!) and the area gets lots — and we mean lots — of snow.

The Balsams also has 90 km. of cross-country trails with one circuit that has a vertical drop of 500 feet more than the ski area (the less daring can ski on the golf course). Trails are 12-feet wide and have two diagonal lanes and one skate lane. The resort also has a topographical trail map, so you should be able to avoid that big drop if you so desire. An ice-skating rink, 30 km. of designated snowshoeing trails, horse-drawn sleigh rides and a natural history program with guided tours round out the outdoor experience. If you still have energy to burn, there's a small fitness center, and the hotel usually offers a morning exercise program.

Lift tickets: $30 for adults weekends, $25 midweek; $20 for children weekends, $18 midweek. (Skiing is complimentary for hotel guests.)
Distance from Boston: About 220 miles north via I-93 (to Exit 35) then Rte. 3 to Colebrook and Rte. 26 to Dixville Notch.
Lodging information: (800) 255-0800, NH; (800) 255-0600, U.S. and Canada.

Mt. Sunapee, Mt. Sunapee, NH; (603) 763-2356

Internet: www.mtsunapee.com

9 lifts; 50 trails; 1,510 vertical feet, 220 skiable acres

New management, the same group that runs Okemo Mountain, has energized family-friendly Mt. Sunapee with a great, cheerful atmosphere and more than $9 million in improvements since 1999. The two most noticeable signs of rebirth are the 25,000-square-foot base lodge with expanded food service and seating, a ski shop, Learning Center desk and Guest Services area, and the high-speed quad that powers skiers to the summit in less than six minutes.

The mountain packs interesting terrain for every level: a special beginner area, 13 novice trails, 24 intermediate and 13 expert trails. On the trails, improved snowmaking delivers 97 percent coverage and a longer season. A fixed-quad chair lift has doubled lift capacity in the Sun Bowl section of the mountain. New grooming machines comb the mountain and a Pipe Dragon groomer creates an enhanced snowboard experience. Mt. Sunapee is a family mountain attracting a loyal following of skiers who like its New England feel and its close proximity (less than two hours) to Boston. The mountain skis a lot bigger than it is, with two different base areas and a separate beginner area. Cross-country skiing is available nearby. Mt. Sunapee is also the base for the New England Handicapped Sports Association (NEHSA), which provides programs for skiers with physical and mental challenges.

Lift tickets: Adults, $47 weekend, $42 weekday; Young Adult (13–18) and Senior (65-69), $41 weekend, $35 weekday; Junior (7-12) and Senior (70+) $32 weekend, $28 weekday. Skiers ages 6 and younger ski free. Every Thursday two out-of-state residents ski for the price of one with proof of residency. Mt. Sunapee has a conditions guarantee. If you are not satisfied with the conditions within the first hour of your ski day, you may return your ticket for a voucher to come visit on another day of the current season.

Distance from Boston: About 100 miles via I-93, I-89 and Rte. 103.

Lodging information: A selection of B&Bs, inns, hotels/motels and condos is available through the Mt. Sunapee refererral service: 877-687-8627.

Ragged Mountain, Danbury, NH; (603) 768-3475 or (603) 768-3600

Internet: www.ragged-mt.com

9 lifts; 50 trails; 1,250 vertical feet; 225 skiable acres

Ragged is a sleeper. This small, but mighty mountain is packed with excellent terrain on three peaks for beginning through advanced skiers. It oozes New England charm. Its white clapboard base facilities resemble a farmhouse complex, complete with barn, and are spacious and comfortable. Good grooming and 98-percent snowmaking coverage provide a memorable experience, and trails run the gamut, from tight and twisting to wide cruisers to glades. There's even a terrain park.

Ragged's owners are committed to building a solid resort, and this season's headliner is a new high-speed six-pasenger chairlift that will whisk skiers to the summit in four-and-a-half minutes. Also new this season are five new trails, expanded snowmaking and the beginning of the Village at Ragged Mountain condominium complex. Ragged has a total of seven peaks peaks to develop, and so far its tackled just three of them.

Lift tickets: Weekends and holidays, Adults, $45, $29 midweek; Teens (13-18) $37, $29 midweek; Youth (6-12), $30, $25 midweek. Skiers ages 5 and younger and 72 and older ski free; Seniors (65-71) receive a 50-percent discount.

Distance from Boston: About 100 miles via I-93 to Rte. 4 West to 104 East.

Lodging information: (800) 887-5464; Ragged Mountain condos: (800) 400-3911.

Gunstock, Gilford, NH; (800) GUNSTOCK or (603) 293-4341
Internet: www.gunstock.com
6 lifts; 47 trails; 220 acres; 1,400 vertical feet
Gunstock is a family-friendly resort with an old fashioned lodge and winter sports that stretch into the night hours for all ages. This is a mountain for those who love to cruise. Trails are maintained by Gunstock's Groom On Demand program; when the mountain needs attention, the cats go out. Advanced skiers can ski through glades on Middle Trigger and find bumps on Red Hat or Flintlock Extension. Intermediate glades can be found on Middle Recoil. Beginners have their own separate area at the Ski Learning Center handletow and the Gunshy chairlift. Snowboarders will find a 600-foot halfpipe and a terrain park. Night skiing is open on 15 trails served by five lifts. Snow tubing is available day and night. Snowshoers and cross-country skiers can enjoy 52 km. of trails for hiking, skating and gliding. The surrounding N.H. lakes region has thousands of rooms and plenty of restaurants as well as other activities such as ice fishing and snowmobiling.
Lift tickets: Adults, $42 weekend, $24-$34 weekday, $20-$22 night; teens and seniors (65-69), $34 weekend, $20-$26 midweek, $16-20 night; Child (6–12) $24 weekend, $12-$16 weekday, $14-$15 night. Skiers and riders ages 5 and younger and 70 and older ski free. The $99 Sunday Family 4-Pack includes two adult and two teen/child tickets; some holiday restrictions apply.
Distance from Boston: About 90 miles via I-93 and Rtes. 3 and 11A.
Lodging information: (603) 293-4341 or (800) GUNSTOCK (486-7862).

Lake Placid/Whiteface

New York

Summit elevation: 4,416 feet
Vertical drop: 3,216 feet
Base elevation: 1,200 feet

Address: Olympic Regional Development Authority (ORDA), Olympic Center, Lake Placid, NY 12946
✆ **Area code:** 518
Ski area phone: 946-2223
ORDA phone: 523-1655
Snow report: 946-7171
ⓘ **Toll-free information:** 800-462-6236
Fax: 523-9275
E-mail: info@orda.org
Toll-free reservations:
(800) 447-5224 (800-44-PLACID)
Internet: www.orda.org (ORDA) or www.whiteface.com www.lakeplacid.com (Lake Placid Visitors Bureau)
Expert:★★★★
Advanced:★★★★
Intermediate:★★★
Beginner:★★★   **Never-ever:**★★

Number and types of lifts: 11–1 eight-passenger, heated gondola, 1 quad, 2 triples, 6 doubles, 1 handle tow
Acreage: about 170 acres
Snowmaking: 99 percent
Uphill capacity: 13,270 skiers per hour
Snowboarding: Yes, unlimited
Bed base: 5,000
Nearest lodging: 1/2 mile in Wilmington, about 9 miles in Lake Placid
Resort child care: Yes, 12 months and older
Adult ticket, per day: $49 (2001/02 price)

Dining:★★★
Apres-ski/nightlife:★★★
Other activities:★★★★★

Strictly in terms of skiable terrain, Whiteface would fall somewhere in the middle of the pack of northeast resorts, but it more than compensates through its dramatic vertical drop, the biggest in the East at more than 3,400 feet. The surprisingly normal and quiet village has been host to two Winter Olympics, 1932 and 1980, and the 2000 Winter Goodwill Games. The memories these stir, combined with the plethora of winter sports activities available set Lake Placid apart as a winter sports Mecca. This season, Whiteface is widening the Thruway trail to a uniform 40 meters to meeet FIS specifications for giant slalom.

From the moment you drive past the dramatic Olympic jumps just south of the village, you know this isn't an ordinary winter vacation spot. The Olympic Regional Development Authority (ORDA) operates the multi-facility recreational area, and more world-class winter sports athletes still train and compete here than anywhere else in the free world. The extent of the facilities also attracts competitions in all of the Olympic winter sports, so athletes of all ages and abilities fill the town throughout the season, constantly renewing the village's Olympic atmosphere.

Like many Eastern mountains, Whiteface stands unshielded, lording over a vast valley of forests and frozen lakes. Its position makes for some of the most spectacular views in the world, but winter winds do whip across that valley and up the walls of Whiteface with regularity. For many veteran Eastern skiers, the complaint about Whiteface has been that it's too often windblown, cold and icy. This is not just myth. The cylindrical building at the summit is a weather research center. Of course, you can't fault any area for bad weather, and on an ideal day, Whiteface comes close to being as good as it gets in the East, and spring here can be especially good.

Whiteface itself is not in Lake Placid at all, but nine miles to the northeast, officially in the town of Wilmington. Most visitors stay in Lake Placid because that is where the major action is. Apart from the shops and restaurants galore, there is Mt. Van Hoevenberg Olympic Sports Complex, eight miles to the southeast. Two big draws: 31 miles of groomed cross-country trails and the bobsled run that offers a half-mile "adrenaline injections" for $30 a pop. For the uninitiated, bouncing off the walls here is not unlike being the pinball in a game played by unseen Nordic giants. Of course, no one in their right mind would want to experience firsthand the thrill of being launched off the 120-meter ski ramp at nearby Intervale, but you can get a breathtaking perspective on that madness by taking the elevator 26 stories to the observation deck at the top. The $7 ticket, thankfully, is round-trip.

Back on Main Street, the town itself is dominated by the arena where America watched its Cinderella hockey team enter the history books with the "Do you believe in miracles?" victory over the heavily favored Russian team in 1980. Wonderfully situated on Mirror Lake, Main Street makes up in charm and bustle what it lacks in quaint. For a relaxing afternoon, take a dogsled ride across the lake or a three-mile walk around. Daytime or evening, many people find both relaxation and exercise on the Olympic oval (where Eric Heiden won five gold medals), lulled into an easy rhythm by the sharp scrape of their skates over the quarter-mile loop. A personal favorite is the nighttime toboggan slide down a floodlit ramp out onto the darkness of frozen Mirror Lake. A word of caution: Wear old clothes!

Mountain layout—Skiing

◆◆ Expert ◆ Advanced: Whiteface is proud of its challenging terrain and is looking for adrenaline seekers to give trails such as Cloudspin and Skyward, where the Olympic downhill races started, a try. For certifiable experts who don't mind a hike to truly challenging terrain, the Slides is the real deal on days when conditions permit. The black-diamond trails off Little Whiteface—Approach, Upper Northway, and Essex—are often left to bump up, providing accessible challenging terrain for **advanced skiers.** Just two seasons ago, Whiteface inserted 13 acres of tree skiing rated black and double black off Little Whiteface Mountain

■ Intermediate: Take the Cloudsplitter gondola from the base or the Little Whiteface double from the midstation to the top of Little Whiteface. An observation platform just off to the left at the top of this double chair gives you an unparalleled view of the lakes and valley. Then try the snaking Excelsior run, which twists back down to the midstation. You can cut the rounded corners of this baby like a bobsled, choosing your own pace.

After that warm-up, tackle Paron's Run or The Follies from the tip-top of Whiteface (Summit Quad). Before this run was added several years ago, intermediates had no way to enjoy either the awe-inspiring view or best-in-the-East vertical available from the top of **the mountain.**

●● Beginner ● Never-ever

These levels have a secluded area, the Mixing Bowl. Novices and families will enjoy the New Boreen trail, cut before the 2000-01 winter, and located below the midstation lodge. The run's average width is 100 feet over approximately a 2,200 foot length.

Mountain layout—Snowboarding

The Brookside terrain park offers 1/4 mile of hits, table tops, rails, picnic tables and other varieties of airtime. Both the halfpipe and terrain park have proven to be quite attractive not only to snowboarders, but to the burgeoning freeskiing crowd as well. You can get a good view from the Valley triple chair; get off at midstation to access it. The halfpipe has hosted events such as the Winter Goodwill Games and the Paul Mitchell Board Frenzy Tour. When cruising down Excelsior, keep up your momentum when you hit the eighth and ninth corners so you can ride out the short flat.

Mountain rating

Whiteface is one of those rare mountains that has more to offer experts and beginners, with less in the middle range for true intermediates. Experts will find much of the upper half of the mountain challenging. Beginners will find anything below midstation much to their liking. Intermediates probably will feel bored by most of the lower half of the mountain and stretched by much of the upper but can push themselves into the advanced stage on Little Whiteface. Be ready for a variety of conditions. The mountain is high enough that icy conditions on the top can give way to mushy corn snow by the time you reach the bottom.

Cross-country and snowshoeing

Adding up all the cross-country trails in and around Lake Placid reveals that the region stands as a major cross-country destination with 455 km. of trails. Foremost is the **Mt. Van Hoevenberg** complex (523-2811), site of the Nordic and biathlon races during the 1980 Olympics. It has cross-country skiing you are unlikely to find elsewhere: 50 km. of marked trails that average 15 ft. wide, regularly groomed and patrolled; bridges built especially for cross-country skiers so you don't have to worry about traffic; snowmaking (5 km.); and emergency phones. The complex has 10 marked loops offering one expert, six intermediate and three novice tours with additional expert skiing on the Porter Mountain racing loops. A trail pass is $12/$9 for a full day/half day; rentals are $16/$12.

The **Lake Placid Resort** (523-2556) has 25 km. of trails and connects with the more secluded Jackrabbit Trail (ski conditions: 523-1365): 50 km. that run from Keene through Lake Placid and Saranac Lake.

Snowshoeing trails crisscross the entire **High Peaks Wilderness** area—get maps and advice at the local Eastern Mountain Sports Store on Lake Placid's Main Street or head to the Dewey Mt. Ski Center that offers snowshoe trails in addition to cross-country skiing. For a more controlled snowshoe experience complete with bonfires to roast marshmallows and educational stops on the trail, stop at the **High Falls Gorge** center. Here you can follow a marked trek around the Ausable River gorge and be welcomed back with complimentary hot chocolate or coffee. Just south of Whiteface, High Falls Gorge is something different for families. Reservations recommended on weekends (946-2278).

Lessons

Group lessons: $25 for 1.5 hours, $55 for three days and $77 for five days. **Never-ever package:** A group lesson with pass and equipment rental is $75 for skiers or riders for one day, $135 for two days and $373 for five days. It puts new skiers on the short skis called Snowblades and guarantees that in five days they'll be able to ski from the top of Little Whiteface.

The Parallel to Perfection program includes rentals, lifts and lessons ($183 for two days; $373 for five days)

Private lessons: $65 an hour, with $45 for an extra hour.

Child care

Ages: 1–6 years.

Costs: $25 per half day or $50 per day per child, with lunch included in full-day price.

Reservations: Recommended; call 946-2223.

Note: The Bunny Hutch is complete with a children's drop-off, adjacent parking for parents, a large nursery, children's rentals and an outdoor terrain garden.

Children's programs: Lessons for ages 7–12 are $45 half day and $75 a full day, lunch included in full-day program. The Kids Kampus and Family Learning Center has its own parking area, base lodge, lifts and trails and is completely separate from the main ski trails of Whiteface, although the lift and trail network allows parents to ski or ride to and from it.

Play 'n Ski is for children ages 4–6. The drop-off area has adjacent parking. Half-day programs are $45. A full-day program costs $75 (including lunch). Reservations recommended. For more about the children's program, call 946-2223.

Lift tickets (2001/02 prices)

	Adult	Child (7-12)	Teen (13-19)/Senior (64-69)
One day	$49	$22	$40
Three days	$144 ($48/day)	$59 ($20/day)	$108 ($36/day)
Five days	$200 ($40/day)	$89 ($18/day)	$161 ($32/day)

Who skis free: Children aged 6 and younger when accompanied by an adult, and ages 70 and older.

Who skis at a discount: Active military pay $25 any day. Super Sunday Specials (Dec. 9; Jan. 6, 27; March 3, 17; April 7) pricing is $25 per adult and $15 for juniors. Ask about lodging packages. Holiday pricing is higher.

Accommodation

Some of the larger hotels centered around the town of Lake Placid tend to be of the modern franchise variety. An important exception is the **Mirror Lake Inn** (523-2544; $$–$$$$ ✕⌂☂P🍴⤵🍷), a traditional lodge right on the lake shore that's probably the finest overnight in the area (it's rated Four Diamond by AAA). The New England-style exterior continues inside with antiques, chandeliers and mahogany walls. The inn also has an indoor pool, whirlpool, sauna, health spa and game room. The two restaurants include one of the best in town, with candlelight dining overlooking the lake.

If snowshoeing or cross-country is your main interest or if you just want to experience the traditional Adirondack Lodge atmosphere, try the **Lake Placid Lodge** (523-2700; $$$$ ✕P🍴🍷); it has cross-country skiing from the door. Expanded from an 1882 lodge, it is filled with the Adirondack twig-and-birch furniture and massive stone fireplaces and has lodge rooms, suites and separate cabins. A little more affordable are the **Mt. Van Hoevenberg B&B and Cabins** (523-9572; $$ ✕☂P🍴⤵🍷), with an outdoor sauna and a games room, and **Trail's End Inn** (576-9860; $$), in Keene Valley, which has a hot tub.

The **Lake Placid Resort Holiday Inn** (523-2556 or 800-874-1980; $–$$ ✕⌂🅿🍷🛏▦▤) in the town center is Lake Placid's largest hotel (209 rooms). All rooms have refrigerators and microwaves, and some have a Jacuzzi tub and fireplace. It has a large indoor pool, whirlpool, sauna, complete health club, 20 km. of cross-country trails and two restaurants, including The Veranda, one of the area's finest. The **Best Western Golden Arrow** (523-3353 or 800-582-5540; $–$$$ ✕⌂🅿🍷▤) is on the lake with spectacular views and has an indoor pool, Jacuzzi, sauna, weight room, and racquetball courts. Also boasting similar amenities is the **Lake Placid Hilton Resort** (523-4411 or 800-755-5598; $$–$$$ ✕⌂🅿🍷🛏▤), with two indoor pools and private balconies for each room with a view of the lake. The hotel's bed-and-breakfast package is quite popular. There is also a **Ramada Inn** (523-2587 or 800-741-7841; $–$$ 🚗✕⌂🅿🍷🛏▤) and a **Howard Johnson Resort Inn** (523-9555 or 800-858-4656) in town.

Skiers on a budget should try the **Edge of the Lake Motor Inn** (523-9430), **Art Devlin's Motor Inn** (523-3700), **Town House Motor Inn** (523-2532), **Alpine Air Motel** (523-9261; $–$$$ ✕⌂🅿✺), the **Econo Lodge** (523-2817; $–$$ 🚗⌂🅿✺), and the **Wildwood** on the Lake (523-2624; $ 🅿🍷✺). Those who want to stay right by Whiteface should try the **Ledgerock** (946-2379 or 800-336-4754; $–$$), a family-owned and operated 19-unit motel, right opposite the entrance to the mountain in Wilmington. The view from the spacious rooms looks just like the trail map.

Dining

For a culinary treat in a quintessential Adirondack setting, head to the **Lake Placid Lodge** (523-2700; $$$$), but be ready for sticker shock. If your wallet can't quite handle it, try just stopping in for an après-ski drink in the fireplaced bar overlooking the lake.

A personal favorite is the **Great Adirondack Steak and Seafood Company** (523-0233; $$) right in the middle of Main Street. Beams, home-brewed beer from the micro-brewery out back and honest hearty food complete the cozy mood.

Every Wednesday the **Alpine Cellar** restaurant has a Bratwurst Night with traditional German fare and oom-pah-pah accordian music, washed down by your choice of 80 different bears.

The **Charcoal Pit** (523-3050; $$–$$$) has been charbroiling steaks and chops for 25 years. **Veranda** (523-3339; $$), next to the Holiday Inn, has a great view to go with fine food.

Nicola's Over Main (523-4430; $$) has wood-fired pizza and a Mediterranean slant. **The Great American Bagel Factory** (523-1874; $–$$) is American-meal-on-the-fly with bagels, specialty coffee and sandwiches. On the way into the village, try the **Downhill Grill** for lunch (523-9510; $–$$). Its menu reflects the decor: old ski memorabilia and Mexican. No ski town is complete without an inexpensive Italian restaurant featuring pizza—**Mr. Mike's Pizza** (523-9770; $) takes care of that craving. Arguably the best burger in town could be had at **Cameron's Restaurant.** It's a hearty Black Angus beef that chef Glen Cameron serves up together with his original soups

In Wilmington, is the upscale and excellent **Hungry Trout** (946-2217; $$) specializing in, you guessed it, fish. In the same neighborhood is the **Wilderness Inn** (946-2391; $$–$$$), where steak lovers will want to try the sandwich on the bar menu.

Dining: $$$-Entrees $20+; $$-$10-20; $-less than $10.
Accommodations: (double room) $$$$-$200+; $$$-$141-$200; $$-$81-$140; $-$80 and less.

 **Après-ski/nightlife**

Lake Placid is large enough to generate its own heat as a nightlife center, drawing not only out-of-town vacationers but also the locals. Because Whiteface lies separated from the town, however, most of the après-ski action is in the base lodge. **Steinhoff's** and **R.F. McDougall's**, at the Hungry Trout, just down the road from Whiteface are also good for an après-ski drink.

Late night, the young and hot of foot head to **Mud Puddles**, on the side street next to the speed skating oval. High-tech disco gear is on full display around the dance floor. Most of the other nightlife action centers around the main hotels. **Roomers** at the Best Western, the **Dancing Bears Lounge** at the Hilton and the **Zig Zag's** are popular spots along Main Street. The **Lake Placid Pub and Brewery**, with its downstairs companion **P.J. O'Neils**, is on Mirror Lake Drive, up from the speed-skating oval.

Anyone looking for a quieter, more middle-aged nightspot should head for **The Cottage,** across the street from the Mirror Lake Inn. The fire's always going, and the sunset view of the lake and mountains is postcard perfect. It also serves good burgers.

 Other activities

Lake Placid is nothing *but* other activities. The half-mile **bobsled rides** at Mt. Van Hoevenberg Sports Complex (seven miles from the village) are $30 per person and a must for any Lake Placid visitor. Just relax and enjoy; they provide a professional driver and a brakeman. Rides on the new combination bobsled/luge track are by reservation only (523-4436).

Tours of the **Olympic Jumping Complex,** with chair lift and elevator ride, cost $7 for adults, $4 for children and seniors. Hours are 9 a.m. to 4 p.m. Tubing, near the jumps, is offered Thursday through Saturday for $6 per person. The **Olympic Speed Skating Oval** is open for public skating 7–9 p.m. daily and 1–3 p.m. on Saturdays and Sundays (523-1655). The cost is $5 for adults and $3 for juniors. Operating hours for the **toboggan run** on Mirror Lake are Wednesday, 7–9 p.m., Friday, 7–10 p.m., Saturday noon–4 p.m. and 7–10 p.m., and Sunday noon–4 p.m. The charge is $3 for adults, $2 for children, and $3 for the toboggan rental. The **Total Winter Passport** includes a bobsled ride, a day of cross-country skiing and admission to the jumping complex, museums and public skating.

Get into the real spirit of things by visiting the **Lake Placid Winter Olympic Museum,** with displays from the 1932 and 1980 Winter Olympics held at Lake Placid. It's open daily. Admission is $3 for adults and $2 for juniors. Call 523-1655 ext. 263 for more information.

 Getting there and getting around

By air: Continental commuter service serves Adirondack Airport, 16 miles away on Rte. 86 in Saranac Lake. Air-ground packages are being developed. Private planes can use Lake Placid Airport.

By train: Trains stop at Westport on the New York City–Montréal line. There has been a shuttle bus from the train station to the resort in the past, but in our experience this is not a convenient way to reach Lake Placid. If you plan to travel this way, ask the Lake Placid Visitors Bureau (phone number in the stat box). Amtrak has ski packages; call (800-872-7245; spells USA-RAIL) for more info.

By car: From the south, take Exit 24 (Albany) off the New York State Thruway (I-87). Take Northway (still I-87) to Exit 30, follow Route 9 north two miles to Route 73 and continue 28 miles to Lake Placid. From the west, take I-90 (NY State Thruway) to Exit 36 (Syracuse) for I-81. Follow I-81 north to Watertown, go east on Route 3 to Saranac Lake, then take Route 86 east to Lake Placid.

Getting around: It's about a 10-mile drive to both Whiteface and Mt. Hoevenberg from the center of Lake Placid. A free shuttlebus connects the town with the outlying facilities.

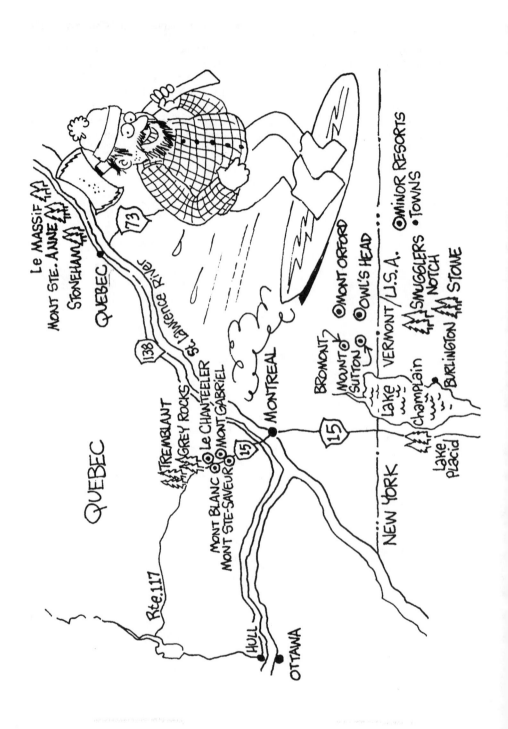

Quebec City, Canada

Mont-Sainte-Anne, Stoneham, Le Massif

Quebec City Facts

Address: Greater Quebec Area Tourism and Convention Bureau, 835, avenue Wilfrid-Laurier, Quebec (Quebec) G1R 2L3
ⓘ **Toll-free reservations:** 800-665-1528
Dining:★★★★
Apres-ski/nightlife:★★★★★
Other activities:★★★★

✆ **Area code:** 418
Phone: 649-2608
Fax: 522-0830
E-mail: bit@riq.qc.ca
World Wide Web: www.Quebecregion.com
Bed base: 11,200

Québec City which was founded in 1608 by the French navigator, geographer and explorer Samuel de Champlain is the only walled city in North America that is north of Mexico. Perched atop a 350-foot-high cliff overlooking the St. Lawrence River, it immerses North American visitors in French history and culture giving them a taste of Europe without jetlag.

Québec is a city that not only embraces winter; it celebrates it. Winter Carnival is a 17-day party, beginning the last weekend in January and presided over by the jolly snowman ambassador, Bonhomme. No matter what the weather, and it's usually but not always frigid in January, the streets are full of colorful locals. Couples stroll arm and arm. Young families tow toddlers on sleds. Singles search for *l'amour*. Everywhere you turn there's activity and music: sleigh rides, ice skating, ice climbing, snow rafting, dog sledding, canoe races across the ice-choked St. Lawrence, cross-country skiing, ice sculptures, dancers, singers, bands and parades. It seems nearly everyone wears the red, white and black sash that is the signature of Quebec and especially Winter Carnival. With all this *joie de vivre*, Québec is an ideal base for a winter vacation.

Don't miss Quebec's little Champs Élysées, Grande Allée, near the Parliament. Private homes once owned by judges and members of Parliament have been converted to discos, restaurants and other outlets for traditional nightlife. Cartier Avenue is great for shopping, and Petit Champlain, a wonderful walking street with many shops and galleries, can be reached by the funicular, a cable car straight down from outside the Chateau Frontenac Fairmont Hotel, for $1.50 each way.

Mont-Sainte-Anne, the largest ski resort in eastern Québec, is 30 minutes away; Stoneham, less than 20 minutes; and remote Le Massif, a little less than an hour. While you can find lodging near all three resorts, none offers the same immersion into French Canadian culture or variety of activities as Québec City. It's an easy immersion; almost everyone on the front lines of tourism speaks at least some English. And here's a real plus: Winter is low season in Québec City; with the exception of Winter Carnival weekends, lodging rates are at their lowest.

A three-area ticket, nicknamed Carte Blanche, offers skiers and snowboarders a multi-day, multi-destination ticket between Mont-Sainte-Anne, Stoneham and Le Massif for only US$30 per day, per adult. With Carte Blanche, visitors staying in downtown Quebec City hotels can also use the Winter Express shuttle to get to the mountains for just a few dollars more.

Mt. Sainte Anne Facts

Summit elevation:	**2,625 feet**
Vertical drop:	**2,050 feet**
Base elevation:	**575 feet**

Expert:★★★★
Advanced: ★★★★
Intermediate: ★★★★★
Beginner: ★★★   Never-ever: ★★★★
Address: 2000, Beau Pre, C.P. 400,
Beaupre (Quebec) Canada G0A 1E0
Area code: 418
Ski area phone: 827-4561
Snow report: (888) 827-4579 or 827-4579
Fax: 827-3121
Toll-free reservations: (800) 463-1568 or
(827-5281

E-mail: info@mont-sainte-anne.com
Internet: www.mont-sainte-anne.com
Number and types of lifts: 13–1 high-speed 8-passenger gondola, 1 high-speed quad with bubble cover, 1 high-speed quad, 1 quad, 1 triple, 2 doubles, 6 surface
Skiable acreage: 428 acres
Snowmaking: 80 percent
Uphill capacity: 18,560
Snowboarding: Yes, unlimited
Bed base: 2,000
Nearest lodging: slopeside
Resort child care: Yes, 6 months-10 years
Adult ticket, per day: $47-$49 (01/02 prices)

Mont-Sainte-Anne

Mont-Sainte-Anne is Québec City's playground. You'll find impressive, big-mountain skiing with an equally impressive lift system. It has super steeps, challenging bumps, expert and training glades, wide cruising runs and gentle beginner trails spread across three faces. All that and an excellent terrain park and monstrous halfpipe make it an excellent choice for all ability levels. Speed demons take note: Mont-Sainte-Anne has 10 F.I.S.-approved race trails. In general, the slopes increase in difficulty as you move from east to west.

The South Side faces the St. Lawrence River, where all base facilities are located. It also bakes under the sun, so the snow is often heavier here, especially on warm days. The North Side, or the back side, has a high-speed quad and a small lodge. The West Side is dedicated to backcountry skiing and riding.

Mont-Sainte-Anne's riverside location delivers plenty of snow, an average of 160 inches a year. When the wind whips up the river, though, it's a bone-chilling and damp cold, so go prepared.

Don't miss the sugar house on the La Pichard trail, where you can taste such treats as maple sugar on snow. This resort lets you get a good taste of winter Québécois-style. You can try paragliding, ice skating, snowshoeing or dogsledding, all served with a French accent. Mont-Sainte-Anne's cross-country center is the largest in Canada and second-largest in North America.

◆◆ **Expert**: West of the gondola on the South Face is an expert's playground, with serious single- and double-black trails and glades. This is steep terrain with a continuous fall line. La Super "S" is long and smooth and steep; its evil twin, La "S," is the same, but with bumps. For even more challenge, head into the woods on La Brunelle. Two lifts – La Trip, a triple, and La Sainte-Paix, a double – service this area, but it's faster to shoot to the base and take the gondola. If you're hot in the bumps, strut your stuff on La Gondoleuse, under the L'Etoile-Filante gondola. For a backcountry experience, head to the West Side.

◆ **Advanced**: On the South Side, take La Crete to La Beauregard for a long, steep, fast cruise. These are two of the 10 FIS-certified race trails on the mountain. La Pionniere, just east of the gondola, has the feel of an old-style New England trail as it twists its way down the upper third of the mountain.

On the North Side, L'Archipel and La Surpremante are good choices. If you want to escape the crowds, take L'Amarok on the West Side, which is served only by a T-bar.

■ **Intermediate**: While experts and advanced skiers head west off the gondola, intermediates should head east, on the South Side, or over the top to the North Side. Warm up on Le Gros Vallon or La Beaupre on the South Side. Be sure to take at least one run on La Pichard to stop by the sugar shack for a maple-syrup treat. On cold days, ride either the gondola, L'Etoile-Filante, or L'Express du Sud, a high-speed quad with a bubble cover to shield the wind.

Venture to the North Side for more cruising trails and open slopes or to play in the intermediate-level glades, La Vital-Roy or La Sidney-Dawes.

●● **Beginner**: The eastern edge of the mountain on both the South and the North sides is where you'll find the easiest trails. Take the gondola up, then work your way down La Familale on the South Side, L'Escapade and La Ferreolaise on the North Side, then return to the South Side on Le Chemin Du Roy, which wraps slowly and gently from the North Side summit to the South Side base.

● **Never-evers**: Choose from three free surface lifts in the ski school area at the mountain's base. After mastering these, take the gondola to the summit and meander down the mountain's longest trail, Le Chemin du Roy.

Mountain rating–Snowboarding

The resort's 282,500-square-foot terrain park, La Grande Allée is perfectly situated under the Turtle lift, a quad chair lift on the South Side. The park has jumps, table tops, banked turns, rolls, pyramids and other features. It is also the site of Dragon's Cradle, a beginners' halfpipe. For serious air, head to the Dragon's Den halfpipe, which is designed according to World Cup standards and has been the site of World Cup events. Both halfpipes and the terrain park are lighted for night riding.

The snowboard park groomers have an innovative approach to jumps. We began in metal gates and immediately shot over two deep whoop-dee-doos, then over a mellow table top that, with enough air, was a comfortable jump to warm-up for spin tricks or just get in a solid grab. This was followed by three quick bank turns which were so tight together they made us feel as if we were entering the gauntlet. At a slower speed one could just make some easy turns through them or step it up a few notches and carve hard high on the banks. After the bank turns, beginners can hook left to ride the beginner's halfpipe. This is a great spot to gain an understanding of how to pump up the walls, without the intimidation factor that is incurred with the speed that is necessary to get out of the lip in a regular-sized halfpipe. After the mini-half, there are hip jumps on both sides so that more advanced riders can aim toward their favorite wall and catch some big air with speed that was gained in the bank turns. These are followed by 11 consecutive whoop-dee-doos. We raced this course three times, and everyone had to speed check at some point when approaching the whoop-dees. The next part of the park has intermediate to advanced tabletops and ends after a long run at the expert halfpipe.

Cross-country and snowshoeing

Superlatives are all one hears for the **Mont-Sainte-Anne Cross-Country Centre**, located 7 km. from the downhill area. With 224 km. of trails through the Laurentian forest, this center is the largest in Canada, second only to California's Royal Gorge in North America, and not to be missed just for the *joie de ski* Canadians exude on cross-country trails.

If you're an intermediate or beginning cross-country skier, don't be intimidated by the large numbers of obvious and very athletic-looking experts in brightly colored Lycra skiing gear. The Mont-Sainte-Anne Cross-Country Centre has plenty of trails for all abilities. A choice of varying length trail loops make it easy to adjust your outing to your ability and stamina. Skating skiers will find a whopping 125 km. of trails groomed for them.

The area's base lodge has an extensive ski school, a small cafeteria, a waxing room and a cross-country boutique with rentals, which include a baby glider to pull along your young-ster if you choose not to leave him or her at the Alpine area day care.

A day trip for the not-faint-of-heart is the trek along the powerline (Sentier du Versant Nord) to the base of the north side of Mont-Sainte-Anne Alpine area. Though it's about a 7 km. trek, all uphill, the reward is the superb scenery along the way and a nice lunch at the Chalet du Versant Nord. And then there's skiing *downhill* all the way back to the base lodge.

Be sure to take the time to look for animal tracks along the trails—they are numerous and varied. An all-day ticket costs $13 for an adult and $4.35 for a child ages 7–13.

Mont-Sainte-Anne also has 20 km. of snowshoeing trails. Try the guided tours with dinner at La Crete summit lodge, on Tuesday nights.

Lodging opportunities at the cross-country area include the unique B&B, **l'Auberge du Fondeur** (827-5281; 800-463-1568) right on the trails, or the **Ruisseau Rouge** and **Le Chaudron** shelters along the trails. These rustic shelters each can accommodate up to eight skiers and are equipped with a wood stove so skiers can cook their own meals. Reservations are required (827-4561, ext. 408) but there is no charge for their use with purchase of a two-day or more ski pass.

Lessons (2001/02 prices in Cdn$, taxes included)

Group lessons: Offered for age 15 and older. Two-hour session is $49 in the morning and $41 in the afternoon. For four days or more, there's a 10-percent discount off regular group rates.

Never-ever package: The Rossignol Beginners Centre has lift tickets, equipment and clothing rentals, and ski and snowboard school under one roof. A one-day program including a two-hour lesson, full-day equipment rental for skis costs $51.

Lesson-only for snowboarders with limited lift ticket is $51 for the first day; the second, third and fourth days are $72 per day and include an all-lift ticket.

Private lessons: Lessons are also available at night by reservation. One person for one hour is $67; a second person is $41; each additional hour is $41.

Special programs: Clinics of the Day are one-and-one-half-hour lessons, offered Sunday afternoons which concentrate on specific conditions and techniques, such as glades, mo-guls or powder. There is also a disabled program.

Child care

Mont-Sainte-Anne's award-winning Children's Centre houses a nursery, day care, ski and snowboard lessons, Kinderski program, equipment rental, indoor and outdoor playgrounds and lunch.

Child care at Mont-Sainte-Anne is wisely split into two sections: the day care center for those ages 2–10 and the nursery for babies ages 6–18 months. Open 9 a.m. (8:30 on weekends) to 4:15 p.m., the Children's Centre is in the same building as the Ski & Snowboard School (note: it is a bit of a climb for a little one). There is at least one caretaker for every three babies, who have their own nap, play and feeding area. The nursery can accommodate up to 12 children daily.

The older children can choose to just play indoors, or they can opt for an outside activity, which can include skating, sliding, skiing or a sleigh ride. Parents may also decide to enroll their child in the Youth Camp program to get them started in skiing.

The cost of day care is $30 per day for the first child in a family (the cost reduces by $5 for each additional child from the same family). Hourly rate is $8. Or $100 for four days.

Children's lessons: Youth Camp and Adventure Camp are programs for youngsters ages 4-14 that keep them occupied daily from 9 a.m. to 4 p.m. (includes lunch): $75, ages 4-7, and $69, ages 8-14, per day. A half day is $52 and $46, respectively. Activities are split up during the day and include getting to know classmates, morning and afternoon ski or boarding lessons, lunch and games. The children in Youth and Adventure Camps also have meeting areas separated by ages.

 ## Lift tickets (2001/02 prices in Cdn $, tax included)

Weekend prices:	Adult	Young Adult (14-22)	Child (7-13)
One day	$49	$40	$29
Two days	$94	$76	$56

Who skis free: Children age 6 and younger ski free anytime. Beginners ski on three lifts at no charge.

Who skis at a discount: Seniors age 65 and older ski for Young Adult rates. Disabled skiers and riders also ski at a discount.

Note: Night skiing, half-day, and four-out-of-five, six-out-of-seven, and seven-out-of-eight consecutive-days tickets are also available.

 ## Accommodations at the resort

Chateau Mont-Sainte-Anne (800-463-4467 or 827-5211; $$-$$$$ 🛁🏊🍽🍷) is a full-service hotel located next to the gondola base and adjacent to the base village. All rooms have balconies and kitchenettes; loft suites also have fireplaces. There's also a health club, indoor pool, restaurant and lounge.

For condominium lodging, try **Chalets Mont-Ste-Anne** (800-463-4395 or 827-5776; $-$$🏊), located next to the Chateau; the ski-in/ski-out **Village Touristique Mont-Ste-Anne** (800-463-7775 or 827-2002; $$-$$$ 🏊); the Swiss-style **Chalets Montmorency** (800-463-2612 or 826-2600; $-$$$ 🏊), 800 yards from the lifts and with a free shuttle; or the stone, Québécois-style **Chalets Village** (800-461-2030 or 650-2030; $-$$$), each chalet with fireplace, double whirlpool or sauna and multiple bedrooms and bathrooms.

Dining

Le Colette (826-1963; $$-$$$), in St. Ferréol-les-Neiges, is an intimate restaurant specializing in French cuisine and game. For European-style fondue, head to **Café Suisse** (826-2184; $-$$), in St-Ferreol-les-Neiges. In Beaupre, **L'Aventure** (827-5748; $-$$) is a lively bar and restaurant with an excellent view of the mountain. It serves an eclectic selection including Mexican and Italian favorites. The best restaurant in the area, and repeatedly listed as one of the top 10 restaurants in the country, is **Auberge La Camarine** (800-567-3939 or 827-1958), in Beaupre, which specializes in progressive French cuisine.

Dining: $$$-Entrees $20+; $$-$10-20; $-less than $10.
Accommodations: (double room) $$$$-$200+; $$$-$141-$200; $$-$81-$140; $-$80 and less.

Après-ski/nightlife

At Mont-Sainte-Anne, the two places to head immediately after skiing are the **ZigZag Bar,** near the gondola base station, and the **Chouette Bar**, in the main lodge at the base of the mountain. Both have pool tables and music, with the Chouette offering dancing to a disc jockey. The deck at the ZigZag is the place to be to meet people when the spring sun lingers later in the day. The **T-Bar** in Chateau Mont-Sainte-Anne is a good spot to stop later on for a relaxing drink in a more genteel atmosphere. On Wednesday through Saturday nights, entertainment is provided by a singer or musician.

Other activities

Mount-Sainte-Anne has a **skating rink** at the base. **Skating, snowshoeing, dog sledding, paragliding** and **sleigh rides** can be arranged at the area. **Snowmobiling** is available nearby. For information on all, call 827-4561.

Getting there

Take Rte. 138 from Québec City to St.-Anne-de-Beaupre, then Rte. 360 to the resort.

Stoneham

Québec locals know that Stoneham is the place to come when the temperatures drop or the wind is howling due to its location in a sun-filled, wind-protected horseshoe valley. The emphasis here is on having fun, whether on the slopes or in the restaurants and bars. Don't let the very English sounding name of the mountain mislead you, Stoneham is très French with many of its patrons speaking only French (most mountain personnel are bilingual, however). But that's good news because as one regular Stoneham skier told our *Ski America* writer, "The French know about food and they know about fun."

Stoneham is not for an advanced skier for a multiday vacation unless he or she wants to keep the family happy (there's always the option to escape to Mont-Sainte-Anne or Le Massif), but it's perfect to try for a day or two of relaxing skiing. Kids will find a lot of activities to keep them occupied both on the slopes and off.

The emphasis here is not on how big the vertical drops are (they range from 1,140 to 1,380 feet), but on how much terrain the connected mountains deliver. And it's a lot. First though, you've got to figure out the trail map. Stoneham lists four mountains on the map, numbered one, two, four and six. One, two and four are developed; number six, with a potential vertical drop of 1,514 is detailed on the map, but the trails aren't cut nor is the lift in. All of this leaves one wondering: So what happened to three and five?

This seemingly haphazard numbering also plagues the trails, which are numbered from 1 to 61. If you actually take the time to count, there are only 30 trails listed on the map. Wait, it gets even more confusing: Plenty of trail numbers are further distinguished by letters. For example there are 1 and 1B, 9 as well as 9B, 9C and 9D. Whatever you do, know which trail 19 you want: There are two, not further distinguished by letters. One is a rambling beginner trail; the other a black-diamond glade.

Sixty percent of the mountain is lit every evening of ski season and that includes two colorfully lighted halfpipes and a snow-tubing area. With its party reputation, a visit for the

Stoneham Facts

Summit:	**2,075 feet**
Vertical Drop	**1,380 feet**
Base	**695 feet**
Expert ★	
Advanced ★	
Intermediate ★★★★	
Beginner ★★★★	
Never-ever ★★★★	

Address: 1420, chemin du Hibou, Stoneham, PQ, Canada G0A 4P0
Area code: 418
Ski area phone: 848-2411
Snow report: 848-2415
Toll-free reservations: (800) 463-6888

Fax: 848-1133
Internet: www.ski-stoneham.com
Number and types of lifts: 9-1 high-speed quad, 3 quads, 1 double, 4 surface lifts
Skiable acreage: 328 (daytime), 183 (nighttime)
Snowmaking: 86 percent
Uphill capacity: 14,200 per hour
Snowboarding: Yes, unlimited
Bed base: 500 at base; 10,000 in Quebec City, 20 minutes away
Nearest lodging: Slopeside
Resort child care: Yes, age 2 1/2 and up
Adult ticket, per day: $39

---

nighttime skiing (because you'd *have* to stop for some refreshments afterwards) is a must for anyone on a ski vacation to the Québec City region.

◆◆ **Expert**: Experts will want to head straight for mountain four. Little grooming is done here, and the trails are steep, skinny and bumped. Trails 47, 48 and 49 are legitimate double blacks. These are left au natural, so you want to be on the look out for stumps, rocks and other such obstructions in lean snow years. You'll have plenty of time to rest your legs after each run, as the only lift to the summit on this peak is a fixed quad.

◆ **Advanced:** Stoneham is primarily a family mountain and even double-black-diamond trails 45 and 46, though steep, are easily maneuverable for upper-intermediate skiers. If you like glades, head for trail 19.

■ **Intermediate**: The entire mountain is an intermediate's playground. Even the bump runs, glades and, as mentioned earlier, the groomed double-black-diamond trails should be tried and conquered. Undulating terrain and wide-open trails call for lots of top-to-bottom GS runs. For challenging fun, ski trails number 41 and 42, both are long with steep pitches that mellow then drop again for little adrenaline rushes.

●● **Beginner** ● **Never-ever:** Peaks one and two, to the skier's right, are the place for beginners to head. Both offer top-to-bottom green-circle trails (piste facile #s 19 to 6 and 6 top to bottom), where those new to the sport can practice turns while making their way down the mountain. The wide open area served by a quad and two Poma lifts right in front of the main base lodge, gives a non-threatening place for beginners to take their first trips up a mountain and their first turns down.

Mountain layout–Snowboarding

Stoneham's parks and pipe are located in the center of the mountain and are easily viewable from the chairlifts. All terrain is accessible via chairlifts with much-appreciated foot-rests, so you can avoid those dreaded T-bars. The parks offer a variety of manmade features, including tabletops, with nice smooth landings and equally smooth takeoffs; nice rollers, for riders off all abilities who wish to practice their bordercross techniques; and plenty of rails and boxes. New school jibbers and bonkers alike will find little reason to leave the parks. The one on 4B is incredibly long, with about 15 consecutive hits.

Trail 10, a double-black diamond glade, takes you to the top of the halfpipe. Unless there's fresh snow, avoid this trail as these glades comprised of a few trees, a bunch of big rocks and a throng of multi-ability riders who are mostly sideslipping (yikes!) their way through the trees to watch others ride the halfpipe. The halfpipe is geared for all ablities. Its short walls are ideal for those getting their first taste of weightlessness.

Our favorite spot by far on the mountain was the *Sous Bois*. This wide, long glade is full of little hits, chutes through the trees, rolling turns and a few gentle moguls. Even two days after a powder storm, we were able to find freshies.

Throughout the season, Stoneham hosts a variety of snowboard contests. These have included Big Air (open to both skiers and snowboarders), Ski and Snowboard Nationals, Clement Cup (for recreational riders age 4-17), Bordercross competitions (some held at night), Snowboard Camp (coached by the 10 best freestyle riders in Canada) and the Snowboard Canada National Jam Tour (which features the ISF Masters and competitions include big air, slopestyle, GS, halfpipe and quarterpipe competitions, and even has DJ's spinning tunes slopeside all weekend long).

Lessons

Group and private lessons: A private lesson is $28.69 per hour and includes the lift ticket for the length of the lesson. A group of four comparable skiers can take an hour's lesson for about $17 per person. (Best deal: a two-hour lesson with a friend; cost is $50.42 for the first person and $21 for the second.)

Never ever: Skiing lessons for ages 7 and older who have never (or hardly ever) skied are affordable and include lift ticket and rentals. They get less expensive at night: $34.77 during the day and $27.82 at night. Lessons for the same times for snowboarding or Snowblading are $43.37 and $33.03 respectively.

Child care

Ages: 2 1/2 and older.

Costs: Cost for the first child for one day is $20 with lunch, with the second child from the same family costing $16. Multivisit booklets offering substantial savings are available. Reservations must be made by phone.

Day care has bilingual caregivers, but most of the children on any given day speak only French. Open from 8:30 a.m.-5 p.m., the center is located just a few steps from the main base lodge. It has a large game room and separate sleeping and eating rooms. For those with younger children, the day care center will arrange babysitting if you call ahead.

Children's lessons: Stoneham offers the Children's Island, a program to introduce young children to skiing. It includes a two-hour ski lesson, indoor activities, outdoor fun in the enclosed Children's Island Park, lunch and snacks for $46.95 per day with multiday rates available. For children just starting out, the ratio is two children per instructor, with never more than four children per instructor as the children progress.

Lift tickets (prices in Cdn$, taxes included)

Weekend prices	Adult	Student (14-22)	Youth (7-13)
One day	$33.91	$25.22	$13.91
Evening	$18.26	$15.65	$10.43
Three days	$93.02	$68.68	$37.38

Note: Because of night-skiing, Stoneham offers a variety of tickets including the longer day ticket (9 a.m.–6 p.m.), a day-to-evening ticket (12:30 p.m.–closing) and an evening ticket that begins at 3 p.m. Consecutive multiday tickets may be bought to seven days.

Who skis free: Children ages 6 and younger.

Who skis at a discount: Ages 65 and older ski at student rates and ages 14-22 need to show an I.D. to get the lower student rate.

Accommodations at the resort

The practical **Hotel Stoneham** is an anchor in the ski area's mini-village and offers 60 spacious rooms where children under age 18 stay for free when sharing a room with their parents. The ski area also rents out about a hundred condos through **Condominiums Stoneham,** varying in size from studios to four bedrooms, located at the base of the slopes. Attractive ski-and-stay packages are available. (Example: two adults, two children for two nights in a hotel for $172.) Reservations at both hotel and condos may be made by calling 848-2411 or 800-463-6888.

If not staying slopeside, the best option is to stay in Québec City, although the nearby town of Ste-Foy (25–30 minutes away) offers a **Holiday Inn** (653-4901; 800-463-5241), a **Comfort Inn** (872-5038; 800-267-3837), the **Hotel Plaza** (658-2727; 800-567-5276), **Hotel Québec** (658-5120; 800-567-5276) and **Hotel Universel** (653-5250; 800-463-4495).

Dining

Stoneham's skiers and slopeside lodgers will find a surprising number of good restaurants despite the small size of the base area. Try the **cafeteria** in the base lodge or **Charlie's Grocery** in the village, which offers freshly baked bread and cookies in addition to cold cuts, cheeses and some take-out. Lunch and light snacks are also available in **Le Bar Le 4 foyers** (the bar of the four fireplaces) in the base lodge, a place for meeting people, dancing, and playing pool.

For more substantial dining, Stoneham offers **Le Pub St-Edmond**, more geared to night-time snacks after skiing than full meals; the Italian cuisine at **Le Capriccio**, which offers 16 different choices of thin crust pizza including the Veniccia with smoked snails and oysters; and **Feu Follet**, with such exotic offerings (the last time we checked) as bruchetta of alligator. All of these options are within easy walking distance of each other in Stoneham's base village. See Québec City dining for some of the best dining choices.

Après-ski/nightlife

Because the base area is so small, it may be hard to believe that the Quebeçois leave Québec City and head here to have fun, but that's what they do. Under new management since the RCR takeover, **Le Bar Le 4 foyers** a funky Irish pub, brings in a wide range of musical performers including the requisite rock bands and a disco night on Thursdays. It serves basic pub fare and screens nonstop snowboard flicks on the TV. There's also a pool table in the back room. Guinness drinkers beware: The beer is so light that you are able to read the paper through the glass! **Le Pub St-Edmond** on the other end of the village (a five-minute walk) offers a little more mellow fare with folk and oldies plus a wide selection of beers. Skiers will find that even with a language barrier – many of Stoneham's regular skiers speak no English – après ski conviviality prevails and trying to make your rudimentary French understood after a few drinks is actually fun.

Other activities

Stoneham has three slopes that are specially equipped for **tubing**, with a lift and a cabin shelter and snack area designed for the enjoyment of this activity. **Ice skating** as well as indoor **wall-climbing** are available. The mini-village has two small **stores**: Boutique Sports Alpins offers gifts and interesting ski items, and La Shop is for snowboarders. Both are fun to browse through, but not designed to occupy truly serious shoppers.

For **snowmobiling**, go to Lac Beauport to Nord Tour (841-2810) for rentals.

Getting there and getting around

Stoneham is 20 minutes from Québec City via Hwy. 73 North, taking the Stoneham exit.

Le Massif

Perched on the edge of the St. Lawrence River, this three-peak area is within a UNESCO World Biosphere Reserve. The natural beauty envelops you. Le Massif's owners have honored this beauty by developing the area in harmony with nature. Lifts, for the most part, are hidden in the trees. Trails rarely intersect and seldom cross under lifts as they plunge toward the ice-choked river. The views are awesome.

Le Massif has the highest vertical drop east of the Canadian Rockies, and, because of its riverfront location, it receives abundant snowfall. Legend has it that when the area's mascot owl, Le Grand Duc, circles, the area will receive at least 30 centimeters of snow within 48 hours. If you visit, don't pack a lunch. The cafeteria food here is among the best and the most reasonably priced we've seen.

Le Massif is one of eastern Canada's great secrets, but that may be about to change. This year, Le Massif will unveil phase II of its development project, a $24.8-million expansion. This includes a summit lodge, easily accessible from the highway, which will eliminate the harrowing drive down the double-diamond access road and through the riverside village of Petite-Riviere-Sainte-Francois and cut the drive time from Québec City by 20 minutes. In addition, the resort is adding a second high-speed chairlift, with midway unloading, on Cap Maillard (a FIS homologated racing trail) site of national training center for downhill and Super G. In addition, are nine new trails and more snowmaking. In addition, Le Massif is extending and improving the double chair. All is expected to be ready by Dec. 1. While we'd recommend a visit to Le Massif in any case, if you're counting on these improvements, we suggest you call before making the trip to make sure they've been completed.

◆◆ **Expert:** Le Massif has two double-black runs, La "42" and Le Sous-Bois. La "42," an ungroomed, natural-snow trail, snakes its way down the eastern edge of the ski area. It's punctuated with bumps, stumps, narrow chutes, steep drops and with the area's trademark jaw-dropping views of the St. Lawrence. New access from the summit cuts out the old skate

Le Massif facts

Summit elevation: 2,645 feet
Vertical drop: 2,526 feet
Base elevation: 118 feet
Expert: ★★★   **Advanced**: ★★★★
Intermediate: ★★★
Beginner: ★★
Never-ever: ★
Address: 1350 Rue Principale, C.P. 47, Petite-Riviere-Saint-Francois, Quebec , Canada G0A 2L0
Area code: 418
Ski area phone: 632-5876; (877) 536-2774
Snow report: 632-5876; (877) 536-2774
Fax: 632-5205

Toll-free reservations: (877)-LeMassif (536-2774)
E-mail: info@lemassif.com
Internet: www.lemassif.com
Number and types of lifts: 5–2 high-speed quad2, 1 double chair, 2 surface
Skiable acreage: 220 acres
Snowmaking: 75 percent
Uphill capacity: 7,220 per hour
Snowboarding: Yes, unlimited
Bed base: 873
Nearest lodging: one-half mile
Resort child care: Yes, 3 years and older
Adult ticket, per day: $42 (01/02)

to this trail. Le Sous-Bois is relatively tame by comparison. In French, its name translates as glades. La Tremblay, a single black, is also challenging since it's rarely groomed. Both of these are accessed by the double chair. For a short, steep thrill, take the plunge on La Pointue.

◆ **Advanced** ■ **Intermediate**: This mountain is nirvana for cruisers. The black diamond and blue square designations here seem almost arbitrary. Most of the trails are meticulously groomed and can be handled by an advanced intermediate. Concentrate your efforts on the quad chair for the best vertical and choice. La Petite Riviere, a blue, is a sweet way to launch your day with spectacular drop-dead views of the St. Lawrence.

●● Beginner ● Never-ever: Previously, we recommended that never-evers avoid this mountain and that only adventurous beginners consider it, but Le Massif has added a new beginner area with its own surface lift at the summit day lodge. From there, they'll advance to the double chair where new beginner trails have been added. Beginners should stick to the upper portion of the mountain until they've built up the skills and confidence to mingle with faster skiers and riders.

Mountain layout–Snowboarding

Le Massif has two terrain parks, one on La Grande Pointe and the other at the bottom of L'Ancienne. However, La "42" and Le Sous-Bois are natural terrain parks. The rest of the mountain is ideal for carving deep arcing turns. For bumps and trees, ride the double lift and spend the day. Save the traverse back for later. Freeriding cruisers will enjoy the terrain in the vicinity of the quad chair.

Lessons

Group lessons: Group lessons: $50 for one hour (3 to 8 persons).
Private lessons: $40 for one hour for one, $15 each additional person.
      Special programs: A 90-minute two-for-one class is $20 per person for class which varies with weather and conditions, perhaps bumps, perhaps powder.

Child care (Cdn$, taxes included)

Ages: Ages 3-6, available weekends and school-vacation weeks, located lower level of base lodge.

Cost: $7 per hour; half-day $12; full-day $19.

Reservations: Recommended; call 632-5876 or 1-877-LeMassif (536-2774).

Children's lessons (ages 6 and younger): $30 for 45 minutes; $10 for each additional child.

Lift tickets (Cdn$, taxes included)

Weekend	Adult	Young Adult (17-23)	Child (7-16)
One day	$42	$34	$24
Three day	$115	$94	$66
Five day	$174	$141	$99

Who skis free: Children ages 6 and younger.

Who skis at a discount: Ages 55 and older ski at young adult rates.

Accommodations near the resort

Le Massif offers skiing packages at bed and breakfasts, inns and motels as well as chalets and villas in nearby towns. Baie-Sainte-Paul is the largest town and offers the best variety of dining and lodging as well as nightlife. For regional information, call (800) 667-2276.

Le Manoir Richelieu (665-3703; 800-866-5577; ⊞⌂⛷✕♨P), located 45 minutes east, is a four-star, five-diamond Fairmont resort with all the amenities you would expect, as well as a casino and full spa. Other onsite activities include cross-country, snowmobile and snowshoe trails, a skating rink, sleigh rides and dog sledding. The resort sits on the bank of the St. Lawrence River, providing magnificent views from many rooms. Le Manoir offers ski packages with Air Canada that include tickets at Le Massif and/or Mont Grand Fonds, see nearby skiing, below.

Getting there

Le Massif is 45 miles east of Québec City on Rte. 138.

Nearby skiing

Parc régional du Mont Grand-Fonds, La Malbaie, Charlevoix (Quebec);
(418) 665-0095

Internet: www.quebecweb.com/montgrandfonds

2 lifts; 14 trails; 1,095 vertical feet

Mont Grand Fonds, located just 15 minutes from the Le Manoir Richelieu, skis bigger that it actually is. Crowds are rare, which is a good thing since there's only one quad and one T-bar. The atmosphere is laid back, the views over the St. Lawrence are terrific, and the trails were cut for maximum sun exposure. Trails to the right of the lifts, as you look up at the mountain, are primarily intermediate, with a few gentle beginner trails, while those to the left provide more challenge. Glades start out open and inviting, but get tighter and steeper as you descend. This is an ideal family mountain, and its proximity to the fabulous Manoir is ideal.

Note: Lifts open at 10 a.m. on weekdays, 9 a.m. on weekends. Grand Fonds also has 160 km. of groomed cross-country trails with four heated warming huts and a special bird-watching area.
Lift tickets (00/01 rates): Adults, $23; Student (6-22), $20; rates include taxes.
Distance from Quebec: 90 miles via Rte. 138.
Lodging information: See Manoir Richelieu, above.

QuébeCity Accommodations

Le Chateau Frontenac (800-441-1414 or 692-3861; $$-$$$$, 🛏🏛📶✕🍷Ⓟ) is the grande dame of Québec City. This Chateau is perched on the edge of the Cap Diamant promontory in Old Québec's upper town. It's historic, formal, elegant and full-service. Rooms vary greatly, from tiny to spacious, some offering magnificent views of the St. Lawrence. Most packages here include the hotel's bountiful buffet breakfast, enough to fuel you through most of the day. Ask about the skiing package, which includes breakfast, lodging and lift tickets for two.

Also full service are the **Québec Hilton** (800-445-8667 or 647-2411; $$-$$$$ 📶✕⌨🍷Ⓟ), and **Hotel Loews Le Concorde** (800-235-6397 or 647-2222; $$-$$$$ 🛏📶✕⌨🍷Ⓟ), both in old Québec, but outside the city walls.

Smaller hotels within the city walls are the **Hotel Clarendon** (888-554-6001 or 692-2480; $$-$$$ 🛏📶Ⓟ), the **Hotellerie Fleur-de-Lys** (800-567-2106 or 694-0106; $$$-$$$$ 🛏Ⓟ), and the **Manoir de l'Esplanade** (694-0834; $-$$Ⓟ).

The **Auberge Saint-Antoine** (888-692-2211 or 692-2211; $$-$$$$Ⓟ), in a restored 19th-century maritime warehouse in the city's Vieux Port area, is an elegant retreat offering the warmth and intimacy of a boutique hotel. Rates include an extravagent continental breakfast and 24-hour snacks.

Just around the corner, is the **Auberge Saint-Pierre** (888-268-1017 or 694-7981Ⓟ). Built in 1821 as an insurance company, today the inn has bathrooms that were once safes. A full, hot breakfast is included in the rates.

Hotel La Maison Acadienne (800-463-0280 or 694-0280; $-$$Ⓟ) serves a continental breakfast and also has packages with Mont-Sainte-Anne.

The recently renovated **Hotel Manoir Victoria** (800-463-6283 or 692-1030; $-$$$🛏🏛📶✕🍷Ⓟ), in the old city, is a good choice for families. Also popular with families is **L'Hotel du Vieux-Québec** (800-361-7787 or 692-1850; $$-$$$ 🛏✕⌨Ⓟ).

Auberge Louis Hébert (525-7812; $$✕ Ⓟ) is on the Grande Allée, the heart of Québec City's nightlife.

Small inns and bed and breakfasts are clustered around the Frontenac and offer simple rooms, usually with breakfast, at affordable rates. Try the **Hotel Manoir de la Terrasse** (694-1592 $), the **Manoir Ste-Genevieve** (694-1666 $-$$) or the **Chateau Bellevue** (800-463-2716 or 692-2573 $-$$ Ⓟ)

For budget lodging, try these hostels: **Centre international de séjour de Québec** (694-0755, $✕), which has a cafeteria and 243 beds in 8- to 12-bed dormitories; **Auberge de la Paix** (694-0735; $), which has 14 rooms with two to eight beds, a kitchen and where rates include breakfast: or **Association du YWCA de Québec** (683-2155; $🏛Ⓟ), a 15-room hostel with shared bathrooms, swimming pool and self-service kitchen.

For something completely different, consider one night at the new **Ice Hotel** (www.icehotel-canada.com; $$$). Constructed completely of snow and ice, this hotel, a sister

Dining: $$$-Entrees $20+; $$-$10-20; $-less than $10.
Accommodations: (double room) $$$$-$200+; $$$-$141-$200; $$-$81-$140; $-$80 and less.

to the original ice-hotel in Sweden, will open in January and close approximately three months later, when it melts. Guests are provided with sleeping bags guaranteed to keep them warm to 30-degrees below zero. Other amenities include a cinema, two art galleries and an ice bar. Rates include breakfast.

Dining in the City

You have to work to get a bad meal in this city. Almost all restaurants post their menu outside the door, and most include a Table d'hôte, or set menu, usually with appetizer, entrée and dessert, for a fixed price.

Aux Anciens Canadiens (692-1627; $$) is located in one of the oldest houses in the city. The Maison Jacquet was built between 1675-76, and its architecture reflects the era, with thick stone walls, solid joints, wainscoting and recessed cupboards. It's split up into five cozy dining rooms on two floors. The fare is traditional Québeçois: pea soup, onion soup, meat pies, fish and game dishes and for dessert, maple syrup pie.

Restaurant Gambrinus (692-5144; $$–$$$), overlooking the Place d'Armes, in Vieux Québec, is an excellent Italian restaurant with a French flair and excellent seafood. A strolling musician performs at night.

Cochon Dingue (523-2013; $$) offers a wide-ranging, bistro-style menu in a busy atmosphere. Good choice for families.

Marie-Clarisse (692-0857; $$$), at the base of the funicular and the bottom of the "Breakneck Stairs," is well respected for fish and seafood.

If you're holding out for a carbo feed, head to the **Place du Spaghetti** (694-9144).

Start the night with dinner at **Louis-Hébert** (525-7812; $$–$$$), on the Grande Allée, and you'll be well situated to enjoy this street's hearty nightlife afterward.

Take in the whole city from **Astral** (647-2222; $$), the revolving restaurant atop Loews Le Concorde hotel. It takes about one hour for it to make a complete circle. A buffet is served every Saturday night, and the Sunday brunch is in a class of its own.

A la maison de Serge Bruyère (694-0618; $–$$$) houses three restaurants under one roof. The most famous, La Grande Table, offers four-diamond fine dining. The others are the Bistro Livernois and the Cafe Bruyère.

The chef at **Laurie Raphael** (692-4555; $$$) was named the best chef in Québec in 1997. You'll quickly agree if you dine at this contemporary restaurant specializing in fresh food and both local and international cuisine.

For more than 45 years, **Au Cafe Suisse** (694-1320; $$) has been serving Swiss fare, such as fondue, raclette and grillades.

For simple, Mediterranean-style fare, head to **Freres de la Cote** (692-5445; $–$$). This lively restaurant has an open kitchen and wood-burning ovens.

If you're a bit adventurous, visit a sugar shack: Follow signs for a cabane à sucre. Most open only when the sap is running. The fare usually includes crepes, eggs, meat pies, meats, toast, baked beans, all topped with maple syrup and flavored with music and dancing.

Québec City Après-ski/nightlife

The **Grande Allée** is lined with bars and restaurants and is the number one choice for nightlife in the city. The **Clarendon** hotel has good jazz music. **St. Jean Street** offers a number of bars with traditional French music. **Le Capitole** features a Las Vegas-style dinner show. Don't miss having a drink at the **Bar St-Laurent** in Le Chateau Frontenac. **Le Pape George** is a bistro with French singers.

Québec City Other activities

Québec City has so much to offer, this is only a beginning.

Shopping: The narrow streets of **Le Quartier Petit Champlain**, in Vieux Québec, are lined with ancient stone buildings housing boutiques with traditional and contemporary Canadian artwork, crafts, clothing and more. Artists sell their work on pedestrian alleyway, **Rue du Trésor**, off Place d'Armes. The **Galeries de la Capitale** not only has 250 shops, but an amusement center.

The frozen falls at **Montmorency Falls Park** are one-and-a-half times higher than Niagara Falls. Cable cars, bridges lookouts and trails make it possible to get close to the falls.

For ice climbing, **L'Ascensation** (647-4422) rents equipment and provides guides.

At **Village Vacances Valcartier** (844-2200), 20 minutes north of the city, go snow rafting, sliding and tubing on 38 slides; skate through a forest; race go-karts on an ice-covered track; snowmobile, ride horseback, dogsled or take a sleigh ride.

On the **Plains of Abraham**, you can go cross-country skiing (649-6476 for information, 648-4212 for trail conditions) and snowshoeing or take a sleigh ride (687-0707).

The Greater Québec area is home to 1,512 km. of **snowmobile trails**. For rentals and guided tours, try Laurentides Sports Service Inc., in Charlesbourg, 849-2824; Location S.M. Sport, in Loretteville, 842-2703; or Dion Moto, 337-2776.

Getting there and getting around

By air: Jean-Lesage International Airport in Québec city is served by Air Canada, Continental, Air Atlantic, American Airlines, Air Transat and Air Nova. A shuttle service operates between the airport and downtown, call 872-5525 or take a cab, call 525-5191 or rent a car.

By car: Stoneham is 20 minutes from Québec City via Hwy 73 North, taking the Stoneham exit. To get to Mont-Sainte-Anne, take Rte. 138 from Québec City to St.-Anne-de-Beaupre, then Rte. 360 to the resort. It's about one-half hour away. Le Massif is 45 miles east of Québec City. Take Route 138 to Petite-Riviere-Sainte-Francois, then follow signs to Le Massif.

Getting around: For those without a car, there is a daily shuttle from downtown hotels to the ski area available from mid-November to April. It costs $22 round trip. Shuttles leave Québec city at 8:30 a.m. and return around 4:30 p.m., or to going in the reverse direction, shuttles leave the ski area at 9:30 a.m. and return at 3:30 p.m. Thursday to Sunday there is an additional departure from Québec at 10:30 a.m. Reservations are compulsory (before 7 a.m. on the day of the trip) and may be made through your hotel. The HiverExpress connects downtown hotels to a number of outdoor activity sites, including Mont-Sainte-Anne and Stoneham, call 525-5191. The Orleans Express operates between Mont-Sainte-Anne and Québec City on Fridays, Saturdays and Sundays; phone 525-3000.

Eastern Townships, Canada

Mont Orford, Mont Sutton
with Owl's Head and Bromont

Eastern Townships Facts

Eastern Townships Tourism Association
Address: 20, rue Don-Bosco Sud,
Sherbrooke (Quebec) J1L 1W4
Email: tce@tourisme-cantons.qc.ca
Internet: www.tourisme-cantons.qc.ca
Phones: (819) 820-2020, 1-800-355-5755
Fax: (819) 566-4445

Quebec Tourism:

Address: P.O. Box 979,
Montreal, (Quebec) H3C 2W3
Email: info@tourisme.gouv.qc.ca
Internet: www.tourisme.gouv.qc.ca.
Phones: Canada and US, 1-877-BONJOUR
(1-877-266-5687); France, 0-800-90-77-77;
Belgium, 0-800-78-532
Fax: (514) 864-3838

The Eastern Townships' marketing efforts would have you believe that the four ski areas in the region—Mont Orford, Mont Sutton, Bromont and Owl's Head—are right next door to each other, but in reality they are anywhere from 20 to 45 minutes away from each other on dry roads. Don't let that deter you, this is a beautiful region for a vacation, and we don't think you'll be disappointed. As with any resort in Quèbec, the French-Canadian culture is everywhere: That means fabulous food, first-rate service, French spoken all around you and an overall feeling of vacationing in France.

The beautiful, rolling countryside is reminiscent of northern New England; you've not yet entered the perfectly flat middle region of Quèbec. The Eastern Townships comprise dozens of quaint little towns, so try to find time to explore in your car. The region is ripe with history. The original residents were Abenaki Indians, and the names they gave to places and bodies of water remain, including Memphremagog, the lake that serves as a centerpiece to the region's winter resorts. Eventually Canada became a British colony and, not surprisingly, loyalists from the American Revolution fled to Quèbec, soon to be followed by other Americans looking for cheap land. It was not until the 1850s that the French-speaking residents arrived and by the early 1900s most of the population was francophone.

That said, each resort has a different feel and flavor. Mont Orford, Mont Sutton and Bromont are dominated by the French experience (in fact, Bromont is rather intimidating because the resort's signs don't have an accompanying English translation, while Sutton and Orford are much more accommodating). On the other hand, at Owl's Head everyone speaks English and switches to French if necessary.

Adventurous intermediates and better who enjoy the challenging terrain at Mont Orford and Mont Sutton should consider spending a day at nearby Jay Peak Resort, VT.

Please make note of the different area codes.

Mont Orford Facts

Summit elevation: 2,800 feet
Vertical drop: 1,772 feet
Base elevation: 1,082 feet
Address: 4380 Chemin du Parc, Orford, PQ; mail:
C.P. 10, Magog,
PQ Canada J1X 3W7
Area code: 819
Ski area phone: 843-6548
Toll-free reservations: (800) 567-2772
Snow report: 843-8882 or (800) 567-2772
Fax: 847-2487
E-mail: info@mt-orford.com
Internet: www.mt-orford.com

Number and types of lifts: 8–2 quads, 1 triple, 3 doubles, 1 T-bar, 1 surface lift
Skiable acreage: 244 acres
Snowmaking: 85 percent
Uphill capacity: 11,400 per hour
Snowboarding: Yes, unlimited
Bed Base: 170 slopeside; 5,000 in Orford-Magog area
Nearest lodging: Condos, walking distance
Resort child care: Yes; 2 years and older
Adult ticket, per day: $29-36 (2001/02 Cdn$)

Expert: ★★★★
Advanced: ★★★★
Intermediate: ★★★★
Beginner: ★★★   **Never-ever:** ★★★

Mont Orford

Mont Orford is operated under a long-term lease on government land within Parc du Mont-Orford. The resort is spread across three separate mountain peaks and has fabulous terrain for all abilities. Adventurous skiers will be challenged here, and you'll be completely surprised by that because at first glance, the mountain looks rather tame. The trails are long, giving skiers and riders maximum use of the vertical drop, and they follow the contours of the mountain. The glades are really tight woods, where trees may be thinned a bit, but the mountain is left alone, like you'll find at Eastern resorts such as Jay Peak and Mad River Glen, VT. Certainly the best time to hit this mountain if you're planning to check out the woods is when there's fresh powder, so keep in mind that Orford gets fresh snow on days when nearby resorts may get rain.

Mountain layout–Skiing

◆◆ **Expert** ◆ **Advanced**: Triple-diamond labels are a bit hyped, but experts won't be disappointed either. Take La Quatuor lift to the top of Mont Giroux, and "warm up" on Slalom: When we skied it, there was new powder and the workout left us huffing and puffing with screaming quads. Riding up Le Quad du Village, you'll realize what you're up for as you look at the bodies littered across Sherbrooke below you (probably thought they'd take a break from the glade skiing—hey, it's a trail, how hard can it be?). Once you unload from Le Quad du Village, you'll find a steep headwall to skier's right. If you're looking for woods (as if you'd be over here for any other reason), stay along the top of the headwall and keep your eyes peeled for the entrance—you'll probably notice people peering down the ravine that gets you into the woods. A new experience for us: Once you're in the woods, you'll see signs for various woods shots off the woods shots. It doesn't matter which way you go, it's all good. Ledges and boulders simply add to the thrill of the woods skiing here. By the way, if it's in-bounds, you can ski it. There are about 12 unnamed glades as well, be nice to the locals, and maybe they'll give you a private tour. Don't miss the glades off Mont Orford either.

For those who prefer trails to woods, don't worry, be happy. Trois-Ruisseaux and Maxi on Mont Orford are especially delightful, and both are groomed in the middle of the day, which is a treat since these are popular trails. Trois-Ruisseaux is a winding trail, narrow in spots with nice steep pitches. Maxi, on the other hand, is steep and goes straight down the mountain. Watch out, you'll pick up lots of speed before you know it.

■ **Intermediate**: The intermediate trails on Mont A.-Desrochers are winding and rolling, sometimes narrow, but with a steady pitch and no unexpected steeps. A wonderful experience! Because the chair is a bit out of the way, you'll find these trails relatively uncrowded. Grande Coulée on Mont Orford is a nice cruiser, but it has a steep section that might intimidate some intermediates (if it's windy, some parts get windswept and icy too). Wondering if you might like woods skiing? Arcade is a gentle glade to skier's right after unloading La Mi-Orford chair. If you're having fun, try Escapade, a short glade.

●● **Beginner** ● **Never-evers**: Talk about being friendly to novices: Beginner trails are groomed during the day if it's a snowy day. The scenic 4 Km. is a narrow cat track from the top of Mont Orford that eventually widens and has fabulous views of nearby Lake Memphremagog and Owl's Head in the distance. A real surprise is that the "north side" of Mont Giroux, which is covered in black on the "east side," has trails that are loads of fun for beginners. Take the Le Quatuor lift and head straight, or skier's right. They're separate from expert trails, so you don't need to worry about hotshots. The learning area is at the base of Mont Giroux and has its own lift.

Mountain layout–Snowboarding

The snowboard park is to rider's right off La Mi-Orford chair. The park was new for the 2000/01 season, and we didn't see many riders there, but then again, it was a powder day so everyone was in the woods and cruising down the trails, leaving rooster tails in their wake. Contour on Mont Orford goes from narrow to wide to narrow and is covered with ledges, rocks and double-fall lines that make it a natural terrain park. Almost all of the glades on Mont Giroux dump onto Passe-Montagne, a long, flat beginner trail that might require some hoofing to get back to the lift. Don't let that stop you if you like glades, some riders say it's a nice relief after the tough workout they just had in the woods! Want to reach warp speed? Head to Maxi and Trois-Ruisseaux.

Lessons (prices in Cdn$, taxes included)

Group lessons: A two-hour lesson costs $25 (maximum of six people).
Never-ever package: Never-evers can take a 90-minute class that includes a full-day lift ticket and rentals, $55. Reserve 24 hours in advance.
Private lessons: One-hour lesson is $36, two hours is $63. Additional skier is $17.

Child care (2001/02 prices in Cdn$ with GST)

Ages: 2 years and older.
Costs: $18 for a full day, lunch is an additional $5.75; $5 per hour.
Reservations: Required.

Children's lessons: Kids 3-6 years old get a 90-minute ski lesson, rentals and daycare for $40 (full day); add lunch, $46. Kids 7 and older get a 90-minute lesson, lift ticket and rentals. Price varies by number of participants: two kids, $57.45 per person; three kids, $45.95; four or more, $34.45. Reservations 24 hours in advance are required for all lessons.

Lift tickets (2001/02 prices in Cdn$ with GST)

	Adult	Junior (6-13)
One day	$36	$21
Three days	$100	$60
Five days	$145	$100

Who skis at a discount: Children 5 and younger pay $5; students age 14 to 21 with I.D. pay $28; seniors age 65 to 69 pay junior rates; seniors age 70 and older pay $5.

Interchangeable Ticket: The "Ski East Pass" is a multiday ticket of four consecutive days or more that offers full interchangability with Mont Sutton, Mont Orford and Owl's Head (Bromont does not participate). It can be purchased at any of the participating resorts. Four days cost $124 Cdn for adults, $80 Cdn for children ages 6 to 13.

Accommodations

The full-service **Auberge Estrimont** (800-567-7320, 819-843-1616; $$$; ✕⌂≋⊡♞♘☺), just minutes away from the mountain, has been under new management for three years and they have made about $1 million in renovations, with more to come. If you don't mind some minor annoyances that haven't yet been repaired, you'll enjoy staying here. Our suite had a sunken living room, fireplace, balcony and small refrigerator. Massage and spa services also are available. The over-priced and uninspired **Manoir des Sables** (800-567-3514, 819-847-4747; $$$; ✕♞♘☺) has 117 deluxe rooms and suites and is set on its own private lake and golf course. Some rooms have a fireplace, Jacuzzi and mini-bar. Service was spotty and lukewarm at best and the atmosphere was similar to a Holiday Inn.

Dining

On-mountain, you'll find a **pub** and a **cafeteria** (there's seating in several areas on different levels, so finding your friends and family is a bit like playing hide-and-seek). **La Loyaliste** at Auberge Estrimont (819-843-1616; $$-$$$) serves excellent regional cuisine in a cozy dining room with a fireplace. If you're a chocoholic, you'll want to order Le Diable, a rich chocolate mousse filled with chocolate sauce—absolutely to die for! We could have eaten here all week, but in the interest of suggesting variety, we forced ourselves to dine elsewhere. **Les Jardins** at Manoir des Sables (819-847-4747; $$-$$$) also focuses on regional cuisine with a French influence. It sets a sumptuous buffet breakfast as well (try the pate). For a much more casual meal, head to **Rôtisserie St-Hubert** (819-847-3366; $-$$). The kids will be happy in the playroom while you drink St.-Hubert private-label beer (on lees, so it's light and somewhat like champagne), munch on the "teaser appetizers" that allow you to sample two or three of your choice (you must try the spicy tortillas—fried corn tortillas stuffed with spiced jalapeño cream cheese) and indulge in their scrumptious rotisserie chicken.

Aprèss-ski/nightlife

The on-mountain **Slalom Pub** has been renovated and has happy hour from 4-6 p.m., dinner, live entertainment and games. Your other choice is to head to nearby **Magog,** where a variety of pubs and restaurants line the main street. Simply walk along until you find a place that meets your fancy.

Mont Sutton Facts

Summit elevation: 3,175 feet
Vertical drop: 1,500 feet
Base elevation: 1,675 feet
Address: 671, chemin Maple, Sutton, PQ Canada J0E 2K0
Area code: 450
Ski area phone: 538-2545
Toll-free reservations: (800) 663-0214
Snow report: (514) 866-7639
Fax: 538-0080
E-mail: Through the Web sites
Internet: www.montsutton.com (resort); www.sutton-info.qc.ca (town & township)

Number and types of lifts: 9–1 high-speed quad, 2 quads, 6 doubles
Skiable acreage: 174 acres
Snowmaking: 60 percent
Uphill capacity: 11,800 per hour
Snowboarding: Yes, unlimited
Bed Base: About 650 in Sutton (275 rooms)
Nearest lodging: Slopeside
Resort child care: Yes; 2 years to 5 years
Adult ticket, per day: $25.21-34.78 (2000/01 CdnS)

Expert: ★★★★
Advanced: ★★★★ **Intermediate:** ★★★★
Beginner: ★★★★ **Never-ever:** ★★★

Mont Sutton

A trip to Mont Sutton is a step back in time. The resort made its debut in 1960 and still has some of its original chair lifts, which you board after working your way through a lift line of wooden fences and passing ticket-checker booths that look like little red-trimmed log cabins. All around you, skiers and riders decked out in the latest gear and apparel chatter away in French. Which reminds us to tell you that Mont Sutton and the nearby town may just be one of the friendliest places we've ever visited. Everyone seems to know everyone, and if they don't know you, they act like they do. By the way, just say *bonjour* or *merci* and everyone happily switches to English (yes, your accent *will* give you away!).

At first glance, Mont Sutton appears to be a small area, but it skis like a large resort. Trails and glades take you all over the mountain before reaching the bottom. Ability levels are generally separated from each other—beginner terrain is on the far right, intermediate terrain is in the middle, and expert terrain is to the far left. Two lifts in the middle of the mountain also serve beginner terrain.

Glades, or *sous-bois,* clearly set this mountain apart from others. They are thinned enough to groom—not often, because they're most fun in the powder. The glades were cut in 1960, long before other resorts even thought of such a thing. Trails follow the true fall line. You're constantly winding your way down the mountain. Trails are also usually left *au naturel*—only 13 are groomed nightly, and fewer than that on a powder day. Are you getting the message yet? This charming retro resort gets a lot of powder, and that's what the skiers here like, so the owners don't mess with it. Speaking of the owners, the same family that opened the resort still runs it, with great affection and respect for the mountain and its guests.

Mountain layout–Skiing

We'd be doing you a real disservice if we told you to use a trail map while skiing this mountain. Our usual MO of telling you which trails to ski and which ones to skip is meaningless.

The locals are proud to say you can ski this mountain for years and never come down the same way. And we believe it! For truly, the way to ski this mountain is to merely follow where your skis take you, and they take you to a different place every time. No one here skis just one run to the bottom, they slip into glades and cut under lifts and dart down the bottom sections of trails and catch air over boulders, usually skiing at least four trails and sous-bois before reaching the bottom. It's an exhilarating experience, whether you're a beginner or an expert. And the separation of ability levels ensures you won't end up somewhere you shouldn't be.

Mountain layout–Snowboarding

Mont Sutton has a Skill Zone, or terrain park, but most riders are here for the natural terrain. You won't be disappointed either: You'll find natural river beds, boulders, drop-offs, trees and dips. And no flats. This mountain really wants you to ride it!

Lessons

One of the country's best technical ski instructors, Guy Duquette, is director of the Ski and Snowboard School. He has been a member of the Canadian Exhibition Team at Interski, which consists of CSIA's top 10 technical ski instructors, since 1987.

Group lessons: A four-hour lesson costs $45.

Never-ever package: The learn-to-ski package costs $29.95 and includes a one-hour lesson, rentals and lifts; learn-to-snowboard costs $39.95. Reservations required. The program allows for three lessons at this price.

Private lessons: One-hour lessons cost $38, each additional person is $12. Also six hours of lessons for the price of five, $190.

Special programs: Ski or snowboard week is 16 hours of lessons, video instruction, racing and awards. Minimum of four per group. $274 for adults, ages 65 and older pay $229.

Child care

Ages: 2 to 5 years.
Costs: Full day, $16; and $3 per hour. Parents are responsible for picking up their children for lunch.
Reservations: Required.
Children's lessons: Kids 3-5 years old are introduced with a daycare program that includes two hours of lessons. Full day, $49 (parents responsible for lunch); half day, $29. Equipment is extra. Kids 6 years and older sign up for adult classes and will be grouped by age (see *Lessons* above). Ski or snowboard week for ages 6-17 includes 16 hours of lessons, video instruction, friendly race and awards. Minimum of four per group. Cost is $229.

Lift tickets

	Adult	Junior (6-17)
One day	$34.78	$24.34
Three days	$88.67	$61.73
Five days	$126.06	$86.94

Who skis free: Kids ages 5 and younger.
Who skis at a discount: Ages 65 and older ski for junior rates.

Dining: $$$-Entrees $20+; $$-$10-20; $-less than $10.
Accommodations: (double room) $$$$-$200+; $$$-$141-$200; $$-$81-$140; $-$80 and less.

Accommodations

You can book your Sutton-area lodging through **Sutton Accommodation,** a separate entity from Mont Sutton, by calling 1-800-663-0214, extension 4.

The only slopeside accommodations are found at a charming 28-room inn, reminiscent of a Swiss chalet, the **Auberge La Paimpolaise** (800-263-3213, 450-538-3213; $; ✕ Ⓟ◉). After a tough day on the slopes, head to the large outdoor Jacuzzi and ask one of the friendly staff to bring you a tasty local beer.

Just down the road, **Auberge des Appalaches** (877-533-5799, 450-538-5799; $; ✕ Ⓟ◉) is a cozy inn owned by long-time locals Micheline Côté and Daniel Martin, who do everything possible to make you feel at home. There are 13 tastefully decorated rooms with private baths and stunning views. The couple guides evening snowshoe tours for guests on Park Sutton's trails, which are accessed from their property. They also have snow tubing and snow volleyball.

The picturesque **Auberge West Brome** (888-902-7663, 450-266-7552; $$-$$$$) is about 10 minutes away in West Brome. This upscale country inn has hotel rooms as well as one- and two-bedroom condo suites with a nice-sized kitchen, fireplace and balcony that are great for families. Some suites also have whirlpool baths. Breakfast is delivered to your room or condo.

Dining

Mont Sutton has four **cafeterias,** two at the summit of lifts and two at the base. Our favorite is Altitude 840 m., where you can have pulled pork and fries in front of a roaring fireplace while you look out at the valley below.

Auberge La Paimpolaise (450-538-3213; $$) is a casual restaurant in a Swiss-style chalet that serves yummy regional and European cuisine. It can get very busy since it's at the base of Mont Sutton, but there's a lively apres-ski bar for a drink while you're waiting. **Auberge des Appalaches** (450-538-5799; $$) is another casual restaurant that serves fine European cuisine. No wonder, the chef is from Paris. Ask for a table next to a window so you can watch the sunset. **Auberge West Brome** (450-266-7552; $$-$$$), a rustic turn-of-the-century farmhouse in nearby West Brome, provides an intimate but casual setting for friends and family. One of our staffer's kids had his first French culinary experience here, and he'll probably never want mac & cheese again. Try the West Brome lamb, which is less gamey than that found in the United States. A wonderful plus, you can choose from five kinds of sauces for your meat or seafood: five pepper, peanut, Thai, satai or Indian.

Aprèss-ski/nightlife

The slopeside **Auberge La Paimpolaise** is the obvious place to head. The apres-ski crowd here is loud and lively. Make sure to ask about the local beers. **Auberge des Appalaches,** just down the road, also has several tasty local beers on hand, plus loads of toys and board games for people of all ages, perfect for families or groups looking for friendly competition and laughter.

Regional cross-country and snowshoeing

Parc du Mont-Orford (819-843-9855) has 87 km. of trails for both classic and skating. Upon entering the Mont Orford entrance to the park, turn right to Le Cerisier Visitor's Center. Trails range from flat and gentle alongside a lake to steep and challenging as they climb up Mont Chauve. Snowshoers and winter hikers are welcome. Cross-country gear and snowshoe rentals are available. Trail fees are Cdn $9.

Park Sutton (450-538-4085) has 20 km. of snowshoeing trails and 40 km. of cross-country skiing trails. Winter hikers also are welcome. The trail network was founded by Daniel Martin, who owns the Auberge des Appalaches just down the road from Mont Sutton. Stop by the auberge to get trail maps (Cdn$3) and access the trail network.

Regional other activities

The Eastern Townships Association puts out a terrific tourist guide, so make sure to pick one up. Here are just a few of the things to do:

There's **tubing** and an **ice skating rink** at the base of Owl's Head. **Au Diable Vert** (888-779-9090, 450-538-5639) in Glen Sutton provides guided snowshoeing, backcountry skiing and dogsledding. **Les Randonnèes Jacques Robidas** (888-677-8767, 819-563-0166) in North Hatley has horse-drawn sleigh rides and dogsledding, by reservation only. Book a half-day or more for dogsledding and learn how to mush your own team.

Local entrepreneur J. Armand Bombardier invented the snowmobile, so there's plenty of **snowmobiling** trails: The most popular is a 466-mile circuit (750 km.) of trails called J.-A.-Bombardier Tour. There's a total of 1,243 miles (2,000 km.) of trails. Pay for an access pass to the trails (your lodging has information on where to purchase one). You'll probably also appreciate the **Musée J. Armand Bombardier** (450-532-5300) in Valcourt, a museum dedicated to Bombardier's life and the sport's history. On weekdays you can tour the adjacent Bombardier factory.

Breathtakingly beautiful **Saint-Benoît-du-Lac Abbey** (819-843-4080), overlooking Lake Memphremagog is where Benedictine monks have lived a contemplative life since 1912. You can buy Abbey-made products such as cheese and apple cider, as well as religious items. Eucharist is celebrated daily at 11 a.m. in Gregorian chant. Winter hours Monday-Friday, 9-10:45 a.m. and 1:30-4:30 p.m.; Saturdays, 9-10:45 a.m. and 11:45 a.m.-4:30 p.m.

There are **museums** for everything from the art of chocolate to the art of communications. Local **vineyards** are open for tastings and guided tours (some have only French-speaking tours). **Shop** till you drop. We found wonderful boutique shops selling everything from antiques to handcrafted items. One of our favorites is **René Henquin's Chocolaterie** on Principale South in Sutton.

Getting there and getting around

By air: Fly into Montreal's Dorval International Airport or Burlington (VT) International Airport. If you arrive from outside Canada, you'll need a passport or birth certificate for customs. You'll need to rent a car either way.

By car: If you're coming from the United States, you'll need a birth certificate to cross the border. The resorts are fairly spread out, and the travel directions vary considerably according to where you're going. The best bet is to ask your lodging for directions and/or print off a map from the resort's or lodging's Web site. Access from the major northeastern U.S. metro areas is relatively easy, via interstates 89, 91 and 93. Here's a general rule of thumb for travel time: The resorts are about an hour from Montreal, one to two hours from Burlington, four to five hours from Boston, and six to seven hours from New York.

Getting around: You'll need a car. Everything is spread out, and you'll want to explore the surrounding area and visit the various resorts.

Dining: $$$-Entrees $20+; $$-$10-20; $-less than $10.
Accommodations: (double room) $$$$-$200+; $$$-$141-$200; $$-$81-$140; $-$80 and less.

Owl's Head; (450) 292-3342

Internet: www.owlshead.com

8 lifts—2 high-speed quads, 6 doubles; Skiable acreage, 86; 1,772 feet vertical

The minute you get off the lift, any lift, you'll be awestruck by the fabulous views from the top of this little mountain that rises above a rather flat section of the region. Lake Memphremagog is below the base, and you often feel as if you'll ski right off the edge of the mountain into the lake. No kidding, the magnificent views are comparable to skiing in the Tahoe region of California. This is a lovely little mountain perfect for families and groups that want gentle skiing and nicely groomed trails. However, it is small, and most will not want to ski here for an entire week unless you have young children. Owl's Head is named after the Abenaki Indian's greatest chief, Owl, whose spirit will live forever through the naming of the mountain in his honor.

◆◆ **Expert** ◆ **Advanced**: Owl's Head has some steeps, but they're short, which means that experts will get bored quickly, but advanced skiers will find a few ways to test themselves. The narrow Grand Allée reaches 47 degrees and "The Wall of Death" on Colorado reaches 43 degrees. Newport Express, a short, narrow double-diamond, is known to locals as Higgins' Hazzard, after an instructor from nearby Jay Peak, VT, who broke body parts several different times here (don't worry, he seems to be the only one who can't get this run down right).

■ **Intermediate**: Lily's Leap is a must-ski: As it winds down the mountain from the top it offers amazing views of the lake far below. Centennial, which meanders across the mountain and provides access to virtually every other run on the mountain, is loads of fun. When you're ready to challenge yourself, try the single-diamond trails.

●● Beginner ● Never-ever: This mountain is well-suited for beginners and never-evers. While some beginner runs feed higher-level skiers to the base, there are no hotshots here. You won't find beginner trails from the top, so head to wide-open Chouette and Panorama for magnificent views of the lake. Proficient beginners will want to go to the top and take Lily's Leap.

For snowboarders, Owl's Head boasts of having the longest terrain park in the Eastern Townships. You'll find a halfpipe, quarterpipes, snow-whales, beams and rails. Carvers will have a field day on this mountain, as most trails are wide-open and some have dips where you can catch air. Lily's Leap has one flat section about a third of the way down, so make sure to carry your speed (you'll see it in plenty of time to prepare yourself).

Lift tickets: Adults, Cdn$30–32, Juniors (6–13), Cdn$20

Lodging information: Owl's Head Auberge (800-363-3342, 450-292-3342; $-$$; ✕ Ⓟ☻) has 20 rooms on the top floor of the base lodge. The meal plan includes breakfast in the cafeteria and dinner in the dining room. **Owl's Head Apartment Hotel** (800-363-3342, 450-292-3318; $-$$; Ⓟ☻) has 36 units, ranging from 1 to 3 bedrooms. Condos have a fully equipped kitchen and fireplace, most have a balcony. Guests have access to a solarium lounge and mini-spa with whirlpool and sauna, as well as a laundry room.

See Eastern Townships Accommodation section as well.

Bromont; (450) 534-2200

Internet: www.skibromont.com

4 lifts—1 high-speed quad, 2 doubles, 1 surface lift; 174 skiable acres; 1,329 feet vertical

This is the place to go if you like night skiing and riding. About 75 percent of the terrain, including the Free Zone terrain park, is lit for night skiing, which goes till 10 p.m. Sunday through Thursday and 10:30 p.m. Friday and Saturday. Its close proximity to Montreal ensures steady business and a lively night life.

Although the trail map is dominated by diamonds, the trails are really intermediate. Experts and advanced skiers will find that the cruisers are a great way to give tired legs a break after skiing hard all week at Mont Orford or Mont Sutton. Grooming is meticulous, and on weekends, trails are groomed three times a day. The mountain has a lower elevation than other resorts in the area, so it often rains here when it snows elsewhere. Bromont gives you 30 minutes to test conditions—if you're not pleased, exchange your ticket for a coupon to return at no extra charge. Most skiers will want to spend only a day here because of limited terrain.

◆◆ **Expert** ◆ **Advanced**: Montreal has a nice steep section, but it's short, plus there's an unnamed woods shot hidden away on skier's right that'll give you a quick adrenaline rush (keep your eyes peeled for the "experts only" warning sign). Don't be fooled by the trail designations. There's no real challenge to speak of here, but you can still have fun if you're with friends and family of a lesser ability.

■ **Intermediate**: Because of the extensive grooming, solid intermediates will be able to ski most, if not all, of the mountain. Coupe de Monde and Knowlton will let you run your skis at maximum speed. Montreal and Cowansville have some surprising changes in pitch that will keep you on your toes. You'll find short sections of some trails are left to bump up, but there's bail-out room if you get intimidated. Head for the bumps at the bottom of St.-Jean to see if you're ready first.

●● **Beginner** ● **Never-ever**: The learning area is on its own peak, Mont Soleil, and is served by a chair lift and a rope tow. The trails here are gentle and will boost any novice's ego. This area gets afternoon sun, a real plus since that's when snow normally firms up on the main mountain. Beginners will want to try Brome, a trail that winds from the top of the main mountain with great views. If you're feeling adventurous, try St.-Bruno and St.-Hubert, which are wide-open, winding trails with pockets of scattered trees.

For snowboarders, the terrain park, Free Zone, has rails, table tops, a quarterpipe and jumps, plus it's lighted for night riding. There's always a lot of activity here, so if you're yearning to learn new tricks or make friends with other riders, this is where you should head. The meticulous grooming on the mountain means lots of fun for riders, whether you're looking to make perfect carving arcs or catch air off plateaus and dips. Beware of the long flat at the bottom of Cowansville and Montreal heading back to the lift. If you're a beginner with some snow time under your belt, you'll enjoy the beginner terrain, which has a steady and sometimes rolling pitch without flats to stop you dead in your tracks. If you're a never-ever, you might want to learn to ride elsewhere so you can avoid the rope tow.

Lift tickets: Adults, Cdn$36; Juniors (6–13) Cdn$21.

Lodging information: Le Château Bromont (800-304-3433, 819-534-3433; $$$-$$$$; ✕⚲⌂🄿🍷🛎🏊) gives you luxury without airs, creating a delightfully elegant atmosphere and experience just minutes from the slopes. Some rooms have fireplaces and whirlpools. Don't miss out on the variety of treatments available at the Spa.

See Eastern Townships Accommodation section for more options.

Tremblant

Québec, Canada

Summit elevation: 3,001 feet
Vertical drop: 2,131 feet
Base elevation: 870 feet

Address: 3005, Chemin Principal
Mont-Tremblant, Quebec, Canada JOT 1Z0
☎ **Area code:** 819
Ski area phone: 681-2000
Snow report: (514) 333-8936 (Montreal)
ⓘ **Toll-free information and reservations:**
(800) 461-8711 or (819) 681-2000
Fax: (819) 681-5996
E-mail: info-sac@intrawest.com
Internet: www.tremblant.ca (ski area) or
www.tremblant.com (region)
Expert:★★★ Advanced:★★★★
Intermediate:★★★★
Beginner:★★★★
Never-ever:★★★

Number and types of lifts: 12–1 high-speed,
eight-person gondola; 5 high-speed quads; 1 quad;
3 triples; 3 Magic Carpets
Acreage: 604
Snowmaking: 80 percent
Uphill capacity: 25,530 skiers per hour
Snowboarding: Yes, unlimited
Bed base: 3,500-plus at resort base
Nearest lodging: slopeside, hotel & condos
Resort child care: Yes, 12 months and older
Adult ticket, per day: $53–$54 (2000/01 prices)

Dining:★★★★
Apres-ski/nightlife:★★★
Other activities: ★★★

Tremblant is a French word that has its roots in Algonquin legend. It means Trembling Mountain. The mountain shook, as though by an angry god, from the Laurentian Shield's release from the weight of the arctic glacier.

This is one of the historic peaks in North American skiing. It began in the 1930s — in 1932, if you count Tremblant's founding from its inaugural Kandahar downhill ski race; or in 1938, the hectic year that Philadelphia millionaire Joe Ryan hiked to the top of Mont Tremblant, purchased it and opened North America's second true winter resort (Sun Valley was the first, two years earlier). Tremblant virtually invented the ski week concept-lessons, lodging and parties all packaged as one fun vacation-and a nearby ski area, Gray Rocks also helps to keep that family package concept alive and kicking today.

Tremblant has been redeveloped as a mountain village, 18th-century French town-style, based on the narrow streets, old buildings, cozy restaurants and quaint shops of Old Quebec City. It was designed and built by Intrawest Corporation, a Canadian company that specializes in developing ski-resort base villages.

The complete resort experience includes the old village of Mont Tremblant and the picturesque town of St. Jovite.This experience also includes the Québecois culture and the French language. Though the employees speak English, the native language here is French, and you will earn big smiles from locals if you give it a try. You get all the fun and excitement of trying out a foreign language with none of the frustration of not being understood. Plus, there's little or no jet lag for North Americans. Keep in mind though, that the summit consistently registers the coldest temperatures south of Hudson's Bay.

Note: In its marketing materials, Tremblant lists most of its prices—lift tickets, lessons, lodging and the like—without taxes added. We have done the math for the lift ticket section, but in most other sections, you'll need to calculate the 7-percent federal Goods and Services Tax (GST) *and* the 7.5-percent Québec provincial tax.

 ## Mountain layout

Tremblant is a hulk of a mountain with skiing on four faces. The trail map proclaims "north" and "south" sides, but these sides would be more accurately portrayed with designations "northeast" and "southwest." It is easy for skiers to follow the sun: Simply ski on the "north side" in the mornings to catch the sun and then move to the "south side" for the afternoons.

Two years ago the resort added a true south face, called Versant Soleil, with 15 intermediate and advanced trails and glades. Most trails are groomed daily, but since fully 60 percent of the new area consists of gladed runs, don't expect buffed snow in the woods.

Most skiers and boarders start from the South Side, where the base village is. However, on crowded days many savvy locals make the 15-minute drive to the parking lot on the north side of the mountain where they can avoid the crowds and get first crack at skiing in the sun.

◆ **Expert:** The most challenging sections of the mountain are in the sectors called The Edge and Versant Soleil. The Edge is reached by the Letendre trail, which starts halfway down the North Side and brings skiers to the base of the Edge fixed-quad chair. This chair serves only expert and advanced terrain. only one trail, Action, is cut; the other descents are through the trees. The gladed skiing in Reaction and Sensation is cut wide enough for strong intermediates, but the glades dropping to the right down Emotion will push experts to their limits. Also on the north Side are Tremblant's major bump runs and super steeps. If you want to drop down steep bumps, try Dynamite, the steepest in eastern Canada, and Expo, beneath the lift and wide enough for big wipeouts. The drop down Devil's River and into the woods at Boiling Kettle also is a rush.

Versant Soleil, accessed by the Le Soleil lift, is 80-percent expert with the bonus of sunshine. Black and double-black runs take you through fall-line glades.

◆ **Advanced:** For the most part, the single blacks are excellent choices for advanced skiers and riders, especially those who are just moving up a category from intermediate. However, we found quite a range among Tremblant's single-black diamond trails: some a challenge worthy of the rating, such as Banzai and Le Tunnel; others that could have been rated blue-square cruisers, such as Géant; and Dernier Cri, that we thought barely deserved a blue rating, at least the day we skied it.

Double-blacks deserve their rating. In the past, Tremblant has used an overlapping double-black diamond symbol that doesn't look that much different than the single black symbol. It looked more like a fat single diamond, or as if the printer didn't quite get things lined up on the second run through the press. Anyway, if you weren't careful, it was possible to end up on something above your ability. We've been told this will not be the case this season, but were warning you just in case the change doesn't get made.

There are steep drops off the catwalk down Vertige (a double diamond) and Dunzee. They are easily avoided, if you prefer. Ryan is one of the original trails, narrow and twisting with short, very manageable stretches of steeps that earn its lower section a double diamond. Ryan is very much like an old-fashioned New England ski trail, but it's nothing compared to Dynamite; consider it a narrow advanced cruiser. But if you think Ryan is challenging at the top, you can bail out on blue-square Charron before you get to the narrow part.

■ **Intermediate:** On the South Side, Grand Prix, Beauvallon and Alpine are great wide-open cruising runs. The Curé Deslauriers trail, toward the lower part of the mountain, has been contoured to form snow waves; it's kind of a skier's terrain park. Kandahar, though rated black, is groomed. It has one fairly steep section, but is a good choice for an upper-intermediates. At the end of the day, Johannsen-a short blue stretch at the base-gets bumped up and/or mushy, depending on temperatures.

The North Side appears tough on the trail map, but is more intermediate than advanced. Stick to the far right or far left and you can't go wrong. Géant, Coyote, and Duncan Haut are all fine for confident intermediates, and in some respects, are better than Beauchemin and Lowell Thomas, which are rated blue and get a lot more traffic.

Intermediates can ski the Le Soleil lift on a blue from the top down Franc Sud and Tobaggan, which runs into Tapecul to the bottom of Le Soleil lift. You can continue down La Carriole and along the run-out, Sentier des Pruches, right to the upper village.

●● **Beginner:** Le p'tit bonheur takes beginners from the top of the North Side to the easiest mid-mountain trails. Still, most will stick to the South Side. From the top of the Flying Mile lift, beginners head left to La Passe and Nansen bas or they can head right down Standard and Biere-en-bas (named after a shortcut secretly cut by a racer when the staff would race down at the end of the day for beers; winner got to drink for free). Finally, take the big step to the top of the mountain and make wedge turns and stem-christies down La Crîte and all of Nansen. All in all this is a fantastic area to start, but stick to Nansen or Roy Scott at the end of the day to avoid the crowds.

● **Never-ever:** Novices start on the free Magic Carpet lifts near the bell (the ski school meeting place). After never-evers master the terrain served by the Magic Carpets, they advance to the Flying Mile lift and Nansen.

 ## Mountain layout: Snowboarding

"Le surf des neiges," which English speakers know as snowboarding, is welcome on all trails, and rentals and lessons are available. Tremblant has Gravity Park for boarders on the North Side. The area is groomed by the state-of-the-art Scorpion snowpark grooming machine and has a halfpipe, rails, tables and jumps and bumps. The park is reached by, and runs alongside of, the Lowell Thomas lift. The end of the run flattens out, so most boarders walk back up. Boarders also ride The Edge and Versant Soleil for the glades.

Mountain rating

Because of the near-continuous fall line with little run-out at the base, Tremblant skis even bigger than it is. The mountain is good for experts, great for advanced and intermediate skiers (though we're still a bit puzzled over some of the trail ratings), very good for beginners and acceptable for never-evers.

We recently visited during February and were impressed with the work of groomers and snowmakers. We heard many stories of days when the mercury drops well below zero (and that's Fahrenheit we're talking about). Bring warm clothes. We've also visited in late January, when the snow phone reported severe winds and only one lift open. Weather can be brutal. Call ahead and be prepared to spa or shop; customer service will give you a break on your lift ticket.

Nearby skiing: Gray Rocks

Gray Rocks is a mouse compared to Tremblant: It has 620 feet of vertical and four chair lifts. When you stand at Tremblant's summit, you can see Gray Rocks' 22 compact runs a few miles in the distance. It may look small, but Gray Rocks is a mouse that roars. Good trail planning and maintenance makes Gray Rocks ski like a much bigger mountain. Trails wrap around the mountain, rather than plunge straight down, and they incorporate the natural features of the terrain.

This is one of the best learning mountains in North America, and Gray Rocks has capitalized on that strength by carving out a big slice of the student skier market. The success of its Learn-to-Ski Week is overwhelming, with thousands of North Americans taking lessons every season. Lessons are not only for timid never-evers. Skiers of every level are faced with a challenging week of perfecting technique. Ski Weeks have been offered since 1951 and include everything: lodging, meals, instruction, video analysis, lift tickets, access to Le Spa fitness center and indoor pool, gratuities, a souvenir pin and photo, and full social calendar and activities.

Part of the success is creating group camaraderie, on and off the slopes. Since people learn best when they are relaxed and having fun, Gray Rocks considers its off-slope program as important as the lessons on the hill. Nightly entertainment, oui. But aprËs-ski also has such creative alternatives as a cooking course, French lessons, wine-and-cheese get-togethers, classical guitar concerts, sleigh rides, a spa and fitness center-the list goes on. Gray Rocks has a day care and "Ski'N'Play" program for children, and it even has a pet kennel.

Gray Rocks also offers an all-inclusive "ski getaway" (room, meals, entertainment, gratuities, skiing, fitness center), with the option to add lessons and clinics.

The best deal here is a package, in which lift tickets valid at Gray Rocks and its sister resort, Mont Blanc, are included (call 800-567-6767 for reservations). Ski Week prices range from $1,125-$1,960 (Cdn$; 00/01 prices) per person, double occupancy, depending on the time of year. (Single occupancy is available for $1,280-$1,955.)

 ## Cross-country and snowshoeing

Canadians have serious winters so they definitely take all of their winter sports seriously. Case in point: the abundant and varied cross-country choices available to visitors to the Tremblant region.

More than 260 km. of cross-country trails are scattered in the region, most of which are found in Parc du Mont-Tremblant (688-2281). A ski pass is $15 at Parc du Mont Tremblant. Trails wind through maple and birch forests and provide views of wildlife and lakes.

There are two networks of marked, patrolled and groomed trails. The La Diable network has nine trails totaling 56 km. with six heated huts along the way. The La Pimbina network has seven trails, 30 km. all together, with two heated huts. Trail fees are $10 for adults and $6 for children younger than 12, those ages 65 and older and anyone in a group of 20 or more. Snowshoeing trail passes are $4. Skis and snowshoes are available for rent, and you can also arrange a trip on marked but ungroomed trails to backcountry bunkhouses.

To get away from all civilization, except for a few strategically located heated huts, head to the Parc du Mont-Tremblant and plan to make a day of it (or two days if winter camping and "an intense encounter with our Quebec winter," as they put it, appeals to you).

This vast reserve offers two reception centers, complete with ski and snowshoe rentals and 150 km. of marked and groomed trails. Pack a lunch and ski out to one of the heated huts;

trail loops of varying degrees of difficulty and length may be chosen. If you're lucky, trail guides will stop by a hut to tell you more about the history and the wildlife of the region.

The Domaine St-Bernard is owned by the Mont-Tremblant Municipality. It offers a network of 110 km. of trails, with 50 km. double-tracked and 12 km. skate groomed. The undulating trails are known for their magnificent vistas, but, alas for the novice skier, the majority of these vantage points are located on diamond and double-diamond trails.

Choose in-village, inn-to-inn trails in the Mont Tremblant/St. Jovite region, a wilderness trek in the nearby Parc du Mont-Tremblant or experience the longest linear park in North America, the 200-kilometer "Le P'tit Train du Nord," that runs from Saint-Jerome through Mont Tremblant to Mont-Laurier. St. Jerome to Ste. Agathe is for cross-country skiing, and Ste. Agathe to Mt. Laurier is for snowmobiling.

Popular choices for the average cross country skier, who will still get his or her share of magnificent views and occasional sightings of wildlife, include the winding Domaine St. Bernard, the Jack Rabbit and skiing on the Gray Rocks golf course. A portion of Le P'tit Train du Nord linear park is also incorporated into these trails.

Lessons (2001/02prices in Cdn$, taxes not included)

Group lessons: $46 for a 90-minute session, two sessions offered each morning; $41 for afternoon. Group lessons are one instructor with four students, making it easy for instructors to give tips while riding Tremblant's gondola.

Never-ever package (lifts, lesson and rentals): Discover Skiing and Snowboarding, also called Magic Trax 1, costs $59 for a morning lesson, $49 in the afternoon. Magic Trax 2 takes beginners to the mountaintop. It's $69 in the morning, $59 in the afternoon.

Private lessons: $89 for a morning hour, $72 in the afternoon.

Special programs: Ski Week is 14 hours of skiing or snowboarding with the same instructor for $217. The program also includes a welcome reception, race, dinner and souvenir video tape. Book at least seven days in advance for a discount.

All private or group instruction can be taken on normal skis, shaped skis, snowboard or Snowblades.

Racing: The Chrono-Course is open every day on Promenade.

Child care (2001/02 prices, Cdn$, without taxes)

Ages: 12 months to 6 years.

Costs: $32 for a half-day, $38 for a half-day with lunch. $49 for a full day, including lunch. Multi-day packages, with lunch, are $45 per day.

Reservations: Call (888) 736-2526. Or, check with the concierge at your hotel or condo for babysitting services that come to your room.

The Kidz Club is at the base of the gondola lift, adjacent to the Magic Carpet beginner's lift and hill.

Children's lessons: Ages 3-12 pay $83 for a full day, including lunch. Tremblant offers Kids Ski Weekends (7 hours over two days) for $166 for 3- and 4-year olds, $153 for 5- to 12-year-olds, lunch included, and Ski Weeks (four days with lunch included) for $287 for ages 3-4, $265 for ages 4-12. Note: you can save up to 13 percent on these programs if you reserve at least seven days in advance. All children's instructors carry radio phones so that they can be located quickly in case of an emergency, and pagers are offered to parents. Prices for all children's programs are lower if pre-booked, call (888) 736-2526.

Lift tickets (prices in Cdn$, with taxes)

	Adult	Child (6-12)
One day	$55	$30
Three days	$161 ($53+/day)	$87 ($29/day)
Five days	$265 ($53/day)	$144 ($28+/day)

Who skis free: Children 5 and younger. The Magic Carpet beginner's lift also is free.
Who skis at a discount: Skiers 65 and older pay $40. Students aged 13–17 ski for $40.
Note: These are prices rounded to the nearest Canadian dollar. These prices include the 7 percent federal GST and the 7.5 percent provincial tax in this section.

Accommodations

Tremblant Reservation Call Center (800-461-8711) can reserve anything at the resort: lodging, lessons, child care, health club. **Mont Tremblant Reservations** can book all lodging and has good travel, lodging and ski packages. Call (800) 567-6760, or dial 425-8681. We list lodging choices in the base-area village, but there are less expensive alternatives nearby.

The lodging-lift package prices we list with each hotel or condo are five-day, per-person, based on double occupancy and do not include taxes. (Two- and three-day packages also are available.) We list a range, based on season and size of unit, from the smallest unit in value-plus season (early December and mid-April) to the largest unit at holiday season.

Staying in the base village is the way to go. At the upper end of the village, the full-service Fairmont hotel, **Fairmont Tremblant** (800-441-1414 or 681-7000; $$$–$$$$ ♿✗⌂🄿🍴🏊🎿🛏), is a magnificent stone and timber structure with ski-in/walk-out access, shops and restaurants, as well as a health club with indoor and outdoor heated pools, whirlpools, sauna, steam baths and an exercise room.

The new **Westin Hotel** (Telephone??; $$$$) is the only five star hotel in the Mont Tremblant village. Opened in August of 2000, this 126-room property has an outdoor saltwater pool, 24-hour room service and a world-class spa.

The **Marriott Residence Inn, Manoir Labelle** (888-272-4000 or 681-4000; $$$–$$$$ ♿✗⌂🄿🍴🎿🛏) is at the lower end of the village.

La Tour Des Voyageurs (800-461-8711; $$$–$$$$) is a condominium hotel adjacent to the Cabriolet lift with ski-in/ski out access, a swimming pool, whirlpool and exercise room.

The **Kandahar Resort Hotel** and the slopeside **Lodge de la Montagne** (800-461-8711; $$$–$$$$), house deluxe condominium units, many with gas fireplaces.

Lining the cobblestoned street that leads from the Chateau to La Tour Des Voyageurs are three- to four-story buildings that house restaurants and shops on the ground floor and condominiums above. The **Saint Bernard, Johannsen** and **Deslauriers** condos (800-461-8711; $$–$$$) are very roomy and beautifully furnished.

Other condo complexes are within two miles and have shuttle service to the slopes. **Pinoteau Village** (800-667-2200; $$$–$$$$ 🚲🄿🍴🎿🛏🍴) and **Condotels du Village** (800-567-6724; $–$$ 🄿🎿) have kitchens, balconies and fireplaces. Pinoteau Village has cross-country trails outside its doors, while the Condotels have a clubhouse with a sauna, hot tub, small exercise room and pool table.

Mont Tremblant Reservations also can book the **Club Tremblant** (800-567-8341; $$$–$$$$ 🚲✗⌂🄿🍴🎿🛏🍴), where rates include breakfast and dinner, as well as lodging and lifts; **Gray Rocks** (800-567-6767; $$–$$$$ ♿⌂🄿🛏🎿), which has its own small ski area

Dining: $$$-Entrees $20+; $$-$10-20; $-less than $10.
Accommodations: (double room) $$$$-$200+; $$$-$141-$200; $$-$81-$140; $-$80 and less.

and specializes in the all-inclusive, heavy-on-socializing Ski Week; the luxurious **Intrawest Resort Club** (800-799-3258; $$–$$$$ ⚥ ⊑ 🄿⚡🆒⊛) or several condos, cozy inns, inexpensive motels and historic lodges in the villages of Mont Tremblant and St. Jovite.

Hotel packages at the resort include a passport in the value season. This includes four hours of snow toy trials, one overnight ski tuneup, 90 minutes of ski tips with an instructor and free Kidz Club for children ages 6 and younger. Advanced reservations are required.

For budget travelers, The 84-bed **Mont-Tremblant Youth Hostel** (425-6008; $) offers four- to 10-bed dorm rooms as well as private rooms; all with shared baths. The lodge is in the village of Mont-Tremblant, just 3 kilometers from the mountain, and a shuttle (fee) stops at the front door. A fully-equipped kitchen is available, but the hostel offers an inexpensive Continental breakfast. Guests can relax in a common room with TV, a reading room with library and Internet access or the English pub with pool table. The pub serves alcohol and is open to guests only.

Dining

Most of the restaurants have moderately priced food, and you can have lunch-type foods for supper, if you like. At the foot of the Gondola Express in the pedestrian village, there are a number of outdoor BBQ venues, in the springtime. At their daily outside grills you can get a hot dog with chips, hamburgers or grilled chicken for less than $5. Most restaurants on the Place St. Bernard have an outdoor grill blazing on a sunny day with snacks and drinks.

Near the Place St. Bernard: At the **Cafe Johannsen at Mt. Tremblant** you can get soups, bagels, salads, beers, coffee and muffins. **Les Delices du St. Bernard** (681-4555; $–$$) is a deli offering cheeses, patés and cold cuts, sandwiches, fresh breads and other dishes.

For the town's best coffee, visit **Au Grain de Café** (681-4567; $) that also serves pastries not far off the plaza.

The atmosphere at **Mexicali Rosa's** (681-2439; $$–$$$) is cozy-ethnic, but the food is fair, especially for those who live in the Southwest. Try the deep-fried ice cream, if you dare, or concentrate on the sangria and margaritas.

Le Shack Resto-bar (681-4700; $–$$) has a breakfast buffet and is *the* spot for people-watching during lunch or an after-ski beer or two. **In Vieux-Tremblant: Cafe Bistro Ryan** (681-4994; $–$$) is for late-night munchies, open from 7 a.m. to 4 a.m!

The three owners of **Creperie Catherine** (681-4888; $) used to cook aboard ships. Now, they offer Bretonne-style crepes with any kind of filling you could possibly dream up in a delightful indoor/outdoor building. It's a great stop for breakfast and desserts. The Chocolate Blast is a favorite sweet crepe.

Microbrasserie La Diable (681-4546; $–$$), or "Microbrewery of the She-devil," serves light meals of European sausages alongside their six unique craft beers, brewed right on the premises. Be sure to note alcohol percentages listed on the menu as well and order accordingly. Don't mistake a 4 percent Diable for an 8.5 percent Extreme Onction!

La Savoie (681-4573; $$) serves traditional French Alps fare in a cozy French Alpine setting. Everything on their menu is "all-you-can-eat" and prices are per person. Strictly for an elegant yet relaxed lunch and dinner. The communal dining experience is great.

La Grappe a Vin ($–$$) is an intimate wine bar where you can order 40 wines by the glass and another 130 by the bottle; choose from 20 ports, 50 scotches and 30 imported beers. In addition an oyster bar, wild game pates, local cheeses, fresh soups and salads are available. It's fun après-ski and perfect for a light dinner.

If you're after a true feast, the high end **Soto** (681-4141;$$$) in the new Westin hotel specializes in Japanese cuisine with emphasis on sushi, sashimi and maki.

The **Pizzatéria** (681-4522; $$) has such enticing garlicky, spicy flavors floating from their doors, you'd be hard-pressed not to stop in. Order to take out or be seen on their strategically placed outdoor deck, perfect people-watching territory.

La Chouquetterie (681-4508; $), which translates as sugar tree. Their specialty is the cream puff, Tropez style. One can hardly bring one's self to bite into such beautiful art.

Queues de Castor (681-4678; $), also known as Beavertails, is a tiny take-out spot. Order the traditional Canadian pastry called a Beavertail (because that's what it looks like).

The **Coco Pazzo Deli** (681-4774; $) is an Italian gourmet deli that sells cheeses, salamis, prosciutto and many kinds of dry pastas. It's around the corner from their restaurant, also called **Coco Pazzo** ($$) where the menu includes roasted rack of lamb, spice rubbed and grilled veal chop and herb-encrusted sea bass as well as an interesting variety of pastas.

Le Gascon (681-4606; $–$$) serves traditional French-style bistro food. Sample offerings at their wine bar or sit outside on their corner terrace overlooking Lake Miroir.

The Laurentians are known for their smoked meats. **Moe's** (425-9821; $–$$) in nearby St. Jovite is rated the best in the region for that specialty.

On the hill: The non-smoking **Grand Manitou**, on top at 3,000 feet (the highest peak in the Laurentians), should satisfy most appetites. It features a meal of the day, for $7 and $10, sandwiches to order, pizza, sandwiches to order, fries and hot dogs.

Après-ski/nightlife

We list these in order from the quieter, mellow spots to the noisy party places. Since many of the hot spots also are restaurants, see the Dining section for more information.

On sunny days, the best après-ski is in the **Place St. Bernard**, where a stage often is set up with a live band cranking out the tunes. People sit in chairs with a brew and enjoy the sun, listen to the music and watch everyone looking for their friends.

La Grappe a Vin is the place to go for fine wine or liquors and light fare.

The mountaintop bar in the **Grand Manitou** is open for après-ski.

Microbrasserie La Diable has canned music, good sausages for late-night snacks and six beers brewed on the premises. Blues bands play every Friday and Saturday.

Le Shack is a bit louder and often has a live band on the weekends. Selected the "wildest après-ski" by *Ski Canada* in 1996, the dancing never stops. Shooters are served in the traditional Québec glass ski boot.

Cafe de l'Epoque in Vieux Tremblant sports strobe lights, loud live music (also CDs) and lots of bodies pressed together on the crowded rustic wood dance floor. OK at night, but a bit of a pit when exposed to daylight.

P'tit Caribou is also in Vieux Tremblant and gets high ratings from *Ski Canada*. Great, live, loud music and bar-top dancing. The people and the noise create the party ambience.

Other activities

Shopping: The village has about 60 shops. Some of the fanciest are in the Chateau Mont Tremblant, with a nice café in the middle of the lobby.

The village also has a two-screen **movie theater**. One screen shows a French film, the other a recent Hollywood release. You also can take a **sleigh ride**, go **ice skating** on Lac Miroir, go for a **dogsled ride** (you can mush the dogs yourself) or **snowmo-**

bile ride. The Fairmont Tremblant has a complete **spa** with facials, manicures, massages and the like.

Visit nearby **Le Scandinave** (425-5524) for the true Nordic experience—spend the day steaming, baking and stewing before taking the plunge in the frozen river that runs through this forest retreat. "Finnish" off your stay with a soothing massage.

The **Spa-sur-le-Lac** at Club Tremblant (425-8341) offers a more traditional experience with eleven body care and aesthetic rooms and a beauty salon.

The Source, billed as "A Lake in the Laurentians," lets guests escape winter. This spa includes an exercise room and a lake created to evoke the Laurentian outdoors complete with beach, waterfall and Tarzan-style rope swing as well as indoor and outdoor hot tubs.

To book any activity, call the MTA central reservation numbers: 800 567-6760 or 425-8681. For more information, you can reach the tourist bureau at Tremblant at 425-2434.

Getting there and getting around

By air: Montréal has the nearest major airport, 75 miles away. Air Canada has many direct or non-stop flights from the United States. Northwest Airlines, KLM and most major airlines serve this major international airport.

By car: From Montréal, take autoroute 15 north to Sainte-Agathe, where the 15 merges with 117. Continue on autoroute 117 north past St. Jovite. About two kilometers (a little more than a mile) past the town, at the light, turn right on Montée Ryan (there's an Ultramar gas station on the left). Follow signs to Tremblant.

Getting around: Most visitors arrive by car, so rent one if you fly into Montréal. And then to get some use from the car, we suggest side trips to Mont Tremblant Village and St. Jovite, or even some of the smaller ski areas in the surrounding area.

Packing tip: Bring shoes with good traction. The cobblestone street is fairly steep. Though it has shallow steps built along each side, most people walk in the street (no vehicles are allowed). It can be slippery late at night and early in the morning when melted snow has frozen again.

Other Laurentian resorts

The Valley of Saint-Sauveur encompasses five ski resorts in a big French café au lait cup: Mont Saint-Sauveur, Mont Avila, Ski Morin Heights, Mont Olympia and Ski Mont Gabriel. These five mountains collectively have 93 runs served by a total of 30 lifts and are linked by a free shuttlebus service. One lift ticket is good at all five areas. With 67 illuminated slopes and 3,000,000 watts of lighting, they make up the largest night-skiing/snowboarding terrain in the world. When the sun goes down, every hill in the valley comes alive with a sparkling circular blanket of light.

All areas offer a variety of well-groomed trails to both challenge experts and comfort beginners making it a true family destination. From expert to novice, each area has its own character and small base village, but they all share extensive snowmaking and proximity to the charming little Quebec village of Saint-Sauveur. More than 60 restaurants feature international cuisine for every budget. Packages are available at most lodging facilities, which range from four-star hotels to affordable condos and family-run B& Bs. Nearly 80 shops, fashion boutiques and warehouses satisfy the need to shop and there are three supermarkets in the village for condo guests wanting to cook in. In the evening, rue Principale is the "buzz" with bars, bistros, discos and live music.

Distance from Montreal: Less than an hour's drive from Montreal's International Airport on the Laurentian Autoroute 15 North, which connects to the North American Interstate highway system.

Information: The Valley of Saint-Sauveur Resorts, Saint-Sauveur des Monts, Quebec (450) 227-4671: This number will link you to anything from mountain info to lodging reservations. Although the message is in French, there is an English option. Internet: www.montsaintsauveur.com.

Mont Saint-Sauveur and Mont Avila

9 lifts; 29 trails; 213 meters (699 vertical feet)

Mont Ste-Sauveur and Mont Avila are considered two separate resorts, but they are actually linked together across the face of three hills with only a property line boundary. Mont Ste-Sauveur is the "in spot" of the Valley with the highest vertical and most skiable acres. It has the most advanced and intermediate trails of the five, with snowmaking on all 142 acres, so if you like to cruise, this is for you. It holds the record for the longest ski season in Quebec with about 180 days thanks to high-tech snowmaking. Mont Avila also has a snow park for snow tubing, snow rafting, ice-skating and snowshoeing. Like many Laurentian ski resorts, this hill opens a window on the Quebequois culture with the Erabliere sugar shack, where traditional maple syrup on snow is served. The village of Saint-Sauveur is at the base.

Ski Morin Heights

6 lifts; 23 trails; 200 meters (656 vertical feet)

Ski Morin Heights is the best-kept secret in the Laurentians. The resort offers a mix of snowsport activities: skiing, snowboarding, back-country telemarking, cross-country and snowshoeing. If you enjoy expert glade skiing, Kicking Horse (skier's right on the edge of the area) will keep you grinning. Or move over a bit to eight more expert runs right next door. Although this hill accommodates all levels, it is best for the advanced and expert skier as it has the most double-blacks/blacks in the five-resort area. The village of Morin-Heights is at the base, adjacent to the largest cross-country ski facilitiy in the area at 175 km.

Mont Olympia 6 lifts

23 trails, 200 meters (656 vertical feet)
Mont Olympia has the best selection of trails for beginners and youngsters. With three double-blacks and three blacks, expert skiers and boarders will also find challenging terrain so it's a great family hill. Most of the runs are greens and blues. Mont Olympia gets more sun than any of the other Valley resorts and is best known for its Snow School and Olympic skier, Jean-Luc Bassard.

Ski Mont Gabriel

9 lifts, 18 trails, 200 meters (656 vertical feet)
Ski Mont Gabriel is the only resort in the Valley to have a dedicated snowboarding mountainside with a terrain park and jumping site accessed by an exclusive T-bar lift. The official site of the Canadian Freestyle Championships, this resort is also a great place to learn. The area between its two mountains (Mountain 1 and Mountain 2) has a big green area for the never-evers and beginners. Mountain 2 is snowboarder's heaven, but there are also some blue runs down from the top. This is the warmest ski area of the five resorts.

Hotel Legend

🚌	Airport Shuttle
🎿	Ski-in /ski-out
〰	Indoor heated pool
🏊	Outdoor heated pool
🏋	fitness center
✕	restaurant
🐾	Pets OK
🚭	No Smoking
💈	In-room Hairdryers
Ⓟ	Parking

visit us online at
www.resortspace.com

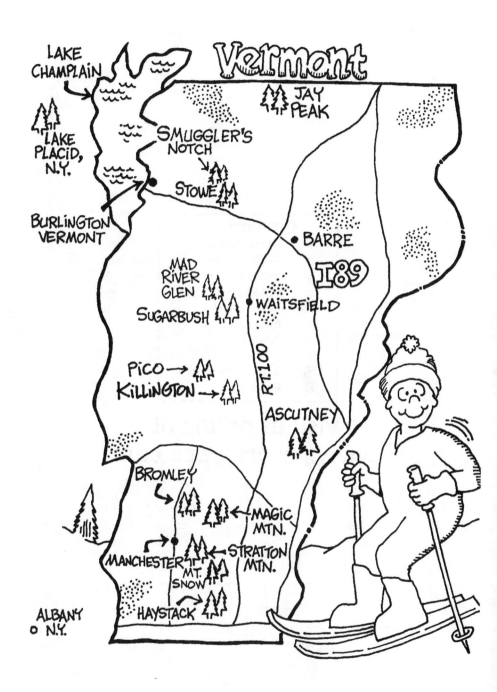

Jay Peak

Vermont

Summit elevation:	**3.968 feet**
Vertical drop:	**2,153 feet**
Base elevation:	**1,815 feet**

Address: Route 242, Jay, VT 05859
✆ **Area code:** 802
Ski area phone: 988-2611
Snow report: 988-9601
ⓘ **Toll-free reservations:** (800) 451-4449 (outside Vermont) or 988-2611.
Fax: 988-4049
E-mail: info@jaypeakresort.com
World Wide Web: www.jaypeakresort.com

Expert: ★★★★★
Advanced: ★★★★★
Intermediate: ★★★
Beginner: ★
Never-ever: ★

Number and types of lifts: 7–1 60 passenger aerial tramway, 1 high-speed quad, 1 quad, 1 triple, 1 double, 2 T bars
Skiable acreage: 385 (plus 150 acres off-piste)
Snowmaking: 80 percent
Uphill capacity: 9,815 per hour
Snowboarding: Yes, unlimited
Bed base: 850 slopeside; 1,500 in area
Nearest lodging: slopeside
Resort child care: Yes, 2 - 7 years
Adult ticket, per day: $52 (2001/02 price)

Dining: ★★
Apres-ski/nightlife: ★
Other activities: ★

If you're looking for some of the East's best woods and most powder, come to Jay Peak Resort. Long before it was popular for Eastern resorts to cut glades, Jay's locals were sneaking into the woods to cut their own lines. It was only after the resort president's 14-year-old son was caught skiing out of bounds that the resort cut some glades and opened them to the public, making tree skiing legit.

Since 1990, the resort has cut 21 glades and two extreme chutes, plus there's an additional 200 acres of backcountry terrain. We strongly suggest you become familiar with Jay's woods-skiing policy, which recommends you be an expert skier/rider in a group of three or more, and clearly states that if you go out of bounds you are responsible for your own actions and cost of rescue. This is serious skiing and riding, with all the ramifications and dangers inherent in backcountry terrain, so always carry a backpack containing emergency necessities in case you get injured or lost and have to stay on the mountain overnight.

As for snow, they call it the "Jay Peak cloud," which hovers over the mountain and dumps a foot or more of snow on days when skies are clear just 5 miles away. The 2000/01 season was a record year for Jay, blanketing the mountain with 571 inches (within two weeks, one storm brought 46 inches and another dumped 54 inches), more than any other resort in the country. In fact, there was so much snow this past season that skiers and riders literally swarmed all over The Face and The Saddle, where normally only the intrepid dare to go because of the granite and boulders that make the very top unskiable. Even in a "poor" snow year, like the 1999/00 season, Jay received 488 inches.

You've heard the old New Englander saying: "You can't get they-ah from hee-ah." While it's a bit of a trek and a lot of back roads to get to Jay, it's well worth the effort. Most of the time, you have the mountain practically to yourself. Even on powder days, you can catch freshies all day long. During holiday weekends, you'll wonder why you ever went anywhere else. Of course, this is when the locals complain about the oh-so-long 15-minute wait to ride up the lift.

People who come to Jay are here for the mountain's challenging and exciting terrain, so this isn't a good vacation for a group that includes non-skiers and non-riders. There's not a whole lot to do in the area; this is rural Vermont at its best, quiet and relaxing, with a focus on outdoor activities and recreation. Come if you want to ski or ride your legs off, settle into a Jacuzzi afterwards, then go to sleep early so you can get up first thing in the morning to do it all over again.

A high-speed detachable quad services terrain on the right side of the mountain previously accessed only from the Tram (which, incidentally, received new cars for the 2000/01 season). Locals refer to the Green Mountain Flyer as the Green Mountain Freezer: You'll understand once you crest the ridge and get a full blast of the wind off the lake. The biggest drawback to Jay's layout is that there are only three ways to work your way across the mountain — Northway, Goat Run and Vermonter — so they can get crowded and the snow gets skied off.

We hope they'll give the base lodges and hotel a facelift soon. If you're here for a week, you might want to consider taking a day or two to ski Quebec's Eastern Township resorts (see Eastern Townships chapter).

Mountain layout–Skiing

◆◆ **Expert** ◆ **Advanced:** Experts who have never been here may very well quake in their boots when they see what Jay considers single-diamond terrain. The Face, The Saddle and Tuckermans Chutes are rock-and-tree-stub strewn, forcing you to pick your way over some gnarly stuff to get to the goods. All this in full view of the folks riding up the Tram. But the real challenge is in the woods. Warm up in Hell's Woods, Buckaroo Bonzai, Everglade and Beaver Pond Glade, then head to Timbuktu and Valhalla. Locals groaned loudly when Jay officially opened Beyond Beaver Pond Glade for the 2000/01 season because it's just about the last piece of "unofficial woods" left on the mountain, but it remains pretty much untouched since you have to hike a bit to get there (or know the shortcut to it, and we're not telling). Keep an eye out for locals, who are more than willing to share their secret stashes if they see that you know what you're doing in the trees. There's plenty of in-bounds woods skiing to keep you grinning for a week, so don't go out of bounds unless you're with someone who knows the area.

Kitzbuehl is a sweet, tight bumped run that'll leave you huffing and puffing. River Quai and Green Beret (when it's open) are both truly hairy trails. Powerline is rated intermediate, but we think its monster moguls and double fall line make it tougher than that.

Advanced skiers ready to push their envelopes will want to take a glade technique lesson and head into the woods. You can always try out the "kiddie" glades mentioned below and see if you're ready first. Tree skiing opens up a whole new world of skiing and riding, it's just you and Mother Nature at her best. One of our expert staffers made her first foray into the woods several seasons ago and now we're lucky when she skis on a trail with us.

■ **Intermediate:** Jay is a great place for intermediates who are comfortable with their ability and want to put themselves to a challenge. Most intermediate trails here would be rated for advanced skiers elsewhere. One writer's niece and nephew, who are used to skiing at Mount Snow, found the narrower trails and wide-open "kiddie" glades (Kokomo, Moon Walk and Bushwacker) to be great fun.

We recommend warming up on Ullr's Dream (slip into Kokomo if you want to avoid the long flat at the end), JFK or Northway to Angel's Wiggle. To take in the amazing 360-degree views from the top to Mt. Mansfield, Quebec's Eastern Townships, Lake Champlain, Mt. Washington and Montreal, ride up the tram and head down Vermonter. Goat Run is another fun trail, but gets iced up and moguled on heavy-traffic days.

Most advanced-intermediates will enjoy the groomed black-diamond trails off the Jet Triple Chair, once they make it past the somewhat-steep top sections. A favorite is Derick Hot Shot, a narrow winding trail that gets moderate bumps on high-traffic days. If you get to the top of the Jet and decide the terrain looks too steep, take Montrealer and choose from some wonderful intermediate terrain like Northway, Paradise Meadows, lower Kitzbuehl and Angel's Wiggle (we wish this area of the mountain were served by its own chair).

●● **Beginner ●** **Never-ever:** Beginners have very limited terrain, with most of it served by T-bars. Once you ride up one of the main chair lifts, you're faced with intermediate terrain that can be very overwhelming if you're not a daring person. The learning area is served by a T-bar—difficult for never-evers—plus higher-level skiers and riders have to use those trails to reach the Tram and Green Mountain Flyer. All this can be very intimidating.

Mountain layout—Snowboarding

Jay has a terrain park on Lower Can Am, but most riders come for the glades, chutes and off-piste terrain. Make sure to read the skiing description, it applies to riders too. Experienced woods riders will quiver with excitement upon discovering the natural halfpipe in Canyonland: We dare you to find it. Ullr's Dream is a great warm-up run, but duck into Kokomo to avoid the lo-o-ong flat at the bottom. Riders coming out of Beaver Pond Glade and Beyond Beaver Pond Glade hook back up to Ullr's, so you'll also want to heed that warning (plus Beyond has its own unavoidable flat that will have you hoofing back to the trails). If you're looking to make sweeping arcs, head to wide-open Jet and Haynes. If they're too steep for your taste, take Montrealer to Angel's Wiggle, then take the Wiggle all the way down or choose from Lower Milk Run and Hell's Crossing to Paradise Meadows. The learning area is served by a T-bar, extremely difficult for never-evers; you might want to learn elsewhere.

Mountain rating

Jay Peak is the perfect mountain for skiers and riders who are adventurous intermediates and better. Most trails are cut classic New England style, meaning narrow and winding. The glades and chutes are so enticing, experts will ski and ride till they drop from exhaustion. Beginners and never-evers should go someplace else to prepare for this mountain.

Cross-country and snowshoeing

Jay Peak has 20 km. of cross-country skiing that network into 200 km. of touring trails in the area. Jay recently purchased new trail-grooming and track-setting equipment. Instruction and rentals are available. A trail pass is $5.

Two-hour, naturalist-led tours on snowshoes are scheduled throughout the week in the afternoons and evenings. Cost is $12 per person and includes guide, snowshoes, headlamps, boots and poles. Check with the Ski School Desk to register. Extended or group tours also can be arranged. For those who want to head out on their own, snowshoe rentals are available anytime through the snowboard shop.

Hazen's Notch Cross-Country Ski & Snowshoe Center (326-4799, email: hazens@sover.net), about 10 miles away in Hazen's Notch, is owned and operated by the non-profit Hazen's Notch Association. The 50 km. of groomed and backcountry trails include 10 km. of snowshoe-only trails. The association plans to add about 16 km. of trails—8 km. of skiing and 8 km. of snowshoeing—for the 2001/02 season. The views alone are worth the trip, plus the high elevation ensures bountiful snow. You'll find ski and snowshoe rentals, plus instruction by appointment. Ask about naturalist-guided snowshoe tours and full-moon snowshoe tours. Adult passes cost $10, children $5 (2000/01 prices).

Lessons (2001/02 prices)

Group lessons: Two-hour ski or snowboard lesson, $25 US/$32 CDN. Multiday packages available.

Never-ever package: Two-hour ski or snowboard lesson with rental and use of T-bars, $39 US/$49 CDN. Multiday packages available. GETSkiing program uses short skis or Snowblades to help you learn to ski or improve technique, $25 US/$32 CDN.

Private lessons: One-hour ski or snowboard session, $48 US/$60 CDN. Private telemark lessons also available.

Special programs: Glade Skiing Techniques are two-hour sessions on days when glade skiing is best and for advanced skiers only, $25 US/$32 CDN. Backcountry Adventure gives guided tours of popular off-piste areas. You must be a very experienced skier or rider; the ski school has the option to disqualify participants, $45 US/$59 CDN. Advanced skiers can go for the First Tracks program with a ticket purchased the day before, getting you up the first tram at 8:15 a.m. weekdays (7:45 a.m. weekends) for a guided tour down the untouched mountain. Cost is $5 US/$7 CDN.

Racing: Racing Camps for recreational skiers feature gate running and on-hill training. JAYSTAR races at 1 p.m. on Thursday, Friday and Saturday, $5 for two runs. Special JAYSTAR Clinic available just prior to race time.

Child care (2001/02 prices)

Ages: 2 to 7 years old.
Cost: $30 all day (does not include cost of lunch); $15 half day.
Reservations: Recommended.

Note: Guests staying at Hotel Jay and Jay Peak Condominiums receive free day care for children ages 2 to 7 years old. Evening supervised dinner is also available. Pre-registration is advised. Infant care is available on a fee basis with advanced reservations.

Children's lessons: Kinderschool Ski Program for ages 3–5, includes lift ticket, $30 US/$39 CDN. Pre-registration is required. Mountain Explorers, a full-day program for ages 5–10 costs $47 US/$60 CDN plus lift tickets. Miniriders is the same program, only for snowboarding. Mountain Adventurers, a full-day program for ages 10–16, $47 US/$60 CDN plus lifts.

Other programs include snowskating, snowshoeing, cross-country skiing, torchlight parades, and First Tracks. Multichild discounts and multiday packages available.

Lift tickets

	Adult	Junior (6-12)	Toddler (6 and younger)
One day	$52	$38	$6

Who skis at a discount: Seniors 65 and older ski for $12 US/$15 CDN. College student with an ID ski for $32 US/$39 CDN. Vermont residents pay $35 for one-day adult, $30 for a junior and $6 for a toddler.

Note: When staying for more than one day, the wise move is to buy a lodging package that includes tickets: Children younger than 14 stay and ski free, teenagers 15–18 stay and ski for $40 US/$50 CDN per day when sharing their parent's room or condo.

Accommodations

Jay Peak Resort assists guests in arranging lodging, air travel, train travel, shuttle van service to the airport and train station and rental cars. Jay Peak is overall a bargain. The best deal is to stay in the slopeside hotel or condos. During non-holiday weeks, children 14 and younger stay and ski free, and teens 15–18 stay and ski for $40 US per day, when sharing the same room or condo with their parents (meals are extra). Five-day stays and longer include a half-day complimentary ticket that can be used on the day of arrival beginning at 12:30 p.m.

If you have kids ages 7 and younger, stay at **Hotel Jay** (800-451-4449 or 988-9601; $–$$). It provides complimentary child care from 9 a.m. to 9 p.m., including a supervised dinner. A sauna, Jacuzzi, family room with fireplace and game room are available. Five-day packages for a family with two adults cost $571 US per adult (includes meals for adults).

Slopeside condos range from luxury to economy. Five-day packages, including lodging and lift tickets, range from $5561 US/$721 CDN to $759 US/$969 CDN per adult. Meal plans are available. Nicest are the recently build **Village Townhouses** ($$). Deluxe accommodations can be found at **Mountainside**, **Trailside** and **Slopeside** condos ($$–$$$). **Mountainside Studios** and **Stoney Path** are perfect for small families or couples ($$–$$$).

There are also a variety of chalets, cabins, motels, hotels, inns and B&Bs in the area. Jay Peak Resort can assist you, or call the Jay Peak Area Association at 800-882-7460.

The Black Lantern Inn (326-4507 or 800-255-8661; $-$$; ⊗ ✗ 𝖯), about 20 minutes down the road in Montgomery, is a beautifully restored stagecoach stop originally built in 1803 and now listed on the National Historic Register. The inn has 10 rooms and six deluxe suites with fireplaces and Jacuzzi bathtubs; all decorated with Vermont antiques.

Phineas Swann Bed & Breakfast (326-4306; $$; ⊗𝖯), a bit closer in Montgomery Center, is an 1890s gingerbread Victorian inn that includes suites in its carriage house with a Jacuzzi, fireplace, queen-size bed and TV/VCR. Gourmet breakfast and afternoon tea is served.

The Inn at Trout River (326-4391 or 800-338-7049; $-$$; ⊗✗𝖯), also in Montgomery Center, is a rambling Victorian with queen-size beds, down quilts, feather pillows, flannel sheets and private baths. The main dining room and sitting room have fireplaces, a Montgomery Soapstone Stove warms up the split-level living room and library.

Dining

Each lodge has a cafeteria that serves breakfast and lunch, and the food vastly improved for the 2000/01 season. For heartier and tastier on-mountain meals, **Hotel Jay** is the place for breakfast and The International Restaurant dishes out a satisfying lunch. Hotel Jay has a fixed-price, gourmet dinner for about $22 that's quite good. Children's menus also are available.

Don't miss dinner at **Zack's on the Rocks** (326-4500; $$), in nearby Hazen's Notch. The dining experience is as much of an adventure as a day on the mountain: You'll feel like you've wandered through the woods and discovered someone's secret garden, complete with vines and flowers draping from the ceiling and employees who remind you of free-spirited wood sprites. You'll first be seated at the piano bar, where you'll find yourself chatting freely with the other patrons as you agonize over the menu. When your appetizers are ready, you're

Dining: $$$-Entrees $20+; $$-$10-20; $-less than $10.
Accommodations: (double room) $$$$-$200+; $$$-$141-$200; $$-$81-$140; $-$80 and less.

led to your table by Zack, ringing a brass bell and usually attired in a purple flowing gown that reminds you of Merlin. And, oh, what a wizard he is in the kitchen!

Several local inns are renowned for their gourmet meals and appropriately, reservations are suggested. Try **The Black Lantern Inn** (326-4507; $$), where the menu changes nightly and is served by candlelight. The food, cozy atmosphere and prices here rival any you'll find across the border in Quebec. **Lemoine's** at The Inn at Trout River (326-4391; $$) is another palate-pleasing experience.

For something less pricey, consider the pub menu at **Hobo's Café** at The Inn at Trout River (326-4391; $-$$). Another good bet is **The Belfry** (326-4400; $-$$), just down the mountain road toward Montgomery Center, where you'll find their extensive menu written on a blackboard at the entrance.

Ask at the hotel front desk to find out about favorite restaurants in nearby Quebec. You'll find French cuisine at affordable prices because of the exchange rate.

Après-ski/nightlife

The **Golden Eagle Sports Bar** and the **International Bar,** both in the Tram base lodge, and the **Sport Lounge at Hotel Jay** are the on-mountain places to head when you quit the slopes. We recommend taste-testing the Vermont micro-brews. Live entertainment, Karaoke nights and theme parties are frequently scheduled. **The Belfry**, just down the mountain road toward Montgomery Center, has a good selection of beers and local microbrews on tap and in the bottle.

Family activities include ice skating, snowcat rides, naturalist-led snowshoeing treks, welcome parties, sing-a-longs and bonfire parties. Teens will find special activities just for them such as movie nights, bowling, snow volleyball and dances.

Other activities

Shopping: There are a few shops in Jay worth visiting, such as The Snow Job (where you'll get the best tunes around) and the Jay Country Store, but if you're planning to take a shopping excursion, we suggest heading to Burlington, Montreal or Magog. In the spring, visit one of the nearby maple sugar shacks. Guided **snowmobile** tours into the surrounding mountains and valleys of the Northeast Kingdom are available for varying lengths of time, with prices starting at $50 single/$70 double for a one-hour tour. Reservations are required, call the Jay Peak reservations line.

Getting there and getting around

By air: Burlington International Airport is served by Continental, Delta, Jetblue, United and USAir. Resort shuttle service and special Thrifty Car Rental rates are available. It takes 1.5 hours to drive from the airport to the mountain.

By car: Jay Peak Resort is on Route 242 in northern-central Vermont, just below the Canadian border, about equidistant between I-91 and I-89. Sample driving times: Boston, 3.5 hours; Albany, 4.5 hours; New York City, 6.5 hours; Toronto, 7 hours; Montreal, 1.5 hours.

By bus: Vermont Transit serves nearby Newport from all major New England points. Ground transportation available.

By train: AMTRAK Vermonter to St. Albans, 45 minutes away. Ground transfers available to Jay Peak.

Getting around: Bring a car if you want to venture off mountain.

Killington/Pico

Vermont

Summit elevation: **4,215 feet**
Vertical drop: **3,050 feet**
Base elevation: **1,165 feet**

Address: Killington Road
Killington, VT 05751
✆ **Area code:** 802
Ski area phone: 422-3333
Snow report: 422-3261
ⓘ **Toll-free reservations:** (800) 621-6867
(621-MTNS)
E-mail: info@killington.com
Internet: www.killington.com
Expert:★★
Advanced:★★★
Intermediate:★★★★
Beginner:★★★★
Never-ever:★★★

Number and types of lifts: 32–2 gondolas,
6 high-speed quads, 6 quads,
6 triples, 4 doubles, 8 surface lifts
Acreage: 1,182 skiable acres
Snowmaking: 70 percent
Uphill capacity: 52,973 per hour
Snowboarding: Yes, unlimited
Bed base: 5,500 (base),18,000 (region)
Nearest lodging: walking distance
Resort child care: Yes, 6 weeks - 6 years
Adult ticket, per day: $59 (01/02)
Dining:★★
Apres-ski/nightlife:★★★★
Other activities:★★

When Preston Leete Smith first envisioned a ski area in the Killington Basin, his vision included more lifts and more trails than any other resort in the East. Although Killington opened in 1958 with only seven trails and two Poma lifts, the resort has truly grown into the "Beast in the East." Today, Killington/Pico sprawls 11 miles over seven mountains (including nearby Pico Mountain, as the resort's name implies), that are crossed by 200 trails and served by 32 lifts, with greater lift capacity than anywhere in the East. From the gentle slopes of Snowshed to the terrifyingly steep pitch of Outer Limits, Killington/Pico strives to be the ski resort that does it all.

Thanks to a vast snowmaking operation, Killington/Pico is usually open longer than any ski resort in the East; sometimes as long as eight months. From the cool days of autumn, when skiers and snowboarders make a few turns down a white strip high on the mountain, framed by fall foliage, to the carefree days of late spring, long after mud season has gone, Killington/Pico attracts those who can't wait for winter and are sad when it's over.

In 1996, Killington added Pico Mountain to its already vast selection of terrain. Eventually, an interconnect will link Pico to Killington, but plans are on hold for the moment. Even if it is 10 minutes away by car, Pico is still worth visiting. Historically significant, Pico was started in 1937 by 1952 Olympic gold medalist Andrea Mead Lawrence's parents. It was one of the first ski resorts in the East and boasted one of the longest ski trails in the country. Considered by many locals as a feather in the "mother ship's" cap, Pico has 2,000 feet of vertical, 48 trails and some very interesting (and often uncrowded) terrain.

A note about Pico: Though we would prefer to give you separate stats for Killington and Pico, the resort's policy is to provide combined stats, as if it were already one resort, so that's what we list. We refer to "Killington/Pico" when we're talking about the whole enchilada (this introduction, primarily), and "Killington" or "Pico" when talking about each one individually. Lift tickets are valid at both areas, but if you plan to ski just Pico, you can purchase a Pico-only pass that's about $15 cheaper than the full pass, and you can order a free Pico card on-line (www.killington.com/html/pico_card_order.html) and use it to take $10 off the lift ticket price. Public transportation between the two is via The Bus, which charges $1 and stops at several locations along the Access Road. Catch it at the Snowshed Base Lodge.

Try as it may, Killington is not all things to all people. Weekend warriors flock to the slopes, and the chaos is sometimes dangerous. Snowshed (the beginner area) is dubbed "Bloodshed" by the locals. Furthermore, navigating the morass of terrain has made more than one skier or rider wish they had their own GPS system. Experts often find themselves zooming down beginner runs because they have missed their black-diamond choice. Worse still, beginners find themselves stranded on black-diamond runs in an attempt to reach their cars at day's end.

Killington boasts five base areas, although the lowest, the Skyeship Base Station on Route 4, is infrequently used. (Note: the Sunrise Base Area on Route 100 is now closed, and lift service is no longer available.) Killington does provide shuttle service at day's end for those who have taken a wrong turn and ended up at a base different from where they parked in the morning. Here's another frustrating aspect of the resort: Only about 1,500 feet of Killington's 3,050-foot vertical drop is "working" vertical. Only three trails, mostly beginner, meander the last 1,500 feet down to the "true" base on Route 4. Unless you're up for a real thigh-burner, don't waste your time skiing or riding here.

To avoid confusion or ending up on those flat run-outs when you'd rather be bashing serious bumps, we recommend signing up for one of the free "Meet the Mountain" tours, which leave from the Snowshed Base Lodge every Monday, Tuesday, Friday, and Saturday at 9:45 a.m., and every Monday afternoon at 12:45 p.m. The tour guides, Killington's volunteer "ambassadors," will show newcomers how to best take advantage of Killington's trails without getting lost or stuck in the thickest crowds.

Mountain layout–Skiing

Killington's terrain is almost too sprawling to describe. The resort has five separate base areas (six, including Pico.) Three are clustered within striking distance at the top of Killington Road. Snowshed and Rams Head are across the street from one another, and Killington base is just a bit up the road. Bear Mountain, home of the famed Outer Limits bump run, is on Bear Mountain Road off Rte. 4. Also off Rte. 4 is the Skyeship Base Station, a good choice for those who don't want to hassle with traffic on the Access Road, but the run down at day's end is less than scintillating.

◆◆ **Expert** ◆ **Advanced:** Between Snowdon Mountain and Killington Peak is some of the toughest terrain. The Canyon quad chair services this area for access to double-diamond Cascade, Downdraft, Double Dipper and Big Dipper Glade.

Skye Peak has proved to be one of the most popular sections of the mountain. Ovation, Superstar, Skye Lark and Bittersweet are all fairly easy expert trails that are covered with plenty of manmade snow. Superstar is usually the last trail to close in the spring and is the scene of the downhill ski leg of the Memorial Day Killington Triathlon.

From the top of Skye Peak, advanced skiers can drop down Skyeburst and Wildfire by following the Skye Peak quad. This connection is not recommended for lower intermediates because it leads to the Bear Mountain quad, which services good advanced and expert terrain.

From the top of the Bear Mountain quad, skiers and riders can descend the double-diamond pitch of Devil's Fiddle or loop in the opposite direction down Wildfire, an easier single-diamond run. For mogul hounds, the real thrill is to drop directly under the chairlift and challenge Outer Limits. If you ski it on one of the rare days it's groomed, if you fall, you may slide all the way to the bottom, much to the amusement of the crowds watching from the base and the chair lift.

After a good snowfall, head to Pico and get fresh tracks down the gnarly Giant Killer or Upper Pike. Upper KA and Sunset 71, narrow trails reminiscent of the early days of New England skiing, wind down from the top of Pico and offer interesting knolls, twists and turns.

■ **Intermediate:** Don't be alarmed by the black diamonds on the Killington trail map. Many of their single-black diamond runs would be blue cruisers at other resorts, and indeed, we've been told that many of them have been relabeled as such.

The Rams Head high-speed quad chair covers mainly beginner and intermediate trails. Capers, a gentle trail, is a good warm-up cruiser. The Snowdon area is another cruiser's delight. It's served by two chairs from the base area and a mid-mountain Poma lift on Bunny Buster. Highline and Conclusion are good advanced cruising runs with excellent pitch. Bunny Buster and Chute are similar but with a more mellow slope.

Needle's Eye drops beneath the second section of the Skyeship gondola and is a nice wide cruiser as is the aptly named Cruise Control. A trip back up the Needle's Eye chair will put skiers back on Bittersweet for a smooth cruise to the Killington Base Lodge or Snowshed.

Pico is home to 49-ner, a cruiser that offers superb views from the top of Pico. Beginners will find the top part of this blue square challenging, though.

●● **Beginner:** Green trails lead from all six interconnected peaks, which allows beginners the panoramic vistas and thrill of skiing from the summit, not possible at areas where the upper-mountain trails are reserved for seasoned skiers, but beginners beware: It's easy to get lost at Killington on these meandering trails. If it's the end of the day, consult your map frequently to make sure you'll end up at the same base area as your car, or be prepared to hop on the shuttle.

● **Never-ever:** Killington, in theory, has a perfect learning area: Snowshed. Served by three chairlifts, this gentle slope is a segregated beginning area. But the top of the trail is accessible from the upper part of the mountain, which can make Snowshed exceedingly crowded and not just with other beginners. Experts often fly down the slope, terrifying those who are less stable on their boards or skis. Consider learning at another resort or head to Pico, where beginners learn at the more isolated Bonanza area.

 ## Mountain layout–Snowboarding

Killington's Superpipe is 450-feet long with 12-foot walls. It also has a terrain park and a skier/boardercross course. Pico has a terrain park on Panhandler and a superpipe is planned for this season. Lessons and rentals are available at Snowshed and Killington base lodges.

Mountain rating

Overall, intermediates won't tire of Killington. Advanced skiers will have a lot of fun in select areas such as Skye Peak, Bear Mountain and Killington Peak. Though experts will find no extreme skiing, they can find glades (called fusion zones) that will test them, such as Low Rider on Snowdon and Julio on Killington Peak. Weekend crowds could prove daunting to beginners and never-evers but if you come to learn to ski during midweek, you will find Snowshed acceptable.

Cross country and snowshoeing

Near the base of the Killington Access Road, **Mountain Meadows Cross Country Ski Resort** (775-7077) has 56 km. of trails meandering across Kent Lake and through surrounding forests. The Center also has a 1.2-km. loop covered by an extensive snowmaking system. When snow is lean, Mountain Meadows is one of the few cross country ski resorts that opens. **Mountain Top Cross Country Ski Resort** (483-2311), in Chittenden, has 110 km. of trails, 40 km. of dual-set tracks and 0.5 km. of trails with snowmaking.

Both areas have rentals, lessons, ski shops and warming huts. Mountain Meadows offers sled dog tours, and Mountain Top offers sledding and horse-drawn sleigh rides.

Trailhead Ski Touring Center in Stockbridge (746-8038) has 60 km. of trails, with 35 km. groomed and 35 km. tracked. In Woodstock, the **Ski Touring Center** (457-2114) has 75 km. of trails, lessons and rentals.

Lessons (2001/02 prices)

Group lessons: The Killington Skier Development Program uses the innovative teaching program called Perfect Turn®. Perfect Turn has 10 levels. For lower intermediates and higher, the two hour clinics, for levels 2 through 8, are offered at 10 a.m. and 1 p.m. and cost $33 for one day. A five-day package including clinic and lift pass is $355.

Never-ever package: The resort has a well-designed Perfect Turn Learn-to-Ski Center at Snowshed. Three-day ($159) and five-day ($279) first-time packages for skiers and riders include lift, clinic and equipment.

Private lessons: A one-hour clinic is $85 for one person, $130 for two. A two-hour lesson is $145 for one, $198 for two. Three- and six-hour clinics also are available.

Special programs: Too many to list here. Among the topics are moguls, women's instruction, racing, adaptive instruction for the disabled and even instruction for instructors.

Racing: None for public participation. Call the Alpine Training Center (422-6797) near the Killington Base Lodge for information on clinics and programs.

Child care (2001/02 prices)

Ages: 6 weeks - 6 years.
Costs: $67 per day (with lunch) and $46 per half day (no lunch). Multiday discounts available.

Reservations: Required; call (800) 621-6867.

Note: All-day programs run from 7:45 a.m. to 4:30 p.m. on weekends, and 8 a.m. to 4:30 p.m. midweek. Parents must supply food and beverage for children 23 months and younger. The Friendly Penguin Children's Center is located in the Rams Head Family Center.

Children's lessons: Programs for ages 2–3 include lessons, lunch and equipment for $97 for a full day, $64 for a half day. Programs for older children, with lessons and lunch but no equipment, run $89 for a full day and $64 for a half day for ages 4–6, and $103 for a full day and $71 for a half day for ages 7–12. Multi-day rates are available. Teens 13–17 can take part in The SnowZone, which offers skiing, snowboarding and skiboarding, and other popular trends in snow sports in either half-day ($26) or full-day ($60) sessions. Prices do not include lift tickets in the SnowZone program. One-, three- and seven-day programs are also available.

Lift tickets (2001/02 prices)

	Adult	Teen (13-18)	Child (6-12)
One day	$59	$52	$36
Two days	$108	$98	$60
Three days	$162	$147	$90
Five days	$250	$225	$140

Who skis free: Children 12 and younger ski free when accompanied by an adult who buys a Monday-Friday five-day pass or longer.

Who skis at a discount: Ages 65 and older, same price as teens. Pico Card holders ski for $10 off the Pico-only lift ticket price of $45 Sunday through Friday, nonholiday. To order a free Pico Card, log onto www.killington.com/html/pico_card_order.html.

Accommodations

Killington is working to create a pedestrian village at its main base area. Killington has very little slopeside lodging and no real ski-in/ski-out options.

You may make reservations for the **Killington Grand Resort Hotel** and all of the following properties by calling the **Killington Travel Service** (800-621-6867). Killington's lodging has a wide price range, with much of it reasonable. Call for specific rate information.

The **Killington Grand Resort Hotel** ($$-$$$$ 丸╳≥P⁊⁊⚇⚇) near the base of Snowshed and is the newest lodge in the area. The hotel has 200 units from hotel rooms to penthouses, and the accommodations are more on par with what you'd find at a Sheraton. The Grand Resort Hotel also has a full-service restaurant, outdoor heated swimming pool, health club and "slopeside" location (in truth, you have to walk across a snowmaking pond on a very long pedestrian bridge to reach the slopes). When you reserve a room, make sure you ask for a "hotel room" or "suite." Most of the "studio" rooms only have sofa or murphy beds.

The top hotel on the mountain road at Killington is **The Inn of the Six Mountains** (800-228-4676 or 422-4302; $$-$$$ ╳≥≙P⁊⁊⚇⚇), with a 65-foot indoor lap pool, exercise room and frequent shuttles to the slopes. Rates include breakfast.

Killington Village has good values and the best location, with nearby athletic club facilities, some nightlife and an excellent shuttlebus system. Of the other condominiums, the **Highridge** units are by far the most desirable. Other good choices are the **Sunrise** condos at the base of Bear Mountain and **The Woods at Killington**, which boasts Jacuzzis and saunas and a complete spa. Both the **Mountain Inn** and the **Cascades Lodge** are very convenient but they are also basic. The Cascades has a nice indoor pool, and the Mountain Inn has some of the best nightlife, when the bar is hopping.

The **Cortina Inn** (773-3333 or 800-451-6108 or cortina1@aol.com; $$$-$$$$ ╳≙P⚇⚇), on Rte. 4, a mile past Pico, is very good. It has a health club, pool, spa, two restaurants, children's activities on holiday weekends, and many large suites. (Web site: http://www.cortinainn.com). **The Vermont Inn** (775-0708 or 800-541-7795 or vtinn@aol.com; $$-$$$$ ╳P⚇⚇), with 18 rooms, fireside dining, and everything homemade, is a charming New England country inn. Breakfast and dinner are included in the rates, and the food is excellent. The inn is located just over one mile west of Pico on Rte. 4.

Dining: $$$-Entrees $20+; $$-$10-20; $-less than $10.
Accommodations: (double room) $$$$-$200+; $$$-$141-$200; $$-$81-$140; $-$80 and less.

The Red Clover Inn (775-2290 or 800-752-0571; $$$–$$$$ ✕🅿🍸🕸✦☺) is five miles from the Killington Access Road and is hard to find, but we think it's the best in the area. Situated on 13 acres, this farmhouse estate has private baths, country decor and hand-made quilts in each room. Room rates, including breakfast and dinner for two, are about $175–$250 on winter weekends, less during the week. The food is superb. Another favorite is **The Inn at Long Trail** (775-7181 or 800-325-2540; $-$$). One of Vermont's first ski lodges, the inn still maintains its cozy, rustic feel. The 19 rooms are small, but the inn has a devoted following. Rates include breakfast and dinner.

Of the other properties on Killington Access Road, **The Red Rob** (422-3303; $$ ✕⛰🅿🕸), **Killington Village Inn** (422-3301; $$–$$$ ✕🅿🕸☺) and **Chalet Killington** (422-3451; $$ ✕🍸🅿🕸✦⛊) rate in that order. The food is reportedly best at the Red Rob, and both the Killington Village Inn and the Chalet have a casual atmosphere. Rates include breakfast at the Red Rob and Chalet, and breakfast and dinner at the Killington Village Inn.

Near the base of the Killington Road is the **North Star Lodge** (422-4040; $-$$ ⛱🅿🕸), which has a pool and shuttle service and is surrounded by good restaurants.

The Grey Bonnet (775-2537; $-$$ ✕⛰🅿🕸✦) on Rte. 100 north received numerous recommendations. There is a nice indoor pool, sauna and pub. Rates include breakfast and dinner. You will need a car to get to the ski area.

A favorite luxury spot of ours is the **Woodstock Inn and Resort** (800-448-7900; $$$–$$$$ ✕⛰🅿🍸🕸✦⛊), about 17 miles east of Killington. Rooms are cozy and beautifully decorated, with hand-stitched quilts on each bed. The dining room wine list has 184 selections, both foreign and domestic. Midweek, the inn has a very attractive package with downhill skiing at nearby Suicide Six or cross-country skiing at the Woodstock Ski Touring Center.

Dining

The Killington area has more than 100 restaurants and bars. The best in the area—ranked among the top in the nation by *Food and Wine* and *Condé Nast Traveler*—is **Hemingway's** (422-3886), one of only two four-star restaurants in Vermont. The Prix Fixe four-course menu ranges from $50-$62.

Our other favorites are **The Summit** (422-3535), an award-winning restaurant with a menu that changes nightly and a great wine list; the top-rated **The Vermont Inn** (800-541-7795 or 775-0708), with fine formal dining; and the award-winning **Red Clover Inn** (775-2290), where the rack of lamb is exceptional. **Jason's** (422-3303) in the Red Rob has excellent Northern Italian food, and **Zola's Grille at the Cortina Inn** (773-3333) serves a blend of Northern Italian, French Bistro, and Mediterranean cuisine in a casual atmosphere. Reservations are required at all restaurants but Zola's.

McGrath's Irish Pub (775-7181) at The Inn at Long Trail serves a wonderful Guinness Stew and shepherd's pie in its funky pub and restaurant built into a cliff. Service can be slow, but the food is hearty and tasty. We have not eaten at **Ovations** (422-5001), at the Killington Grand Resort Hotel, but it advertises a family-oriented menu. At **Charity's** (422-3800), the bar is cozy and welcoming, the portions healthy and the menu of steaks, BBQ and Italian dishes such as Tortellini Siciliano and Shrimp Diavlo can appease virtually any hungry skier's appetite. Avoid the prime rib though; it's tough.

Choices (422-4030) on the Killington Access Road is recommended by lots of locals.

For restaurants a bit kinder to the budget: **The Wobbly Barn Steakhouse** (422-3392) is known for steaks and a great salad bar (no reservations). **Mrs. Brady's** (422-2020) serves the "basics" (salads, burgers, roast turkey and monster sandwiches). **Pizza Jerks** (422-4111) and the **Outback Pizza** (422-9885), both on the Access Road, serve decent 'za, but the best pizza in the region is down in Rutland at **A Crust Above** (747-4700). Head west down Rte. 4 and look for the sign on the left after Pizza Hut.

If you're looking for a good cup of coffee or a quick breakfast, head a mile up the Killington Access Road to **Crazy Mountain** (422-2113). This cafe serves the best coffee on the mountain. Fill up on delectable muffins and pastries or hearty fare such as bagel-and-egg sandwiches or breakfast burritos. It also makes great sandwiches, such as chicken with sundried tomatoes, basil, mozzarella, and pesto, if you want to buy something for lunch and steer clear of the banal and expensive base lodge fare.

Après-ski/nightlife

Killington's après-ski scene, strung out along the Access Road, is often voted number one in the nation, with the atmosphere generally raucous and young, and the festivities often driven by excellent bands, some nationally known. Après-ski at the mountain includes the **Mahogany Ridge** at the Killington Base Lodge, the **Long Trail Brew Pub** at Snowshed and the **Bear Mountain Lounge** at, you guessed it, the Bear Mountain Base Lodge.

Immediate après-ski action on the Access Road can be found in **Charity's**. **Outback Pizza** is highly recommended for its happy hour(s) as well. It's a favorite locals' hangout on weekdays, with $5 all-you-can-eat pizza on Monday nights; entertainment and dancing extend into the evening on weekends. A new local hotspot is the **Lookout Bar and Grill**, where Skiddy, one of Killington's best local bump skiers, rules the bar. For rowdy après-ski and then dancing to loud music, head to the **Wobbly Barn Steakhouse**. Big name bands often lead the line-up on busy winter weekends at **The Pickle Barrel**, which has a lively happy hour with dancing later in the evening. It's a favorite among the young college crowd.

Those over the age of 30 may want to opt out of the mosh pits at Wobbly Barn and the Pickle Barrel, and head down the road to **The Grist Mill**. This restaurant/bar has earned a reputation in recent years as the place for slightly "more mature" skiers, but don't let that fool you: maturity at Killington is strictly relative. The place rocks on weekends, when live music and dancing is featured, and its circular bar and layout is perfect for checking out the action and general people-watching. Plus, for our money the Grist Mill makes the area's most toe-curling Goombays, a local concoction of fruit juices and various shades of rum. Two Goombays and you'll understand why this rates as the unofficial drink of the official après-ski/nightlife capital of the East.

Casey's Caboose is a favorite locals' haunt with killer spicy buffalo wings. An older, quieter set meets at the **Summit** for happy hour. When the bar at the **Mountain Inn** has live entertainment, it's great fun.

From Pico, head a few yards up Rte. 4 to The Inn at Long Trail, nestled right into the apex of Killington Pass. McGrath's Irish pub here serves Guinness ale on tap. Live entertainment, performing on a stage built right into the cliff, keeps the bar full on weekends at St. Paddy's Day.

Other activities

Shopping: The Killington Shops at the Shack, several outlet-style stores now owned by the ski resort, are at the intersection of Rte. 4 and the Killington Access Road. In Killington, stop at the Greenbrier Gift Shop for handcrafted items and gourmet ware. Nearby Bridgewater has an old mill that now houses about 10 shops including a bookstore, Miranda Pottery and Charles Shackleton Furniture. Woodstock, about 17 miles east of Killington on Rte. 4, is one of Vermont's most beautiful villages and is packed with art galleries and shops. Even farther east on Rte. 4 in Quechee is the Simon Pearce glass blowing workshop and store.

Snowshed also has an **indoor rock climbing wall** that's open daily. Call 773-3343 for more information. The **Killington Peak Restaurant** at the top of the K-1 Gondola serves dinner Wednesdays only. The fixed-price dinner, ($30-or-so for adults and $15-or so for children) includes a ride to the top in gondola. Reservations are required, 422-6780. Farther down the Access Road, an **outdoor skating rink** can be found below the Summit Lodge on Grist Mill Pond. For **snowmobiling information** call the Cortina Inn, 773-3333, or Killington Snowmobile Tours, 422-2121.

Getting there and getting around

By air: Major airports are located in Burlington, VT, Albany, NY, and Manchester, NH. Burlington is about a 90-minute drive from Killington, while Albany and Manchester are each about 2 hours. Green Mountain Limousine Service (773-1313) runs transfers from the Burlington airport for $330 for two, round-trip, plus 15-percent driver gratuity. Thrifty Rental Cars has an office at the Inn of the Six Mountains. Major car rental companies are also available at the Burlington, Albany and Manchester airports. Other airports with commercial service are Rutland (USAir Express), 30 minutes away, and West Lebanon, NH (Delta), a 45-minute drive.

By car: Killington is at the intersection of Rtes. 4 and 100 in central Vermont near the city of Rutland, about three hours northwest of Boston. Pico is located about three miles west of the Access Road on Rte. 4.

By train: Daily service is available on Amtrak's Ethan Allen Express from New York City to Rutland, with bus service or car rental to Killington. Train-lodging-lift packages are available. Call (800) USA-RAIL (872-7245) for train info, or Killington Travel Service (800-621-6867) for package info.

Getting around: Bring or rent a car or use the Killington Shuttle bus service. Though you may not use your car to move between your lodging and the slopes, Killington is very spread out, and you may want to visit the attractions nearby.

Mad River Valley
Sugarbush & Mad River Glen

Waitsfield/Warren Region
Vermont

Dining: ★★★★
Apres-ski/nightlife:★★
Other activities:★★
ⓘ Toll free reservations: (800) 828-4748
Internet: www.madrivervalley.com

Sugarbush

Summit elevation: 4,135 feet
Vertical drop: 2,650 feet
Base elevation: 1,485 feet
Expert: ★★★★★
Advanced: ★★★★
Intermediate:★★★★
Beginner: ★★★★
Never-ever:★★★★
Address: 2405 Sugarbush Access Road
Warren, VT 05674-9572
☏ **Area code:** 802
Ski area phone: 583-6300
Snow report: 583-SNOW
ⓘ **Toll-free reservations:** (800) 53-SUGAR
Fax: 583-6303
Internet: www.sugarbush.com
Number and types of lifts: 18–4 high-
speed quads, 3 quad chairs, 3 triples,
4 double chairs, 4 surface lifts
Skiable Acreage: 432
Snowmaking: 61 percent
Uphill capacity: 24,363 per hour
Snowboarding: Yes, unlimited
Bed Base: 6,600 (2,200 on mountain)
Nearest lodging: Slopeside
Resort child care: Yes, 6 weeks and older
Adult ticket, per day: $41-$57 (01/02)

Mad River Glen

Summit elevation: 3,637 feet
Vertical drop: 2,000 feet
Base elevation: 1,637 feet
Expert: ★★★★★
Advanced: ★★★★
Intermediate:★★★
Beginner: ★★★
Never-ever: ★
Address: PO Box 1089
Waitsfield, VT 05673
☏ **Area code:** 802
Ski area phone: 496-3551
Snow report: 496-3551
ⓘ **Toll-free information:** (800) 850-6742,
area Chamber
Fax: 496-3562
E-mail: ski@madriverglen.com
Internet: www.madriverglen.com
Number and types of lifts: 5–3 double
chairs, 1 single chair, 1 surface lift
Skiable Acreage: about 115
Snowmaking: 15 percent
Uphill capacity: 3,000 per hour
Snowboarding: No
Bed Base: 6,600
Nearest lodging: About a quarter-mile
Resort child care: Yes, 6 weeks and older
Adult ticket, per day: $32-$42 (01/02)

Once the playground for the well-to-do, the out-of-the-way Mad River Valley gradually fell out of favor with the "in" ski crowd and became the place that time forgot. This has been a good thing. The valley remains free of large chain hotels and other ski resort sprawl, and the ambiance is classic New England: clapboard houses, quaint inns, restored barns and picture-postcard downtowns in the two villages that make up the valley, Waitsfield and Warren.

Purchased by the American Skiing Company in the mid-1990s, Sugarbush once again attracts the "in" crowd, not the Kennedys and Hollywood starlets, but people who really know how to ski and ride. ASC added high-speed lifts, more snowmaking and new trails, but they (thankfully) left the soul of Sugarbush untouched.

The first indication of this is that base area does not have an ASC trademark Grand Summit Hotel. The only slopeside lodging is condos, and these are well hidden in the trees. What's plainly obvious on the drive up the access road is that Sugarbush's trails, at least many of the ones in the Lincoln Peak area, are steep and narrow. It's no wonder that the resort is home to extreme skier John Egan of Warren-Miller-movie fame. This is old-time New England skiing at its finest.

Serious skiers will find more of the same seven miles up the road at Mad River Glen. The Alta of the East, Mad River Glen is the way skiing used to be. Home to one of the few single chairs left in the country, Mad River has almost no snowmaking and no condos. Narrow trails cut down the thickly wooded mountain are merely suggestions of where to ski. Diehards ski all over Mad River Glen, through trees, over frozen waterfalls and down cliffs. Its terrain attracts such a devoted following that Mad River is America's only skier-owned, nonprofit cooperative. For co-op share information, call the resort.

But beginners, don't despair. Both Sugarbush and Mad River have plenty of trails marked with green circles and blue squares. And everyone will enjoy the relatively uncrowded slopes, because the valley is still off the beaten path.

 # Sugarbush
Mountain layout—skiing

Sugarbush is divided into two separate areas, Lincoln Peak and Mount Ellen, connected by a 10-minute ride on rollercoaster-like high-speed quad chair lift. Each of these mountains is then subdivided further into ski areas with their own distinct flavors. Lincoln Peak alone has four separate mountains, ranging from the extreme runs of Castlerock Peak to the relatively gentle slopes of North Lynx Peak. Mount Ellen, one of few mountains in Vermont over 4,000 feet, has three double-diamond runs plummeting off its summit complemented by good cruising terrain below.

◆◆ **Expert** ◆ **Advanced:** At Lincoln Peak, the runs served by Castlerock lift are very black and no place for the timid. The entire Castlerock area offers narrow New England-style steeps, and if you are lucky the Castlerock run will occasionally be groomed, making for a heavenly smooth steep. This year, the Castlerock double chair was replaced with a new, yet still slow, double. It is popular with those in this ability level, so be aware that sometimes there is a wait, usually not more than eight to 10 minutes. The benefit is that these narrow trails do not fill up with yahoo skiers. You have to want to be there to end up at Castlerock.

From the summit of Lincoln Peak and the top of the Heaven's Gate triple, experts can drop down Ripcord or Paradise, two double-black-diamond runs that frequently bump up. The more wide-open Organgrinder (the old gondola lift line), which we dubbed "Organ Do-nor," is a wide, steep run that dares you to ski fast. Stein's Run, accessible by either the Super Bravo Express or the Valley House Double chair lifts, is another long, steep, bumped-up run. Egan's Woods, to skier's left of Stein's Run, is no doubt where extreme skier John Egan plays.

Mt. Ellen is primarily an intermediate playground, though the double blacks at the top—F.I.S., Black Diamond, Exterminator and Bravo (the latter a single diamond)—are among the toughest in New England.

■ **Intermediate:** Intermediates should start at the Super Bravo chair on Lincoln Peak, then traverse to the Heaven's Gate triple. Once at the summit, take Upper Jester, a run full of fun switchbacks that take you back to the top of the Super Bravo lift. From here, choose from Downspout, Domino, Snowball, Murphy's Glades or Lower Jester. On a busy day, these runs are crowded with skiers. Intermediates also tend to flock to the North Lynx triple on the upper part of North Lynx Peak. Here, the views are good, and the runs sometimes bump up.

The slopes tend to be less crowded on the lower part of North Lynx Peak and parts of Gadd Peak. Eden, a tree-skiing area on Gadd Peak, is the place to learn to navigate glades. Spring Fling is wide-open and attracts few skiers and is great for long, fast turns.

Mount Ellen also has wide-open cruising runs. On the map, the intermediate runs from the top of the Summit quad chair seem relatively short, but the map is misleading. The Rim Run, connecting to Upper Lookin' Good, Lower Rim Run, Cruiser and Straight Shot, is one of the classic cruising runs in the United States. The other intermediate section is Inverness, served by a quad chair.

●● **Beginner:** North Lynx Peak on the far right side of the Lincoln Peak is a good place for beginners. Start on Pushover and Easy Rider and then graduate to Slowpoke and Sleeper. At Mount Ellen, Walt's Trail is a long green run from the top of the Inverness chair.

● **Never-ever:** Lincoln Peak has Easy Rider, a gentle slope served by a double chair. Mount Ellen has Easy Street and Sugar Run, off to one side and also served by a double chair.

 ## Mountain layout—Snowboarding

Sugarbush has moved its terrain park and pipe to Lincoln Peak and is adding a beginner park and pipe in the Gate House area. The only trail that will leave you hiking here is Lower FIS; even if you hold speed you'll be booting out and kicking. It's worth it on a powder day, because this is a quiet trail that holds freshies late, but you will have to hike out. There are a few traverses where you'll need to keep up speed: Bailout from Castlerock Run to Heaven's Gate is not all that bad, a little speed will get the job done. The Northway that goes from Exterminator over to the Inverness lift at Mount Ellen is long and somewhat flat as well, but speed should carry provided the surface is groomed, otherwise, you'll hike. Reverse Traverse, from the top of Stein's Run over to Murphy's Glades, is tough because you really can't get a lot of speed to go the distance. Instead, head down Snowball to Spring Fling.

 ## Lessons (2001/02 prices)

As part of the American Skiing Company, Sugarbush uses the Perfect Turn® program.

Group lessons: Group clinics are $30 for all levels except never-evers. A Value Pak of 10 two-hour clinics costs $200.

Never-evers: Learn-to-Ski or Ride clinics include lesson, lifts and rentals and costs $70 for the first day and $75 for the second and third times on snow. Or you can buy all three days for $150.

Private lessons: $75 an hour.

Special programs: Sugarbush offers a morning powder clinic and afternoon clinics for bumps or steeps. Multi-day clinics for snowboarders, women and expert skiers or riders, called Snow Sports University, are also available. Call 888-651-4827 for reservations.

Child care

Ages: 6 weeks to 6 years.

Location: Sugarbush Village (a group of condos to the far right past the main parking lot at Lincoln Peak).

Cost: Day Care Cubs (6 weeks–6 years) get a non-ski program for $59, $49 for a half day. Reservations required; call 802-583-6717.

Note: You can park at Sugarbush Village, but make sure you have a lift ticket already and be prepared to push and skate your way uphill to the lift.

Children's lessons: Children are divided into age groups for instruction. Microbears for 3-year-olds combines day care with some skiing: $75 full day, $49 half day. Minibears for 4-6-year-olds combines ski lessons with play activities: $77 full day, $49 half day. Sugarbears, ages 7–12, get ski or snowboard lessons: $85 full day, $59 for half day. Children's programs include lunch and lift tickets, plus equipment for the age 6-and-younger crowd. Reservations required; call 888-651-4827. Lessons for every group but Microbears start at the Gate House Lodge at Lincoln Peak. Microbears are located at child care.

Lift tickets (2001/02 prices)

	Adult	Young Adult (13-18)
One day	$57	$49
Three days	$135 ($45/day)	$117 ($39/day)
Five days	$205 ($41/day)	$185 ($37/day)

Who skis free: Children ages 5 and younger.

Who skis at a discount: Sugarbush lowers ticket prices for adults in its Value Season, (opening through mid-December and in April). Ages 65 and older ski for the child's price.

Note: The Valley of the Giants, a joint ticket for Mad River Glen and Sugarbush, is available when skiers purchase accommodation for three nights or more in the valley. The joint lift ticket allows skiers to choose where they want to ski in the valley each day. Make sure to ask about this special lift ticket when you make reservations.

Mad River Glen
Mountain layout—skiing

Mad River Glen or MRG is a throwback to earlier ski days, and as one of our contributors put it, "It's the type of skiing that made my mother give up the sport." The ski area prides itself on being tough, and the bumper sticker, "Mad River Glen: Ski It If You Can," is all-too-true. Trail ratings are not inflated, and even the beginner trails here might be graded intermediate elsewhere. But MRG fans love this area and have shown their devotion by buying shares of this now member-owned ski resort. And yes, we mean ski resort; snowboards are not allowed. MRG is traditional (it's one of two areas in the nation with a chair lift for solo riders), natural (little snowmaking, combined with plenty of tight tree skiing), hard-corps (the ski shop at the base sells T-shirts with the slogan, "Friends, don't let friends get first track") and homey (skiers with serious tracks to carve have got to love a cafeteria with peanut-butter-and-jelly sandwiches to go). It's a mountain for serious skiers, not posers. Leave your Bogner suit on the hanger and don some wool pants. You'll fit right in.

◆◆ **Expert** ◆ **Advanced:** Experts will be happy just about anywhere at Mad River glen, especially after a snowstorm when the bumps become gigantic. One nice feature that's a throwback to tradition is the area's refusal to make much manmade snow. All of the expert terrain is covered with natural snow (when it falls), so it bumps up nicely and doesn't get as icy as the East's other resorts.

While the line for the single chair is usually about 10 minutes long, it can approach 45 minutes on peak holidays and good powder days, and the real experts happily wait. From the top of this historic lift, experts can immediately drop down the Chute under the lift or traverse to Catamount Bowl, one of the most wide-open runs on the mountain. For more of a challenge, find a guide or hook up with a local and venture into the area called Paradise, entered by dropping down an 8-foot waterfall. Ask around for Octopus's Garden and the 19th and 20th Holes. If you look like you know how to ski, a local may direct you to these.

At the single chair's midstation, tree skiing beckons through the Glades to the right as you ski off the chair. Experts with tired legs can traverse on Broadway and drop down wide-open Grand Canyon.

■ **Intermediate:** Mad River glen is not known for its cruiser runs, and if intermediates find themselves at the top of the single chair, they have only one route down, upper Antelope, which splits into Catamount after a few turns. Both runs are quite narrow, and intermediates should beware: About halfway down, antelope veers off into the woods and gets steeper, and, hard to believe, even narrower. Unless you're up for a challenge, follow Broadway under the lift, and head to the other side of the mountain.

Intermediates will find a better selection of terrain off the Sunnyside Chair. Quacky to Porcupine is a nice run. Bunny will also take you from Quacky to the base. To the right of the chair is a series of expert trails, Panther, Partridge, Slalom Hill and Gazelle, most of which empty into Birdland. Confident intermediates will find these runs challenging, if not downright scary, and a missed turn may mean you have to side-slip into a trail.

If you feel like you're ready to tackle MRG's classic terrain (i.e., the woods), give yourself a sampler. From the top of the Sunnyside chair, take Fox to the big intersection and traverse straight into the woods. The trees soon open up into the Glades. If this trail seems fun, congratulations! You're ready for the tough stuff. If you're intimidated, bail out on Bunny.

●● **Beginner:** Birdland is ostensibly the beginner area, but to get there, you have to have good route-finding skills. Otherwise, you'll find yourself at the top of an overly-moguled expert pitch vowing to give up the sport. Take the Sunnyside chair to the top, then follow Fox to Snail, catwalks that will take you to the land of green circles. Granted, Duck, Lark, Robin, Wren and Loon are for beginners, but intermediates will find the pitch is comfortable. Learn to ski here, and little will daunt you elsewhere.

● **Never-ever:** Mad River Glen is not the best place for a first-timer

Mountain layout—Snowboarding

Snowboarding has been banned at Mad River Glen since the 1993/94 season, when some impolite boarders ticked off the owner. That policy is unchanged. The co-op membership vote on allowing snowboarding failed, with 86 percent voting against sharing the mountain with snowboarders.

Lessons (2001/02 prices)

Mad River Glen has a ski school that, like the area, marches to its own drummer. The Beginner You Can Learn to Ski Package, including a beginner ticket, a two-hour lesson and rentals, is $55 for either alpine or telemark. A follow-up two-hour lesson on the same day costs $35. Private lessons cost $55 for one hour, $90 for two hours.

Child care (2001/02 prices)

Ages: 6 weeks to 6 years.

The Cricket Club Nursery (496-2123) offers infant care to 18 months for $45 for a full day, $30 for a half day. Ages 18 months-6 years cost $40 for a full day and $25 for a half day. Ski and Play programs are $55 for a full day with lunch and $35 for a half day. The Nursery does not take reservations, but if you check your child into the nursery on Friday and pay for 2 days, you're guaranteed a spot on Saturday. Or if you call at 8:15 a.m. and say you're on your way, they will hold a spot for your child. Call 496-3551, ext. 20.

Lessons: Ducks is for first-time children ages 6-12; Chipmunks is for ages 4-7; Panthers is for ages 7-12. Programs run from 10 a.m. to 3 p.m. and cost $60. Lunch is included but a lift ticket is not. A half-day is $30, without lunch. Kids who know how to ski can sign up for the Freestyle Team and learn to attack Mad River's moguls.

Mad River Glen lift tickets (2001/02 prices)

	Adult	Junior (6-15)
One day, midweek	$32	$23
One day, weekend	$40	$26
One day, holiday	$42	$30

Who skis free: Ages 70 and older. Children 5 and younger are issued a free ticket when skiing with a paying adult.

Who skis at a discount: Ages 65-69 ski at junior prices. If you buy a two-day ticket, you get $2 off the price each day. For a three-day or longer ticket, you get $3 off the daily price.

Note: Ski the Valley is a joint ticket for Mad River Glen and Sugarbush available when skiers purchase accommodation for three nights or more in the valley. Make sure to ask about this special lift ticket when you make reservations.

Cross-country and snowshoeing

The **Blueberry Lake Cross Country Ski Center** (496-6687) has 23 km. of trails, beginner to expert, groomed for skate skiing and classic. Dogs are permitted. **Ole's Cross Country Center** (496-3430; near the airport) has 50 km. of groomed trails on rolling terrain. Ole's also has snowshoeing and a Rossignol demo center. The **Inn at the Round Barn Farm** (496-2276) cross-country area, with 15 km. of groomed trails, is linked with Ole's.

Snowshoe treks are available from the summit of **Sugarbush**'s Mount Ellen to Lincoln Peak. Free, guided treks begin at the base of Lincoln Peak. **Mad River Glen** has just under five miles of snowshoe trails on the mountain. These trails connect with Vermont's famed Long Trail. It also offers snowshoe naturalist programs. Or arrange **treks** through Vermont Pack & Paddle (496-7225) and Clearwater Sports (496-2708). Snowshoers who want to strike out on their own can take advantage of a variety of **backcountry trails** in the region; a trail map is available from the Sugarbush Chamber of Commerce.

Accommodations

This area has some of Vermont's finest country inns and B&Bs, all of which can be booked through Sugarbush Chamber of Commerce (800-828-4748; spells 82-VISIT; or www.madrivervalley.com), Sugarbush Central Reservations (800-537-8427; spells 53-SUGAR) or call the inns directly.

Topping the list, **The Inn at the Round Barn Farm** (496-2276; $$–$$$$), a mile from Rte. 100, across the covered bridge, on East Warren Road is one of the best B&Bs we've seen anywhere in ski country. The farmhouse has been made into an elegant, spacious, 11-room bed-and-breakfast. It is peaceful and quiet, strictly No Smoking, with children discouraged. The stunning Richardson Room with Vermont-made canopied king bed, skylights, gas fireplace, oversized Jacuzzi and steam shower is top-of-the-line. There are 30 km. of cross-country tracks outside the door.

The Pitcher Inn (496-6350 or 888-867-4824; $$$$) is luxury in the tiny village of Warren, with eight rooms in the main inn and two suites in an adjacent barn. This is a member of the Relais & Chateaux properties.

Tucker Hill Inn (496-3983 or 800-543-7841; $-$$), two miles from lifts, has 22 rooms and a steakhouse restaurant. **The Waitsfield Inn** (496-3979 or 800-758-3801; $-$$), in the center of Waitsfield Village, started life in the 1820s as a parsonage, was a sleeping-bag dorm for young skiers in the '60s and '70s and is now a quaintly elegant 14-bedroom B&B. It now has restaurant, too.

The Sugartree Inn (583-3211; $$) has award-winning breakfasts and a collection of rooms, ranging from large with canopied beds and/or fireplace to small; all are most pleasant. The inn is only a quarter mile from Sugarbush's slopes. **The Featherbed Inn** (496-7151; $$), on Rte. 100 only a stone's throw from the resort access road, is a restored 1806 house with 10 spacious guest rooms, all with private baths and luxurious featherbeds, plenty of space to spread out and to-die-for breakfasts.

West Hill House B&B (496-7162; $$-$$$) has seven bedrooms all with private baths. **Beaver Pond Farm Inn** (583-2861; $-$$) is right on the cross-country trails of the Sugarbush golf course. **1824 House Inn** (496-7555; $) has eight rooms just north of town with featherbeds and an outdoor hot tub.

The nicest full-service hotel property is the **Sugarbush Inn** (583-6114 or 800-53SUGAR; $$) on the access road. The inn and its 46 rooms are well-kept but nondescript.

Closer to Sugarbush resort you'll find **Sugar Lodge** at Sugarbush (800-982-3465; $-$$), only a half mile from Lincoln Peak. The **Weathertop Lodge** (800-800-3625, 496-4909; $-$$), on Rte. 17 between town and Mad River Glen, is an affordable B&B.

The **Inn At The Mad River Barn** (496-3310; $-$$) has rustic but spacious rooms and some of the best lodging food in the valley (both in quantity and quality). To stay here is to step into a wonderful 1940s ski lodge.

Families will want to check into **John Egan's Big World** on Rte. 100 (496-5557; $-$$) or the **Hyde Away** Inn and Restaurant (496-2322; $-$$) on Rte. 17. Both are great spots for children and close to the slopes. The Hyde Away has become the favorite locals' hangout for shooting pool.

Of the Condominiums in the **Village at Sugarbush**, the most luxurious are the **Southface Condominiums** with hot tubs in each unit and a shuttlebus ride from the slopes. The Snow Creek condos are ski-in/ski-out, but you have the noise of snow guns at your back window during snowmaking operations. The **Paradise** condos are newer but a good walk from the slopes; however, they have a reliable, free shuttle service. The **Summit** units are roomy, and **Castle Rock** condos are close to the slopes. **Unihab** looks like boxes stacked on one another, and the small **Middle Earth** condos are 10 minutes from the lifts. Rates range from $145 for a one-bedroom in value season to $635 for a four-bedroom during holidays. Guests may use the indoor pool, tennis, racquetball, squash courts, aerobics, Jacuzzi, steam room and Nautilus equipment at the Sugarbush Sports Center for an additional fee.

Almost as close to the lifts as Sugarbush Village units is **The Bridges Resort and Racquet Club** (583-2922 or 800-453-2922; $$-$$$$), with tennis courts and an indoor pool. These units are quieter than the mountain units and have wonderful amenities as well as a regular shuttle.

Skiers heading for Mad River Glen should check into the unfortunately named **Battleground** condos on Rte. 17 (496-2288 or 800-248-2102).

 Dining

The Mad River Valley has more than 40 eating establishments, many of them offering excellent food. Most of them require reservations, so call before venturing out.

The top of the line is **Chez Henri** (583-2600; $$-$$$) in Sugarbush Village at the base area of Lincoln Peak. The oldest restaurant in the valley, it captures a true French bistro feeling, with low ceilings and a flickering fire. The owner, Henri Borel, personally greets guests and makes them feel at home. He also supervises the excellent wine selection. Chez Henri features lunch, fondue in the late afternoon, then dinner until 10 p.m.

The **Spotted Cow** (496-5151; $$-$$$), run by Jay and Renata Young, has gained a reputation for some of the best food in the valley. Pricey to be sure. Don't miss the Bermuda fish chowder; it's worth the trip to Waitsfield.

The **Pitcher Inn** Restaurant (496-6350; $$$) has courted the gourmet crowd, but to mixed reviews. Meals here are served in an attractive traditional dining room overlooking the Mad River in Warren Village. The wine cellar boasts 3,500 bottles.

John Egan's Big World Pub & Grill (496-3033; $$) serves excellent food and is a great place to bring the family.

The **Common Man** (583-2800; $$) has attracted a faithful clientele and has a reputation for good food, but for the money, it's not quite as "common" as the name implies. The atmosphere is what might be called a New England Baroque barn with crystal chandeliers.

The **Warren House** (583-2421; $$), down a driveway to the left as you approach the Sugarbush parking lot, has developed lots of fans and offers an eclectic menu rivaling any in the area, along with a good wine list.

Michael's Restaurant (496-3832; $$), at Powderhound Lodge on Rte. 100, serves dishes such as Grown-Up Grilled Cheese, Lobster Shepherds Pie and Green Mountain Jambalaya.

The **Steak Place at Tucker Hill** (496-3025; $$) serves beef in front of a flickering fireplace under a beamed ceiling. It also has light apres-ski and late-night fare.

Millbrook Country Inn (496-2405; $$), on Rte. 17, has a small fireplaced dining room with original art and antiques. The meals are prepared from local organic produce.

Miguel's Stowe Away (583-3858; $-$$) serves plentiful Mexican food at affordable prices, guaranteeing that this place is normally packed.

Mad River Barn Restaurant ($) has a popular Saturday buffet and serves dinners Sunday through Friday from 6:30 to 8 p.m.

A Sugarbush tradition worth the effort is the **American Flatbread Kitchen** (496-8856; $), open only on weekends, at the Lareau Farm Country Inn. Be ready for a long wait (anywhere from 30 to 90 minutes).

For families out to stretch the budget and still get good wholesome food, try the **Hyde Away** (496-2322; $-$$), on Rte. 17. **BonGiorno's** (496-6265; $), also on Rte. 17, is the place to head for pizza and affordable pasta, with delivery as well. For simple quick food, try **The Den** (496-8880; $-$$) on Waitsfield's main street. Jay's (496-8282; $) doesn't claim to be anything fancy but is a good spot for family fare.

For breakfast, try the **Hyde Away** or **Pepper's Restaurant** (583-2202; $) at Pepper's Lodge. The Mad River Barn lays out excellent homemade muffins and jams and serves only real maple syrup.

New this year is **Pete's Eats,** located in the same building as the Mad mountain Tavern. You can get breakfast while having your skis tuned at the shop next door. Try two eggs, coffee, toast and hash browns with a quick edge and wax for $10.99.

The **Valley Pizzaria** (496-9200; $) makes real brick-oven, hand-thrown pizza. It's as close to Jersey pizza as you'll ever find in Vermont, one local tells us. Seating is limited; get it to go.

Condo dwellers can pick up basic staples, baked goods, beer and wine at the **Paradise Deli & Market** (583-2757) on the access road. The deli also has dinners-to-go. There are two supermarkets in town. Shaw's is to Sugarbush as Mehuron's Market is to Mad River Glen. Shaw's has the better produce. Mehuron's is the local's choice, the bonuses here are the butcher and fish departments.

Après-ski/nightlife

Après-ski starts at the base lodges, which do booming business at the bar as the lifts close. Chez Henri's Back Room is the on-mountain après-ski hangout and can rock all evening. The Hyde Away is where you will find the locals; the Blue Tooth on the access road is most popular with tourists. On weekends try the Sugarbush Inn for a slightly more upscale, older crowd.

The base area bar at Mad River Glen, General Stark's Pub, follows the retro atmosphere of the area with plenty of fun in an old-time bar. After leaving Mad River Glen, the next place to stop is the Mad River Barn. The bar there looks like an old Vermont bar should look: moose head hanging over the fireplace, hunting scenes on every wall, big couches and stuffed chairs, wood paneling and bumper pool or shuffleboard.

Gallagher's recently had a much-needed facelift. In the evenings, it has dancing with a mix of music from rock to country-rock and an interesting crowd. Mad Mountain Tavern, across from Gallagher's, is popular with the dancin' crowd because of live music on weekends.

 ## Other activities

Shopping: Waitsfield and Warren have art galleries, country stores and antique and collectible shops that are fun for browsing and buying. Most shops in tiny Warren Village are within easy walking-distance of each other.

Dining: $$$-Entrees $20+; $$-$10-20; $-less than $10.

Accommodations: (double room) $$$$-$200+; $$$-$141-$200; $$-$81-$140; $-$80 and less.

The Sugarbush Sports Center and the Bridges Resort and Racquet Club have various **sports and exercise facilities.**

Winter Wonderland (800-53-SUGAR), owned by the resort, located at the Sugarbush Golf Course on Golf Course Road, offers evening sleigh rides for $10 a person or a **sleigh ride/dinner combination** for $40 a person. During the day they have **snowmobile rides,** cross-country skiing on the golf course and **snowshoeing.**

Snowshoe treks (583-0381) are available from the summit of Sugarbush's Mount Ellen to Lincoln Peak. Snow tubing is also available at Lincoln Peak Thursday through Sunday from 10 a.m. to 5 p.m. and on Wednesday and Saturday at night from 6–9 p.m. Treks are also offered by Vermont Pack and Paddle and Clearwater Sports (496-2708). Mad River Glen offers snowshoe naturalist programs.

Sleigh rides and skijoring (496-7141) can be arranged at the Vermont Icelandic Horse Farm in Waitsfield. (Skijoring here involves being pulled behind a horse or snowmobile while on skis.) Other farms offering sleigh rides are the Mountain Valley Farm (496-9255).

Ice skating rinks are at Tucker Hill Lodge, Sugarbush Inn, Sugarbush Health and Racquet Club or the Skatium next to Grand Union in Waitsfield.

Mad River Flick (426-4200) has first-run **movies,** plus something at the concession stand most movie theaters don't offer, beer and wine.

For the perfect way to unwind, head to Mad River Massage (496-5638) on Rte. 100 just south of the intersection with Rte. 17 and get the kinks kneaded out of your body. While you are there, explore their unique gift store with potions, lotions, aroma therapy candles and hand-crafted jewelry.

Getting there and around

Getting there: Sugarbush is off Rte. 100, about 20 miles south of Waterbury. Burlington airport is about an hour away. Amtrak offers train-ski-lodging packages, with daily service from New York, Philadelphia and Washington, D.C. For information and packages, call (800) 237-7547; (800) 872-7245 for train only.

Getting around: The valley offers daily public buses that run from Waitsfield, to Warren as well to the Sugarbush base areas and Mad River Glen. Schedules can be obtained from your lodging or online at www.madrivervalley.com/transportation. For a one-time visit to town it's okay, but for more frequent visits, bring or rent a car.

Mount Snow

Haystack

Vermont

Summit elevation: 3,600 feet
Vertical drop: 1,700 feet
Base elevation: 1,900 feet

Address: Route 100,
Mount Snow, VT 05356
☏ **Area code:** 802
Ski area phone: 464-3333
Snow report: 464-2151 **Weather:** 464-4131
ⓘ **Toll-free reservations:**
(800) 245-7669 (245-SNOW)
E-mail: info@mountsnow.com
World Wide Web: www.mountsnow.com
Expert:★
Advanced:★
Intermediate:★★★★
Beginner:★★★★
Never-ever:★★

Number of lifts: 23–3 high-speed quads,
1 quad, 10 triples, 4 doubles, 2 surface lifts,
3 magic carpets
Snowmaking: 78 percent
Trail acreage: 750 acres
Uphill capacity: 36,252 per hour
Snowboarding: Yes, unlimited
Bed Base: 10,000
Nearest lodging: Base area, condos, hotel
Resort child care: Yes, 6 weeks to 6 years old
Adult ticket, per day: $49-$55(2000/01)

Dining:★★★★
Apres-ski/nightlife:★★
Other activities:★★

For those living in the Northeast's major metropolitan areas, Mt. Snow, with a summit elevation of 3,600 feet, is the closest big mountain resort. Its proximity to major metropolitan centers means the resort attracts crowds on weekends and holidays. During these times, smart skiers and riders head to nearby Haystack. As the crow flies, Haystack is 2.5 miles from Mount Snow's southern end, but by car, it's 5 miles up Handle Road, which runs parallel to Rte. 100. Of note, the two resorts are not connected by trails or lifts, and Haystack is only open on weekends and holidays.

Mount Snow's height allows it to live up to its name. As weather moves up and over the mountain, snow often drops from the clouds. When nature fails, the resort, like its American Skiing Company cousin Killington, makes prodigious amounts of snow. Although it's big, Mount Snow is also surprisingly flat. Almost all the runs spilling down the front side from the summit are beginner or intermediate trails, and it's possible to ski top to bottom on the well-groomed runs without breaking a sweat. Not a favorite mountain for experts, Mount Snow is a Mecca for intermediates. Those who have always struggled in the bumps or trees might find the resort's terrain a great place to improve these skills.

Mountain layout—Skiing

◆◆ **Expert** ◆ **Advanced:** Aggressive skiers and snowboarders looking for a shot of adrenaline should head straight for the North Face area, a group of isolated steeper runs, some of which are allowed to bump up.

With a 37-degree pitch, Ripcord is the steepest, but Jaws, Plummet, Nekole's Way and Fallen Timbers also provide fine steep turns. The steep glades at The Plunge, Epiphany and The Trials will challenge any expert. On the opposite side of Mount Snow, the Sunbrook area has mostly cruisers, but Beartrap, the one advanced run, is a haven for bump skiers, in part because of its sunny face and snowmaking coverage. Beartrap has its own double lift, and the resort pumps out loud music from 900-watt speakers to get you in the spirit.

At Haystack, advanced skiers and snowboarders should head for The Witches, a separate area with trails named Merlin, Wizard and Warlock's Woods.

■ **Intermediate:** Other than the North Face, the rest of Mount Snow is a cruiser's delight. You can carve hero turns down just about any trail on the mountain. Be sure not to miss Snowdance, a trail as wide as a football field is long off the Canyon Express chair lift. The Sunbrook area, located off the south side of the summit, is an ideal spot for lower intermediates. With its southern exposure, it's also a great place for catching rays. Although the resort's glades are all marked with black diamonds, Claim Jumper and Sap Tapper aren't steep and are good places for skiers and riders to learn or improve their tree skiing.

At Haystack, stick to the Hayfever lift (for time reasons if nothing else; the Barnstormer triple chair is long). Last Chance usually has some good bumps to warm up on, and after a little practice, the intermediate skier or rider will probably be ready to try his or her hand at The Witches.

●● **Beginner** ● **Never-ever:** First-timers can start at the Launch Pad area outside the Perfect Turn® Discovery Center on the right side (looking up the mountain) of Mount Snow's main base area. This area has its own lifts: two Magic Carpets, a rope tow and a triple chair. From the summit, beginners will feel comfortable on Deer Run and Long John, two trails that make wide traverses of the mountain.

At the south end of the resort is Carinthia, which offers long mellow runs for advanced beginners, lower intermediates and anyone else who wants to have a playful cruise. There are enough zigs, zags and small drops to keep a skier awake. But snowboarders flock to this area and can fly by slower skiers, unnerving those who are still learning the sport.

At Haystack, beginners can start on the Skidder handle tow and graduate to beginner/advanced-beginner trails such as Last Chance and Outcast.

Mountain layout—Snowboarding

Mount Snow and Haystack both have great trails for boarders of all levels, as well as four excellent terrain parks of varying difficulty. Un Blanco Gulch, located on the Canyon Trail, has a quarter-pipe, spines and plenty of jumps. But the real center for snowboarders is Carinthia. The Gut is a competition-sized halfpipe. Terrain parks at Carintha include Inferno, Mount Snow's longest terrain park with a double-diamond rating, and the more mellow El Diablo, which feeds into the Palmer Boardercross course. A new kid's terrain park, Grommet, is designed for those 12 and younger to let them get their taste of jumps and hits.

Mountain rating

The emphasis is definitely on the intermediate level. Advanced skiers and riders can try some of the relatively tough runs on the North Face, but if you are an expert, don't come out of your way to ski these; they're not that tough. Beginners, get ready to improve; this mountain has just your kind of terrain.

Cross-country

The Mount Snow Valley has four major ski touring centers. The largest is **Hermitage Cross-Country Touring Center** (464-3511), on Road in Wilmington, with 50 km. of trails that form a circle from the warming hut to Mount Snow and back. **Timber Creek** (464-0999) and the **White House of Wilmington Cross Country Ski Center** (464-2135) offer more than 60 km. of trails skewed toward the intermediate Nordic skier. Advanced cross-country skiers can ski the one-way, 2.5-mile Ridge Trail connecting the Haystack and Mount Snow summits. The Ridge Trail fee is $10, which includes a lift ride to the summit.

 ## Lessons (2001/02 prices)

Lessons and equipment rentals for skiers and riders age 13 and older are offered out of the Perfect Turn® Discovery Center, located on the north side of the main base area at Mount Snow.

Group lessons: The Perfect Turn® instruction program offers several levels of clinics. For lower intermediates and higher, the clinics have a maximum of six people and normally last two hours. Skiers and riders watch a short video that demonstrates various levels of ability, then place themselves into the proper clinic. Morning and afternoon sessions are offered and cost $33.

Never-ever package: Learn-to-Ski or Snowboard for first-timers is a half-day program employing the Guaranteed Learning Method, meaning the resort guarantees new skiers and riders that they will be able to ride a lift, turn and stop by the end of the clinic. The package includes lessons, equipment and beginner lift ticket . Level 1 costs $70. Packages for Levels 2-3 (those skiing or riding green-circle trails) cost $75. Reservations are required.

Private lessons: $80 an hour. Private lessons at Haystack cost $60 an hour.

Special Programs: Women's programs, family ski/snowboard clinics and senior programs are available. There are also separate clinics available for advanced skiers and snowboarders. Call the resort.

Child care (2001/02 prices)

Childcare is open 8 a.m.-4:30 p.m. on weekends.

Ages: 6 weeks to 6 years.

Costs: $64 for a full day with lunch; $320 for five days. Discovery Camp, an introductory ski program for 3-year-olds registered in full-day childcare, costs an additional $20 with rentals.

Reservations: Required; call (800) 889-4411 or 464-4152.

Babysitting: Mount Snow Child Care has a few babysitters who will come to your vacation home, condo or hotel room. Cost is $10/hour for one child, $1/hour for each additional child (rates do not apply New Year's Eve); call (800) 889-4411 or 464-4152. Baby on the Go (464-5475) rents baby needs, such as cribs, strollers, car seats and high chairs. Delivery and set-up are available at an additional charge.

Children's lessons: Perfect Kids programs are available for ages 4-12. Ages 4-6 enroll in Snow Camp. The full-day cost is $81, including lessons and lunch, but no equipment. Ages 7–12 enroll in Mountain Camp or Mountain Riders. The full-day cost is $69 for lessons and lunch but no equipment. Lifts are covered while kids are in lessons, but half-day enrollees will need to buy a lift ticket if they want to continue on their own. Half-day costs are $38 for Snow Camp and $31 for Mountain Camp or Mountain Riders.

Lift tickets (2001/02 prices)

	Adult	Junior (6-12)
One day* (00/01)	$58	$37
Three days	$154 ($51/day)	$104 ($35/day)
Five days*	$246 ($49/day)	$165 ($33/day)

*Note: Prices are rounded to the nearest dollar to include the 5% Vermont sales tax.

Who skis free: Children ages 5 and younger. Children 12 and younger ski free when their parent buys a five-day midweek lift ticket.

Who skis at a discount: Ages 65 and older ski for junior prices; ages 13–18 pay $138 (includes tax) for three days; $218 (includes tax) for five days.

Mount Snow tickets also are valid at Haystack. Tickets to ski Haystack alone cost about $40 for adults (older than 13) and $30 for juniors/seniors a day, everyday, for everyone.

Mount Snow/Haystack is one of the American Skiing Company resorts, most of which are in the Northeast. For a description of discount programs that give benefits at all the resorts, see the Lift Ticket section in the Sunday River chapter.

Accommodations

Condo projects and a lodge at the base area have shuttle service to the slopes. Most of the other lodging lines Rte. 100 between the slopes and Wilmington,, with some tucked on side roads back into the foothills.

Rates vary, depending on season and the size of the unit. Per-person rates start at about $132 for two-day weekend packages; five-day midweek packages (Sunday through Thursday nights) are a bargain—some as low as $35 per person per day. A new one-night package combines a night in a hotel with a day of skiing starting at $44 a day (another bargain).

For a **vacation planner** with descriptions of most area properties, write: Mount Snow, Rte. 100, Mount Snow, Vermont 05356, or call (800) 245-7669 (245-SNOW), e-mail: vacasvs@sover.net.

Condominiums

Rates are based on the size of the unit and number of bathrooms. They start at about $250 on the weekends; half that midweek.

The Mount Snow Condominiums (800-451-4211 or 464-7788; $$$–$$$$ P✺) are at the base of the lifts, but only the Seasons complex is actually ski-in/ski-out. Seasons' condos are the most highly recommended with an athletic center, indoor pools, saunas and hot tubs. Two-bedroom/two-bath units cost around $800 for a weekend. Call (800) 245-7669 for information on all condos near the base area (shuttle service to the slopes).

Timber Creek Townhomes (800-982-8922 or 464-1222; $$$$ ✕ P✺) are luxury condos across Rte. 100 from the ski area. They have a fitness center and 18 km. of cross-country trails just outside. Shuttlebuses run between the complex and the ski area.

Greenspring at Mount Snow (800-247-7833 or 464-7111; $$$–$$$$ ♿ ≥ ⌂ P▮) are upscale condos a mile from the slopes. This complex has the best athletic center in the area.

As an ASC resort, Mount Snow also has a **Grand Summit Resort Hotel & Conference Center** (464-6600 or 800-845-7690; $$$–$$$$ ✕ ♿ ≥ P✺▮) a ski in/ski out full-service resort hotel with 200 rooms in the Main Base Area.

Inns

Snow Lake Lodge (800-451-4211 or 802-464-7788; $$–$$$) is a sprawling 92-room mountain lodge near the base of Mount Snow. While still fairly basic, the lodge does have a fitness center, sauna, indoor hot tub, outdoor Jacuzzi and aprés-ski entertainment. The Sundance lift is a 300-yard walk or a free shuttle ride away. The lodge is excellent with children.

The Inn at Sawmill Farm (802-464-8131; $$$$ ✕ ℗ ⛄ ✿ ⊟), is one of the nation's top country inns and is in a class by itself. Entry is through a portion of the former barn. The inn is not suitable for children, nor does it take credit cards.

Less than a quarter-mile from Mount Snow, the **Yankee Doodle Lodge** (800-388-5591 or 802-464-5591; $$$$) is family-friendly and comes highly recommended by the locals.

The **Lodge at Mount Snow** (800-451-4289 or 802-464-5112; $$$$ TfN) is on Rte. 100 near the entrance to the resort and has midweek packages that include free lodging for kids 12 and younger.

Andirons Lodge (800-445-7669 or 802-464-2114; $$ ✕ ⛰ ℗ ✿), on Rte. 100 in West Dover, is just two miles from the lifts. While somewhat short on hospitality, this motel offers low-cost lodging in simple paneled rooms with double beds; some have additional twin beds. There is an indoor pool, a sauna and a newly refurbished game room called the Billiard Sanctuary. The attached Dover Forge restaurant serves affordable meals.

Nordic Hills Lodge (800-326-5130 or 802-464-5130; $$$$ ✕ ℗ ✿), on 179 Coldbrook Road in Wilmington, has cable TV. Rates include breakfast and dinner.

Gray Ghost Inn (800-745-3615 or 802-464-2474), on Rte. 100, West Dover, is a large country inn operated by a British couple. Many rooms have smaller beds or bunk beds for children. Rates include breakfast.

Trail's End (800-859-2585 or 802-464-2727; $$–$$$ ℗ ✿ ❂), Smith Road, Wilmington. This inn has 15 country-style rooms. Meals are served family style at three round tables, so visitors probably will return home with new friends.

Old Red Mill (800-843-8483 or 802-464-3700; $–$$ ✕ ℗ ✿), Rte. 100 in Wilmington, was created from a former sawmill and is one of the bargains in the region. Rooms are small, only about 7 by 12 feet with a double bed, but all have TV. Larger rooms are available for families. The common areas are rustic.

Horizon Inn (800-336-5513 or 802-464-2131; $–$$$ ✕ ⛰ ℗ ✿ ▮ ❂), Rte. 9 in Wilmington, has an indoor heated pool, whirlpool, sauna and game room.

Best Western—The Lodge at Mount Snow (800-451-4289 or 802-464-5112; $$$$ ✕ ℗ ✿), at the base of Mount Snow, has midweek packages that include free lodging for kids 12 and younger.

The White House of Wilmington (464-2135; $$–$$$ aTBGfN), Rte. 9, Wilmington, is an upscale, romantic 23-room inn serving breakfast and dinner. An Editor's Pick by the Yankee Travel Guide, the inn has an indoor pool.

Bed & Breakfasts

Mount Snow also has a group of charming and elegant bed-and-breakfast establishments with rates starting at about $125 per night on weekends and $70 midweek. These B&Bs are smaller, most with fewer than 15 rooms.

The Doveberry Inn (800-722-3204 or 464-5652; $$ ✕ ℗ ✿ ❂) on Rte. 100, West Dover is run by Michael and Christine Fayette, both culinary-school-trained chefs. This inn is not suitable for young children.

Dining: $$$–Entrees $20+; $$–$10-20; $–less than $10.
Accommodations: (double room) $$$$–$200+; $$$–$141-$200; $$–$81-$140; $–$80 and less.

West Dover Inn (800-732-0745 or 464-5207;$$ 🛏 ✕ Ⓟ ✀), Rte. 100, West Dover, is an historic country inn built in 1846. It has 12 elegant rooms furnished with antiques, hand-sewn quilts and color TVs, as well as two suites with fireplaces and whirlpool tubs.

Deerhill Inn (800-464-3100; $$–$$$$ ✕ Ⓟ ✀), Valley View Road, in West Dover, is a chef-owned romantic hillside inn with panoramic views of Mount Snow and Haystack.

The Red Shutter Inn (800-845-7548 or 464-3768; $$–$$$ ✕ Ⓟ ✀ Ⓢ) is on Rte. 9, Wilmington. This 1894 country home has been converted into an elegant country inn with nine guest rooms.

The Nutmeg Inn (464-3351; $$–$$$ Ⓟ 🍷 ✀ Ⓢ) is on Rte. 9W, Wilmington. Built in the 1770s as a home, this inn is decorated with country accents and quilts and has 10 rooms and three fireplace suites.

The Orchard Inn (464-7147) on Rte. 100 just north of Wilmington, has seven rooms. The restaurant, Piero's Trattoria, serves the most authentic Italian cuisine in the valley..

The Inn at Quail Run (800-343-7227 or 464-3362; $$$$) is recommended by locals and welcomes both children and pets. Its brunch is considered the best in the valley.

🍴☕🍴 Dining

The top dining experience (and the most expensive) is the **Inn at Sawmill Farm** (464-1130; $$$-$$$$), which holds a Wine Spectator Grand Award..

The Hermitage (464-3511; $$–$$$) serves excellent meals at less stratospheric prices. A very large dining room was the world's largest collection of hanging Delacroix prints. The wine cellar has 30,000 bottles of 2,000 different labels. All game birds and venison are raised on the premises, and the jams, jellies and maple syrup are homemade.

For other fine dining try **Betty Hillman's Le Petit Chef** (464-8437; $$–$$$), **Two Tannery Road** (464-2707; $$$), and **Gregory's** (464-5207; $$–$$$), next to the West Dover Inn. **Doveberry Restaurant** (464-5652; $$$) is small and intimate with husband-and-wife chefs, culinary school graduates who have worked in Nantucket and San Francisco. The menu is Northern Italian. **The Deerhill Inn and Restaurant** (800-626-5674 or 464-3100; $$$), on Valley View Road, in West Dover, features award-winning American cuisine and a strong wine list.

Fennessey's (464-9361; $$) serves up consistently good food at reasonable prices according to locals. **The White House** (464-2135; $$) serves a great Sunday brunch with a 30-foot buffet table. Dinners are excellent and are served in a nice setting overlooking Wilmington. Locals tell us **The Inn at Quail Run** (464-3362; $$) serves the best brunch in the valley.

The Roadhouse (464-5017; $$) is normally packed. It serves the basic stuff skiers love, such as steak, chicken, ribs, swordfish and trout, in large portions. **Dot's of Dover** (464-6476; $) in the Mountain Park Plaza next to the movie theater, serves breakfast, lunch and dinner daily, plus an excellent Sunday brunch. The chili has won awards, and it gives you your O.J. in a jar. The ownership also serves dinner daily at **Dot's Restaurant**, on Rte. 9, in Wilmington (464-7284; $).

For economical eats, try **Poncho's Wreck** (464-9320; $$), a local institution with an eclectic dining room serving Mexican food, steaks, lobsters and fresh fish. **Anchor Seafood** (464-5616; $$), specializes in surf and turf. **Alonzo's Pasta & Grille** (464-0123; $$) at Crafts Inn in Wilmington is another local favorite. **Cafe Tannery** (464-2078; $-$$) offers lighter fare such as burgers, burritos and salads and does take-out.

The Vermont House (464-9360; $-$$) on Wilmington's main street, serves good food for cheap prices and is one of the locals' favorites. Head to **Deacon's Den** (464-9361; $) after skiing for pizza, burgers and sandwiches. **TC's Tavern** (464-9316; $–$$) has inexpensive family fare. For Chinese food, try **First Wok** (464-5861; $-$$) in the Mountain Park Plaza, West Dover.

For groceries, head to Shaw's on Rte. 9 in Wilmington, east of Rte. 100.

 ## Après-ski/nightlife

The **Snow Barn** features live music most weekends, sometimes with up-and-coming national acts. It has a separate area for pool and other games, with a central stone fireplace and a pizza window. Both Snow Barn and **Deacon's Den** usually have cover charges.

Après-ski at **Cuzzins** is a wild affair where the DJ gets folk up and dancing on the tables. The line is long, but the fun is worth it. **Walt's Pub**, at the Snow Lake Lodge, has a quiet, family-style atmosphere with "unplugged" music on Saturday nights and Pub Night on Mondays, featuring a special beer on tap and 10 cent wings.

One of the most popular nightspots, the **Silo**, is actually in a converted grain Silo (in the Silo Family Restaurant on Rt. 100). It caters to a young crowd and has practically a monopoly on nightlife for the snowboarding set. Locals head to the Silo every evening for 10-cent wings from 4-6 p.m. Downstairs is a smoke-filled cigar bar for aficionados. The **Dover Bar & Grille** (464-2689), across Rte. 100 from the Silo, is another local hangout.

 ## Other activities

The Mount Snow Valley is reportedly the busiest area for **snowmobiling** in Vermont. Try High Country Snowmobile Tours (464-2108 or 800-627-7533), which operates from the base of Mt. Snow, Wheeler Farm snowmobile tours (464-5225) in Wilmington and Stizmark (464-3384). **Dog-sledding** is available through Snow Doggin' (464-1100 ext. 4618). Adams Farm (464-3762) in Wilmington offers sleigh rides.

Mount Snow runs a lift-served tubing hill open Friday and Saturday evenings. Rates are $18 per four-hour session or $13 for those with lift tickets.

A **movie theater**, in the Mountain Park Plaza on Rt. 100 in West Dover, shows first-run movies. The **Snowseum** in the main base area covers the history of skiing through Mount Snow's eyes using old equipment and photos. The Grand Summit Resort Hotel now has a **spa** offering massage therapy, facials and body treatments. Reservations are required; call 464-6600, ext. 6005. **Shopping**: Wilmington Village has a few quaint shops, but this is not a major activity at Mount Snow.

 ## Getting there and getting around

By air: The closest airports are in Albany, N.Y. and Hartford's (C.T.) Bradley International, both less than a two-hour drive.

By car: Mount Snow is the closest major Vermont ski resort to New York and Boston. It is on Rte. 100, nine miles north of Wilmington.

Getting Around: A car isn't completely necessary, but it is pretty helpful, especially at night. During the day, take shuttle buses to and from the lifts; at night, take the MOOver, a free shuttle that serves much of the Mount Snow Valley from the resort down into Wilmington. It runs late on weekends. Ya can't miss it: The buses are painted like Holstein cows.

Okemo Mountain

Vermont

Summit elevation:	**3,344 feet**
Vertical drop:	**2,150 feet**
Base elevation:	**1,194 feet**

Address: 77 Okemo Ridge Road
Ludlow, VT 05149-9708
✆ **Area code:** 802
Ski area phone: 228-4041
Snow report: 228-5222
Fax: 228-4558
ⓘ **Toll-free reservations:**
(800) 786-5366 (800-78-OKEMO)
E-mail: info@okemo.com
Internet: www.okemo.com

Number of lifts: 14–3 high-speed quads,
4 quads, 3 triple chairs, 4 surface lifts
Snowmaking: 95 percent
Skiable acreage: 520 acres
Uphill capacity: 23,650 per hour
Snowboarding: Yes, unlimited
Bed Base: 10,000
Nearest lodging: Slopeside, condos
Resort child care: Yes, 6 weeks and older
Adult ticket, per day: $54–$59 (01/02 prices)

Expert: ★
Advanced: ★
Intermediate: ★★★★★
Beginner: ★★★
Never-ever: ★★

Dining: ★★★
Apres-ski/nightlife: ★★
Other activities: ★★

Okemo towers over the Vermont town of Ludlow, one of the few communities in the state that was home to viable industries before the resort opened in 1956. Home to 2,700 permanent residents, Ludlow now has a reputation as being a full-service resort town with quaint Victorian structures, a handful of shops and several excellent restaurants.

Okemo Mountain itself is known as more of an intermediate skier's mountain, despite having the highest vertical drop in southern Vermont at 2,150 feet. Ribbons of trails stream from the peak with amazing consistency in width and pitch, and they rarely intersect, which allows you to enjoy them without having to slow down at trail junctions. Strategically placed high-speed lifts power skiers uphill and keep lift lines to a minimum. Everything is smooth, from the excellent grooming and snowmaking to the slopeside accommodations and ski school.

To add some challenge to the mountain, Okemo opened a new alpine terrain park last year. The Nor'Easter trail offers rollers, whale backs, knolls, and hits all sculpted by groomers on this intermediate run. The groomers also work on bump runs (yes, you read that right), notably on the Ledges trail, where Okemo stages mogul competitions.

Okemo is larger than many skiers think; along with its impressive vertical drop, it has significant breadth. From the South Face to the Solitude Day Lodge is two miles "as the bird flies," but you can ski from one side to the other without taking any lifts.

Okemo's popularity is straining its support facilities. If you are renting equipment, get there early, very early. We received reports of a family with two children arriving at the rental shop at 9 a.m. and not making it to the mountain until closs to 11 a.m. This is not an isolated report. Rent ahead of time or be ready to wait.

Mountain layout—Skiing

The mellow skiing and most of the beginning ski school action takes place on the gentle rise served by two quads, South Ridge Quads A and B. These two quads also provide access to several clusters of condos and townhouses slopeside as well as serving as the gateway to the rest of Okemo's lift system from the Base Lodge. There can be a slight logjam at these two lifts, but once up on the mountain you can ski to a triple chair, a fixed quad or a high-speed quad that take skiers to the upper trails.

The Northstar Express high-speed quad draws the biggest crowd but moves skiers up-mountain in a hurry, unloading at a cluster of black trails on the left, blues on the right. A less crowded option is to ski down another 100 yards to the seldom used Sachem quad, which serves a few intermediate tune-up runs or the Glades Peak quad, which allows skiers to access the South Face area with its cruisers, bumps and glades.

◆◆ **Expert** ◆ **Advanced:** There are no true double-black trails on the mountain. Outrage and Double Black Diamond are both gladed and not particularly precipitous, but enjoyable and challenging with proper snow conditions. The best challenges for seasoned experts are the glades that have been opened recently to skiers. Forest Bump is 16 acres of tree skiing off the Rimrock trail. Loose Spruce and Stump Jumper provide tight and not-so-tight glades just to the right of the South Face high-speed quad. The other way that Okemo created above average skiing conditions is with bumps. Wild Thing, Blind Faith and Punch Line are often left to bump up, but when they are groomed with the bumps cut down, they are delightful cruising runs. Elsewhere on the mountain, you can often find bumps on Sel's Choice and the Ledges. If air is what you desire, head to the terrain park right in front of the Sugar Shack.

■ **Intermediate:** Overall, the pitch on this mountain is so consistent and the trails are so similarly cut, a skier would be hard pressed to describe the difference between Dream Weaver at one side of the mountain and Heaven's Gate on the opposite side. This is not a negative, just a fact of life on this mountain. At Okemo, intermediates should choose their trails based on crowds. Our experience has been that while a cruise down groomed Punch Line and Blind Faith may be crowded, wide arching turns can be made down Upper and Lower Tomahawk and Screamin' Demon without another skier in sight. As its name implies, the Solitude area is often the least crowded and has a bounty of intermediate terrain.

●● **Beginner:** The 4.5-mile Upper (and Lower) Mountain Road is the easiest route from the top. But beginners can ski virtually anywhere that is marked intermediate on this mountain. The Green Ridge triple and the Solitude Peak high-speed quad have many runs for beginners. The trails are wide enough to allow traverses and the pitch is mellow enough for them to maintain control.

● **Never-ever:** Okemo has a learning area near the base lodge, served by two quads and two surface lifts. Riding the surface lifts is free. Unfortunately, the post never-ever lessons take place in an area that is crisscrossed by more advanced skiers moving between lifts and condos. The child-care area is tucked away from other skiers.

 ## Mountain layout—Snowboarding

Okemo has a large snowboarding community not confined to the young and restless. Gray-haired ski patrollers and instructors foster a pro-boarding attitude. The mountain has two halfpipes including a Super Pipe and a quarterpipe as well as a half-mile-long snowboard park. A boardercross track is featured in Okemo's second terrain park on Nor'Easter. A sound system cranks out tunes at 900 watts.

Rentals are available on the mountain, at the board center in Ludlow at Sport Odyssey, Totem Pole Ski Shop and Northern Ski Works.

Mountain rating

If you're an expert or advanced skier, Okemo won't offer enough of a challenge unless you yearn for bumps or glades. But beginners and intermediate skiers and snowboarders will think they've died and gone to heaven. Never-evers might want to look for another resort with a separate learning area, but Okemo is designed to bring never-evers up onto the mountain very quickly. This mountain can be a great ego boost to every skier.

Cross-country and snowshoeing

The **Okemo Valley Nordic Center** (288-1396), set along the Black River, only a half-mile from Okemo Mountain, has fine facilities with 28 km. of trails, a rental and repair shop and a restaurant. Instruction is available. It also has 10 km. of dedicated snowshoe trails. Changing rooms with showers are available. The center is open from 8 a.m.-4 p.m. on weekends and holidays; Monday through Friday, it opens at 9 a.m.

Lessons (2001/02 prices)

Group lessons: $30 for a 1.75-hour lesson. Seniors pay $15.

Never-ever package: For skiing or snowboarding, packages include lesson, rental equipment and beginner lifts, and cost $50 for ages 7–12 and $59 for adults. Second lesson, same day, is $25. First Tracks is available in a two-day option for $109 for adults, $95 for juniors.

Private lessons: $65 per hour, each additional hour is $55, and each additional skier is charged $40 per hour.

Special programs: Upper-level groups concentrate on various subjects, such as moguls, black diamonds, parallel turns or learning how to use shaped skis. Three-day adult snowboard camps cost $369. Okemo also has an Adaptive Program for skiers and riders with disabilities (advance reservation required). Women's Ski Spree is a multiday indulgence for women of all abilities. Cost is $525 for the five-day program, $369 for the three-day.

Child care (2001/02 prices)

Ages: 6 weeks to 8 years.

Costs: $60 for a full day with lunch. Half days are $40. Sunday morning, 8 a.m.-1:30 p.m., $50, with lunch.

Reservations: Recommended; call 228-4041 and ask for the Penguin Playground DayCare Center.

Note: Every Saturday evening from January through March, Okemo has Kids Night Out, an evening child care program. It costs $35 for the four-hour session per child, or $60 for up to three children. Okemo also sells an unlimited season child-care pass for $1,295 or $1,595 with introduction to skiing lessons as well.

Children's lessons: Children ages 4–7 enroll in Snow Stars. The program is $78 for a full day with lunch, $47 for a half day; multiday discounts are available. Okemo has Snow Star riders at the same prices for ages 5–7 who want to learn to snowboard. Small-sized boards are available for rent at an extra cost. Young Mountain Explorers and Young Riders, ages 7–12, have supervised lesson programs for $70 a day or $135 for two days (lift ticket is additional) with discounts for additional days. Teens, ages 13-16, have their own lessons, Get

Altitude, $30 for a 1.75-hour lesson, either morning or afternoon. A one-hour Parent & Tot program allows kids to learn with Mom and Dad for $80. The instructor will leave parents with tips on helping their child improve on the slopes.

Lift tickets (2001/02 prices)

	Adult	Young Adult (13-18)	Junior (7-12)
One day: weekend/holiday	$59	$50	$38
One day: midweek	$54	$47	$35
Three days: weekend/holiday	$148/$165	$127/$141	$95/$105
Five days	$227/$255	$192/$215	$147/$155

Who skis free: Children ages 6 and younger, or those riding beginner surface lifts.

Who skis at a discount: Ages 65-69 ski for Young Adult rates; ages 70 and older ski for Junior rates.

Sunday morning discount: Ski from 8 a.m.-12:30 p.m. for $47 adult; $42 young adult and $29 junior/super-senior (ages 70+) and hit the road before the rest of the traffic.

Note: All listed prices include Vermont sales tax.

Accommodations

Okemo has many **slopeside condos and townhouses** (800-786-5366). Per-person rates vary widely depending on proximity to the slopes and size, but a range would be $375–$850 off-mountain to $450-$1,000+ slopeside for a five-night ski week. Kids ages 12 and younger stay free at Okemo Mountain Resort condos. As always, ask about packages.

The Okemo/Ludlow area, including Chester, Springfield, Weston, Plymouth and Proctorsville, has more than 50 country inns, B&Bs and motels. **The Governor's Inn** (228-8830 or 800-468-3766; $$-$$$$) is located right on Main Street and is one of Ludlow's nicest lodges. All rooms have private baths and are furnished in Victorian fashion, complete with puffy comforters. Rates include breakfast only or breakfast and dinner. The six-course dinners are preceded by hors d'oeuvres in the den. Right at the base of Okemo's Mountain Road is the **Andrie Rose Inn** (228-4846 or 800-223-4846; $$$-$$$$), considered one of the most romantic inns in Vermont. Most rooms have Jacuzzis, and the suites have fireplaces. The inn also has well-appointed family suites.

The **Echo Lake Inn** (824-6700 or 800-356-6844; $$–$$$$ ✕ ℙ ❀ ❋), north on Rte. 100, is a rambling New England inn with an excellent dining room and cozy public rooms. Presidents Coolidge and McKinley slept here. Rates with breakfast only or with breakfast and dinner are available. **The Inn at Water's Edge** (228-8143; $$$-$$$$ ℙ), also located north on Rte. 100 on the shores of Echo Lake, opened in the fall of 1999. The owners completely refurbished a 150-year-old Victorian home and made a romantic inn with eleven small rooms complete with antiques, private baths and Jacuzzis. Rates include breakfast, dinner served fireside and afternoon tea. After dinner, relax in the traditional English pub. Of note, the inn caters to couples, and children are discouraged. **The Hawk Inn and Mountain Resort** (672-3811 or 800-685-4295; $$$$ ⇌ ✕ ⇲ ⌂ ℙ ❧ ❀ ▦) has luxury country inn and townhouse facilities. This complex features indoor/outdoor pool, sauna, Jacuzzis, sleigh rides and fine dining. Rates include breakfast. **The Castle** (226-7361; $$$$) is a gracious, turn-of-the-century former Governor's mansion. New owners have painstakingly preserved the old-world standard for luxury and ambiance and have furnished the entire mansion with period furniture. The food is exception and the dining

Dining: $$$-Entrees $20+; $$-$10-20; $-less than $10.
Accommodations: (double room) $$$$-$200+; $$$-$141-$200; $$-$81-$140; $-$80 and less.

room is extremely romantic. The **Cavendish Pointe Hotel** (226-7688 or 800-438-7908; $–$$ ✗⌂Ⓟ⌐◁)) offers the full service of a 70-room country-style hotel, restaurant, indoor pool, lounge and game room. The hotel is on Rte. 103, two miles from Okemo.

The **Best Western Colonial Motel** (228-8188; $$–$$$ ✗⌐Ⓟ⌐✻) offers very afford-able lodging within walking distance of Ludlow's shopping, nightlife and dining. **Happy Trails Motel** (228-9984 or 800-228-9984; $–$$$ Ⓟ◁▣) in Ludlow offers great bargains with a good hot tub. **The Shoestring Lodge** (228-6217) offers a quiet, no smoking, family environment for those on a budget. Rooms with private or shared bath are available. It is both on the Okemo shuttle bus route and within walking distance to town.

Dining

On mountain, don't miss **Gables** ($–$$) in the Solitude Day Lodge. This ski-in/ski-out restaurant is now run by the New England Culinary Institute and puts typical ski lodge fare to shame. Lunch delicacies include Tuscan bruschetta, butternut squash ravioli, and portobello mushroom sandwiches. Prices are reasonable, and the restaurant already has a steady following. Hours are 11 a.m. to 3 p.m.

Upscale restaurants that serve dinner in the area include the **Echo Lake Inn** (228-5585; $$–$$$) north of town, where Chef Kevin Barnes has been creating gourmet delicacies for over a decade, and **The River Tavern Restaurant** at the Hawk Inn and Mountain Resort (672-3811; $$–$$$), which serves delicious meals. The Tortilla crusted Lamb Chops with tart cherry chipotle sauce are wonderful and reminiscent of a European gourmet platter.

The following restaurants are not as upper crust, but serve excellent affordable meals perfect for families. **Nikki's** (228-7797; $–$$) at the foot of the Okemo Mountain access road has a very good reputation and is a favorite among locals. Nikki's is moderately expensive, but its Osso Bucco con Orechiette or steamed whole Maine lobster are excellent. **Willie Dunn's Grille** (228-1387; $$) at the Okemo Valley Golf & Nordic Center offers superb affordable meals. The Shrimp Puttanesca with capers and olives in a red sauce is excellent. **Sam's Steakhouse,** formerly Michael's Seafood & Steak Tavern, (228-5622; $$),on Rte. 103 just east of Ludlow, serves a filet mignon so tender it can be cut with a butter knife, as well as seafood, chicken, sinful desserts and an incredible salad bar.

D.J.'s Restaurant (228-5374; $–$$) gets high marks from locals for its prime rib, steak, seafood, pasta and fabulous salad bar. **Cappuccino's** (228-7566; $) also gets raves for chicken and pasta specials as well as beef, pork, veal and vegetarian meals.

The Combes Family Inn (800-822-8799; $$$) serves a single-entrée dinner at 7 p.m. each evening. Call for the day's menu and to make reservations. **The Ludlow Cooking Company** (226-7251; $) in town also has sandwiches, deli items, rich desserts, and something handy for condo dwellers: meals to go, mostly of the Italian variety, but also great Homestyle Stuffed Cabbage for any homesick Polish skiers. **A State of Bean** (228-2326; $) at the base of the access road has overstuffed chairs and couches, and serves fresh-baked muffins and pastries, homemade soups, sandwiches, salads, desserts and, of course, a variety of coffee drinks. North of Ludlow on Rte. 103 is **Harry's** (259-2996; $–$$), an understated place that has a high repeat business because of its moderate prices and international cuisine. Try the burrito if you want the best (and most!) food for the least money.

In nearby Chester, stop and have a meal at **Raspberries and Thyme** (875-4486; $–$$).

Breakfast and lunch are always good. Dinner is served Wednesday to Sunday. For the best breakfast values head to Main Street in Ludlow to **Cafe at deLight**, **Mr. B's** or **The Hatchery**. For pizza, try **Christopher's** (228-7822) or **Wicked Good Pizza** (228-4131).

Goodman's American Pie (228-4271), on Main Street, serves wood-fired pizza. New in Ludlow is **Al Dente** (228-7400), which serves affordable pasta specials.

Aprèss-ski/nightlife

For après-ski on the mountain, try **Sitting Bull Lounge,** with a wide-screen TV, après-ski parties, $1 draft beer day on non-holiday Wednesdays and live music on weekends; **Gables** with its gourmet appetizers or hot cider with Wild Turkey. Locals say **The Loft**, a popular après spot, serves the best wings in town. Down the mountain, head to **Willie Dunn's Grille**, at the Okemo Valley Golf & Nordic Center, or Archie's Steakhouse for its chicken wings and draft beer specials.

Later in the evening, **The Pot Belly** has country rock, '60s and '70s classics with a great bar and a big TV. Watch out when ordering their wines by the glass—they simply recork any leftover bottles each night and save them for the next day, so only order the wine if you can see them open a new bottle. **The Black River Brewing Company**, now located on Rte. 103 outside Ludlow, is one of the best deals in town. The home-brew is good and other local microbrews are available.

Other activities

Shopping: Ludlow also has a wide array of specialty shops with clothing, antiques and gifts. One of the best browsing stores in the Northeast, the **Vermont Country Store**, is in nearby Weston on Route 100. It's full of useful little items that are hard to find elsewhere, such as pant stretchers (wire frames that help natural-fiber pants dry without wrinkles) and Vermont Bag Balm, which helps heal sore cow udders and chapped hands. **The Green Mountain Sugarhouse**, three miles from Ludlow on Rte. 100, is the spot to get those Vermont maple syrup gifts. In downtown Ludlow, don't miss **Chapter 14**, which mixes books with women's clothing, jewelry and an eclectic gallery upstairs, or **Blue Sky Trading Company** for jewelry and gifts.

The Okemo Valley Golf Club has opened a new indoor **Golf Operations Center** (228-1396) that features a 4,200-square-foot indoor practice area, a large putting practice area, indoor golf swing stations, a full swing golf simulator and a pro shop. Golf clinics are offered year round. **Ice skating** is free under the lights at Dorsey Park, but you need your own skates.

For **hot tubs and spas** head to Knight Tubs (228-2260) in Ludlow, open from 3–11 p.m.

Getting there and getting around

By air: Colgan Air/US Airways Express offers four flights a day from nearby Rutland (25 miles away) to Boston, but the airport sometimes closes in bad weather. The nearest major airports are Burlington, Vt.; Manchester, N.H.; or Hartford, Conn., all about two hours away.

By car: Okemo is in south-central Vermont on Rte. 103 in Ludlow, about two hours from Albany, N.Y.; three hours from Boston; and 4.5 hours from New York City.

By train: Amtrak has service from New York's Penn Station to Rutland, 25 miles to Okemo. Thrifty has a car rental office at the train station in Rutland.

Getting around: We recommend a car. But unless you are staying on-mountain, beware, parking at Okemo can be a bear. You will most likely end up parking almost in town and taking a shuttle to the base area. Two free shuttlebuses are available. The Village Shuttle operates on weekends and holidays serving area towns. The Okemo Trolley operates Dec. 17 through March 31, daily into the evening, and accesses all of Okemo's properties.

Dining: $$$-Entrees $20+; $$-$10-20; $-less than $10.
Accommodations: (double room) $$$$-$200+; $$$-$141-$200; $$-$81-$140; $-$80 and less.

Smugglers' Notch

Vermont

Summit elevation: 3,640 feet
Vertical drop: 2,610 feet
Base elevation: 1,030 feet

Address: 4323 Vermont Rte. 108 South Smugglers' Notch, VT 05464-9537
✆ Area code: 802
Ski area phone: 644-8851
Snow report: 644-1111
ⓘ Toll-free reservations and information: (800) 451-8752
Toll-free from the United Kingdom: 0800-169-8219
E-mail: smuggs@smuggs.com
Internet: www.smuggs.com/
Expert:★★★★
Advanced:★★★★
Intermediate:★★★
Beginner:★★★★
Never-ever:★★★★★

Number and types of lifts: 9–6 double chairs, 3 surface lifts
Acreage: 264 acres marked trails; access to 750 acres of woods
Snowmaking: 62 percent
Uphill capacity: 7,400 per hour
Snowboarding: Yes, unlimited
Bed base: 2,2000
Nearest lodging: walking distance, condos
Resort child care: Yes, 6 weeks and older
Adult ticket, per day: $48 (2001/02)

Dining:★★
Apres-ski/nightlife:★
Other activities:★★★

Smugglers' Notch has earned bragging rights as the best family resort in North America. In fact, it's the only North American resort that guarantees your family will have fun. If any family member participates in one of the resort's programs and doesn't have fun, Smugglers' will refund the entire program portion of that family member's stay. One of our staff members put that guarantee to the test: Her boyfriend's 16-year-old daughter hadn't skied in several years because she decided it wasn't fun anymore, but after her lesson here, she couldn't be dragged off the mountain. And her skiing improved dramatically in one day!

The family market has been the resort's focus for the past decade and the dividends have been exceptional. *Family Circle, SKI, Skiing, Travel & Leisure, FamilyFun and Better Homes and Gardens magazines* and *AOL's Family Travel Network* have all given Smugglers' #1 ranking for family vacations. The commitment to families is total: pedestrian-friendly village with stores, restaurants, an outdoor ice rink, sledding hill, indoor pool, saunas, steam baths, outdoor tennis, massage, crafts classes, sleigh rides, movies, parties for kids and adults and the largest licensed day-care facility in New England. Smugglers' even offers a study hall for youngsters ages 7-17 who need to keep up with classwork while on vacation. The popular Club Smugglers' package includes lodging, lift tickets and daily lessons, and you can add day care and special activities to the package. Vacation packages can be crafted to include lodging, lift tickets, ski school and day care in any combination. Once families arrive and pick up their welcome packets, most will never have to deal with additional payments except meals.

If you're an advanced or expert skier, Smugglers' is a well-kept secret. Its 2,610 vertical feet places second behind Killington for Vermont's longest vertical descent. Smugglers' has three mountains, one of which, Madonna Mountain, gives a 2,130-foot drop off one chair. You normally will have the mountain almost to yourself, and the steeps, bumps, glades and unofficial woods skiing and riding will keep you satisfied for a week-long vacation. Granted, the lift system is old and seems to creep up the mountain, but the time on the flanks of Sterling and Madonna is worth every minute of lift time. New this season are additional glades on all three mountains and a new Learn-to-Ski Development on Morse Mountain.

Incidentally, the area was named for the smugglers and bootleggers who brought in forbidden English goods during the War of 1812 and booze during Prohibition, storing the contraband in caves between Madonna Mountain and Mt. Mansfield, the latter one of the peaks at Stowe. Though Route 108 passes Smugglers' and continues through the notch to Stowe, it is closed in winter.

 ## Mountain layout—Skiing

◆◆ **Expert** ◆ **Advanced:** The real challenge is from the top of Madonna Mountain. Smugglers' lays claim to the East's only triple-black-diamond trail, The Black Hole, which is in the woods next to Freefall. Smugglers' doesn't usually overhype its skiing, but this tight, steep, gladed run is no tougher than what you'll find at nearby Stowe Mountain Resort or Jay Peak Resort. Four legitimate double-black-diamond trails also beckon. The icefalls, ledges and stumps on Upper Liftline will make even true experts hold their breath. Freefall is just that: The turns come quickly and you drop 10 to 15 feet with each turn. Upper F.I.S. sports a 41-percent gradient, and with the addition of top-to-bottom snowmaking it has become a tad more civilized than in the past.

If you're hooked on glades, you'll want to check out Doc Dempsey's. It lost some trees in the ice storm a few years ago, which just gives it more character: It's become a winding, narrow New England trail dotted with groves of trees, and the bumps in spring make it extra fun. We just wish it were longer. If the top of Doc's is closed because of lack of snow, follow Catwalk to Upper F.I.S., take about 2 turns and drop into the set of tracks on skiers' right, bypassing the cliff band at the top of Doc's. Another quick adrenaline rush is Highlander Glades on Sterling Mountain. Tree skiers will be awed by the amount of uncut terrain within the resort's boundaries: Keep an eye out for locals who might share their secret stashes. (Smugglers' off-trail policy requires you enter and exit from open trails; you are solely responsible for yourself). An unofficial easy glade that makes for a great first foray into the woods for kids is off the top of the Practice Slope Extension. In all, five new glades have been opened.

The best bump runs are F.I.S., the middle portion of Upper Liftline, Smugglers' Alley and Exhibition. The snow on Madonna Mountain takes longer to soften, so warm up on Sterling and head to the Madonna 1 chair after 11:30 a.m. or so.

■ **Intermediate:** Fifty-three percent of the trails are rated intermediate, and many are well suited to recent ski-school grads. Intermediate runs are concentrated on Madonna and Sterling peaks. Two favorite routes for lower intermediates who want to get a sense of big-mountain skiing are off Sterling: Upper Rumrunner to Lower Rumrunner, and Upper Rumrunner to Black Snake to the bottom of Treasure Run to Lower Exhibition. The views are spectacular both ways.

For advanced intermediates who want to test their mettle, try Chute on Sterling Mountain. It's a short advanced run that's steep with some bumps and stumps, especially in the spring, but the 15 to 20 turns it takes to get down make it perfect in case you decide you're in over your head.

●● **Beginner** ● **Never-ever:** The third mountain at Smugglers' is Morse, with 17 trails ranging from beginner to expert. It is the ski schooler's mountain. You won't find any hotshots here. Morse also is home to Mogul Mouse's Magic Lift, a half-speed double chair especially kind to beginners and young children. From the top of the lift winds the Magic Learning Trail, with nature stations, exploration paths and ski-through "caves." Morse Bowl is served by the Highlands double chair and has five trails for beginners and advanced beginners and a separate base lodge.

Mountain layout—Snowboarding

Prohibition Park on Madonna has a 400-foot superpipe with a 17-foot radius as well as multiple hits, spines and rolls, and piped-in music. The Night School of Boarding meets three nights a week at Sir Henry's Hill & Fun Park at the base of Morse Mountain. The three-hour sessions are open to novices ages 6 and older. New this year is a Bombardier Super Half Pipe Grinder for grooming. Meadowlark trail from the upper base lodge back to village has a gentle grade, if the snow is fast, it's fine; if its spring and sticky take the shuttlebus. Three, open-to-anyone pipe jams are held during the season.

Mountain rating

Smugglers' is good for all types of skiers and boarders. Kids swarm over Morse Mountain, center of ski school classes, après-ski bonfires and hot chocolate, making it a magnet for those who revel in a family atmosphere. Experts and advanced skiers/riders should head to Madonna Mountain. Intermediates can cruise down Sterling. A warning to anyone who might be afraid of heights: The Madonna 1 lift is high off the ground and is surrounded by some intimidating cliffs. Smugglers' has no high-speed quads or triple chairs, which sometimes contributes to long waits at the lift loading area on weekends and holidays. The trade-off is that the trails are not congested.

If you're a day visitor of intermediate skiing ability or better, don't turn in to the main village. Continue up the hill to the top parking lot. Here you'll find fewer cars and a short walk to a point where you can ski to the lifts on Sterling and Madonna. Best of all, you can ski back to your car at day's end.

Cross-country and snowshoeing

More than 23 km. (about 14 miles) of scenic cross-country skiing on groomed and tracked trails, plus 20 km. of snowshoe trails, are accessible from the main Smugglers' area. **The Nordic Ski and Snowshoe Adventure Center** offers rentals, lessons, backcountry and night tours as well as snowshoe rentals and tours.

Lessons (2001/02 prices)

Snow Sport University (Smugglers' ski school) Director Peter Ingvoldstad has been acclaimed as one of the most innovative teachers in the country. Lessons are included with most Ski/Snowboard Week packages.

Group lessons: One-and-one-half hours, $29.

Never-ever package: $49 for a 1.5-hour coaching session, rentals and lift ticket valid on Morse Mountain on Saturdays and Sundays.

Private lessons: $65 per hour.

Special programs: Classes on style, terrain tactics, halfpipe tricks, family tours, night snowboarding lessons and programs for skiers 55 and older.

Racing: A race course, the Madonna Mountain Carving Course, is located on Lower Liftline on Wednesdays, Thursdays and weekends. Two runs are $4. On Saturdays and Sundays, Smugglers' has a free family fun race with prizes on the Carving Course.

Child care (2001/02 prices)

Ages: 6 weeks-6 years old.
Costs: $55 per day or $235 for five days.
Reservations: Make them when you book your vacation, either with your travel agent or by calling the toll-free number listed in the fact box.

Note: Alice's Wonderland Child Care is a major reason why *Family Circle* magazine chose Smugglers' as the top family resort for three years running. The facility is staffed with professional caregivers who may also be hired for evening babysitting.

Every night except Monday, Friday and Sunday, the center has Parents' Night Out, with dinner and activities for ages 3–12, at $20 per child, so Mom and Dad can have some fun on their own.

Children's lessons: Kids and teens are divided into the following age groups: 3–5, 6–10, 11–14 and 15–17. The teen program allows that age group to meet new friends with whom they can hang out at the supervised evening teen activities.

Though lesson registration now is done when you make your initial reservations, getting rental equipment is probably the only remaining hassle you will encounter after resort registration. As anyone with kids can imagine, it's a zoo. If possible, try to pick up rental equipment the afternoon before lessons start. Once kids are assigned to a class, forms are filled out, clothes tucked away and ski boots are pulled on, the instructors get the kids busy with coloring books and games, and young children are given their own trail map and journal in which they can record their ski or snowboard progression. That's a good time for parents to get lost.

Smugglers' has a "Mom & Me/Dad & Me" program that teaches parents how to teach their youngsters to ski. These lessons, essentially specialized private lessons, are for children aged 2 or older and a parent of at least intermediate skiing ability. Parents are taught games to make learning fun, and safety tips such as how to ride the lift with kids.

Young Boy Scouts who are guests at Smugglers' can earn merit badges in alpine and cross-country skiing.

Discovery Dynamos is full-day for kids 3–5 for all ability levels and encourages confidence with lunch included for $69 a day with multiday rates available. Adventure Rangers for ages 6–10 has discovery programs and snow treks for $69 a day. Mountain Explorers for the 15–17 group lets teens cruise in groups for only $29 a day.

Lift tickets (2001/02 prices).

	Adult	Youth (7-18)
Anyday	$48	$34
Multiday	*	*

Who skis free: Ages 6 and younger and 70 and older.
Who skis at a discount: Those 65–69 ski for $36 anytime.
Note: *If you're staying for more than one day here, the wise move is to buy a lodging package that includes tickets and lessons.

Accommodations

At Smugglers' the primary and desirable place to stay is in the **Resort Village**. More than 2,200 beds are within walking distance of the lifts. Prices start at $495 per adult and $425 for youth for a five-day Club Smugglers' package, including lifts and lessons (packages for fewer days can be arranged). Children aged 6 and younger ski and stay free. Packages also include a welcome party, use of the pool and hot tub, family game nights, outdoor ice skating, family sledding parties, a weekly torchlight parade with fireworks finale and a farewell party. Showtime Theatre, nightly teen activities and adult entertainment (don't get overwrought; it's clean adult fun) are also available. Condos at Smugglers' are spacious, clean and family-furnished.

Smugglers' central check-in area is designed around the concept that once you check in, you have everything you need—lift tickets, instruction vouchers, rentals and day care. Computers at the front desk are tied to key areas such as the rental shop to make the resort very guest-friendly. We give Smugglers' credit for continuing to improve the check-in system, but the check-in area can get a bit backed up; sometimes a lot backed up. Plan to have one parent stand in line while the other takes fidgety kids for a walk in the Resort Village (if you check in at night, one parent can take the kids sledding or swimming, a resort spokeswoman said). Remember, the payoff comes later—once you check in, you won't have to wait in line again for tickets or lessons.

Dining

You never have to leave the Village to eat. For home-baked breakfast treats and giant cookies, try **The Green Mountain Deli and Sweet Shoppe** (ext. 1141; $)with fresh-roasted coffee, espresso or cappuccino. Lunch favorites include chili in a bread bowl, spinach salads and made-to-order deli sandwiches. The **Riga-Bello's Pizzeria** (ext. 1142; $–$$) offers daily specials, pizza, salads, calzones and stuffed breads with meat and vegetable fillings—for eating there, taking out or delivery to your condo. The **Mountain Grille** (ext. 1247; $–$$), with a view of the slopes, is open continuously for breakfast, lunch and dinner, including light fare entrées. Kids on the FamilyFest Package get two free kids' meals from a special buffet of family favorites like hot dogs, chicken, potatoes and macaroni and cheese at the Mountain Grille when parents order a meal.

The **Hearth and Candle** (644-8090 $–$$$) is a privately operated restaurant in the Village with a friendly, though more formal, atmosphere. Families are served in the cozy Hearth Room, and couples desiring a quiet atmosphere are escorted upstairs to the adults-only Birch Room. Entrées range from steak and pasta to exotic preparations of fish and game. A new entertainment and dining feature is **Smugglers' Adventure Dinner.** Lift transportation to the top of Sterling Mountain brings guests to The Top of The Notch, a mountain hut lit only by candles. The renowned Hearth and Candle serves a gourmet venison stew appetizer, a choice of three entrees and its famous apple crisp. Snowshoeing on Sterling Pond under a starlit sky settles the hearty meal.

Restaurants dot the route between the resort and Jeffersonville, five miles away. Some examples: Across from the entrance to the Village Center is the ever funky **Cafe Banditos** (644-8884; $–$$) with low-cost Mexican food, hickory-smoked chicken and ribs and a children's menu. The **Three Mountain Lodge** (644-5736; $$) serves eclectic dining in a classic log-lodge atmosphere. The night we were there, an acoustic blues guitarist provided entertainment. **Angelina's** (644-2011; $–$$) in Cambridge has great pizza, with a thin crust that's crispy on the bottom and soft on the top and loaded with sauce. Our kids, who consider themselves pizza connoisseurs, gave it an 8 out of 10.

The **Hungry Lion** (644-5848), at the Smugglers' Notch Inn, five miles away, is a popular family restaurant that offers daily specials, vegetarian dishes, homemade breads and desserts, and a "cubs" menu. **Dinner's Dunn** (644-8219; $–$$) at The Windridge Bakery meets all appetite styles with simple soups and homemade breads baked in an old oven that's part of the decor, to traditional chicken and beef favorites. It's open for breakfast and lunch. The newest restaurant on the route is **The Yankee Smuggler** (422-5511; $–$$), which serves traditional American cuisine and a nontraditional dish or two each evening that's "smuggled" in from a foreign country.

 ## Après-ski/nightlife

Smugglers' has great nightlife. It's family oriented, but even our childless staffers who have visited here end up having more fun than they initially imagined. Activities provide fun for all ages; for example, a family sledding party on lighted Sir Henry's Hill, evening snowmobile tours, big screen movie night, bingo blast and a pizza-and-ice-cream-sundae party.

For more traditional fun, try **The Mountain Grille** for après-ski and nighttime entertainment such as karaoke on Tuesdays and dancing to DJ music on Saturdays. A magician entertains on Wednesdays. Teens have the nightly **Outer Limits Teen Center** with music videos, snacks, and dance parties. Surprisingly, our teens had more fun at the **FunZone**, an indoor playground for guests of all ages that includes miniature golf, basketball hoops, and inflatable attractions like a 22-foot giant double-lane slide and a padded jousting ring.

Other activities

Shopping: The Village Center has a few shops, stocked with necessities and typical T-shirt/hat/pin souvenirs and children's games.

Don't miss a visit to the **Boyden Valley Winery**, 8 miles down the road in Cambridge. This fourth-generation Vermont farmer makes award-winning wines using Vermont apples and berries and his own grapes and maple syrup. Tours and free wine tastings will convince you to buy a case of each and you'll find Vermont specialty products, an artisans' gallery, handmade furniture and gift baskets. You won't leave empty-handed!

If you want handmade Vermont crafts, you also can make your own. Smugglers' has an unusual activity, **Artists in the Mountains**. Local artisans teach classes in traditional New England crafts, such as tin punching, basket weaving, stenciling and dried flower arranging. The classes include materials and cost $35–$40.

As already noted, there are kids' parties, karaoke, sleigh rides, snowshoeing, sledding, a swimming pool, hot tubs, and ice skating.

 ## Getting there and getting around

By air: Burlington International Airport is 40 minutes away. Shuttles are available (24-hour notice required; book it when you book lodging).

By car: Smugglers' Notch is on Route 108 near Jeffersonville in northwest Vermont.

Getting around: Everything is within walking distance at the resort or ride the free resort shuttle. If you want to visit some of the restaurants in or on the way to Jeffersonville, you'll need a car. A local taxi service also is available.

Dining: $$$–Entrees $20+; $$–$10-20; $–less than $10.
Accommodations: (double room) $$$$–$200+; $$$–$141-$200; $$–$81-$140; $–$80 and less.

Stowe

Vermont

Summit elevation:	**3,640 feet**
Vertical drop:	**2,360 feet**
Base elevation:	**1,280 feet**

Address: 5781 Mountain Rd.
Stowe, VT 05672
✆ **Area code:** 802
Ski area phone: 253-3000 or 800-253-4754
Snow report: 253-3600
ⓘ **Toll-free reservations:**
(800) 247-8693 (24-STOWE);
for slopeside lodging only, (800) 253-4754
Advance Ticket Sales: 888-253-4TIX
Fax: 253-3406
E-mail: info@stowe.com
Internet: http://www.stowe.com
Expert:★★★★
Advanced:★★★★
Intermediate:★★★★
Beginner:★★★★
Never-ever:★★★

Number and types of lifts: 11–1 high-speed
quad, 1 eight-passenger gondola, 1 triple,
6 doubles, and 2 surface lifts
Skiable acreage: 480 acres
Snowmaking: 73 percent
Uphill capacity: 12,326 per hour
Snowboarding: Yes, unlimited
Bed base: 5,000+
Nearest lodging: Slopeside, hotel
Resort child care: Yes, 6 weeks and older
Adult ticket, per day: $55 (00/01)

Dining:★★★★
Apres-ski/nightlife:★★
Other activities:★★★

The skiing and riding at Stowe Mountain Resort is spread across two peaks: Mt. Mansfield, the highest in Vermont at 4,395 feet, and Spruce Peak. The first sight of towering Mt. Mansfield, with its snow-capped summit above treeline, is breathtaking. Stowe has an undeniable blue-blood lineage as one of the oldest and most distinguished Eastern ski resorts. Its ski patrol, founded in 1934, is one of the oldest in the United States, and its winter carnival is the longest-running such event in the nation.

Stowe has made a concerted effort to retain its long, narrow, twisting runs cut close into the surrounding forests; runs that are an important part of making Stowe a classic New England ski experience. Ski publications repeatedly bestow various accolades on the resort, giving it top marks for overall experience, for its adventure, backcountry and vintage Eastern flavor and for its tree skiing. Stowe's lodging and dining also have received repeated recognition from national publications.

Stowe's best-kept secret is its tree skiing. It's best-kept because the resort has an official policy of not acknowledging its unofficial trails, glades and out-of-bounds terrain. Also the locals are extremely reluctant to share their secret stashes with outsiders and we don't blame them one bit. If you decide to ski or ride on unofficial terrain, you are responsible for your own safety.

The town of Stowe, with its charming, white-steepled church and main street lined with historic buildings, is about seven miles away from the ski area. To truly enjoy all this area has to offer, you need a car.

Mountain layout—Skiing

◆◆ **Expert:** Part of the legend of Stowe revolves around its Front Four, and the fact that it features some of the steepest and most difficult runs in skidom. Having descended the Front Four is a badge of honor for Northeast skiers and deservedly so, given the nature of Goat, Starr, Liftline and National. Besides being steep, the headwalls are frequently draped with vintage New England ice and the trails are liberally moguled. Experts who are gunning for all four should begin with National and Liftline. The resort's winch cats allow groomers to prepare these two from time to time, so this is a good place to get used to the considerable steepness of the Front Four. Starr is not groomed, and the view from the top of this run, as it disappears in a steep dive toward the base lodge area far below, is one you won't forget. If you haven't met your match by this time, then you're ready for Goat, a moguled gut-sucker no more than three to five bumps wide.

Expert tree skiers and riders will want to start in the woods off Bypass, where there's a steep, tight drop-in that opens into perfectly spaced trees. Once you dump out on Nosedive, you'll find plenty of places to slip into the woods. Skiers and riders are known to hike the Chin (4,395 feet) and put their mettle to the test on its out-of-bounds terrain, but we suggest you hook up with someone who's familiar with the area. The cliff bands and tight chutes are really nasty stuff, plus you can easily end up on the backside of the mountain with no clue how to return to civilization.

◆ **Advanced:** A very nice section of glade skiing through well-spaced trees is just off the top section of Nosedive. Chin Clip from the top of the gondola is long, moguled, and moderately narrow, but it does not have quite the steep grade that the Front Four boast.

■ **Intermediate:** This group can enjoy nearly 60 percent of the trails, including much of Spruce Peak. At Mt. Mansfield, ski to the right or left of the Front Four. Advanced intermediates will probably want to chance the tricky top part of Nosedive for the pleasure of skiing the long, sweeping cruiser that beckons further down. Going left from the top of the FourRunner Quad, take Upper Lord until it leads you to a handful of long excellent intermediate runs all the way to the bottom in Lower Lord, North Slope, Standard and Gulch.

From the quad, reaching the intermediate skiing under the gondola presents a problem. The connection between these two parts of the mountain is not convenient unless you are willing to take a run down Nosedive, rated double-black at its top. (Yes, it's narrow with big moguls, but there's enough room to pick your way down. We got our advanced intermediate staff member down it before she realized its rating.) If you don't want to chance Nosedive, it's a hike from the quad area over to the gondola, or you can take the green-circle Crossover trail toward the bottom of the mountain, which allows skiers to traverse directly across the Front Four to the gondola base. If you want to work your way back from the gondola to the quad, take the Cliff Trail, which eventually hooks up with Lower Nosedive and dumps you at the base of the high-speed chair.

If you feel as though you need a little elbow room after too many tight New England trails, try Perry Merrill or Gondolier from the gondola, or cut turns about as wide as you want down Main Street on Spruce Peak, across the base parking lot. Upper Spruce Peak is like skiing was in the old days, which means "no snow from heaven, no skiing." The Big Spruce double is an old and cold lift. When the snow is good and the wind isn't blowing, though, the mountain is a cruiser's delight, and powder days are a real treat.

Intermediates may also enjoy Stowe's night skiing. The upper portion of Perry Merrill and all of Gondolier are lit Thursday through Saturday until 9 p.m. The ride up is in the warm gondola.

●● **Beginners:** One route we would recommend to all levels is the four-mile-long, green-circle Toll Road, which starts at the top of the FourRunner quad. This is a marvelous trail for lower-level skiers, but the more proficient probably will enjoy it too—more for its beauty than for its challenge. You will pass through a canopy of trees, where you can hear only quiet sounds, such as birds chirping or snow plopping from the branches. A little later you'll find the small wood-and-stone Mountain Chapel, where on Sundays at 1 p.m. you can attend an informal church service. You just won't find this type of intimate ski trail out West.

● **Never-evers:** First-timers should start at Spruce Peak base area, then work up to the runs off the Toll House chair (Chair 5), then advance to Chair 4.

Mountain layout—Snowboarding

Stowe has been a leader in the growth and development of snowboarding in the United States. In fact, it's Jake Burton Carpenter's home mountain and Snowboard Life magazine ranks it #1 in the East. The resort's terrain park, The Jungle, is a great place to find Burton employees and riders, who hang here in their free time. Stowe also has a halfpipe on the lower section of North Slope.

On the mountain trails, beginners should focus on Lower Spruce, then head over to Mt. Mansfield for long carving runs on Gondolier, Perry Merrill and Sunrise. As the day progresses, advanced boarders should move from Liftline and Nosedive to Hayride and Centerline, then North Slope.

Cross-country

Stowe has one of the best cross-country networks in the country. Four touring areas all interconnect to provide roughly 150 groomed km. of trails, and an additional 110 km. in the backcountry. Plus there are a slew of trails for snowshoeing.

The Trapp Family Lodge (253-5719; 800-826-7000) organized America's first touring center and has 55 km. groomed and machine-tracked trails that connect to another 100 km. in the Mt. Mansfield and Topnotch Resort networks. Trapp's also has 45 km. of backcountry trails. The fee is $12 a day for adults, $2 for children, free for those younger than 6. Rentals and instruction are available. See Accommodations and Dining for more information.

The Edson Hill Touring Center (253-7371) has about 50 km. of trails with 35 km. trails groomed. Elevation varies from 1,400 to 2,100 feet. The fee is $10 a day for adults, $5 for children, ages 6 and younger are free.

Stowe Mountain Resort (253-3000) has 80 km. of trails, 35 km. of which are groomed. The daily fee is $12 for adults and $8 for children.

The Topnotch Resort (253-8585) has 20 km. of trails, most of which are groomed and tracked. Trail fee is $10 for adults, $6 for children.

Lessons (2001/02 prices)

Group lessons: $33 for 90 minutes.
Private lessons: $80 an hour, with multihour and multiperson discounts.
Kids Super Start, for children ages 3–12 years, costs $50.

Special programs: Women in Motion, all-day program costs $60 per day for one to three days and includes a lesson (off-piste, bumps, racing, etc.), rental of the newest demo equipment and lunch.

Note: Telephone extension for the ski school is 3680 and 3681.

Lift tickets (2001/02 prices)

	Adult	Child (6-12)
One day (00/01)	$55	$35
Three days	$141 ($165/holiday)	$90 ($98/holiday)
Five days	$214 ($275/holiday)	$138 ($163/holiday)

Who skis free: Children ages 5 and younger with paid parent or guardian.

Who skis at a discount: Ages 65 and older ski for the same price as children. Multiday, non-holiday tickets can be bought by phone, three days in advance.

Note: Non-holiday night skiing is $20 for adults and $16 for children. A twilight ticket, valid from 1 to 9 p.m., is $42 for adults, $30 for children. All prices include Vermont sales tax.

Child care (2001/02 prices)

Ages: 6 weeks through 6 years.

Costs: Full day with lunch is $68. Half day with snack is $48. Children ages 3 and older can have an optional ski lesson for an additional $20.

Reservations: Required; call 253-3000, Ext. 3686. The Cubs licensed day care facility is at the Spruce Peak area.

Children's lessons: Headquartered at Spruce Peak, full-day Adventure Center ski programs with lunch are $85 for those ages 3–12 years. Snowboarding programs are the same price but limited to children ages 6–12.

Accommodations

When staying at least three days, ask about the Stowe Value Packages. Extras include night skiing, extra half days, lessons, etc. Your lift tickets will be waiting for you along with your room key, so there's no need to stop at the ticket window on your way to the trails the next morning. Call (800) 247-8693 (24-STOWE).

When the Trapp Family's life was dramatized in *The Sound of Music,* their everlasting fame was guaranteed. **The Trapp Family Lodge** (253-8511 or 800-826-7000; $$$$ ✕⌂⌂🏠🅿🍴🎿⛄), which they established near Stowe upon arriving in the United States, is a legend in its own right. Although, the original building burned down in the late 1970s, it was rebuilt. It is still the most popular and upscale place to stay in the area and is still in the family. It's now run by a son. This is a self-contained resort with an excellent cross-country center. The collection of restaurants is among the best in the area, and a modern pool and fitness center provide excellent amenities. Make reservations early because this lodge is normally full throughout the season (Christmas reservations should be made about a year in advance). Rates include breakfast and dinner.

Not as famous as the Trapp Family Lodge, but much closer to the lifts and the town, **Topnotch at Stowe Resort & Spa** (253-8585 or 800-451-8686; in Canada 800-228-8686; $$$$ 🛏✕🏠🅿🍴⛄🎿) boasts an excellent fitness center and spa. Topnotch has rooms and condos, along with excellent meeting facilities. It also has the only covered tennis courts in Stowe.

Dining: $$$-Entrees $20+; $$-$10-20; $-less than $10.

Accommodations: (double room) $$$$-$200+; $$$-$141-$200; $$-$81-$140; $-$80 and less.

The Inn at the Mountain (800-253-4754 or 253-3000; $$–$$$$ ⚿✕⌐🅿🍷🏊💡) is part of the Stowe Mountain Resort. This beautiful inn and the surrounding condominiums (available through the same telephone number) make up the only ski-in/ski-out facility in Stowe. The flavor is country New England. The modern Fitness Center across the parking lot is free to all guests. The Fireside Tavern is the perfect place to unwind after a day on the slopes. Room and condo unit rates include breakfast and dinner

The best family accommodations in Stowe are at the **Golden Eagle Resort** (253-4811 or 800-626-1010; $$–$$$ ➡✕🏔🅿🍷🏊💡). This sprawling complex has more than a dozen buildings and facilities, from motel rooms with kitchenettes to apartments. The complex has one of the best fitness centers in town, which includes an indoor pool. It is all unpretentious and affordable. Because there are dozens of pricing options, the best bet is to contact the property and explain your needs.

The Stoweflake Mountain Resort and Spa (253-7355 or 800-253-2232; $$$–$$$$ ✕⌐🏔🅿🍷🏊💡), down the road a bit from the Golden Eagle, recently added a spa and sports club as well as a new wing of deluxe rooms with fireplaces and mountain views. Rates include breakfast and dinner. The Stoweflake also manages a nice group of townhouse condominiums with studio to three-bedroom units.

Ye Olde England Inne (253-7558; 800-477-3771, toll-free in the U.S. and Canada; 0-800-962-684 toll-free from the U.K.; $$–$$$$ ✕⌐🅿🍷☻), is on the Mountain Road. Bigger than a country inn and smaller than a full-fledged hotel, it has an English country motif and lavish Laura Ashley touches. Every room is decorated differently. The Bluff House, perched on the hill behind the inn, has luxury suites with unobstructed views over the valley. Room rates include breakfast.

Stowe Inn at Little River (253-4836 or 800-227-1108; $$ ✕⌐🅿), right in the middle of town, has expanded beyond its 1814-era colonial roots with more modern units across the parking lot, giving a total of 43 rooms. For atmosphere opt for the Main Inn with its wide-planked floors and four-poster beds. The restaurant is an excellent place from which to watch the village light up at night.

Green Mountain Inn (253-7301 or 800-253-7302; $$–$$$ ✕🅿🍷⚲💡☻) on Main Street is a charming old inn with a super location in the middle of town. The wide-planked floors are pine, as is the furniture, with many antique, four-poster canopied beds. Rooms that front on the street may be noisy for light sleepers; delivery trucks start to rev their engines at the nearby stop light at about 6 a.m. The hotel has an annex that is not quite so quaint but is off the main road. Rates include breakfast.

Ten Acres Lodge (253-7638 or 800-327-7357) is on Luce Hill Road. This country inn was converted from an 1840s farm house. Rooms vary in size; those in the main lodge are relatively simple, but the common areas are beautiful. Eight modern units, called the Hill House, are tucked into the woods behind the old farmhouse. These all have fireplaces in the rooms and share an outdoor hot tub. Rates include breakfast.

The Gables Inn (253-7730 or 800-422-5371; $$–$$$$ ➡✕🅿🍷🏊☻), on Mountain Road, is a real lived-in house, which helps everyone have a good time. The breakfasts are among the best in Stowe, and guests wouldn't think of eating anywhere else for dinner either. Rates include two meals.

The newly built **Stone Hill Inn** (253-6282; $$$$; ☻🅿🍷) is an exquisitely luxurious getaway designed for romance and comfort; no kids allowed. The nine rooms, each decorated differently, include a king-size bed, a cozy sitting area, a fireplace in the bedroom *and* in the bathroom and a Jacuzzi for two. Prices include breakfast, evening hors d'oeuvres and unlimited soft drinks.

The **Mount Mansfield Hostel** (800-866-8749 or 253-4010 $), at the foot of Mount Mansfield, offers bunk-style sleeping with shared bathroom facilities. Bring your own sleeping blanket and towels. Nothing's fancy here, but there are a couple of common rooms, one with a large hearth. Breakfast and dinner are available. The dorm is locked from 10 a.m.- 4 p.m. Another dorm that specializes in youth groups is **The Round Hearth at Stowe** (253-7223), with prices similar to the Mount Mansfield Hostel.

Dining

Stowe has long been famous for its cuisine. **Ten Acres** (253-7638) and **Isle de France** (253-7751; $$$) are considered by most to be the top gourmet spots around. Many locals consider the innovative fine dining offered at **Blue Moon Café** (253-7006; $$–$$$) the best in the area.

The **Trapp Family Lodge** (253-8511; $$–$$$) puts on an excellent Austrian-style meal for a fixed price of about $36. There normally is a choice of about a dozen entrées.

For alternatives that aren't budget-busters, try **Miguel's Stowe Away** (253-7574; $–$$) or the **Cactus Café** (253-7770; $–$$) for Mexican food, **Restaurant Swisspot** (253-4622; $–$$) for fondues and decadent Swiss chocolate pie, and **Gracie's** (253-8741) for great burgers and meat loaf. **The Shed** (253-4364; $–$$) has a microbrewery and is a great spot for steaks and prime rib. **Foxfire** (253-4887; $–$$) has good Italian food, as does **Trattoria La Festa** (253-8480; $$). **The Whip Bar and Grill** (253-7301; $$), in the lower level of the Green Mountain Inn, is a good place for a light dinner or sandwiches. **Mr. Pickwicks Polo Pub** in the Ye Olde England Inne (253-7558; $$) serves excellent game.

The **Fireside Tavern** (235-3000; $$) in the Inn at the Mountain at the base of the Toll House lift, serves moderate continental cuisine as well as hearty lunches.

On-mountain, there are several choices for lunch and snacks. The **Midway Café** in the Midway Lodge has fresh-baked pastries and muffins and gourmet coffee. The **Cliff House Restaurant** at the gondola top has a nice upscale atmosphere.

A breakfast favorite is **McCarthy's,** next to the movie theater, adjacent to the Baggy Knees complex. Also the breakfast at **The Gables** shouldn't be missed, especially on weekends.

Après-ski/nightlife

The ingredients that make the perfect après-ski spot are all there in just the right measure at the **Matterhorn Bar**. On the mountain road, this raucous little roadhouse is packed and rollicking after the slopes close. There's a dance floor, a disc jockey, loud music, a rectangular bar that makes for easy circulation, pool tables, big-screen TV. More low-key après-ski at the mountain is in the **Fireside Tavern** at the Inn at the Mountain.

The **Rusty Nail** is the "in" spot for dancing and live music, frequently blues. **The Mountain Road House R&B Grille** has live rhythm and blues.

Mr. Pickwick's at Ye Olde England Inne gets a good pub crowd with its 150-plus different beers, and the bar at **Miguel's Stowe Away** seems to be a singles meeting place.

Other activities

Shopping: Stowe has over a hundred shops and art galleries for browsing, most in town. Shaw's General Store is a century old and was the town's first

Dining: $$$-Entrees $20+; $$-$10-20; $-less than $10.
Accommodations: (double room) $$$$-$200+; $$$-$141-$200; $$-$81-$140; $-$80 and less.

ski shop. Other unusual shops are Moriarty Hats & Sweaters, for knitted goods, and the Stowe Craft Gallery for handcrafted, contemporary works.

Indoor tennis can be played at the Topnotch Racquet Club on the Mountain Road. Four Deco Turf courts are available as well as lessons for hourly fees. In the Village, Jackson arena has an Olympic-size **ice skating** rink (253-6148). **Swimming** open to the public, can be found at the Golden Eagle Resort (253-4811), Mountaineer Inn (253-7525), Salzburg Inn (253-8541), Topnotch Resort & Spa (253-9649) and the Town & Country Motor Lodge (253-7595).

Rent **snowmobiles** at Nichols Snowmobiles (253-7239) or from Farm Resort (888-3525). the Sterling Ridge Inn (644-8265), in Jeffersonville, offers snowmobile tours of Smugglers' Notch. Get **Snowshoe** rentals and guided tours from Umiak Outdoor Outfitters (253-2317). **Horse-drawn sleigh rides** take place at Edson Hill Manor (253-7371), Stowehof Inn (253-9722), Pristine Meadows (253-9901), Charlie Horse (253-2215), Stoweflake (253-7355), the Trapp Family Lodge (253-8511) and Topnotch (253-8585). Stowe also has **horseback riding** at Edson Hill Manor (253-7371) and Stowehof Inn (253-9722).

Ben and Jerry's ice cream factory (244-5641) is just down the road in Waterbury and has tours that include samples. Winter is not nearly as busy as summer, so it's a good time to visit. **The Cabot Cheese Factory** (563-2231) is also open.

Special events include the Stowe Winter Carnival in January, the country's oldest winter party; the Mountain Adventure Fest Tour de Stowe cross-country races as well as the Stowe Derby—the country's oldest combination downhill/cross-country event, both held in February; a Sugar Slalom race with maple-sugar-on-snow at the finish line and the Stowe Snow Beach Party, both in April.

Getting there and getting around

By air: Numerous flights arrive at the Burlington International Airport, which is 45 minutes from Stowe. Most hotels have a transfer service; you can also rent a car. The Stowe Area Association provides discounts on flights and rental cars when you make your hotel reservations.

By train: A romantic trip aboard Amtrak's Vermonter offers private berths, cocktail-bearing attendants and the incomparable sensation of watching the moonlit landscape of New England whirl past your window to the lonely call of the train whistle. You arrive in Waterbury, 15 miles from Stowe, early in the morning (the Stowe trolley meets each daily arrival and departure). Reservations required. The Stowe Area Association offers 10 percent off Amtrak tickets with no date restrictions.

By car: Distance from Boston is about 205 miles; from New York, 325 miles. The resort is a few miles north of Waterbury Exit 10 on I-89.

Getting around: You can manage without a car, but we recommend one. We realize that this will only contribute to increased street congestion, but the alternative is the Town Trolley, which runs between the village of Stowe and Mt. Mansfield. It provides, in the words of a British journalist who begged a ride back into town with us, "an epic voyage." The trolley. Makes. A lot. Of stops. Between town. And. The. Mountain. It costs $1 per single ride and $5 for a week-long pass. It is fine for *short* jaunts and operates until 11 p.m.

Stratton Mountain & Bromley
and the Manchester area
Vermont

Stratton Facts

Summit elevation:	3,875 feet
Vertical drop:	2,003 feet
Base elevation:	1,872 feet

Address: RR1 Box 145,
Stratton Mountain, VT 05155
✆ Area code: 802
Ski area phone: 297-2200
Snow report: 297-4211
ⓘ Toll-free reservations:
(800) STRATTON (787-2886)
Fax: 297-4300
E-mail: skistratton@intrawest.com
Internet: www.stratton.com
Number and types of lifts: 13–
1 twelve-passenger gondola, 4 six-passenger
high-speed chair, 4 quads, 1 triple,
1 double, 2 surface lifts
Skiable acreage: 583 acres
Snowmaking: 85 percent
Uphill capacity: 29,550 per hour
Snowboarding: Yes, unlimited
Bed base: 8,000 in region
Nearest lodging: Slopeside
Resort child care: Yes, 6 weeks and older
Adult ticket, per day: $55-$61 (00/01 prices)
Expert:★ Advanced:★★★
Intermediate:★★★★
Beginner:★★★★
Never-ever:★★★★

Bromley Facts

Summit elevation:	3,284 feet
Vertical drop:	1,334 feet
Base elevation:	1,950 feet

Address: P.O. Box 1130,
Manchester Center, VT 05255
✆ Area code: 802
Ski area phone: 824-5522
Snow report: 824-5522
ⓘ Toll-free reservations: (800) 865-4786
Internet: www.bromley.com
Number and types of lifts: 9–1 high-speed quad,
1 quad, 5 doubles, 3 surface lifts
Skiable acreage: 300 acres
Snowmaking: 84 percent
Uphill capacity: 9,045 per hour
Snowboarding: Yes, unlimited
Nearest lodging: Slopeside
Resort child care: Yes, 6 weeks and older
Adult ticket, per day: $25-$46 (2000/01 prices)

Expert:★ Advanced:★
Intermediate:★★★★
Beginner:★★★★
Never-ever:★★★★

Manchester Region
Dining (in region):★★★★★
Apres-ski/nightlife (in region):★★★
Other activities (in region):★★★

Manchester is a hub for skiing in southern Vermont. The town itself, made over as the quintessential Vermont village, complete with white-spire churches, manorial hotels, gourmet dining and antique and craft shops, as well as factory outlets and Orvis fly fishing on the Battenkill River, could take up another entire chapter. Instead, we focus in this chapter on the areas closest to the ski areas.

Stratton, 20 miles from Manchester, is the largest resort in the region and also the chicest. With a car-free base village full of stylish shops, gourmet restaurants, slope-side condos and even a Bavarian-looking clock tower, Stratton does indeed feel like Vail. The cobblestone walkway through the village is even heated. Intrawest just keeps making Stratton bigger and better. New this year are two more six-passenger, high-speed chairs. One services the Sun Bowl; the other goes from the top of the Sun Bowl to the mountain's summit.

Bromley, six miles east of Manchester, is more of a no-nonsense, function-over-fashion ski resort. Its base area consists of a lodge. Period. Nearby are a hotel, some condos and a few private homes but no stores or restaurants. People come to Bromley to ski, ride and hang out with their friends and families on its sunny (one hopes) slopes. Although significantly smaller than Stratton, Bromley has trails for everyone, from gentle beginner runs that wind down the mountain through the woods to expert pistes with shots through the trees.

Stratton
Mountain layout—skiing

One of few eastern resorts with its own base village, Stratton caters to a tony down-country clientele who want convenient amenities and manicured slopes. Excellent grooming on the mostly intermediate terrain makes Stratton one of America's best ego-inflating resorts. Experts can find some good challenges, but don't expect to be pushed; come here to get pampered, and feel good about your skiing.

◆◆ **Expert** ◆ **Advanced:** The pitch for cruising here is nice enough that no expert or advanced skier will complain. Ducking from the trees onto the groomed provides a nice change of pace. For the more challenging terrain, head straight to the summit on the gondola. Polar Bear, Grizzly Bear and Upper Tamarack, all served by the Ursa Express six-passenger chair, are narrow runs in fine New England tradition with good vertical. Upper Kidderbrook to Freefall provides another good advanced cruiser on the Sun Bowl side. Upper Standard, right under the gondola, starts steep but mellows at the bottom. Upper Spruce is the easiest of the double-diamond trails with tempting glades to the right, but none of the double diamonds is really worth of that rating. For bumps, head to World Cup.

■ **Intermediate:** The upper mountain has some steeps for advanced intermediates. Upper Lift Line to Lower Lift Line, the longest fall-line trail on the mountain, is made for big giant-slalom turns and Upper Drifter to Lower Drifter is the same. Racers from the Stratton Mountain School are often carving turns on these trails, as well as North American, off the Ursa Express The Sun Bowl chair has excellent cruisers down Rowley's Run and Sunriser. On the lower mountain, Yodeler is a good warm-up run.

●● **Beginner:** Stratton has a Ski Learning Park with 10 gentle trails and its own lift. This park includes a terrain garden, where the mountain staff sculpts bumps and rolls, so beginners can practice their balance and independent leg action. A long top-to-bottom trail West Meadow to Lower Wanderer makes beginners feel like champs. In the Sun Bowl area head to Lower Middlebrook. The other beginner trails, 91, Big Ben and Main Line, are only reached from intermediate trails.

Mountain rating—Snowboarding

Stratton, one of the pioneers in snowboarding, has four terrain parks, two halfpipes and ever-changing obstacles, including rails, spines, tabletops and quarterpipes. The beginner terrain park on East Meadow allows those new to snowboarding thrills suitable to their skill level.

Lessons (2001/02 prices)

Stratton has an on-mountain Adventure Center where you can try telemark skis, a snowboard, Snowblades or freeride skis designed for fun and tricks, especially in the halfpipe and other places frequented by snowboarders. Begin at Village Rentals in the Village Lodge in the Courtyard. From here, you'll be sent onto the mountain to the rental tent to pick up your equipment, then finally up to the Ski & Snowboard School. Give yourself plenty of time or you'll miss your lesson.

Group lessons: $29 for 1.75 hours.

Never-ever package: $89 includes beginner lift ticket, lesson and equipment; $83 for children ages 7–12.

Private lessons: : $70 per hour

Special programs: Stratton has women's ski and snowboard camps during the season designed to boost confidence and enhance strength, style and technique.

Child care (2001/02 prices)

Stratton: 6 weeks to 5 years. The Childcare Center in the Village Lodge is open 8 a.m. to 5 p.m., and drop-off is under the upper parking deck. A full day costs $89, lunch and snack included; half-day costs $50. Reservations required; call (800) 787-2886 (800-STRATTON).

Children's lessons: Little Cub snow school programs for ages 4–6 run full ($89) and half-days ($50). The program for age 7–12 is all day and costs $109.

Lift tickets (2001/02)

(weekend/weekday)	Adult	Child (7-12)	13-17 and 65-69
One day (00/01)	$59/$55	$42/$40	$52/$48
Three days	$143/$129	$117/$104	$126/$115
Five days	$185/$178	$147/$142	$174/$162

Who skis free: Children younger than age 7.

Who skis at a discount: Those 70 and older ski for children's prices.

Stratton and Okemo have joined forces on a multiday lift ticket plan that permits skiing or riding at either resort. For details, call either resort.

Bromley

Intimate in atmosphere and size, Bromley is perfect for those who prefer not to sweat when skiing. There is some advanced stuff. Most of the 42 trails come down blue from the summit, leading into gentle cruising greens; perfect practice runs for intermediates and beginners but hardly deserving of names like Shincracker.

◆◆ **Expert** ◆ **Advanced:** When it is open, The Plunge provides gladed thrills. Pick your own level of difficulty. Even the best will find challenges. A few seasons ago, Bromley added some black runs to the mountain's steeper east side. Short and sharp with a double fall line, the longest of these challenging runs—Stargazer, Havoc and Blue Ribbon—bring you down to the Blue Ribbon Quad. There is more tree skiing between Pabst Peril and Avalanche.

■ **Intermediate:** This is a perfect mountain for every level of intermediate. The mellower trails are to the right of the high-speed quad (looking down the mountain). The black-diamond trails offer advanced-intermediate skiers excellent challenge.

●● **Beginner:** A good beginner area with a closed never-ever section of the mountain.

Mountain rating: Snowboarding

There is a terrain park, called Snowboard Heaven, on the Lord's Prayer run. The park has all the right stuff: pipe, rolls, jumps, its own T-bar and loud music. The halfpipe is big, and claims to be the steepest in Vermont.

Lessons (2001/02 prices)

Group lessons: $35 for a 1.75-hour lesson.
Never-ever package: Called The Beginners Circle and Snowboard Starter programs are for ages 15 and older. The $65 cost includes a 1.75-hour lesson, equipment and a beginners lift ticket. The two-days cost $99.
Private lessons: $70 per hour, $35 per extra person. Multiple-hour discounts available.

Child care

The Bromley Kids' Center accepts children ages 6 weeks to 6 years. Half day $28, full day $49. Call 824-5522 for reservations and information.

Children's lessons: The Mighty Moose Club (3–5 years) includes playtime, skiing sessions and equipment for $50, half day; $91 full day. Pig Dog Pups (5-6 years) and Pig Dog Mountain Club (7–12 years) includes lift tickets, lessons and lunch but no rental equipment for $80 per day; $91 with equipments.

Lift tickets

	(weekend/weekday)	Adult Child (7-14)	Teen (13-17)
One day	$49/42	$34/$32	$42/$36
Two days	$82/$70	$57/$55	$72/$65

Holiday rates are approximately $5 more per day.

Who skis free: Children ages 6 and younger ski free everyday; ages 70 and older ski free on weekends and holidays.
Who skis at a discount: Ages 65–69 ski for $33/$29.

Cross-country

The Manchester area offers an excellent series of trails.
Hildene (362-1788) in Manchester Village has 15 km. of trails through the pine-covered estate of Robert Todd Lincoln. There is a warming hut in the carriage barn, with rentals, trail tickets and light refreshments.

Nordic Inn (824-6444), just east of Peru, has trails that wander into the Green Mountain National Forest.

The **Stratton Ski Touring Center** (297-4114) at the Sun Bowl has 20 km. of tracked cross-country trails and 50 km. of backcountry skiing. Lessons and guided tours are available.

Beginner terrain and great views are available at the **Nordic Center** at the Stratton Mountain Country Club. Stratton offers Tubbs snowshoe rentals here and at its mountain summit, backcountry Nordic skiing, and moonlight tours; call for prices and details.

Viking Ski Touring Center (824-3933) in Londonderry provides 30 km. of groomed trails through woods and open fields, best suited for intermediates, but with some advanced trails, too. This is one of the oldest cross-country centers in North America.

Porc Trails (824-3933) are a series of ungroomed trails maintained by the West River Outing Club of Londonderry. If you intend to use them, make sure someone knows where you are and when you intend to return because the trails are not patrolled daily. Call for directions and parking locations.

Accommodations

The town of Manchester is a tourism Mecca with accommodations from giant resorts and B&Bs to a slew of lesser-priced roadside motels. The Manchester and Mountains Chamber (362-2100) and the **Londonderry Chamber** (824-8178) can help with arrangements. The hotels and B&Bs listed below are near the ski areas.

At Stratton: Lift and lodging packages (midweek, non-holiday) begin at $49 per person, per day, based on double occupancy. The new **Long Trail House** units will comfortably house a family for an extended stay, with an outdoor heated pool, hot tubs and underground climate-controlled parking. The **Village Lodge** (297-2500) is smack in the middle of Stratton and is the premier property for location: Walk out your door and you are 100 yards from the gondola. It has no pool, dining room, or lounge; for those, take the shuttle to its larger sister hotel, the **Stratton Mountain Inn** (297-2500). The **Liftline Lodge** (297-2600; $–$$) provides Stratton's most economical lodging on the mountain and has many of the resort's restaurants. Stratton Reservations has plenty of condos all within easy reach of the slopes. For reservations at any of Stratton's lodges, call (800) 787-2886 (800-STRATTON). Note: Stratton Mountain packages offer great discounts. Children younger than age 6 stay and ski free anytime. Children 12 and younger stay free in the same room with their parents.

At Bromley: All accommodations are in condos and private homes (up to 4 bedrooms), either slopeside or fed by a shuttle to the base lodge. Best deal: three-day midweek special of $75 per person per day including lift ticket and lessons (based on four people in a two-bedroom condo). No pets. A special midweek deal at the **Sun Lodge** (824-5458 or 800-865-4786; $–$$$ ⚹✕🏔️🅿️✻) provides excellent value.

Between Bromley and Magic Mountain, on Rte. 11, try the **Swiss Inn** (824-3442 or 800-847-9477; $–$$). It has basic rooms but a wonderful restaurant. For an upscale B&B experience, call **The Meadowbrook Inn** (824-6444 or 800-498-6445; $$–$$$). Both are convenient to the Green Mountain National Forest with 26 km. of cross-country trails.

The Londonderry Inn (824-5226; $–$$ ✕🅿️✻), on Rte. 100, a *"Yankee Magazine* Editor's Pick," has 25 individually decorated rooms.

These property management companies deal with condos throughout the area: **Alpine Rentals** (800-817-4562, 824-4562), **Bondville Real Estate** (800-856-8388; 297-3316) or **Winhill Real Estate** (800-214-5648, 297-1550).

The cheapest lodging is the **Vagabond** (874-4096), a hostel on the way to Jamaica (a nearby town, not the island in the Caribbean).

Dining

Dining in the region surrounding the three ski areas is excellent and eclectic. Those looking for a quaint and romantic atmosphere can find it, and those searching for family bargains will not be disappointed.

At Stratton Mountain:

Season's (297-2600; $$), in the Liftline Lodge, has great crabcakes. **Cafe on the Corner** (297-2600; $), also at the Liftline Lodge, has a good breakfast and nice lunch sandwiches. **Sage Hill Restaurant** (297-2500; $$$), in the Stratton Mountain Inn, has great views and a good kitchen. The lunch and dinner menus are creative, well prepared and wonderfully presented. Great Italian food seems to be the main theme on the mountain with **Mulberry Street** (297-3065; $$) serving basic pastas and pizzas and the cozy **La Pista** (297-2343; $$) featuring trendy Italian cooking.

Mulligan's (297-9293; $$) serves moderately priced, basic American fare with a good kids' menu in a loud, TV-in-every-corner atmosphere. Cider's (formerly The Roost; 297-4492; $), right at the base of the slopes, gets rave reviews from families for great breakfasts.

Out Back at Winhall River (297-3663; $$$), just south of the access road, has phenomenal lobster bisque together with other casual fare. Tell the kitchen to go slow on the salt and order red wine by the bottle rather than by the glass. **The Three O'Clock Inn** (824-6327; $$$) serves gourmet fare in an old restored farmhouse in South Londonderry. **Meadowbrook Inn** (824-6444; $$$), between Bromley and Londonderry, open weekends only, is romantic and cozy with continental cuisine.

The Frog's Leap Inn (824-3019; $$$), in Londonderry, serves creative meals by candlelight. **The Garden Cafe** (824-9574; $$$), at the junction of Rtes. 11 and 100 in Londonderry, has been serving upscale meals for more than 15 years.

For fondues and other Swiss/German entrées, head to the **Swiss Inn** (824-3442; $$). **Grant's Tavern and Restaurant** (297-3500; $$$), in Bear Creek, two miles from the Stratton access road, serves meals ranging from crispy cod in a Chinese bean sauce to Fra Diablo. **Foggy Goggle** (827-1300; $$) has steak and seafood in a tavern atmosphere.

The Red Fox (297-2488; $$-$$$), in Bondville, was recommended by about every local for Italian food. **The Noodle Room** (824-4122; $$), at the base of the Magic Mountain access road, has lots of pasta and doesn't take credit cards. **Johnny Seesaw's** (824-5533), just down the road from Bromley in Peru, serves enormous portions. **Jake's Cafe** (824-6614; $) serves pizzas and sandwiches.

Après-ski/nightlife

At Stratton, après-ski is on the deck of **Grizzly's** with entertainment almost every weekend, in **Mulligan's** with its 50 different types of beer or **The Tavern** in the Stratton Mountain Inn. In the evenings, the action on the mountain continues in the **Green Door Pub** in Mulligan's, with live entertainment on weekends, and at **Snyders,** a tap room in Cider's, with live music. Off the mountain, try the locals' hangout, **Red Fox** in Bondville, for live music Fridays and dancing. The **Foggy Goggle,** also in Bondville, is rockin' on the weekends with live bands and free pizza from 4–5 p.m. daily. If you're into the cigar and martini crazes, head to **Mulberry Street.**

Other activities

Shopping: This is a major non-ski activity in the Manchester region. About 40 factory outlet stores, including Coach, Brooks Brothers, Cole Hahn and Garnet Hill, are spread throughout Manchester, along with boutiques and shops with handcrafted regional gift items and unusual clothing.

The **Stratton Sports Center** has indoor tennis, racquetball, indoor pool, hot tubs, saunas, fitness center, tanning salons and massages.

Stratton offers **mini-snowmobile** rides to kids in the base area.

A run-down **movie theater** in Manchester has two screens. For **ice skating**, head to the Riley Rink (362-0150) in Manchester. **Sleigh rides** are offered by Horses for Hire (297-1468) in Rawsonville, just south of Bondville on Rte. 30, Karl Pfister's Sleigh Rides (824-6320) in Landgrove, near Bromley, Sun Bowl Ranch (297-9210) at Stratton and Taylor Farm Sleigh Rides (824-5690) in Londonderry.

Getting there and getting around

By air: Manchester is about 90 minutes from the Albany, N.Y. airport and requires a car for easy access.

By car: Manchester Center is at the intersection of Rtes. 7A and 30 in southwestern Vermont, about 140 miles from Boston and 235 miles from New York City. Stratton is on Rte. 30 about 20 miles east of Manchester. Look for the Stratton Mountain Road from Rte. 30. If you're heading straight for Stratton from I-91, take Exit 2 at Brattleboro, follow signs to Rte. 30, then drive 38 miles to Bondville and the Stratton Mountain Road. Bromley is six miles from Manchester traveling on Rte. 11, eight miles west of Londonderry.

Getting around: Bring a car.

Nearby skiing

Magic Mountain, Londonderry, VT; (802) 8244-5645

Internet: http:// www.magicmtn.com
4 lifts; 135 skiable acres; 1,600 vertical feet

Magic has the most challenging terrain in the region — and often the most challenging conditions — and is called the Mad River Glen of southern Vermont. Stratton and Bromley groom their slopes perfectly. Magic grooms, but not with a fine-tooth comb. Most of the trails are classic New England: narrow, fall-line and full of natural obstacles. Back to basics is the rule. It's the only mountain we've seen that lists the width of its runs on the trail map. Double diamonds fully deserve the ranking, and the trees everywhere are skiable for experts. Riders will find a half-pipe and terrain park.

Lift tickets: (00/01) Adults, $38 weekend/holiday, $28 weekday; Teens (13-17), $34 weekend/holiday, $26 midweek; Juniors (7–12) $02 weekend/holiday and $24 midweek. Children ages 6 and younger and seniors 75 and older ski free everyday. Seniors 65-69 ski for $20 any day; Seniors 70-74 ski for $15 any day. College students ski for $32/$26.

Distance from Boston: about 140 miles. Off Rte. 100, on Rte. 11, west of Londonderry.

Lodging information/reservations: Dostal's Resort Lodge (824-6700 or 800-255-5373; $$ TGfN) is the most upscale and has an Austrian flavor. The Blue Gentian Lodge (824-5908 or 800-456-2405; $ fNo) has basic double rooms with an Austrian flavor. For Trailside Condominiums, call 824-5620.

Dining: $$$-Entrees $20+; $$-$10-20; $-less than $10.
Accommodations: (double room) $$$$-$200+; $$$-$141-$200; $$-$81-$140; $-$80 and less.

Other Vermont Regional Resorts

Ascutney Mountain Resort, Brownsville, VT; (802) 484-7711; (800) 243-0011
Internet: www.ascutney.com
5 lifts; 55 trails; 1,800 vertical feet
Ascutney, located just off I-91 on the New Hampshire/Vermont border, is a mid-sized resort that appeals to young families with a variety of activities both on and off the hill, including tubing, ice skating, pizza parties, torchlight parades and a good children's ski school. Last year, the resort added a high-speed quad to a new summit. This year, the resort is improving its snowmaking and enhancing its children's learning area. Ascutney's terrain is a good mix for advanced and intermediate skiers and riders, with plenty of narrow, twisting old-style New England trails. There's a separate beginner area that's perfect for learning or for skiing with little ones. The base area is anchored by a 240-room ski-in/ski-out hotel.
Lift tickets: Adults, $49 weekend/holiday, $44 weekday; Juniors (7–16) and Seniors (65–69) $35 weekend/holiday and $31 midweek. Those 6 and younger and 70 and older ski free. Half-day tickets are available.
Distance from Burlington: About 105 miles south I-89, I-91, Rte. 5 and Rte. 44. Ascutney is about 130 miles from Albany, NY, and about 130 miles from Boston or Hartford, CT.
Lodging information/reservations: (800) 243-0011.

Suicide Six, Woodstock, VT; (802) 457-6661, Ski Reports (802) 457-6661
Internet: www.woodstockinn.com/skiatinn.html
2 lifts, 1 tow; 23 trails; 650 vertical feet
Suicide Six is part of the Woodstock Inn and Resort. Though small, it has limited terrain for every ability level, including a double-black diamond glade. The resort also has a halfpipe for snowboarders. The Woodstock Inn boasts one of the better cross-country skiing trail systems in the state, with 60 km. of trails. It also has an excellent indoor sports facility.
Lift tickets: Adults, $42 ; Children and seniors, $26. Half-day tickets are available. Lodging and lift packages are the way to go here; call the inn for more information. Skiing is free for inn guests midweek/nonholiday.
Distance from Burlington: About 100 miles via I-89 and Rte. 4. Suicide Six is about 125 miles from Albany and about 150 miles from Boston.
Lodging information: Woodstock Inn, (800) 448-7900 or (802) 457-1100.

Snowshoe Mountain
West Virginia

Summit elevation:	3,100 feet
Vertical drop:	1,500 feet
Base elevation:	1,600 feet

Address: 1 Showshoe Drive,
Snowshoe, WV, 26209
✆ Area code: 304
Ski area phone: 572-1000
Snow report: 572-4636; (800) 258-0330
Reservations: 877-441-4386 or 572-1000
Fax: 572-5636
E-mail: info@snoshoemtn.com
Internet: www.snowshoemtn.com
Expert: ★
Advanced: ★★
Intermediate: ★★★★★
Beginner: ★★★★★
Never-ever: ★★★★

Number and types of lifts: 14–2 high-speed
quads, 2 quads, 7 triples, 3 surface lifts
Acreage: 224 acres
Snowmaking: 100 percent
Uphill capacity: 22,900 per hour
Snowboarding: Yes
Bed base: 1,500 condominium units; 285 hotel/inn
rooms
Nearest lodging: Slopeside
Resort child care: Yes, 12 weeks and up
Adult ticket, per day: $45-$57 (01/02 prices)
Dining: ★★★★
Apres-ski/nightlife: ★★
Other activities: ★★★

"Northern exposure with southern hospitality" is the way Snowshoe folks like to describe themselves. While a vast majority of the nearly half million skiers who come here annually live well south of the Mason-Dixon line, this southern ski area gets nearly 200 inches of annual snowfall so you've got to admit they've got a point. In actuality, Snowshoe encompasses three areas: Snowshoe, Silver Creek and The Western Territory. Snowshoe has three distinct sub-sections. Silver Creek Resort is a terrific family area, with night skiing, a terrain park and snow tubing. The Western Territory has two expert runs served by a high-speed quad. Though the areas are separate, a shuttle bus efficiently transports skiers the short distance between them, and one lift ticket is good at all.

Snowshoe, owned by Intrawest, is an "upside down" resort: The base facilities are at the summit. A mountaintop village has been under construction for several years, and a new lodge, condominiums, restaurants, shops and other base village facilities have been, and continue to be, added. It's the most elaborate and extensive resort in the South, and a vast majority of the skiing/riding is aimed at intermediates. Silver Creek is less crowded, and the slopes are wider and better designed than at Snowshoe, but the skiing is less challenging.

Mountain layout—Skiing

Expert ◆ Advanced ◆◆ : To reach The Western Territory, site of the expert terrain, you must cross the street. Literally. It's located across the access road from Snowshoe. Given the predominance of southern, once-a-year ski-weekers among the clientele, this section is usually least crowded, but it consists of just two runs, Cupp Run and Shay's Revenge, which take advantage of Snowshoe's total vertical drop. Both trails are worthy of their black-diamond rating. At moments along Cupp's, nifty little places can be found to zip into the trees, and one section of Shay's is significantly steep and often bumps up.

Silver Creek holds two trails marked black, Flying Eagle and Bear Creek. While these have short sections that present some pitch, competent intermediates can handle them.

Intermediate: More than one-third of the runs here are rated in the blue-square realm. At the Snowshoe area, the best runs are Ball Hooter and Skip Jack, which lead down to the Ballhooter and Grabhammer (why the run is denoted in two words and the lift in one word is anybody's guess) chairs respectively. Traffic can be a problem here, however, as these lie at the heart of the hill. Another interesting, less traveled option is the Upper Flume/J Hook/ Lower Widowmaker route, which is found all the way at skier's right off the Widowmaker chair and combines easy with intermediate sliding on both narrow and wide trails.

At Silver Creek, Fox Chase-to-Laurel Run offers the most extended blue-rated run. Cascade and Slaymaker-to-Spur also present good cruising. None of these is particularly long.

Beginner: The resort caters to green-level skiers and riders. At the far left, off Snowshoe's top ridge, the resort created the Northern Tract, a comfortably isolated group of a half-dozen easy trails that gives green-trail skiers their own lift-served real estate off the Powderidge chair. The trails are wide enough to be reassuring, but meander a bit to lend texture.

Silver Creek's green-rated runs are generally short but very welcoming, presenting a good place for never-evers to begin the transition to more general terrain. Cubb Run gently hugs the far right edge of the area and allows access to three chairlifts.

Never-ever: The good news is that the Skidder area for never-evers is located just a few steps from the Shavers Center, home to the ski school and rental shop. The bad news is that it's laid out laterally on the ridge top and can become a bit frenzied and turbulent with skiers and riders passing through en route to other parts of the hill. The terrain itself is conducive to learning: short, wide and gentle.

Mountain layout—Snowboarding

Snowshoe has embraced riders with open arms, creating at Silver Creek the Ruckus Ridge Mountaineer Terrain Park, a very popular attraction with both riders and freeskiers. The park includes a 450-foot halfpipe that the resort boasts to be "the largest all-snow halfpipe in the region." At least a dozen features fill the park, including berms, tabletops, banks and various jumps. It runs top-to-bottom on the Mountaineer trail which, although rated black diamond, isn't significantly steep. The resort's terrain is generally snowboarder-friendly, with a minimum of crossover trails and relatively few spots that require unstrapping and pushing. Riders can add some texture to the general cruising nature of the main mountain by taking the short detour onto the Knot Bumper/Glades combination off the Ball Hooter chair. The resort stages a variety of competitions and other events throughout the season.

Mountain rating

Snowshoe does very well by its core customers: Southerners who ski once or twice for a week-long vacation or long weekends each season and families who come from the Washington, DC, and Baltimore areas or from Virginia cities. The terrain is largely approachable with superb snowmaking and snow grooming that allows low-intermediates and intermediates to have a good time. The Silver Creek area presents an excellent venue for families, especially those with younger children, with its combination of single-facility, ski-in/out lodging, night skiing, terrain park and snow tubing. Pickings are slim for the true advanced and expert skier.

Cross-country and snowshoeing

The resort's cross-country skiing operates out of the **Snowshoe Outdoor Adventure Center** (572-5477), between Snowshoe and Silver Creek. The trail system covers 40 km. along the Cheat Mountain Ridge Trail, as well as through the nearby backcountry. The center is fully equipped with rentals and offers instruction.

The **Elk River Inn** (572-3771),in Slatyfork about 5 miles from the bottom of the Snowshoe access road, has a touring center and immediate access to 5 km. of adjacent groomed trails. Another 35 km. can be accessed nearby. The Inn offers ski rentals and will give instruction by appointment.

Lessons (2001/02 prices)

The Snowshoe Ski and Snowboard School operates out of the Shavers Center in the main resort complex, and out of a building adjacent to the Silver Creek Lodge on the Silver Creek side.

Group Lessons: Two-hour, adult group lessons for ages 13 and up (skiing or snowboarding) for Levels 1-4 are scheduled daily at 9:30 a.m. and 1:30 p.m. and cost $30. Multi-day lesson packages are available for $25/day. Two-hour afternoon ski clinics are offered daily for adults skiing at Levels 5-9 at 1:30 p.m. for $40 each. Similar sessions are offered for more advanced snowboarders.

Never-ever packages: Magic Trax is specifically designed for first-time skiers and is available during non-holiday periods. It utilizes Rossignol Short Cut skis. A two-hour session costs $30. Equipment rentals and beginner-area ticket are included.

Private Lessons: All-day costs $340, plus $100 for each additional person. Half-day is approximately $195, plus $75 per extra person. One-hour sessions are offered at 8:30 a.m. and 12:15 p.m. and 3:30 p.m. at a rate of approximately $75 per person, plus $35 per additional participant.

Special Programs: Special programs include Women's Clinics and Night Moves. Women's Clinics, designed for women skiing or riding at Levels 1-4, meet from 9 a.m.-1 p.m. on Mondays and Saturdays and cost $90 per person, which includes lunch. Night Moves is a family-oriented, learn-to-snowboard program for ages 7 and older that meets at Silver Creek from 6-8 p.m. on Tuesdays, Thursdays and Saturdays. Restricted to never-ever riders, the program costs $30 per person, including rental equipment.

Child care (2001/02 prices)

Ages: 12 weeks-10 years.
Costs: Ages 2-10, $45 per day, 8 a.m.-5 p.m., including lunch; $20 per half-day, 8 a.m.-12 p.m. or 1 p.m.-5 p.m., without lunch; or $5 per hour. Younger than age 2, $60 per day, $24 per half-day or $6 per hour.

The Kids' Night Out program is offered Mondays, Wednesdays and Saturdays from 6-9 p.m. for ages 5-12 for $35 and includes arts and crafts, snowshoeing, bonfires, story telling, and other indoor and outdoor activities.

Children's lessons: Full-day and half-day ski and snowboard programs are offered for ages 3-12, with groupings broken into ages 3-4 and 5-12, based also on ability level. Full-day programs run from 9 a.m.-4 p.m. Ages 3-4 cost $75 per day, or $67 per day for a multi-day package; ages 5-12 cost $60 and $57 respectively. Half-day sessions run from 9 a.m.-12 p.m. and 1-4 p.m. The fees for ages 3-4 are $45 per day and $43 per day for multi-day packages;

for ages 5-12, fees are $35 and $33 respectively. These rates do not include lift tickets or equipment rental, but all-day sessions do include lunch.

Lift tickets (2001/02 prices)

Snowshoe provides a variety of pricing modes. Below we quote prices for weekends.

	Adult	Junior (7-12)	Student/Sr. (65-69)
One day	$53	$35	$48
Multi-day	$44	$29	$35

Who skis free: Children 6 and younger.

Who skis at a discount: Seniors 70 and older ski for $27 for one day; $26 for multi-day. Weekdays cost $45 for adults, $30 for juniors and $36 for students and seniors (65–69).

Note: Snowshoe sells tickets for night skiing, 4:30-10 p.m. for $27 adult, $19 junior, $23 student/seniors (65–69). There is a Twilight Skiing pass valid 12:30–10 p.m. and an Extended Day ski pass good 8:30 a.m.–10 p.m.

Accommodations

Intrawest is in the process of creating one of its signature base villages (in this case, a mountaintop village) at Snowshoe. The resort holds a vast array of housing of all types, including some 1,500 condominium units and, at the base of the access road, a nice but basic motel. Call 877-441-4386 or 572-1000.

Rimfire Lodge ($$-$$$$; Tqf) is one of the newest facilities, set in the heart of the pedestrian village. It has hotel rooms, plus studio, one- and two-bedroom units. Typical of Intrawest properties, accommodations are comfortable, but smaller units can be a bit cramped. Most units have kitchens, all have gas-fired fireplaces, and guests get the advantage of underground parking. The intra-resort shuttle stops at the door.

Highland House ($$-$$$$; qft) overlooks the Ballhooter lift and is the resort's latest expansion. Units run the gamut from hotel rooms and so-called deluxe hotel rooms to two-bedroom condos with a den.

Silver Creek Lodge ($$-$$$$; TqBft) is the 240-unit, self-contained base facility at Silver Creek. Accommodations range from studios to four-bedroom condos, plus a penthouse. This is an ideal site for families with young children, as the tubing hill, night skiing, terrain park, kids' ski school, child care, rental shop, pool and other amenities are right there.

Spruce Lodge ($-$$; q) is the on-hill "no frills" lodge, offering double rooms, some with bunk beds. It's low-budget, but located smack in the middle of things.

Inn at Snowshoe ($-$$; TB) sits at the base of the access road 6 miles from the summit village. A 150-room hotel, it has some one-bedroom suites.

Off the mountain, the area boasts a handful of nice B&B's. The **Elk River Inn** (572-3771; www.ertc.com; $-$$$), with 10 rooms in the inn, a five-room farmhouse with three shared baths and kitchen, and five kitchen-equipped cabins, is 5 miles from the access road and offers breakfast, an excellent restaurant and on-site Nordic skiing, as well as its own snowboard shop. **The Morning Glory Inn** (572-5000; www.morninggloryinn.com; $-$$) is brand new and located just 3 miles from the access road. It has six large bedrooms with oversized Jacuzzi-tub bathrooms, a large, homey public living room and a full breakfast that's substantial and homemade. The **Brazen Head Inn** (339-6917; $-$$), 7 miles north of the mountain on US Rte. 219, offers comfortable B&B lodging and dining. The 20-room roadside lodge also offers daily dining and features an Irish style pub.

 ## Dining

On-mountain, the number of eateries is expanding rapidly. **The Red Fox** (572-111; $$-$$$) remains the long-standing benchmark for on-mountain fine dining. It features "Mountain Alpine" cuisine, which consists of a lot of meat and wild game specialties, presented with an unusual combination of European-style service and American/mountain casual ambiance.

The **Junction Restaurant** (572-5800; $$) is one of the newer entries, a result of the base village expansion. The decor hearkens back to West Virginia logging boom times and the heyday of Shay steam locomotives, featuring memorabilia from the nearby Cass Scenic Railroad. The food is classic American fare, and reasonably good. The **Foxfire Grill** (572-5555; $-$$), another new entry in the Rimfire Lodge, features live blues and barbecue, as well as burgers. For something simpler and faster, **The Cheat Mountain Pizza Company** (572-5757; $-$$) serves pretty good pizza, from plain to gourmet, as well as salads, calzones and other Italian fare. One meal that's fun and recommended is the terrific waffle breakfast at **The Boathouse** (572-1000; $), a rustic day lodge set at the base of the Ballhooter Lift. Lunch is also available.

Off the mountain, the **Restaurant at the Elk River Inn** (866-572-3771 or 572-3771; www.ertc.com; $$-$$$) serves a changing menu of truly gourmet regional and international dishes, superb desserts and a nice selection of local microbrews. Reservations are recommended.

 ## Aprèss-ski/nightlife

A surprising amount of activity goes on here after dark, including night skiing. If you're looking for a bar scene or club, you can easily find it. **The Connection** is the hottest spot on the mountain. Yes, it's located in the Shavers Centre base facility, so there's nothing exotic about it, but the upstairs club scene really does rock. Live bands and a DJ are a regular feature, plus there's pool, foosball, some video games and a large-screen TV. The partying usually lasts well into the night. A particular favorite of ours is the **Comedy Cellar Bar** (572-5440 for performance info), squirreled away in the basement of the almost dorm-like Mountain Lodge. The bar itself is small and intimate and open nightly; on Tuesdays-Saturdays at 9 p.m., however, local Roy Riley (not a bad performer himself) shares the small stage with one or two pros who frequent the national circuit for a full evening of stand-up comedy. It's definitely adult entertainment, and it's lots of fun.

Rosa's Cantina, found a bit out of the way at the top of the Widowmaker Lift, serves unremarkable burgers and Mexican fare, but somehow manages to have one fine bar. Gregarious bartenders, good brew and an altogether very friendly, locals' atmosphere make it a good spot for a drink. The **Foxfire Grill**, although new, manages to generate a nice sense of atmosphere, and frequently offers local, live music that's a kick to stomp the feet to. If you're staying over on the family-oriented Silver Creek side, you have two choices right in Silver Creek Lodge. The **Bear's Den** is on the second floor, a fine spot to take in a quiet beer or hot drink on a cold day. At the **Red Oak Pub**, you can quench your thirst while playing billiards or fooseball.

Other activities

Snowshoe Resort has just recently begun to offer snowmobile touring. **Mile High Snowmobiling Tours** is located near the Cross Country Ski Center,

Dining: $$$-Entrees $20+; $$-$10-20; $-less than $10.
Accommodations: (double room) $$$$-$200+; $$$-$141-$200; $$-$81-$140; $-$80 and less.

and reservations can be made at the Adventure Center in the base village. The cost for a one-hour tour is $50 per driver, plus $15 per passenger. Another relatively new offering is a **Sunrise Country Hut** dinner. You can only get there by snowmobile or all-terrain vehicle (it's a two-mile ride), and you get a good country meal (steak, salmon or chicken; wine included) in a beautiful, isolated setting for $75 per person.

While at the Adventure Center, you can also sign up for a **dogsledding** outing. The cost is $49 per couple. Two **horse-drawn sleigh ride** options are available. A short ride on the Skidder beginner slope (great for small children) costs but $5. One-hour ride will run you $60 for two passengers; one or two other passengers over age 12 can join you for $10 each.

The tubing hill at **Ruckus Ridge Adventure Park** is found at Silver Creek. The cost runs $12 per person for two hours, or $15 for an all-day pass.

Shopping: Nobody is going to mistake this place for a shopper's paradise. The expanding base village represents an attempt to bring in some interesting retail, but it's minimal at best. We like **The Chocolate Factory** (572-1289) because, well, who doesn't love a store that sells chocolate? **The Red Fox Mercantile**, at The Red Fox Restaurant is also interesting for its proprietary sauces and such. You can also pay premium prices for high-quality clothing and accessories here. **The General Store** sells provisions for your condo, but beware the high-elevation prices. If you're heading to a condo, best to pack in supplies from your local supermarket, then add absolute necessities, or must-be-fresh stuff here. It also rents videos and VCRs, sells gas and makes some pretty good sandwiches.

Getting there and getting around

By car: You're going to end up driving here, even if you fly, since the nearest sizable airport is nearly two-and-a-half hours away. The resort is located on Route 66 off Route 219, about 45 miles south of Elkins, WV. It's rather remote no matter from which direction you approach. From the south or the west, exit I-64, at White Sulphur Springs, then take Highway 92 and 39 to Marlinton, until you see the Snowshoe signs. From the north, exit I-79 at Weston (Highway 33 at exit #99), go to Elkins, then south on Highway 219. From the East, it's I-81 to Staunton, Route 42/39 west to Route 28 south; or, from Harrisonburg, VA, take Route 33 west to Route 28 south.

By plane: Roanoke, VA, airport is approximately 2.75 -3 hours from the resort, and is served by US Airways, Delta, American and United Airlines. Yeager Airport in Charleston, WV, is about 3.5 hours away and served by US Airways, United Express and Delta's Comair. Closest is Greenbrier Valley Airport in Lewisburg, WV, approximately 1.5 hours from Snowshoe, which is only served by US Airways but offers the Greenbrier Valley Airport Shuttle (536-1193) for those who choose not to drive.

Getting around: As long as you're on the mountain, the shuttle bus will reliably get you where you need to go. If you want to go off-mountain, you're going to need that car. Parking is a bit chaotic; however, the newest lodges, Rimfire and Highland House, offer underground parking.

Other Eastern and Midwestern Regional resorts

Note: We have not listed lift ticket prices for these resorts—virtually none had been finalized by press date. Call or use the internet before visiting. In most cases the prices will be in the $35–$45 range depending on whether skiing weekends or weekdays. Most of these resorts have excellent learn-to-ski programs as well as good instruction to allow skiers to make the breakthrough from beginner to intermediate to advanced.

Massachusetts Regional Resorts

Jiminy Peak, Hancock, MA; (413) 738-5500; (888) 454-6469

Internet: www.jiminypeak.com
9 lifts; 40 trails; 1,140 vertical feet

Brodie Mountain, Hancock, MA; (413) 443-4752

Internet: www.skibrodie.com
6 lifts; 40 trails; 1,200 vertical feet
Jiminy Peak caters to families and intermediates with terrain that isn't too steep and isn't too flat. The Berkshire Express, a high-speed, six-passenger chairlift, gets to the summit in five minutes, where Hendricks Summit Lodge stands as the only ski area summit lodge in the region. Night skiing takes place on 19 runs, including New England's longest lighted trail, Left Bank. A terrain park and halfpipe are located on the green-rated Grand Slam trail, and are served by their own rope tow.

Jiminy is one of the strongest proponents of GETSkiing—a program specifically designed for never-evers that utilizes Elan short shaped skis to make starting easier. Program participants also receive a GETSkiing Card, good for other discounts. Shuttle bus service is offered on weekends from the Albany, NY, area and from Long Island.

The day-care center takes infants as young as 6 months. Jiminy has comfortable slopeside lodging at the Country Inn, an all-suite hotel with outdoor, heated pool, indoor and outdoor whirlpools, exercise room and game room. Two- and three-bedroom condominiums are also available.

Jiminy's owner acquired nearby Brodie Mountain, just 3 miles away. The area operates Wednesday-Sunday from mid-December through the end of March and is open seven days a week during holiday periods (Christmas, Martin Luther King Day/mid-January and Presidents Day/mid-February). Brodie is a family favorite with an Irish flavor, and St. Patrick's Day (actually it's a week-long celebration) here is not to be missed, whether you're Irish or not. A new tubing park opened last year. It operates nightly Wednesday-Friday, and all day and night on weekends and holidays

Distance from Albany, NY: About 40 miles via I-90, Rte. 43 and Brodie Mountain Rd.
Lodging information: (800) 882-8859

Wachusett Mountain, Princeton, MA; (978) 464-2300; (800) 754-1234
Internet: www.wachusett.com
6 lifts; 20 trails; 1,000 vertical feet
   Wachusett is the highest mountain in central Massachusetts. It has some decent advanced trails dropping from the summit. All are groomed several times a day. The good news about that is that the snow is kept in excellent condition despite heavy traffic. The bad news: the bite is taken out of most anything that may have been tough. There usually is, however, a machine-made bump field on 10th Mountain Trail. In recent seasons, the area has implemented a number of improvements, including two triple chairs, a 10,000-square-foot addition to the base lodge, upgraded rental equipment, two intermediate-level, lower-mountain trails and an alpine park.
   If you want fast cruisers, this is the place to strap on your boards. Try Conifer Connection or Challenger for intermediate cruising. Head to 10th Mountain for those bumps. Beginners stick to the cluster of Easy Rider, Sundowner and Indian Summer. Night skiing is open from 4–10 p.m. A cross-country operation is based at the Wachusett Village Inn.
Distance from Boston: About 50 miles via Rtes. 2 and 140.
Lodging information: The Wachusett Village Inn, (978) 874-2000, is about four miles from the mountain and runs a shuttle service.

New Jersey Regional Resorts
Mountain Creek, Vernon, N.J.; (973) 827-2000
Internet: www.mountaincreek.com
11 lifts; 47 trails; 1,040 vertical feet
Location, location, location. Those are the three words responsible for the rejuvenation of once neglected Great Gorge and Vernon Valley into the almost all new Mountain Creek by ski area developer Intrawest. More than $40 million—$8.6 million on snowmaking and $8.2 million on ski lifts alone—has been invested in recent years in this four-peak mini-resort located within 75 miles of 22 million people. The changes, which include two high-speed quads, an eight-person "cabriolet" (stand-up gondola), an expanded children's center and enhanced snow making, are all for the best. A major new real estate development has begun that will create a destination-resort ambience.
   Don't let black diamond designations scare you off, here, even if you're a lower-intermediate skier; these designations are all relative, and they are just the steeper trails at the area-although Pipe Line, rated double-black, challenges with some true steep, albeit if only for a short distance. Cliff Run, too, is relatively short, but a sweet black-diamond. For the most part, however, the mountain is mellow and a great place for cruising without dealing with the long commute to the bigger mountains.
   Mountain Creek's two terrain parks and two half pipes, called Uncommon Ground, have proven a major magnet for riders, and about 40 percent of the clientele are snowboarders (with night skiing every night, it's a great place to keep teenagers busy). On Vernon Peak, the park runs top to bottom, reaching nearly a mile in length, and ending in a user-friendly "family" section. On South Peak, the park is built in four distinct sections, one of which is designated as "family" terrain.
   The resort offers Kids Kamps, MagicTrax first time skier packages and Phat Trax for first-time riders. A snowtubing park rounds out the activity options.

Distance from New York: 47 miles. Take Lincoln Tunnel to Rte. 3 west to Rte. 46 west to Rte. 23 north to County Rte. 515 north to Rte. 94 south. Or Take George Washington Bridge to Rte. 80 West, Rte 23 north to County Rte. 515 north to Rte. 94 south.

Distance from Philadelphia: Approximately 130 miles. Take N.J. Turnpike to Rte. 287 to Rte. 23 to County Rte. 515 north to Rte. 94 south.

Lodging information: Mountain Creek Lodging (on-mountain condominiums), (888) 456-9998; Legands Resort, (800) 835-2555; Apple Valley Inn, (973) 764-3735; Wooden Duck B&B, (973) 300-0395; Chateau Hathorn, (914) 986-6099.

New York Regional Resorts

Hunter, NY; (518) 263-4223
Internet: www.huntermtn.com
10 lifts, 1 tow; 53 trails; 1,600 vertical feet

Ski Windham, NY; (518) 734-4300
Internet: www.skiwindham.com
6 lifts, 1 tow, 34 trails; 1,600 vertical feet

These are the two closest large ski areas to New York City, only a two-and-a-half hours' drive north. These resorts are in the midst of the rocky Catskills, home to such legends as Rip Van Winkle. As far as skiing goes, the region woke with a vengeance almost 30 years ago. Trails were dynamited and bulldozed through rugged mountains, and snowmaking became an integral part of Eastern ski resorts.

The villages surrounding the mountains reflect the personality of their respective resort. Hunter and nearby Tannersville are one-street Adirondack towns with supermarkets, bars, pubs, discos, hotels and homes. Windham is the quieter sister, with a more manicured look; delis rather than supermarkets, country inns instead of hotels. On the slopes, weekend crowds at Hunter reflect a mostly singles, Generation X heritage (with more families, recently). Windham is a family resort, and its skiers are far more sedate. In Hunter you may hear the bass throb of a disco beat and other sounds of merriment. The streets teem into the small hours. In Windham the loudest midnight sound may be the snow guns, a passing car or water gurgling downstream.

Hunter Mountain and Ski Windham are only 10 miles apart. Both have the same amount of vertical but Hunter is a major leaguer, by far the bigger operation. It has become one of the snowmaking champions of the Northeast, shooting out mountains of snow and continually upgrading the system. When conditions are poor everywhere else in the region, this is where the skiers come expecting snow. Hunter West creates that big-league sensibility. It only has a few runs, but four of them—Annapurna, Westway, the Colonel's Alternate and Claire's Way—are accurately rated double-black. On the main face, double-black K-27 has long been one of the East's most challenging runs. Hunter One provides well for intermediates and beginners.

Hunter's commitment to snowboarders is strong. Last season it began employing a separate a Terrain Park Staff to keep the park in top shape. A fully-functional Yurt, popular with riders who only want to play in the park, is operated on the weekends and holidays, and the resort is committed to increased freestyle features.

Snowtubing and snowshoeing are fairly recent offerings. The snowtubing park has its own small lodge. A small, lift-accessible network of snowshoeing trails has been laid out at the top of the mountain, with access to a wider range of state maintained trails, as well.

Hunter can be crowded on weekends, and that the main mountain's trail layout can lead to traffic problems. This is, however, the place to be if you want to be where the action is.

Ski Windham offers good skiing but doesn't have the extent of its neighbor's snowmaking or as much difficult terrain. Each area has a high-speed quad pumping skiers up the mountain and keeping lines manageable. A small handful of trails off the top provide adequate steeps, but they quickly flatten out. The area began offering weekend and holiday night skiing on limited terrain a few years ago, which has proven popular. The base lodge is modern and user-friendly. This is definitely a family-friendly place to ski or ride.

Windham has created at least five terrain parks on all levels of terrain, so that riders and free skiers can chose the challenge that suits them. The snowtubing park features DiscountNight on Fridays. Also, demos are available not only for skis and snowboards, but also for Snowblades, Big Feet and snowshoes. On peak season Fridays, Saturdays and Sundays, the area offers First Tracks, a chance to ski for an hour before the lifts open to the public. Cost is $14 per person.

Distance from New York: 120 miles north of the city; take I-87 to Exit 20 at Saugerties, and follow Rte. 32 to Rte. 32A, then 23A west to the area. To reach Ski Windham, turn north on Rte. 296 off of Rte. 23A or, if coming on the N.Y. thruway, take Exit 21 in Catskill, and go west on Rte. 23 for 25 miles.

Lodging information: (518) 263-4641 or (800) 754-9463.

North Carolina

Beech Mountain Ski Resort, Beech Mountain, NC; (828) 387-2011

Internet: www.skibeech.com

1 highspeed chair lift, 6 chair lifts, 4 drag lifts; 17 trails; 830 vertical feet

This is the highest ski and snowboarding area in the eastern United States with an elevation of 5,505 feet. If you want to ski or ride in North Carolina, this is the place to come. Beech Mountain has 100 percent snowmaking coverage and excellent learning programs for adults and children, and one of the best adaptive skiing programs around. There is a halfpipe and a terrain park for boarders. And all slopes are lighted for night skiine.

Distance from Asheville, NC: About 80 miles (about a two-and-a-half hour drive).

Lodging information: (800) 438-2093

Pennsylvania: The Poconos

Honeymoon hideaways, major highways and big-city accessibility have made the hills of the Poconos in Northeastern Pennsylvania a convenient weekend retreat for some of America's largest metropolitan areas.

The region has long had a hot honeymoon/weekend-getaway reputation with lodges offering heart-shaped beds and in-room spas. Beds of all shapes are not in short supply—you'll find 80,000 within an hour of the hills.

Weekends tend to be crowded, very crowded. However, most areas have 100 percent snowmaking and state-of-the-art grooming, so surface conditions are reasonably good. Groomers will freshen up and snow guns fire if conditions fall apart too quickly. Most of the terrain is intermediate, with a few short-but-sweet black diamonds to keep the hot skiers happy, and plenty of beginner areas, often set apart. Each mountain maintains a hill specifically for never-evers.

Blue Mountain, Palmerton, PA; (610) 826-7700; Snow report (800) 235-2226.

Internet: www.aminews.com/bluemountain

7 lifts; 75 acres; 1,082 vertical feet

This ski area is closest to Philadelphia, and offers the highest vertical drop in the Poconos, 1,082 feet on Challenge. The pitch is steep and steady with moguls and a headwall near the bottom that will challenge the toughest. With ideal conditions, you might think you were skiing Vermont. The area features night skiing seven nights a week and tickets are sold according to the hours you want to ski. Blue Mountain prohibits snowboarding.

The resort has no cross-country skiing. However, many state parks and nearby resorts have cross-country areas. The Pocono Mountain Tourist Bureau at (717) 424-6050 provides a cross-country report.

Distance from New York or Philadelphia: About 100 miles. Skiers heading to Blue Mountain should take the Northeast Extension of the Pennsylvania Turnpike to Exit 33 or 35 then follow the signs.

Lodging information: (800) 762-6667; (800) POCONOS.

Jack Frost/Big Boulder, Blakeslee, PA; (570) 443-8425.

Internet: www.big2resorts.com

14 lifts; 155 skiable acres; 600 vertical feet (Jack Frost)

These two areas, marketed as the Big Two Resorts with an interchangeable lift ticket, are on opposite sides of Rte. 940 and a few miles from each other.

Big Boulder was one of the first Poconos ski areas and one of the first to cover its trails with machine-made snow. Today beginners and intermediates practice their skills day and night on its 2,900-foot-long, 475-foot-high hill. If you arrive on a Friday night, you can ski until 10 p.m.

The Jack Frost lodge is at the top of the mountain. The 21 slopes and trails are straight, top to bottom, with variety in pitch. Both mountains have lift-served slopes for tubing.

At Big Boulder snowboarders are welcome to ride, hop, slide and jump at the Bonk Yard with its boxes, rail slides, barrels and truck tires. Jack Frost snowboarders have two halfpipes, 400 and 500 feet in length.

Distance from New York: About 100 miles. To reach Jack Frost/Big Boulder from New York, take Exit 43 from I-80. Jack Frost is five miles north by Route 115 then west on Route 940. Big Boulder is south of the interstate via Routes 115 and 903. **Distance from D.C.:** About 60 miles by I-10, I-215, Hwy. 30, Hwy. 330 and Hwy. 18.

Lodging information: (800) 468-2442.

Camelback, Tannersville, PA; (570) 629-1661; snow report (800) 233-8100.

Internet: skicamelback.com

12 lifts; 139 skiable acres; 32 trails; 811 vertical feet.

This area is the closest to metropolitan New York, and only about 20 minutes further from Philadelphia than Blue Mountain. It is an intermediate cruising heaven with 32 trails and two fairly new high-speed quads.

Although Margies and the Hump are rated expert, they tend to get slick early. The best skiing is on the intermediate trails, such as Interstate and Marc Antony. With the Stevenson high-speed quad three new trails were added, including black-diamond 5,000-foot Cliffhanger which is FIS rated (proper length, width and pitch to hold a professional race).

The trails are lighted for night skiing. Cameland, a special learning area, was created for children ages 4–9. This season Camelback will add a tubing park with six runs and two lifts, shaped-ski rentals, and a new learning area for never-evers. There is also a snowboard park with a halfpipe.

Camelback has no cross-country skiing. However, many state parks and resorts near the ski areas have cross-country trails. Call Pocono Mountain Tourist Bureau for a cross-country report at (717) 424-6050.

Distance from New York: About 100 miles. To reach Camelback, take Exit 45 from I-80, then follow signs.

Lodging information: (800) 762-6667; (800) POCONOS.

Other Pennsylvania resorts

Elk Mountain Ski Area, Union Dale, PA; (570) 679-4400

Internet: www.elkskier.com
6 lifts; 25 trails; 1,000 vertical feet

This is, for Pennsylvania, a tough skier's mountain. The slopes are good for advanced skiers and solid intermediates who want some practice. The beginner trails can be difficult on an icy day. There is no real resort area, but the region has about 50 hotels. Elk is in the northeast corner of Pennsylvania near Scranton. Night skiing and child care are available.

Distance from Scranton: About 26 miles via I-81.

Lodging information: Special packages are offered at nearby motels. Best accommodations are at Nicholas Village in Clarks Summit.

Seven Springs, Champion, PA; (814) 352-7777

Internet: www.7springs.com
11 lifts and 7 tows; 30 trails; 750 vertical feet

Hidden Valley, Hidden Valley, PA; (814) 443-2600

Internet: www.hiddenvalleyresort.com
6 lifts and 2 tows; 17 trails; 610 vertical feet

These resorts are about three and a half hours from Baltimore and Washington and an hour from Pittsburgh. Seven Springs has the best base facilities and more difficult trails, and Hidden Valley offers quieter surroundings. Trails at these two resorts will keep beginners and intermediates happy for a day or two. Both areas have child care (starting at "walking age" for Seven Springs; 18 months and older at Hidden Valley) and night skiing.

Distance from Pittsburgh: About 55 miles east via the Pennsylvania Turnpike.

Lodging information: Hidden Valley, (800) 458-0175; Seven Springs, (800) 452-2223.

West Virginia

Canaan Valley, Davis, WV; (304) 866-4121

Internet: None found.
3 lifts; 34 trails; 850 vertical feet

Timberline Four Seasons Resort, Davis, WV; (304) 866-4801, (800) SNOWING
Internet: wvweb.com/www/timberline.html
3 lifts; 35 trails; 1,000 vertical feet

A long time favorite ski area for D.C.-area skiers, Canaan (pronounced Kuh-NANE) Valley ski area is located in a pristine wilderness area. Deer stroll in front of the park hotel. Terrific cross-country skiing is nearby. The downhill skiing is good for all levels.

Timberline was one of the first in the country to welcome snowboarders. It is a small family area, boasting a two-mile long beginner's run. It's usually uncrowded compared to next-door Canaan, and many of the skiers are resort property owners.

Distance from Pittsburgh: About 145 miles southeast.

Lodging information: Canaan Valley, (304) 622-4121; Timberline, (800) 766-9464.

Virginia/Maryland

Wintergreen, Wintergreen, VA; (804) 325-2200

Internet: www.wintergreenresort.com

5 lifts; 17 slopes and trails; 1,003 vertical feet

Wintergreen is less than an hour south of Charlottesville along the famed Skyline Drive. While natural snow is limited, the manmade variety is religiously pumped out day and night. The lodge is rather upscale with boutiques and antiques. Most skiing is mellow, but The Highlands offers a thousand feet of bumps with limited crowds, thanks to the ski patrol. Night skiing and child care are available.

Distance from Charlottesville, VA: About 45 miles southwest.

Lodging information: (800) 226-2444.

Wisp, McHenry, MD; (301) 387-4911

Internet: www.gcnet.net/wisp

7 lifts; 23 trails; 610 vertical feet

Located above scenic Deep Creek Lake, Wisp is the closest thing below the Mason-Dixon Line to skiing Lake Tahoe. A solid family ski area with terrain for all levels; intermediates will especially enjoy cruising on the back side of the mountain. Night skiing is available, but no child care for children younger than 4.

Distance from Pittsburgh: About 125 miles southeast via I-79, I-68 and Rte. 219.

Lodging information: (301) 387-4911.

Midwest

The biggest Midwestern ski areas may not have the great verticals of mountains to the east and west, but they have enough terrain, fine facilities, and uphill capacity to tune anyone up for bigger adventures. The following are the best Midwestern ski destinations.

Michigan's Lower Peninsula:

Boyne Highlands and Boyne Mountain,

Harbor Springs and Boyne Falls MI; (800) 462-6963 (GO-BOYNE)

Internet: www.boyne.com

22 lifts, 82 trails, 520 vertical feet

The Mountain and **Highlands**, situated about 30 minutes apart, are near Petoskey and Harbor Springs, two towns that are New England lookalikes and have been a Midwest winter vacation area since the 1920s. The Mountain's steep chutes and mogul fields are legendary among flatlanders. In an effort to soften its tough image, a large new beginner area and tow were added in '95. This is a Midwest classic with sweeping bowls and Eastern-style trails that slice through the hilly hardwoods. An intermediate mountain by reputation, it recently added some tougher terrain. If advanced skiing is what you seek, head for the Mountain.

Both areas feature a high-speed lift, unusual in the Great Lakes states. (Boyne Mountain has one of just four 6-person chairs in the U.S.) Each resort has an uphill capacity approaching 22,000 skiers per hour—tops in the Midwest. Boyne's snowmaking capabilities are well known among Midwestern skiers. The Mountain routinely stays open on weekends through April, and has extended into May on a couple of occasions—most recently in 1996.

Plenty of lodging and amenities exist at the resorts and in the area. Many skiers choose to stay in town and day-trip to the ski areas. Call Boyne Country CVB at (800) 845-2828.

Nubs Nob is just across the valley from the Highlands. Nubs offers the best trio of advanced slopes in the Lower Peninsula. Recent additions of intermediate and beginner terrain help round out the variety. It's the locals' choice. Most skiers up for an extended weekend will add a day of skiing at Nubs.

Crystal Mountain, Thompsonville MI; (616) 378-2911

Internet: www.crystalmtn.com
7 lifts, 22 trails, 375 vertical feet

Crystal Mountain skis much bigger than its 375-foot vertical. It's a great family area that offers solid intermediate slopes and lots of lower-level trails. As evidence of its appeal, Crystal ranks annually among the top 10 resorts for overall NASTAR participants. It has a variety of lodging and a fitness center with a pool.

Shanty Creek/Schuss Mountain, Ballaire MI; (231) 533-8621; (800) 348-4440

Internet: www.shantycreek.com
9 lifts, 30 trails, 450 vertical feet

These two resorts offer a nice weekend retreat. They are about five miles apart but are now operated as one with interchangeable lift tickets. Shanty has the nicest lodging, but Schuss has the better skiing—a good skier will get bored quickly at Shanty.

Michigan Upper Peninsula:

This is a rugged land of dense forests, long winters, deep snows and a collection of ski areas called Big Snow Country. The region receives over 200 inches of snowfall annually. Resorts listed here are all located near Ironwood and Hurley, about a seven-hour drive from Chicago or four hours from the Twin Cities. These areas have enough variety and are close enough together to keep skiers happy for a weekend or a midweek trip.

Indianhead Mountain, Wakefield, MI; (906) 229-5181; (800) 346-3426

Internet: www.indianheadmtn.com
9 lifts, 22 trails, 638 vertical feet

Indianhead runs are wide boulevards. It's an intermediate's dream—long, smooth runs—but they all look the same. The skier who likes a good challenge may get bored here, but it is a great family area. The lodge and compact ski area sit atop the mountain. Runs fan out into the deep forests below, but all the lifts funnel back to the lodge on top. The main lodge was originally a dairy barn, part of a hilltop farm dating from the turn of the century. It's quite rustic and charming. A new pool and fitness center were added in recent years.

Blackjack, Bessemer, MI; (800) 848-1125
Internet: skiblackjack.com
6 lifts, 20 trails, 465 vertical feet
Blackjack appeals to intermediate and advanced skiers, befitting its brawny lumberjack image. They will enjoy busting down some of the wide bump runs or exploring the many narrow chutes and trails that fork off the boulevards. The Black River meanders through the valley—very picturesque.

Big Powderhorn Mountain, Bessemer, MI; (906) 932-4838; (800) 222-3131
Internet: www.bpla.com
9 lifts, 24 trails, 600 vertical feet
This area offers a good variety of trails and the most uphill capacity in the immediate area (9,600 per hour). It has tree-lined trails, open bowls, rambling runs and narrow chutes to explore, plus the most slopeside lodging, restaurants and après-ski activity in the area.

Minnesota

Blessed with superb ski terrain and consistently cold temperatures, northern Minnesota has some of the best snow conditions east of the Rockies, and the northwoods scenery is spectacular. What's here? Three excellent ski areas with big vertical drops (for the Midwest)— Giants Ridge, 550 feet; Spirit Mountain, 700 feet; and Lutsen, 800 feet. They are around Duluth and within an hour or so of each other.

Lutsen, Lutsen, MN; (218) 663-7281, (800) 360-7666
Internet: None found.
8 lifts, 48 trails, 800 vertical feet
About an hour north of Duluth on Hwy. 61 (immortalized by Bob Dylan in the 1960s), Lutsen is the closest thing to true mountain skiing in the Great Lakes area. It has the only gondola in the Midwest and the skiing is off of four peaks (*à la* Killington). It will remind you of a New England ski area—long rock-ribbed trails flanked by birch and pine, and tight short headwalls. Moose Mountain offers the best cruisers between the Appalachians and the Rockies. The many Lake Superior views are magnificent. A variety of accommodations exist at Lutsen Mountain and along the north shore—rustic to plush, simple to gourmet. Cross-country skiing also is plentiful throughout the area.

Spirit Mountain, Duluth, MN; (218) 628-2891;(800) 642-6377
Internet: None found.
8 lifts, 21 trails, 700 vertical feet
Spirit Mountain has good vertical, long runs, snowy winters and great views of Duluth and the harbor perched on the Superior shoreline. The skiing is long on intermediate and beginner runs, without much variation in pitch and few twists and turns. A high-speed covered quad services the beginner trails—nice on cold days. An expert won't find much challenge here.

Giant's Ridge, Biwabik, MN; (218) 865-4143
Internet: None found.
5 lifts, 19 trails, 500 vertical feet
About an hour's drive northwest of Duluth, this area is not as crowded as the other two. The trails soar off the crest and are varied in pitch, with a headwall here, a bowl there. The day lodge is first class, and so is the cross-country skiing.

Wisconsin

The skiing here has a certain ruggedness that you won't find in Michigan's Lower Peninsula. It doesn't receive the natural lake-effect snow that Michigan gets, but the areas do an adequate job of snowmaking.

Devil's Head, Merrimac, WI; (800) 338-4579 (DEVILSX)
Internet: None found.
15 lifts and tows, 21 trails, 500 vertical feet
In the beautiful Baraboo Bluffs overlooking the Wisconsin River Valley, this area has excellent beginner and intermediate skiing. One of the beginner runs is nearly two miles long. Its drawbacks are limited advanced terrain and not much variation. It is a full-service resort with a country-club atmosphere. Weekend crowds can be huge.

Located just down the road is **Cascade,** with 460 vertical feet and a wide variety of skiing. It's straightforward skiing, with solid cruising and hefty faces for the bumps. It has more uphill capacity than Devil's Head (14,000 per hour), but weekend lines can still be long. These two resorts, just three hours from Chicago, are together consistently rated the top day-trip destinations in the Midwest.

Rib Mountain, Wausau, WI; (715) 845-2846
Internet: www.ribmtn.com
4 lifts, 13 trails, 624 vertical feet
Rib is the most European-feeling setting in the Midwest, with the city nestled at the base of the mountain. It offers no-frills skiing with wide trails, but with narrow chutes off the Rib to entice advanced skiers. Lodging is available in the city.

Mt. La Crosse, La Crosse, WI; (800) 426-3665
Internet: None found.
4 lifts, 17 trails, 516 vertical feet
Skiers will find most of this area's runs are cut through rocky bluffs providing headwalls and chutes. Mt. La Crosse sits high atop a rugged cliff overlooking the Mississippi River. It has the only true double-black slope in the Midwest—Damnation.

Whitecap Mountain, Montreal, WI; (715) 561-2227
Internet: None found.
8 lifts, 32 trails, 400 vertical feet
Whitecap has had a facelift in recent years. Several new shops and a conference center have been added to the day lodge, but the expansion still preserves the Old-World charm. The most interesting mix of trails in the area drops down three peaks in every direction. It's the one place in the Midwest where a trail map comes in handy. Located in the Pekonee Mountains, it's in sight of Lake Superior on a clear day.

Index

downhill and cross-country resorts alphabetically